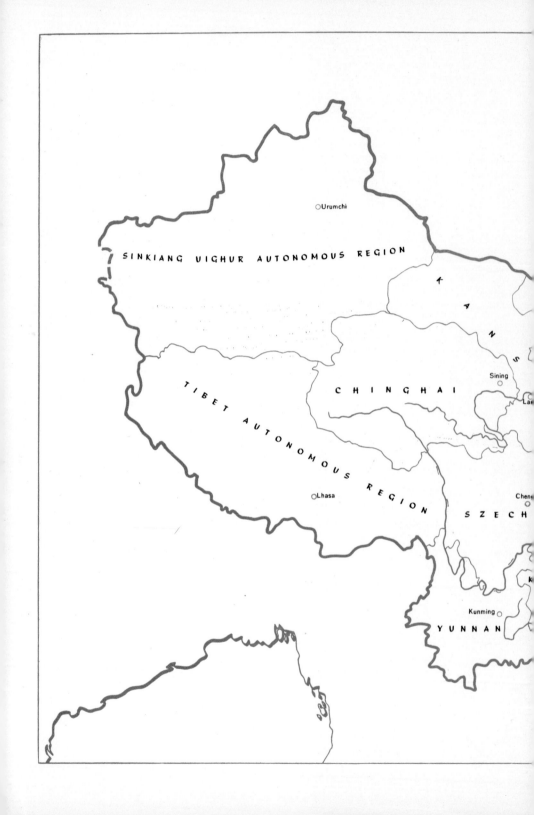

Urumchi

SINKIANG UIGHUR AUTONOMOUS REGION

K
A
N
S

CHINGHAI

Sining

Lan

TIBET AUTONOMOUS REGION

Lhasa

SZECH

Chen

YUNNAN

Kunming

HEILUNGKIANG

Harbin

KIRIN

Changchun

Shenyang

LIAONING

INNER MONGOLIA AUT. REGION

Huhehot

Peking
Tsunhua
Chinwangtao
Tientsin

HOPEI

Hsinhsien
Taiyuan
Shihchiachuang
Yentai

SHANSI

Yellow River
Tsinan

SHANTUNG

Sian

SHENSI

Chengchow

HONAN

KIANGSU

ANHWEI

Hofei
Nanking
Soochow
Shanghai

HUPEH

Yangtze River

Wuhan
Hangchow

CHEKIANG

Nanchang

Changsha
Shaoshan

KIANGSI

HOW

HUNAN

ang

Chingkangshan
Juichin

FUKIEN

Foochow

KWANGSI
CHUANG AUT. REGION

KWANGTUNG

TAIWAN

Nanning
Pearl River
Kwangchow

Nanning
Kwangchow

Tungsha Is.

Chungsha Is.

Sisha Is.

Nansha Is.

Tsengmu Reef

South China Sea
Islands

TRAVELS in CHINA

1966-71

TRAVELS
in CHINA
1966-71

Rewi Alley

NEW WORLD PRESS PEKING
1973

First edition 1973

Printed in the People's Republic of China

CONTENTS

Introduction

There has been, and will be for some time to come, a good deal written on the China of the past half decade, for the changes during that time have been both fundamental and dramatic. This record, based in the main on my notes of travels during the 1966-71 period, takes us into factory, school, forest and commune in many parts of the hinterland. As cities and towns are now much more than before integrated with and servicing the back country, some visits to organisations even in the bigger urban centres have been included. Most of my travels were made to communes, organisations and other units which were considered to be models for work at that particular stage of the Cultural Revolution. Each step forward, however, showed up new steps that had to be taken to consolidate the position gained, and to insure that the idea spread to other brigades, communes, counties and provinces. One model piece of work cannot stand by itself, can only be considered a pilot-undertaking if others follow on, as they have done in the case of the greatest model of all, Tachai of Shansi. The subsequent years of the Cultural Revolution ensured that conditions were created which made it possible for all units to become pilots for others and to catch up with and learn from the more advanced. The negative results which followed the enforcement of the revisionist line of Liu Shao-chi will be seen from my notes on such brigades as Taoyuan in Funing county, and Hsihoying near Tientsin, which will be described in the chapters on Hopei and on Peking and Tientsin, respectively.

Prior to the Great Proletarian Cultural Revolution, the Socialist Education Movement had uncovered much work that was poor in the countryside and had already generated a widespread desire to study Mao Tsetung Thought and to apply it in practice. Thus it had given some considerable basic political education to many people in the rural areas and raised understanding which with the beginning of the Cultural Revolution resulted in immediate progress. It has been the aim of these notes to show some of these developments in Chinese life and the influence of Mao Tsetung's writings on the thinking, habits and work of the people.

Though the gigantic struggle that the Cultural Revolution brought to the whole superstructure, especially in the great cities, is not gone into in these pages, journeys reported on may help the reader to a better understanding of the common folk's will to keep on working creatively all through the immense changes of those years. Not only was production maintained with increased vigor, but also the peasants seized hold of politics in a new way, a way that has greatly affected the thinking of those who struggle for advance not only in China, but also in the rest of the world.

Subsequent events in the revolution decided whether or not the lessons taught by these models could become the accepted norm in the commune organisation. Of course the fundamental question has been and always will be, whether the correct line is being followed or not, and all results must be measured against this standard. Do they conform to the basic political demand that they serve the people (the workers, peasants and revolutionary soldiers)? This has been called the struggle between the two lines — the line of Mao Tsetung of serving the people and building socialism with your own strength and resources, building it greater, faster, better, and with less waste, and the other, the revisionist line of relying on outside help, serving the interests of only a minority and in short re-introducing, with "enlightened self-interest", a new bourgeois class.

Many chapters are based on articles which have already appeared in "Eastern Horizon" or "Ta Kung Pao" in Hongkong. Others are from unpublished material. The reader may tire a little of the stress laid on work in the rural areas. He may even be a little irritated by weights and measures being expressed in the common Chinese forms, the "jin" which is half a kilogram, or about 1.1 pounds, and the "mou" which is one sixth of an acre, or one fifteenth of a hectare. These, however, are the measures in which the Chinese people think and which they feel are best to describe work on intensively cultivated land. As for the emphasis on commune work, it will be realised that of the over 800 million Chinese people around 80 percent work on the land and that therefore its productivity and man's organisation for its proper use are fundamental to China's progress today and basic to the success of her revolution, which has so great a meaning to the working people of the whole world.

Chapter 1

The Beginnings of Change.

Socialist Education Movement in the Countryside

It was spring and early summer in 1966. Amongst the commune brigades then visited were those in north Kiangsu, Shantung, and two counties of Honan. Let us first take the one at Yangchow which is a famous old city in northern Kiangsu situated on the Grand Canal. Well known for its scenery, its commerce and its handicrafts, it is now fast becoming a rising industrial centre. In its vicinity below the old Tang dynasty wall lies Shuangchao Commune, which has nine brigades. It was a bright spring day when I went to visit the particular brigade that had through its good work in the Socialist Education Movement become a model for others. I met and talked with the commune chairman and two of the brigade leaders. The two latter were very different types. One brigade leader was tall and taciturn, making his words count, while his companion was short and peppery, a man who described things exuberantly. Both were in their ordinary work clothes, wearing straw sandals on bare feet. Their land was previously some of tho poorest around Yangchow, mostly yellow clay and sand, which then gave only meager crops. The membership of this brigade when first organised was poor and badly housed. Its leaders looked the situation over and said: "The first thing to be done is to raise the fighting spirit of the people by deeper and more intensive political study. Only that will allow us to go on and take the necessary practical steps to pull ourselves up. And what do these steps consist of? We must carry in good soil, and then get enough fertiliser on the land so that it will grow more. We have but 1,200 mou and over 2,000 people so that there is not much more than half a mou per person. We can get supply contracts from the city for all the vegetables we can produce, which gives us a chance to do our duty and support growing industry. The needed soil can be got from waste land around the city, and then we can dig out a lot of mud from canals for fertiliser and soil as well. We must fetch still more house refuse out of the city to go into our compost pits. We must plow under green manure. We must spend what we can on chemical fertiliser, and we must select and raise our seedlings by the most modern methods, protecting them against bad weather with glass houses, glassed over or plastic-covered beds, so that we can be right on time with continuous crop rotation. We must make our land give its utmost — never let it rest!" And this they have done. On the 500 mou on which they have planted grain, they gained a record crop of 1,360 jin a mou in 1964 and have kept to that since. They confidently expected to exceed that amount in 1966. They have 700 mou in vegetables on neat, rectangular lots. To get their land this way took a terrific amount of spadework in levelling, cleaning away all ancient grave mounds and all the old-time tiny fields, filling in hollows, and making the whole as smooth as the top of a table. Then for the rice paddy that succeeds the wheat there had to be water brought in, which meant digging laterals and connecting up with a larger scheme. It all took patient, hard toil and a whole lot of determination. But they have found the way, and the once poor land has become rich land, dry land has become irrigated. New homes have been built for many members. Now there is no worry about livelihood, for there is a good grain surplus and a continuous demand for their vegetables.

Many other commune farmers come to see their brigade and all marvel that so poor a place can now do so much. The membership says it can do a great deal more yet. The head of the production team, the peppery little middle-aged man with spectacles and a lot of energy, said, "In the old days, the peasant was isolated. All we had was a continual stream of tax collectors, landlord bailiffs, and so on. We faced flood and drought alone. Now," and he pointed to the fluorescent light in the room we sat in, "we have electricity laid on. The whole county is covered with electrically powered pumping stations. We have part-work, part-study middle schools whose graduates come to our production teams. Agricultural college students come and work along with us to find out better ways of doing things, better seeds, better fertilisers. The people in the city are behind us, often coming out to the countryside on mass work. Our government sends many to work on water control, so that even in drought we are certain not to be without water and can get rid of it in flood. Everyone now studies Mao Tsetung Thought, which gives us a way to work together."

Chufu in Shantung

Chufu, a county in Shantung, is well known to the students of ancient China as being the home of the philosopher Confucius. It is situated off the north-south railway, in loess soil country.

Going out of the city down the cypress-lined avenue that leads to a walled-in enclosure in which lay many graves, we turned to the left and drove out into the countryside, passing through several villages until we came to the one from which Hsiachiatsun Brigade of Hsiatsun Commune operates. It had become a model in putting Mao Tsetung Thought into action during the Movement for Socialist Education. The brigade leader, Hsia Chi-seng, met us. A medium-sized, rugged-faced farmer who though he did not waste words, was yet most convincing. He told of the 120 families of the brigade, 600 people in all, who with their labor strength of 220 of whom 160 could do full, permanent work, farmed 782 mou of flat land the brigade owns. How in the last year of the old society it had produced but 180 jin of grain a mou, and that two landlords took most of that. Five rich peasants did well and the 11 middle peasants with their families did not starve, but for the 53 poor peasant families the outlook was grim, and 15 of these families were reduced to begging. The usual way out for young men over twenty from poor families was to join a warlord or Kuomintang army and hope for a relatively kind officer. Some would return when they were old, but most died and were never heard of again. In the 'fifties, village reorganisation was made, and by 1957, a total of 310 jin of grain a mou gained. 'Fifty-nine, '60 and '61 were drought years, but much was done in well digging, a permanent supply of excellent water being found at 60 feet. The drought years with the new organisation brought greater determination to overcome such misfortunes in future. Now in the brigade are 12 good wells, nine of which are equipped with electrically powered pumps. More wells are being dug. In 1963 a mou of land yielded 665 jin of grain. In 1964, it was 872. Then in 1965 production shot up to 1,158 jin a mou. In 1966, it was expected to gain 1,220 jin, and as I looked at the growing crops it seemed certain to me that such a hope would become a fact. Pulling down old cottages and building bright new ones has made old walls available to go into the compost heaps, as do the cleanings from the new pig sties where 260 pigs are now kept. The aim is to have one pig for each person in the brigade within the next five years, and new houses for all inside three.

Each person in the brigade, old and young, averages a cash income of 88 yuan a year. Over and above the grain they sell to the state, they have already 150,000 jin in store in jars in their own homes and expect to add to this, always maintaining a full year's supply in hand in case of any emergency. They have 150,000 yuan in the bank, and with it they are going on with their program of house building, and of underground irrigation canals. Deep ditches take up a lot of land. Better have the water run in pipes three feet underground to where it is wanted, and use the soil above for planting. Much work has gone into making the cropland level, ancient graves having been removed and small fields made into large ones. The brigade already has bought a tractor and expected soon to be able to buy a truck. It could now make its own flat-topped carts that have pneumatic tyres, which families often own individually. The parts of these carts that seem to be in most need of replacing are the sturdy spokes, supplies of which I noted on the shelves of the brigade general goods store. It was an interesting store for a commune brigade. I noted especially many of the big-size thermos bottles costing 1.32 yuan without outside container. The need for such could be seen when one looked at the brigade hot water service. In charge of a jovial 78-year-old man, it kept a supply of boiling water going all the day, so that housewives could pop in and get thermos bottles filled at any time. I talked with the boy in charge of the store, a 16-year-old graduate of the upper primary school. Then to the old man who boiled the water, from them going on to the small electrically operated grain mill, another facility that means a lot to everyone. People bring in their supply of grain in their household wicker basket and put it in the line waiting. The old man in charge of the mill grinds it, and adds the basket to the pile of waiting ones that will go home with boys coming from school, or elders coming in from the fields.

There are three primary schools in the brigade. These are lower primary only. For the upper grades, children go to a school in a nearby village which three units combine to operate. Two village boys had come home from school and passed us as we were talking. One of them was the crack marksman of the younger set, though only fourteen. Everyone learns to shoot nowadays, old men as well as youngsters. I took their picture as they came along, arms around each other's neck, and deep in some serious discussion.

The brigade operates its own brick and lime kilns and has a black-smith's shop which turns out farm and household articles, as well as doing cart and implement repair. It has a tailor's shop and electricity. The wheat crop is harvested in June, and then the second crop of maize or kao-liang (sorghum) is planted at once. Some fields are planted in cotton, but grain is the main crop. A small area in millet and one in medicinal herbs is also harvested. They have 50 mou in experimental plots for dif-ferent strains of wheat and other seeds, which is watched carefully by all, it being now well understood how important the best possible seed is to the brigade plans to raise production.

In addition to local group meetings, there is a general meeting of the whole brigade twice a month. All kinds of matters come up that have to do with the community, for now there are so many more things to do. Soon the brigade will have its own meeting hall. An evening school will be organised, and an upper primary day school also. The three small clinics operate all right, but there is the need for a local bath house that is now being met. Homes that have straggled out past the village outskirts are being rebuilt inside the village area where there is a good deal of empty ground, while the area encircling the village proper is being turned back to become fields again. It is interesting to note that all these decisions and many major problems which crop up are discussed in general meetings.

Lankao County in Honan

In the past, whenever the Yellow river flooded, which was often, it affected the area now occupied by Lankao county in northeast Honan. After repeated floods, big sand dunes were left, and much alkaline marsh covered the landscape. In the mid-'sixties it leapt into national notice as the place where the late Chiao Yu-lu, good student of Mao Tsetung, was Party secretary.

One morning we set out from its county seat, crossing what was during the Ming dynasty the bed of the Yellow river, then going on over that where the same old Yellow Dragon flowed in early Ching. Taking a road that cut through the old dykes, we came to a broad expanse of country studded with freshly forested hills that had not so long ago been sand dunes. The cultivated land lay in strips separated by deep ditches, and on one rise we saw the village of Changchuang, headquarters of the brigade of that name which worked the countryside. It is a brigade of 1,570 people, one of the 24 of Tsaoyin Commune. In 1963 it had gained a harvest of 91,000 jin of grain and 5,000 jin of peanuts. Then in 1965, it harvested 610,000 jin of grain and 204,207 jin of peanuts. These figures are almost unbelievable, coming as they do from a place whose energy and hopes were curbed so long and so bitterly by great sand dunes, sand from which the winds would lift and plant where it listed, alkaline marsh where the thick white dust would glitter, mocking man's efforts. Then Chiao Yu-lu came, charged with the spirit of the Thought of Mao Tsetung, a thinking that took difficulties simply in its stride. Chiao Yu-lu found an old peasant who showed him how he had stabilised the grave of his mother by putting a layer of good sticky clay dug from the marsh over the sand. Chiao Yu-lu tried it on sand dunes, and it worked. He mobilised the people and in six months had covered every big sand dune including those which had once swallowed up three villages, and then after covering them over planted dates and other trees on them, along with deep-rooting grasses. Then he with his folk turned to the waterlogged land and dug in the alkali, putting it a good three feet down, then ditching each reclaimed strip on either side. It worked, and wheat grew well.

A Soviet expert had been called in in the 'fifties for his advice on how to deal with the sand. He said that it would cost 260 yuan a mou to spray bitumen on the dunes, and during the process nothing should be planted on them. The figure did not include the cost of the equipment for spraying. As there were over 22,000 mou of sand dunes in Changchuang Brigade alone, this idea was not taken up. The brigade had no financial resources, only the thinking Chiao Yu-lu brought to it, giving it the leadership and the spirit to carry the thing through.

The work done in just one half year out of the 15 months Chiao Yu-lu spent in Lankao county was previously estimated to have to be carried out in several stages, taking five years in all. In the spring of 1966, the brigade had its first income from forestry products, a forestry farm by the Yellow river buying 20,000 young trees from the big nursery the brigade had set up. There are 380,000 people in the 188 brigades of the ten communes in Lankao, farming its 1,100 square kilometres of land. There are few who have not made a trip to Changchuang Brigade to see what has happened there, for it is a real demonstration of man's ability to cope with bigger things and put into practice the Mao Tsetung essay "The Foolish Old Man Who Removed the Mountains".

I went through many of the homes in Changchuang. All were proud of their own grain stored, most having enough for their families for a year.

Then there is their production team store, and their brigade store, all over and above the surplus grain they sell to the state. To people who have so often faced tough times, not knowing how they would be able to even survive, this means much.

The young folk told us many stories of the old days when the sand dunes dominated their lives. How for instance a concert party whose visit they had looked forward to once got lost when the dunes obliterated the roads.

Chiao Yu-lu was a name that brought immediate response from all of the brigade, one old man saying how in the old society a man had to stand with bowed head in front of county officials, but how now Chiao Yu-lu and his assistant Chang Hsin-li were one with them. Chang Hsin-li had come with us on our trip, and he certainly was on the closest terms with them all, knowing them all by name and appreciating the struggle each and every one of them had put up. Some of the old men, he said, were so full of the onslaught against the sand dunes that they would go on working long into the moonlit nights of winter. People really gave everything they had in that particular fight and came out of it more closely knit than ever before, also with a new appreciation of their own strength and of the value of the teaching of the philosophy of Mao Tsetung.

All of the brigades in Lankao acknowledge much help from the life and work of Chiao Yu-lu. But there is one more which needs a special note. In Changchuang, the main problem was sand. In Chinsai over by Kuyang, which was old Kaocheng, there was a stretch of land of over 5,000 mou into which the Yellow river swept in 1932, scooping up the good soil and sweeping it away, mockingly leaving in its place a deposit of heavily alkaline soil. Only 800 mou of the brigade land was relatively free of alkali. In 1962 only 120,000 jin of grain was gained, so that 350,000 jin had to be sent in by the government as relief grain for the 593 families, totalling 2,569 folk in all, who lived in the several villages around Chinsai. In 1964, 86,850 jin still had to be sent in as relief grain, but by 1965 the brigade, by almost superhuman effort, had produced 970,000 jin, enough for themselves and some to be sold as well. They expect to gain 1,800,000 jin in 1966, and 3,370,000 in 1970. To do this, they are swinging together in the way they have devised, to bury the alkaline surface soil under 1.2 metres of earth with an impervious layer of clay on it to prevent its rising again. They are sinking wells, which are being mechanised, planting trees, digging irrigation laterals and all the rest. 364 families are those of formerly poor peasants, 195 are middle peasant, 18 landlord and 50 rich peasant, in the old order. Everyone works. Even old women, old men, school children — all of them together. A local slogan for those not so strong as others, says, "If you cannot work a whole day, then work half. If you cannot fill a whole shovel with earth, then lift just half. Be like a silkworm munching mulberry leaves, one mouthful after the other until a whole leaf is gone. If we all keep at it there will be no alkaline land left." Looking over the same landscape in the summer of 1966, one says, "What a beautiful countryside!" The tens of thousands of trees planted by old dykes and on hills, the well laid out new fields, the cotton coming along well, all these have come as the result of a major struggle, inspired by ideas that can really remove mountains. Little wonder that it was made a model to be studied during the Socialist Education Movement.

Linhsien

Linhsien has now become nationally known as the heroic county at the foot of the Taihang mountains and too as a great object lesson in the Movement for Socialist Education in the countryside. Whereas Lankao suffered from too much water, Linhsien never had enough. In the old days, it was a well-known famine area whenever one of the all too frequent droughts came to Honan. It lies where Shansi, Hopei and Honan meet. Once the poorest of the poor, the county of Linhsien has pulled itself up by its own bootstraps and now is a model for both forestry and water control. Coming to it in late June of 1966, we branched off from the main highway and went through some very rocky hills, until we turned off and rose up a steep slope to the Tumen Brigade office of Tsaisang Commune. This was a noted bad area in the old days, as there are no natural underground water resources, and the place is too high to be reached by any of the new canal systems which have irrigated some 330,000 mou of the county, once dry. The people here would often have to vacate their homes in drought years and go and try to live in some place where there was water. Several tries were made to have circular tank detention pools made. A few worked, but most leaked. The brigade is one of 1,450 people and farms 1,715 mou of land built high on the hillside with stone terrace wall facings. Water would often have to be carried ten Chinese li, over three miles, simply for household use. Some catchment wells had been dug, but the task was tough, asking almost too much of the strength of anyone. And anyway, labor power was needed in the fields all the time. Then yet again, as they studied the Mao Tsetung essay on contradiction they realised that they must together face up to the main one, lack of water.

At a meeting one night after listening with increasing impatience about the old man who removed the mountains, Wang Dao-yun, a 57-year-old, was the first to take up tools and start to cut a new water storage well out of the rock. Three feet in diameter on top, 20 feet deep, and 15 feet in diameter at the base. There are always a few wild storms in the summer months, more than enough to fill such wells, which keep water sweet and clean without trouble. Wang walked out of the meeting and promptly went to work with his hammer and chisel. Three days later he had only got down one foot and his arm and hand were swollen. Some advised him to quit the mad idea. He was too old, they said. He went on though, and moreover in time completed the well. Next, was a 16-year-old boy and his 14-year-old sister who lived nearby. They got along so well that a third man started building himself a two-story house with the stone cut from his well. A half blind and nearly deaf man of 75, with a totally blind son of 40, next took up tools. Their progress was slow, but their determination great. Their well was a complete success and the drama of it really moved the village to action. All over the hillside around in the nights after field work was over could be heard the sound of tapping on stone, as the people put out their strength. At the time of my visit there were already 630 wells in use, while eight new catchment reservoirs had been constructed. One well can materially assist three mou of land and ensure a crop, but the plan now is to have one well per mou. Soil on the best land is not thick, only 600 mou having above three feet. Yet with water and fertiliser, much can be done. In 1949, the average production of grain per mou was 190 jin for the whole year. In 1965, a drought year, it was 550 jin. 1966 promised much more. First the people grew persimmon trees in suitable places. Now the drive is for walnuts in all places where the tree will grow. People are rightly proud now of what they have done, and everyone lifts his head higher. Confidence has come where there was little confidence before. With the right way of thinking and out of their own strength this has come about, and all smile.

Datsaiyuan Brigade

Datsaiyuan Brigade of Chengkwang Commune near Linhsien city has good land. It is some of the best irrigated in the county. All of its 1,415 mou are now served by new canal laterals, and there are also many wells that reach down to a good water table. Its 1,289 people live in two villages, 274 families of them. Certainly it has known hard times. In the old society it never gained more than 270 jin a mou a year, 150 in the spring and 120 in the autumn. In 1942, around 700 people were left destitute by an utter crop failure. Many died, many took to the roads as refugees. Liberated away back in 1944, by 1950 it gained for the whole year 350 jin a mou, 500 in 1960, and then after a period of political study in the '62-'63 winter, it harvested 600 jin in all. In 1964-65 the pace was lost. Production went down to something over 400 jin for the whole year. There were internal wrangles, some saying that they knew the best way, others saying it was best to go one's own path, and so on. County cadres who came to the villages were received coldly. There was evidently something wrong.

In the 1965-66 winter a study course was started. It ran from November 1965 to February 1966. Everyone had a chance to bring up all his or her troubles. All could discuss the way forward together. For study material, several of the most pertinent of Mao Tsetung's essays were chosen. That on Norman Bethune, that on serving the people, that on the Foolish Old Man who removed the mountains, and then the one "On Practice". The results were startling. The first crop of 1966 averaged 410 jin a mou, and the second will not be far behind. Something definitely has happened in Datsaiyuan. We went from one house to another talking to the folk. There was the brigade leader, a quiet, slow farmer. He had been so moved by Mao's works that he had long determined to become a servant of the people with all his heart. But his wife did not like the idea. She badgered him to give up the job. Live quietly. Don't always be going to meetings. Stay at home and shut the gate. Play with the children. She carried on a war to make him resign. She cooked his food badly. Left it to get cold. Did not do his mending properly, and scolded him all the time. But when the movement started she could not keep away, so she joined to hear what was being said. Then she found herself memorising some of the passages, if only to keep up with other women. But they kept coming to her mind when she was back at home, and the more she thought them over the more sensible they seemed to her. Then the realisation came that she was wrong. First she set about and did all the things that would make her husband feel better, then she told him that he was right — she had been wrong. He was deeply stirred and said, "Now we shall be a united revolutionary family."

We met Tien Ching, a woman of 75, hale and hearty, with a good firm hand grip. "Yes," she said, "they said I should stay at home. But I am still strong. When I learn of that old man and the mountains, I realise I can do a lot for people yet. I like memorising the words of Chairman Mao, and the youngsters help me to get them right." Though she is illiterate, she knows the places in the book where the passages she wants are written, and bails up school children to read them to her to see if she has them quite right.

A pretty girl of 21 told how she did not like work, only wanting to do herself up and make trips to the county city. How after the last movement she found the way ahead and is now known as the "iron-armed lass" because of her ability to do so much. A young married woman with two children, wearing plain homespun, told how she had gone with her husband to Taiyuan for five years. She did not work there but had many pretty clothes. She loved the buses, trains and bustle of a city, so that when activist workers like her husband were advised to send family members who were unemployed back to their communes to help with basic production there, and he told her she must go, she stormed, threatened divorce, and all manner of things, but in the end she went. When she finally did get to the village she refused work and just wore her pretty clothes every day until the village girls called her "that clothes rack". When the study period started she went along. The way everyone wanted to transfer words into action impressed her. The more she read the more she wanted to memorise, and soon was helping those who were illiterate with their memorisation. Then she tore up the letter she had written her husband asking for divorce, and instead wrote one telling him that he was right, and that she looked forward to his coming home on leave. She is happy to be back as one of the group and now wonders how she could have been so foolish as to make all those distressing family scenes.

So does the ferment go on through Datsaiyuan, catching hold of everyone, old and young. The children help the old people, the old ones help the young, and everyone is determined that they will make their land do more and even more yet. It will not be easy for many in the West to understand the power of the application of the thinking of Mao Tsetung, but it is a fact that it is bringing immense results, not only in production, but also in building a new people. It is in this light that a new estimate needs to be made of it by all who would understand what is happening in the Chinese countryside of today.

Such then is a brief introduction to some of the model brigades in the stage that immediately preceded the Cultural Revolution, the struggle for socialist education in the countryside.

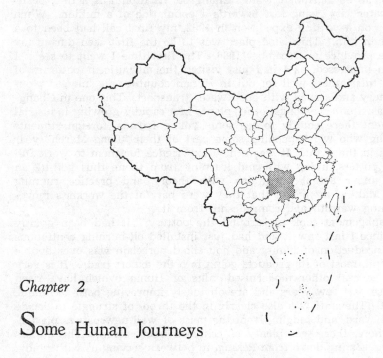

Chapter 2

Some Hunan Journeys

In the summer of 1966, the storm of the Cultural Revolution broke and the streets of the cities were filled with marching youth. In the early winter I went to Hunan to see some of the work there that was being held up as model for communes everywhere to learn from. Journeys were made into northeastern, eastern and northwestern Hunan, some time also being spent around the provincial capital Changsha, and also Shaoshan, the birthplace of Chairman Mao, which had become at that time a great youth centre. From their first determination to get to Peking and other big cities as soon as possible to take part in the Cultural Revolution, the students had by now more and more gone on the march, emulating revolutionary Long Marchers of the past and taking their message far and wide throughout the countryside, while they themselves toughened up as they went. To the passing visitor, they almost seemed to be the predominant feature of the countryside at this stage, so many were there on the roads at this time.

The last visit to Hunan was made in 1970 during a study tour on the life and work of Chairman Mao.

Hunan Return

It was good to be in Hunan again. Changsha, its capital, is a fine, beautifully situated city rising fast towards a population of a million. When I last came on a writing expedition in 1962, my final call had been to a city porcelain kiln. This same place was to be the first seen during my stay in the province in December 1966. The first time I went to see it I was not so impressed, as I had just visited the magnificent potteries of Liling and then others well set out in Hunan counties, all amongst wonderful scenery and served with good water transport. This one in Changsha city was situated amongst other plants in a rapidly growing industrial area. I went there chiefly to see some young friends, foreign students from Peking who were spending some part of their "Long March" year as workers in the plant. It was a new experience for them to work full days with potters, living with and learning from them, thus getting an education under actual conditions with theory and practice running together. Making them feel that they were part of the worker's movement, gaining warmth and comradeship from it.

The management took me around the pottery. It had been greatly enlarged since I last saw it and had just installed oil-burning continuous kilns. Its production of high-grade household porcelain was over double the 1962 total, most of its products going into the export trade. It is very similar to several other modernised kilns of Hunan which have risen during these past few years and are obviously improving both technique and output. The staff was also clearly in the throes of struggle to decide the way forward, and judging from the mass of wall newspapers plastered everywhere, there was plenty of criticism being given. The hostess on the plane coming down from Peking, in between serving us with candy, tea, fruit and periodicals, and in reading some of the Mao quotations from her Little Red Book, had taken time to teach the passengers a new song, with words from Chairman Mao's essay "Serve the People": "If we have shortcomings, we are not afraid to have them pointed out and criticised, because we serve the people. Anyone, no matter who, may point out our shortcomings. If he is right, we will correct them. If what he proposes will benefit the people, we will act upon it." Set to a rollicking tune, it was soon being sung by all the passengers. Judging from the wide smiles seen around the pottery on our afternoon visit, a good deal was being said there that pleased the workers mightily. There was no time to discuss internal politics with the young workers however, even if they had been willing to do so. They were obviously busy and did not like to stop and talk while others were working.

Changsha had over 200,000 Red Guards and other students visiting during the first days of December, all of them going on to see Chairman Mao's home at Shaoshan, 100 kilometres away. Marchers with their packs, indeed, were everywhere. Packs are tied up in colored plastic sheeting, reds and blues predominating. Hunan winter weather is mostly overcast with plenty of rain, fog and snow. The young visitors' numbers in Changsha, however, were small in comparison with those of Peking,

11 million students having gone through the capital since summer, and three million still there at the end of November when we left. Yet for Changsha, a city of only around 800,000 population, 200,000 visitors is quite a lot. The Little Red Books which all carry and read together and to others are full of down-to-earth, common sense politics, which leaves its impact wherever they go. The posters will be blown down, the youngsters will move on out into work or back to their schooling, but the message they have brought will remain in people's minds. Everywhere there has been a definite rise in political understanding. The fight against revisionism is definitely on.

A Rubber Factory

This was brought out well in the second visit made to a Changsha enterprise. Back in pre-Liberation days, on the outskirts of Changsha, a revolutionary underground centre was established on a hill amongst scattered old grave mounds. At Liberation, the place was cleared and converted into the site for an Army clothing factory. The underground branch messenger became a worker there. In 1958, in spite of the fact that a good deal of the rubber had to be imported into China, the factory changed its line and started to make rubber shoes which, with improving livelihood, were in great demand. The old Army personnel who had operated the clothing plant took over the new production line after workers and staff had received training in other rubber factories around the country. But somehow their products did not make the grade very well. They built up to 2,000 workers, but quality grading on the national basis remained low. This was so until 1964, when after a period of intensive political study and criticism, which brought in its wake much streamlining and better method, by the end of 1965 it hit the highest grades in China for its two chief products, the overshoe and the cloth shoe with a rubber sole. The study period also led workers to go out into the country and size up needs of workers in communes. They found many with feet which did not fit into any of the regular shoes made. One lad of 18 had a giant's feet. The factory decided to make moulds for special cases such as his and turn out shoes for all at the same prices as for the regular sizes, though the cost of making such individual ones was many times higher than the price asked for them. "Ours is a socialist country. Of course we have to do things like this," they said. They also made waders for farmers in those regions where schistosomiasis was prevalent, putting them out as cheaply as possible. Now that the rubber used comes in the main from China's own rubber plantations, the factory is no longer so dependent on imports. The old management is still in charge, confessing that it had become proud and over-confident, thinking that a project could be bullocked through if enough managerial drive was available. Now after the study period and the consequent modernising, 1,850 workers produce better and more efficiently than the original number, and there is so great a demand for their product that the factory is being enlarged. The old underground messenger has recently passed away, but his son is an up-

and-coming member of the factory working force. New automation cuts out much of the drudgery, so that the whole enterprise itself proceeds with an absence of commandism or hurry, in neatness and precision, with better understanding between all who work there.

A Shoe Factory

Changsha before it was burnt by the retreating Kuomintang army in 1938 was a wonderful old city of handicraftsmen. Many survived the wars, and on Liberation groups of the shoe makers were collected to make one big enterprise where there would be some mechanisation and where working conditions would be good. They picked a hilltop area rather higher than that of the rubber factory, and built themselves fine airy workrooms there. By dint of much struggle they have made a name for themselves both in the local and export trade. Not a big place, it has some 380 workers who use some of the leather made by Miao folk in the hills and convert it into the long horseman's boots eagerly bought by the folk in Inner Mongolia. They also turn out lambskin-lined children's high boots for Switzerland and Sweden, sharp-pointed style shoes for Hongkong and Singapore, and rubber-soled shoes for the local market. The work is careful and the resulting product pleasing in its fine craftsmanship.

Memorial Park

I had last visited the memorial park in summer, when there were masses of youngsters swimming and boating in the lake. Now in the first stage of winter, with a cold wind coming down from the north, it was still attractive, the grass still green, and many trees still with leaves. A 16-year-old Red Guard lad from Chienyang in west Hunan had marched to Changsha with 13 others. He walked along with us for a while, but no, he would not have his picture taken. A smaller local one with a cheerful smile obliged, however, and moreover introduced four companions who were equally willing but not so photogenic as he was.

Changsha Return

After two weeks out in the countryside we returned to Changsha, finding the struggle still proceeding. Turning on the radio that evening, one heard a Moscow report to the effect that the aim of the Cultural Revolution was to turn the Chinese people into robots, dumbly obeying orders. Actually, the exact opposite is the case. It is first and foremost revisionism, then autocratic commandism and the dictator type of leadership that is being challenged by the young people, who are determined that the purity of Mao Tsetung Thought will not be taken over by the real opponents of such and used as a baton to hold the people down, and so divert the revolution on to a non-revolutionary road.

We climbed up the Tien Sing Ke, a pavilion on all that remains of Changsha's city wall. There is a pleasant public garden here, with plenty of flowers even though it was mid-December. The place was thronged with youngsters from county middle schools who had marched into Changsha to learn all they could, see all they could, and especially to go to Shaoshan. Down on the river bund, a new boulevard replaces the old sloping riverbank that was my first memory of the place. The river was busier with boat traffic than I have ever seen it. Changsha is changing with accelerating speed.

Changsha to Shaoshan

Though Hsiangtan is a separate city and Shaoshan, the birthplace of Mao Tsetung, is under its jurisdiction, it is today almost a suburb of Changsha, so well is it joined up by a modern macadamised highway and by the now well bridged Hsiang river. Just over 100 kilometres from Changsha, Shaoshan is easily reached by car in a couple of hours. On our way, we passed marchers both going and coming. Some were primary-school children, others on and all the way up to university students. Then too, there were groups of Changsha working people joined together to take part in what has been a continuing demonstration ever since the Cultural Revolution started. In all 1963, around 40,000 people came to Shaoshan. Each day in this 1966 autumn, some 50,000 arrived, making a total of two and a half million by early December. By mid-December, a mere 10,000 a day were coming in, but these were enough to make the whole highway from Changsha bright with their red flags and eager faces.

It had been seven years since I was at Shaoshan last, so that the new improvements were impressive. A new highway into the town, hills either forested or else in orchard trees. A fine main irrigation canal leading down from a reservoir on a tributary of the Hsiang river runs over a magnificent aqueduct and branches off into laterals. It irrigates a million mou of land in three counties. A well laid out exhibition hall and a new guest house for foreign visitors — 3,000 have come in 1966 — are set amongst trees on the hillside overlooking the town. When we came, the mild Hunan winter had not cut the leaves so that the maples glowed red amongst tall bamboo, and some young gingkos gave a great splash of gold to the scene. The old guest house where I stayed in 1959 had been changed to become a Red Guard hostel and around it milled the crowd of youngsters from many provinces. They were warm and friendly. In the exhibition galleries, as well as in Chairman Mao's old home into which they crowded, they were fascinated by the exhibits. There are indeed many moving family and revolutionary pictures, the pictures of the six members of the family killed in the revolution being especially so.

There are many good stories about young marchers who have come in. Indeed, one can guess at many a one by a few simple questions. "How old are you," I asked a barefoot bright-faced boy. He said he was 14 and had come from Yoyang, a good four days' hike. "It has been good. We are all together, and we sing songs," he said. Friends told of how at one stage, when the place was literally filled to the last corner, a group had arrived marching from Chuehshan, a hill county in Honan. It had taken them a month to come. The oldest was 14, the youngest 13. They looked around, saw the exhibition hall and the home of Chairman Mao, but were then told that as there was a big crowd that day there were no billets available for them and they would have to return to Changsha. Their leader saluted and turned to his group and told them to put on their packs, as they were marching back immediately. There were no demurs. In the meantime, however, the matter had been reported and a cadre came down to the reporting station just as they were leaving, to take them over and find places for them in the cadres' own quarters, which would ensure that they had a couple of days' rest. But stories of good spirit shown are legion. A new kind of youth has emerged. It is they who will decide events in the last three decades of this millennium.

Evening in Shaoshan can be very beautiful. Mist through the pines on hilltops and down valleys. There has been much written about the place already, and there will be much more in future. For from here the East started to grow red. Confucius, so long ago, preached for the rulers decorum, filial piety and all the rest of it. His teachings were avidly taken by the ruling class and served to make feudalism last as long as it did in China. But Mao Tsetung puts his trust in the people. It is the people who are the deciding factor, he says.

To Northeast Hunan

When we left Shaoshan in the morning it was raining. Lines of trucks and buses were taking on their passengers, and columns of marchers were setting out for home, or to march on elsewhere. We took the road north to Ninghsiang, where we joined the main highway west. There were more marchers coming down through the rain to Shaoshan than there were going away from it. Their number rather increased as we went on to Yoyang and then crossed the Li river on to Changteh. One column was headed by a square-cut little boy who could not have been more than nine. Pack on back and swinging his arms across his body, he certainly looked the part. Many had put their shoes in their packs and were marching barefoot.

On the ferry crossing the Yuan river to Changteh, a whole bunch of little girls of about 11 or 12 came on the ferry, packs complete, but also with enamel basins and other odds and ends. "Yes," they said in a matter-of-fact way, "we have been out in the country helping with production for a few days. They said we were too small to march to Shaoshan, so we have been out to do five days' work instead." In the days not so long ago they would have been chaperoned by teachers and would have felt that they were doing a big thing. Now they take for granted the whole trip out and back home again.

When I came here seven years ago, there was but one modern factory — a cotton mill — set up on a hillside near the Yuan river. Now the place has quite a sizeable industry. There are some handicraft factories in the town itself and we saw one making shirt buttons from shell and other black coat buttons from plastic. Leather belts are made here for export, and there is both glass and pottery produced. Here the charcoal brazier is a great high bowl of a good brown glazed pottery of the kind that, along with lacquer and the Japanese wooden sandal "geta" and much else, went down from these areas and across to Japan in the very early days to become part of domestic living there.

Changteh, as it borders Tungting Lake, is rich with aquatic products. Its paddy fields give 1,000 jin of grain a mou each year, and 90 percent of the county is flat. The municipality including suburbs, has around 200,000 people. Changteh county has 640,000.

Down by the edge of the river we saw an old timer with a long, thin, wickerwork basket, closed and about three feet long, swung from a tripod by a rope and operated by a long handle. The operator swung it low so that it struck the water and the contents, which were root crops, were in time nicely skinned, with much more economy than trying to pare them, a process unsuitable for knobby, under-water roots. It had "always been done" this way the old man said and, as results are so efficient, it will probably be the way it is done for a long time to come yet.

The middle portion of Changteh has been made over anew, with wide, macadamised streets and well-set buildings. The old, all-wood type house of west Hunan has largely gone from the middle of the city. As the capital of a prefecture of 4,500,000 people with a rising standard of living, it may be said to be but at the beginning of change.

Leaving Changteh, we went through the hills south until we came to Peach Blossom Springs, made famous by the poem of Tao Yuan-ming around 1,600 years ago. The beauty of this place shows what a piece of mountain valley and hillside can become if left to grow tall bamboo and great trees, a fine example for all forest lovers and water conservation experts to come and learn from. Amongst the varieties of bamboo here is a queer one with a square instead of a round trunk. The old images of the poet have been removed as he was portrayed in court robes, whereas he hated the court and left it to go back amongst the farm people to live and work. Were he alive today he would be pleased to see the quotations and poems from the works of Mao Tsetung in gold and red on the walls of the old buildings here.

It was well into the afternoon before we got to beautiful Yuanling, where we crossed the Yuan river and went to stay in the county offices. Yuanling is a county of 330,000 people in the Chienyang prefecture. It is 70 percent mountainous, but there are still over 650,000 mou of land, valley and hillside that can be cropped. The Yuan river makes a good transport artery down to Tungting Lake, a wooden boat taking five days to make the journey. At low water, however, there are some tough rapids to negotiate, though with the blasting away of dangerous rocks these have lost much of their hazard.

We went up through busy streets to the martyrs' memorial, set on a scenic hill at the back of the town. A mass of children just out of school scampered along beside us, thinking that perhaps there might be something unusual on foot, but all that happened was that I took several snaps of them clambering up the steps, admiring the bounce they had, and their freshness.

The local leading cadre here was a Peking ex-soldier who came south with the Liberation Army 17 years ago. His assistant and the county head are both local men. They have plenty to do, for in Yuanling, like everywhere else in hinterland China, there are new things being put into operation all the time. Tea plantations to be made, new forests planted, irrigation, power and transport to be worried about. Then too, the political understanding of a whole population needs always to be deepened. Six hundred local youngsters went to Peking to see Chairman Mao in the autumn of 1966. Several hundred more have already gone off on long marches. A great many have visited Shaoshan, and now the line of marchers coming down the streets from Kweichow province in the west, on their way through Hunan to Chingkangshan in Kiangsi, seems never ending. In the streets of Yuanling they are already taken for granted, wending their way single file through, without attracting more than a glance. The new power station here is a modern one burning local coal, and the town, now on both sides of the river, shows up well at night with plenty of street lamps. In public works in the winter of 1966-67, a good-sized reservoir is being built that will irrigate 100,000 mou of previously dry land. It is expected that all canal digging work will also be completed before the spring. Highways to the communes in this country are not so easy to make, there being so many steep hills and rivers, but yet a good deal of work is being done on such projects also. The people are all Han, though there is one hill area where folk count themselves as Han yet speak an old and different language amongst themselves. Experts have decided that it is somewhat akin to the Tu language spoken in the Tu-Miao Autonomous Chou, which it neighbors.

While travelling between counties in the hills of the Tu-Miao Autonomous Chou at the end of December, snow fell thickly on the higher ranges. This was a real test for marchers coming down from Szechuan, many with thin, unlined cotton trousers, already somewhat too short as with growing youth, no socks but with rubber shoes. Their padded coats and mufflers did not keep the cold from nether portions, but they were gaining a real feel of what the Long March really meant. A precious bit of education in struggle, each mile a rich lesson.

After a couple of weeks in the Chishou region we rejoined the main highway above Yuanling and went through Chenhsi, Shupu on overwooded hills down to Ankiang, more often called Chienyang, where the headquarters of the prefecture of that name are located. On the way we passed many young marchers who had come across Kweichow from Kunming in Yunnan. They planned to march on to Peking, and as they had been a month on the way already and were feeling well, they thought that they could make it all right. Cost for a marcher is nine yuan a month for food, and maybe a few fen (one hundredth of a yuan) a day for other things. It is said the winter of 1966-67 is just the trial period. By the spring of 1967, they said, the whole student body of China from middle school up will be on the move. However that may be, at the end of December 1966 numbers on the roads seemed to be increasing all the time.

Chienyang has become a modern city since my last visit, with a broad city street and newly constructed shops and office buildings. Its cotton mill, machine shops and fertiliser factory serve the countryside, and the advent of the water pump turbine has enabled much dry land previously out of reach of irrigation systems to get its share. Consequently the 80-day drought of 1966 did not adversely affect the crop yield. A new hydroelectric power station will soon make the present coal-burning steam power plant obsolete.

We spent the evening on the street, watching marching youth crowding into the stores. The stall where water bottles for marchers were sold was well patronised. Seven thousand Chienyang youth went to Peking in the autumn, being taken by trucks over Hsuehfengshan to the rail head now at Shaoyang.

When we tackled Hsuehfengshan — Mountains of Snowy Peaks — the going was not so easy, for the steep incline was frozen over following first rain and then snow. We halted by one incline on which it was too slippery for me even to walk to put on tyre chains, and to say good-bye to the old cadre from Chienyang who had farewelled us so far. An old Long March fighter, he had been as he put it "going around China with Chairman Mao" since boyhood in Chaling, below Chingkangshan. A boy of perhaps 17, who looked very honest but a bit lost, came up and, pointing to the outsize rubber overshoes he was wearing, said it was too slippery to walk, and was there a place in the car for him over the snowy summit of the 2,000-metre-high road. "Put out your determination," the old cadre said sternly. "Learn to get over difficulties! Have you your book of quotations?" The boy pulled out his Little Red Book and just stared at it for a moment. Then swiftly pulling some dried grasses, he tied them around his rubbers and plodded gamely enough off uphill. One meets all kinds on the roads, though. One group stepping out freely and fast turned out to be a teacher and three students from a Kunming middle school. The advance party for a big group, they were off by forced marches to get to Shaoshan and arrange for quarters for the others, doing 60-70 kilometres a day, and part of the night. They looked as though they were thoroughly enjoying the experience, as indeed did the big majority of the marchers we saw. These Kunming ones were planning to go to Yenan after Peking, then to walk through the Tsinling mountains down to Chengtu and finally back to Kunming. A whole year of walking, learning all the time.

Coming out of the Hsuehfengshan mountains at Tungkou, we noticed that the river had been dammed there and water pump turbines were throwing the water 46 metres up the hillside to an irrigation system high above. Tungkou is in the Shaoyang prefecture, but it was evening before the old pagoda that rises over Shaoyang town came into sight. Shaoyang is now a place of 140,000 people, capital of a prefecture of 6,300,000. These have a labor force of 2,500,000. Meeting the leaders of the prefecture after supper that night, I learnt that one million commune members are now busy on winter water conservancy tasks, and that 800,000 mou of land will be added to the 5,500,000 mou already irrigated in the prefecture for the coming year.   Inside two years 2,400,000 mou will be added.   The one big project which entails leading water through many hill tunnels is being worked on.   There are 10 medium and 40 small projects either completed or else being worked on now.   All agreed that the arming of the people with Mao Tsetung Thought had been a strong activating force and had brought to effectiveness much latent potential in the people, a fact that they illustrated with many fascinating stories.

Old Shaoyang was just one very long street, a little back from the riverside.   A big new bridge over a tributary river has just been completed, allowing the city to spread farther uphill.   The orange groves I so admired in 1962 have been greatly extended, and new industry has come in.   After looking at the bridge, and then stopping at times to talk to the young marchers on the roads, we were soon going through the counties that separated Shaoyang from Changsha.   Marchers look their best winding amongst the trees on hinterland roads.   By the time their stream got to Hsianghsiang, and then to Hsiangtan, they were apt to get lost in crowds of country folk, some of whom were holding demonstrations of their own, with banners, drums and cymbals.

By the time they got to the great wide highway that runs from Hsiangtan to Changsha they were relatively only small groups amongst the crowd and the traffic.   Then at Changsha, where big street demonstrations were in progress, they simply became one with the mass of people about them.   It was said that more and more marchers were coming into Changsha all the time.   Nothing like the numbers there were when train and road traffic was free of charge to them, but still leaving a steady 140,000 to 150,000 in the city all the time.   It is certainly a time of high adventure for Chinese youth, a preparation for tougher struggle maybe yet to come.

The new year had come in when we spent the last day in Changsha and went over to Yuloushan, where many of the "Long Marchers" were billeted in schools.   A new highway to the summit has been made since I was last here, and the old images taken from the temples.   They had long lost any meaning to the people and remained just pictures that today's youth disliked as being a part of the old they wanted to get rid of.

The Hsiang river was gay with red flags from all the shipping there, and the setting sun lit all with its radiance.   Soon there will be a high great bridge spanning the two forks of the river and the Island of Oranges in between.   It will rise above the water high enough so that boats can go under it in the highest water of summer.   People now are out to get the kind of thinking that gives them confidence to do anything they set their hands to.   Anyone who does not realise this does not understand modern China.

The Tu-Miao Autonomous Chou of West Hunan

On leaving the main highway about half way between Chishou, capital of the Tu-Miao Autonomous Chou in west Hunan, and its county of Feng-huang, then taking a road that leads into the partially wooded hills of the

Shanchiang district, one finds that the population here is all Miao. After passing through several villages, one finally comes to Huangmaoping, a relatively fertile area, now converted into paddy fields following the construction of the Shanchiang reservoir and other water conservancy projects.

This was once one of the poorest of Miao districts, and certainly in the old society one of the most cruelly oppressed. We sat a while around the blazing spruce wood fire of a middle-aged local man, listening to him tell of some of the things that had happened in the past 30 years. He started with the period when an influenza epidemic swept the countryside, followed by cholera and dysentery, which cut the number of families in Huangmaoping alone from 42 to 22. Bandit plagues killed also, and there arose a bandit chieftain, a certain Lung Yung-fei, who was out to defeat another bandit, Lung Chi-fen who already held the peasants of Huangmaoping and surrounding villages in thrall. Lung Yung-fei attacked the whole widespread area seven times, each time burning the poor thatched houses of the peasants. Finally he won supremacy, and then set out to build himself a headquarters, to fully subjugate the people.

Near where we sat talking was a deep pit that ran down through the limestone to an underground river. Into this pit Lung pitched those who in any way displeased him. A stone tablet now marks the spot. One of the old thatched cob houses has been left there, our host told us, to show the next generation how their fathers had to live.

In the meantime the village has changed to become a modern one, a model from the health standpoint, with a small hospital and modern medicines. In the old days, a sick peasant could only call in the "'wu shih" — also called "shen han" if a man, or "wu po" if a woman. Such a magician would have to be given one jin of pork, one chicken, and an envelope containing ten coppers. Only then would he or she go through the prescribed incantation.

New homes have now been built, there is a school for children. Youngsters play, sing the new songs of the day and recite Chairman Mao's quotations in high ringing voices. They have all learnt to swim in the new reservoir not far from the village. None could swim before. I passed one group who had with them a blind man who once made his living telling fortunes. The children had taught him to recite Mao's essays, and now he goes around teaching them to old folk who cannot read.

We went up into Lung's former citadel, a great sprawling house set on a hillside with two fort towers, one at each end of it. Lung typified all that was worst in a rotten society when almost every county was controlled by a similar robber baron. One step higher on the ladder was Chen Shin-shen, the "west Hunan king" in Fenghuang, who tried to eliminate Lung. But Lung was too strong, so Chen made friends with him instead. The Kuomintang nominated Chen a lieutenant-general, and Lung a major-general, in charge of "bandit suppression" forces. As we sat listening, the voice of the head of the district went on quietly, telling us some of the notorious acts of Lung that make his memory hated. The builders of his towers took six months to complete the task. When they asked for their wages, Lung laughed coldly and said, "You have kept me waiting for six months! Well, I will give wages to anyone of you who climbs up the outside of the tower you have built." One of the youngest took him at his word and was actually half way up the vertical face when Lung shouted to his men, "See, he is a bandit. Can climb walls. Shoot him." So the boy was shot and his body thrown into the death pit.

The masons who did intricate carving on doorway portals for him he paid, but then sent one of his men to kill them on the road and bring the money back. His worst atrocity, however, was carried out on a tailor. It appears that there was an itinerant tailor named Tien Se-hung living in a village nearby, who had five dependents. Lung ordered him in, and for three months the man worked for Lung's three wives, children, and retainers. When he asked for wages, Lung said that he would be paid when he finished everything that was required of him. So the tailor just went home and then off to other jobs that would give some income to support his family. In the meantime, Lung sent men to find him, and finally once when he came back home they got him. Lung had him stripped, nailed to a young forked tree with big nails, and then slowly had him skinned alive, each bit of skinning being done at half-hour intervals. The place was by the roadside along which the people were going to market, so that everyone saw what was meant for them to see. Lung, by the way, was the friend and confidant of a certain American Catholic missionary whose Chinese name was Wu Ke-lan, and who was stationed in Yuangling. Wu Ke-lan had very close relations with all west Hunan bandit chiefs. In later years, Lung began to be called the "Miao king", and his authority increased over a wide area right up until Liberation, when he took to the hills but was captured, tried and executed in 1950.

In Huangmaoping, he had an execution ground made on the road not far from the tree where he had Tien Se-hung, the tailor, skinned. A little field called "Death Flat" where his executioners slaughtered as many local people as he willed. His wives were as much hated as he was, fiends in their own right. When the day of judgment came, the people would have none of them either.

Today the big house is the office of the district and also of the local commune. Tien's wife and two of her children survived. Both children have grown up and are married and working, with children of their own. The head of the poor peasants' association, a middle-aged woman, invited us into her home for a while. A strong hard-working person still, she gave us some of the more graphic details of the tragic old days. When we were going out of Shanchiang, we met her coming down the highway with a big load of fuel on her back.

Epidemics and bandits played greater havoc amongst many hill villages than even around Huangmaoping. Many of the families simply ran away, and for most of these it meant starvation on the roads, and death. In the Shaoshenlung Brigade area there were in the 'thirties 100 families. By Liberation, not one was left. Later nine families returned. In the Tsaosan Brigade area there were 145 families. Only 11 survived until Liberation. In Ladu, out of 104 families but five were left. No wonder the people have erected a monument by the tree against which Tien the tailor was nailed, and in simple, moving words have recorded the outstanding facts of this particular incident in the class war.   They have erected a pavilion there also, and today many groups of marching Red Guards and students come and read the inscription, and hear from the people themselves some of the bitter story.

Shanchiang Commune now has 18 brigades with 2,040 families, a total of 8,260 awakened Miao people.   With their own hands they have carried through water conservancy projects that could hardly have been dreamt of in the other day.   They know from experience how without the bandit chieftains the Kuomintang could not have held the west Hunan areas, and how foreign imperialism, backer of the Kuomintang, had its part in the upkeep of the feudal order.

Today the people there not only support themselves in grain but also sell a good quantity to the state — a million jin in 1966.   Every person in the commune gets 500 jin of grain a year.   They own 240 cattle and 3,200 pigs.   When Lung the bandit ruled, many of the people had to leave the valley and go up into the hills, living together there in a big cave until six years after Liberation when they felt secure and confident enough to come down, build houses and live a normal life again.   Such is a little fragment of the story of the Miao folk of Shanchiang.

From Chishou one takes the road direct north to Huayuan, another well-known Miao centre.   The first part of the road is scenic, with tall mountains rising through clouds, and green waters of rivers deep below. We passed through Aitsai, a Miao village I had visited in 1959.   Considerable changes had been made.   Water pump turbines brought up water to hillside fields and provided power for milling rice and so on.   A big new school and many new dwelling houses had been built.

Then the highway took a steep incline into the mountains, winding in many bends until we finally came to hilltop country with terraced field valleys between.   Snow fell, adding to the beauty of the scenery.   The highway is one that was built to enable the Chiang Kai-shek government to evacuate to Chungking in the War of Resistance days, and Huayuan, our objective, is a county town in the middle of a high mountain plateau, only 25 kilometres from the Szechuan border.   The road now has become a main route for the "Long March" youth who hike down from Chungking into Hunan on their way to Shaoshan, so that we passed many groups of them on the way.

Huayuan is a Miao county, with a minority of Han people living mainly around the county centre.   Until recently it was not prosperous, the people subsisting mainly on corn and sweet potatoes, the land being too dry for paddy fields.   Then early in 1965 the people drove a tunnel 1,010 metres long, 2 metres wide and 2 high, through a mountain, dammed a river on the other side and brought the water through to run in two main canals around the rim of Huayuan's central valley fields for irrigation. Many other irrigation projects were also completed.   In consequence, a rich crop of rice was gained in 1966, and the whole nature of the place changed.

A county leading cadre accompanied us on our visits. He was an old Red Army fighter who had been on the Long March. A local Huayuan lad of 16 when he marched off, he has had a lifetime of struggle in the revolution. Something indeed to see some of the things fought for come true: Miao, Tu and Han getting on well together; water pump turbines coming to every village where there is water enough to turn them; the land being made to produce in an unheard-of way, and bare hills starting to turn green again. Schools and hospitals for everyone, and the flame of revolution as bright as ever.

The Huayuan county centre is a pretty place. Most of the buildings are new brick ones with tiled roofs. The place lying considerably higher than Chishou, the temperature in winter is a good deal lower, yet it is pleasant enough. Huayuan county centre has a tractor station.

We spent our first afternoon in Huayuan making closer inspection of the tunnel conservancy project of which people are so proud. They are rightly so for, done as it was with local resources, it is an epic piece of work, and one that has started many another tunnelling project throughout other hill counties. We went up into the hills and then down a valley to the edge of a reservoir made by damming up what used to be called the Miao river, running as it does through Miao country. It has now been renamed "Brothers' River" on account of new relations between Han and Miao. Here the water flows into the tunnel with a volume and head enough to generate 1,000 kws of electricity in the newly built little powerhouse. The first unit of the power scheme is already working and provides lighting and daytime power for the city. Once the people have water they find they can bend it to their will. There have been 27 kilometres of main canal and 48 of laterals dug and in operation already, irrigating 50,000 mou of land, converting it from a corn and sweet potato economy to one of rice giving two crops a year. This all has been done at a cost of 15 yuan a mou, less than US $40 an acre, including viaducts, siphons, power station and all other construction.

There were many incidents during the tunnel-making operation. The mountain above was too high to make air vents through, so the fumes from explosions took a long time to clear. A mountain spring was uncovered in the work, which made for more troubles. Workers who had started off by doing five or six metres a day while the going was good now did less and became somewhat dispirited. "It will take many years to get through at this rate," they said. In one team of 14, 11 fainted in one day. Then work was stopped for a while, so that the three short essays of Chairman Mao ("Serve the People", "In Memory of Norman Bethune" and "The Foolish Old Man Who Removed the Mountains") could be studied, better ways thought up and a new attack made. As a result they were able to drive ahead at the rate of 11 metres a day, so that in eight months and eight days the main task was done, and people came from all over the countryside to join in a big celebration. Ten thousand had been expected, but actually around 30,000 arrived on the spot, some walking over 100 li (three li to an English mile) to get to it. Grandchildren helped old people along to clamber around and look. It was an exciting thing, all in all, and 1966 crops which brought in 1,020 jin of grain a mou instead of the old 300 proved its value to the lives of the people. Of the over 10,000 small and medium water utilisation projects that have been carried through in the autonomous chou in these past few years it stands out as being exceptionally successful.

One morning later, we set out and crossed the bridge over the river that separates Hunan from Kweichow and Szechuan. The bridge is at a village called Chadung, and is one that was burnt by the retreating Kuomintang but rebuilt by the Liberation Army when it crossed here in the struggle for the liberation of Szechuan. It is a roofed wooden structure resting on the ancient stone supports, but will shortly give place to a high-level modern bridge. The price of deforestation over the centuries is that floodwater comes up so high at times that low bridges are liable to be washed away. On the Szechuan side, it is Hsiushan county. On the Kweichow side, the Sungtao Miao Autonomous County. Just where the three frontiers converged was a place where, in Kuomintang times, fugitives from law would sometimes run and escape the authorities of all three provinces.

We took a boat here and went upstream to where 1,300 commune farmers were building a dam to hold back waters which will operate three pump turbines to force water up cliffs 38 metres high and irrigate 13,000 mou of land. They have borrowed 70,000 yuan to do the job, so that the cost of getting water onto the land will be less than six yuan a mou. Then on the way back to Huayuan we went up a valley to see where the waters of the western branch of the big main canal have been siphoned across a valley with a reinforced concrete structure built on the spot. Another valley further east has been crossed by a reinforced concrete aqueduct, expensive, but so much superior to the wooden ones that continually have to be changed.

The next morning in looking back, one thought of the magnificent scenery, then of the lines of young marchers so fresh and cheery, cloth red stars sewn on their caps, coming down from Szechuan to spread through the counties of Hunan on their way to Shaoshan and Chingkang-shan. Then of the young workers on the dam, some stripped to the waist despite winter weather, putting their very best into the task in hand. Of the red flags in front of a line of school children marching to the project to assist it, then of the Miao woman standing in the door of her house with a bowl of food inviting me to come in and have "a-ba" — the first meal of the day. Along the main highway to Szechuan and beside the county centre, most of the people are Han. Further back off the road in amongst the hills, almost all are Miao.

One afternoon we spent our time with two Tu minority nationality families. Tu people mostly live in Paoching, Lungshan and Yungshun counties of the Tu-Miao region, but these families had moved down to Huayuan when the highway was built in search of some way to live. Both had the surname of Tien. In the first, it was a daughter who brought notice to the family. She joined in with three other girls after a study course in the works of Chairman Mao, and despite a good deal of opposition from other members who said cotton could not be grown in Huayuan, succeeded in producing a high-yield crop from 40 mou. The girls had their first experience in working together when constructing a dam in mid-winter, when it was necessary to stand in the water in the first stages. When others said it was too bitter, they led in doing the job. It was their success on this project that gave them confidence to go further. The family is a poor peasant one, but its members now know a great deal about the world, for as they sit over the open fire let into the stone slab floor looking out on little limestone mountaintops past a pomelo tree, the daughter keeps them all up to date with what is going on in Vietnam, and how important the principle of self-sufficiency is these days. She is a quiet, determined lass, one from whom much more will be heard as she and her companions continue to achieve what was said to be impossible.

The other Tien family, consisting of an old mother, a 45-year-old son, his wife and six children, is an "all red" family. Their house, set amongst other farmhouses, is neat and clean. Old Five, who is a bright youngster of seven, greeted us. The father, mother and one daughter were at home. They all understand well how it is they can get along as happily as they do. From their earnings they have 600 jin of grain each per year. They all have things to do. One daughter who was shy did not like to go out to militia meetings at night, but the father said, "In the old days who would ever have invited you to such a meeting!" She went, and now has become an ardent militia member. Everyone in the family studies and everyone finds ways to do things for other people.

As we sat, the mother brought us a big bowl of steaming hot sweet potatoes, which people here like to eat in winter sitting around a fire, and which they at times further roast in the hot embers. "It was not always like this," the father said. "It was not easy to get rid of old capitalist ideas, for in the old society we had learnt that we had to grab what we could. Then we had to unlearn all that and find out that only by working and studying together, helping each other, could we play our part properly." Then he went on to cite instances to illustrate his point with simple, but graphically told stories. They were nice people to have met, and it was pleasing to note that the brigades to which they belonged have trebled their production in these past few years despite insect pests, drought and so on. They are now digging laterals for the better utilisation of irrigation canal waters, which when completed will give them added strength.

The leader of the Huayuan county irrigation work, a quiet and very convincing expert named Shih, accompanied us deep into the hills to the site where the medium-sized Taiwu reservoir in the Siaobaiwu commune area is being built. It is a project on which 8,000 members of five communes are taking part, and which will irrigate 50,000 mou of dry hillsides by the end of 1967. Eleven million cubic metres of earth have to be moved, and a total of 2,800 metres of tunnelling done. We saw how work on the 40 kilometres of main canal was already under way. Siaobaiwu village has to be moved uphill, and the brigade of the commune with headquarters there promises to do this task and build a kilometre of main canal also. When we visited, work was being done in mud and slush near where the foundations of the dam will go, and where a coffer-dam was being built to divert the river waters through the longest tunnel, then near completion. It was cold and sleet was driving down, the higher hilltops around having snow on them, but work went ahead with considerable zest, a cheer-leader giving a quotation from Chairman Mao which all would repeat as they worked, girls and boys, old and young, men and women.

We sat for a while in the brigade headquarters in Siaobaiwu and listened to some of the tales of construction that always fascinate. The dam will be 38 metres high, constructed of earth and faced with stone blocks. 101 families in the village have to move away, and 500 mou of valley land will be lost. A relatively small price to pay for what will be gained.

From this project we went down the highway a mile or so, and then climbed up a slippery stone block stairway path into the hills until we came into the area of a project that was completed in 1959-60, which entailed leading a canal around a perpendicular cliff face over 400 metres high, and then out onto 6,000 mou of previously dry land.

It was an ambitious task to conceive, said the now 64-year-old Miao who was then the leader of one work group. We sat in his home around a blazing fire while he told of what had been done, and how the completion of the work had inspired all the Miao folk in the hills. At the beginning, a technician was brought in from outside. He looked at the proposal, then resigned and went home. The people carried on. They let workers down the cliffs on long ropes. Party members paid up their dues before they started, as they might not live through until the completion of the job. Five in all lost their lives before the work was finished. One was a lad who diverted the course of a boulder which would have crashed into a work group of his fellows, but himself was carried down the cliff with it. Another, a girl, was crushed by a rockfall; and then three were killed in the course of using explosives, caught as they were being hoisted up.

Engineer Shih translated while the old man spoke in Miao quietly and with considerable dignity. Yes, the project was a huge success. Grain totals like 1,300 jin a mou were being gained. The allowance of grain per member of his family was now 800 jin a year. The brigade has been able also to sell 40,000 jin to the state. No, he himself was not able to marry until late in life. A schoolboy son of about 12 came up the hill and into the house, red scarf on, and a cheerful smile. It was obvious the old man was very proud of him. The boy could not speak the common language yet but was learning, he said. Away from the main highway, everyone speaks Miao in these parts. The old man reached for a tobacco leaf, put it in his pipe bowl and then thrust the pipe bowl into the red hot embers of the fire we sat by and, puffing on the long bamboo stem, went on with his tale. "Twelve thousand metres of canal around rocky faces, and 4,000 of us Miao working on it was not a simple thing. Yet in 1966 we had 80 days of drought at the time we needed water most. In the other days we would have starved. But in 1966 we took in the biggest crop we had ever seen — all because we had made that canal!" They have good reason to be proud of the Wulungchun project, as it is called. I looked around the house as he spoke. Strings of peppers hung from the ceiling. Leaves of dried tobacco, neatly folded and tied in bundles put behind the low chair father sat in. A stoutly built house of good timbers, it replaces the wild grass thatched hut which was the best the poor Miao of the old days were able to provide themselves with. "Yes," he said, "tiles are much better than thatch. There are no leaking roofs now. It's a comfortable home. Neighbors helped us to build it in 1953." His wife gave me what was obviously a cherished possession, a Miao silk belt she had woven herself when younger, she said.

Huayuan county has carried through many public works in these years, water conservancy projects naturally being in the lead, so much so that it is not easy to find labor power always to do other things. Though the region is mountainous, yet highways have been constructed to all county "chu" subdivisions, and by the end of 1967 all 20 communes will be joined to the highway system. "Never enough people for all the things we have to do," county leaders complain.

For a little while we sat around a charcoal brazier after breakfast on the morning of departure. The county cadre who had been on the historic Long March spoke of how so many Miao and Tu people had joined with the Red Army. In his long years away his speech had changed to that of the Northwest, and though he had always registered himself as Han, maybe his family was Tu, he was not sure. As a 15-year-old boy fighter then, he had not thought much about it. What other comrades were, then that was what he was also.

Snow had fallen through the night, and the mountains were white. On the way to them we halted for a while to take a picture of a contingent of Miao commune farmers, on their way to Siaobaiwu. They carried their bedding, their vegetables, cooking pots, their red flag, and the frame for Chairman Mao's picture, which they had taken off to protect the picture from sleet which still drove in with the wind. A Miao woman headed the party, her silver ear rings glistening, and a strong smile on her face.

The higher we went the deeper the snow lay, youngsters having a high old time on ancient home-made skis. Apparently these are kept in the houses, have been handed down from father to son, and are well made. The two sticks are of bamboo. The boy crouches down and first propelled by his sticks, comes whizzing down an incline. On one bridge by a school the boys had improvised skis made by splitting up green bamboo and just twisting the front end up — not so broad or so nicely upturned as the proper hilltop home-made ones. The game with these was for a whole bunch of boys to get on the incline above a bridge, one on the skis and another pushing him, then tear through the melee, padded clothing saving many who tumbled over from scratches.

We descended out of Huayuan county into Aitsai in Chishou and then cut back into Huayuan for a second visit, going up a valley road beside a river. Here the scenery was something almost out of this world, with all kinds of hill shapes and mist effects.

At the terminus of the road we crossed a river and climbed around a hill face to where we could get a good view of the waterfall called Dalungdung, which comes out of a hole on an almost perpendicular cliff face and dashes down 150 metres into a deep pool below. Work was going ahead to cut off the waterfall and divert it down pipes to a hydro-electric station by the river bank, which will give Chishou another 5,000 kws of electricity when it is completed in 1967. The work entails the digging of a 400-metre tunnel from where the cave dam will be made out to the cliff where it will make a descent to the turbines with an excellent head. The tunnel was nearing completion when we visited, it being 2.4 metres wide and high. The work was being done by the Miao folk around.

Down in the depths of the pool below the waterfall live the "wawa" fish, a four legged fish that can come out and walk on land — those captured being around three feet long and well able to bite. They lie on the floor of the pool and wait with open mouths for small fish to enter, it is said. They are scientifically an interesting survival of the time when fish began to leave the water and live on land.

On the 22-kilometre stretch from Dalungdung back to Aitsai, we noted no fewer than three dams under construction in the river by the brigades we passed through, which will enable pump turbines to be installed. On inquiry, I found that in the whole Tu-Miao region there were already over 1,000 such pumps in operation, and that by the end of 1967 there would be 3,000. One sees them beside the highways everywhere up amongst the hills, waiting to be taken down to some places in the valley below where a dam can be made and water forced up to hillside fields above. Their installation started in 1964, and after they were successfully used on rivers like the Milo in Pingkiang, their use spread up into the hills. They are helping to solve the grain problem in no uncertain way, and when their installation is complete, along with all the other bigger conservancy projects like Siaobaiwu, a mass of labor power will be released. Labor power which will be needed for the more speedy reforestation of the hills, to halt the floods which can so easily threaten the defiant hands of people out in rebellion against the domination of nature over their lives.

In Northeast Hunan

We did not pick quite the nicest part of the year to come to Maotien. The December day was cloudy and chilly when we struck north from the old Red Army revolutionary centre of Pingkiang in northeast Hunan to come 140 kilometres over the mountains into Yoyang county, then down to the village of Maotien by the banks of the Sha river. To get there, we left the main highway and then crossed over the river, after which we drove for 17 kilometres along one of the newer highways until we came to Maotien village. On the highway after leaving the Pingkiang border we had passed through Yuehtien, Huangtien and Kungtien, the "tien" being the word for fields. There are so many hills here that each piece of valley land amongst them takes on considerable economic importance. Maotien village is headquarters of one of the "chu" of Yoyang county, which has four communes with, in all, over 40,000 people in its area. Once a desperately poor region, it has pulled itself up by its own bootstraps to become nationally known. I had heard of it during a meeting in Peking explaining the Cultural Revolution, it simply being said there that it was in a back hill area in Hunan, which naturally excited my curiosity only more. I asked to visit it, and then found out that it was well away in the hills from Yoyang city, which lies by the great Tungting Lake. Yoyang is a place well known through the long history of China. It was not to write my thoughts on climbing Yoyang Tower as did the old poets that I came to this county, however, but rather to see what the hill village folk had done in these years under the inspiration of their Hunan fellow countryman, Mao Tsetung. We had hardly started to come down the highway into their area when change met us. Words in explanation are hardly necessary when one comes to Maotien, so clearly does the picture speak as one looks around. Hills recently barren and eroded are now tea gardens fringed with fruit trees with their trunks whitewashed. Hill terraces remade with precision and new strength, new housing, new schools, new cooperative marketing agencies. Outside one of the schools the students were waiting for a visiting middle school to come in. We had passed their long columns on the road and guessed it would be dusk before they got to Maotien. Youngsters from the county town aged between 11 and 16, they seemed, all very fresh and well scrubbed, unlike the dusty older ones who have come long distances and who bring much color with their red flags and different shades of clothing, packs encased in blue plastic sheeting, and a colored picture of Chairman Mao carried in front of them. The stream of youth was never ending, those on their way north, then those from the north coming down through Yoyang and Pingkiang to Changsha and Shaoshan. Most tried to look as much like the old Red Army as possible, some even copying the uniforms used in the mass opera, "The East is Red", down to red puttees, light-blue uniforms and a red star sewn on their caps. Even those with sore feet looked determined and pushed on rapidly. Certainly it is a great period of toughening up for them all, as well as being a piece of practical education in the human and physical geography of their land.

But to return to Maotien. Its four communes radiate out a distance of 30 li from the centre, the two most distant being in high mountain levels. It seemed best, due to the limited time available, that we concentrate our visits on brigades of the communes nearest the village centre.

A winter evening these days in a country village is an experience. People eat around dusk, then meetings and militia drill start, and the place is full of activity for the next few hours until bedtime.

The "chu" Party secretary, who then was also deputy secretary of Yoyang county's Party committee, was young, short and sturdy — a typical Hunan type. He is a native of Maotien, and an obvious leader. Sitting together over a charcoal brazier, he told me a good deal of the past. Raids of the Japanese imperial army with their burn all, kill all and loot all policy, the Kuomintang terror, then stories of guerillas who fought back, struggle after struggle, until we came down to the last years in which the people have gained the confidence they need to remake their land and their lives. How grain production is now double what it was in 1949 and what are the problems of farming a light, lateritic red soil with hills of white, coarse sand above. How if people only had the spirit to try, there were many sources of income they had not thought of. In addition to hill and forest products, gold dust in the streams, small mineral deposits and so on, which could be dug and marketed.

The first morning in Maotien we spent in looking at the remoulding of the terraced fields which was under way. Previously of all heights and sizes, they were now being made into rectangular terraced lands that will permit mechanisation in the future. In the old days, when a landlord owned many pieces and demanded 60 percent of the tenants' crops, no farmer could even dream of carrying through such a plan. Now all together, with members of other brigades in the commune, a thousand folk get out and really make over their land anew. When they have finished this they have their eye on a spur that runs down between two valleys, with the general idea that they will remove the whole thing. They even talk of removing the village completely from rich valley land to higher levels. In 1959 they built a dam which holds back a reservoir that irrigates several valleys and for two thirds of the year provides enough electricity for the township. The first part of the winter is usually dry, and reservoir waters are low. It is then, though, that most of the bigger fish that breed there are caught. They grow to remarkable sizes and make excellent eating.

We halted for a rest at one farmer's home. His wife, who brought in the tea, was simply but beautifully dressed. Yes, they were getting on very well. In grain they had 500 jin a year for each of the six members of the home. The eldest boy had been accepted as a soldier, while the younger ones were still at school. They got around 100 jin of sweet potato and about the same amount of rough grains also, and then too other necessities, such as tea and cotton. Once it had been said that these hill districts would not grow cotton. It would not flower, the old folk said. For many years after Liberation, cotton needed for padded clothing and bedding quilts was brought in. Now the commune here not only grows what they need but also sells a good deal to the state. Tea is also a new product, and then too the fruit, mainly pears and oranges, which is exported as far as Hongkong. Certainly it is a changed place, with the fields around Maotien village bringing in 1,300 jin a mou a year, as against the one-crop economy of the other days when 300 jin a mou was the best to be hoped for. Now better farming, better fertiliser and better seed selection, as well as better spirit, enables three crops to come off the same land each year, with plans being made for even higher totals yet.

I asked the old farmer about family income before change came to Maotien. He said that the family then never had more than half a jin of grain a day, and that the rest was vegetables or sweet potatoes. "You should have seen our land here then! All tiny plots. Hilltops like a bald man's head. The rest was vegetables or sweet potatoes. We attacked the hills and terraced them, carried up earth to start tea plants growing, orchard trees and cotton, and now even those white quartz sandhills are producing wealth! When the masses take charge, change comes."

Early one morning we went out to watch the commune members in action in field work and study. Later we passed a group of around 50 formed into a special class to be study leaders. Then when passing a primary school we went in and found all learning to recite the Little Red Book there. There is no question that this winter in the countryside is going down in history as the one when the people really got a grasp of just exactly what the quotations from Chairman Mao's works mean to them and their work and future. All over the hillsides could be heard songs like "The East is Red" and "The Helmsman". Everywhere red banners streamed. Houses had framed pictures of Chairman Mao. A very different scene from that in the miserable old days of landlordism. The farmer we had tea with in the morning was a man of 56. He remembered well the Japanese kill and burn expeditions, the bound conscripts of the Kuomintang of whom few if any ever came back home again. The pitiful life of the farmers, and the brutality and callousness of the old ruling class.

"Hunan is Chairman Mao's home province. We ought to do better here than anywhere else, if only in gratitude to him for holding to the revolution and finding the way forward for it," he said. We walked into the big and well appointed marketing and supply agency in the village, finding business brisk. One section is devoted to buying things the people bring in either from their homes or from the hills, articles from wild animal skins and medicinal herbs down to discarded bits and pieces of worn-out household goods.

As we looked around, we saw several groups of Red Guard marchers going single file on paths around the hillsides, come to learn from the communes here, their red flags winding in and out of plantations of young trees like something of old Red Army days, when in the period of the Great Revolution of 1924-27 this area was under the Hunan-Hupeh-Kiangsi border region. It was also said here that the locality could not grow many valuable trees such as spruce, walnuts, and so on, but now planting of such is being done on quite a large scale. At the entertainment given by the commune's concert party there was an act which told of a man who had left Maotien because of famine and had gone to live in Hupeh. After many years his son asked him to come home again. He set out with cotton, rice and other goods on his carrying pole, but when after carrying them for two weeks he arrived home, he was surprised to find that Maotien now had a surplus of all these things, cheaper than in Hupeh.

One easily understands the reason why, in the old days, the "mao" character for wild grasses, "maotsao", was used for the "Mao" of Maotien. Today the "Mao" character has been changed to that of Chairman Mao's name. But when one goes up the valleys and sees the wild grasses waving on parts of hillsides not yet planted with tea bushes, spruce, tung or fruit trees, one realises how pervading the wild grasses must have seemed to the farmers of older days. There are around 40,000 mou of paddy fields in the four communes of Maotien. To this amount has been added the 15,000 mou of terraced fields snatched from the hillsides for wheat, vegetables, cotton or sweet potatoes, and then another 15,000 mou for tea plants and orchard trees, and one begins to get an overall picture of the new economy. Spruce plantations border and crown the terraced hillsides, and tung oil trees are planted by borders and in odd corners. Other hillsides have been converted to orchards. Climbing up a hill ridge now covered with tea bushes in neat rows, we could look down on the fields green with winter wheat, or vegetables, and then up to hill ridges at the rear where spruce plantations were growing well. A morning amongst the brigades of Nanchung Commune showed us from where the mainstream of activity comes. Each and every brigade has its Mao Tsetung Thought study room, bright with red posters, charts, essays and pictures. Each has its study leaders and its study models like, for instance, Tso Teng-yang, who is a woman of 38 with five children. Once thought rather stupid, she has through her study really taken hold of life again. Though her oldest child is but 11, she has arranged her home tasks so that she can take part in the work of the brigade, actually gaining over 2,000 workpoints in the last year. Her husband, who works full time in the fields and man-like, does not feel that things in the house are his concern, gains no more than 3,500 workpoints a year. Then in one of the brigades I met Kuo Shih-chin and his wife, now in their late fifties. They are prime foresters and pig-raising experts, giving their all for the commune. Their story was met by many others, folk who gave the best room in their house for a study room, putting out their strength without limit as the desire to do more for the others came to them. Everyone is trying to find new ways of helping others, there being a wealth of examples. It always seems that it is the poorest place that becomes the most outstanding the quickest. Maotien is a good example, and even in such a generally poor place it is the once poorest unit which does best. The sour soil of Janfang Brigade was the poorest in Maotien. 183 families, 806 people in all, till 763 mou of paddy and 120 mou of dry land there. At the end of 1966 there were 11 Party members, and 30 of the Communist Youth League. 635 of them took part in the work of the brigade, and 550 were enrolled in classes for the study of Chairman Mao's works. 180 families had Chairman Mao's picture. There were then 300 copies of Chairman Mao's works in the brigade, and 900 copies of his three short essays: "Serve the People", "In Memory of Norman Bethune" and "The Foolish Old Man Who Removed the Mountains". There were eight meeting rooms and 165 study activists. Methods of working the soil and in fertiliser have brought good results, so that the brigade was able to get as much as 1,280 jin of grain a mou as against the 300 of poorer days. Members came off relief grain for the first time in 1965, and by then were also self-sufficient in cotton. Everyone now has all the cotton needed for padded clothing. As a matter of fact, the padded clothing of the Maotien farmers must be considerably above the average for even city folk. Youngsters feel like throwing some of it off on a warm winter's day, as the weather became after a day or two, following the cold snap from the north which had welcomed us here. Many too would prefer the good bare feet to the rubber sports shoe on fine days. But now they feel they must look their best, and for the moment that means clothes for formerly poor people.

One warm afternoon, however, we went up one of the side valleys to where remoulding of terraces was being done. There was a row of rubber sports shoes neatly arranged along a path beside, and the younger workers were stepping lightly and freely without them. A 15-year-old actually seemed to be flying, his quick feet hardly seeming to touch the ground as he returned with empty baskets and his carrying pole to get more. In the penetrating cold of a wet Hunan day in winter however, or on a winter's frosty morning, socks and water-tight shoes are real comfort, which everyone now has.

In the headquarters of Nanchung Commune to which 12 brigades as well as a forest farm belong, we found a staff of 14, the duties of each being to act as the connecting link between the brigades, collect their statistics, arrange for mutual help, and so on. One cadre for each brigade. Brigade cadres work along with other members. The commune cadres stick to their travel and office work, and do practical work only in rush seasons. Three of them are girls, and are local middle-school graduates.

One may see discarded around houses in Maotien the old stone-cut tubs and stone fixtures for husking rice. A brigade tractor hitched up to a small rice mill now does the task swiftly and efficiently. A new diesel powered rice mill is now being put up in Maotien village, able to handle much more. Mechanisation will not halt now. People are used to electric lighting already. The truck, the tractor, the rice mill, the mechanised oil press come to even so remote a spot as the hill village of Maotien, where once there was so little to mitigate the sheer bitterness of a deadeningly monotonous fight against tyrants, drought, flood, and pestilence. The interchange of youth between town and country, the cinema and radio, all bring in new ideas. Reinforced concrete bridges make highways more permanent. Maotien youth hikes six days and gets to Shaoshan to see Chairman Mao's old home. There he meets other young folk from all over China. Into Maotien, now made famous because of its successes, hike students from Changsha and Yoyang, staying a few days, usually being able to give concert performances in the evenings. I met a group of them in a hillside village. They were reading chapters of a new novel to the older villagers around their homes. The present stage is certainly bringing a great merging of town and country in a new way.

It is not so far to Hsiangsse Commune from Maotien. Only nine kilometres. But the way lies over a range of mountains through which the commune members, using a ton and a half of explosive most of which they made themselves, blasted a road a couple of winters ago. It not only connects the commune with Maotien, but also with another highway that leads into Tungcheng county of Hupeh province over its border. From the range summit where one crosses over, a wonderful view of each valley can be obtained.

Hsiangsse Commune has newly built offices, a meeting hall and another fine view — across the valley to the bold outlines of Hsiangsse mountain beyond, the slopes of which are a forestry farm. We called in on several of the 11 brigades which till the 11,500 mou of valley land and 1,600 mou of hillsides, besides carrying out small mining ventures and planting hills with spruce and tea bushes. Hard to get at, this commune area was once desperately poor. Even many landlords and rich peasants of the past did not live nearly so well as do the commune members of today. Eighty percent of the people however had been poor peasants who had a truly miserable livelihood, for not much more than 200 jin a mou was ever harvested. They had cut all the timber on the hills to burn charcoal, and for them each year had been poorer than the last.

With the new day there came a sharp turn for the better. With their three-crop economy they now average around 900 jin of grain a mou. They have dug 850 reservoirs, big and small. One of these is quite a large-scale one, the others mainly ponds. Ten thousand mou of their paddy fields can now be irrigated automatically. We walked through a good spruce forest which covered one hill, a few years ago devoid of any vegetation at all, then up others where tea bushes were growing well. We ate apples, pears and oranges which had been grown here, and saw a whole hillside covered with chestnuts, which were coming along well. Before, no walnuts were grown; now those planted eight years ago are already starting to bear. It is something for a people to get together as they have done here and plant eight million trees of economic value and then see that they grow to bearing.

As in the terraced valley lands around Maotien, the paddy field is being remoulded this winter. As some of the hills are steeper, terrace walls on upper levels are higher, many stone faced, and a good ten feet high. Down in the valley bottom, there is another problem which has had to be met. Around 2,000 mou of the paddy fields became muddy to such a depth that they were not easily workable. Indeed, one farm lad was drowned in them. The problem has been solved by taking off the earth necessary for cropping during the slack season of winter, then making a base of stone and sand below, finally just putting the whole field back on a solid foundation. Cooperation and the right spirit has enabled this to be done in these past few years. Opposite the commune offices, a hill was being levelled to make a place for a new grain store. "No, while we have hills we shall not give an inch of ground that can grow crops for buildings. Moreover, we plan to move the old homes which still stand on such land back to the hills," they say.

Too much water, too little water. Even amongst these hills there is this problem. Drainage ditches must take off water that might drown rice seedlings. Five diesel engine operated pumps come into operation if paddy field water is not enough, and swiftly flood where necessary.

Everywhere the strong, clear ideas of Mao Tsetung are being taken down to mass level in no uncertain way. At one home, a boy of six recited for me the whole of the essay "Serve the People". Hands in pockets, he seemed to do it effortlessly. Then when we asked how he put it to practice, he pulled out some castor oil plant beans from his pocket and said, "I collect these . . . and I swept the kitchen for the old woman who lives near us . . . and I minded the babies . . . and . . . and . . . I collected castor oil beans." Then with a radiant smile he scampered off. As in the brigades of Nanchung Commune, each of these in Hsiangsse has stories of folk who have given their all to others. But all well realise that it will be through their collective work that they can give most. Their studies teach them that. Houses down the valley road have big red wall murals with gold lettering on them of quotations from Chairman Mao's works. Everyone knows the current songs of the day. The movement is like a strong wind blowing through an old countryside, bringing understanding and the urge for change, along with the determination not to bend before imperialism or revisionism in any shape or form.

On the way back to Maotien, we stopped for a while at a part-work, part-study agricultural middle school newly built on the side of a hill, where there is ample space around for practical work in planting many kinds of trees, and making many new terraces. Most of the students were off on a march to the Chingkangshan mountains, the old revolutionary base, a gathering point for most of the middle-school students of central China this winter, after they have first visited Shaoshan. Those who remained were doing practical work helping to bring in materials for school building construction. After graduation, students will go straight into commune brigades, able at once to take part in practical tasks, and to carry what they have learnt on to others. First of all, they learn the lesson, "What do we live for?" Getting that settled in their minds, they then go ahead.

All good things come to an end. The five days around Maotien too soon came to a close. On one of the last evenings we again sat over a brazier of charcoal, and the local leader summed up some of the things that had been accomplished. How even in 1966, a rich harvest year, there had been many difficulties to overcome. A late snow in the spring which froze many shoots. A deluge in June that flooded and brought much sand down from the hills. Then a four months' drought at the end of the year which would have been serious but for the 380 wells which had been sunk, the 44 reservoirs, and 6,500 pools dug.

We talked of people's livelihood, and of how the old tung oil lamp with its dim light had now been replaced by electric lights in the four communes. How everyone had mosquito nets and bedding quilts, enamel basins, good porcelain and what not, when before such things were for landlords only. Very touching were the stories of old men who refused to be laid off but who kept on working and getting good results. One of 84 years who kept up with the youngsters on earth shifting. Then another strong old one with two hefty sons, who always demanded the heaviest work. He was 72 when he first became a labor hero, is 76 now and still working. Then too, of things people are doing for each other. Taking in old folk who have no dependents, giving blood to the sick who need it in hospital. The old man Hsueh Heng-lin who put his arms around the necks of two cows the other members wanted to slaughter, saying, "I will take these and look after them. They will breed. We must have more animal power in the days to come." He is 72 now, and for the past eight years has put his whole energy into looking after these cows and the calves they have had, so that everyone is grateful to him. With the new work that has come to be done, the cattle have been essential so that he feels he has given much strength to his fellows. The idea of not stopping doing things while any health remains is firmly embedded here. Local stories of instances are legion. There are five health clinics in the Maotien district with a staff of 84. Most of the sicknesses that were prevalent have now been pretty well cleared out.

We talked for a long time into the evening about the new highways that have been made, the mountainsides that have been turned green again, the way the whole district goes to school and studies the road forward, the production and use of fertiliser, and of how all the old images in people's homes and in wayside shrines, ancestral temples and so on have been discarded, and the weight of superstition removed from the minds of at least the whole new generation.

On our last day we paid a visit to the third of the four Maotien communes. It takes "Maotien" for its name, and has 11 brigades. Its conditions are much the same as those of the two already described, being notable in addition, however, for its handicraft industry. In its metalworking shops it turns out 185 kinds of articles for daily use, mainly farm tools and kitchen utensils. It also produces a rubber-tyred handcart with a sturdy hardwood frame, then a range of bamboo articles in everyday use on the farm and in the home. The big problem here is the control of the Sha river, which when it floods covers much of the valley land. This river has been dyked, but there are many problems concerning it still to be met. More forestry in the hills, a new course for the river to be dug so as to straighten it out, a control dam in the hills, sand dredging and so on are all being worked on. We saw a new road being made into the mountains, and men carrying up big reinforced concrete pipes to a small power and pumping project in the hills. Seven men to each pipe of 700 jin. Few people around the world have realised the incredible effort that has gone into the remaking of the Chinese countryside in these years since Liberation.

There is much to be done yet in Maotien, many problems to be solved. The old methods of house heating in winter, for instance, make for too much smoke in the home, which is not good for the people's eyes. New sources of fuel will eventually have to be found. Still more afforestation has to be done on upper hill levels in particular. The further completion of Hunan's great resources for hydro-electric power, and extension of the power grid into the hill counties will, after other major problems have been settled in the course of not too long a time, solve the problem of smoke in the homes, and so also that of afforestation. At present there is a great contradiction still between the gatherers of fuel and the planters of trees, which the addition of some other fuels and later the introduction of the more common electric heating appliances in the home will eventually erase.

More mechanisation too will come to the villages and to the land. There is little doubt, however, that all of these problems will be solved and that the people who have done so much already will together go on to do things on a still grander scale. The answer to each and every problem is the way the people look at it. For the rest, to be enjoyed even if not spoken much of, there were all the simple things of Maotien — the sight of children competing with whipping tops, the six workers in the oil press driving wedges in the time-honored old way, yet aware that mechanisation of their task was just around the corner. The womenfolk with laughing fat babies. The feet of youth stepping lightly, ready to tackle any new long march into the future with the same disregard for self as their fathers had. Maotien, a real Tachai of Hunan, was good to have visited.

Pingkiang

We had passed through Pingkiang in northeast Hunan and had a meal and a rest in its county seat on our motor trip from Changsha to Yoyang. Then it was clear but cold. A week later when we returned there was a warm southern glow which covered the mass of hills and brought a light blue haze, with rain starting to fall on the last hour of our journey. The long lines of youth marchers could be relatively easily distinguished as to place of origin. Those from local counties around about would have children of all sizes as well as teachers, with some of the bigger ones taking along a bit of extra camping equipment on carrying poles. Hunan, Kiangsi and Cantonese students from middle or upper schools would have oiled paper umbrellas of a deep red. Those from north Hupeh, yellow oiled cloth ones. Northern students again are used to a long dry winter, and after having come a very long way usually travelled light and fast with small packs. They were at a disadvantage with the southerners in footwear, having cloth shoes and socks, while the southerners often went barefoot or in straw sandals. The second time we came into Pingkiang, the town had turned out to welcome home the 900 youngsters who had gone to Peking to see Chairman Mao and who had returned together, full of their adventure and the glory of achievement.

It is good that the revolutionary youth of Pingkiang carries on the traditions of the county. In the late 'twenties and early 'thirties, when the Hunan-Hupeh-Kiangsi Border Government had its headquarters in Mufushan in the northeast of the county, there were some 600,000 people in Pingkiang. Then came the Kuomintang suppression with its kill all, loot all and burn all policy. Whole hill areas were depopulated, 120,000 people known to have lost their lives, while many more fled to other parts of the country. At the time of Liberation the population was something over 400,000; in 1966 it was 638,000. Slowly the hill areas are reviving. Better irrigation and better crop yields have helped to fill up the villages in the richer portions. The county has an area of 6,978,000 mou, of which 4,800,000 are mountainous. There are 770,000 mou of cropping land, around 600,000 of which can be used for paddy fields by the 54 communes which now produce over 400 million jin of grain a year. Also produced are 20,000 dan of tea (one "dan" = 100 jin or 50 kilograms). Other major production items are spruce timber, bamboo, tea oil and medicinal plants — especially the wood of a tree called the "Bai", peculiar to this locality.

The problem of irrigation was one that faced the people after their new organisation. There was a long history of crops being destroyed by drought, and indeed had it not been for the work already done there would have been a poor result in 1966, which saw three months without rain in the autumn. The main river of Pingkiang is the Milo, which runs into Tungting Lake. It is famous in China as being the one in which Chu Yuan, the statesman of Chu in the Warring States period of the 5th century B.C., is said to have drowned himself. Then there is the Changkiang which has waters so calm and translucent that they gave the name to the county, the "Ping" in Pingkiang meaning in this case peaceful or calm. The problem was how to raise the waters of these and other rivers so that they would irrigate the dry lands above. Work already done on a plan due to be completed by 1969 includes the installation of 365 turbine pumps. These have been set up in groups by low dams already built. At present they help a great deal to give the county its 270,000 mou of newly irrigated paddy. They also already give the county 2,000 kws of power for operating 350 small rice mills and other mechanisation projects. By the completion of the plan there will be 8,000 kws from this source, giving power to 2,000 small commune enterprises. The method chosen is economical. Everything is made in the province and the machinery is relatively simple. Maintenance is easy and the commune members can look at the task with confidence, knowing that they can carry it through. By 1969, there will be 220 pumping stations, each with 20 pumps. This will make a very basic contribution to the solving of the problem of better livelihood.

We went out one morning to see one of these groups in action. After about an hour's drive from the city, finally cutting across some camellia-studded hills — camellias in full white blossom, petals falling on the bright red earth below — we came to one of the middle reaches of the Milo river over which a 200-metre dam had been thrown, diverting most of the water into a canal ripped through a range of hills on the opposite bank. By the side of the river where we started to cross was one battery of little turbine pumps, which when put into operation threw water up into the canal above. There were four of them and they were installed vertically. Then we walked a mile or so from the intake of the canal which takes the major portion of the river water through the cut in the hills to a combined power and pumping station. Here the turbine pumps are installed horizontally. Both pumping and power systems can be run at the same time or separately, just as the need arises. Pumping is essential in August, September and October for the late rice crop, and the water at that time is thrown up 15 metres to a hillside canal system which irrigates 10,000 mou. For most of the rest of the year, power is more important. What strikes one is the economical way the whole project has been done, all with resources of the commune brigades around. Then the careful use of the power produced. Though it is only around 250 kws, yet it can spare 51 kws for the little complex nearby which operates small-scale flour milling, rice milling, oil pressing, pig fodder preparation and cotton carding. The longest line of folk waiting with their baskets was at the rice milling unit. The cost of milling 100 jin is 30 fen. This would take a farmer a long day's work to husk by manual labor. For his day's work in the commune he would get 70 fen to one yuan. It is obviously better then to have the youngsters bring in the rice to the complex and have it done so swiftly and well there. In addition to its work in the countryside, the project supplies power to the city for a repair shop, a winery and, in season, a tea-curing plant. At night it gives lighting to Pingkiang city. The project, by taking off the Milo river waters, cuts off a big bend, shortening its flow down the valley by 30 li. The next stage of the project entails diverting the whole of the Milo river waters into the new canal and building a lock for rafts and boats. At present enough water is left in the old bed to take timber and bamboo rafts or small boats, as they come down. A runoff from the main canal has been converted to be a testing place for various sizes and models of turbine pumps. For these are just one of the new tools the city has been able to give the countryside, and though it has already been proved an immense success, there are still improvements which can be made and new models provided for various peculiar situations.

On our way back through the hills from the project we met five youngsters of about 15 on the path, long-march packs on their backs and a smile of triumph on their faces. They had been all the way to Peking and were returning to tell their people all about it. The pumping project leader who came with us had many good stories of construction. The dam was built in the three winter months, and the 300 men of one brigade who did the job had to work in cold water with bare feet most of the time. The whole project, started at the end of 1964, was finished in seven months — on May 22nd, 1965. "If we say 'Serve the people', then this is our way," they said, and got right down to the job. Chu Yuan, the Warring States poet, drowned himself in the Milo river in despair. Tu Fu, the Tang poet, died in sickness and melancholy near it 1,000 years later. It took another millennium to produce a people's leader in the region around these streams that flow into Tungting Lake. Today, Mao Tsetung, poet and rebel, is certainly in the hearts of the people of the countryside.

Amongst the camellia bushes we saw a good number of commune youth levelling off old graves, the remains from which are reburied in places where they will not interfere with production for the living. To have been able to reach this stage in the old countryside means much. Pingkiang in some ancient time was called Lo Tse Kuo, the state of Lo. But that was a very long time ago. Now it has a pleasant county seat that is set on hills with clean concrete paved streets and big camphor trees around. Shops contain almost everything one can get in the big cities, and in the way of varied foods a good deal more than most big centres can offer. "Long Marchers" coming down from the north like to stay here for a few days for rest and study before going onwards.

In Pingkiang we talked with a Red Guard of early revolutionary days. Huang Tu-fang, now 65, short, active, and with a heavily scarred face, the result of just one of the three wounds he received when fighting on the side of the people in the struggle around Pingkiang from 1926 to 1939. In 1926, he and eight others in his family joined the revolution. He himself was then 15. There came early organisation, many mistakes, defeats and then victories. The details as he saw them in 1927-28 were fascinating. He went to Chingkangshan with Chairman Mao but later was sent back to carry on activities in Pingkiang, mainly in the Mufushan region. In 1935 the regular troops went off to join in the Long March northwards, and guerillas were left. These became the regular troops that in 1938 went to make up the New Fourth Army. Again he was left to carry on the local struggle. After the Chiayi Incident in Hunan in 1939, however, the Kuomintang literally stuffed the area with troops, carrying out their policy of devastation in guerilla-held areas so that it was not possible to live there, for after burning the homes and forests, draining fish ponds and breaking any irrigation work, they would even shoot at anything moving. Huang and his comrades were told to disperse, each one carrying on his activities, ready to come together later. He went to Kiangsi and worked as a farmhand then, until Liberation in 1949 when he could return to Hunan and renew connections with comrades and those of his family who had come through the wars. He still takes active part in revolutionary work. Still thinks of the old fights and analyses the causes of victory or defeat. How each directive that came from Mao Tsetung would be correct and to the point. How vacillation brought troubles. How the Kuomintang would kill the people but not stand up to the Japanese. All this and much more he goes over and over again with old comrades, and then too with the younger ones of a new day.

That the spirit of the old revolutionaries is still alive and active was shown in the autumn of 1966. In one of the communes on the slopes of Mufushan a forest fire became a serious threat and endangered a big stand of pine on the other side of the commune. The youngsters of the commune took off and fought the fire in the most strategic place, despite the hazards. Eleven of them were cut off and lost their lives. The youth of China is not afraid to die these days, when there is a cause to fight for.

It is 35 kilometres from Pingkiang city to Chiayi. It was here that in July 1937 the old Liberated Areas set up an office, for their guerilla troops were in strength the country around. In 1938, when guerilla fighters were incorporated into the New Fourth Army and moved away, work in the countryside continued and a New Fourth Army office was left. On June 12th, 1939, because the Communist cadres were paying due attention to popular front rules, the Kuomintang soldiers were allowed to pass in the usual way. That particular day, however, under orders from their general, Yang Sen, they suddenly halted and surrounded the New Fourth Army office where six cadres led by Tu Cheng-kun were working. A Kuomintang aid de camp came in and Tu walked with him to the front door of the old temple then maintained as an office. The Kuomintang opened fire and Tu was killed. The others were captured. One Wu Yueh was executed in public, shouting slogans as he was put before the firing squad: "Down with Japanese imperialism! Death to traitors who sell their country! Long live the liberation of the Chinese people! Long live the Communist Party and Chairman Mao!"

The Kuomintang did not attempt any more public executions after that, but buried the remaining four captives alive at the foot of what is the Martyrs' Memorial. The widow of Tu, who escaped along with her two-year-old son, walked up there with us. She is a quiet woman of 59. Her son is a cadre in the county government with a growing family so that she has now three grandchildren to comfort her. After we had seen the memorial, she led us down to an old folks' home below. Most of the inmates were old women, survivors from the wars, "bandits' wives", as the Kuomintang called them. They have no families and have made up a family of their own in a pleasant building, still doing what they can to support themselves. A group of Peking University students were visiting when we were. They had put wreaths on the memorial and were paying respects to Tu's widow. The Fire God Temple, which was once the office of the New Fourth Army, has disappeared with the years.

We went down the village street to see another pumping and power station similar to that at Hungtsa. This was further upstream on the Milo river and needed but a 90-metre dam. With a 1.8-metre head, and in spite of low water, the volume was still sufficient to operate five turbine pumps which could throw water up nine metres and so irrigate 4,000 mou of paddy, as well as operate a good assortment of processing mills. The cotton carding unit here was quite large. There was also a noodle-making machine, which turned out noodles for commune folk at five fen a jin. Going to look at this piece of work, we were joined by a group of Wuhan students, living in the district offices nearby, and by a bevy of children, so the place was full of songs and laughter as we went around. On the way back to Pingkiang we stopped at another unit situated on a little tributary of the Milo. It had two pump turbines, which also operated a rice mill and a 5-kw. generator for local lighting. Here the water head was lower than that on the Chiayi installation, only 1.7 metres. So today has this revolutionary bit of farm machinery, the little pump turbine, spread like wildfire over north Hunan. Easy to instal, cheap to buy, it so effortlessly does the work that was a burden to many. Just one of the good things new to the countryside that the sacrifices made by the older generation have brought to the people.

In the village we looked at some of the old crafts and saw with pleasure the popcorn-making machine that heats the corn in a little container revolving over a charcoal fire. And then the old man operating the machine takes the lid off, lets the contents explode with a terrific bang into a sack, much to the delight of the younger generation waiting expectantly around. The village was very clean and bright with slogans in red and gold lettering on newly whitewashed walls, as will be seen everywhere in rural China this year end of 1966.

We spent an evening in Pingkiang looking at the lantern slide exhibition arranged for propaganda work on the harnessing of the Milo river and the use of the pump turbine. Amongst the other guests were a group of students from Hunan Agricultural University, taking the opportunity of marching to see advances being made in each and every county. Their books will certainly be more meaningful to them when they start in with them again.

Some of the bigger pump turbine stations are those on the lower reaches of the Milo river as it flows down to the town of Milo west of the county. We visited two of these sites, one under construction at Huangtan, and the other at Chinchungkou still further downstream.

At Huangtan, some 700 members of Wukou Commune were building a dam across the river, and a channel to take the pump turbines. They were ripping down rock from the hillsides and carrying huge chunks of it downhill to the job, with relays of workers and carrying poles. Ten pump turbines were being installed here. The work has been going for a month now, and the members expect to get it done and operating by the spring of 1967. It will give some 650 kws of power. Then further down river we came to the completed Chinchungkou project which throws water 45 metres up a hillside and supplies canals that irrigate 80,000 mou of paddy fields. It was started in September 1965 and finished by members of Fengkung Commune ten months later. It has 22 pump turbines, most used solely for pumping, there being but 250 kws of power generated here to supply power for the commune productive enterprises by day and lighting by night. A shipping lock runs through the dam. The dam across the river is 167 metres long. Like all dams on these pump turbine projects, the high water simply flows over its top. The big thing about the Chinchungkou installation is the amount of water it can hoist to run around hillside fields, over reinforced concrete aqueducts, and out onto land that was once subject to every drought that came along. The powerhouse, service buildings and housing for the various little mills make quite a new village, a popular halting station for student marchers. One such school we inquired from had been on the road for nine days, having made a big circle through the hinterland country. It would still be several days before the students returned home.

We climbed up a hillside above the project and admired the work done, the long tunnels made through some of the hills there to take the canals, and the way canal sides were being planted with trees. It was very impressive to see the winding canals so full of water flowing gaily and swiftly. When the whole Milo project is finished and all rapids have been done away with, it will be possible to bring relatively large boats through what will be a series of quiet lakes almost up to Pingkiang city. It is planned to plant bamboo on both sides of the river, making each reach between the dams beautiful in a new way. Actually, the whole area is a lovely one from the point of view of scenery, forests, hill and pellucid stream blending harmoniously.

We went on down river from the project. A teachers' training college was building a branch school on a piece of once waste hillside. Further along we came to the tea plantation of the county, also occupying a large area of what was once waste land. It takes five years for tea bushes to come into full production here. The three-year-old bushes were doing well and the youngsters who were operating the farm were youth from the cities of Hsiangtan and elsewhere come back to the hinterland to open up such lands. They all seemed to be thriving on the toughening up they are getting on the new plantation, for in their work they have a definite aim — to create something where there was nothing before except a continuing process of desiccation and denudation.

A great amount of new roading has been done in these recent years in Pingkiang. It is now possible for trucks to get to almost every commune in the county. The tractor with one or two trailers carrying away produce is now a familiar sight on back roads. Some of the roads made through back area have required immense work, carving their way through rough country with deep cuttings through the hills. The thing that strikes one about Pingkiang is the immense work that has already been done in all areas in these years, basic work that will permit so much more to be completed in the future. Many little pictures rise in one's mind as one thinks back over what has been seen in the days spent in Pingkiang. The sturdy city lad who had joined in with commune farmers carrying down rock in Huangtan. Shirt-front open, barefoot, he swung along with the seven others, moving in their rhythm. The eagerness in the face of the girl when asked how the new rice milling helped her. "See, the husks are ground to powder! It would take us a long time to do all that! Take it back home and mix it with slops and the pigs will eat it greedily!"

The last of the pump turbine installations we went to see in Pingkiang was not far away from the city. It cuts in across the hills from the Changsha highway, over a great stretch of waste hilltops which for centuries have been used as grave mounds, and then drops down to the Milo river again. Here at Yenchiatan, a 123-metre-long, 2.7-metre-high dam has been thrown across the river, on the south side of which is an installation in which four sets of turbines do pumping and operate commune processing machinery. Then there is a shipping lock, and one crosses over the dam on a bridge to where six sets of turbines pump water for the town water supply and also help with the town electricity. They pump water up a 28-metre hill. Some of it goes to the town reservoir, and the rest around hillsides in canals, irrigating 9,000 mou of paddy fields and 3,000 mou of reclaimed hilltop land. A feature about the dam is that it is mainly composed of the gravestones of the centuries, the pompous tablets erected by past officials to their own glory, and such. The graves themselves are being taken away and the waste area converted to tea plantations. A bunch of "Long Marchers" from Chengtu in Szechuan had notebooks out and were studying the dam and turbines with deep interest. An old pagoda on a hilltop nearby cast its reflection meditatively into the clear dam waters. One of the new water turbine pump experts educated by installing and operating water turbine pumps, just as Red Army generals were educated by fighting, was busy on the installation of a new unit. It was another pleasant memory to take away, as we sped down the highway out of Pingkiang county to Changsha.

The stream of marchers had increased in the two weeks we had been in northeast Hunan. A light rain was falling, but the stream never stopped. I loved the pictures presented. One group had green plastic raincoats. The next blue, but most had either an umbrella or just a strip of colorful plastic around their bedding pack. One boy with a fine keen face, well patched light-blue clothing and bare feet, carried the flag at the head of his group and really looked like some old Red Army fighter all over again. Our car pulled onto the side of the road to allow a line of trucks to pass. From under one big Cantonese umbrella looked up two of the sweetest faces we had seen in a very long time — girls of about 15, barefoot also, packs carried jauntily, and smiles that lit the way.

Hunan 1970

We now take a leap into time, coming right up to the summer of 1970 and back in Hunan again.

> One plane wing dips;
> Chu-tze-chou, the Isle
> of Oranges, lies below,
> and we come down to the Changsha
> where a farm boy grew
> to manhood, bringing such change
> that today the whole world
> rocks under its impact.

So we came to the go-ahead Hunan capital city of Changsha one early summer's morning, 23 of us, members of Afro-Asian and other international organisations in Peking, to study together some of the early struggles of the Chinese Revolution.

About Hunan

For the benefit of those of us who were not familiar with this southwest China province our host from the provincial Revolutionary Committee, set up in April 1968, explained that Hunan now had a population of over 38 million. About one fifth of its area, he explained, is arable land, on which 3,200 communes with 45,000 production brigades produce the food and cotton necessary to support a rapidly growing industrialisation. On being asked how Mao Tsetung Thought had taken hold of the people, he replied that it now — especially in the last four years — had indeed struck deeply into daily life everywhere. No fewer than eight million copies of the works of Chairman Mao have been printed and circulated in the province, while 31 million Little Red Books of quotations have been produced and distributed in addition. Smaller pamphlets of his three short, most-read essays and such other popular works are in every hand. Propaganda groups include 750,000 activists in Mao Tsetung Thought.

With theory put into practice, it can be said that the rise in public health work has been positively phenomenal. Eighty-five percent of the production brigades have instituted the cooperative health scheme, and all brigades now have "barefoot" doctors who are able to take care of common sicknesses. Since education has been given over to worker and peasant leadership, double the number of children are in primary and middle schools as there were in 1965. Every brigade has its own primary school, and all communes operate their own middle schools. Besides its predominantly Han population, Hunan has also Yao, Tung, Miao, Tu as well as other minority nationality peoples who today join eagerly in the surge forward.

Changsha

Changsha and its industrial satellite town of Chuchow are swiftly being industrialised, factory production in the first quarter of 1970 exceeding that of the last quarter of 1969 by 45 percent. Then out on the land, the problem of bringing in new paddy fields and increasing the area that will grow rice has been met well. In 1969 alone, throughout the province no fewer than 574,000 water conservancy works have been undertaken, and 360 million cubic metres of earth has been moved to make them possible. Though Hunan has a magnificent inland waterway transport system, that of the highways has not been neglected either. From the products of Hunan's steel industry, serviceable trucks are being made to render the road transport system more self-sufficient. This will perhaps be enough for a general outline to a very big subject. To get along with the story, we did not rest long in the guest house, but were soon out visiting places of revolutionary interest around the city, the first being Chingshuitang.

Chingshuitang

Chingshuitang means "clear water pool" in English. There is a big fish pond there that gives its name to the locality. When I first visited the place during the mid-'fifties it was still a very humble affair in the suburbs of the city. Standing amongst its vegetable gardens, it had once housed the headquarters of the Communist Party of Hunan. Formerly a barren area amid many old grave mounds, the surroundings had been built in a good deal even by the time of that visit. Then, an old vegetable gardener neighbor had come in and told us how he had known Chairman Mao when he lived here as a young, energetic revolutionary of a very revolutionary period. Now the old man had passed on. The house where Chairman Mao lived and worked has been repaired. The vegetable gardens have been improved, and farmers were tending almost incredibly neat rows of tomatoes and other vegetables. But the biggest change was at the entrance out by the main street where a colossal statue of Chairman Mao now stands, backed by flag poles from which red banners fly. Across the pond which reflects its face is a big new building, constructed to house a historic exhibition which in due time will be opened.

Inside the historic Party headquarters the old furniture was in place and things were very much as they had originally been. A photograph of Chairman Mao's first wife, Yang Kai-hui, and their two children was on the wall. The eldest of the two little boys, Mao An-ying, was to die later in the revolution, as a soldier fighting in Korea.

The girl museum guide told how in the 1922-23 period Chairman Mao had been active in both the trade union and youth movements. How he went from here to Anyuan and how he urged the workers to strike when Liu Shao-chi thought they were too immature and tried to halt any such action. The Anyuan workers, however, followed Chairman Mao's directive and gained what was really at that time an earth-shaking victory for Chinese labor. She told how Yang Kai-hui had been a very loyal and able comrade to Chairman Mao all through the years until 1930 when she was arrested by the warlord Ho Chien, tortured and then murdered.

A Revolutionary Centre

A quiet little house, this. Yet one from which so much that mattered went out. There came from it the beginning of the great peasant revolt of Hunan. Lu Tung-sung was sent out from here to Hengyang and its environs where 100,000 peasants were organised, with the first headquarters of the peasant movement at Hengshan. Kuo Liang was sent out to lead railway workers on the Hankow-Canton railway in support of the great railway strike. From here too, a workers' college was planned. Contacts were maintained with every progressive force in Changsha, so that this quiet little country cottage became a hive of activity. Workers at that time were often pessimistic about their lot.

"Gung" (工) is the character for work, they would say. But put your head outside it, and the character changes to "tu" for earth (土). In other words, we die and are buried. But Chairman Mao laughed and said that was not the case. Put the characters for "gung ren" (工人), or worker, together and you get "tien" (天) or heaven, the worker with head up to the heavens and feet solidly on the earth. In other words, he is master of the situation. He can overthrow the mountains that hold him down and create a new world.

Workers' College

We went to see Workers' College, which too has been beautifully restored. It operated in 1921-22, was suppressed but opened up under another name and went on until the Great Revolution of 1924-27, when its staff and students all went off to join in the fray. It was not big, never exceeding 200 students, yet amongst its graduates are six famous martyrs who gave their lives gloriously for the revolution. Mao Tse-min, a brother of Chairman Mao, was one of them. Hsia Ming-han another. His poem written before his execution is well known in China today. It runs:

> Execution, after all
> a small matter! The big thing
> to believe in the truth!
> Just kill me, Hsia Ming-han,
> but know
> there will be many
> to follow me.

As principal of this college, Chairman Mao was able to put into practice his ideas about how education for the task he had in hand should go — lively and vigorous, with the students taking a full part. His aim was to build a leadership for the worker-peasant united front. The general ideas of Marxism were brought out in such a way that they would come home to everyone, for all knew well it was the mass of the peasants who grew the food the upper class gorged themselves on, and it was these peasants who died of starvation. That those who wove cloth often did not have enough clothing to keep out the cold in the bitterness of winter. The essential role of the poor and lower-middle peasant in the Chinese revolution was studied and discussed. All of this was tied in with the problem of how to overthrow imperialism and the reactionary warlord regime. How to transform education, literature and art so that they would serve the people. The magazine the college published was called "New Times" and Chairman Mao wrote an editorial in its first number on "Foreign Powers, Warlords and Revolution". In it, he called upon the people to rise and overthrow the reaction. Little wonder that the local warlord, a certain Tsao, closed the college down in 1923, though he was unable to prevent its being set up with renewed vigor elsewhere under the name of "Hsiangkiang Middle School".

Our Guide

Our guide at the restored buildings of the college was a Hunan lass who certainly knew her job. In the courtyard outside, a big rosebush spread its color. Sunlight shone through the grapevine trellis making patterns on the ground outside the open doors. Yes, life is warmth, color and light and a striving always for these. Not to revolt when revolt is required is not to be true to the best one knows. The people she talked about — so many of them have paid the price. Ho Shu-heng, who worked with Chairman Mao to lead the work of the college, was killed in battle at Changting in Fukien in 1935. The list of its graduates who have given their all is long. To really serve the people is not an easy thing.

First Normal School

We spent a whole afternoon at the reconstructed First Normal School, in which Chairman Mao was a student, then teacher. This school was one which had been set up by the Hunan provincial government for the training of primary-school teachers. Chairman Mao passed the entrance exam and enrolled as a student when he was a studious country boy, a great reader, and already very patriotic and dissatisfied with things as they were in China. There had been the overthrow of the Manchus in 1911, and increasingly youth felt that new ways had to be found to meet new situations. He was a student for five and a half years. In 1918 and again in 1919 he went to Peking with the object of connecting up the Hunan youth movement with that in Peking. Returning to Changsha, he became. principal of the primary school attached to the normal college, a position he held until the middle of 1921, when he went to Shanghai to attend the First Communist Party Congress. When he came back he taught one of the classes in the normal college until he set up in Chingshuitang, thereafter putting the whole of his energies into Party work.

Cold Bath Daily

Many stories about Chairman Mao are current at the First Normal School, for though the old buildings were burnt by the Kuomintang in the anti-Japanese War of Resistance and the old staff scattered, yet the stories remained. We went through the whole establishment, an exact replica of the old one, looking at the places where Chairman Mao had worked or lived, right on to the big well in the back courtyard where he took a cold sluice-down every day in all seasons, for he was a great believer in physical culture. As we talked and looked, the sound of singing from the classrooms came in. So full of spirit and with so great a revolutionary quality, its emotional impact struck one strongly. For here are the results of revolution. Not the old droning classes memorising and memorising, dulling the minds of students with repetition drilling in the teaching of the old order, but here something with the lid taken off, and a new potential showing itself.

To Shaoshan

It was a magnificent summer's morning when we went across country to Shaoshan, the birthplace of Chairman Mao and where he spent his first 16 years. People were out transplanting rice, with everything calm and peaceful yet filled with energy and purpose. We halted a while by one of the 19 viaducts which are part of the main irrigation canal. This canal runs 370 li up into the hills and brings water to 100,000 mou of ground in three counties thus helping to make yields increase from but 300 jin per mou a year to 900. Shaoshan is 104 kilometres from Changsha, and has now a very resplendent railway station and rail connection with the provincial capital, making it easy of access for the million people a year who come from all over China, and too, from all over the world, to visit this place. Here in the peasant house was born in 1893 the boy who achieved so much and who was to become a world figure with a vast and still growing influence on the thinking of mankind.

We walked from the newly constructed guest house set up on the slope of a wooded valley over to Chairman Mao's boyhood home. He worked on the land from the age of six, then at eight he went to primary school off and on until he was 13. He studied and worked again until the age of 16, after which he set out to gain more education and succeeded in passing the entrance examination to the normal college in Changsha. Then another five and a half years of study helped to prepare him to enter the intense struggles that faced the youth of that period. From practical experience he knew what the lives of the working people were like. What it was to be wet and cold, how it felt to transplant rice, the bite of the sun. What it meant to have the cooperation of one's fellows. Who were the enemies of the poor and who were their friends. Obviously, from all accounts, he had a wonderful mother. When she died in 1920 he made his first trip back to Shaoshan after last seeing it in 1913. In a family meeting with his two brothers and one sister he persuaded them to join with him in revolution. In 1925 he came back and organised the first Party branch there, so that it was at Shaoshan that the peasant revolution really started. Of the original group of Party members 32 were later to die in the revolution, including the branch secretary, whose son is now the Party secretary of that branch. Chairman Mao also set up the Peasant Association in Shaoshan during that visit. He did not come again until 1927, when it was in connection with his inspection of the Hunan peasant movement.

Shaoshan Stories

There are many stories told around Shaoshan of his early days. How he loved to swim in the pond below his home. How he organised the buffalo boys into a cooperative working unit. How he would hang the coverlet of his bed over his door so that the light of the oil wick lamp he read by would not get through and worry his mother who feared he read too much with so poor a lamp. The trap door into a loft where he held the first Party branch meeting. Stories of a boy who went out to become a student, which in the eyes of the people of that time meant to achieve fame and fortune, but who came back home a revolutionary, with an already developed conviction that in Marxism-Leninism there was a way, and that such a way would have to be followed if China was to be saved.

Exhibition Hall

There has been built a fine exhibition hall in Shaoshan where pictures and relics of early revolutionary days are shown. It has been greatly enlarged since my last visit at the beginning of 1967, and much new material added. I shall describe some of it.

Mao Tse-min

Included there are mementoes of the immediate family of Chairman Mao who sacrificed their lives for the revolution. The portraits and the written history. They start with the picture of Mao Tse-min who joined the Party in 1922, was sent to Anyuan and struggled against the line of Liu Shao-chi. In 1925 he went to Shanghai where as head of the establishment known then as the Yangtze Bookshop he headed the publishing branch of the Central Committee. Later he went to Canton, afterwards making his way to south Kiangsi where he took a prominent part in leading the economy of the old Liberated Areas. After the Long March he took up similar work in the Yenan Border Region, afterwards going to Sinkiang where, under the name of Chou Pin, he played a leading part until a Kuomintang coup arrested all Communist workers, he being executed in September 1943.

A younger brother, Mao Tse-tan, stayed behind in the border region after the departure of the Long March army, leading a guerilla detachment. He was betrayed and killed.

Chairman Mao's Family

Yang Kai-hui, the wife of Chairman Mao, was 21 when she came to the Party, working in Shanghai and Canton, and then losing her life after being arrested by the Kuomintang in Changsha in 1930. Her son, Mao An-ying, arrested at the same time as his mother, was saved and sent to Shanghai, where he had a bitter life as a paper seller and wanderer on the streets until found and sent to Yenan in 1936. He went with the Chinese People's Volunteers to Korea, and was killed there in 1950.

Mao Tse-chien was Chairman Mao's adopted sister — really a niece whose parents had died — who was sent by him to the Changsha normal school. After graduation she became a leader of a group in the Great Revolution but was wounded near Leiyang and later killed by the Kuomintang. This was in 1928. Then there was Mao Chu-hsiung, a nephew whose picture shows a high-spirited lad. He took part in a group action against a south Hunan landlord in 1946 and lost his life. He was but 19.

Such are those of Chairman Mao's intimate family who have made the supreme sacrifice. Those of his close comrades who have done so are, of course, too many to count easily.

Ever Vindicated

There is an oil painting of Chairman Mao as a boy standing in the Hunan library looking at a map of the whole world, and then realising how small Hunan was on it. Hunan that had been his whole world hitherto. His passion to rid his native Hunan, and then the whole China from the crude exploitation its people suffered from, grew with his increased background knowledge that continual peasant and worker investigations brought him. Then when, through his organisation of students and people, he found the way ahead he took to it with immense vigor and ability. His hand now could be seen in so much. In Peking in 1918 and 1919, carrying some of the fire started amongst students in Hunan there where it culminated in the May 4th Movement, backing the New People's Society of Shanghai in 1920. Getting bookshops opened in different parts of Hunan. Going to Shanghai for the First Party Congress, then returning with fresh drive, determined to organise both workers and peasants and succeeding remarkably well, both at the Anyuan coal mines and in his own Hunan countryside. Then as the Communist Party grew, dealing with the reactionary line formulated by Chen Tu-hsiu and Chang Kuo-tao, who must have looked down their intellectual noses at this tough Hunan countryman who so sturdily opposed them, ever backing his words with solid achievement in the field of practical revolution. He has never winced in the face of internal struggle, always meeting it as it has come, holding to principle and ever being vindicated in the end.

New Highlights

While we were in Shaoshan the political leader of the Army unit stationed there, a keen student of Mao Tsetung Thought, spent a day in discussion with us and gave many highlights which had been missed in shorter visits here previously. With 80 percent of China's population belonging to the peasantry, the young man Mao Tsetung quite early felt that he had to know more about the peasant problem. He became used to going into the countryside making detailed investigations, and he spent the whole of the summer vacation with another student, tramping for 40 days through five counties and covering 500 kilometres. He had asked for a grant from the provincial department of education to make the investigation trip, but it was refused. He made it anyway, doing things for the peasants in lieu of food payment — writing letters or couplets for the doors of homes provided a way in many places. Carrying an oiled paper umbrella and wearing straw sandals, the two young men required little. Later in the same year, out on a weekend peasant investigation, he and his companions wanted to sleep in a temple but the monk in charge refused to have them, so they went to sleep outside. At midnight the priest relented, came out and invited them all in.   In January 1918 Mao Tsetung went on a hike into the hills of Liuyang, feeling that the complicated terrain there made it an excellent place for building a revolutionary base, which a decade later it proved to be.   Then he went up the Dawei mountains, part of the Chingkangshan range, and later hiked up from Liuyang all the way to Chingkangshan.   It was mid-winter and he took a bath in the snow, which impressed the peasants around greatly.   He also planted a chestnut tree there which is still bearing. Later on, he went to Peking.   On the way the train broke down in Honan, so he had some days to undertake an investigation into the life of the peasants there.   Increasingly, it became routine for him to make frequent trips into the countryside and find out the actual situation in the rural economy.   Bringing the lessons of the exemplary Hunan youth movement to Peking with him and with his policy of action, he became a very vital and powerful element in the May 4th Movement of 1919, although his name did not yet come so much into the limelight.   In a like way his ability to bring people together and unite them around a cause was one of the most important factors in the setting up of the Communist Party in Shanghai in 1921.

Workers' Movement

From July 1921 to the middle of 1923, Chairman Mao concentrated his energy on the workers' movement and worked in the fields of education and organisation.   Beginning with the summer of 1923 the stress was laid on the worker and peasant united front.   In 1924-25 the great thing he felt was to arouse the peasant masses, where such a vast reservoir of strength lay.   These three periods represented different stages of the revolutionary development and revolutionary action.   His Workers' College for instance, had students from 34 of the counties of Hunan who prepared themselves to go into the countryside and arouse the people.   After the suppression of the great railway strike of February 7th, 1923 by the warlord Wu Pei-fu, increased work in the countryside became necessary.

Contradictions now showed up in the Communist Party leadership, which was dominated by Chen Tu-hsiu, an intellectual who increasingly came to dislike Mao Tsetung and hated the peasant movement.   Chen Tu-hsiu was backed in those days by other intellectuals right down to Liu Shao-chi.   Mao Tsetung had already by then come to the conclusion that the united front must consist in the main of a worker and peasant alliance, and that the peasants must be armed as they were the main force in any democratic revolution in China.   He maintained that the oppressed peasantry, demanding revolution as a way to solve their difficulties, was the main force in China's revolution.   He envisaged a peasant movement which, though not spontaneously rising, would develop under the leadership of the proletariat.   This was the raison d'etre for Workers' College in Changsha.   His aim was to educate the proletariat on the importance of the peasantry and how to give it leadership.   In June 1923, the Third Congress of the Party was held, and Mao Tsetung's line, the worker-peasant united front line, gained victory over the extreme leftism of Chang Kuo-tao and the rightism of Chen Tu-hsiu. The revolutionary upsurge now began to take more definite form.

Mao Tsetung returned to Hunan from the Central Committee in Shanghai and threw himself into the task of organising the nucleus of the great peasant movement of that province with immense enthusiasm and ability. So for example in February 1925 he went to Shaoshan where he worked on promoting a real model for the peasant movement with the help of his newly organised Communist Party branch. Later in the year he went to Canton to head the Peasant Institute which had been set up there, and where he wrote his treatise on the analysis of classes in Chinese society. Steadily he educated his trainees to rely on the poor peasant, ally with the middle peasant and eliminate feudalism and exploitation. The first step, he taught, was how to carry through land reform work, and thus develop agricultural production with a resultant rise in living standards. There were the completely destitute, and the less destitute, he said, but these two groups together made up 70 percent of China's population. To win over these two groups, he advised his students, was a prime necessity. When going into the countryside not to make friends with rich peasants, not to go and eat chicken in landlords' houses. It was quite true, and not only at that time, that if a revolutionary came to the village in leather shoes and nice clothing, the peasants would simply look contemptuously on him as a landlord's bailiff, a gentleman or some running dog of the officials, and have nothing to do with him.

Ever Mao Tsetung stressed the importance of bringing over the wavering middle peasant and building unity against the big exploiters, and in this he succeeded. The people of Shaoshan still have the saying that on every road in the area you can see his footprints, in every paddy field lies his sweat, and that in every home you feel the warmth brought in by him. He led the struggle first against the biggest landlords. Chen Hsu-sheng for instance had 3,000 mou of good land. Every time Chen opened his front door he looked gloatingly out on the 800 mou of especially fine paddy fields he owned. He was not only rich, but also a despot.

Mao Tsetung, for the purpose of struggle, divided the landlord class up into big, middle and small landlords, despotic or not. Chen was the worst of the big ones, so the first struggle was led against him and succeeded in July 1925. Another bully and tyrant was named Tang Chun-yen, who from 1913-25 had killed no fewer than 50 people, and who became the next target of the struggle. A third was Yin Tien-li who was also bitterly hated by common folk around. The successful fight against these three heightened the spirit of revolt amongst the peasant masses and led them to take the initiative in the revolution themselves. Mao pointed out that some of the children of landlord families and city intellectuals supported the Communist Party or student movements in cities, and he asked that those who with complete sincerity did oppose foreign aggression and who stood with the progressive forces be welcomed and helped to remould themselves. Ever he pointed out that we must believe in the people, who are the motive power in history. Never look on them as backward, on the contrary, that we should criticise ourselves if our methods are backward in dealing with them.

Resistance

As in the days of the Great Revolution, the situation in the world at large remains the same. What is the strongest thing in the world? It is the strength of the masses. Though oppressed by the reaction, the mass movement of the peoples will ever forge ahead with the immense strength of a Yangtze or a Yellow river in flood, breaking down all barriers. In the latter part of 1926 and the spring of 1927, Chairman Mao called on the people of Hunan to rise in resistance, telling them that they must form self-defence corps, and that their weapons should come by taking them from the landlord-controlled militia. He advanced the idea that if we want to correct a social wrong we must set up the absolute authority of the masses and not be scared of violence. Against this, Chen Tu-hsiu and some of the intellectuals who had learnt their Marxism only from books were scared and condemned all that happened in Hunan. When Chou En-lai headed 800,000 workers in Shanghai, Chen Tu-hsiu's main thought was how to disarm them and pass all power over to Chiang Kai-shek, who had actually already betrayed the revolution and gone over to the side of imperialism.

Peasant Investigation

Mao Tsetung came back to Hunan from Wuhan where he then was, and made a 32-day investigation of the whole peasant movement. He was immensely pleased with its strength and vigor. This movement was a great school for the revolution, a way to crush the rotten old order and to build a new one. Here the rebels learnt to fight by fighting. Mao Tsetung also stressed the need for organisation at this time, knowing that such a process was truly that of liberating. Difficulties there were, the deeper the work went. For instance, dialects differed sometimes from county to county. Most of the peasants were quite illiterate. But against this, landlord families led a soft life, ever having to be carried in sedan chairs by the peasants. The peasants grew toughened feet and could move fast over great distances. They could be taught Marxism, if it was given them in a popular, understandable way and if it touched directly on their own problems. To teach was hard and dangerous work, for the running dogs of landlords and officials were everywhere. In underground work there were many possibilities. Meetings of clan friends and relatives could be made a cover for political meetings. Some organisers learnt a trade to cover their activities, others went out as pedlars selling cloth and needles. There were those who became barbers or knife grinders to find the right opportunity to bring their message home. The enemy had his network, the people could have theirs also, and there were so many ways to penetrate the strongholds of the old system. Some revolutionaries became traditional doctors, letter writers, story tellers, or even masqueraded as fortune tellers. Whatever ways were found, the message did begin to get across, and broke the stranglehold the many long years of feudal tabu and Confucian ideology had laid on the minds of ordinary working people.

Chen Tu-hsiu Ousted

The fall of the Wuhan government brought on the ouster of Chen Tu-hsiu, but the new leadership of the Central Committee of the Communist Party was in the hands of Li Li-san, Wang Ming and others who in turn opposed Mao Tsetung, the man on the spot, the practical revolutionary who carried the brunt of things. In September 1927 began the Hunan Autumn Harvest Uprising led by Chairman Mao. There had already been the Nanchang Army uprising in Kiangsi led by Chou En-lai, and its troops were moving southwards. State power in China, with the help of foreign imperialism and the Chinese reaction had been seized by the Kuomintang, so that the Great Revolution period came to an end. It was to be followed by the whole Chingkangshan epic, which makes another chapter to this piece of revolutionary history. The Kuomintang at this time marched into north Hunan and massacred some 330,000 people labelled as Communists, in their efforts to stabilise their rule. The ten-year period of Kuomintang terror set in and, to give just one instance of it, one can point to the village of Shuangtung in Hunan where there had been a population of 3,000, with only 32 remaining after the killings.

Yet Chairman Mao was anything but a defeated man. Even as the Great Revolution was crushed was he thinking of how to rebuild the Party and people's army so that it would carry the revolution through its next stages, and rebuild them he did. There are stories told of him at Shaoshan when he was a boy out herding buffaloes. How he would organise the other buffalo boys and all go to pick fodder together, and then divide it up equally before they all went home with it at night. His talent for organising and of applying Marxist theory to practice has stood him in good stead. When he left the country and went to Changsha to be a city student, then teacher and Communist Party organiser, he had often to deal with intellectuals who had been ruined by the old society's educational system. Opportunists, careerists, those without any sense of responsibility to public affairs, those who ever struggled for place and position and who were full of emotional contradictions between themselves. All of these he must have met and had to deal with in his task of organising revolutionary work.

Autumn Harvest Uprising

In the Autumn Harvest Uprising, the Hunan revolutionaries were to meet a good deal of tough struggle. Hsia Tao-yin, a commander of Kuomintang troops who had been taken over, deserted with his troops to the enemy, which taught the lesson never again to depend on such forces. Only after reorganising them into different units, after education and remoulding, should such be done. Other lessons were bitterly learnt also. Never try to hold a captured city if superior forces come to lay siege. Liuyang city was taken, held, then besieged and lost to the enemy with heavy losses to its garrison of good troops. But over all these and other setbacks, Chairman Mao kept the morale of fighters up. At a summing up meeting at Wenchiashih after the battles, he put the position clearly. Do we push the revolution through? Do we dare or not? So on out of Hunan into the mountains of Chingkangshan the remnants of the people's armies moved, beginning on September 20th, 1927.

Revolutionary History

Aspects of this piece of revolutionary history will be discussed for a very long time to come yet. We were glad for the leadership in our discussion and for the answers which came so directly and with such clarity. One would need to write a book in many volumes to put them all down, and then to get them properly understood one would have to give immense background also. So this brief sketch of only some of the aspects has here been attempted.

Hunan Potters

We did not leave Changsha without having a peep at a little of its industry. The chief centre for making porcelain ware in Hunan is out in northeast Hunan at Liling, but right in the industrial section of Changsha city there is also a big factory with 1,700 workers, whose products go to 34 countries abroad. I had visited it several times before, for it was first set up in 1956. For some time its products were not of high quality, all going into the rural market. Now the rural market is being met by new commune and county potteries whose standards are also rising fast, so that the one in Changsha can now go ahead producing superior products with a modern, streamlined production line. The continuous kilns I saw being installed in 1967, the last time I visited, are now in operation, and over 15 million pieces a year are being produced. Costs have been cut, especially with the many work innovations that have come in. Just one thing, a differently designed sagger has led to a 60 percent saving in the use of materials for firing. Under its new organisation, evolved during the Cultural Revolution, work is going ahead fast and new targets are being set.

To Chuchow

We took the train from Chuchow late one evening. As we had approached it by the big wide highway from Changsha, it had been a maze of lights, its many big industrial plants being on their night shifts. Industrial workers are now taking the place that Chairman Mao planned for them, helping to provide the means for better agricultural production, workers themselves going out from cities into the countryside in increasing numbers leading in new crafts and learning from the people of their needs and how to fill them.

So did we leave Hunan, with all its memories of struggle and revolution, its immense accomplishments and the feel of the bright future which now opens up in front of it in the era of the ever victorious Mao Tsetung Thought. For now the scope of the revolution reaches out far beyond the borders of Hunan and all China, right into every land that the young Mao Tsetung looked at so intently on the world map in the Hunan library over half a century ago. The movement for basic social change is now an enormous and swiftly growing one, mankind's answer to the oppression, exploitation and the threat of endless new and more horrible wars which the warlords of the old order devise. The great mass of the working poor of our world demand the kind of society in which it can express its full potential in confidence, dignity and the freedom to grow into the more creative man to be. Here in Hunan was born one who has given such leadership that his whole people has been able to forge a revolutionary base of immense value to the whole of struggling mankind.

Miao school boys in Chishou, west Hunan.

HUNAN

Miao commune folk marching off to winter work, west Hunan.

Hunan student marchers, 1967.

Shaoshan — youth marchers at Chairman Mao's childhood home.

Student long marchers from the north in Shaoshan, Hunan.

Lock, west Hunan.

West Hunan.

Siphon over valley, west Hunan.

New canal, Shaoshan, Hunan.

Where tailor Tien was skinned alive. "Never forget class bitterness, the debts of blood and tears," the tablet reminds.

Dam for turbine pump, west Hunan.

Over new canal at Shaoshan, Hunan.

New country bridge, Hunan, built of stone on old model.

Miao village, west Hunan.

Revolutionary Museum
buildings, Shaoshan,
Hunan.

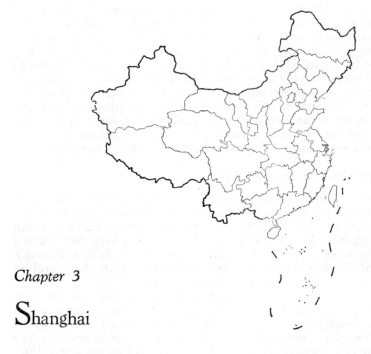

Chapter 3

Shanghai

Modern Shanghai was founded by get-rich-quick foreign imperialist adventurers and opium traders who needed a place of their own exempt from Chinese supervision, safe and well-controlled by their own council, administration and police. A place from which to carry on their nefarious business. Based on predatory imperialism, it was a city of great wealth and vast poverty, developing certain types of industry, especially textiles, when cheap Chinese labor from a rotting hinterland became available. Chinese men, women and children, underpaid, often enough starving, many actually slaves, came to man its factories, create its amenities, and serve its every need. When wars and peasant risings made life for landlords and other exploiters in China less pleasant, Shanghai became a place of refuge and a haven for them. The Chinese underworld too found its paradise here. Shanghai ended up before Liberation as a city of extreme poverty for the many and extreme wealth for the few. It was a happy hunting ground for gangsters, pimps, prostitutes, adventurers and other exploiters, Chinese and foreign; a place where millionaires were made, and the beginnings of great foreign fortunes amassed.

61

After Liberation in 1949, its function changed. Now increasingly it became a place in the service of the hinterland. Its workers went to set up factories in the far interior. Its students went to border areas on distant frontiers. Shanghai dialect began to be heard around places like Lanchow in Kansu, Harbin in Heilungkiang, Urumchi in Sinkiang. Though its export trade kept up and its shipping increased, with its harbor remaining one of the great ones of the world, yet its face was now definitively turned towards the interior, and the Yangtze river carried increasing tonnage of Shanghai-built shipping loaded with Shanghai-built machinery year after year. A changed city now, with new destiny beckoning it ahead. A city that entered the Cultural Revolution with zest and fire, and one which has come through the struggle fresher and stronger than ever. This then the city, now so much part of the hinterland, where the following visits were made in the years of the Cultural Revolution.

Shanghai in the Summer of 1967

It had seemed to many not so important that some people who looked backward liked the old opera better than the new, preferred light literature with middle-class values to realistic, down-to-earth writing that was meant for the working folk. But as the Cultural Revolution of May 1966 stormed ahead, the need for a new look became clear, and with it a thorough reappraisal of the whole superstructure of society, with the object of bringing it closer to the Thought of Mao Tsetung.

We came to Shanghai from Peking, and one evening saw the new opera "The Red Lamp-Shade" which was the story of the women's section of the Boxer Rebellion, and then the play "Rent Collection Courtyard", both of the new type, and both then highly popular in Shanghai. The stress in such new productions as in the whole field of art and culture lies obviously on service to the workers, peasants and soldiers. The new model operas like "Shachiapang" and "On the Docks" I had seen in Peking but was glad to see again in Shanghai. These new works impressed with their change in ideological content and their closeness to contemporary life, as advocated by Chairman Mao in his Talks at the Yenan Forum on Literature and Art in 1942. It became evident now, however, that the revolution was spreading far beyond the confines of art and literature, right down into society and was tackling very basic issues. Perhaps it would be good to look back a little to understand the main one, the struggle against revisionism.

In the 'fifties, after the defeat of the U.S. in Korea, things in China had gone along as planned. Though there had been the great Yangtze flood and other tough problems, all had been surmounted. On the international front, imperialism was held back and the attempted blockade of China had failed. The Vietnamese people on China's southern border had been able to throw out French imperialism, and the socialist world had unity. Then came the Bandung Conference, and the enunciation of the principle of coexistence. It did seem queer, to say the least, that the USSR should at once take hold of this idea and begin to expand it into something quite different, into one which meant cooperation with American imperialism.   Soviet delegates and their supporters began to talk speciously about world disarmament and peaceful transition as the only way forward.   But then again many who had all their lives accepted the Soviet Union as the leader of the world revolution felt that surely after so many bitter struggles the USSR could not go the road of betrayal.

In 1959-61 a vast natural calamity hit China which made the Chinese people need all their friends.   This was the time cynically picked by the new revisionist leadership of the USSR to wield the big club and try to force China to submit to the revisionist camp.   It was then that the true essence of revisionism began to be better understood by real revolutionaries as simply another facet of bourgeois ideology and the handmaid of imperialism.   The various international conferences during the following years made this alliance only too manifest.   For the revisionists no tricks were too dirty in the effort to try and smash revolutionary China. Still raising revolutionary slogans from time to time, they always were willing to appease American imperialism and even to side with the American aggressors.   They became simply a gang without honor amongst the advancing peoples of the world, their presence in any revolutionary situation a sign of disaster — many countries showing clear evidence of this.

In the USSR, with the gap in wages and living standards between the common worker and peasant on the one hand and the engineers, the scientists, administrators, in short, the intelligentsia on the other always widening, there has appeared in the Soviet Union a divergence of interest. Those who are economically prosperous, have a certain social position and are able to send their children to university and high school, are no longer interested in the revolution; they want peace above all and are quite prepared to sacrifice other people and other peoples to rapacious American imperialism.   "To hell with you, Jack, I'm all right," is their thinking.

In China one had become used to the idea that there existed unity against revisionism.   The Leap Forward did much basic construction work throughout the country which was later to bear rich fruit.   Chairman Mao had said that the class struggle would continue under socialism, but most people felt that this struggle would not have to be very severe. Then there came rumblings, as proofs of new class distinctions began to manifest themselves.   It became evident that there was also a trend towards revisionism in China, and that there were some in positions of great authority who favored the idea of peaceful transition towards socialism, which in essence as we have seen in Russia meant capitulation to capitalism.   In the service of their theories, the most powerful of the revisionist group found a valuable ally in art and literature circles, and in the field of education.   Art and literature for the working people had since the Yenan Talks of 1942 in principle followed the teaching of Chairman Mao.   In practice, however, it did the opposite.   Part-work, part-study schools were accepted in theory, but no real effort was made to put them into widespread practice.   As far as was possible, education in its higher branches was reserved for the children of the intelligentsia. Inevitably a new class stratum began to arise, as it had in the USSR.

No one realised this better than Chairman Mao himself. But the question was how to bring the whole thing home to the people and cause a thorough heart-searching that would show up mistakes and revolutionary backsliding even in the highest places. During the past 17 years, Mao Tsetung had brought up the question of the need for revolutionary changes in the cultural field, in art and literature and education, but these suggestions were either ignored or sidetracked as has now, during the Great Proletarian Cultural Revolution, become apparent from the exposure of the activities of the capitalist roaders.

The resistance to cultural revolutionary change during the post-Liberation years finally led Chairman Mao and those responding to his direct leadership to launch the battle for men's minds and souls which is the Cultural Revolution. . . .

The opening salvoes of the Cultural Revolution were launched with the publication of an exposé in the Shanghai press. A protest movement against the anti-Mao Tsetung line then current in the Peking and Tsinghua Universities followed. As the Cultural Revolution got further under way and the first bastions of revisionism had been conquered, the first Red Guards were formed. This ardent student youth produced the young leaders who then, with the support of Chairman Mao, began to take a good look at certain self-styled "authorities", certain habits and customs and, in general, to question the old. Their function became important, for it was they who at that stage could move out to the countryside to propagate Mao Tsetung's revolutionary line in the communes. For a time it seemed to a certain group of people as if the old established forces, headed by some who were quite evidently taking the revisionist road, might win. Due however to Chairman Mao's leadership and to the energy and sense of organisation of rebel youth, workers, peasants, and the People's Liberation Army, the fight for the future was won by the anti-revisionists.

It is true that some class enemies and some ignorant elements took advantage of the movement, and donning red armbands carried out excesses in its name. Then too, sometimes young people were used by others who belonged to the reaction. But by and large, this youth, many of them sons and daughters of the revolution, did galvanise the rising generation of the whole country to a sense of their own responsibilities. The spark they ignited spread. They themselves travelled great distances, first by public transport and then by hiking. Young people in factory and farm, in city schools and county administration met and discussed things together. It was perhaps the greatest interchange of ideas and experience amongst the youth of China in history.

This mobilisation of the youth to criticise and rebel was a bold stroke. Its effect was dramatic. The Thought of Mao Tsetung penetrated deeper than it had ever done through the ranks of society. Privileged positions began to be abandoned, and closer touch with the people resulted. Struggle assumed various forms, but always the effort was made to keep it on the ideological rather than the physical fighting level. Its effect internationally was great. The controversy made more and more people see problems through new eyes. The oppressed and the exploited everywhere felt the freshening wind, gaining encouragement that those who fought for the success of the continuing social revolution in China were doing so for the oppressed people everywhere. The revisionists and their allies and friends became frightened and screamed that it was they who were leading the have-nots, that it was they who were on the side of the sweating lad pulling a cart over a hot city street or up a country hillside. That it was they who stood beside the child burnt to death in Vietnam. It was they, they claimed, who were with the liberation fighters in Africa and Latin America, with the Negro freedom fighters in the USA and the other poor there in the grip of monopoly. But increasingly the two thirds of the world who have to struggle for their daily food began to look towards the China that did not hesitate to turn against revisionism wherever it raised its head, even if it was amongst those who occupied the highest places in her own land. Soon the true position became clear for all to see.

The workers and peasants, the soldiers and the youth of China have done an immense task. Things will never be the same again. The young will have to return to their studies and the older ones to work, but the thing they have started will lead to new strength in a revolutionary way. The wisdom of Mao Tsetung has triumphed again.

Shanghai, the largest industrial centre of China, and the city where the most intense struggles were carried on, is also one of the places where the various stages have been brought to a triumphant ending and where new difficulties that have arisen are being successfully surmounted. Not all youth realises that revolutionary work must go stage by stage, and, while disorder in a certain situation when the class interests of the working people are threatened, is a good thing, it cannot be tolerated when rebels have taken power and the new three-way alliance between rebels, PLA (the People's Liberation Army) and old cadres has taken place. Industry is interdependent and nearly all factories rely for supplies, raw material, power etc. on other factories, mines, communes and so on, which are sometimes situated in other areas of the country. But difficulties in supply arising from the uneven development of the Cultural Revolution in different parts of China have been very quickly surmounted by the uncovering of new supply sources and, secondly, by the practical application of the slogan: Grasp revolution, promote production.

But there are other problems. There is the need for intense study by the incoming group, study of Chairman Mao's works, with resulting criticism and a repudiation of the bad practices of the past.

The revolution has clearly shown that not so many people are needed in the superstructure of administration as there were before, and even better production results can be obtained with less red tape. In order to have a real understanding of the problems on the production line, all administrative personnel must take part for a certain time in production along with the working force. Politics, not the profit incentive, must be the leading factor, but that does not mean that production should lag. On the contrary, politics is the key to success in production. Some of the industrial plants where the best production results have been gained are those where the rebel groups first took power. Yet again, the solution to the problems the revolution has raised will have to come from the people themselves. There are over 8,000 factories in Shanghai. There are also many schools, universities, hospitals and institutes. Army men cannot go to all and be the fairy godmother to solve everybody's problems. The young rebels will have to go back to their schools or to work, and anyway, their first year of struggle in the revolution is just a beginning of revolutionary struggle in their lives compared with the long years the old cadres have had. The revolutionary old cadres must continue to learn and at the same time give leadership, relying on the Thought of Mao Tsetung and the wealth of their own experience, but by and large it will be the working people who will take the major hand in shaping their own destiny, in an organised, disciplined way. The complicated picture of groups, some good, some good in some ways, bad in others, some outright bad, accorded very much to the class struggle in society. There are also people who have been fooled but who now see and there are those who are still influenced by middle-class thinking. But all these groups and people will learn a lot from the discussions still going on, still obviously not all problems will be solved and so the struggle must go on. Many will accept bitterness now, cutting out other bitterness that would come to those who follow. The revolution is not just an exciting day out. It is a long-term struggle involving all the people in our world. As Chairman Mao has said: "A revolution is not a dinner party, or writing an essay, or painting a picture, or doing embroidery. . . ." Rather is it a thing where successes are gained at the expense of many mistakes, whose victory has to be paid for — and that does not come for nothing.

A Shanghai Commune

One of the chief revolutionary organisations of Shanghai had a member-ship of only 3,000 at the time of the January 1967 seizure of power. Now it has two million. As the veil lifts and people begin to understand that there were some people actually trying to lead them back to the old order, there comes a good deal of gratitude to the rebels for the positive things they have done. This was further brought out during a visit to a commune on the outskirts of Shanghai where a rebel group which included the old commune Party secretary had taken over and had had to deal with various new situations. A group of the sons of old landlords and rich peasants actually tried armed rebellion, their first object being to kill the commune militia leader. He was too quick for them. But it went to show that though a string of garlic hung up under the eaves has lost its roots, its heart remains as bitter as ever, as the militia leader told us when we went to see him in his tiny, neat home.

He talked too of the old days when three swords were always hanging over the heads of the poor peasants — land rent, land tax, and high interest on loans they were forced to take. How then there often seemed but three roads open to them — drowning in the river, hanging, or being jailed. Poor peasants joined the rebel groups as soon as they understood that the new revisionists had planned to reintroduce such things as private trade, bigger private plots, permission to hire labor in order to help the privileged. Production in this past year on this commune has risen to well over 1,000 jin a mou. There has been rebellion, while crop totals were the highest ever.

We walked around and looked at their piggeries, their cow sheds, the small handicraft industry they had set up, and then into the faces of the alive, well-nourished children, realising that indeed the countryside was a going concern these days. "In the old days we went to the pawnshops with tears in our eyes," they said. "Now we go to the banks with joy to put in deposits." The commune has nearly a million yuan in the bank as savings. It has around 22,000 people, and this last season had an increase of 30 percent on harvest totals. It gets three times as much cotton per mou now as it did in 1950. It is entitled to talk proudly about the achievements during the Cultural Revolution, as these have been won by hard work and study and not through the exploitation of others.

Shanghai No. 1 Steel Mill

The Shanghai No. 1 Steel Mill is a giant concern employing 12,000 regular workers, with installations which spread over a great area. There was a small Japanese plant on the site during the War of Resistance which produced 3,000 tons of steel a year. The present one turns out around 3,000 tons of steel and steel products a day. We went through some of the shops seeing big Bessemer and open hearth furnaces, and then on to watch seamless steel tubing being turned out under modern conditions in great high shops. It is an impressive plant. Most of the chimneys that used to belch forth dank black smoke have now, I was especially glad to note, been fitted with a recovery system which puts the chemicals in the smoke to good use, allowing no poisonous material to escape and pollute the air.

This mill was enlarged to its present size as a Leap Forward project in 1958. Its technical progress has been rapid — in 1958 only one kind of spring steel was produced. Now it makes 70 kinds. Products like stainless steel, once imported, now come from this mill. Workers are pleased with what they have been able to do. It was a surprise then, when the administration in Peking sent down an inspector who reported unfavorably on their work, saying that there was no good mass line, etc., etc. Chen Pei-hsien, for a time Party secretary of Shanghai, supported this report. The workers thought this strange, for had not Chairman Mao visited the works in 1959 telling them that they had done well and had a great future? Then too, how could a mill whose workers had installed a big furnace in 47 days, a world record, have a bad mass line? Actually, it was easy to understand why the report was made. Certain authorities, now proved to have been following the capitalist line, were then out to disparage Leap Forward work and brand it as useless. They wanted the "single sheet of paper" style of work which is the Chinese way of describing the method of issuing orders from above which are supposed to solve everything. They wanted a capitalist rather than a socialist type of enterprise. Hearing the story, many things became clear to me, for I had travelled over 15 provinces seeing Leap Forward work and was saddened later to see that many promising industrial projects had been abandoned for no apparent reason. Now the reason was clear. There were people at work to blacken everything tried out in the Leap Forward. If it was revolutionary, they wanted to smash it.

The work team sent to the mill in 1966 from Peking called black white and white black, and used its power to fight and suppress revolutionaries. But as the truth of the matter began to be understood by the workers, they supported the rebel organisation to such good effect that now the three-way alliance of old cadres, rebels and Army are giving the leadership needed and work swings along in harmony, with practically the whole work force now in the rebel group. For them now that particular struggle is over and they can look back on the things said and done and analyse them. They laugh particularly at one story. The mill had a good worker, an old Shantung man, who was very much against waste. He collected the broken ends of rubber pipes, cut off because they no longer fitted tightly, and stored them in an empty shed until there were enough to be taken away by utilisers of such material. The work team reported that there was such waste in the mill that tons of rubber piping could be picked up and stored away at any worker's pleasure. They could not conceive of a man who would do a thing for the good of the mill with no thought of self-interest!

Shanghai Railway Administration

I spent a fascinating afternoon at the offices of the Shanghai Railway Administration. I reminded the rebel youth group there that I had seen some of the events of 1927, '31 and '37 in this historic spot, and how good it was now to see new history being made. The leader of the rebel group is a 23-year-old lad from Shaohsing in Chekiang province. Around him he has a good leading group of old cadres, young rebels and Army helpers. He has been able to give such good, direct leadership that problems are now swiftly solved and the whole railway administration has now returned to normal. The tough times, however, were quite tough. On December 26th, 1966, the old guard headed by Chen Pei-hsien, the Shanghai authority, commenced its attack against the railway system, realising that if it could paralyse this, things would soon grind to a halt amongst Shanghai's factories, wharves and so on. It issued cheques to many of the workers and sent some off to Peking. It called away the railway administration. Mountains of goods soon collected and passengers were crowding the railway station, the administrative offices and other premises so that nothing could move.

This was the situation the rebels faced and which had to be solved against resistance by inside forces and from outside. Student Red Guards asked people not to go to the station, brought in food for those already there, got them off the railway lines, and started some of the 46 trains parked on various sidings along the line moving again. It was not a swift victory, however. By January 9th the "black liners" had halted all trains, and 80 percent of the ships in the port were lying idle. The combination of the rebel group with the workers, the gaining of worker understanding, was the thing that ended this "black line" scheme. The old administration had agreed that 35 million yuan could be used, actually to buy up the workers. 350,000 yuan had already been distributed. But now many workers came to those who had passed out the cheques and tore them up in their faces. Others who had cashed the money brought it to the administration. Rebels told them, "You can buy a sewing machine or a radio, but if we all go back to the old society, then what will any of us have?" Workers saw this point very clearly indeed and their response was immediate. The rebel group now went to deal with 400,000 tons of accumulated freight and soon had it moving off at the rate of 80,000 tons a day. Rebel leaders worked day and night, everyone concerned throwing himself into the struggle so that by April not only had the whole backlog been moved but also freight trains were running better than they ever had done. We were taken to the railway control station and watched the operators checking on the various trains, putting their position and times on their graphs. We met old and new workers and admired the high spirit prevailing all around. The rebel leaders told how excited they were when they got the first Peking through express train running again. Many wept at that time. Now not only those who are students at the Tungchi Engineering University of Shanghai, but also railway cadres and workers look at politics in a new way and more than ever trust in the guidance of the Thought of Mao Tsetung. The policy of trying to buy over workers by money has been thoroughly exposed.

We talked for a while about the political ideas of the ex-administrative leader of the railways here. When he himself was asked what his objects were, he said simply 1. to increase rail transportation, 2. to push the technical revolution and 3. to increase workers' welfare, which his hearers thought was a statement that might have come from any capitalist or revisionist chieftain anywhere. He did not support the rebels. For a time, the rebels had a stiff fight and had to build their own support. Then on January 12th came a message of congratulation from the Central Committee of the Communist Party in Peking and all were immensely encouraged.

A Shanghai Ship-Building Yard

We spent a morning down on Point Island in the Yangtzepoo area at a ship-building yard which I had visited several times since Liberation, even knowing of it in the 'thirties in its very early stages. It covers around 60 acres of land and now has a working force of 4,000. It built

80 boats in 1965, 102 in 1966, and plans for 120 in 1967. Mostly small craft for rivers and big canals, but also sea-going dredges and 3,000-ton cargo ships. It also does machine construction for industry — a rotary furnace for a cement works abroad was being completed and a part for a big machine in a synthetic fibre factory we noted as we went around. When a piece is too big to bring into the shops, and there is no machine tool big enough to do the job, then a crane simply picks up the finished ship part and puts it into place. The plant has many bits of Shanghai workers' creativeness like this.

I was interested in its part in the Cultural Revolution. Actually, it had carried out a campaign for socialist education between October 1965 to October 1966 which had resulted in finding that the two managers and the Party secretary had the wrong class viewpoint and in consequence had been discharged. Then, as the new movement gripped the working force they split into 80 groups, which after considerable discussion joined together in four, then again came together in one of 3,000 people and took power. The rebel group still leads in the administration but all old cadres are at their tasks, though supervised by the new group. There is no official three-way alliance yet — but workers are all satisfied that what they have now in their new unity is what they want, and work goes ahead well in all sections. The principle of "wendou" (verbal struggle) has been respected and there were no fights between the various groups even when there were a whole 80. In the designing rooms designers clipped plastic sheets spread out over floors, on the wharves 1,000-ton dredges were being completed, while many smaller craft destined for the Yangtze were on the slips. Everything the vessel needs is made on the spot — engines, propellers, superstructure and all fittings. Workers smiled greetings as one passed, and there was a general air of activity and good spirit about the whole plant. It had achieved a grand unity. Everyone knew the political issues, why he was working, and for whom. No wonder they showed it in their faces and in their work.

Second Radio Factory

We spent one morning at the Second Radio Factory of Shanghai. It was a place that had been converted from a textile plant to its present use and employs 1,600 workers who make radio sets and a range of transistors, in 1966 to the tune of 85,000.

The situation in the plant had been confused. It was a special pet of the old Municipal Party Committee, which used it as a kind of trying-out post. The Party secretary relied on old landlord elements, and had brought no fewer than 27 of them into the factory leadership, and many also into the Communist Party. His chief favorite was a landlord who had owned no less than 3,000 mou in Tsingpu county near Shanghai, and who right up to 1965 was still collecting house rents from town housing he owned that had not been socialised. Another landlord was made headmaster of the factory school and also a Party member. This group joined together to throw out real revolutionaries, including one very good

old cadre who had been in the Party since 1938.   One woman landlord
had written a letter of congratulation to Chiang Kai-shek on his 60th
birthday in 1946.   She had kept a copy and hoped to use it if the Kuomintang ever came back.   The Red Guards found it hidden in the wall
behind a mirror in her house.   She had also been admitted to the factory
Party group.   This Party group, with outside help including that of an
official work team, tried all kinds of ways to upset the rebel group which
had been formed.   They had made "black files" (secret reports on the
rebel workers) and tried in every way to intimidate them.   They tried
economism — buying over workers — they tried to throw the whole place
into chaos by various devices, but the rebel group which had emerged
by November 14th, 1966 was able to successfully take over on January
15th, just two months later, with the help of the majority of workers
in the plant.   Then they had to work hard to completely expose the old
leadership and make workers understand fully all the ramifications.   Production lagged in the last part of 1966, and quality suffered on some of
the products.   This has already been corrected, and in 1967 the planned
production for the year will be 30 percent higher than that of 1966.   It
is a beautifully streamlined factory, and the old cadres with experience
who have come over to the rebel side have shown great ability in technical
advance.   The factory machine shops build the special machines needed
for high polish and so on, and the whole plant swings ahead with the
precision of a well-ordered machine.   Many of its products go to the
fishing fleets off the coast, and to stock breeding farms in the far hinterland, Chinghai, Sinkiang, Mongolia. . . .

Two Scientists

During our stay in Shanghai, we spent a morning with two scientists.
They are well-known figures in Shanghai life, for they were brought
to public notice by Ko Ching-shih, an old revolutionary who was Shanghai's mayor and a strong supporter of the Mao Tsetung line.   Ko Ching-
shih died a few years ago.

The first scientist, Peng Chia-mu, a Cantonese by birth, created much
comment in the Academy of Sciences when he led in insisting on research
that had to do with the needs of the people, not research for research's
sake, or for following through some line divorced from reality dictated
by the foreign professor that the scientist had studied under abroad.
Peng was one of the group that took part in the synthesis of insulin.   He
went wherever there was the greatest need, spending some time in distant
Sinkiang.   Then he was told he was threatened with a swift death from
a malignant tumor in the chest.   In hospital, he found great strength
and determination in reading Chairman Mao's works, which both he and
his doctor believed helped to tide him over times of crisis.   Anyway, to
make a long story short, he has had no recurrence, and has been able to
make a considerable contribution in the years since recovery.   When the
Cultural Revolution broke in Shanghai, however, he first permitted himself to be organised into the group that supported the principal authority

in Shanghai. When rebels accused him of not supporting the Mao Tsetung line, he was furious. "Cut off my head if you like," he said, "but I will never acknowledge that I have left the teachings of Mao Tsetung." It was some time before he could see that there were those who were using him, hypocritically employing "left" language to fight the rebels. Actually, the Academy of Sciences branch in Shanghai was not counted as a school or as an official organisation, so did not get the material on the movement that such did. It was some time before they received Chairman Mao's Sixteen Points for the Cultural Revolution, even. Peng went to Peking and saw Premier Chou En-lai who told him that the Academy was both a school and an organisation, and must in future be treated as such, and that they could all make revolution. The old authorities in Shanghai had kept control by making big grants to the Academy for projects, but as he and others joined the rebel group, a new wind spread through the institution and the rebels came to power.

The second scientist, Tsai Tsu-chuan, is a native of Yuhang in Che-kiang. When his family was beggared by the Japanese invasion, he walked the roads with them until he was 14. Then an elder brother who was an apprentice in Shanghai found him a boy-worker job making ampules in a glass factory. That was in 1940. Now at 43 he is a member of a research team in Futan University, with a growing family of his own. He became famous by inventing a new type of lamp that replaced the imported bulbs for street lighting, thus making China independent of imports. Today the country has even become an exporter of such lamps. As a worker he was immensely popular, for he has a very pleasant personality as well as an inventive brain.

With no formal education and coming up the hard way, he has achieved results that are the envy of many a scientist in this field. It was not that his fame had gone to his head that made him take the conservative side when the rebel movement started. Rather was it pressure brought about by other scientists around him who said that it was really they who were for Chairman Mao, and not the rebels. They exhorted him to throw in his lot with them and go the whole way never dallying, as they said, like a Sukarno until disaster hit. So he was beset from many sides. In his own family his children criticised him. The rebel students criticised him, and the authorities tried by all means to hold him with them, so that with a book of Mao's Quotations in hand he was left to think the thing through for himself. He did, and came out on the side of the rebels. There were many big character wall posters against him, but after he had taken the step he became more and more sure that he was right, wondering now why he did not see everything clearly at first. The poorest of workers must surely stand with their own class, he realised as the issues were put in front of him.

Reinforced Concrete Boats

The last morning of visiting we spent in the Reinforced Concrete Boat Factory at Kiating, once a rural county, now one of the new suburbs of expanding Shanghai. The factory was not a big one, like the ones of Wusih and Yangchow I had visited a year ago, but it was one of special interest at this time of the Cultural Revolution. Its 344 workers had taken the movement seriously. The general manager had organised some Scarlet Guards and had given them preference, trying to crush the two real rebel groups that had arisen.

In the course of the Cultural Revolution a very clever operator, an ex-capitalist who had become wealthy in the old days renting out boats to farmers, and who had come in here as a wooden boat-building worker after he changed his domicile, was perhaps the most objectionable element the movement uncovered. He studied the movement closely from the beginning and thought that here now was the time when he could cash in and give vent to his hate for the Communist Party. With an inborn contempt for his fellow workers, he thought to use them and get all the leading cadres of the plant dismissed. At first it seemed in the general confusion that he might succeed. But in his enthusiasm he overplayed his hand. The workers too, saw that their production was lagging — it was January 1967 — and became keen to see their plant go forward, not backward. They investigated him and found the truth. At the time of our visit, more was still being found about his past. Quite cleverly and for a long time he had been setting workers against each other. When the Scarlet Guards found how they had been fooled, and after discussions together, the great unity victoriously emerged, only the general manager and his assistant being laid aside for the time being. The Party secretary and the assistant manager remained at their posts, and the rebel committee ably took over policy functions of the general manager.

The plant had originally been making and repairing wooden boats, and some of these continue to be made. The main product, however, is the five-ton reinforced concrete boat, which, selling at less than half the price of the wooden one, is in high demand. In 1966, 1,714 boats were made and the plan is for 1,960 vessels in 1967. Soon eight- and 12-ton boats will be built, so successful have the five-ton ones been. At first, the farmers looked at them questioningly, fearing that they would sink. As we watched the morning's launchings, one sailed past with a good five tons of chemical fertiliser and a production team of six seated on top of it. Before many years are out the cement boat will be the most common type of boat on the vast network of canals and rivers of the Yangtze delta. Cheap to repair, easy to operate and with a strength superior to the wooden ones, they give new freedoms to the commune folk whose main system of transport is by canal. Production fell short during the hectic month of move and counter-move in January 1967, when but 90 boats were built instead of the 150 planned. But the loss is being rapidly made up. Costs have gone down from 448.39 yuan in January to 397.51 in May of 1967. In 1966, it took six workers — mostly commune lasses — to turn out a boat. Now eight of them can turn out two in the same time. New economies are being found and better work done than before the Cultural Revolution stormed in. The whole place is alive with its responsibility of putting Mao Tsetung's essay "Serve the People" into action.

During our stay in Shanghai our group split up, going to various places and meeting the participants in the stormy struggles. The veteran American correspondent Anna Louise Strong went to see things she liked, Sudanese friends to others. All of us were accompanied by the young rebels of Shanghai who were our hosts, and now had done so much to bring understanding where it was needed over the past year. Shanghai, a revolutionary city, will stay revolutionary — there is little doubt about that.

The next visits to Shanghai came in the spring and autumn of 1969 by which time the Cultural Revolution was firmly under the direction of the working class. In the spring I visited factories, two of which I have written something on.

Diesel Injectors in Shanghai

The working class of Shanghai can be rightly proud of its achievements. It has a glorious revolutionary tradition, and as an increasingly creative and class-conscious group it has learnt and is learning through struggle to analyse problems in the fields of politics and production and to act in the light of the Thought of Mao Tsetung, which presents so great a challenge and inspiration to them.

Anyone who has worked in the far hinterland of China with diesel trucks and tractors knows the importance of two things: good crankshaft bearings, and efficient oil injectors. How many a driver in the 'fifties has cursed the Soviet-made spare oil injector he used to replace a bad one when he found the spare no better than the part replaced. A new one that had come in exchange for a very considerable amount of pork that had made it perhaps the most expensive injector in the world, even though other foreign ones imported through Hongkong cost the Chinese worker an ounce of gold!

It was, therefore, with considerable interest in the late spring of 1969 that we went out into one of the northern suburbs of Shanghai to see a place where the resourcefulness of the Shanghai workers had flowered and these products were being successfully made; good crankshaft bearings which had been made in quantity for quite some time and, as a new product, injectors for diesel engines that conform to international standards and are sold per unit for just 4.40 yuan — under two US dollars!

The factory was the Shanghai Bearings Works, one of 658 workers and set up in 1955 as the result of 28 smaller shops being brought together. Under its direction at that time it turned out 1,500 bearings a shift, rising to 3,000 in 1960.

When the Cultural Revolution started the workers of the plant formed opposing groups, but united in September of 1967 and set up their three-way committee of old cadres, rebels and PLA men by the end of that year. Then study became vigorous, and by the beginning of 1968 the whole factory force had intensively studied and were using the three short essays — "Serve the People", "The Foolish Old Man Who Removed the Mountains" and "In Memory of Norman Bethune". All, too, had studied the directives that had come from Peking and all had joined groups for an extended study of Chairman Mao's works. From this period there have come to light many stories of the devotion to study. There is the woman worker Chia Shan-hsi, for instance, the wife of a cadre in the factory. She had been given away by her parents when she was a child. Her husband had been a buffalo boy before he became a small factory apprentice. She set up a study group with her husband in their home, and their increased determination as real activists became a great source of inspiration to all who worked around them. Chang Ming-rei is a deaf-mute. Yet he studied and used the Thought of Chairman Mao so well that people were influenced to tackle their work as he did. Though he could not talk he could write long passages from memory and was always optimistic, resourceful and keen. As a result of the new acupuncture treatment he has learnt now to say "Long live Chairman Mao", and he can also hear a little.

When a new production plan was being made, the quota was raised. The factory management thought that the only way to fulfil it was to add another shift and engage more workers. But the workers themselves in their political study groups asked whether this was not just carrying on the Liu Shao-chi revisionist policy. Not the real way out. This in turn led to a deeper study of revisionism by all, and a thorough criticism of the method was suggested. Groups studied their equipment, their methods, and went to work. On every side, now that worker inventiveness was brought to the fore ways were devised to do the job better and cheaper. Production for one shift went up to 3,600 bearings. Then it went on to 4,000, to 5,000, 6,000 and finally to a dramatic 10,300. At the same time, production costs were lowered by 53 percent, and the work was done by 13.5 percent less workers. The 1969 plan envisages raising production by a further 20 percent.

Now the workers were able to turn their attention to starting on the manufacture of injectors for diesel engines, and one third of the work force began work on the design and construction of 70 sets of machinery for this purpose. They had become used to getting over difficulties, especially in the struggles of 1968 when, due to the shortage of coal, the factory could not get the 30 tons of coal a month it needed for heat treatment necessary during one stage of the process, and in consequence had to devise a cold treatment which actually has turned out to be better, faster, and cheaper. Then too, there developed a shortage of tin and alloys which became for a time unobtainable. They searched through their own stores and found 20 tons of useful scrap which had been piled away. They visited all similar factories and talked and persuaded the workers to help them to meet the shortage. In consequence, there was no stoppage at all as they got all that was needed. Workers did overtime on their shifts without any complaint, scared neither of fatigue nor of the sub-zero weather of the early 1968 winter, putting in the automation that enabled the work to be done. One worker actually stayed on the job continuously for 48 hours, and almost had to be forced to go home and rest. Said one, "If there was no coal to cook, what would we do? Starve? Of course we'd find a way!" And in that spirit they went about setting up the production line for injectors. They knew that the Chinese people had been forced to pay heavily for injectors in the past, and willingly took on their shoulders the responsibility of making so precise an appliance. Accepting the challenge they went right out to meet it. Workers in other factories gave them old machine tools they could convert. Some of these machines look their age, but all have been remodelled so they do what is required of them accurately and efficiently. There are too, of course, many of the new streamlined machines as well, and then there are the worker adaptions for such processes as heat and cold treatment, testing and so on which are a joy to see. Like the struggle to alter the production line for the bearings, the setting up of this new production line for injectors took all the thought and energy workers were able to give it. One man who got sick went to the doctor and was given time off from work for a rest. He put the slip in his pocket and went back to work anyway. Workers said, "We don't need any kind of material incentive, no prizes or honors. We just want to be really loyal to the thinking of Chairman Mao and make our factory truly serve the people better." Time taken to complete various tasks shrank as enthusiasm grew — what once took 45 days is being done now in four or five. What took another factory making injectors three months to do was done here in 33 days. By October 1st 1968, the first injector was made and sent to Peking as a present to Chairman Mao. In two and a half months the workers had constructed 47 machines, and the production line through its 80 processes was working well enough so that, in January 1969, 150 injectors were produced. In February, 250; in March 2,605 and April promising a total well over 3,000 — our visit came at the end of the first week of that month.

The leader of the Revolutionary Committee is a 22-year-old worker who came to the factory in 1965. With him is an old cadre, and it was obvious that the two were working extremely well together. Most of the working force of the plant are young lads and lasses, and all seem determined to push ahead and gain still greater victories. Experimentation on adding automation to machines was still in progress, as we noted in passing. Now, in the next stage of Chinese industry, the world will be amazed at the pace with which advance is being made.

Handicapped Workers

Another factory visited in Shanghai was an unusual one. Each of the 13 districts of Shanghai municipality has its factory for handicapped people — the blind, deaf and mute, and those who are crippled in some other way.

The factory we went to see was out in the Hsuchiahui (Siccawei, in Shanghai dialect) district, and was called the Deaf and Mute Workers' Electrical Appliance Factory No. 2. A young worker who was head of the Revolutionary Committee told us the story. The factory, it seems, was set up in the Great Leap Forward, in 1959, and has grown from small to big, its products going into the internal and also to the export market.

After greetings, Sung Ya-ying, a blind woman worker, took the floor. She was young, strong, and good-looking, with beautiful eyes though they did not see. She told us to mention a quotation in the Little Red Book, which we did. She and her two companions then swiftly turned up their big braille books and read it off without a mistake. Braille is written in an alphabet, and the language is the Chinese common one so that all speak with a perfect accent, at times correcting their other Shanghai comrades for their use of dialect forms. She told us that the factory started with eight workers: four blind, four maimed in other ways. Now there are 320 people working in the plant, half of whom are blind. There are around 100 deaf and mute, then some who have crippled legs. The workers in the plant's machine shop are healthy and not handicapped people. Most of the blind were fairly old, and had known something of the bitterness of the old society where for those afflicted like them there were only three ways to try to make a living: tell fortunes, beg, or else take a clapper or fiddle and stand at street corners trying to amuse people and get a copper or two. Always dressed in rags despite winter rain or snow, ever having to be on the job — ever feeling they were a nuisance to their home folk, not as much use as a dog who could at least watch the door. Ever being looked on with contempt by the more fortunate around.

When they first started work, they had only bench tools. Following the principle of self-reliance, they built their own machine tools. "People who are exploited," she said, "cannot give up their lives to the exploiters. They have to make their own way ahead. Our technique was not good but our spirit was high," she went on. "We could reach after economic independence we had never been able to dream of obtaining, an independence with all the respect that brings. Our workers who could see went to other factories and learnt. Every machine we have in the plant we have made ourselves, and in doing this we have changed our own thinking and have grown in political understanding and ability. No longer are we "waste products", but are responsible members of an advancing society. This means a great deal to those who have felt the weight of a policeman's baton, or the kick of a Kuomintang soldier in the old society. When we came to study the short essay "The Foolish Old Man Who Removed the Mountains", our determination stiffened. Each and every word struck deep into our being. Now we can analyse in the light of all we have learnt, realising that all difficulties are but paper tigers if one meets them together and with an iron will.

"Yes, at first we blind had to carefully feel the driving belts and machines, listening, memorising, taking machines to pieces, then putting them together until we could do this correctly. We had to learn the names of parts, what they are made of, where they go, all with infinite patience, and then each motion of the production process. Even on Sunday rest days the workshops would have many of the blind coming in and working away mastering their machines. Now ever since we have been mechanised, we have not had a single industrial accident with our blind, though, as you see, the machines are fast-moving ones, and our production does not falter. Because our blind folk have had to be so dependent on touch, they are clever with their hands, and so can easily repair a machine when it develops a fault. There is not more than a three per 1,000 wastage in production. We have the sympathetic assistance of factory leaders in all we try to do, and we deal now with every difficulty as if we were facing the enemy.

"When we first came to the factory, we were full of happiness at being able to get wages. Then as we studied and learnt the real meaning of life, we came to feel that we are truly part of the world revolution, and that our chief function is to serve the people regardless of self. In 1964 we got a contract to make materials for Vietnam. Then we felt that the bitterness of the people of Vietnam was our bitterness and so put our whole heart and soul into doing the task as well as it could possibly be done, the workshop becoming our battleground. Though we cannot see, yet in our mind's eye we can look out over the whole world where there are people like ourselves and do all we can to liberate them. We have studied revisionism and now know just where that leads, ever hating the Liu Shao-chi line and ever determined to hold more closely to the Thought of Chairman Mao. No production quota has ever been given us that we have not fulfilled, and we think of our factory as not only a place where we produce, but also as a school for political study."

The leader of the deaf-mute group then took up the story, speaking dramatically on his hands, his face full of expression and lighting up as he made this exciting point, then that. He told how formerly a group of medical experts, nurses and many appliances had been brought to the factory, how experiments were made on the deaf and mute to see if the appliances would produce results. After a month and a half the specialists went off, leaving a nurse in charge. Then she too went, and no one was in any way cured. Now, since the successful application of an acupuncture theory by a certain PLA medical unit, an Army medical group came in, armed simply with the acupuncture needles. They carefully asked all the deaf and mute the reasons for their condition, visited their homes and talked with their people. After they had given a medical check-up they started treatment. Their course runs to three periods of 60 days each, there being sub-periods of ten days' needling, followed by three of rest inside each major period, each course separated from the other by a rest.

"The PLA medical workers come into the factory to do the needling," he said, "and we deaf-mutes just leave our benches and go to them for a little while until the needling is done, and then return to work without any fuss." Five of the younger ones are already speaking and hearing quite well. Ten sing many songs, while 50 can say "Long life to Chairman Mao". After he told us all of this, he and his companion sang us many songs and made us a speech that was clear and understandable. They were both at the beginning of the second course.

When we visited the factory it was turning out wall fittings for sockets needed in connecting up motors in industrial plants, parts being made out of plastic, porcelain and brass. It made one feel humble to see quite old blind women taking fine screws and drilling hole centres so exactly and so swiftly. In the factory too, were a group of Shanghai school children who had come to do practical work during their school day and to learn from the handicapped how to make struggle a meaningful thing. They were very well dressed and perky, and sang us a couple of songs while they worked. One felt that they were privileged children indeed in being able to come to such a factory that was so filled with expression of working-class spirit at its best.

In November of 1969 I came to Shanghai once more, spending some of the bright autumn days seeing more of what had been done.

Shanghai, November 1969

Perhaps no place in China changes so rapidly as does Shanghai. One of the great industrial cities of the world, its factories are manned by a working force which now so rightly feels itself to be victor after the struggles of the Cultural Revolution. A force fired with the determination of Mao Tsetung Thought to carry on the revolution and produce all the things which the revisionists said were out of reach of Chinese industry at this stage. A morning spent going from hall to hall of the great Shanghai Industrial Exhibition gave a first overall impression of how well they are succeeding. I had been to see the exhibition in its early stages in other years, but got a considerable surprise coming this time and finding so much that was new. Amongst the exciting things we saw was new style automation machinery controlled by computers that not only record and control, but also do repairs in some cases. Many different processes in machine-building were thus fully automated. New kinds of generators, turbines, new steel furnaces, giant trucks, an electron microscope that enlarges up to 200,000 times, down to the most modern electrical watches and delicate measuring tools — all were there. There was also mention of plants that used part of their waste for fuel. The spirit the demonstrators put into their task was contagious. They were anxious to have visitors feel as they did, that what has been done was in the main a result of advances made in political understanding, which was indeed the case. The visit was an excellent preliminary to a closer view of some of Shanghai's factories in this present stage.

Truck Plant

We went out into industrial Shanghai one morning to look at the plant that had turned out the 15-ton truck which we had seen in the industrial exhibition. We found it was called the "Shanghai Truck Manufacturing Works", and was where 1,200 workers turned out four-ton gasoline-engined trucks for use mainly around Shanghai. In the old days of foreign settlements, the site had been a garage and repair shop operated by a foreigner. Then, after the Japanese defeat, it had been used as a storehouse by the Kuomintang. With Liberation it became a truck repair station. At that time China had to use existing vehicles all of which had been imported, so that in all 151 kinds of trucks were serviced — the different vintages of 26 foreign brands. Parts often had to be made, as none were available any longer in Shanghai. Then came the Great Leap Forward, and workers decided that they must step out and make a serviceable truck themselves. So early in 1959 a total of 54 days was spent in producing a four-ton model. This somewhat confounded the critics who said that before a truck could be attempted three to five years would be needed to draw up proper plans and have them approved. They also said that without capital and sophisticated tooling it was unlikely that a working truck could ever be turned out. Workers, however, kept on with this production in addition to their repair work, raising the power of their new truck engine from 80 to over 100 h.p. But it was not easy to expand. There were Liu Shao-chi supporters who were against workers stepping out and making trucks, and who would not give more working space or better tools. Workers did not have the right kind of steel for the whole of front and rear axles, so had to tap on the parts which would carry the wheels and weld them into position, after the 26-lb. manually operated hammers had driven the sleeve on. Many kinds of such innovations and extemporisations had to be made all along the line, but in the end the workers did succeed in creating a production line, building the machines they wanted and turning out the kind of vehicle that is in so much demand around the city.

Then came the need to produce a 15-ton model tip truck for mining work, with the result that the first models of this vehicle were turned out in time for October 1st, 1969. Some 71 other plants contributed in helping to provide parts for it, an example of what cooperation can do under socialism. The new truck is a diesel oil burning model, and has passed exhaustive tests well.

The production of the four-ton model has gone up 20 percent since the start of the Cultural Revolution in 1966. Seventy percent of all parts needed are made in the factory. One 8-hour shift is worked, with two in a few of the busier departments. Over 60 percent of the workers are men. In the Cultural Revolution the administration was heavily cut down, with those who remained also taking part at times in actual work in the plant.

We went through the various shops and enjoyed having workers explain their innovations and how much these had saved in work time. As the factory has just grown and grown from small to big on whatever land has been available, there will soon come the need for a completely new plant, with automation playing a bigger part and production more streamlined than it has been possible to make it at present. With a politically working force such as the factory has now nearly anything can be done.

Lathe Part Factory

This was also shown well in another factory visited in Shanghai. An unusual place out past the pagoda at Lunghua, situated by a canal, it was once the forwarding station for coffins being returned to the country-side. As most of the people of Shanghai have their original roots in the country, and according to custom wanted to be buried in their home village, the receiving and forwarding of encoffined remains assumed large proportions and a station was set up to carry on this work, its workers being some of the very poor of Shanghai. When the appeal to get rid of old customs came in 1966 at the beginning of the Cultural Revolution, the whole business was stopped. Remains were then cremated and that was that. The authorities at that stage in Shanghai, however, were out to create confusion and halt the Cultural Revolution if they could. They simply closed the station and threw the 160 employees out of work. At that moment the PLA stepped into the picture and had the order reversed. But what were such unskilled workers to do? After making inquiries they found there was room for a factory cutting up metal ingots and steel plate to required sizes for industry. An overhead crane was needed to get metal sheets up to the shearing machines. A suitable disused one was finally found, then at midnight when the streets were clear it was hauled all the way across the city and out to Lunghua. But before this was done, the whole of the big yard had to have its level raised and be paved, filled in with stones and rubble, for it was at paddy field level and in times of rain a sea of mud. Workers went out to all sorts of places collecting concrete and brick rubble. Many of them were women, and the way they threw themselves into the task alongside the men was epic. All kinds of methods had to be thought out to get the heavy machines loaded, brought out and then unloaded, installed and put into production. Despite the fact that the big majority of the workers were illiterate and not a few getting on in age, every single problem was solved and first production targets were successfully met. Then someone heard a story about Japanese traders joking down at the Canton (Kwang-chow) Fair. Lathe chucks, the line centres of the face plate for holding the piece being machined, were being purchased from Japan. The traders said, "Why, the Chinese can make hydrogen bombs, but they can't make their own lathe chucks." This story went around, and finally it was decided that it would be a good idea if one plant specialised on these. So the story was told to the sheet-metal cutters and they were inspired to start in on the task. At first they bought old machine tools that were being discarded as scrap and remodelled them. With factory workers' advice which they sought they improvised all kinds of substitute methods, but they made chucks, and very good ones too. Then when it was seen what an excellent product they turned out, modern grinders, better milling machines and shapers came in. Some of these machines had come before the construction of the new shop to hold them was finished, so they were being operated under temporary shelter while the building of the shop went on overhead, enclosing the shelter as well as the machines, we noted. Other shops already constructed were being re-tooled.

We looked at the discarded Japanese-made chucks that had been brought in as specimens from various factories after a year of use, and then at some of those made here which had been used for a similar period. There was considerable difference in favor of the latter. It is estimated that chucks now being produced will last, doing their work precisely, over three times as long as foreign models that have been imported. At the testing bench, each of the parts of the chuck is exhaustively tested for accuracy. I talked to a woman operating a new grinding machine. Yes, she was an old worker of the plant, had come up through its struggles and was proud of it. "We have a very good future in serving the people in this way. We are all happy with it," she said quietly and sincerely.

With each change, groups of workers have been sent to big Shanghai factories to learn for periods of from one to three months, and it is amazing how fast the workers have mastered technique by concentrating on their work, discussing it with work comrades and setting themselves definite goals. Quite a few of the menfolk were once refugees from rural north Kiangsu — "Kompo-nying", in Shanghai dialect — the poorest of the poor. But given a chance to fight their way clear of their old condition they set about it in no uncertain terms. As soon as it is found that, with innovations and through mechanisation, fewer workers are required, more work is sought, more machines glide up the canal alongside and are hauled up to be installed and made to work for the good of the people of China. The work force has now been joined by some new middle-school graduates.

Pharmaceutical Factory

Pharmaceuticals for Western medicine in the old days were largely imported. A foreign firm, "Kofa", had a small factory in Shanghai which made up a few household remedies like eye drops, cough mixture and first-aid medicines, all from imported materials, but that was about all. Now spreading out from the old "Kofa" plant is the Shanghai Pharmaceutical Factory No. 4, just one of the many Shanghai plants that supply modern drugs to the hinterland. After Liberation installations were quickly planned and erected here for the manufacture of the three most commonly used antibiotics, which were consequently produced in great quantity and marketed cheaply. In the three years of the Cultural Revolution, four more antibiotics were mass-produced in this one plant, and others which are now being experimented with show great promise. In this past year, prices for antibiotics made here have been cut by 40 to 60 percent. "Serving the people does not mean taking excess profits from them," one of our hosts said. "With better methods, we can now do the job more cheaply."

The Revolutionary Committee feels that it can now advance more swiftly than ever before, as full play is being given to ideas of the workers. Formerly, worker innovations when suggested were simply put aside and not bothered with. "What can mere workers understand of higher chemistry!" was the usual comment. The revisionist line then in power believed in relying on expertise only. But now workers are determined that they will go into new fields, that no problem will be too big for them to tackle. "The bigger they are the harder they fall" is their attitude. "Difficulties are made to be brought down!" Of the 1,600 workers in the plant, 600 are women. Three 8-hour shifts are worked in the more important shops. One hour's political study is done every day after work.

It is a big plant to go over. One climbs up many iron-rung stairways, wends one's way through a veritable forest of pipes, around great containers until finally, down on the ground floor again, one looks through the glass panel of a door and sees the product coming down like white snow before going on to an automated bottling and packing line prior to being sent out.

A Shanghai Hospital

I went to one of the old Shanghai hospitals to see medicine in action. It was once part of a Catholic Mission, set up in 1907 and named Kuangtzu. It then had three grades of accommodation but made its income mainly from the top grade, which catered for officials of the old French Concession where it was situated, rich Chinese and so on. In the third-grade wards, ordinary people came and, as ample proof shows, were often used for experimentation. No doctors or nurses were on duty at night, the place being left in charge of ward servants. In just one day, as records show, there were 20 deaths in the poor wards. In 1951, the whole place was taken over and made into the hospital of the Second Medical College of Shanghai. Its beds were increased from 700 to 1,100. Staff members were added as the hospital was given new duties — it had to keep clinics in 30 factories it served, to assist in commune clinics in counties around Shanghai, and provide teaching staff for the medical college built next door. So the staff of 300 went up to 1,700. In place of 30 doctors, there were 300, the number of nurses went up from 40 to 480, of technicians from 70 to 200. The 13 subdivisions of the hospital were increased to 20.

In the Great Leap Forward, the whole medical staff set out to raise standards, achieving bigger successes in their work. In the Cultural Revolution, they set out to get rid of old worship of foreign expertise and method and make a closely integrated working unit, to clear the minds of the older staff of revisionist or reactionary ideas, and to step forward on both feet. Pharmaceutical and instrument-making factories cooperated by giving them drugs, equipment, and instruments better and cheaper than those which had been imported at so great a cost. We went through the seven big operating theatres and watched operations being done. Equipment bought from abroad at a cost of 5,000 yuan was being replaced by some which cost but 500 yuan and did the job better.

Some of the most dramatic things that have been done are in the realm of burn surgery. We looked through a window at one patient who had 99 percent of his skin area burnt. A 19-year-old worker burnt by chemicals, he had lived eight days already and the hospital was optimistic about his chances. His own spirit was high though he lay prone and naked on a special bed. We then talked with three others, the most severe case being that of a Hupeh iron worker who had 89.3 percent of the skin surface burnt and had had both hands amputated, lips and ears burnt away. With the aid of a rubber band with a holder on it that kept a pen in place, the man could write. Indeed he had written a long poem in praise of Chairman Mao and then proceeded to show us how he did it. He had learnt how to do many things for himself, and was full of spirit and the will to live and do things again.

The hospital has achieved considerable success with replacing completely amputated limbs. The seven done already have been entirely successful. The eighth seemed to be much more of a problem on arrival. A young collier from coal mines in Anhwei had his leg run over by a coal truck down in the mine and completely amputated. The bone was crushed for the width of the section of the wheel that cut it through. It took 24 hours to get him down to Shanghai, and the blood vessels were not all joined up finally until six hours later, making it 30 hours in all since the accident happened. His name is Wu Shao-chen, and he is a Shaohsien man from Anhwei, 23 years old. He told us his views, stating them quite clearly and with much determination. All for Chairman Mao. He expects to get back to the coal face and put Mao Tsetung Thought into action again. Yes, one leg will be a bit shorter than the other, but he can wear a thicker boot to compensate, he feels. He also feels that he owes the people a great deal and wants to pay some of the debt, at least. His leg was still in plaster, but he could get around already on crutches.

Doctors and nurses are now not so sharply divided as they were in other days. Once there were several grades of both doctors and nurses. Now such practice is out. Doctors encourage nurses to learn and do, and to gradually become doctors in turn. Quite a few of the young-looking members of operating teams we watched had been nurses who had learnt. Amongst recent operations such teams have carried out was one on a nine-year-old boy with a malignant tumor on the lung. They successfully removed it, and the child has become well and has gone back to his village, there being no recurrence.

So does the old superstructure now come to be a thing really in the service of the people. A process that has started here in China, yet one with a world-wide application as the people take power. The overall impression of this institution after the Cultural Revolution was that it had become a youthful, dedicated, well-integrated group with a well-defined common aim and increased technical ability.

Satellite Town

It is good to go back to one of the new satellite towns set up around Shanghai in the Great Leap Forward of 1959, and see how people there have fared.   Pengpu is a housing estate with 3,600 families, 16,000 people in all, in flats contained in four- and five-storied modern buildings, 120 rows of them.   Fifteen factories have their workers' housing here, many of the workers being steel mill men.   There is a street of shops where almost everything which can be bought in the city is obtainable, and there are housing estate factories for workers' dependents, making small transistor radios, plastic parts for the electrical industry, doing clothing repair, shoe making etc.   There are two middle schools with a total of 1,000 students and two primary schools with 4,000.   There is a hospital with some 50 doctors and nurses and a kindergarten for 300 children. For women who work in factories there are nurseries in the factories themselves, but many of the homes have old people who take good care of the children there.   Now too, with the growth of Mao Tsetung Thought study groups, these older people are looking around for useful things to do for other people to put theory into practice, and to see to it that there is no hardship incurred when both husband and wife are away.   Study groups arrange for people to take turns helping a household when a mother is sick, for instance, and has to go to hospital.   They encourage old people to take part in collective living instead of just idling away the days of retirement, to fill them with some purpose, even if it is only helping the children to sweep the yards, tidy the gardens, and so on. Study groups too, get them to make themselves available as speakers at group meetings, to tell of the horrors of the old society.   They also mem-orise Chairman Mao's poems and teach them to youngsters.   Study groups can help many a family with human problems that arise and in encourag-ing health work.   Most of the older people in retirement have had a hard life and have been through heartbreaking struggles.   Yang Si-mei, a widow, lived for many years in a shack made out of split-open gasoline tins.   It was built up on the drying stage over the top floor of an alley-way house, the bare stage being sublet for the purpose by the subtenants of the two rooms below.   Her first eight children had all died.   At last she had a boy and girl whom she managed to keep alive until Liberation. These now both work in factories around and have started families of their own.   Families have their heroes — this one an eldest son killed fighting imperialism in the Korean War, that one with a daughter work-ing on a state farm away on the Sinkiang border.   Children now get a thorough training in socialist morality.   They find something that has been accidentally dropped, and it gets back to the housing office at once. Pocketbooks, watches, fountain pens are just some of the things which have been returned.

Not only do study group leaders, school teachers and parents help to instil the ideas of service to the people into youngsters, the old folk who help with sweeping also play their part quite naturally.   They tell the children, "See, your skin has never been broken with beating.   But your present has not been easy to obtain.   It has come only after many have fought for you.   So we must carry on and follow Chairman Mao. There are many people in the world still to be liberated!"   Youngsters have been good in finding ways to help.   Slide rubbish baskets down from top flats, put boards on the stairs, pave muddy paths with stones they collect, wash the lost handkerchiefs small children have dropped and put them out to dry on bushes so that mothers can see them and take those which are theirs away. Some old women have been illiterate, only learning characters when they have come to study groups. One of these visualises characters when she goes to bed, then in the night awakes and finds that she has forgotten how one or two of them are written. She gets up, puts on the light and finds the place in the book. Then, satisfied that she will now remember them, goes back to sleep. In the Cultural Revolution, a new appreciation of class struggle is being gained and people's vigilance against class enemies is being raised, a leader of the Revolutionary Committee of the estate, a sweet-faced woman named Shih Ching-pu, told us. When we said good-bye, after having seen the kindergarten children perform items in each of their classrooms, and having visited several flats and talking with the folk there, she wished success to revolutionary work in New Zealand. The trees between the blocks of housing were rich in autumn colors. The place was alive with children who also came to shake hands. So many small, eager hands! The river of change flows deeply and strongly in Shanghai, one felt as one drove back to the city. In another ten years it is certain all will have changed again.

The Shanghai Machine Tools Plant

The Shanghai Machine Tools Plant is not a small concern. It employs 3,400 workers who operate the rapidly modernising plant for three 8-hour shifts a day. Way back in 1942 the factory was founded by a Japanese capitalist who started to make armaments for the Japanese forces then in occupation of Shanghai and so much of China. When the Kuomintang returned, the militarist Tang En-po took over, but employed only a mere skeleton force of workers, the place being mainly used for getting hold of raw materials for speculation. Anything there was an offer for, would be sold. So when the people came to take over there were but 24 workers and 20 machines left. With these, however, lathe, shaper, and milling-machine cutters were made. In 1952, some new buildings were constructed, the work force increased and more essential tools turned out. Said a factory leader in effect, "We had grown between 1949 and 1956, using collective leadership and depending on our work force helping to solve problems, doing so with considerable success. In 1956, however, there came down directives from Peking embodying the Liu Shao-chi line. We were asked from then on to study USSR methods and to listen to Soviet experts, a group of whom were sent to the factory. They set up a bureaucratic control system, a single chain of command that had to be obeyed. Workers were not given their head as before, it being impressed on them that nothing they had to say was of value anyway. Workers were not to bother about the factory affairs, but go out and amuse themselves. So all kinds of material incentive were offered, this being labelled 'progressive'." Innovations suggested by practical workers now were turned down as being no good. Soviet methods of prizes, fining and firing were introduced. Then came the Great Leap Forward of 1958-59. Again workers came to the fore and production rose 100 percent. A big success was made in the manufacture of fine drills for watch-making and other similar instruments. Previously all such things had been imported. A worker, Tse Fu-lin, made 280 experiments before producing one high-precision machine. But it was so excellent that Ko Ching-shih, revolutionary political leader then of Shanghai, named him "worker-engineer", and he met Chairman Mao. Thirty kinds of new fine tool accessories were turned out. By 1960 production had gone up seven times. Then came the bad years. The worst period was 1962-64 when the Liu Shao-chi line came back in full force. Masses of rules came down to be applied to workers, and all kinds of bureaucratic procedures seemed designed to make workers servants of their machines. They were told to operate only inside the maze of rules. Any kind of innovation had to be passed first by the shop foreman, and then go on up through administrative channels through all departments before it came to the chief man. The leaders at that time were mostly old Kuomintang people with poor political understanding. In consequence of all this, during 1962-64 production fell 30 percent. Not only the management but also the Party group in the factory supported the Liu Shao-chi line. There was a growing confusion in the minds of many workers as a result of all this. Then, in 1966, the drama of the exposure of intrigues of the reaction in cultural circles got started. Following this, and as the Cultural Revolution began to gather force, many opinions were expressed in the factory. There were many meetings and much argument. Some groups went this way, some that, until in January 1967 one rebel group in the factory seized power. There were over 100 groups of workers then organised, but on June 5th they all came together in the grand alliance. Then in September 1967 the Revolutionary Committee was set up and took over. It is well worth recording that all through this very tough struggle production did not halt for one day. After the Revolutionary Committee took over came the period of struggle, criticism and transformation, combined with an intensive course of study in Chairman Mao's works. Workers here are preponderantly young, a great many 18-year-olds being added in the 1958-59-60 period, and then many from the factory's own middle school and college during the Cultural Revolution. Forty percent of the total number of workers are women.

We went around the plant, finding that it covered considerable acreage. It took over what had been a storage place for coffins, for it had been the custom of people from distant parts of China to pay storage on the coffins of the departed until such time as conditions in the interior or their own financial position permitted the remains to be sent back there. Shanghai had been a place of refuge for many landlords and rich people of the interior, and they were content to pay even quite high rent for a place to deposit their dead comfortably. This kind of business was definitely not included in the new day, so this factory fell heir to a big area on which to build new shops, making an attractive garden of the central part. We watched as we went around, bright little shafts of steel being carried by automation into machines, electrically heated, then cut, finally becoming beautifully made machine drill bits dropping nonchalantly into a container below. Much automation was being put into effect. More will come as a scheduled complete re-tooling is finished. The products being turned out are of high standard and able to compete internationally. The circular saws for cutting steel plate have been considered by foreign traders better than British models.

The factory is playing its part in helping to change education in schools around the neighborhood, and has its representatives in worker groups going to the big universities. Looking back, there is a good deal of questioning of the kind of education the Soviet experts advocated. One factory technician, a college graduate, worked on making a tool from Soviet specifications. Its production record was poor; moreover, over 25 percent of its output was defective. A similar machine tool made by workers did the job better and produced less than five percent rejects. Technician Mei Yao-hsing was a good worker, a graduate of a middle school. Showing much ability, he was sent to Harbin Technical College to take a course. He stayed four years out of the seven-year course, but considered he was not getting as much real education as he would have been getting in the factory itself. Apparently, while the Soviet experts were in the factory they tried to build a machine to send back to the USSR, if successful. It was kept a great secret. Try as they would, however, they could not get it to work properly. After they left, workers constructed one which did the job they set out to do, properly. Small wonder, then, that the problem of how to educate the next generation for industry comes up in their minds. If a certain sort of education is of no use to the people, then what is it good for?

Shanghai Electric Meter Factory

One morning we went out into the Hongkew area of Shanghai, coming to a building that was once a Japanese army headquarters. A big, three-floored place round an internal compound. Here today are situated the shops of the Shanghai Electric Meter Factory, employing some 800 workers, building various kinds of meters, from big sets to be installed in the Mao Tsetung Hydroelectric Factory in Albania down to small voltmeters for common diesel engines. It was first established by bringing together the workers of some 20 small street workshops. In the Great Leap Forward, many kinds of meters were turned out and there was a big surge ahead, with workers pressing eagerly forward. Then after 1960 came the bureaucratic, revisionist Liu Shao-chi line, which the factory leadership rigidly enforced, and when the Cultural Revolution came there was considerable struggle. The Party leader posed as an old revolutionary and had quite a following who believed him largely for that reason. For a time the working group was split up and there was much in-fighting. Finally the PLA came in, and more investigations were made into just who was stoking the fires of internal strife. It was found that the "old revolutionary" was really a Kuomintang agent in disguise with a long history of counter-revolutionary work. It had been his policy to divide. To cut a long story short, however, after the Revolutionary Committee of ten which included three old cadres, one old worker and the rest young workers was set up, production went ahead rapidly. Today 80-90 kinds of meters are made, the products being used not only in Shanghai but also in 30 foreign countries. In 1968 production was 23 percent above that of 1966, and in 1969 the year's plan already reached was 20 percent above that of 1968. Many new innovations have been put to use, including some automation. Russian meters had proved to be defective and all needed replacing in big Shanghai factories. This is being done. One big steel mill which had its representative working and observing in this plant has made the change-over of its Russian meters to Shanghai-made ones already. There were three difficult meters to make. One for recording generator revolutions, another for kilo-amperes, and another a special voltmeter. Experts reckoned it would take two to three years to plan and produce them. A group of workers came together, brought their bedding to the factory and went all out, day and night experimenting and discussing until they had the answer. For the most difficult meter, that for recording generator revolutions, it took two and a half months to iron out difficulties and build. All kept up with political study, gaining in determination as they did so. Fifty-six percent of the work force are women, 58.4 percent of them are under 30. We noted one pretty lass working on a complicated task who was already on the way to becoming an old-timer. She was 19 and had been in the plant for a year now. Then there was one really old worker, a technician who was a sturdy, capable 59 and to whom much credit is due in helping to make new innovations. He was invited to Peking for the 20th celebration of the founding of New China on October 1st and felt very privileged to have seen Chairman Mao at close hand. Something indeed for a one-time child slave worker, sent from Nantung to Shanghai when he was 13 to work in the cruel machine-shop industry of that time.

One of the girl workers who is on the Revolutionary Committee and who had taken part in the group which had fought to produce the meters needed, said that the most important thing was to convince everyone that they could do the job, and that for this the study of Chairman Mao's works was invaluable.

Wrist Watch Factory

Almost every visitor who comes to Shanghai and is invited to see some of the outstanding work done, is taken to the plant where wrist watches are made. The wrist watch is so personal a thing — of interest to everyone. There is a terrific demand for good wrist watches in China, especially in the hinterland communes, and this plant is the pioneer in the land. Soon a second one will come into production in Shanghai, and there are already plants in both Peking and Tientsin. This Shanghai plant, now getting old, was started in 1955, and made its first watch for October 1st of that year. It had many faults, of course, as a first model would. However, with better equipment and materials available, a big production drive began during the Great Leap Forward, and much modernising was done. By 1966, 900,000 watches a year were produced. So far in this one year of 1969, 1,500,000 have been made. The 1966 model was corrected to a variation of 45 seconds in 24 hours. The 1969 model has a variation of not more than 30 seconds. The number of parts has been cut down from 154 to 137, and standards have been raised. Before 1960 the plant had to get hair springs, main springs and watch jewels from the USSR. Many of the springs were faulty. Now these three parts are produced up to standard in Shanghai. This year two new models have been made, an electrically operated watch and then an automatic, waterproof model.

In 1958, some automatically operated Swiss machines were bought and installed in the former tobacco factory nearby, which had been taken over and which had large modern workrooms. Today, 70 percent of all machines used are made in either the factory or else by supporting plants. Surely there have been many difficulties. In the early stages, Shanghai did not produce fine drills. Steel sewing needles had to be machined to make drills fine enough. 146 small workshops in the Hongkew and Yangtzepoo districts helped to get the first mechanisation going, but now the factory with its own machine shops and its seven other big production departments goes ahead on its own steam.

It was a pleasure to go around, first seeing the long lines of automatically operating machines working along by themselves, dropping tiny parts into trays. Then, how impressive it was to see the lines of workers testing and sorting parts, all working with modern equipment! We put on white coats and wore rubber slippers when we went into the final assembly room for the thrill of seeing all those parts come together in a nicely working watch. New kinds of automation are being tried out here. As in the electric meter factory, research work is not being done in distant laboratories but right on the spot, as is designing. In one department we noticed many primary-school boys who were being given tasks to make up their afternoon's practical work. The factory leadership is now a Revolutionary Committee of 11, set up in December 1967 and consisting of revolutionary old cadres, a factory militia representative, and workers. All do a period each week on bench work. The administrative cadre group of 300 has been cut down to 100, and every effort is being made to close the gap between cadre and production worker.

Watch Jewel Factory

Closely associated with the wrist watch factory is the plant which produces the jewels for watch bearings. Work with such tiny necessities is no less difficult than that for any other high-precision machining. In this age of chemicals the stone for the jewel can be made as hard as necessary, is sliced off a block, made into tiny shafts from which the jewels are cut, and then goes on down through a whole line of processing until the final product comes out, needing to be looked at through a microscope in order to appreciate the machining which has been done.

We visited this plant out in the western district of Shanghai.   Up until 1960 it had made fountain pens, with 700 workers.   Then it went on to filling the need for good jewels, since it was becoming difficult to buy any from the USSR and much of what was bought was defective.   The beginnings were tough, for whole sets of machinery had to be devised. Sometimes several kinds of machines to do the same process were built to see which one operated best and which could be still further improved upon.   The old workers showed much skill in this.   The result was that a minimum of machinery was bought from abroad, and now by 1969 there is no longer the need to bring in any more, for many kinds of automation are being successfully introduced, the machinery for it being made by the plant itself.   The very expensive foreign diamonds needed for cutting have been dispensed with, and diamond sand which is easily available in China at a very low price substitutes well.

In 1965, a modern industrial building was erected with good lighting and facilities. Many young people, graduates of schools, were taken on as workers, bringing the number of workers to around 1,000.   Eighty more young people have been taken on from schools during the Cultural Revolution.   Research and experimentation are now done on the job, and inspection testing is done by a group of old workers rather than by technicians sent down by an old-time manager.   In 1964-65 and 1966, production remained about the same each year — 700,000 sets of 17 jewels each.   In 1968 it had risen to a million sets, and by the beginning of November 1969 to two million, it being expected that by the end of the year it will have gone to 2,500,000 sets.

The factory management formerly were keen worshippers of everything foreign.   Right down to the forceps used to pick up tiny jewels, they insisted that foreign makes only could be used.   The new Revolutionary Committee went to a medical instrument factory and had them made at a fraction of the cost of the imported, and every bit as good in use. Better, the workers say.   The synthetic jewels are a glittering red, so workers say with pride that their watches have a real Chinese red heart.

In the Liu Shao-chi period, when factories were ordered to go right out for profits, the bad custom of keeping everything secret arose in some places.   Obviously, why share methods with other plants, which under revisionism would become competitors rather than brothers?   Now that idea has been well and truly smashed.   Every success, every better way discovered is eagerly shared with every plant in the country doing like production.

Aerated Water Factory

Down in Yangtzepoo is an old aerated water factory operated by foreign interests in the other day. It had been established in 1923. Its work was seasonal, so there was a good deal of hardship amongst employees when they were laid off each winter. It was a typical foreign enterprise operated to gain the maximum profit in the shortest time. Now as a socialist plant it has arranged to have regular work for its 1,800 workers throughout the year. In the summer time all are busy with the various kinds of drinks, while in the winter the making of confectionery and glucose takes precedence. Production rises fast, the 1969 output being 74 percent over 1966. As well as the aerated waters, fruit cordials are also made, as is the edible rice paper used as inner wrapping of some sweets. In some big Shanghai industrial plants where work is done at high temperatures and where there is a great deal of sweating, a lemon drink is prescribed by the doctors. So big beer bottles are filled with this for summer-time factory demand. 5,500 tons of sweets were made last winter and 15,000 tons of glucose, much of which goes into the export market. During the Liu Shao-chi period, an expert was sent in to assist the plant with new products. He ignored asking the opinions of workers and fussed away with one or two technicians. Busy for almost three years, still he produced nothing. Now, as one goes around the plant he sees that since the whole business of automation and technical innovation has been thrown open to the workers a whole range of new methods has been introduced. The Revolutionary Committee here was set up in September 1967 and has 14 members. Five are old cadres, two factory militia representatives, and seven workers.

Chi Yi Commune

Like all China's industrial centres, Shanghai has to depend on the countryside for its food. The role of the rural commune in city environs, therefore, is an important one. The first commune ever organised here was one southeast of the city. It is Chi Yi Commune set up in 1958. It has 11 brigades, eight small factories, two middle schools, several primary schools, and a hospital. It is electrified and mechanised with eight big tractors and 20 small ones. It has 230 pumps operated by electric motors.

It was a warm autumn day when we went to visit it. The leader of the Revolutionary Committee was an upper middle-school graduate who had come to work there during the movement for socialist education in the countryside. He spoke proudly of results that are now being gained. Of the 20,800 mou, in round figures, 10,000 are in grain, 6,000 in cotton and 4,000 in vegetables. The Cultural Revolution saw the complete ending of the old grave mounds, so that they no longer stand in the way of tractors. Also irrigation canals have been put underground and the land they once occupied put into production. By this underground pipe method there is a considerable saving in water. Air vents like chimneys rise at places along the line of the canal, but they are easily passed by mechanisation, so do not offer any obstacle. The commune itself makes the needed reinforced concrete pipes. Grain production in the brigade has gone up from 400 jin a mou in 1950 to 1,200 jin in 1969. On cotton fields, production has increased five times in the same period. In the Liu Shao-chi years, some cadres tried to push for his revisionist line of working for swift gain. Vegetables, they said, bring more profit. "Let's grow more of them and not bother about grain or cotton," they argued. But the commune leadership went on with the original plan, and the brigades followed suit. Now the commune supports itself in grain, sells its quota, sets aside its own stores on commune, brigade and production team levels, and then sells a considerable surplus to the state.

We went to the commune implement repair works and, in addition to seeing the various repairs being made, watched the young people making electrical motors for the countryside. Last summer there was a flash flood which inundated a good deal of the land around Shanghai for some hours. But with everyone jumping into the waters and saving things that were floating off, and then with pumps pumping out, no great damage was done. The biggest crop in history was later harvested.

We visited the dairy farm, the piggeries, the poultry farm and the mushroom-growing houses where nine floors of mushrooms were happily sprouting, and then went to sit for a while in a farmhouse. The old man was out in the fields but his son and the son's wife entertained us. There also was a smiling and charmingly friendly four-months-old baby. They were ex-poor peasants, and he had come out of the Army a year or so ago to go back to his commune work. He now supervises primary schools for the commune. His wife works in one of the production enterprises. They talked about the importance of political study, which indeed is a way of life for all these folk now. They study in their production teams and in their homes, in school and factory. "We have to step up our vigilance, and we have to prepare against war," the commune leader said. There is no question but that that is being done.

For the rest, the most important victory that has been won, perhaps, is that against liver fluke, which in the bad old days infected 80 percent of the population. Swollen stomachs, early death, childless women, list-lessness and misery were some of the things the disease caused. Formerly, the carrier of the disease, the "ting lo" snail, was to be found everywhere. Now it is hard to find one. In the commune hospital there is a staff of 60, of whom 40 spend a great deal of their time going around the brigades and helping there. Each brigade has its two "barefoot" doctors who do many of the simple treatments and take an active part in preventive work. We visited the kindergarten where some 200 young hopefuls sang and danced for us. Now there is no apparent difference between the well looked after city child and his fellow in the commune around, except that the country one is healthier and better complexioned due to fresh air and sun. Food on the commune is varied and ample. There are three large peach orchards and 500 fish ponds. Much of the higher land is in mulberries. There are 2,000 stall-fed sheep and 20,000 pigs, 13,000 com-mune-owned and 7,000 owned by commune members. Around 10,000 jin of compost is used per mou for fertiliser, and there is as much chemical fertiliser available as the commune wants.

Shanghai Scenes

So came to an end one more visit to Shanghai. I walked in the parks, watched cadres being sent off to work on the harvest in the countryside. Noted that new buildings were going up in what had been the old British consulate gardens. How the old British lions had vanished from what was once the Hongkong and Shanghai Bank. The old imperialism has had its day, and today the people militant are keen to show what they can do, filled with the spirit and the determination of Mao Tsetung Thought.

One bright afternoon was spent in former Hongkew Park. Masses of children were there, marching in school by school, then disbanding to play before marching away again. They are different children from those of former times. Today they see older brothers and cousins, family friends and graduating students of their schools packing up and going off into distant parts of the hinterland to state farms and communes or other places of work. Going happily and with great promise in being able to make a revolutionary contribution. Going because Chairman Mao has said that youth must be prepared to sacrifice and show determination if the revolution is to succeed. Probably around half a million Shanghai youth have gone to the hinterland already during the Cultural Revolution. Many more will go. In the next stage the Chinese people march forward together.

The old Hongkew Park reminded me so much of Lu Hsun, the revolutionary writer of the early stages of the revolution, that I wrote these lines:

> So near where he once lived
> the statue of Lu Hsun sits
> quietly in its chair
> of bronze, daring new generations
> to live as he did, give as
> he gave; his head erect
> and as challenging as he
> ever carried it, while now
> on the grass in front of his likeness
> the oncoming youth swarms around;
> two groups organise a tug of war;
> pull, how they pull! So many feet
> running to join the excitement
> laugh with victors and vanquished,
> until a whistle blows, shouting stops
> they fall in then march off singing
> and to me the face of Lu Hsun
> whose spirit so pervades this place
> seems more serene than ever,
> well satisfied.

Machiao Commune in 1971

Not far from where the smokestacks of Minhang, the satellite city, showed up on the skyline, we left the main highway and cut across country to Machiao Commune, a famous one amongst those that encircle the great industrial city of Shanghai. I had come last in 1967, mainly to see the small industry of a commune farming 40,800 mou of rice flatland by 7,500 families, making up 35,000 people. In that year the 20 brigades of the commune in all averaged 1,012 jin of grain a mou. In 1970 they averaged

1,452 jin, and expect to exceed 1,600 jin in 1971. Around 1,000 of its members work in the commune's small industry. The last time I had come, the industrial side was insignificant. The few concrete boats being made under a shed by a canal were at that time a defiant protest against the Liu Shao-chi idea that communes should not try to carry through industrial processes that were the prerogative of large-scale industry, — that industry was industry and agriculture was agriculture and never the twain should meet. Concrete boats in the 1966-67 period were just beginning to capture the imagination of Yangtze delta farmers, and the demand for them was far greater than the supply. The Mao Tsetung idea of all possible self-sufficiency at every level made the membership decide to try to meet their own commune demand themselves. So the first four-ton farm boats were built, succeeded, and quickly led to a demand for more. In May 1971, when we came again, we were surprised to find big new modern workshop buildings erected and two long lines of boats under them in various stages of completion. They were mainly of the eight- and 12-ton variety, to be used as sailing or motorised junks. In the canal were several having their wooden superstructure completed. Evidently the immediate demand for small farm boats has been met, and now come requests for craft for the bigger canals, and for Huangpu and Lower Yangtze shipping. Twelve tonners made here sold for yuan 2,500, and eight tonners for 1,200. For the whole year, the commune averages one daily launching. Most of the workers I saw were women from the commune brigades. The building of smaller craft can now be done at brigade level, if necessary, the commune plant being reserved for bigger orders. After seeing all this we took a road that ran straight across country to another village, a road that had originally been an irrigation canal, whose water now ran in pipes beneath it. In this village steel wire was being drawn, reeled and woven on a loom. Then on the slips nearby were some 60-ton reinforced concrete lighters being constructed for heavier river transport. Rather staggering to see commune folk so casually constructing boats like these and to realise the implications. For what one commune can do, so can another, and when a base is laid for people's industry with already existing urban industry assisting rather than trying to halt it, then the mechanisation of agriculture and the further integration of factory and farm take on a new dimension. More of the creative potential of the people in the countryside is used, with people growing in ability to cope as livelihood improves and the old terrors are trodden down. Commune leaders also were very proud of what they had done in carrying out innovations on a new rice transplanter which their machine shops had built. In 1970 they sowed 200 mou with the best type of transplanter yet evolved around Shanghai, interested to find that the experimental area's yield in grain was somewhat better than that carried through on the hand-transplanted fields. In the new model they have built, various defects discovered in the last season have been corrected, and they were about to put it to work. Up to the present in the commune, plowing is done by tractors, but both sowing and reaping are still done mainly by hand. The commune machine shops also turn out the transformers and other equipment required for rural electrification. The commune has built its own machine tools and most of the machinery the other commune factories need — cement mixers, a crane for launching concrete boats and so on. The biggest of the seven commune industrial plants is the chemical fertiliser one which, in cooperation with two other communes, has 400 workers.

Before leaving we talked a bit about the advances in public health. For cooperative medicine, members pay two yuan a year per person, which gives them free medical attention and medicine for that period. There are three "barefoot" doctors to every brigade clinic and a health worker for every production team. The commune has its own hospital and four clinics for its special services. As the average yearly income per person for all 35,000 commune folk, old and young, is around 137 yuan, people feel that the two yuan each is well invested, and certainly they look to be a very healthy lot as one passes amongst them today. They have done something for health by sinking wells for drinking water instead of using water from the canals as in the past. Water coming into wells, filtered through sand and gravel packed outside the perforated intake well pipes which are laid on the well bottom, is much cleaner and sweeter than the water used formerly which was boiled in the main, but still carried a good deal of disease.

The crops certainly looked lush as we saw them. Wheat about to be reaped, oil seeds ripening, and rice planting beginning. But the old humdrum struggle of the peasant has changed now, and life for everyone in Machiao takes on new meaning as deeper understanding of work and its responsibilities comes home to all. In the old days, people here would be fortunate to get the equivalent of 200 jin of grain each per year. Now they get 540. Physically and mentally they are today more able to cope with the tasks that lie so tantalisingly in front of them. The commune has two middle schools, and all children go through the eight-year schools, the last two grades of which are of lower middle-school level. Practice in line with Mao Tsetung Thought dovetails with theory so that schooling is an assistance to them in entering commune work, rather than something that cuts them off from it. Serving the people not just as a slogan, but as a down-to-earth, practical thing, that is the result desired in education today.

SHANGHAI

Shanghai is a place where youth learn by practice.

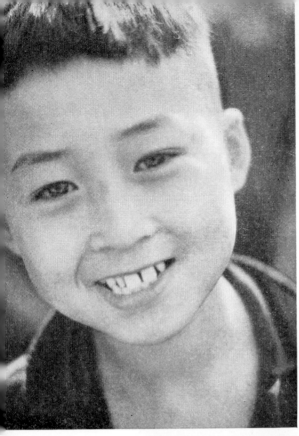

"I am going to work in a generator factory." Shanghai.

Sweet and 12 already, Shanghai.

Children in a Shang-
hai rural commune.

School propaganda group
gives concert, Shanghai.

Shanghai-made tugs now take big lighters (also Shanghai-made) up the Yangtze and through the gorges.

Concrete boats under construction in a Shanghai suburban commune.

The four-ton truck made in Shanghai.

Shanghai-made 15-ton tip truck.

A Shanghai commune turns out transformers for rural use.

Dairy stock in a Shanghai commune.

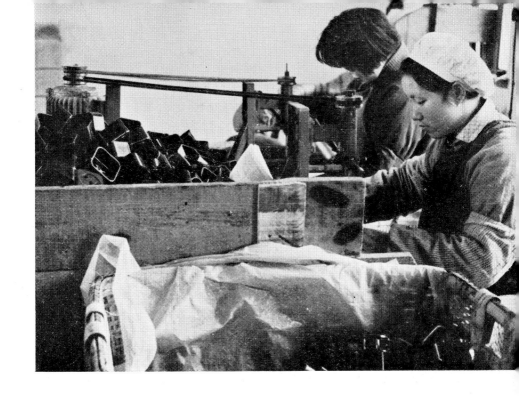

Factory for handicapped people, Shanghai.

Shanghai commune makes a mechanised rice transplanter of improved model.

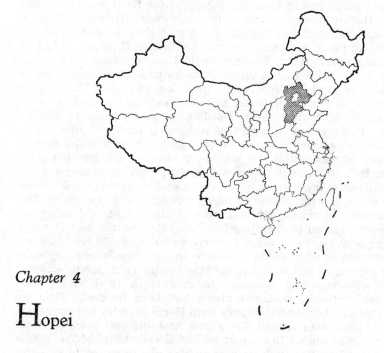

Chapter 4

Hopei

These accounts have been selected from amongst those written on places visited in Hopei province over the past five years. They do not include the municipalities of Peking and Tientsin, which are dealt with in another chapter.

Hopei, with its capital at Shihchiachuang, is a province of around 41 million people who for the most part farm an area of 190,000 square kilometres. The province includes a big section of the north China plain, as well as rugged mountainous regions adjacent to the Great Wall.

We start our account with mass work on water conservancy, which at the end of 1966 was in high tide. For in 1963 the whole of the vast plain of Hopei was flooded due to heavy downpours in the mountains to the west.

"The Hai river must be brought under permanent control!"

Down in south Hopei in the autumn of 1966 much was being done on irrigation, measures against waterlogging and flood control. Leaders

97

declared that in the previous winter as many as 100,000 commune members had gone up to work on the Hai river conservancy projects in the area below Tientsin, as this work affected all the southern portion of the province. In the past there had been but one outlet for flood waters and that through the Hai river, which flows to the sea through Tientsin. When all the five rivers that flow into the Hai along with their host of tributaries were in summer flood, the one outlet was far from sufficient, and in consequence many areas around Tientsin would become lakes. Further upstream, the water which backed up would cause widespread inundation of the vast plains of southern Hopei and a great loss in crops. The inability of the Hai river to take all the water had also rendered useless large areas along the east coast which, due to flooding, became marshy or alkaline wastelands. There was no prospect of reclaiming this until new outlets to the sea were dug, river channels widened and deepened, and a modern system of control locks built. It was an immense challenge — to carry out in a few bold strokes with the power of the people measures by which some of the damage brought on by centuries of deforestation and erosion could be done away with. A daring move, relying on the strength of Mao Tsetung Thought in raising the initiative of the people and using experience already gained in operating huge projects over the past 17 years.

In Peking newspapers of early winter we read how 300,000 commune farmers had come to areas around Tehchow in Shantung where they were working on deepening and widening the Machia and Tuhai rivers, quadrupling their water-carrying capacity. In addition a 150-kilometre-long drainage canal between these two rivers had been finished. Then we also learnt that another 300,000 diggers from Hopei counties had converged on the Tzeya river area around Tsangchow near the east coast of Hopei province for similar work. In the past we had already heard of Tsangchow occasionally in connection with its pears which were reputed to be extra large and juicy, its dates which had much flesh but a small stone, and its marvellous acrobats. Actually today it is an up-and-coming prefecture of 14 counties and one municipality, with its seat at Tsanghsien, a city of 100,000 situated on the Tientsin-Shanghai railway. It was obviously the nearest place to go and catch a glimpse of the struggle on the battlefront against flood.

Trains being crowded because of the masses of Red Guards coming and going to and from Peking, we set off by car on a mid-November morning, with the frost showing white on the big cabbage crop then being taken in. We passed groups of students marching out to help farmers in the fields, and then more and more groups of around 20, mostly Red Guards with bedding packed on their backs and a determined look on their faces, setting out on their stint of the "Long March" program now developing.

Leaving Tientsin, we struck down the coast through the lake and fen country, passing numbers of commune folk already at work widening riverbeds, building dykes, and doing other construction jobs for the Hai river conservancy project. Chairman Mao had said that the Hai river must be controlled. Every commune worker coming to do this is given an enameled badge with these words on it, and everyone wants to make them come true. After the many years of flooding which have caused such tragic losses to many millions, farm folk are grateful for the leadership they get now in their rebellion against the domination of unruly nature. They move into the construction sites swiftly, erecting their own quarters in a practised, orderly way. The 15 men who will live in one hut can carry in on their pneumatic-tyred carts the timbers and the heavy reed matting needed for its construction and quickly cover the walls and roof with a mud plaster. Such huts are far more serviceable than the much more expensive tents. Cook-houses and other service buildings are set up at the same time. Electricians bring in lighting, and red banners stream everywhere.

Entertainment groups sing or lecture over loudspeakers. During the daily eight-hour work period breaks are made also for reading quotations from Chairman Mao and for singing. Then shovels flash again, and the little steel handcarts in their tens of thousands run up inclines. In the winter of 1965-66 a great deal was done towards the completion of the earlier stages. The 1966-67 winter will see very much more, while by the end of 1967 this part of the whole project will basically be completed.

With the work done already much flood damage can be prevented, though there are still problems with the silt of rivers that flow down from the Taihang and Wutai mountains. Of the five tributaries of the Hai river the Yungting is the longest, having as its upper reaches the Sangan river of north Shansi. The Hutuo river from Wutai flows into the Tzeya. The Chang river winding out of Linhsien in Honan after coming down from the Taihang mountains changes its name to Wei when it comes into Hopei. A canal to take its surplus waters to the sea was dug in the 1954-55 winter. Soon there will be six outlets for these rivers to the sea, instead of previously one. The immense flood of 1963 was the biggest in 180 years. Should a similar flood come again, the widening already done or projected together with all the new outlets will take care of it.

In addition to the problem of getting rid of the water, that of land reclamation is also being attacked. Many tens of thousands of acres of once alkaline waste or marsh along the coast are now growing good crops of grain, much of it rice. More is being brought in all the time. In the Tsangchow prefecture grain totals are this year 30 percent higher than they were in the good year of 1965.

One liked the look of the commune youth on the roads marching to the worksites. Most were in their twenties. Few if any over 40. A youth that has none of the hopelessness of the old days lined on their faces, but rather one that knows where it is going and why. "First this Hai river job, then after that there will be a bigger one," they seemed to say. Certainly there are bigger difficulties to be met yet. Back in the mountains of Wutai and Taihang billions upon billions of trees have to be planted, millions of small check dams to be made to halt the erosion that brings the silt down and halt the rush caused by summer rainstorms. There is plenty of challenge for a long time to come yet, so there can be no resting on laurels.

We went south of Tsangchow to where the waters of the internal canal system are carried under the Grand Canal. What has been done here is certainly impressive. A control dam with 22 sluice gates, electrically controlled, expels water at a high rate when necessary. During our visit there was little water in the Grand Canal, it being cut off by works being done in the Tehchow area of adjacent Shantung province. Of all Hopei areas those of Tsangchow and Hengshui were always considered the poorest, because of their difficulties with alkalinity and water control. Way back in the Han dynasty, when the mountains from which the rivers rose bore forests, life was thriving along the seacoast. Amongst the earth thrown up by the digging of the new Nanpai river, one noted plenty of Han dynasty shards, as well as some Tzechow ware of Sung. But down through the last few centuries, with their ever recurrent floods and droughts, the people became poorer and poorer.

Now the turn upward is being made. Alkaline lands are changed into "tai tien" — raised rectangular fields with ditches around. Both drought and flooding are being met on many large fields by deep ditches for taking off floodwaters, and right alongside and on a higher level run irrigation canals. At one village I talked with an old man leading a donkey which was pulling out a small cart of compost — around 700 lbs. of it — to a field. Yes, he was old. Over 60, but his teeth were those of a youngster, every one bright and intact. And he enjoyed working. Everyone should work as long as he was able, he thought. Otherwise there was no meaning to life. How could one "serve the people" by making the people serve him? he wondered. This new consciousness that now fills the hearts of country folk is something that the West has not caught up with yet. They know of the overseas Chinese, hard-working, frugal, patient and devoting their whole energies to competing in the struggle for livelihood and to bringing up their children. But they do not know of the tremendous and ever increasing number throughout this quarter of the world who have found a new meaning to life, and are living in accordance with it.

While in Tsangchow, we went some 15 miles southeast to see the old city. It was founded in the Spring and Autumn period of Chou, and existed right up to the beginning of Ming, when the Prince of Yen, later to be the third emperor of that dynasty, ordered it to a new location, probably following high tide or a flood. Folklore says he burnt the city. Possibly this was to enforce the move. Anyway, all that is left standing now are parts of the walls, some five miles around, and in the city by what was once a temple a huge iron lion, perhaps the biggest of its kind in China. Not far away is the place where the image was evidently founded, iron cash having been used as the material. We picked up many of these old coins as we went around, most in big chunks of half-melted-together pieces.

There are some characters under the neck of the image saying it is the Lion King. Its casting in Latter Chou, around 950 A.D. in the Five Dynasties period, was possibly conceived as a metaphysical measure to hold back the high waves from the sea, at that time a good deal nearer to the place than it is today. The image, 17 feet high and 16 long, was blown over by a typhoon in the Chia Ch'ing period of the Ching dynasty, so that its head and tail were broken. Otherwise it is intact. A railed-off pavilion now protects it as an ancient relic.

All through the old city are layers of pottery shards. Where ditches have been made around raised fields one can see shards of the lower strata of the Chou and Han dynasties, mostly grey pottery. On higher levels are masses of Sung Tzechow, Sung Ting, and Sung and Yuan Chun. Then there are blue-and-white shards of early Ming. Nearby is an old folk's home from which an old man came over to watch us. He was 84, and though the picture of health, said, "I'm only fit for looking after the children now." Two youngsters came to join the lookers-on. Despite the early winter day one had his upper garments off and tucked up under his arm.

It was really something to see the Tsangchow acrobats. Many of them in the troupe that put on a show when we were in the city were youngsters who were marvels in steadiness and precision. The old peasants who sat in the front row with towels on their heads, north China fashion, must have thought of the other days when Tsangchow little boys and girls went out with some master to other towns doing acrobatics in street side shows or on vacant lots, getting a few coppers to hold body and soul together because there was no living in the countryside, and folk had to think up some way. These poised, healthy and confident children of today are something for the older generation to be proud of. Like everything else in art and culture today in China, the main theme running through the performance was preparation to resist aggression and carry through construction centred on Mao Tsetung Thought.

We spent a morning going north of the city to a worksite where many thousands of commune farmers were on the job. Going through the living quarters they had erected, we saw how comfortably they were arranged. Actual cost for the housing for three months is around 20 fen a man. The kitchens for each row of houses face the road. Cook-houses were clean and with cooks in white aprons. In one we saw them making an artistic job of vegetarian dishes that looked like meat. But what the workers like mainly is plenty of hot steamed bread and a good heavy soup.

The particular task these workers were on was the digging of one more outlet for the Tzeya river waters to the sea. The Peipai river work at the point we visited consisted not only of digging the new channel, but also of building a long new highway bridge over it, and then the construction of an aqueduct over which the Grand Canal will run, while crossing underneath will be the new outlet canal.

In the winter of 1965-66 the first stages of the work were done, consisting in the building of a new 1,880-metre railway bridge and the ramps leading up to it. One approach of these ramps was put in by Tientsin students and the other half by the people's militia. Commune members who come to winter conservancy work are always anxious to take part. It is exciting to join so big a movement and to participate in making history. The workers do eight hours work each day and then take part in the sessions of the "Mao Tsetung University", classes being arranged for the evenings. Many of them also learn new techniques, as the mere handful of city technicians only act as teachers and the commune members themselves make all the steel forms needed for reinforced concrete structures, as well as many other things.

Between visits to look at Hai river conservancy work at Tsangchow, we spent half a day seeing two local enterprises. The first was a handicraft unit which took in the straw braid made by local housewives and made it up into elegant-looking shopping bags lined either with plastic or cloth. These bags show artistic patterns made up of the dyed sheath leaves of corn cobs. Properly mechanised, the factory has 150 workers and is highly productive. These workers are as warm and pleasant a bunch of people as one would wish to meet. Their products go to 21 foreign countries.

The second establishment makes a kind of pickled cabbage. The white of the local Chinese cabbage is used for this. It is chopped up and then dried, after which it is pickled and left some months in vats to be cured and then sent abroad in little brown jars — mostly to Singapore and other Southeast Asian lands. As the main pickling work can only be done for a month in the autumn and then for another month when the cabbage comes out of winter pits in spring, the factory has another line — preparing for export three date products. Really all are prepared from the same kind of date, the Chinese jujube — "Zizyphus Jujuba" — which grows very well in Tsangchow, one of the over 70 varieties found in Hopei. Picked green and processed with sugar, it makes sweet honey dates. De-stoned and processed another way, it makes a small round red date, a popular Peking winter delicacy. We tasted all three kinds, I hope not too long or too heartily, but they were so good it was not so easy to stop. The manager kindly insisted that I take two of the little brown pots of pickle with me, so I departed with them in the straw bag the bag-making factory had sent me off with, feeling a bit of a robber but happy to have them.

On November 17th, Tsangchow had a big celebration in honor of the anniversary of the statement by Chairman Mao that the Hai river must be controlled. Streets were alive with banners and drums.

One of the leading cadres on the conservancy work told me of one commune member who had come carrying an old basket. His friends did not know why he had brought it along until there came the time in an evening discussion meeting to explain. He told how his parents had been driven away by flood, and how with this basket they had wandered over the land in bitterness, begging what they could. How the father had died in those tough days, but how his mother had brought him up despite all. How his mother had asked him to take this basket to where the conservation work was being done, and to tell his fellows about it all. He himself has become a very purposeful worker shifting more earth than two or three others, having found out that there is a technique that helps, if the spirit is eager and "on the ball".

"Yes," said another, "there is a plan. But what we want is to fix this excess water business as soon as possible." Soon there will be new highways running beside wide dyke tops. There will be new forests as windbreaks beside them. There will be more alkaline fields turned into "tai tien". The scenery of the land will change. And the people will change again.

One early morning we went along the Paoting highway west into Hochien county, and then struck north across country until we came to the big new canal being dug, the communes of one county each responsible for one section. The section allocated to Ankuo county had been finished and commune members had gone home except those who were planting trees up the ramp. Ankuo is a famous county where traditional medical practitioners from all over the country once came to buy their medicines at the huge temple to the God of Medicine. The God has gone the way of all gods in today's China, but someone said jokingly, "Ankuo herbals must be good. The people from there have finished their task before any of the others!"

It is an imposing canal. Many good strong reinforced concrete bridges have been erected across it for farm tractor and other traffic, and on one of these we crossed, looking at the wide highway that runs alongside its northern ramp, and at the built-up fields where surplus earth is going into what was once alkaline waste. A leading cadre from the provincial seat at Paoting and one from the county were both working with the commune folk, sleeping in the same shelters, eating the same food, and seeing that everything was going to plan. The canal is one of the big ones that drain off the waters of the Tzeya before they get to the Hai river. Highly dyked on both sides, these new channels will take the waters from any ordinary big flood. To prepare for extraordinary flood, another dyke was being built a mile or so south, making a kind of detention basin which could be used when necessary. Villages in this area will be moved away to the perimeter next year.

All across the countryside were the banners of commune brigades where folk were busy either digging ditches or raising fields, or both. Each winter that passes now sees a great leap forward in conservancy and reclamation work. The making of the Grand Canal in ancient days was a puny piece of work compared with what is being done now. "What Chairman Mao says, we do," the people say. A plan? Good, but we shall not wait for any plan to finish its time limit. Right into work we shall go until we finish it! Then after that, we'll go straight up into the tiger's lair and deal with the silt problem at its source! There is a note of supreme confidence reigning in the whole countryside today, the feeling that all difficulties are just paper tigers if tackled the right way together. The crops have been good, the children are full of health. We crossed over the Heilungkang river which had been remade, passed many primary schools filled with children, crossed some of the 700 new bridges over newly remade or dug waterways and went over macadamised highways. Everywhere change is well on the way.

In the first days of Liberation, engineers would put in big budgets and many demands. Now the work is done for a fraction of the cost, and with a general raising of morale at that. In no country of our world perhaps can so great a number of people converge on a task, erect quarters for themselves and get a job done so fast as is being done on the Hai river conservancy today, finish it and thoroughly enjoy the doing of it.

It is not easy work, especially when the water table is reached and the last part of the digging has to be done in mud. The loads on the little carts are then heavier, but workers have found a way. They jack up a handcart on the top of the dyke, take the tyre off one wheel, and use that as a pulley for a wire rope that is attached to the front of the cart. Two hefty men with shoulder harness attached to the rope running down the ramp give a welcome hand to those pushing the cart up. Tractors are mainly used for tamping the earth on the dyke as it is brought up by the small carts.

The last evening in Tsangchow we were entertained by a young people's volunteer concert group which had been out on worksites giving performances for each section of the workers. They wore daily travel clothes, patched as is the fashion with a youth that is one with its ordinary folk. Their spirit was high, and the items went off with machine-gun rapidity. Naturally, the main theme was support for the Hai river project, and the strength of Mao Tsetung Thought which gives folk leadership, cohesion and a determination to fight through at all costs.

We had seen the more bare and desolate areas of the Tsangchow prefecture in coming down from Tientsin to Huanghua county and then on to the prefectural seat. On our return home, we took the easy way of going by the modern highway from Tsangchow to Paoting and then up to Peking.

In Hochien county we saw the middle stages of the digging of the Peipai river. It was sunny but with a cold wind which, however, did not stop the commune workers from throwing off their upper clothing as they pitched into the task. An interval would come and then the county health workers would shout over megaphones, "Put on your jackets when you rest. Don't get a chill!" Each county apparently brings its health workers to the worksite. Elsewhere all across the wide plains well-drilling was in progress, as was the raising of the level of the land which was formed into rectangular fields surrounded by drainage ditches. Some of the completed areas, with the winter wheat showing green on them, looked like a big garden backed by windbreaks. Old people and children were doing autumn tree planting everywhere.

The whole country was hard at work. A mobilised country is the China of today, able to move its people easily and efficiently. Certainly the commune farmers of the 67 counties who have sent their workers onto the Hai river project will not only change the face of the land but will themselves not be the same after they have completed their job. It is a considerable satisfaction to them to know that they will have been able to extend their control over the runoff from 50,000 or more square kilometres of land, which includes some of the five million acres they themselves farm.

Back in Peking, I thought back over the countryside seen. The tens of thousands of banners streaming along high points of construction sites, and then those alongside all the other digging going on all over the plains.

Of the marchers going south reminding one of the times of the War of Resistance and old revolutionary war days, knowing that the present change will sweep on like a great wave, taking away all that stands in its path. A new era is swiftly coming in.

Peking to Hsingtai

We left Peking to go south from Hsichihmen railway station rather than from the main one, the extra traffic caused by the coming and going of hundreds of thousands of Red Guards from all over the country making it necessary for every station possible to be brought into use.   Over a 1966 autumn countryside, groups of commune members were busy with the autumn harvest or irrigating the freshly-sown winter wheat. The city of Hsingtai, reached six hours later, is one of around 120,000 people and to us quiet after a crowded Peking.   In Manchu dynasty times it was called Shunteh Fu, and was a major centre in south Hopei. Today it has broad streets and new buildings and an air of serene prosperity, for harvests around have been good since the great flood year of 1963, despite the terrific earthquakes of March and April of 1966.

On the wall of my room in the guest house were words of Chairman Mao. "All reactionaries are paper tigers. . . ." Subjectively, the great flood and the big earthquakes were fierce enough, making for a stern battle, but objectively they were also paper tigers, leaving the people after their passing stronger and better knit together than they had ever been. More sure of themselves and more able, and after seeing what has been done when Mao Tsetung Thought was applied, keener than ever to master all of it they can.

To Earthquake Areas

It is something over 40 miles from Hsingtai city past the Jenhsien county seat and then on by a commune cartroad formed on dyke tops to the villages of Paichiachai and Malan, both the headquarters of brigades in Paichiachai Commune in Lungyao county. These were the two villages which were the epicentre of the first of the great earthquakes of March and April of 1966. The first caused the most damage to people, as it took place in the early hours before dawn on March 8th, when there had been a fall of spring snow and people were still sleeping comfortably in their bedding quilts, wearing nothing as is the so scientific northern China peasant custom. The jolt came like a hammer, and the two villages were completely wrecked. Those who got out of the ruins had to dig out their fellows. People's Army units who by a forced march arrived with doctors and help assisted also in digging out survivors. In Malan village everyone who got out of his home needed some kind of medical attention, but Paichiachai was almost as bad. Helicopters took the seriously wounded to hospitals, but those who could get along with bandages set about building shelters. As soon as that had been done they went out to their fields, jumping over the wide fissures and attending to the crops. Through holes in the ground and up wells the earthquakes forced up masses of sand and water.

The water was quickly channelled into the fields of winter wheat and proved a great help, for the spring rains did not come as usual. A month after the first shock a bigger one came, knocking down the first temporary homes. Despite all the bitterness, however, the first crop of wheat proved to be a good one. The second of kaoliang and corn had an insect scourge attack it during the summer, making for a 12-day-and-night fight by all the people of the two brigades with insecticides to beat it. Despite all damage, the 1966 harvest showed a more than 26 percent advance on the 1965 one, and in 1966 both brigades will be able to sell grain to the state and come off the relief grain they had been getting since the great flood of 1963, which covered the whole region for a considerable period. The area has had a long history of both drought and flood.

Paichiachai Brigade has 654 families, 2,053 people in all, in 18 production teams. They farm 7,600 mou, some of which is marshy or alkaline land and 2,600 mou of which is irrigated. Malan has 1,392 people left of whom 330 are permanent workers. 430 others, old and young, help in rush periods. The brigade leader, a tall, serious, bearded farmer, had his whole family of six killed in the earthquake. Losses amongst the people were more serious than at Paichiachai. They farm 2,400 mou of relatively flat arable land, having brought in some waste land during this past year.

In neither of the villages were there carpenters, masons, lime-burning or brick kiln workers, well sinkers or the like needed for the work of reconstruction. The three-year plan of rebuilding, however, has progressed, all new houses being strongly constructed, low in stud and of solid brick, all put up by the people themselves. Mud-brick houses all fell, but the well constructed brick ones of old landlords usually remained at least partially intact. Folk now think that the entire rebuilding will be completed by the end of 1967 instead of 1968. Every bit of the rebuilding work they have done themselves. Some of the people even refused to take relief goods the state sent in. "Give them to someone who needs them more," they would say. But state help with implements and tools was gladly received and put to use, as was the gift of horses from the Tibetan region, which a delegation from there brought down. Both brigades had lost practically all of their working stock when stables collapsed. Everyone was full of admiration for the PLA fighters. They came in on the double immediately, giving clothing and bedding to people who needed it more than they did. Until all the people had shelters built for them, the soldiers slept out in the open despite the weather. They helped to build the lime and brick kilns, and to do everything else that was needed until the people themselves could take hold of their future confidently again. Folk speak of them with great warmth and admiration.

When I visited, both brigades were deep in the study of the works of Mao Tsetung. Study books were beside the fields, and in homes by the streets. Texts were on the walls and everywhere else they could be painted. Red Guards from Hsingtai schools were leading many of the youngsters in study. There were red flags everywhere. Everywhere the song, "The East is Red". Everyone we met talked about the big difficulties of flood, insects, drought and earthquake, told how study helped him or her, giving the clarity and determination needed to carry struggle through still further. Paichiachai is a bigger village, and its construction is further ahead than that of Malan, but both are something to see and be happy with, for here is the best that is in man coming to the surface and expressing itself. A determination not to let any difficulty stand in one's way, together with a belief in and regard for each other. The spirit of sacrifice for the people as a powerful force.

There is plenty of coal nearby, so it is used for house fuel, allowing corn and kaoliang stalks to go into compost heaps. A yellow lupine which can be grown on the waste alkaline land is also a valuable component for compost. But the most valuable thing to add to compost is the mud bricks of "kangs" (brick beds) in destroyed homes. Paichiachai has a group of small factories for flour milling, grain processing, timber working, all operated by electricity. With a belt taken from a power saw pulley, two youngsters were milling millet. The brigade is proud of its team of six girls who have opened up some wasteland and converted it to rice paddy. They are certainly a tough six with a wholesome belief in the future and of their place in it. I watched them harvesting kaoliang, admiring their clear, decisive strokes. These increasingly will be the people who will matter in the China of the next stage. For the young ones, the future is theirs. The many old ones who can keep up will add the experience of the past. The long years of resistance to the Japanese, when the area was a guerilla base, bred a husky independence. Two youngsters were wrestling, going about it in a swift business-like way. I asked the victor, a slip of a boy around 12, if he dared take me on. "Yes," he said, and immediately started to encircle me, waiting for my two feet to come together so that he could dive at them. On its better irrigated land, the commune grows vegetables for export to cities. I stopped by a field of eggplant, seeing a little old lady working there. I found that she had the small feet of the old days, a bright cheerful face under white hair. She was over 60 but did not like to miss a day at work.

Leaving Malan, I looked back. The new street was hidden by a fold of the downs, and all that could be seen was a village that looked as if it had come through the wars, the ruins of houses standing up starkly. There have been eight years of war with the then strongest power in Asia plus famines, floods, earthquakes, insect pests. Grimly, folk here have buried their dead. Cheerfully, they come together now and throw themselves into the fray again. No wonder the Little Red Book, the red and gold text pinned on their chests, the red and gold slogans that meet one's eye all through their village which reflect the red and gold in their hearts, are precious. They give the clear way forward so that all shall become increasingly masters of their destiny.

Nanhui Brigade

Hsingtai county is one of the biggest of the 17 counties in the Hsingtai prefecture. It stretches well into the Taihang mountains until it reaches the Shansi border at Hohsun county. A rugged area, mostly of barren hills, it was the scene of many a bitter struggle in the War of Resistance days, when Japanese columns would drive in against the Eighth Route Army units which held it. The limp of Wang Tse-chi who met us outside the gate of his village of Nanhui was a reminder of those days in which he too, was a fighter. Now he is the leader of Nanhui Brigade of Hsihuang-tsun Commune, in these Taihang mountains. The village is one of well built, stone-block houses, looking gay in autumn with richly loaded persimmon trees around. The brigade entertained us with bowls of hot water and a plentiful supply of this year's walnuts. There were 194 families living in the village, 784 people in all. They farmed 960 mou, the bulk of which was rich valley land and the rest small terraced plots on adjacent hillsides.

After the end of the Resistance War, people who had run away returned. Earth was cut away from the loess cliffs which still existed at lower hill levels, and more of the valley was reclaimed. They had fields on both sides of a river which flowed through them peacefully enough. It was lined by persimmons and walnuts, 600 richly bearing trees in all. A water wheel did the brigade's flour milling. Each year saw increases in crop yield, until some fields were giving 1,000 jin of grain a mou. Then on August 4th, 1963, at ten in the morning, during an incredible rain that covered the whole mountain area and later inundated the plains, a wall of water 30 feet high swept down. It had carried away a dam up in the hills. Its force swept all before it. The 600 big old persimmon and walnut trees vanished, as did the water wheel and flour mill. Spreading right across the valley, all that the flood left of the once rich fields was a desert of sand and stones. The rich soil was simply scooped up and carried away. So were 28 of the village homes. A 70-ton segment of the dam up in the hills was deposited on what was once cropland, as if to make mockery of man's efforts. The people and their animals escaped up the hillside, as all village homes that were not swept away were inundated.

And so, the people wondered, what next? Some were for dispersal, to make an effort to become integrated into other communes. What grain they had stored was lost. Soon autumn would come and clothing would be needed. A farmer must have land. Without land, what can he do? Wang Tse-chi limped over the valley and surveyed the damage. "Not so bad, not so bad! The river is now back within its banks. Now we shall start right away and get rid of the sand dunes that have planted themselves where once our best land was, and so shall we make all anew. We have had no one killed. We have all our animals!" People at first did not feel they could do it, but the rubber-tyred handcarts got to work and slowly by day and night the valley was cleared of boulders and sand. Then earth had to be brought down to make fields, stone walls of fields built to hold it, as well as a stone dyke to protect against the river. It was hardest when winter came and the frost began to bite. At first work seemed to go so slowly that some began to get dispirited again and wonder if, after all, it was possible to do the thing they were trying to do. They stopped a while and studied the Mao Tsetung essay "The Foolish Old Man

Who Removed the Mountains", and then began planning restoration of
their land in five years.   Actually they have done it in three, though they
have planned some extension that will take them two more winters to
complete.   Reclamation has to go on at the same time as ordinary production, and it has been the long winter evenings that have been utilised for
the earth-moving work.   The best score they had was putting a good,
heavy working layer of three feet of earth on 32 mou in 18 nights. Children
came along with elders.   Each attack was carefully planned, with everyone
knowing exactly what was expected of him or her, problems having been
raised and debated in the preliminary meetings held prior to each major
effort.   The new earth, of course, had to have a good deal of compost
fertiliser added to make it do all that was required.   By the autumn of
1966 the brigade was already selling a surplus of grain to the state.   The
battle had been won.   When I went around on a bright mid-October
morning in 1966, the place seemed most prosperous.   The crop of sweet
potatoes being harvested was a rich one.   New homes had been built for
many, and the children were a joy to see.   Wang Tse-chi talked of plans
to almost double production by the end of 1967, and treble it by 1970.
I said good-bye to the 20 "iron" girls, the 260 model workers, and all the
rest, looking back in some amazement at them as they saw me off.   Ordinary folk who have found the way, and have made it do so much.

Hochialou Brigade

It was a lovely autumn morning when we set out to go to the Hochialou
Production Brigade, situated on the Hopei-Shansi border in the upland
hills of the Taihang mountain complex.   Jagged mountaintops and then
hills in blue streamed past us as we forded sparkling streams and sped
over passes separating one valley from another, until we finally took a
cartroad running up beside a mountain stream and came to our destination.   Folk were out to meet us, a goodly portion of the 129 families with
the 664 people who make them up, carrying pictures of Chairman Mao or
streamers with slogans on them.   It was a stone-built village set on a
hillside, whitewashed walls looking neat with the red and gold texts from
Chairman Mao's works painted up on them.   The brigade owns only 506
mou of flat farmland, most of it in the riverbed, or on terraces up the
gullies. Less than a mou per person. One of the gullies was called "Death
Gully" because it was once so desolate.   The brigade made it their hinterland to expand into.

They did not start gingerly from the bottom.   Instead they went to the
ridge of the range of hills behind, and started afforestation in semi-circular
sweeps right across the gully and up either side of it.   They put pines,
oak and ash up high, then chestnuts, then lower down apricots with persimmons and walnuts in the richer part of the valley.   Then as they came
still further down, they had stone check dams made in the little stream,
one every 100 yards or so to hold the water in pools so that it could be
used for irrigation.   Beside these they cut out terraced fields to grow grain,
and also to plant apple or peach orchards.   At the entrance to the valley

is an apiary with some 70 hives of bees. No sheep or goats are kept in the brigade, priority being given to the 143 pigs and the 73 work animals, whose refuse so much assists the compost heaps. Consequently, the wild grasses up the steep hillsides each side of the valley grow well and check erosion.

What Trees Can Do

In the terrific downpour of 1963 the value of these grasses and of the trees so heavily planted showed up well. There was no great flood in "Death Gully", though many other valley floors in nearby ravines were completely washed out. So does "Death Gully" stand as an object lesson for all to come and see. Under the ripening apples, folk working there put on a concert for us. Children and youngsters dancing and singing. Then the 12 girls who make up the "iron girl" team of the brigade put on their items. They are famous figures locally, for they have learnt how to chisel holes on hill faces out of the rock, then fill them with earth to plant trees in. Tree roots, after they have a start, make their way through interstices in the rock and grow well. The brigade was selling around 14,000 jin of apples to the state in 1966, and already had sold a similar amount of peaches in the preceding summer. They are getting an increased number of walnuts and chestnuts all the time as trees planted ten years ago come into fuller bearing.

The brigade is famous also for its small industry that helps to make it self-sufficient. Some of the water from a canal turns a generator which operates a number of machines in the daytime and lights the village at night. The rest of the water drives a flour mill. There are even machines for making bean noodles. Manually operated machines include those for cutting sweet potatoes into slices before drying them, and for threshing kaoliang heads. Motors operate chaff cutting, a corn-cob husking machine, and a little sawmill. As not many of these machines are used at one time there is enough power to go around. In the winter when the water freezes, a diesel engine powers the generator.

Woman Leader

The head of the Women's Union invited three of us to lunch at her home. Simple food, but very tasty. She had five children, four of them boys. The second eldest, a 12-year-old, had lunch with us. I asked him what he would like to be when he grew up. Quite simply and without hesitation, he replied "a revolutionary". Later in the day I passed him on a terrace up in "Death Gully". He was leading a pair of donkeys which were pulling a potato digger, knowing well too that this was revolutionary work.

Handicapped Man

An outstanding member of the brigade was Yao Chu-dui. He lost a hand in the wars but came home and took part in everything he could, making one hand do better than many with two. I meant to have asked him which war it was, though judging from his age I guessed it to have been the one in Korea. He puts his whole heart and soul into giving leadership in the toughest work, breaking stone and planting trees, and is admired by all. Ninety-one percent of the women of the commune take part in work along with the men, old divisions having been dropped. Wang Huai-hsien, the brigade Party secretary, said seriously, "We think of what the USA is doing in Vietnam as we work, and we feel all we do is for the revolution. We try to more completely arm ourselves with the kind of thinking we know will carry us through." I myself felt when looking over what they had done, how important an object lesson this work was to folk up in the country that comprises the basin of the Yellow and Yangtze rivers for, surely, if erosion and silting is to be halted, the same kind of thing that has been done here will have to be done in millions of gullies all the way through the Northwest.

Yungfuchuang

We went out to visit the Yungfuchuang brigade of Jenhsien county. Yungfuchuang is a big village, and the line of welcomers streamed long. Children brightened the morning, youth gave it determination, and the old folk, dignity. The brigade has 1,200 families, 5,400 people in all, working 19,000 mou of land. Subject to flooding, yields have been poor. Before 1964, they were only about 80 jin of grain a mou. In 1964 production rose to 174 jin a mou, despite the second flood which came in the spring of that year following the vast one of 1963. There was no wheat harvested that spring, but beans were planted and gave a rich crop.

The land was flat, but a great deal of it was covered in reeds. An attack was made on this land, ditching it and digging out the reed roots, around half a million jin of such roots being removed. When plowed and flattened out, it makes rich-looking fields, glinting with the green of winter wheat. One stretch of 800 mou was being sown while we were there. Tractors, horses, and people all pulled drills. The tractor drills did the main job, people and horses doing the sowing of border edges and headlands not easily reached by the broad machine drills. Tractor drivers were all youngsters who have been trained in the local tractor station. They are ordinary brigade members, getting no additional pay for their work, the effort now being made to avoid having special technicians who will be more and more cut off from the affairs of the brigade. When plowing, for instance, was done by the tractor station, it cost 75 fen a mou; now it is done by brigade members themselves at a cost of 51 fen a mou. The old system led to many of the more conservative to resist mechanisation. The new one gives a wider interest in it, as an essential part of brigade activities. Everything else done in the brigade is the same. Health clinics, schools and small industries. All who work in such are simply commune members with like pay and like benefits. Chao Mi-kwei, a tough-looking but quiet-spoken man, told of the struggle to dig wells. Though flood is the worst menace to the land here, drought comes next, and drought has to be met. Two thousand wells had to be dug to solve the drought problem in the 1965-66 winter, some over 60 metres deep. Well sinkers had to be trained on the job. Youth, barelegged and barefooted, padded pants discarded when necessary, right in the pit of a freezing winter, went down into the slush in well bottoms. Grabbing some sleep in the early hours of the mornings, they would then get back to the work again. Their struggles made 5,000 more mou of wheat possible in 1966 than would have been the case had the wells not been dug. The 1965 harvest with 189 jin a mou totalled a good deal more than the 1964 one, but the 1966 one will double that of the previous year, despite drought, insect pests and the earthquakes. The first crop of 1966 alone gave 300 jin and, as we saw, the autumn harvest was coming in richly to add to the total.

We halted when out in the fields to see the big pumping out station which with its long line of high-powered pumps, throws out floodwaters into a drainage system. It had been badly shaken by the earthquakes but had remained intact nevertheless, and able to operate. Many of the workers in the fields were students from the schools of Hsingtai who had come out to assist production in the countryside.

Part Work, Part Study

The last calls in the commune were made at the part-work, part-study agricultural middle school, and the brigade's modern little flour mill, then the paper factory. The school has 100 mou of land itself, and does a good deal of experimentation with seeds and insect control. It also operates a small modern loom-weaving factory operated with motors. It is hard to estimate the creative ability of a youth group dressed in their best and standing in line to meet their visitors, but I guessed from their faces that there were a good many here who would not be scared to go down freezing wells on a dark winter's night. We made a visit to the marketing and supply store on the main street of the village. It looked as up-to-date and efficient as any in a city, with as well stocked shelves.

Paper Factory

The paper factory is a modern one under construction. Most of the machinery for a two-ton plant has been installed. Buildings are simple, erected by the young workers themselves, who learn as they go with the aid of workers of other paper factories which have helped in providing and setting up equipment. With each step forward the commune becomes more and more self-sufficient. We saw modern rifles stacked by one working field group which were also commune militia. Education, commerce, medicine, industry and mechanisation, along with defence, all integrate into the commune system now. It is the flowering of an idea that started to operate in 1958 and which has come a long way since, passing through its period of experimentation, and now, with a closer understanding of Mao Tsetung Thought since the Cultural Revolution sweeps in, all are more than ever confident that things can be changed for the better, and that though the road forward might be hard, victory can be won.   In 1964, through its own efforts, this commune brigade was able to come off state relief.   In 1966 it is able to sell the state considerable quantities of grain, thus getting the satisfaction of being able to take part in the revolution in a meaningful way.

Lu Yu-lan

Lu Yu-lan is a name that has come before the people of China today as one deserving respect.   A person whose life and struggle is an example for the young all over the country.   It took us over three hours after leaving Hsingtai city to arrive at her home in Tungliushanku Brigade of Shaposi Commune in Linhsi county on the Hopei-Shantung border, driving through the counties of Nanho, Pinghsiang and Weihsien.

Still unmarried at 26, Lu Yu-lan was at 15 the leader of the local elementary cooperative.   She is now concurrently Party secretary for the brigade as well as for the whole commune.   Her brigade has 344 families in it, 1,448 people all told, with a regular working force of 576.   They were completely inundated in the flood of 1963 and badly rocked in the earthquakes of 1966, when a part of Lu Yu-lan's own home was wrecked. They fought the insect pest successfully, and in 1966 doubled their 1965 crop, which at 250 jin a mou was over three times the 70 jin a mou the area gained in 1955.

Lu Yu-lan's struggles, however, were long.   She was young, and she was a woman.   A few of the older men ganged up against her and led in stormy criticism meetings against her.   She went calmly on with her work in production, gaining a good deal of support from the women and young people.   With their help, she planted a big stretch of sandy wasteland with trees as a windbreak and to halt sands shifting, after the appeal had gone out from Peking to do this.   The leading group did all they could to stop her.   Then, when after a few years the trees had grown well, they and their gang cut them down on two nights in 1959.   Lu Yu-lan and her helpers, after their daily work, went off and planted the whole area again. Then came the great flood of 1963 and washed the young plantation away. For a third time she and her supporters planted.   Again her detractors tried to halt her.   But this time they did not succeed.   She had such popular support and so much clear right on her side that she was able to expose the bad elements and even bring one of their leaders over to her side, to leave the ranks of administrators and become a hard-working farmer again. When her group struggled against him everyone came forward, right down to an eight-year-old Young Pioneer, and told of the things about him which everyone needed to know.   The result was that Lu Yu-lan got all the help needed to get her 250,000 trees planted, and to carry through changes needed to raise production.   There is plenty of land, around 5,000 mou of it. 2,100 mou is in crops and 700 in fruit trees, vines and such. The brigade has 129 draft animals, the chief of the stables being an old man with a 16-year-old son making two enthusiasts whose whole life is bound up in their work.

With considerable pride, Lu Yu-lan showed us the exhibition her group had made of the high-bearing varieties of kaoliang, corn, wheat and cotton which the brigade had produced. Then she took us to see experimental beds and her young forest spread over land once held to be useless. Trees were all deciduous, quick growing evergreens suitable for this particular alkaline wasteland and climate apparently not being yet available. Nevertheless, a good deal of the sandstorm nuisance the village suffered from for so long has already been cut out. Tree roots have halted it. We went out to the cotton fields and met the older women who were leading there. Some were in their sixties, one even in her seventies, still quite hale and hearty. Lu Yu-lan had many stories of their self-sacrifice and of the way they memorised and re-memorised the three short essays of Chairman Mao in their last study period. Along with the menfolk and the youth of the brigade they had taken part in the attack on the revisionists in cultural circles in Peking at many meetings at the beginning of the 1966 summer. Over 20 articles had been written by them on the subject for the newspapers.

During the War of Resistance the area was administered from the South Shantung Region Administrative Office, then at Weihsien near Linhsi. The struggle against the Japanese and their puppets was fierce in those years, and little could be done then to attack the basic problems of the countryside. Many of the young men went off to fight in the War of Liberation which followed. The reorganisation of the whole system of land ownership and the struggle against feudal and capitalist philosophy followed. The mass study which has gone into making up a new understanding, has made big strides forward possible. Lu Yu-lan's village reaps six times as much grain as it did in 1955. The hearts of the village folk are more than six times as confident. Lu Yu-lan gave me a "yu-lu-pai" (quotation badge) to pin on my coat. The people all wear one made of red cloth with gold letters sewn on. Mine was one she had been given in Peking, and was a metal tab bearing the characters meaning "Service to the people of China and those of the whole world". I was proud to have it from so distinguished a fighter for the same cause.

While in Hsingtai we went to a performance of the "Hopei Bangtze" form of opera. The theme was one set in the New Fourth Army areas in the War of Resistance, "Shachiapang". It was done with the usual singing and acrobatics of old-style opera, but with a rousing action story that obviously pleased the crowded audience. A new culture is coming in, and though much of the old still remains in the thought of people, the new is so strong it steadily erodes all that is unscientific, all that holds back the creativeness of liberated minds.

Some Fighting Communes of Tsunhua

It was a bright, warm early autumn afternoon in 1966 when we left the quiet beauty of Peitaiho beach and took the train for industrial Tangshan.

At Liberation not a single man, woman or child could read. Now the village has 200 graduates from primary or higher schools, and most of the older folk have learnt to read well enough to understand the passages in Chairman Mao's works on which they rely so much for the inspiration in their work and struggle. Really, in Shashihyu it has been very much like in the tale of the Foolish Old Man in Chairman Mao's works who said he would remove the mountains. Here, in fact, the task was in some ways harder than in the removal of the mountains which stood in front of the old man's house. Here, the stones and the bigger rocks had to be upended and built into terrace walls, then earth had to be carried long distances from down the valley and the strips already terraced filled in with it. Much of the work had to be done outside the ordinary hours of productive work so that nights were full of the sound of toil as the whole village, old and young, with incredible energy, persistence and determination worked together to build a little heaven on earth out of their collective spirit.

It was not easy. At first, many thought it could not be done. Then a start was made on one field, it taking 90 evenings to get 3.3 mou completed. The youth of the village did a field and the brigade put up a tall stone slab beside it with a poem praising their spirit. This started a competition. The village lasses, the old men, the old women now all wanted to show what they could do. One thing led to the other. New fields began to climb up the rocky hillsides. Some of the brigade members went off to see the famous Tachai brigade in Shansi, and studied what had been done there. They came back with many new ideas and were able to carry their enthusiasm to those around them, so that now hillside faces began to turn to grain fields everywhere. In a very heavy summer downpour a portion of one area was smashed by a landslide, but yet the work went on of patiently restoring, patiently bringing new areas in on land which in most parts of the world would be looked at as totally unusable, utterly worthless, and quite unable to support stock or human life.

The brigade in the past had always used the stalks of kaoliang or corn for winter fuel. This denied them the value these are in compost heaps. So on areas too steep for terracing and on others near hilltops members have planted trees for fuel which, properly conserved, will be able to take care of at least some of this need. They received a directive to plant a large number of apple trees. But at a meeting members agreed that they could not use their already terraced land for that. So they set about bringing in a new hillslope, making terraces, digging into the rock and making holes to be filled with earth for fruit trees, and in the end were able to plant millet between the trees. They thus increased their annual grain total rather than diminished it, as some members had feared.

The problem of water was as great as that of earth. They solved it in part with the construction of a reservoir cut into the rock high up on the hillside amongst their terraced land. This reservoir took 13,000 man days to make, and was completed with but the ordinary village tools. It does not leak, stores the summer rainwater, and has pipelines leading to it from a hill spring as well.

But it was a cold, wet morning that greeted us the next day when we set out across country for Tsunhua county, rain that abated when we had passed through Fengjun county and had entered the hills of Tsunhua. We took a side road leading off from the main highway and struck into the area farmed by Yuehkechuang Commune, then again branched off on a narrow road that forded a stream and wound through the hills until we came to the village that is the headquarters of Shashihyu Brigade. Thirty to 40 years ago there was not even a good hill track to this village. At that time it did not even have a name and was not marked on any maps, and in the period of Japanese occupation anything that was not on the quite detailed maps they had been preparing for so long simply did not exist for the Japanese, so that the village was not bothered even by enemy cavalry probes. From 1933 onwards it was well known to guerilla forces as a safe place to stay and got its name in 1943, when the Eighth Route Army men came and went.

Shashihyu

We were met by a brigade leader who was one of the 78 families, 68 of whom once lived on wild herbs, scraps of grain, hiring themselves out as carriers, or simply becoming beggars in the bad seasons. They cut what scrub remained on the hills and sold it for fuel. In the worst times they were even forced to sell their children. Liberation came to the whole area by 1947, when they started to put their collective house in order, thinking it good that by 1950 they were able to reap 84 jin of grain a mou a year from their 780 mou of land. In a bad year, they still had to ask the government for relief grain, as for example in 1953 when they received 90,000 jin. But from the years 1956-66 they have been able not only to keep themselves but also to sell to the state over 400,000 jin of grain and a million jin of fruit. The broad valley facing south is situated in the upper hills with steep ridges rising on both sides. The brigade owns 2,400 mou, of which 1,200 mou can be used for grain or orchard production — 800 in grain, and 400 in fruit trees amongst which millet is grown. By 1965 the grain land had been made to produce 560 jin a mou. From the way it looked at the time of our visit, the 1966 total would be higher. How then has this miracle been made to take place in a valley of which people sang, "Earth here is as rare as precious pearls, water as precious as oil, the whole hillside is but a mass of great rocks," and then, "No lass wants to be married into a Shashihyu home where there is only rock and no earth, folk living on wild vegetables and bran, through all the nine cold periods of winter no padded clothing." It was not that the people did not work hard. They had with great industry managed to till 2,300 plots of ground, but the old way of living, with each man rather grudgingly helping the other in mutual-aid teams, and then the first cooperative stage, did not bring out their full potential. Middle peasant families then averaged a yearly income of 37 yuan a family. For poor peasants it was but 17 yuan. In 1965, the whole population of the 109 families now in the brigade, 598 people in all, averaged 114 yuan per person for the year.

In their great struggle, the villagers were building better than they knew. What they had done was soon understood throughout many parts of China, and other commune farmers came to study and learn. Then the brigade stepped out into the international field as a teacher, for it proved that even in the face of such immense difficulties and such impossible natural conditions the food problem could be solved anywhere in our world today, if people are armed with the kind of thinking these people have put to use. A helicopter landing field has been constructed and Chinese leaders with state guests from such lands as Albania, Mali and Zambia have flown in. Now the village youth who keep on bringing up earth know that they have an international role as well as a national one. Throughout the village new homes are being built, looking very charming in early autumn with tall hollyhocks and sunflowers, the gold of ripening pumpkins, and the mass of greenery around. Walnuts and Chinese dates hang richly from trees around each home. Pear trees are loaded down with fruit. The 101 children in the local primary school come running down the stone-flagged path with happy abandon. "What a rich and happy village this is," one would say even at a casual glance, especially if one came at this time of year. A great many of the houses are newly built — 280 of them. Clothing is adequate for all seasons. Among the 109 families there are 90 new bicycles and also many transistor radios and sewing machines. 210,000 yuan has been spent on better farm equipment for the brigade since 1956 — carts, horses, and so on. Orchard trees, including walnuts and dates, number 103,000. The 920 mou afforested in fuel trees is being rapidly enlarged. It was not just a case of planting and then the job was done. Many of the first experiments in tree-raising failed, and the work had to be done over again after causes for the failure had been analysed. Folk have shown that just ordinary farm people can be real heroes with an influence on history if they but find the correct way and follow it. Those quiet Hopei girls, whose grandmothers had bound feet, now go right out and build a dam by themselves which they call March 8th Dam in honor of International Women's Day. There are 31 lasses named "iron", or really sturdy. 70 "iron" men, 17 "iron" middle-aged women, and ten old labor heroes — so named because of their long years of self-sacrificing toil. Then too, there is much concern about the next generation, not to let it become soft and self-indulgent. "There is plenty of room for improvement in Shashihyu," they all say, "and we want our youngsters to make it in a tough, creative, revolutionary way!" There is no room for revisionism here.

Tsunhua Town

It rained so hard while we were there that we beat a swift retreat in the afternoon to the Tsunhua county seat, determined to come again when the weather cleared and finish the tour. It was good to spend the evening in town, however, meeting local friends and talking about Tsunhua in general, thus gaining a valuable background for better evaluating Shashihyu. The county is described as being one of 1,940 square kilometres, 47 percent of which is hills, 20 percent downs and 33 percent flat arable land. It was first liberated in 1945, but then the Kuomintang with their new U.S. arms drove in, only to be thrown out in 1947. It has a population today of 485,000 people, divided into 45 communes and 692 brigades. The 830,000 mou of arable land raises today an average of around 500 jin of grain a mou. There are four ordinary and 80 part-work, part-study middle schools, and 1,136 primary schools with 117,000 pupils. Twenty percent of the land is cultivated by tractors. Draft animals and plows now come to back villages where not so long ago the big hoe was the only tool used for breaking open the ground. There is a drive for better fertiliser which with better seed selection, improvement of strains, closer planting, and better irrigation makes the land produce around five times as much as it did in 1947. Not so much chemical fertiliser is used as yet, the great bulk being house and pig manure composted, the mud bricks of the sleeping "kangs" in houses being added each spring and making a valuable component. Each mou of heavy ground must get 5-6,000 jin of compost if it is to produce 500 jin of grain. If another 1,000 jin could be added, the grain total would rise an additional 100 jin. In addition to the grain sold to the state each year, over two million jin of cotton, and over two million of peanuts, as well as around 14 million jin of fruit are sold also. In the old days the farmers had a rhyme which said that folk in Tsunhua had one suit of clothing every three years and only one poor quilt for every two persons. Today on a holiday, with everyone wearing his best and the streets full of spanking new bicycles, the countryside takes on a new look. A people who were the backbone of the last stages of the War of Liberation are looking after themselves economically as well as politically. But let us take another look at the marginal lands, lands that no one wanted, where refugees and beggars once lived, grimly holding on through evil days.

Hsipu Brigade

One goes out of East Gate of Tsunhua county town then heads towards a range of hills south of Shashihyu. Finally after crossing a flooded river we arrived at the village of Hsipu, situated just at the foot of the hills. So much planting has been done on the Hsipu side of the village that it is almost hidden from view, and one arrives without realising it. We were met at the office of Chienming Commune by Wang Kuo-fan, its Party secretary, who at the same time is Party secretary of Hsipu Brigade of that commune. He is also a member of the National People's Congress and a well-known figure in rural China today. A tall, rather gaunt Hopei peasant of 46, he has had a hard past. The good land in Hsipu in the other days was mainly landlord owned. There were many beggar families amongst the very poor. Wang Kuo-fan was amongst them. These went to the more distant mountain valleys to cut fuel in winter, hired themselves out when they could, while many went begging when there was no other way out. It was 13 families of such folk that Wang Kuo-fan organised into a mutual-aid team in 1951. Together with four other families they raised enough money to buy a donkey. The mutual-aid team owned three legs only, which meant that they could use the donkey for but three quarters of its time. But still, all were proud of the purchase. Then the mutual-aid team changed to become an elementary farm cooperative and such was their spirit for the struggle that they prospered fairly swiftly and, when the stage of early, then of higher cooperatives and finally the commune arrived, they were in the lead in village affairs. When the Hsipu brigade of the commune was created, members began to look around for new resources. Surely there was plenty of land that could be terraced on the downs below the steep hill faces, but the soil was just decomposing red rock which changed to a sticky clay and would not take a crop. Experiments were made in using the loess sand out of the riverbed together with it, and it was found that the mixture with the addition of compost fertiliser made an excellent soil. It was quite a way up the hillslope from the riverbed, but then a road could be made and the commune rubber-tyred carts could be used, as well as the ordinary small carts of the brigade folk. At first slowly, and then with greater speed as all pitched into the task, new fields rose above those in the valley. Fields that soon filled with crops just as heavy as those on the flat land below. Then above these fields came plantations of walnut and chestnut trees — 40,000 of them — apple and peach orchards, then pines and cedars. Many of the trees are too small yet to show up much but all are growing well. Naturally, Wang Kuo-fan is proud of them all, though he did not say very much about them, not being given to long explanations. The look on his face when he pointed them all out was enough however.

As we went uphill, an elderly man with two young cowherds passed us, all swinging along behind their animals. He gave me a warm handshake in passing, and an encouraging word or two. Though he was dressed like an ordinary farmer, it turned out that he was an old Red Army fighter with 20 years' army experience. After being wounded he was demobilised and came home wearing a metal support around his waist. Minding stock, that was what he wanted to do. The two lads help him and together they make a good team, all very happy together.

It was fascinating to stroll around Hsipu. Yes, there was the donkey, still working well. And, here is the primary school. It has 340 pupils. Every youngster who ought to be in school attends. It does not matter what he wears or does not wear. If he is in the first grade of primary school and has no slate then it is all right to chalk characters and figures on the desk top for a blackboard. They can be wiped away as easily as those on a slate, and can be made bigger anyway. They are a merry bunch of healthy children, and it was a real delight to move amongst them, listening to their singing and watching them at work. In the village also is a commune middle school, and an agricultural part-work, part-study middle school of 80 youngsters that has now been operating for the past three years.

Chienming Commune of which Hsipu Brigade is part, is one of 21,000 mou of land worked by 13,400 people from 2,340 families. Its area is 30

Chinese li long, and ten wide (2 li = 1 km). In the landlord-ridden days it produced around 70-80 jin of grain a mou each year. Villages here averaged around 30 deaths a year, most of them due to malnutrition. For a considerable time after Liberation the population had to be given relief grain and relief clothing. This was especially so of Hsipu which then had 154 families with 454 people in them. Today it has 210 families with 1,018 people. During the past year only two have died, and those of old age. The brigade is one of the 187 in Tsunhua county which are electrified, so that there are plenty of electric lights and motors. Besides many head of cattle it has 37 donkeys, 14 mules and horses, 12 big rubber-tyred horse carts, 40 donkey carts, and 30 rubber-wheeled pushcarts. Coming down the main village street, I saw a grandfather of over 60 and his 15-year-old grandson, both riding new bicycles. The brigade sells to the state grain, peanuts, cotton and fruit in large quantities now, reserving for its own use 414 jin of grain per person per year. A crop of 628 jin a mou was gained in 1965.

The hills above Hsipu, the lower slopes now rich with crops on newly terraced fields and the higher green with orchard or forest planting, were not always so attractive. The Japanese army, maddened by continual guerilla attacks on them, made the whole area into a no man's land — on which to be found meant execution. They burnt off the forests, all homes they found, and tried to make a complete desert there. All this, however, simply meant that the people went to the Eighth Route Army and fought together with them, until in the end the Japanese retreated.

I liked the scientific way the whole business of composting was done in Hsipu. The big pits where house manure was first kept, then the well-made compost heaps to which it was added. The brigade has constructed its own reservoir which irrigates 6,000 mou. Summer storms make the river swell dangerously at times, but the 10,000 willows that now grow in the Hsipu village border have protected it so far. Wang Kuo-fan was very insistent that the mainspring of _all_ that has been done is the fact that every effort has been made to get all to understand the content of the works of Mao Tsetung, and that in these there is an answer to the way forward for everyone. He interspersed many instances of actual happenings in his village as he said all this, giving the now so familiar sentiments new flavor and weight.

On the way back to Tsunhua town we passed many groups of school children organised with sticks to go out amongst the cornfields after a borer that needs finding and eradicating. Two of the bigger boys of one group carried a blackboard in front, with a piece out of Chairman Mao's works written on it. The way this group marched though, would have been a credit to any army unit. They really did look like a people out for action. Wang Kuo-fan had said that he and his comrades were determined that they would do everything in their power to prevent the next generation in their commune from becoming revisionists and taking a path away from the revolution. These youngsters, heads up and bodies swinging along together gave a strong feeling that things were going the right way in this old countryside.

Malanyu

Before leaving Tsunhua we took a tour out to the hot springs not far from Malanyu and the Eastern Tombs of the Manchu dynasty. Here the springs that were once used by Manchu courtiers, and even by the famous Ming general Chi Chi-kwang, are now part of a rest home for workers.

We had a bathe and then visited the local general store next door. Like many another village store around hinterland China it had become the local social centre. People liked coming, bringing their produce for exchange. They enjoyed looking at the new stock and generally having a pleasant time meeting their friends. The area around here had been badly struck by a hailstorm in mid-June. But no one was prepared to yield to despair and give up. The land was swiftly plowed again and a new crop of corn and beans planted, which will be about a month behind the main crop but was doing very well nevertheless.

Shashihyu Again

We took care that is was a fine, bright day when we made the second visit to Shashihyu, going to parts of the brigade area we had not visited on the first occasion. The geological formation of the slopes at the rear of the village is one of slabs of conglomerate, piled one on top of the other, interstices being filled with a sticky clay. It is not the kind of rock easy to make a reservoir in, the danger of leakage being so great. But compared with the big round rocks of the area in a western valley which had been reclaimed, the going has been relatively easy, though the back-breaking task of carrying up earth from the valley bottom has been the same. We went over rocky paths, past the brigade office manned by two lasses who were not up to the heavy hill reclamation work. Then we crossed a causeway which had been built by the old men of the brigade who had then reclaimed some ravine land above it. These fields had a high stand of corn. Then we came around a hillside and great boulders raised their heads everywhere. It was here the apple orchard has been planted, and heavy heads of millet bend under fruit-laden trees, as if this was the richest land in Hopei instead of being former marginal land not wanted by anyone. Apples were being picked and packed into wickerwork baskets which donkeys were carrying away suspended from pack saddles. The work that has been put into making these terraced fields is almost incredible. The brigade leader said, pointing to an especially rugged bit of hillside, "Someday, we shall complete taming every single bit of this land and we shall have a highway coming through here so that we can get fruit out more easily."

We went to the school. A very simple one tucked away under a hill with three teachers, one lad and two lasses. The children were a live, happy bunch, singing songs, doing skits and farewelling us with a good deal of warmth.

A 1968 Visit to Shashihyu

The year 1966 went by, and so did 1967. In January 1968, we returned to Shashihyu. Mid-winter, and with the red earth lying fallow beneath the rows of fruit trees or around the narrow terraces, it was a completely different picture. A new water supply system has been built by the commune, it now being piped by 1,000 metres of earthenware pipes from a reservoir the commune can pump up to, using the electricity from the new power line that has come into the village. No more apple or pear trees were being planted, new plantings now consisting of walnuts, dates and trees for fuel and timber. During the first part of the Cultural Revolution, visitors helped to reclaim some 50 more mou of terraced hillside land, carry up the earth, cut out the stone, and bring in the fertiliser. The brigade now hopes to work towards better preserving the summer floodwater, halting erosion and utilising every bit of available fertiliser. Hopes are that in 1968 each mou will yield 600 jin of grain. The 1967 crop suffered because of a big hurricane that came in with an early summer storm, wreaking havoc amongst the standing grain and the fruit trees. "We have to be prepared to meet enemies like these," the brigade leader said philosophically. Food, however, was enough, and through the Cultural Revolution study and work have gone on together, rising to new levels during the time we were there. The grand alliance, then the three-way alliance of old cadres, new rebels and militia has been working well, and there is every hope that with determination and spirit it will be possible to carry through work already started, and bring new results. We looked at the new cooperative store and were impressed with the range of articles in supply there. Many of the homes have been rebuilt and all have tiled roofs. Living standards have obviously risen since the summer of 1966. Many visitors have come and have painted their impressions on stones, the many large flat ones around being admirably suited for this. In the Cultural Revolution there was not quite the same amount of class struggle as in richer villages, for here the people had all been so very poor. There were no landlords and but one rich peasant family. The revisionist line of increasing private plots had not been carried out either, the size here being not more than a quarter of a mou per family. The original idea of working for the common good had gone deep. But there was plenty to do in studying how to combat selfishness and oppose rivisionism. Homely examples were quoted and analysed and then related to actual conditions around. There were 104 children in school, not counting some who had gone on to the middle school at the commune headquarters in the valley below. People all knew about the war of aggression against Vietnam, and indeed one of the largest of the inscribed stones was that written by a visiting group of young Vietnamese people.

Tungling Commune

After coming back to Tsunghua from Shashihyu, we went out to the Eastern Tombs of the Ching dynasty, now a national monument kept well in repair. Near there we called on an old revolutionary, a Manchu, in Tungling Brigade of Tungling Commune.

He was around 70, slight of build, but very straight and dignified, with white whiskers and a small beard. Yes, his life had been hard. After the 1911 revolution, suddenly difficulties crowded in. His folk tried tilling land around the tombs, but had to bring in poor Hans to learn from them how to do it. Landlords and rich peasants came in, took over their land and enslaved them. The Japanese imperial army marched in and drove them away making a no man's land of the only place they knew as home. Driven out, they dug holes in the ground, covering them with cornstalks for roofing. They carried fuel to the cities, earning barely enough to exist. Many sold their children, many gave up the struggle and died. Then finally in 1947 Liberation came, and old and young were assured of food and work. Four sons his wife bore him. One is now a PLA man in Inner Mongolia, while the other three have all gone through middle school and are in his commune brigade. One of them, a teacher in the local school now, is married and there are two grandchildren to cheer him up. "And you know," he said, "we can say anything we like to the cadres or any leaders." And he smiled at the Han brigade leader, a tough strong-looking peasant type who was sitting with us, who smiled pleasantly back.

It was hard to believe that the old man had gone through all those hardships. He was quiet spoken, full of old-fashioned courtesy, gentle yet very direct. He had been a cadre until he had retired, but the affairs of the brigade still had a deep interest for him. He knew a lot about the path to revisionism and in a few direct words stated his views. After all he and his have gone through, they are all for the way forward together with Chairman Mao. He is proud of the fact that Tungling "bai", which is the name of a special corn raised in his commune, is now eagerly sought after, both at home and abroad. It is a high-yield, especially good-tasting variety which with proper fertiliser brings in 1,000 jin a mou of good white grain. The brigade leader then came in with some words about what had been done in these years since Tungling Commune had been set up. Their brigade had 2,000 mou of land for the 975 people from 210 families. More than half of them are Manchu. Their fields lie on hillside, plain and the borders of the riverbed beside the towering mausolea of the Eastern Tombs. In 1967, an average yield of 516 jin a mou of grain was gained and for each of the 975 people, old and young, there is 414 jin a year. 1965 was a drought year, but despite the 265 days without rain a big harvest was gained. The brigade has 550 orchard trees, mostly pear and persimmon, and 550 pigs.

As was the custom of Manchu Bannermen here, all old housedoors face east, not south. The old man finished our talk by saying that his people had come down into the Ming empire and had lived idly for generations. Now with the realisation that all peoples were one in China and with a secure future ahead of them, they find new strength. Yes, they have a brigade school and a clinic. The medical cadre works half time in the fields, as there are not enough sick people for him to attend to full time.

We asked about other difficulties, and he said that the main one was the corn weevil which bored into the corn stalk so that it easily blew over in the wind and broke off. The attack on this pest has been a mass campaign. As the weevil hibernates amongst the corn stalks left in the ground, these are dug up and used for fuel. In spring an onslaught is made with insecticides against this enemy, along with the pests that attack sorghum and millet. Many hands have made light work, and again the people have won.

Hsipu, 1968

We went back to see Hsipu Brigade, interested to see what had happened since our last visit in 1966. Wang Kuo-fan was away at a meeting in Tangshan but his deputy, another ex-pauper, Wang Yung, received us. The talk started off quietly with a simple statement of results gained. Grain at 628 jin a mou in 1966, with 105 of cotton and 216 of peanuts a mou. The 1967 figures were 697 jin of grain, 115 of cotton and 216 of peanuts. Then we went back to August 1966, when I had come last, for what had happened since then. It appeared that Wang Kuo-fan and his ex-pauper friends thought that there would not be so much class struggle, for had not everyone worked hard to get the results that had come to them, all the way up from the three legs of that donkey? But Wang still had a bitter lesson to learn. There was a certain local family called Tu. And amongst the Tu clan was a Tu Kwei, an "operator" whose ambitious schemes included getting rid of Wang Kuo-fan. The Cultural Revolution provided him with the opportunity to try, and he soon made up his own organisation, giving it a high-sounding revolutionary name, and then put up a big wall poster which listed "14 crimes" of Wang Kuo-fan. These so-called "crimes" were actually either sheer inventions of Tu Kwei, or else ordinary mistakes highly magnified. Wang Kuo-fan was hauled in front of this organisation no fewer than 20 times to face accusations and criticism. His home was ransacked several times, his Party membership was cancelled, and his 67-year-old mother died, mainly because of anger it was said. Tu Kwei was relentless. He had the bit between his teeth and was going full speed ahead. At one point he tried to accelerate, saying that Wang Kuo-fan ought to be killed within five days, so Wang's old friends had to come around to protect him and set up their own organisation. Tu Kwei had the support of all the ex-landlord families and those of the rich peasants, as well as many who had some kind of a past they wanted to conceal. Some schoolboys attached themselves to him also, fooled by his high-sounding flow of revolutionary words. There was no physical struggle, but the battle of words continued, with Wang Kuo-fan's group steadily gaining ground. Two PLA men came to observe, and soon learnt things that showed up the whole matter in a new light. Tu Kwei had tried to muddy up Wang Kuo-fan's past, saying that he was no true Party member at all. Tu Kwei, it now came out, had been a member of the "Red Eyes", a landlord self-protection corps, and was trying now to prevent the uncovering of others who had also been so associated. Tu Kwei hated Wang Kuo-fan amongst other reasons for not helping to save Tu's cousin, Tu Chih, executed as a counter-revolutionary in 1951. Before Liberation, in the War of Resistance, it was proved, Tu had stolen cotton needed for making explosive. He got hold of a KMT cart left in the village and sold the cotton for himself for the equivalent of 1,000 yuan. In 1955 he had managed to get away with 2,000 jin of grain, and was in the habit of lending out money to those over whom he had some control, at 30-40 percent a year interest. His lies about Wang Kuo-fan's party affiliations were soon completely exposed as pure inventions. All of these as well as many other facts were gathered about Tu Kwei, which showed him up as a thorough enemy. Whereas Wang Kuo-fan's mistakes all came under the heading of "contradictions amongst the people", those of Tu Kwei showed him up as a real class enemy, completely unprincipled and very cunning.

"I don't know much about 'general direction'," Wang Yung said, "but I do know that Wang Kuo-fan led our 34 beggar families and 73 who had to earn their living from what they could carry on their backs, up from tumble-down thatched huts to decent homes. That his spirit and energy gave the leadership we needed to get the results we have." Then he went on to outline some of the more dramatic results, the 60 rubber-tyred carts, the 137 bicycles, the radios and sewing machines, then the crop totals. "I was eight years a beggar. Now I am with Chairman Mao. In the War of Resistance Tu Kwei sold out Chang En to the enemy and then put the blame on Wang Kuo-fan. We can learn something from that and so much else. Who the true revolutionaries are and who the phonies. Deeds count." Then he went on to describe how the head of the militia who supported Wang Kuo-fan had been seized and stripped naked, but not caring about that, how he had shouted back the quotation from Chairman Mao's works on paper tigers. Tu Kwei thought that he had military power when his group seized the arms of the militia, but he calculated wrongly. Yes, a lot had been done after the take-over from Tu Kwei at the end of January 1967. People put out their best. 110,000 trees were planted. A brigade piggery was established, new pieces of terraced land brought in on the hillsides. "Now," he asked, "who spreads poison, and who does not?" referring to the fact that Tu Kwei had told others that the two Army men had come into the commune to spread poison.

There has been an exhibition set up of the rise of Hsipu Brigade, well illustrated. The donkey whose three legs were bought now gets light work only and for most of the day is tethered near the exhibition hall. We left after a warm farewell, pleased to have caught up on what has been happening in this little hinterland village, and of its meaning to poor folk everywhere.

Coming back to the Tsunhua county seat, looking over the fields under a light fall of snow and at the rugged mountains that rose behind them, one could not help thinking back on the final visit paid while we were in Hsipu. It was to the home of an ex-pauper, who had been blind but whose sight was restored with an operation after Liberation. The home was a newly built, strong one, with the sun streaming in through glass windows onto the kang where his wife played with a child. He still had something of the look of a blind man, but when he spoke of the new life that had opened up for people like himself, he was enthusiastic. "There is my old hut," he said, pointing to a tiny thatched shed in the garden now used to store odds and ends. "The thatch leaked always. We kept as warm as we could on the kang it covered, always cold in winter, never with enough to eat. Our world has changed."

Chienhojan

One morning we set out from Tsunhua going north and soon entered the hills. After a while we came to one more well-known no man's land created by the Japanese imperialists in order to fight the guerillas. An area where all villages were levelled and burnt, and any living thing was shot at. Steadily we climbed, beyond a reservoir and high up into the mountains, where we found the villages of Chienjan and Hojan, which together make up Chienho Brigade of the local commune. Originally so poor that its people had to be fed by relief grain from outside, it has in these years achieved an economic independence that is truly surprising.

There was no water. Each mou of terraced fields brought in only 30-40 jin of corn or millet a year. A great deal had been done with planting some 50,000 chestnut, 10,000 pear and 500,000 fir and ash trees on the rocky slopes. But how to get water and so obtain enough grain was the major problem. Eighteen young people of the militia came into the fray. They worked steadily for 18 months, diverting the water from a stream that runs through the Great Wall. One hilltop had to be cut through and 100 metres tunnelled through rock for the canal to carry the water around the terraces of the Hojan production team land. The task took such a long time because the rock was hard, and experience had to be gained during work. 1967 was the first year of irrigated terrace land, with a harvest of 480 jin a mou, some of it from new rice paddy. For the 744 people in the 131 households there was 360 jin of grain each for the year. Last year they also had a crop of 140,000 jin of chestnuts and 30,000 of pears. They have built a highway that runs through their brigade and goes on to Chengteh, the prefecture to the north. The houses are mainly new brick and tile homes, replacing the old thatched huts. The children were delightful as they crowded around and sang songs for us. It was the week before Spring Festival, and a holiday feeling was already in the air.

We went through the break in the Great Wall which the new highway had made, and saw how the old barracks there had gone and chestnut trees stood on the old house terraces. "One hundred jin a tree," folk told us. They look forward to the time when their young trees will be as big as these. Each year they plant all they have time to, and plan for the time when they will have all the available hillsides covered with food-producing trees that will be growing while people rest.

In Tsunhua before we left we passed some thousands of commune folk who marched through the city — delegates from Mao Tsetung Thought study groups from all over the county. Soon they would go back to their locations fired with new enthusiasm, prepared for the big task of 1968. It was good to have come to this rural centre set amongst the mountains and catch some of the enthusiasm that warmed even the coldest day. Tsunhua is indeed a happy memory.

Shashihyu where
a rocky hillside has been made
to grow grain and fruit; Hsipu
where beggars, fuel carriers
and the other poor, gathered
making the old land bloom
in a new way; again fighting
the class enemy when
once more he raises his head;
at Tungling we sat with
an old Manchu farmer, listening
to him tell of the struggle
against insect pests, and of
the success of the local corn
they call Tungling "bai";
watch the long lines of farm folk
coming over a snow-covered land
to the fair in Tsunhua, then
go through the mountains
to Chienhojan Brigade,
where under the shadow of
the Great Wall, eighteen youths
fought for as many months,
ripping through the mountains
bringing in water to irrigate
all their terraced fields;
then after looking at so much
relaxing in Tangshan springs
awhile before returning in
an evening lit with the glow
of a setting sun, which dyed
snows red, playing tricks
in pastel shades with mountains
in blue and valleys where
a pregnant earth awaited spring;

so many thoughts,
so much change that comes
to the huts of the once
denied; Tsunhua a book
with its lessons printed
clearly for all to see.

Changli Communes

Changli is a county in the Tangshan prefecture of Hopei, with a long coast-line on the Gulf of Pohai. Once the sea came right up to the mountains, but river deposition of loess has pushed the coastline eastwards, making for a relatively fertile area of rolling country and plain on which are dotted the villages of the brigades and production teams of 39 communes. It is not an easy area to farm, for the treacherous Luan river flows down through it, at times bringing great floods when there are cloudbursts up in its vast deforested watershed region.   Then, too, many of the fields along the coastline have high salinity. Much of the soil is light and sandy, and in drought years suffers. Nevertheless, in these years the people, ap-proaching half a million in number and farming an area of over two mou of land each, have raised production on the saline lands from around 100 jin of grain a mou to three times that amount, and have been able to assure an annual distribution of around 400 jin of grain per capita for the population, besides building up reserves. The once saline areas now, after treatment, have been changed into rice paddy fields. Corn, sorghum, wheat, beans and sweet potatoes are also grown, while there is a high yield of chestnuts, dates and walnuts from the higher hilly lands and one of grapes and orchard fruits from the lower ones.

We came to Changli in the summer of 1968 by car through country roads lined with tall crops, passing through villages where young life looked healthy and happy, and where the fields were being constantly attended to by lines of production team members working together.   Ar-riving, we put up in the Fruit Research Institute of the Hopei provincial government which is situated here, comfortably set amongst proud or-chards. Certainly a good place to visit when in mid-summer peaches ripen and the first crop of early apples comes from the trees.

Wuliying Brigade

Running through the old city of Changli, now indistinguishable from its suburbs as the city walls have all been removed, we went off to spend some hours with Wuliying Brigade of Shihlipu Commune. It is a brigade of 2,221 people who live off 2,146 mou of arable land and who have a work strength of 756, divided into ten production teams. Once the place was chiefly noted for the poverty of the people, 70 percent of the land and the best at that being owned by a tiny group of landlords and rich peasants. There were 36 beggar families, and 300 families in all living below suste-nance level, so much so that each year there would be some of the hungry eating wild grasses who died from eating poisonous herbs. In 1943 alone, 100 families emigrated to the Northeast to try to make a living. Even after Liberation when the land was divided, some had to sell their newly ac-quired land to live. The land they had did not produce more than 120 jin a mou, while from their vineyards they had poor yields. Only slowly and painfully they made progress. With Liberation there came a demand for stone slabs from the hills. Some said, "Let us just make money from this work, and not bother too much about the land because we cannot do much more with it." This was especially after they had two failures on trying to get better irrigation. In the first, the idea was to blast open a spring which supplied a small stream coming out of a cave. The pressure of the water showed that there was more behind it. But the blast they set off opened up a fissure down which all the water drained, so that they lost even that which they had.

The second scheme was to build a reservoir, but a cloudburst came and took the dam away. The third was more ambitious. It was to raise water from the Yinma river for over two li and channel it into canals that would supply vineyards, paddy and grain fields. For a raised causeway carrying the water across country, for aqueducts, check dams and the like an enormous amount of cut stone was needed. So instead of selling slabs for ready cash, they had to work all out to supply their own needs. It meant a struggle on the ideological front, for the road forward depended on collective effort. The communists won, and the work was successfully carried through. The brigade now has 25 pumps driven by electric motors. Vineyards have spread, stone slabs making effective vine supports. The brigade now sells a million jin of grapes a year, some of this going into the export trade. Well worth putting up 6,200 metres of canal for, they feel now.

In the years following Liberation, members looked at 400 mou of their land which was semi-waste, being mainly waterlogged, and wondered how they could bring it into better production. A brigade leader suggested making it into rice paddy, but experts called in said this was not possible. The soil was all wrong. It was just sour swampland, and that was that. Undeterred, the brigade leader and some activists went on trying, sending members to work for a while on similar projects in neighboring brigades where marsh was made into paddy, until in the end they had enough experience and succeeded on their own. Surely, some soil had to be carried in. A proper blend of fertilisers had to be experimented with and put into use, and there had to be enough water at the right time. With quiet, determined leadership all of these difficulties were mastered, so now the brigade is getting 700 jin a mou of rice off what was once their most hopeless land. Each year the paddy fields are being improved and give higher yields.

I was interested in seeing the 350-pupil school, where the teachers did not get the usual salaries but were simply on a workpoint basis like all other commune members. The same thing was the case in the brigade clinic. In this latter place, fees for medical attention and the cost of medicines were entered into an account to be met when commune distribution of funds came each autumn.

The brigade had in its stables 108 horses, which were mainly used for pulling 36 big rubber-tyred carts. It operated a small machine shop, a little flour mill, and various similar enterprises. One of its production teams, with 14 members, did electrical repairs and kept all electrical installations in order. A permanent stone-cutting team provides material for house reconstruction and for sale outside the commune. New housing is being built fast now. It took 17,000 man days to build the irrigation system, levelling being done by members themselves using the old local carpenter's method of putting a basin of water on a table and then sighting across it. The result of all this endeavor has been that there are now many more experienced men amongst the commune members who look around to see what more they can do.   They have built many terraces in the style of Shashihyu, the model backhill brigade in Tsunhua county, which quite a few have been to inspect and learn from. They have planted 5,000 walnut trees, 4,000 chestnuts, 200 mou of pines, and 24,000 fuel trees in good places amongst the hills.   Now, feeling the need for better technique, they are promoting their own agricultural middle school due to start this autumn with 70 students and scheduled to be enlarged to more than double that number in future.

Yearly income of brigade members has grown from 73 yuan each in 1956 to 143 yuan in 1967. At the time of the efforts of the revisionists to start on the road back to capitalism, the membership closed ranks and stood against some of the proposals which came down to them. Since then, they have entered the struggle of the Cultural Revolution with all their hearts. They have organised themselves into 368 study groups which find time each and every day to meet together, if even only for relatively short discussion. The new way has obviously penetrated into these homes quite definitely, carrying with it the determination to fight through all difficulties and to create anew.

The Revolutionary Committee of this commune brigade is an impressive group. The old brigade Party secretary is its chairman, and with him was an able young woman of the militia, then a good, steady-looking old farmer obviously with a wealth of experience, another a tall, strong practical-looking Hopei peasant type, and lastly a precise-looking accountant-book-keeper. The brigade leader told how all realised that in making their vineyards, their terraced fields, their irrigation and their paddy, they were helping also to make China more secure and helping the world revolution. That they were working for everyone of their class everywhere. One had the feeling that he was very sincere in this. I think I met most of the children. A good, tough-looking bunch of young hopefuls, who sang the songs of the cultural movement with a fine swing and much enthusiasm.

Chengmingshan Brigade

The commune brigade visited on the following day had a committee of similar composition, except that the two leaders were rather older and the militia representative a man. The girl member — a teacher — was dressed in a pretty summer blouse, had fine teeth and a strong, purposeful face. As we sat in the brigade headquarters in a spick and span newly built stone building under mountain crests, we could see right out across the plains below to the sea. In the same compound was one of the brigade schools, and as we came into it the pupils gave us a wonderful welcome. They will be those who will carry on the work of Chengmingshan Brigade when they grow up. A brigade with a fighting tradition; one that was a forward post of the Eighth Route Army in War of Resistance days, when by determined struggle they kept the enemy at bay. The speaker described some of the engagements of those days and the heroism of the militia in its various battles. In the Kuomintang period the new enemy drove right in and burnt many of the houses, but did not break the people's spirit. In both the War of Resistance and War of Liberation, landlords and rich peasants sided with the enemy, consequently the people were under no delusions about them. Class struggle in the Cultural Revolution therefore was more or less plain sailing for them all, though it led to more intensive political study by everyone, of course.

Chengmingshan village has its families scattered around the hillside, so that each night after supper people concentrate in little groups in nearby home centres agreed upon by all and take up their study, relating it to their work of the day, the ideas that have come to them since the last meeting, and to the text of the study material. One can go on talking on the subject of "serving the people" for quite a long time, while the slogan "Struggle against selfishness and criticise revisionism" offers endless possibilities for discussion. Actually, revisionism did not strike Chengmingshan Brigade in such a big way. The revisionist directive to go out and bring in waste land to add to the private plots, however, did find some adherents, all of whom since have "cut at the root of revisionism", as they say, and have handed over the land they reclaimed to the brigade.

The general description of any commune brigade is interesting, for the farm commune is a new thing for the world, and in many ways a pattern for the future. As it becomes more self-sufficient and raises the standards of livelihood along with its standards of education, it will go on evolving. First steps are of necessity slow, as so much tough basic work has to be done. The commune does not alter the livelihood of the masses instantly. For instance, we visited one home in Chengmingshan that had been burnt by the Kuomintang in 1946. It was not properly rebuilt until 1960. Brigade work came first.

Cheng Village faces due north and south. Its mountains are rugged with ridges on which ancient pines stand against the winds. It is one of the brigades of Liangshan Commune which lies northeast of Changli. In its nine production teams there are 251 families, 1,150 people in all. People of poor and lower-middle peasant stock number 707. Arable land is made up of terraces on the rocky hillsides and some rolling country at the foot of the mountain, 1,888 mou of it. The terraced land accounts for 750 mou of this. It has 50,000 fruit trees — apple, pear, peach and apricot, and in addition walnuts, chestnuts and black dates. None of the land has very good soil, most of it having a heavy admixture of coarse sand. Boulders from the hillside are to be found in plenty, strewn all over the lower portions on which the layer of soil is quite thin. At Liberation, around 40 jin of grain a mou would be harvested when there was enough rain, the main harvest being from fruit, which then brought a crop of around 300,000 jin for the whole region. Last year, 258 jin a mou of grain was gained, and the fruit harvest was 1,200,000 jin. At Liberation, there was almost total illiteracy. Now all children are in school, while the brigade has already produced seven university graduates and 47 middle-school graduates from its numbers. Its clinic has one Western and one traditional Chinese doctor, both of whom stem from commune ranks. Looking back while in study discussion, people over and over again ask themselves what force pulled them out of the slough in which the landlords held them. Landlords owned 81 percent of the land at that time and had the power to treat the big majority of the people as beasts of burden.

"After we got rid of the landlords there were still two great difficulties — to get enough to eat and to get water to drink." The water problem had the highest priority, because drought would leave people with no crops at all. Drinking water had to be hauled all the way up from a well down below the village. When drought came, the whole village would turn out with shoulder poles to carry water day and night to save the crops. In 1956-57 they built two hill reservoirs with a capacity of 65,000 cubic metres of water, enough to irrigate 600 mou of cropland and enough too for 8,000 fruit trees. In 1966, it was decided to dig a big open well where three tiny springs emerged from the rocks. Some people said the project would surely be a failure. To work the rocks was tough, and there was the chance that there might be no more water at all down there. To try and dig an open well 24 metres long and eight wide, down until they got the water, did not appeal to some. But under the direction of the brigade militia commander the work was done. After 1,500 man days had been spent in the 80 days following February 10th, 1966, water was struck, the whole well having been faced with cut stone. Enough water came in to ensure irrigation for 150 mou of hillside terrace land, as well as enough for 1,500 fruit trees. They called it "the foolish old man who removed the mountains" well. Water is pumped out by a small electrically powered pump. Electricity came to the brigade in 1961, and all homes now have electric lights.

The Cultural Revolution has affected everyone, of course. Especially many of the old who had just been sitting around, but who were now stirred to come back and help. Some insisted on going out to work weeding, sitting on the ground as they went about their task! One small-footed old woman, too crippled to go out, made it a daily task to clean the pictures of Chairman Mao around the place where she lived. She says, "If I forget to do this, I forget him, and if I forget him, I might as well forget everything."

"What do you think our people would do if there was no rain at all?" the girl on the committee said when she was giving details about the brigade. "Would they just give in? Our people who have fought the Japanese imperial army and kept them off, who have fought against the Kuomintang, and who now do all they can to help Vietnam, and to pull down revisionism — for us there is no surrender. We shall fight on." And looking into the faces of the youngsters who lined the village street to farewell us, one quite believed her.

Out on the plain again, and looking back at Chengmingshan, the flat-roofed stone houses attractively whitewashed and standing amongst rich summer greenery looked almost idyllic. One was glad of the visit made which took one inside the lives of the people, their struggles and their enormous achievements, treasuring the memory of keen young faces now rising to carry the struggle into new stages.

Other Changli Events

While at Changli we attended an unusual theatre performance. It was put on by a concert party composed of 19 young people, one from each of 19 communes in the county. They had come together in Changli, and after some practice together were giving a series of entertainments around before dissolving their group and each returning to his or her commune again. It was not a long show, but there was no pause at all between the items which followed one after the other with immense verve and energy. The young people were all in the 18 to 25 age category, and their items brought terrific response from the audience, most of whom were also young. They just loved it. All themes were on the Cultural Revolution, and all instruments traditional ones. Especially impressive was a drummer who beat out his accompaniment with much precision on three types of old-time drums.

We spent a final morning in Changli looking at the 1,800 mou of orchards of the Hopei Fruit Research Institute, which grew out of a combination of two fruit orchards operated by railway companies during the late 'thirties. Here the most suitable varieties for commune use throughout the province are experimented with and perfected.

Pohai Commune in Funing County

Being anxious to see some more of the work in making saline marsh into the high-class paddy which we had noted at Wuliying Brigade, we went out to the seacoast in Funing county where Pohai Commune had done such work on a grand scale. It was a fascinating experience to look over the great wide fields of growing rice, knowing that so short a time ago they had been a saline waste.

Shuitien, Korean Nationality Brigade

The commune has its headquarters in the village of Hsihonan with 3,800 families of 18,300 people who farm 39,000 mou of arable land, 24,000 of which is now in rice paddy. It has 18 brigades, one a fishing unit and another, Shuitien Brigade, is a Korean minority nationality one. To find Korean nationality units northeast of the Great Wall is common, but to come across one in Hopei is unusual. It appears that the founders were among those who had left Korea in 1909 when the Japanese were taking over, and had settled in various parts of the Northeast. After Liberation, the first 12 families who had been isolated in various areas were brought south, the number being added to each year until there are now 73 families in all. The state has built them a pleasant living compound and a good school for their 92 pupils in six classes, where both Chinese and Korean is taught. The state also helps when small difficulties arise. For instance, the Korean national costume for women needs more cloth than the cloth ration provides for. Korean women also like a special type of rubber shoe. The state supplies both of these from the Korean Autonomous Region of Yenpien in the Northeast. The Koreans brought along their know-how in making rice grow well in cold areas, and with the help of the commune and other brigades they have gone from success to success, averaging 820 jin a mou from their fields in 1967. They sold the state 410,000 jin of rice in 1967, 5,600 jin from every family, which must be a record grain delivery in China. Per capita population, they have an income of 240 yuan a year. In rural China, as prosperity grows, the families first buy bicycles, then a sewing machine, then a radio, and then wrist watches. Shuitien Brigade is well into the wrist watch stage. In the Cultural Revolution they all have been active and have come to a clearer understanding of what revisionism is, and of the correct political line. The strength of the new ideas is great, and now practically everyone belongs to one of the political study groups.

We visited the Korean compound and met many of the folk in their homes, then while out in the fields we stopped by a field kindergarten which looked after the little ones of working women there. By the way, one of the things the Cultural Revolution has done has been to break down some of the traditional local attitude of men towards the women — lording it over them, looking down upon them as those born to do all the toughest work. There had been the custom, in the period of the promotion of incentives to working, of giving as many as 25 points for work in the cold water during rice transplanting. Now all members agree that they should go back to ten workpoints, the customary total for an adult doing a full day's work.

Rice paddy took quite a long time to get started in Pohai Commune. As the water buffalo does not do well in the north, the Koreans have brought down the draft cattle they were used to in the Northeast for paddy field work, using these for their rubber-tyred transport carts also. They struggled with the bad salty swamp for some years, but did not get much more than 300 mou producing well, until a big reservoir in the hills was finished during the Great Leap Forward and supplied enough water not only to combat drought but also for washing out the soil. Then the whole commune too, got to work, and all the marshes changed to become a great sea of waving grain, like a miracle in a folk tale. In 1961, when the Yangho reservoir had just been finished, there were 700 mou in paddy. By 1962, this had grown to 2,600. In 1963, to 9,000 mou; 1964 to 18,000; 1966 to 21,000 and 1968 to 24,000. The big reservoir was but one of the projects that the commune helped to put through. For instance, the commune borrowed 100,000 yuan from the state to do a water diversion project that ended in complete failure, making the second attempt to do it out of the commune's own strength more difficult, as so many were dead against another try. Finally, however, the forces for progress won out and the task was successfully completed. Such a success made it easier to win approval of the masses to complete a big drainage canal 2,400 metres long. Now, big projects for each winter, the off season, are the expected thing, and approval for the organisation of this type of work is relatively easy to get.

Collective morality has improved a great deal in the progress of the Cultural Revolution. One carter picked up a bag with 9,000 yuan in it on the road. He took it to the brigade who found out that it belonged to a neighboring commune brigade and was for a division of profits among the membership there. The people were overjoyed when it was found. Other lost articles found on roads are also regularly returned. A carter with a load of cement covered it with his bedding when a night rain came, and went cold himself rather than let any of the cement get spoilt. Many such stories now go the rounds of the study groups, with everyone commenting on them. Stories of fighters on the Long March, of commune members like themselves in Tachai, in Shashihyu and other model brigades are also often told, inspiring all.

"We have made a great salty marsh give good harvests for the country," they say, "and we can do so much more yet!" They go back over their own struggles and analyse. "Why did 130 families leave farm production altogether one season in the 'fifties, and go off to get a living from the sea?" "Why did Party secretary Liang Lin oppose brigade leader Chang Yu-hen who took seed rice and gave it out to the membership in one time of grain shortage? Who was right?" Then they turn to affairs in their own prefecture of Tangshan, going over the case of Wang Kuo-fan of Hsipu Brigade, and following his struggle and success during the Cultural Revolution. The study group is really a way, especially with people who are putting theory into practice each and every day. They know, too, many stories of the miserable past when the taking of a new concubine by the local landlord meant so much bitterness for the many who would have to pay for the days of feasting. Then a good year would give 120-130 jin a mou, and most of that the landlords and officials demanded. Now with production coming up to 1,000 jin a mou in good grain alone, with 4,500 pigs in their commune piggeries, with a labor strength of 7,000 strong, properly nourished members, 800 draft animals and 200 rubber-tyred carts along with their first big tractor, the old is hard for the young to even visualise.

Taoyuan "Experience"

Yet the struggle does go on, in one form or another, as it is bound to do as these once poor and denied more and more take hold of their destiny. Nowhere in all these Pohai Bay communes has this been dramatised more starkly than in Luwangchuang Commune in Funing county. One of the brigades in this commune is called Taoyuan, now known nationally, and even internationally as the one which China's chief revisionist, Liu Shao-chi, sought to hold up to the people as one which should be considered the national model, using the rural Socialist Education Movement to carry through what was a purely revisionist line in its reorganisation. It was to be Taoyuan that would lead in the future, not the self-sufficient, sturdy Tachai in Shansi or Shashihyu and Hsipu in Hopei. Taoyuan, in which the chief revisionist's wife Wang Kwang-mei with her strong backing personally maintained control by a reign of terror, accusing the good leading cadres of crimes that they were then called upon to prove they had not committed, and raising the most corrupt elements to be her minions. With the help of the Taoyuan experience, it is easier to understand the struggle that has taken place over China in these last three years.

As we sat in the brigade meeting room in Taoyuan, listening to Wu Chen, head of the Revolutionary Committee, tell about conditions in the brigade, it was hard to realise that the struggle for the socialist road had been so bitter. Almost mechanically one put down the figures Wu Chen gave — how there were 249 families with 1,220 people who have a working strength of 501, cultivating 2,127 mou of good flat land, 78 percent of which is irrigated with 16 power pumps. One would have thought that the most bitter era of struggle would have ended when the eight landlord and five rich peasant families had control wrenched from their hands. In their day, production never rose over 246 jin a mou. But by the mid-'fifties in the farm cooperative period, it had risen to 410 jin, while in 1967 it was 619 jin, with 1968 promising well to exceed that figure, for this year people have worked better than they ever have. The standing crops we passed through bore testimony to that.

Wu Chen became the Taoyuan brigade leader when the commune was first set up. He was of poor peasant stock, and once carried fuel for a landlord. Then, in the bad year of 1938 he joined the stream of refugees to the Northeast, where for three years he was a carpenter's apprentice, coming back home after the Kuomintang entered Changchun and started conscripting young men of his age as soldiers. Liberation came to Funing county in August 1948, after which he threw himself into the work of organising mutual-aid teams. He was made a Party member in 1949, and successively head of the militia and head of production. Though he had the support of the big majority of the people, yet too he had an enemy, a certain Kwan Ching-tung. This man, an upper middle peasant, wormed his way into favor quite cleverly. He was made a cadre in 1953 and, in the time of the setting up of cooperatives, organised a middle peasants' cooperative which had a simple formula for discarding applicants for membership — the three "not haves", it was called. If you did not have carts or horses, if you had no capital, if you did not have good land with proper title, then this cooperative wanted to have nothing to do with you. Wu Chen at this time was leading a poor man's cooperative with considerable ability and in direct opposition to the methods of Kwan. Nevertheless Kwan somehow or other became a Party member and a cooperative head. When the lower type cooperative was merged in the higher, he had the rich man's co-operative's bull killed rather than let it serve poor men's cows. He divided lower cooperative funds rather than let them become part of the capital of the higher cooperative into which it had merged. All the way through the movements of the 'fifties he showed that he was against the cooperative movement, against the grain policy and against the Great Leap Forward, yet somehow he could always talk his way through and somehow or other gain a higher position. Then the commune was set up, and he got himself in charge of promoting irrigation, electrification, mechanisation and chemical fertilisers, with many opportunties for making a little money on the side. Actually, in cooperation with three others, he sold 400 jin of high tension power line belonging to the commune and pocketed the proceeds.

In 1961, the administration of communes was reduced in size and many cadres were sent down to the brigades. Kwan came to Taoyuan Brigade, taking the post of militia head and chief of the security section, always looking for new opportunities of squeeze. He found one for example when going out to buy sweet potato shoots, on which deal he made a cool 1,000 yuan. He would even make use of his position to go out and steal from the standing crops and in 1962 set up a gambling centre in his home, out of which he made some 400 yuan and added many noted local scamps to his group. Why then did he have so great a daring in front of the people? The answer takes us back to 1958, when Liu Shao-chi and his wife came to visit Taoyuan, and Kwan Ching-tung was their guide. The wife was immediately attracted to him, and both she and her husband swallowed his talk hook, line and sinker when he calmly told them that Taoyuan gained no less than 15,000 jin of kaoliang a mou — exactly ten times the amount actually harvested even in the best year!

When the movement for socialist education of 1963-65 started, Kwan Ching-tung was made a target for criticism, but in November 1963 Wang Kwang-mei under the name of Tung Pu, member of the Public Security Bureau of the Hopei government, came in with a work team. Using the power which the work team possessed, she stopped all criticism of Kwan Ching-tung and, saying that all the cadres and Party members in Taoyuan were no good, discharged 22 Party members, suspended three and gave many of the rest bad marks. Of the 47 cadres she overthrew 40. Her adviser in all of this was Kwan Ching-tung. Carrying out her husband's revisionist policy, she had the brigade toe the Liu Shao-chi line and borrow 640,000 yuan from the state for making roads, installing power and so on. Actually the commune had already bought a good deal of electrical equipment out of its own funds and was adding to this, so that with a policy of self-reliance it could carry through electrification for irrigation and reconstruction out of its own resources. Roads and power are good. Loans on a revisionist basis are bad. Kwan sold the material which the commune had already bought and no one was able to say what happened to the money. Specious slogans were put out that now all Taoyuan would use coal for fuel, eat white rice, have electric light and radio music, and would achieve greater prosperity with the new line the revisionists proposed. The old leader, Wu Chen, was demoted and sent off to the "reform-through-labor" gang. Kwan Ching-tung with his big patron was now all powerful. He lost no opportunities for attacking the revolutionary line. The fact that rice could now be eaten, he said, was due to Wang Kwang-mei, not the Great Leap Forward reservoir on the Yangho. He had a monument put up, out of the capital the commune had borrowed, with the words "Never forget" on it, the inference being that none should forget Liu Shao-chi's wife's beneficence.

Actually, while in Taoyuan, Wang Kwang-mei put on quite an act. Never once really joining the physical labor of the farmers, she had 270 pictures of herself taken in 20 days, most portraying her "at farm work". She propagated the writings of her husband, taking care that the works of Chairman Mao, to whom she gave outward deference, should not circulate. Kwan Ching-tung had the house in which she lived declared a museum, to be entered with reverence. Only just before she left the brigade did she tell her real name. When she went back to Peking she wrote a report called "Experiences in Taoyuan" which was widely propagated all over the country. In it, she opposed the Mao Tsetung line for commune construction, replacing it with the one her husband proposed. She was out against all old cadres and Party members. She told many lies, some of which were so glaring they caused widespread comment. For instance, she said that a certain brigade member, Wang Ching-yuan, died of the bitterness he was made to suffer. Actually, Wang Ching-yuan is still very much alive, and when he heard of what she had said, he shouted, "She can die, but I'll not die yet." She also said that a member, Chao Tieh-chin, was deaf and mute before the movement started but was so influenced by it that he learned to speak and could hear. Actually Chao Tieh-chin has never been afflicted with deafness or dumbness, and he laughs at the story. She took considerable pains to prevent her report from reaching Taoyuan, though Kwan Ching-tung made three journeys to Peking to take her presents and tell her of developments.

In the meantime, to maintain his sway Kwan instituted a reign of terror against the old cadres and their supporters. For instance one old cadre who had made some minor mistakes but was criticised and cleared in the Socialist Education Movement, was attacked viciously again. He was roped up and confined for 38 days in a small room, while an old aunt, over 70, who looked after him was treated so badly she died. Another bad case was that of a good honest member everyone liked but who was against Kwan. He was arrested as a counter-revolutionary. These things struck fear into the hearts of many old cadres and for a time paralysed action. Kwan Ching-tung talked in high-sounding revolutionary terms and obviously had all the backing needed from the then most influential quarters.

When the Cultural Revolution broke out, however, one of the old Party members and cadres organised the May 4th Movement rebel group to criticise him and his outfit. The revisionist backing becoming less and less influential, the mass of ordinary people gathered behind Feng Ai-chung, leader of the rebels. People could say what they wanted now. They could point to the scamp Yao Shu-tien, whose mother was called

"Tigress", and who himself had well earned his nickname "Wan Ren Hen" — "Hated by Everyone". They now at last got rid of the "marriage section" by which Wang Kwang-mei, Liu Shao-chi's wife, had tried to institutionalise the feudal habit of young men giving presents to their brides amounting to 800 to 1,000 yuan each!

Soon the walls of the village were covered with big character posters as the people poured out their feelings. Over 20,000 were written, as well as some 300 drawings being made, all quite graphic. The first 200 big wall posters in criticism of Wang Kwang-mei and her followers were put up on the 11th of October 1966. On the following 24th of January a big meeting was held denouncing her, people from all the counties around attending, so that many learnt just what revisionism actually entailed in the practical field. How it was merely an extension of the class struggle that had to be fought out. Then on April 10th 1967, a group of PLA men came in to assist the rebel group. They called study meetings of old cadres, rebel groups and poor peasants and went over the whole struggle, analysing and clearing up. Wu Chen was completely exonerated on April 23rd after having done forced labor for three years. At a big meeting the people enthusiastically agreed with this action. No, he had never operated an opium den as Kwan Ching-tung had charged. No, he had never belonged to the Kuomintang or been a counter-revolutionary. Now the tables were turned, and Kwan found himself under arrest as charge after charge was levelled against him, all of which had ample proof behind them. Wu Chen became chairman of the Revolutionary Committee, and was also made deputy chairman of the Funing county Revolutionary Committee. Feng Ai-chung acts as first assistant to Wu Chen now, and the people show their happiness with the leadership in the way they rally round and work in high spirit. No longer is Taoyuan the plaything of the chief revisionist and his wife, their capital in spreading their poison. Again the people have won a victory.

One reflects over revisionist tactics as shown up in Taoyuan. Thirty workpoints were given to some for just half a day of high-pressure work, while others steadily working from dawn to dusk got only the normal ten points. People were told to eat their fill, use up all the grain in the granaries and let the state supply the deficiency. Huge loans were sought which, if accepted as planned, would have made the farmers not self-reliant but simply slaves of the big city banks. The lure of bigger and better private plots was dangled in front of them, along with all the other rigmarole that the revisionists use to lead the people away from the road forward. Despite all this, the people have, under the leadership of Mao Tsetung, resolutely taken the correct way forward and in so doing have inspired their kind all over the land.

Chengchuang Brigade

It was one of the hottest days of a hot summer when we struck across country from the main highway near Funing city. Old men were fanning themselves in the shade of trees; youngsters were finding streams, pools

and canals to luxuriate in. In the fields, production teams kept doggedly on under their big peasant straw hats. Carters on the road taking
white chemical fertiliser in shiny plastic bags provided a new note —
fertiliser going to supplement the compost that had started the rice
paddy to grow a deep rich green, the mark of a good crop to be. Rice
is a new thing in this part of Hopei, and now Funing county alone
has 80,000 mou in it, all high yielding.

Our road was a winding commune-made one that led us around
some hills until, through a vista of trees and mountains, we caught a
glimpse of red banners and knew that there would be the young people
of the place making a welcome party for us. It was the village of
Chengchuang Brigade, now famous for its success in pulling itself up
by its own bootstraps, as it were, and for the way it has fought for
the thinking of Chairman Mao through the Cultural Revolution. The
leaders of the Revolutionary Committee, one woman and four men, were
impressive, the woman clear-minded and concise, the men strong, hard-
bitten poor peasant types. They told the story, as most communes do,
from as far back as they could remember. The Resistance War, when
the village was in the Eighth Route Army area, occasionally being raided
by Japanese troops out to burn and loot, then into the War of Liberation,
when it played its part too. Of the early struggles against three landlord despots, each one of whom more or less controlled one of the
divisions, or "pa", into which the straggling village of Chengchuang
was divided. That they were cruel and ruthless, as evinced by the stories
told, is an understatement. But in spite of all this, Cheng Kuo-chu,
the son of one of the worst exploiters, and a very good talker, proclaimed
himself converted to the new order. Passionately he would denounce
his father Cheng Feng-jui. Yet the people did not trust him very much
and were on the point of denouncing him when another swift operator
and glib talker entered the scene. He was Teng Hsing-ho who had been
a local official under the Japanese but who beat his breast declaring
that in his heart he had been with the people all the time. Liberation
came early to Chengchuang, for there had been underground and semi-
open Communist work going on from the end of the Resistance War.
But now the armies and cadres moved on to help with the liberation
of all China, and more local cadres had to be trained to take over.
Teng Hsing-ho managed to get accepted as a member of the Communist
Party and was assigned cadre work. In his official capacity, he was
now able to save Cheng Kuo-chu from the anger of the people and to
send him for training till finally, in 1950, he got him accepted into the
Communist Party. Cleverly these two built up their own group in
Chengchuang and organisations in the areas around. Quite early they
became close followers of Liu Shao-chi in Peking, carrying out his policies
as best they could.

In one case Teng gave a man 30 workpoints for doing just two hours'
work, from 5-7 in the morning. . . . Quietly both he and Cheng carried
on opposition to the policies of Chairman Mao, deriding the Great Leap
Forward, the expansion of the cooperative movement, and all the rest.

In quite a clever way they had a great many trees felled and then, when the timber was sold in other places, coined in liberally on the proceeds of the sales. Teng then accused one family of stealing trees and had them fined 1,000 yuan. But even with everything they owned being sold, the family could not pay the fine. The injustice of the whole business was so great that the old peasant's daughter tried to hang herself. Largely as a result of the rule of Teng and his group, production fell badly. Weather conditions had something to do with it, no doubt, though the main trouble was lack of spirit amongst the people. But there the facts stand.

In 1964 the Socialist Education Movement started, and the people were able to show up Teng and Cheng to such an extent that they lost their position, and a real poor peasant leadership came in. The people were now organised for production, and the land responded. Then the Cultural Revolution started.

In 1966 Teng and Cheng watched what was going on very carefully. They went around and saw their friends and started to hatch plans which ripened in February 1967, when they emerged again at the head of some schoolboys and others they had fooled, declaring themselves to be leading a rebel group dedicated to getting rid of all old cadres and Party members. But they operated a scarce three months. The people had had plenty of time to compare notes, and much more was known about them now than was the case during the Socialist Education Movement. The people already had had an intensive course of study of some of Chairman Mao's works. They stood up together. Teng and Cheng were detained by the militia, and all struggled against them with such effect that their whole line was completely exposed and mass understanding of revisionism and its agents grew. The people promptly set to work now and made many changes. They looked with new eyes at a swamp of 325 mou that had hitherto lain unproductive; they now have it growing rice, with the full expectation that in 1968 it will bring in a crop of 600 jin a mou or more. Last year the people each had 414 jin of grain. Ever setting higher targets, they hope to do better as they go on.

They made an overall plan for the complete reorganisation of their farmlands and the construction of a reservoir for 65,000 cubic metres of water in a basin at the foot of their highest mountain. There are many stories of how the new thinking has affected families. For instance, one woman told her son to collect the beans sown on their private plot and sell them for making beancurd. They boy added a shovelful of sand to the beans and then showed them to his mother. She looked long and hard, saying, "Son, people cannot make beancurd out of sand! Adding sand to increase weight belongs to the old way of doing things we do not want now."

The boy clapped his hands happily. "Mother, you've passed! You've studied the essay on Norman Bethune well! I was testing you," he said, and together they cleaned the beans of the sand. Another local story was of an ex-landlord, notoriously lazy, who had to go out to work each day with a woman and three boys. One day he said he had to ease himself, so went off over a rise. Out of sight he walked a long way, lay down and went to sleep. After a while the boys went out to look for him, but the landlord grumbled that his leg ached and he could no longer work. The woman reported this to the brigade meeting in the evening, then the truant was sent for. He said his leg was too bad to walk, so came whining on all fours. Peasants reminded him of the time when the landlord group owned 2,568 mou in the brigade and the poor peasants 220 mou. How many had been beaten and killed by such as he! Then they told him to go home and do better the next day. Still on all fours, he went out. But when the lad who was going with him got tired of the slow pace and went on ahead, the man jumped up with surprising agility and ran off home, caught in the act, however, by another small boy who was following on behind and who afterwards told the tale, with actions included, to an amused audience.

There was something big and heroic about these people who lived amongst rugged mountains making their land bend to their will. No longer do pitiful bands of starving refugees wind over the landscape either to be beggars around cities or else emigrants to the distant provinces of the Northeast. Now they are standing up and taking responsibility, knowing the score and where they are going. They showed me the model of their commune as they envisaged it by 1970, ambitious but perfectly feasible. The Cultural Revolution has carried them quite a few steps forward on their journey, and for them life opens out in a way it never did before.

The Yangho Reservoir

Leaving Chengchuang, we went back to the main highway and sped up the river valley to the Yangho reservoir, a big one that holds 300 million cubic metres of water normally after summer rains, and then stores it for spring use in the commune below. It was one of the projects carried through in the Great Leap Forward of 1958-60. This year it has been invaluable, for the season has been one of drought. Without its water, some 200,000 mou of land would have suffered badly. Its dam, 1,600 metres long and 64 metres high, was completed in a little over a year from commencement of the work in 1959. In 1967, during the Cultural Revolution, one of the main canals was extended, and we went across country to see some of the long aqueducts of reinforced concrete that were built at that time. Each winter still sees mass work on extending the laterals. There is yet some construction work needed around the main dam, and there will be a good deal still to do in extending afforestation schemes in the basin through which the headwaters of the river which supplies the reservoir run.

Lulung County, and a Peep into the Future

The bare hills of China's hinterland seem endless. In loess country the erosion is seen to have started just below the ridges, forming valleys which, gradually widening until near the base of the hills, are barren wastes of sand and stone, the original loess of the hillside having long ago been washed away. Most of the time dry, these products of many long centuries of deforestation are devastated year by year by silt-charged, torrential rivers in times of heavy summer rains.

The 129 families that make up Fushenchuang Brigade of Hsiehchia-chuang Commune in Lulung county, Hopei, depended on such land for their livelihood. The land owned by the village is situated on a promontory encircled by the Chinglung river on three sides. As the Chinglung riverbed widened and the floods became more severe, summer floods forced the evacuation of the village no less than three times, until in 1950 it reached its present location. The terraced fields on hillsides gave very low yields — around 60 jin per mou a year. Any relatively good land was formerly owned by landlords. When a unit of the Eighth Route Army came to Fushenchuang during the War of Resistance, there was not enough grain in the village to spare even one meal for the troops. People then lived short lives, most trying to get jobs as hired workers for the rich. In one year two families starved to death. Though the first Communist Party group was formed in 1943, not much attention could be given to economic problems, for the Wars of Resistance and Liberation had to be fought, and many youths went off to take part in the struggle. In 1947 Land Reform was carried out, but after a big flood in 1949 no less than ten families sold the land they had been given and went away. Again class differentiation waxed stronger. The rich became richer, the poor, poorer. Things got better when cooperatives were formed, but the state continued having to send in relief grain until 1957, when by good work and the commune organisation which then came in, Fushen-chuang became self-sufficient. In 1958 they harvested 290 jin a mou. In 1967, 463 jin while in this 1968 they expect to get over 500. In 1967, they not only sold 80,000 jin of surplus grain to the state, but also put another 80,000 jin into their own brigade granary for emergency use.

"If our fighters come again, we shall have enough for them to eat," said the tall, thoughtful Chen Hui, chairman of the brigade Revolutionary Committee. Quite a person is Chen Hui, who formerly was brigade Party secretary and who has the strong support of his fellows because of his determination to serve the people, his ability and his qualities of leadership. When the pessimists said it was no use building a buttress into the riverbed to protect their shores because the river would sweep away anything man could make, then it was he who told his brigade, "Just let us put our determination into the task! Built thoughtfully and strongly enough, using the proper material, and the thing will stand." Seven metres high and 80 long, its headworks made from cut stone which members brought down on ice sledges in the winter, it has stood up against some of the biggest floods the place has experienced. It has also allowed an area of 100 mou of good flat land, previously waste, to be made into excellent farmland, sorghum and corn standing high on it at the time of my visit. It was Chen Hui too who, reading of how pump turbines had been so successful in Hunan, had one brought in and led in installing it on the river edge. The first pump was too small to drive the water up the 48-metre hill, though it was big enough to give sufficient power for village lighting. A bigger one was being installed while I visited, which will do the job better. The turbine pump is a new farm implement, which in the last three years has covered the hinterland of south China. It was the first time, however, I had seen it being used in north China. It pumps water up steep hillsides, provides power for lighting and for running food-processing machines, is inexpensive and easy to instal. A real mechanical wonder, though in this area still needing the know-how of a Chen Hui to adapt it to local conditions.

We went uphill and saw how the irrigation canal wound around the little peaks like a snake, and then we came to the head of the biggest valley, where seven young militia men had taken over the task of revamping the land and making a vineyard and orchard there. The valley had check dams running up it, each creating a little reservoir, big enough however to hold any rainwater. We sat under the vines there and had tea, while the lads told us how they had made fields and planted peaches, apples and grapevines. They grow all the vegetables they need for their own use, but give all the eggs their chickens lay to the brigade for sale. One of their number is the cook. The others all work outside. They had planted zinnias around their housing so that the place had become a real mountain of flowers and fruit. All land is used, and the bigger ponds grow fish. The wide barren space of valley floor at the foot of the hill has been covered with two metres of loess soil carted in and made into a grain field.

Looking at the promontory when coming by road, it is seen to be quite covered with vegetation. Date trees grow on the terrace fronts, and walnut trees are put in waste corners wherever they will grow. The main fruit crops are peaches, grapes and apples. There are 40,000 fruit trees in all. The people do not have big private plots, just the little vegetable gardens around their houses. They have wholeheartedly entered into the spirit of the Cultural Revolution, increasing their own knowledge and morale and being now able to make a new assessment of the class struggle.

There are many stories told of how the movement has affected them. For instance, there is the one of the steer which was in the habit of coming over from a neighboring brigade and feeding on precious wheat shoots. Some young Fushenchuang members beat it so hard it died. For a while members of the two brigades were not on speaking terms because of this incident. The Fushenchuang people were first to make amends. They sent over an animal to replace the dead one, with apologies. But the other brigade sent the animal back, saying "It was we who were wrong for letting our animals stray!" — A six-year-old child found a five yuan bill in the dust of the highway. He took it straight to the brigade office, without telling anyone first. — A commune member driving a cart over a frozen river felt the ice giving way. Both horses and cart would have been lost if he had not jumped down and, though falling into the water and putting himself in great personal danger, saved the lot. — The truck garage caught fire, but despite the danger a member rushed into the burning building and rolled out a full drum of gasoline that was stored there.

The stories reporting people's loyalty to their collective, rather than the old tales which stressed filial piety, are those that circulate most these days. Loyalty that extends from the production team to the brigade, from the brigade to the commune, from the commune onwards, finally encompassing the poor and oppressed throughout the whole world, as they proudly say.

Soon the communes along the Chinglung river will band together and, damming the river higher up in its course, make a big reservoir to further protect themselves from drought or flood. This, however, will not be enough unless the silt problem is adequately dealt with. Inevitably, then, will the myriad hill valleys of hinterland China begin to take on the same appearance as those of Fushenchuang. The devotion and organisation needed to carry through such a task will be tremendous, but basically the problem of silting up riverbeds can only be dealt with in this way — through the conservation of the little rivulets and tributaries over vast areas. So, seeing the hills of Fushenchuang today, one is really glimpsing the future. Within sight of the village is the Great Wall, streaming over mountaintops. Now a new great wall is being made, a green one that will effectively halt the monsters and demons that for too long have ridden unchecked down over widening riverbeds in the eroded lands of north and northwest China.

The sun was setting as we left Fushenchuang to return to the Lulung county seat. Red rays lit up the villages and shone through the ranks of tall kaoliang on the ridges, glittering on vistas of the Chinglung river below. Fushenchuang is just 50 li from the city, the way lying over some quite steep hills. It is only one of the 557 brigades in the 34 communes of the county with its 320,000 people. Lulung itself is one of the 13 counties of the Tangshan prefecture. Practically all the arable land of Lulung is rolling country, once much subject to drought, flood, cyclones, hailstones and crop pests. A well-known place for poverty, it rarely averaged more than 100 jin a mou from its land. Its strategic position in the ancient north China defence line made it an important outpost as far back as the Chou dynasty in the first millennium B.C. A prefectural seat in the Ching dynasty, it has learnt something first hand of foreign imperialism, having been occupied for a time by foreign troops during the Boxer Rebellion. The French put some of their Boxer indemnity money into building a huge Catholic Mission with high walls and an imposing church, where arms were stored in the cellars of the living quarters, and the old ruling class was strongly supported, even when the ruler was the infamous Japanese puppet, Yin Ju-keng who seized 22 counties with the help of his masters, delivering them over to Japanese imperialism. People's resistance started in the summer of 1937 and continued with quite a number of victorious battles right up to the end of the anti-Japanese War of Resistance. Then the fight turned against the Kuomintang puppets of American imperialism. On their first attempt to occupy the region, these puppets were promptly chased out. Coming a second time in force, they were able to hold the county seat for 11 months before they were forced to retreat to Luanhsien.

After we had sat a while in one of the spacious compounds of the old Mission, one part of which is occupied by the county Revolutionary Committee, we went out to look at the environs. A primary school and some Mao Tsetung Thought study classes for county cadres were busy in the various compounds. On the high earthwork where the old magistrate's yamen had once stood, university students from Peking were levelling earth, prior to being sent out to brigades to learn from the people while working with them on daily tasks. The slim, delicate Liao period stone pagoda nearby still stands, with bells hung from its upturned eaves tinkling in the wind. Yes, communes suffer from hailstones and cyclones at times. Some floods and drought still occur. But the arable land in the county has been increased by 140,000 mou, and with 250 new wells, 130 dams in the hills, mechanised pumps, and a 1967 production of 328 jin of grain a mou, with other crops like peanuts and walnuts (600,000 jin exported in 1967) coming along nicely, people have the strength to push forward, beat down insect pests, infectious diseases and a good many other afflictions of the past.

They have a glorious tradition, being one of the four counties around here that during the darkest period set up an anti-Japanese autonomous government. Then their people went with a rifle in one hand and a hoe in the other, carrying on the fight as well as maintaining production. Now, after their Revolutionary Committee was set up in March 1968, they have organised 26,500 Mao Tsetung Thought study groups which deepen the common folk's understanding of political issues while, at the same time, they work hard together for higher crop yields. People often read together the first quotation of the Little Red Book, "The force at the core leading our cause forward is the Chinese Communist Party. The theoretical basis guiding our thinking is Marxism-Leninism." The struggle against revisionism has laid bare wrong policy and resultant abuses that were creeping in. The fight against selfishness comes into every home, to people of all ages. For instance, brigades in the past usually allowed one yuan a day for travel expenses when sending members out on work. Now people find that they can get along with 50 fen a day, so return half to the brigade. Wang Chung-kwei of Taling Brigade picked up a bowl in the marketing and supply agency, adding it to his purchases without paying for it. It worried him badly as he thought it over later. That evening in his family study group he criticised himself, then writing out his self-criticism he took it with the money to the agency the next morning. Such instances as these are legion. They are part of a changing countryside. When, as is the case with the 120 families of Fushenchuang, people are trusted to assess their own workpoints for their day's work, change has really taken place that will lead to still more changes in the future.

Going out of Lulung down the highway east, these lines came to me:

> The wonder of a great people
> on the move; a cantata
> to the accompaniment of waters
> rippling through new canals,
> bees humming amongst the blossom
> of new orchards, the fire
> of new thought spreading
> over an ancient countryside
> that has renewed its vigor,
> each morning
> a myriad hinterland towns
> and villages, like Lulung
> and Fushenchuang
> vibrant with the message
> of the day, their sound
> and that of singing
> echoing against old hills
> drifting among redoubts
> of the Great Wall
> moving hearts and hands
> to action; the once
> oppressed now
> masters of all.

From Lumber to Matches in the Class Struggle in a Hinterland Town

Lumber of many kinds comes down from Northeast forests through the Great Wall at Shanhaikwan, part of the rising industrial port of Chinwangtao on Pohai Bay of north China. Three varieties of it go into the manufacture of match sticks and match boxes. Poplar and Manchurian linden timber for the match sticks, silver birch for the match boxes. In the old days, two small capitalist enterprises made the sticks only, distributing them to various match factories in different parts of the country. They were joined after Liberation by five more, all using local capital. Then when privately owned plants were taken into equal partnership by the state in 1956, they were all combined into one. Production swiftly went up from a total of 700 tons of match sticks a year to 2,300 tons. In 1958 came the General Line forward which laid stress on local sufficiency, so that match factories in other provinces started to manufacture their own sticks. The role of the plant now became that of supplying the 13 counties of the Tangshan prefecture of which Chinwangtao was a part with good matches at the right price. As the plant rated only as local industry, not national, it had to depend on its own resources. It went to older established match factories and procured some discarded machines which it repaired in its own machine shop, and finally by

1960 its matches appeared on the local market. Though a good many of the processes were manual, 30 million boxes were made that year. To be making the complete match, instead of just part of it, pleased the working forces, making good workers try harder.

Chinwangtao in the old days was a place with very little industry of any kind. With Liberation, however, many new factories were set up. A new working class began to develop which, because of its prestige, attracted many from the old society it could have well done without. Little officials who had worked with the Japanese or Kuomintang, discharged or deserting Kuomintang soldiers, landlords and rich peasants who had run away from the villages at the time of Land Reform and now sometimes used assumed names, looked for jobs as factory workers. In the match factory the situation was more complicated by the fact that the man who had cleverly talked his way into the Party and had become the first Party secretary, was a strong rightist and actually an ex-landlord, a fact that he had managed to have kept quiet, while pushing his way ahead. He liked to get hold of opportunists like himself. The managers of the old small capitalist enterprises had been kept on in leading administrative positions, and these soon began to combine with those who also had poor political backgrounds amongst the workers. The Party secretary was exposed and reduced to the status of ordinary worker in 1960, but still the old group had enough power to hold on. When the Cultural Revolution began, they entered boldly into the struggle and tried to seize power for themselves and their like in their own and neighboring factories. The ex-Party secretary came forward as a group leader. This group tried to halt production so blatantly that the other workers organised against them, and soon the tide of struggle was turned against those with mysterious connections who had shown by their actions that they were against the interests of the people, the plant and its work force.

On the 31st of March 1968, the Revolutionary Committee was set up. Administrative staff was cut down. Though there were few old technical workers, the plant went ahead with its own automation, buying some machines but building most itself. The 463 workers now had learnt who was with them and who was against them, who were their friends, who their enemies, and what their responsibility was as a vanguard force. They have cut out piecework, which the old management liked. With no added material incentives, the plant which had a plan for 140 million boxes in 1968, will actually make over 150 million. The good people whom the bad old management fired are having their cases reviewed in a new light by real working folk, not by this or that kind of clever operator with vast personal ambition, but no loyalty to the working class. The storm was quite fierce while it lasted, but now that it is over all see better, and all are enthusiastic about the future of their plant. They have a good deal of local support, as the making of match boxes is a task that is given out to families around the factory who can swiftly put them together from already crinkled and cut wood slices. Family members who cannot leave home because of children and other tasks

all gain some income from this work.   Castings for the plant's machine
building are turned out by a neighboring foundry, otherwise all work
is done in the plant.   It is fascinating to watch the women workers
packing matches into boxes.   Their fingers move with lightning rapidity
and incredible precision.   Soon, however, this process will be done with
machines, which are already being tried out and perfected.   Match sticks
are now taken through their various stages by conveyor belts and blowers.

Steadily the work force advances step by step towards higher mechanization, cutting costs and producing what the people need — a good
quality article at the price anyone can pay.   Scrap wooden sheets are
cut up to make wood wool to send to the Tangshan potteries for packing
material.   In all, not a very unusual story from today's China, maybe,
yet still quite an illustration of what has been going on in the smaller
local plants in provincial cities, where people feel they have to know
the full score before proceeding any further.   The next long-range step
perhaps is increased afforestation of the hills left bare for so many centuries in the counties of the prefecture so that, in the spirit of Mao Tsetung,
new local sources of timber will be available and another step in self-
sufficiency will have been taken.

Loting and the Good Militia of Chaotan

In the last days of July 1968 we left the main highway by the bridge
over the Luan river in northeast Hopei.   A wild, turbulent river usually
at this time of the year, this summer the Luan was not more than a placid
stream flowing quietly down a rather empty riverbed.   It had not rained
in any quantity since October 1967, and there had been no snow in winter.
Some of the crops were obviously thirsting for water.   Others irrigated
from wells looked a rich, healthy green in contrast.   As usual, the sight
of the children was lovely.   The little ones in the wonderful freedom
of a coat of suntan only, stood by wells where electrically powered pumps
brought up streams of water.   With the tall green corn behind them and
their golden skins they made a perfect picture.

Finally we got to Loting county, the birthplace of Li Ta-chao, one of
the founders of the Communist Party, who was later murdered by the
warlord Chang Tso-lin.   Loting actually was once a great Kuomintang
haunt, many of its officials and army officers coming from the outsize
landlord population it then possessed — one that had once numbered 6.5
percent of the population, there being around 5,000 families of landlords
and rich peasants out of a total of 88,000 families in the county.   They
then owned 70 percent of the land.   Middle peasants held 16 percent,
while the bulk of the people who were poor peasants had to be content
with 14 percent, though they numbered 74 percent of the population.
In good years, the poor would get around 150 jin of grain a mou.   In
the bad ones, many would have to leave and go as refugees to the distant
Northeast to find a way to live, or else hire themselves out as carriers.

Loting is in the Tangshan prefecture, and is an almost flat county,
running down to Pohai Bay.   Today it has 34 communes and one township,

the old county town. It produces wheat, rice, maize, cotton, kaoliang, beans, peanuts and millet. After Liberation, the land was redivided and the first elementary cooperatives formed, which resulted in so much better spirit that grain totals leapt to 294 jin a mou. Progress since then has been steady and yields have reached 435 jin in 1967, with the area of arable land much extended through the inclusion of once waste sandhills and salty marsh. Electrification has allowed for the installation of power pumps at wells, which explains why so much crop has been saved this year. Mechanization comes in fast. There are 75 tractors in the county which till 70 percent of the land. Threshing machines are used now instead of the old stone roller being pulled over the threshing floor. Both irrigation and drainage canals have been dug. In the winter of 1958-59 alone, 80,000 commune members moved four million cubic metres of earth during such construction work. Not that every big flood can yet be fully dealt with, but the 70 drainage canals already dug can manage anything that does not exceed 3,000 mm. of rainfall affecting the 300,000 mou of low-lying land in the county.

In electrification, the county has installed 330 kilometres of high voltage wiring, and 650 kilometres of low, as well as 250 transformer stations. Though most of the work in mechanisation is done by electric power, there are still 170 diesel engines working in various communes. Rice is not grown so much as in the Changli and Funing counties to the north. And far less than further south, where there is a huge pioneer rice paddy farm which uses Luan river water diverted into a canal running across Loting.

The county has 440 health workers, each commune brigade having a member who goes out to the fields to work, but who has had some training in treating common diseases in county teaching classes. In each commune there is a larger unit, which sends any difficult cases to the county hospital to be dealt with. There are 296 schools, with 70,000 students, 5,000 of them being in middle schools. 280,000 people in the county have been through a course of study in the thinking of Chairman Mao, and many now lead in their family groups. A vastly deeper understanding of politics has come during the past two years of the Cultural Revolution. Private dealers have gone, and finished are the fortune tellers and all the rest of such gentry who battened on the peasant. In the wheat harvest of early summer 1968, work on a total of 250,000 mou that usually dragged out over 20 days was done in four and five, and a cleaner harvest has never been seen. The various policies of Liu Shao-chi in Peking have been completely overturned, and there is widespread criticism of revisionism. The Cultural Revolution unearthed many enemy agents in its cleansing process, including the local head of the Kuomintang Youth Corps, who had successfully concealed himself through the years. One KMT army officer of high rank, who was a graduate of the Whampoa Military Academy, had gone to Peking and had become a factory worker. Fearing exposure there he came back to Loting where he had many friends. A noted killer, he had been responsible for many murders in his career. However, the net was thrown wide in Loting, and the catch was big, including him.

We had come to Loting mainly to visit Chaotan Brigade, one that has done many of the things that Chiao Yu-lu did in Lankao, Honan. We found that it lay some 30 li from Loting city, on a dusty commune road that wound through the crops and villages of Wangtan Commune. Getting to it we were met by most of the people of the village in a very warm reception. Just as at Lankao, the Honan model reclamation county, it has been good leadership that has done much to pull things together and make them work. It was a leadership that depended mainly on the good, determined head of the militia and an old experienced Party worker who worked well together. The head of the militia has now been made a member of the Revolutionary Committee of the province, and was away for meetings when we came so that his deputy, a member of the brigade Revolutionary Committee, gave us the story of the place as we sat in the spick and span new brigade office. Militia are usually thought of for their military side, but here the good militia of Chaotan have been leaders in so much more.

It was one of those stories that thrill anyone. There has been strong organisation of the people for self-defence, in the realisation that their beach frontage was where some of the foreign armies that marched on Peking in 1900 at the time of the Boxer Rebellion landed. "We have to guard the front door to Peking, as well as make these sandhills and these old, salty lagoons produce all the food we need," they say. "We also have to build houses that are fit to live in, though there is no timber here, no stone." These are the sentiments of the local population. There are 1,291 people in 286 families who are organised into six production teams to farm the 3,715 mou.

In the usual manner, prior to Liberation the 36 families of landlords and rich peasants, owning all the good land, lived on the labor of the poor peasant majority. But just dividing the land again and giving everyone a share did not solve the whole problem either. Before the first elementary cooperatives were organised in 1952, 11 families had sold their land, and four others had sold all the farm equipment they had been given. At first but five cooperatives were organised. Though there was an immediate bettering in production, it was evident that Liu Shao-chi and his group in Peking were against the rapid spread of the cooperative movement, while Chairman Mao was for it. Chairman Mao won. Intensive education in Mao Tsetung Thought started in 1962 and has gone on until the present, the whole militia force taking the lead as teachers. "If we are to fight a people's war properly, we first must have the clear understanding amongst all the working people around us," they say. The old conservative peasant has in consequence changed to become an eager progressive. Both mentally and physically he has changed. To see the young people of Chaotan is to see the children of the poor in fine mental and physical shape, glorying in their work and in their lithe strength.

In this drought year all come together in the evenings to carry water to the higher land where it is needed. The millet will be harvested soon, the corn and kaoliang before the end of August. Then comes the preparation of land for winter wheat, followed by peanut and sweet potato harvest, as autumn draws in. Finally the supply of winter cabbage is grown and brought in. In everything now, the group with its discussion meetings leads. Study groups organised by the militia take up many evenings. In the 'forties, the highest production here was 120 jin a mou. In 1967 it was 541 jin. The people got 520 jin each for the year. The quota for selling to the state for that year was 420,000 jin. Actually, 530,000 jin was sold. Income per capita of population in 1967 was 105 yuan. Instead of bringing home a pathetic few yuan to help his family get over the new year, the family heads think of a bicycle, a radio, or a sewing machine, if they do not have these already.

For the militia when it was re-formed in 1958, the line was clear. Imperialism lords it over much of the world. In Vietnam it is carrying out ferocious aggression against the people. Two thirds of the world are not yet liberated from oppression. In serving the people, we must encourage them to follow the pattern set by Tachai in Shansi, and by Lankao. Our best weapons in this are the three short essays of Chairman Mao. Be prepared against war and famine, and all for the people! Though the village is stretched out, three li long and with 11 roads, the whole militia group can concentrate in ten minutes. 135 of their members have passed the test as sharpshooters. All study world events and their relation to China with avidity. We visited one compound in the village in which four families live, with six militia members amongst their number.

The brigade decided that to have bricks for building they would have to build a brick kiln. With the militia they did the work together, and the only money spent was seven fen for nails to repair an earth rammer. Over a million bricks have been burnt for new housing. We visited the place and the workers, with a big red flag, climbed up to the kiln entrance to pose for a picture. Then we went around the fields and saw the modern insect-killing incandescent lamp hung amongst the corn to kill pests, the sandhills growing peanuts well, the old marshy lagoons transformed into grain fields, and the 200 mou of bad land put into orchard, with grapes and apples predominating. Chopped up corn and kaoliang stalks added to compost helps much in converting saline country.

There are 240 children in the brigade school. Those under age and those who have finished school come into special classes that members of the militia lead at certain times. Busy people are those militiamen. They do their ordinary farm work and their military training as well as acting as activists on political study. With electric light in the homes, evening study is facilitated for the 120 study groups in the brigade. They are all sure that the study group is the way.

We talked for some time about well-digging, marsh-draining, saline soil washing and on anti-drought methods. It was clear that there had been much discussion already on these points. The old Party secretary, now one of the Revolutionary Committee leaders, felt that it was his task to bring on able youngsters to do the work he had been doing, all the time giving the benefit of his experience. The revisionist directives that had come from Liu Shao-chi had resulted in some members reclaiming waste land to add to their private plots, but all of this was soon passed back to the brigade and organised into the big rectangular fields now high with the standing crops of the collective.

As we went on, the evening sun shining through the dust our car raised as it passed through villages, one wondered how many people amongst all those "China watchers" abroad realised what was happening in the Chinese countryside where a new strength is developing in so basic a way, and where now change follows so rapidly on change, as the people re-orient themselves to the China of the era of Mao Tsetung.

A Glass Fibre Factory in Chinwangtao

One would hardly think to find in so small a town as Chinwangtao, known mainly for its harbor, so modern a plant as a glass fibre factory. A factory moreover that takes the process through to spinning, weaving and to the manufacture of substitutes for steel, piping and plastic material. But here, set amongst the fields of tall, waving corn outside the old town is such a plant. Started in 1958 during the Great Leap Forward, its first buildings were designed by Russian experts who also brought in some of their machinery for the first processes of producing the thread. In these latter years, however, the first buildings have been vacated as being unpractical, a new modern Chinese-made plant was erected and the old imported machines have been removed. The new ones which have been substituted from the growing machine industry of China have been found to be much more efficient.

It is not a very large plant. There are 1,400 workers and staff in all. We met some of the members of the Revolutionary Committee composed of the Army representative, old cadres and young workers. It is by and large a young people's factory, 85 percent of its work force being under 25. Some of them are students who have been sent here to work to finish their education. Then there are the youngsters from the Yenan Middle School of Chinwangtao, a school that the factory leads, who come here in groups of 150 for two weeks' training as workers. The output in 1970 will be double that of the first year the factory went in production. There are over 100 activists in the propagation of Mao Tsetung Thought, and over 500 cited as good workers and staff members. Especially in the past two years all production targets have been overfulfilled.

The over 20 different products of the plant are sold in 17 of China's provinces, and are exported to five foreign countries. Workers work in three 8-hour shifts, so that the machines never stop. Each worker does an hour's political study each day. All are loud in their praise for a middle-aged technician sent down to the factory from a higher level. He has been able to give leadership and technique that has resulted in improvements to 15 products. One machine alteration by his group has enormously increased its productivity. Some advised him, because of his age and health, to retire and take more care of himself. But he says that so long as he can work he will keep going, for without work his life would hold no meaning for him.

When workers heard that 600-count very fine glass fibre was being imported and that the cost was great, they set to work to produce it in their factory and have succeeded very well, so that this line now goes into production. All of their products are in great demand, especially the ordinary cloth that can be made into bags for packing chemical ferti- liser, the fibre being resistant to corrosive chemicals. The electrical industry has many demands on products, as has the machine industry. Interchange of ideas and technique from other glass fibre factories in different parts of China makes one innovation that is successful soon common to all.

It is quite fascinating to watch the bags of glass marbles which are the raw material going through a washing machine, and then on to receptacles above the long melting furnace into which they are dropped, and then to come out as long silken threads to be wound on reels and go on to the spinning and weaving shops.

Despite the fact that Chinwangtao is a rising port and a new industrial centre, one somehow cannot forget its so recent past, when it was a small, sleepy place from which Kaiping coal from the British-controlled mines nearby was exported to the great U.S. monopoly enterprise, the Shanghai Power Company. Foreign monopolies have gone from China, and now each area, each organisation, tries to make itself as self-sufficient as possible, as part of general preparations for any emergency. This one knows well, yet as one looks out over the rich summer harvests around the plant it still seems to be somewhat miraculous that plastic substitutes for steel, for instance, can be made so efficiently in this quiet rural setting.

Summer 1969 in North Hopei

We sat together on the grassy side of a hill. A thin, quiet man of 66, a group of boys with baskets, and around us the goats they were out grazing. One of the smaller animals came up and lay down close to a boy, putting its head in his lap as it chewed its cud contentedly. "Yes," said the old man, "there have been many changes along this coast. In the old days we had far too much bitterness. Do you ever drink goat's milk? It's good and clean! We carry back enough fodder to feed the animals until tomorrow morning, when we will come again. Some of the boys collect the kind of plants pigs do well on. Those two there," he said, pointing to a couple in neat town clothes, "are children of cadres who have come to our brigade to work. They collect pig feed first, and maybe will learn how to take care of goats later. These two," he continued, indicating the couple nearest him, "will soon be big enough to join the production teams in the fields." I asked the latter what they would do when they grew up. Most boys a while ago if asked the same question would have said that they wanted to be something a bit romantic, but these two answered without hesitation, "working people". It is very evident that the status of working people has risen in these last three years.

The old man asked me if I had ever been to Sinkiang, and if I knew of a county called Chaosu; he was pleased when I replied that indeed I had been to, and did know of, such a place. His son, he said proudly, worked there. It was right next to the USSR, and he was glad to have him in so responsible a place. The new day evidently brings a new kind of unity amongst China's working folk, as they go from coast to hinterland. It was getting near mid-day as the group shouldered their big baskets filled with grass and, along with their charges, moved off at a smart pace to the brigade village a mile or so away over on the other side of the valley, leaving one with the feeling of having met some good, genuine people.

Going down a simple north Hopei village street one halted at a typical local building, curved roof, low stud, with coils of wide strips of thin willow wood resting against its walls. Inside were piles of racks for steaming bread or other foods, the type that goes over the iron cooking pans. There were steamers for the big cooking pans of organisations, and then those for family use, tiers and tiers of them. Inside was a workroom, where a middle-aged man with a black beard was adroitly drilling holes and lacing the circles of already treated wood together with strips of wicker vine. Each circle of steamer tier fitted precisely on top of the other. The man's hands moved deftly, and one complimented him on his skill. "It is just serving the people, and fighting for the world revolution," he replied in a matter-of-fact way, never pausing in his task. Some foreign folk may wonder why they don't use pressure cookers. But steam cooking has been going on in China since before the Han dynasty 2,000 years ago, and this kind of "loong" as it is called, has evolved, suitable for the most universally used cooking pans and fuel available. It is cheap, made on the spot and can be used to cater for groups of all sizes, simply by adding a tier or two.

It was just a year since I had gone to Funing county where, in Taoyuan Brigade of Luwangchuang Commune, the revisionists Liu Shao-chi and Wang Kwang-mei, his wife, had tried to create a "model" for the regime they proposed by using the weapons of terror and money. Once again I met Wu Chen, the brigade leader, as strong and vigorous as ever, and saw the newly organised exhibition of the dramatic events that went with the down-to-earth struggle between the two lines here during the Cultural Revolution. Then I went to see the wonderful crops, new orchard and river plantations along by the Yang river. Following the best wheat harvest ever gained, the autumn crops of sorghum, corn, peanuts, beans and sweet potatoes were magnificent. "No, we do not use chemical fertiliser with sweet potatoes. People say it alters their taste, so only compost is used with them," the members said. For the rest of the crops, the piles of snow-white fertiliser in plastic bags one sees everywhere are now a feature of this countryside.

On our walk we came to one of the brigade workshops. It made wicker baskets and wooden farm implements. At the time of our visit, three workers were making wooden three-tyned harvesting forks out of willow wood, grown by themselves in their own plantation. Quite a process of stretching the green wood to the required shape, later using fire to straighten, and finally working the tynes through holes in a block of tough date wood, but in the end producing a familiar light and serviceable tool of the kind commune farmers around all welcome.

To Changli

The summer heat lay heavily when we drove again to Changli county. There had been heavy rain, and some ponds were left beside the fields, making new pools for youngsters to splash in with delight. At Changli the many fruit trees gave a pleasant shade, and we noted changes that had taken place since our last visit of a year ago. Much had been done on the county overall plan of finalising anti-erosion work on terraced land, on afforestation to halt shifting sands from the sea beaches, and on straightening and eliminating field borders and levelling the land, making easily worked rectangular fields, and converting marshlands from alkaline waste to rich paddy fields. Also, by October 1st 1969, all of the 37 communes in the county will have been joined to the electric power grid, the 35,000-kw. plant having been completed and 80 kilometres of high transmission line already laid. So all homes of the 420,000 inhabitants of the county will have electric light this winter and there will be power for pumping and food processing. There has been no question of neglecting the political needs of society here. We visited the county printery in the city. Once it had done small jobs only, mainly such things as accounting and other forms needed, with a small number of workers. Now in the past three years, its working force enlarged to 103, it has printed 7,300,000 copies of the Little Red Book. We watched them turning out the latest edition, smaller and thicker than the first ones, and with a very glossy red plastic cover. It included not only the original quotations, but also five important essays and Chairman Mao's poems. The workers were being assisted by primary and local middle-school students who were doing their half day practical work in this way. The books are well used. Some 80 percent of the population of the county are in study classes of one kind or another. Even one old woman who has reached the ripe old age of 104 has learnt to sing "The East is Red".

After a cool, restful night, one was awakened at five in the morning by a mass of sound. The news, and then extracts from the "Red Lantern" opera with piano accompaniment came through the big trees surrounding the compound in which we were living. Then at six, quietness descended only to be broken by cicadas, and the pleasant restful feeling of a north Hopei summer's day. The crop of millet beside our house stood high and proudly. A 400-jin-a-mou crop, friends felt. The revolution was won on millet, they say, so the more of it the merrier.

Holiangshan Brigade

It was an experience to leave Changli city and go out to visit Holiangshan Brigade, for it has done so many of the things once thought to be impossible. It is not a big brigade, just 196 families in all, totalling 985 people. On dry, hillside land, it has concentrated on fruit production. Trying to get the very best advice possible, it invited a Soviet expert as consultant during its cooperative stage. He said that it would be impossible to grow grain between the trees, and that the brigade would have to depend on the state for that. But now, 400 jin a mou of grain a year has been taken from orchard land, and the trees have borne more richly than they have ever done. The Soviet expert also taught a system of pruning that was said to be the world's most advanced and most successful. But the peasants have discarded it and have gone ahead with one which gives better results. Pear trees producing 1,000 jin each of high grade export "Tientsin" type pears, and giving around the same total each year without any "small" or "big" years as was once thought to be inevitable, is a record to be proud of.

However, behind that success there has been much putting of heads together of old and young, discussing fertilisers, pruning, tree diseases, and so on. One was impressed by the way the membership had added to the look of their village by planting a double line of trees down its main street, and too, by planting chestnuts and walnuts up on the higher ground above their orchard and cropland. Of their 1,487 mou of rolling country, 1,200 mou is in apples, pears or peaches, from which they market 1,200,000 jin a year. The main problem on so high a piece of land is naturally irrigation. Around the same time as they invited the Soviet expert they also brought in a group of well sinkers led by a college-trained technician. This group spent 8,000 yuan but did not find any water, reporting that it was unlikely any would be found in such a locality. So then the membership started well-sinking on their own. They went down through rock for 80 metres, and then struck it in plenty. Encouraged by this success, they dug 12 more all around the same depth, and so the problem of water began to be solved. Before 1958, the state had to supply the brigade with 60,000 jin of grain a year. After they had struck water and carried out their plan of growing their own grain inside their orchard, they were able to sell the state a surplus of 84,000 jin of grain a year. They also put down 3,500 metres of underground piping to carry water to irrigation ditches. Then, to cap their efforts, they went to work in 1967 and built a water tower from the stone they cut from their own hillsides. They reasoned this way, "Others said we had no water resources. We have proved that we do. They said we could not grow crops in our orchards. That, however, we have done. We have all seen water towers on railway stations and in towns. Some of us have even cut stone for them and helped to build them. Now that electric power has come to us, why do we not build our own water tower, bringing running water to our homes as well as to orchard trees and crops? Why say that because other brigades do not have water towers is a good enough reason why we shouldn't have one?" So all went right ahead and built their own tower, making it as firm as any one would wish to see. Everything they did themselves, cutting the stone, hauling it, and then carrying through the construction job. It is a good, sturdy, high tower that can store 25 tons of water which is pumped by an electric pump from the well beside it. Two more wells have been dug near enough to the tower so as to serve it if anything goes wrong with the well at present in use. So now all dwellings have running water nearby. It is fun to see the children in the brigade kindergarten splashing around in the sump of running water that serves their vicinity. Nearby too, was the brigade seven-year school, allowing us a glance at a lively bunch of youngsters. From school and kindergarten we went on to see the livestock section where the worker in charge is also a veterinary surgeon, much in demand by other brigades in the vicinity. The brigade breeds all its own draft stock, of which it owns 43 head. It also has its own considerable store of grain over and above the amount sent to the county granaries. And each household stores grain against any emergency.

After we had gone around and seen some of the achievements in Holiangshan, we went out of the sun into the cool brigade meeting room and met a group of leaders from Chengmingshan Brigade, which is further up the valley in the hills. I had visited this place last year, once the poorest in the locality. In the interval, there had come the taking over of education by the brigade leadership, and friends from there had come down to give us their experience, for their school is now counted as being one of the most successful around.

Previously, Chengmingshan Brigade had two lower primary schools, one on each side of a deep cut valley. Pupils who wanted to go on to the upper primary school had to walk two miles down the valley, while to the nearest lower middle school they would have to go four and a half miles. Then also, to go to the middle school needed an outlay which was often out of reach for many peasant families. All schools were under the direction of the central school of the county, and an educational establishment was thus created, teachers being quite apart from the people. There were many entry rules with respect to age, examination marks and so on. Everyone knew Tsao Kwei-lin as a good boy of strong character. He failed by one mark in one subject to get into the middle school. But then he went to a People's Liberation Army school, and did very well there. Actually 43 percent of primary pupils from poor families who were keen to go to middle school were unable to do so.

In consequence, and during the Cultural Revolution, the brigade leadership realised that the decisive issue was the question of who should have the power, and were delighted when they heard the directive from Chairman Mao that schools in the countryside should be directed by the poor and lower-middle peasants. In consequence, in the autumn of 1968, they set about carrying through their educational revolution, building a new school with a seven-year course, which takes the pupils from primary through the lower middle school, in place of the old system which took nine years to get the same result. 92.5 percent of all brigade children attend, 236 of them. Teaching methods too have changed considerably. Poor and lower-middle peasants give lessons, as does the head of the militia, the brigade electrician, the accountant, the orchard technician and the brigade "barefoot" doctor.

Before, students might sit in classrooms for ten years and not know what the different crops were and what were the problems concerning them. None knew how to measure output of fruit correctly. Few could be bookkeepers. They had a horror of things considered dirty, so that while they kept their clothing immaculate, their minds often became dirty. Many of the old teachers looked askance at poor-peasant teacher Chao Yen-yi, who always came to school early and employed the time before classes in cleaning out the school latrines. Or Chung Yu-chang who always carried out nightsoil to the compost heaps before coming to class. But perhaps the best object lesson was given by the old peasant Chao Cheng-yi, who saw students and teachers standing around looking down into the deep pit of the school latrine, into which a small pig had fallen. Chao without hesitation went right down after the pig and saved it, and then went off to clean up afterwards. A lesson that no teacher or student forgot. Said the brigade leader, "We do not try, as the old schools did, to find and push on the ones who can memorise glibly. What matters to us is whether we get a body of young people coming out of our school who understand the meaning of Chairman Mao's Thought and can apply it. In the past, the so-called very clever students who were sent on to college began to think that they had special rights, were entitled to ask for more, and often did not like coming back to their home villages even for a visit, because they felt that the villages were too dull, dirty and commonplace. What we want to do in our school is to raise our own standards, do the things ourselves which no one else can do for us, and in so doing make our contribution to proletarian internationalism. Our young folk must learn how to meet the challenge of the countryside, carry on the revolution and rebuild the land that is theirs. There is so much to be done!"

Leaving Changli county, we took a road across country one wet afternoon, and by evening were pulling again into what was once a huge Catholic Mission compound in Yungping Fu which is now called Lulung. It was my second visit to the place, and it was good to hear how much had been done in the intervening time. Lulung is an ancient city, having been first mentioned in history in the year 586 A.D. In its long existence it has been a battleground many times, for it borders on the Great Wall. In the early 'thirties when Japanese aggression placed it under the puppet regime of a certain Yin Ju-keng, it provided Japan with a duty-free area from which to dump goods into China, and gave Japan control of Chinwangtao port. But in the Wars of Resistance and Liberation the people's forces were so active that the enemy was denied any real control in Lulung.

The county is mainly high rolling country and hills. Bounded by the winding Chinglung river to the west, it is 1,200 square kilometres in area and is farmed by 35 communes. Since Liberation, all the usual stages have been gone through, Revolutionary Committees having been established on all levels by 1968. Then started the struggle-criticism-transformation movement, and a cleansing of revolutionary ranks, both amongst old cadres and new rebel groups, which has strengthened the militant ability of all to put Mao Tsetung Thought into action. Three new small-scale reservoirs have been completed in the early part of 1969, extending the area of irrigated land by 14,000 mou. Preliminary work has started on the big Chinglung river dam, which will benefit many counties when completed.

The first evening we spent at Lulung was an eventful one, for we were invited to a performance put on by local youth in the big auditorium of the county upper middle school, a hall which had been built by Red Guards in 1967. Like the performance we had seen at Changli one evening, this one went with a good deal of swift action, and reminded me of some I had seen in Yenan in the days of the War of Resistance.

The next day despite bad weather, we set off for another visit to Fushenchuang Brigade, situated in the bend of the Chinglung river some 30 kilometres north of the city. This brigade is quite famous for having taken a range of hills and converted them into rich terraced fields and orchards, and for having raised the living standards of the poorest village of the region to one where there is plenty for all. Chen Hui, whom we met again, is quite a leader. A quiet, middle-aged man, he has been the one who so ably led the brigade to overcome much. The water turbine is now a common enough farm tool in south China, where low dams can be made over rivers and the power used for pumping water up, as well as for local electric power needs.

There must be literally tens of thousands of them in southern and southwestern provinces now, but their installation in silt-bearing rivers that rise swiftly when summer rains fall over the deforested, eroded lands they drain is rather more difficult. Especially when rivers freeze over in winter. Certainly, had the people been content to wait until the overall plan for Chinglung conservancy was carried through, their problems would have been less. But they wanted the water here and now, as well as the power for lighting and milling. Chen Hui found a place against a projecting cliff into which a channel of water diverted from the main river could run, and where even in winter there would be enough water under the ice to keep the turbines moving. He succeeded with his first turbine in 1968, and in 1969 has put in a bigger one. The people have dug all the laterals necessary, many of them having had to be chiselled through the rock. The rock on these hills is of the kind that cannot be blasted without making cracks through which water would leak, and water is too precious for that. An aqueduct has had to be made over a road, and for that workers in a Tangshan factory have helped by finding a big iron pipe from their waste heap, which when tarred and given a solid bearing at each end does the job admirably. We asked the commune members what changes have come to them in the revolution.

"You know," they said, "things are different with us now. We were glad before to come from poverty to plenty, but all thought still about personal interests. Now we feel that we are living for the revolution, and that what we are doing here is a part of the world struggle." In pre-Liberation days the fields here averaged 60 jin a mou. Last year, the harvest was over seven times that total, and this year will be far better. There has been a crop of winter wheat grown for the first time in the brigade, later giving place to the usual one of maize and beans, millet and kaoliang. In the 'fifties the brigade had to get a subsidy of 25,000 jin of state grain a year. But in the three years of the Cultural Revolution they have given the state a surplus of 210,000 jin, as well as putting 100,000 jin into their own brigade store. None of the young people know the taste of bran and bitter herbs the old people once ate, unless at times a special meal of such is prepared for them so that they will understand what their elders have come through. A measure of progress can be gauged from the fact that before folk came together collectively there were but five quite small donkeys as the only means of transport, other than the man with the carrying pole. Now six rubber-tyred carts that can carry a ton and a half each are busy all the time, while there is a beginning of mechanisation in the one tractor and the 15 other machines including a diesel engine which operates food-processing machinery. The brigade also has 73 cattle and 210 pigs. "Yes," they say, "we have fought against barren hills, erosion, flooding, drought, and the class enemy. And in all these struggles we have learnt that Mao Tsetung Thought really does help us to win." The old landlord and rich peasant families who had educated people amongst them and still felt quite superior, had looked down on Chen Hui and the middle and poor peasants, saying, "Look at them! They think they're going to lead water up all those hills, the poor fools. And as for generating electricity from our mad river, that is clearly quite impossible. The only way to get water up a hill is to carry it there. As for lighting at night, why, they had better use the moon!"

A little group of 11 of the younger members have set up an orchard in one of the gullies, putting check dams in steps across it, thus holding the water in ponds which they use for irrigation or just for ducks to splash in and vegetation to grow around. They have many peach trees, and quite a hillside of grapevines. They are growing walnuts and chestnuts now on higher levels, and have planted some 7,000 trees in honor of the Ninth Party Congress, as well as digging 3,100 metres of canal to commemorate that event also. Their 3,700 fruit trees and 400 vines are bringing in a record crop this year, and they are happy that their production will very materially help the brigade to carry out new plans.

There are 21 students from Chinwangtao city high schools allocated to the brigade. Fifteen are girls. Their leader, Meng Hsin-ying was a young woman now 21. She spoke well and directly, telling that she came from a worker family, which had rather spoilt her, as she wanted to go through the educational system and become an important person. As a graduate of an upper middle school, with a good working-class background, her family had expected her to become a college graduate after another five years' schooling. Now here she was, in a small commune brigade, her speech already becoming like that of the local folk, her hands hard, but very much a person after the year she had spent with her comrades facing up to the difficulties the new kind of life entailed. Quite simply she spoke of the problems that had come up, frankly admitting that she and all her fellow-students who had come were full of old middle-class ideas. How at first they felt so ineffectual beside others when they used shovels and picks, how their hands blistered and then the blisters burst and left raw patches of flesh. How their backs ached, and how poor the food tasted, especially when those of their number whose turn it was to stay at home and cook did not make a very good practical job of it.

"Yes, during our old school period, we had been out into the country for a day's work at times — two or three times a year — but that was more like an excursion," she said. "Coming to Fushenchuang was the real thing. There were times when the group vacillated a bit. That was before they became toughened up to the work and conditions. Then there came the news that many of our classmates had been sent to factories to work. They could live at home, do eight hours work only, have good food, and go to night classes. How simple this was compared with getting up in the middle of a stormy night to go out in the mud and save the stacks of kaoliang that were being blown around! Or to stand in the bitter wind of early winter slicing up sweet potatoes to put out to dry. Or to have shoulders red and sore with carrying poles. But we came together and fully discussed our situation, and turning to relevant passages in the Quotations from Chairman Mao, felt that we after all were on the right line, realising that if we could not integrate and work with the peasants we really knew nothing.

One of our number was something of a bookworm. He had studied many texts on plant diseases and the various kinds of harmful insect life. So when he was told that there were pests appearing in a millet field he went there to look for them. But search as he would, finally with his face right down to the ground, he could not locate the trouble, until the next day the team leader came and showed him the insect that was causing the damage and where its eggs were. We discussed this incident in our evening meeting and came to the conclusion that had we gone on with that higher school education for still another ten years we should only have become more foolish year by year. In the past at times, someone would come and tell us about our 'glorious future'. We were to be the 'future rulers of our land', and so on. Now we have discussed together what our future should be, and all have agreed that life only has meaning for us if we can really serve the people. But how can we really serve the people if we do not know them? If we have not worked with them? Mountain paths and city streets are not the same. It is out amongst the hills and streams of the hinterland that the big majority of our people live and work, and all depends on the food they produce. Now in our first year at Fushenchuang we have improved in physique. We are no longer afraid of getting our clothes dirty — only of having dirty minds that are proud and selfish. One of our number was given the job of making the sugar mash from fermented threshing-floor waste which is a very economical fodder for fattening hogs. He did not like doing this at first, scared that the news of his becoming a keeper of pigs would make people back home laugh at him. He was frightened too of pig lice, and of collecting pig manure. But the others all helped him, studying the essay on Norman Bethune together, so that he went and put his whole heart into the job. Others started calling him by a new nickname, "General Sugar", and he laughed and liked it. "Raising pigs for the revolution is good," he wrote home.

Actually, all of the home folk of the 21 are now proud of them and what they have been able to do and learn. "Every day we learn something," Meng Hsin-ying said, "especially we learn how the commune folk put brigade welfare before their own, how helpful they are to each other, how frugal, and how sincere. To give one little instance. We were digging irrigation ditches with some of the brigade members. One of our number came across two big sweet potatoes that had not been dug up in the harvesting. He thought of taking them home to feed the pig our kitchen was raising for itself. Then one of the brigade members also dug up a big one and, it being sundown, we walked down to the village together. But when we got to his home he did not go in but went on down to the brigade office, to pass in the potato there. So small a thing, yet how indicative of clean thinking. Sunflowers always turn to the sun, and the people must always turn to Mao Tsetung Thought. The brigade member had taught us a lesson, one of the many of the kind that made us blush when we realised their significance. We realised how easy it would have been for us to stay in the city and talk revolution, yet ever expecting the peasants to support us better. How this would have taken us straight into the camp of revisionism, which always uses the red flag to try and beat down the red flag."

When Meng Hsin-ying finished, she said modestly that she was sorry she could not explain better. The square-set little figure, her directness and obvious sincerity unmarred by any spurious emotionalism made a deep impression on her hearers. She had said her piece and had said it well.

The next speaker was a "barefoot" doctor of the brigade. She was Hsin Tsui-huan, a rather heavily built peasant girl from Liangchiayu Brigade a little to the north of Fushenchuang where, it was agreed, the work of the "barefoot" doctor had shown the best results in brigades around. Like that of Fushenchuang it was not a big brigade, just one of 177 families — 842 people. She herself had started medical work by becoming an apprentice to a traditional doctor after four years' primary schooling in the village school. Then she worked for a while in the local commune hospital and local health station, after which there came a PLA medical team which gave a six months' intensive course to commune medical workers. Still in her early twenties, she has in the main gathered her medical experience from practice. Most commune members prefer traditional medicine, so she has led in going to the hills and helping to gather the various kinds of herbs needed.

With the coming in of the cooperative medicine scheme, whereby each family pays a little to the clinic to help to keep them well, she maintains close touch with the people. She and two others operate the clinic. One is there all the time, while the other two are either out gathering herbs, visiting families, or else working in the fields with the production teams, always carrying their box of medicines along with them to the worksite. Most of the complaints are respiratory, and for these there are many good local herb medicines. Then there are the common rheumatic disorders which answer well to acupuncture — she and her two comrades have learnt enough of it to be able to give such treatment. Hsin Tsui-huan had done a course in midwifery and can give help in this. Cases which are difficult can be sent to the commune hospital, which is not much more than a mile away from her village, but what most people want is treatment on the spot. Her clinic boils up the herb mixtures and sends them hot in small thermos bottles to the people in their homes, which is much appreciated. People most fear having to go to a county or city hospital, where many expenses will be incurred, and where they may have to wait some time for their turn for treatment. Many troubles, when caught at early stages, are easily cured, and in this she and her clinic can help a lot.

Dentistry? No, complicated dental work is better done in the commune or county hospital. But just for pulling teeth, an agonising process as well as an expensive one in the old-time village, why, she and also both of her fellow workers can deal with that relatively painlessly. Preventive medicine is important in the village, Hsin Tsui-huan thinks. So she gives health lessons to the children in the brigade school on the dangers of intestinal parasites and body lice, and on the importance of fresh air and water. People in her village mostly live several families in one compound, so she sets out to train one health worker for each compound. Before, the local children would go to collect herbs to sell to the Native Products Co. and get money for sweets. Now she organises them to do the work more thoroughly as part of their education and as a practical way to serve the people. Before, many children would die of recurring local epidemics, but since the brigade clinic has started none have. One old man of 60 had so bad a rupture he was bent double. He had no money to go to the county hospital for an operation, but then a travelling Army medical aid team came during the Cultural Revolution and gave him the operation on the spot, so that he walks erect and happy again. Then after citing some other instances of this kind she went back to the subject of traditional medicines used, saying that one of the main troubles was cutting them up, weighing them, and packaging. "We blister our hands at times chopping up those roots, for the work has to be done finely, but we are rewarded when people thank us and we see them able to go out with their production teams as usual." Modestly Hsin Tsui-huan closed with the words: "Though I have been able to do very little, I am very happy at heart."

It was evening when we left Fushenchuang and started back over the 30 kilometres of country road to Lulung. The afternoon had been overcast, but now the rays of the setting sun struck red across the Chinglung river and against the towers and ramparts of the Great Wall that streamed across the blue hills to the north. At household doors in the villages through which we passed people stood waving farewell to us, Little Red Books in their hands. Brave, tough people who so courageously work towards a new dawn.

Changli — 1970

In the old days of U.S. missionary enterprise, Changli was well known as a mission centre. Situated on Pohai Bay in northeast Hopei, it is now famous for some of its vanguard commune brigades which have made the forbidding foothills of the rugged mountains there bear both fruit and grain, giving the once poverty-stricken people self-sufficiency and a new dignity.

We spent one hot summer's morning in one of these brigades, the Holiangshan. I had visited it a year ago and was surprised at the changes that had been made — the new stables, pig sties, 5,000 more metres of underground piping — pipes from the glass fibre factory in Chinwangtao — laid for the high-pressure water supply gained from the water tower built, and so on. In the last three years, 42 wells have been dug, at depths from 60 to 70 metres each. Eighteen produce water, so that now drought as an old enemy is about mastered. They had some losses this summer from a terrific windstorm, and now lay plans to meet future attacks by windbreaks. Some of the wells are held in reserve, and more are being dug. It is an untold epic in determination and patience to dig down through all that rock, not find water, so start again in another place, and find no water there either after weeks of back-breaking work, then on to another site. The workers in the brigade repair and construction shop had their working surroundings conveniently fixed up, tools well looked after and each in its proper place. They looked after the motors, the pumps, the sprayers, and village electrification. In busy periods they went out to work with the other production teams unless urgently needed on repair jobs. We looked in on the brigade plant research station, finding that every conceivable kind of moth or bug found amongst the grain had been collected, as well as many specimens of orchard tree disease. All of this material was not only used in finding out more about pest eradication but was also valuable teaching material for the brigade primary school, all children being taught about those things which affected their livelihood.

Most of Changli's around 900,000 mou of agricultural land is relatively flat, lying on the strip between the mountains and the sea. 300,000 mou of it, once largely alkaline land, now grows rice, the rest the usual winter wheat, then the summer crops of corn, kaoliang, millet and beans, peanuts and sweet potatoes. Much of this land is divided into irregular fields just as it was when there was the old individual land ownership. Now this coming autumn, in the 50 days after the harvest and before the ground freezes, there is to be a grand onslaught on levelling out the land and making large rectangular fields more suitable for mechanisation. Everyone will take part, townspeople, people in organisations, old and young, and already preparatory steps are being taken to ensure success. In this past year and a half there has been the movement for well digging, which resulted in the total number of deep wells in the county being raised from 1,100 to 2,500, and as a result a much greater freedom from the danger of drought.

Before leaving Changli we visited a commune old folk's home. Nicely set in one of the town's big compound houses, the old folk cultivated their little plots of vegetables and flowers, and seemed a very contented little band indeed. They were not in any way cut off from the life around them. The harmony with their group was enhanced rather than in any way impaired. They were still part of Chengkwan Commune of Changli.

On the way north from Changli we travelled through Funing county. Then on the road we passed a long line of rubber-tyred carts, each with big rolls of machine-made paper on them. The kind that was once imported from abroad, because China could not meet its own requirements. They came from the new Funing county paper mill, one more expression of local self-sufficiency that is so heartening to see everywhere in China today.

Panchiayu Brigade in Northeast Hopei, 1970

A heavy downpour had slightly cooled a really hot night. In the early morning as we prepared to set out, the rising sun began to peep through a light mist and shine on cobwebs spun over the top of hedges, making the dewdrops on them sparkle brightly. A huge spiderweb hung between two apple trees like a great banner shining in the rays of dawn. We went north from Tangshan city, a modern northeast Hopei municipality with a population of a million, and soon were passing through the streets of the Fengjun county seat. Amongst the 48 rural communes of this county lies one which is called Huoshihying. Huoshihying has 13 brigades, the most famous being Panchiayu. The 600,000 people in Fengjun county, which consists in the main of flat farmland or rolling country, gain outsize crops these days, thus providing much surplus grain for the state. Huoshihying Commune, however, is in the hills northeast of the county seat. Rugged, rocky, eroded hills these, from which most of the soil has long since been washed away, and on which the goats owned by generations of farmers down the years have halted any young trees from growing. A poor area. Some would have said a hopeless one.

We drove up a narrow mountain road, previously a water course, until we got to Panchiayu, finding it a village nestling in a gulch between the hills. On arrival we were brought to a new, well-built meeting room, where a profusion of fruits — apples, grapes, peaches, plums and walnuts — were spread out in welcome. A group of old men greeted us warmly, but before we got down to the dramatic story they had to tell, we heard something of the Panchiayu Brigade of today.   It has 15,000 mou of rocky hill land, 6,500 of which it has planted in trees or orchards, and 2,000 — mostly stone-faced — terraces on which it raises its grain.   In the spirit of Tachai the brigade has gone ahead with terracing work, carrying up soil to its new little fields which in this year 1970 look extremely prosperous.   The village, too, is beautiful.   It has whitewashed stone walls, over which summer vines run in profusion, tall sunflowers standing behind, grapevines running over trellises in every courtyard, and a gay little stream that flows in from the hills beyond, making a place for children to paddle and women to wash clothes.   On a terrace above the stream in one place, quarters have been built for the group of students allocated to the place from city schools.

When the Japanese drove in during the years 1937-41, all of the land which was any good was owned by a little group of landlords and rich peasants dominated by their chief, Pan Hwei-lin, who had a big house and compound surrounded with a high stone wall.   This Pan Hwei-lin, however, found the activities of the people of Panchiayu not to his liking, so he went off with his bailiff and henchmen to join the Japanese.   At that time, there was no highway into Panchiayu, just narrow hill tracks over which enemy troops with their pack horses would come on marauding expeditions.   Despite enemy pressure the people never gave them grain, money or fodder voluntarily.   They fought back, laying mines on the mountain path and in concealed positions as snipers picked off enemy leaders.   There were in those years no fewer than 138 enemy forays into the hill villages here, and 54 times the Panchiayu village militia gave battle.   They became close to Eighth Route Army groups in the hills, and at times fought together with them.

The Japanese and their puppets finally came to the decision that of all the hill villages, Panchiayu was their most implacable enemy.   They did not have the high flying super-fortresses, the blockbusters and napalm the USA uses on such hamlets in South Vietnam, Laos and Cambodia, but they felt they could do what the U.S. army was later to do at Song My.   So they assembled an expedition from the garrisons of many of the towns around, with orders to meet in the vicinity of Panchiayu. There were 3,000 Japanese and 2,000 puppet troops engaged in the operation, and marching through the night they concentrated before dawn in the vicinity of Panchiayu, led by the traitor Pan Hwei-lin's men.   On January 25th 1941, just two days before the lunar New Year for which each family was preparing, they surrounded the village and herded the people, most of whom were still in bed, out of their houses onto the frozen surface of a pond.   Shivering in the bitter cold, old folk, women and children were then driven at bayonet point into the compound of the landlord Pan Kwei-lin, where the three courtyards had been filled with straw over which gasoline had been poured.   This was then set on fire, while at the four gates of the compound troops fired into the mass of the people.   There were 241 families, 1,703 people in all, and 1,230 were killed.   Some escaped through a hole made in the compound wall, including Pan Kwang-lin who told us the story, a man who at that time was still young but whose voice still trembled when he spoke of it all. Another, Pan So-hsin, whose home was on the northern perimeter of the village right against a mountain, downed one enemy soldier with a stone, then grabbed his weapon and killed two others, right in his doorway. He then escaped with his wife and two small sons up the mountainside. He was one of the group who welcomed us, and is now a slight, rather bent man of small stature in his mid-sixties. He still works with stones, now using them to make terrace faces, and still can eat two jin of grain a day. Counting grandchildren he now has 13 in his family.

There were many acts of heroism. Young boys stood up and cursed the enemy. Pan So-mi, a mother 50 years old, caught a grenade the enemy had thrown into the compound and, hurling it back before it exploded, landed it right in the middle of a group of them just as it went off. Pan Fu-ting took 29 people, mainly men, into the landlord's grain store, which had strong walls and doors covered with iron plates, with windows of skin instead of the usual paper. The enemy tried climbing over the walls but was beaten back each time, anything that could be used as weapons being brought into play including the arm of the big weighing balance. Jabs of bayonets into the iron covering of the doors and bullet holes are remaining scars of struggle there. The Japanese set fire to the village before leaving it in the afternoon, but the granary escaped destruction and all its defenders escaped. On the short winter's day the enemy was most anxious to depart early, rightly fearing that Eighth Route Army units would catch up with them if they lingered. As it was, the Eighth Route Army men did get to the village quite soon and joined in with the survivors and the people who came in to help from other villages around, to save what could be saved. Sometimes the living were found under piles of dead. Most were badly wounded. Food and shelter had to be provided and the dead buried. The Eighth Route Army gave of its resources, and the villages around gave of theirs, so that a new Panchiayu arose on the ashes of the old. The savagery of individual enemy soldiers showed itself when they bayonetted children in the stomach and killed nursing mothers. One hates hearing of such horror stories as they show man at his lowest level, the level that imperialism forces him down to. All imperialisms have done and are still doing these things, but the stories of them are always revolting, whether these atrocities happened on the bloodstained snow of Panchiayu or in jungle villages down along the Mekong river.

The menfolk who escaped the massacre at Panchiayu formed themselves into a revenge corps. Soon it had taken part in a score of actions against the enemy and had killed over 100 of them. Before the end of the War of Resistance in 1945 it had raised that total to 1,021, including in that number puppet agents as well as Japanese. The corps then joined the Liberation Army as a regular army unit and fought many battles in the Northeast, afterwards going with the forces that swept south all the way to Hainan Island.

The dead of Panchiayu were buried under four mounds, two for the men, one for the women, and one for children. A memorial hall and plinth have been erected in front of these, while behind them a permanent exhibition hall is being completed. This will preserve the memory of the events of that cold winter's day for the youth of tomorrow, in case they take too much for granted and forget the things that imperialism is capable of doing to those it would make its slaves. There are many stories of the period prior to the massacre, too, that need preserving. On one of their forays the Japanese had arrested a disabled veteran soldier, stripped him and beat him to try to make him tell who were Communists. He died without answering them. To his defence strode out of the peasant ranks old Pan Hwei-min, who was really a Communist Party member. Trying to stop the beating, he roundly cursed the enemy until they seized him too and beat him the same way then used fire to burn him, hoping to extort a confession which he would not make. He also died, but his image lives on.

The brigade now harvests some 500,000 jin of fruit a year and has raised its grain production from the 100 jin a mou at Liberation to 500 jin, using both its compost — 5,000 jin a mou — and the chemical fertiliser made in the county chemical plant. The enemy had burned some 1,300 "chien", or housing units as they are calculated in China, but over 2,300 have been built since. Counting village people who have gone to outside organisations to work, there are in all about as many as there were on that fateful day in January 1941. The children charmed us with their songs, the girls obliging with some newly composed ones. Amongst them a six-year-old gave us a long narrative piece, and then a bunch of boys, not to be outdone, complied with our wish that they too sing, doing a very considerable section from the modern opera "Taking Tiger Mountain by Strategy". The boys were very proud of their Liberation Army caps, and reminded one strongly of the "little devils" of Eighth Route Army days. We met various groups of them, one very attractive bunch standing under the big ash tree that was planted in the Yunglo period of the Ming dynasty. It was nearly destroyed in the burning of the village but has since grown a new stem from the old roots. The hollow old trunk still stands. It was the secret storehouse for written materials of the Party through many years, and so has quite a distinguished place amongst the sights of the village. Sometimes visitors from Japan come to visit Panchiayu and the people welcome them, knowing that there is a people's Japan as well as an imperialist one, and that people's Japan is on their side.

Practically every family name in the village is Pan, those of the new village holding the name as a badge of honor, as well they might. They are the people who fought back, and they are those who now are keenest to build the new day. Today power lines cross the hills and come down to Panchiayu, so that every home is lit on dark winter nights and motors turn the food-processing machines. There is a good brigade school that gives junior middle school courses as well as primary ones, and a brigade clinic with two "barefoot" village doctors. In the old times of the 'forties, few of the people had even been as far away as the county seat of Fengjun. Now the public bus from Tangshan, 120 li (60 kilometres) away, comes in once a day. Rubber-tyred brigade carts take the fruit crop out to be marketed by the state. Forty percent of the households in the village have sewing machines and radios.

There are 149 activists in the propagation of Mao Tsetung Thought. Much has been done to make irrigation of terraced fields possible, everyone joining in the task — even old women and an ex-soldier with one leg who refuses to be left out of anything and pluckily gets up the steepest slopes with his wooden stump. Three hundred mou of new land have been reclaimed in the last four years, and give good crops. Reclamation here means fighting for every foot. Soil has to be carried in, stone terrace faces built. Never has the spirit of the people to do things been higher than it is now. New trees are being planted all the time, especially walnuts, chestnuts, pepper and dates. Goats are being kept away from the new plantings, whitewashed stone markers being set out to show goatherds just how far they can let their charges roam. The task of planting trees is not easy, by the way. Holes have to be made into the rock, filled with good earth, and the young trees in their early stages nursed through times of drought. But they grow surprisingly well despite the hard, barren nature of the mountain slopes. One slope I noticed was marked with white stone as having been planted in commemoration of the Ninth Party Congress in 1969. The young trees were just visible from the highway.

"We will make these rocky mountains support us. Our will is stronger than theirs," the people say. Such then is some of the story of Panchiayu.

Something from Nothing — Paichia Paotze Brigade

He was tall and handsome, with a serious though quiet expression on his face as he explained the situation with regard to Paichia Paotze Brigade of which he was the leader. The brigade was one of the 14 of Chienkechuang Commune in Funing county. A small brigade — just 56 households with a total of 310 people in all, working as one unit and with no production teams. Tucked away under the stony peak of Horse Mountain, the little community has but 418 mou of land, all of mountainside slopes. From Liberation up to 1967 it was in receipt of relief grain, though in those years it had planted some 3,500 fruit trees which are now bearing well.

"Look at that field of cotton," a young man who had come with us exclaimed. "It's all growing on rock!" The terrace face was rock all right, but soil had been brought up and spread over its surface when it was terraced. Ten thousand jin of compost per mou is added each year, as well as chemical fertiliser. Funing county, by the way, has its own chemical fertiliser factory which produces enough for all its communes.

But back to the brigade leader, who is that in his capacity as chairman of the Revolutionary Committee. His name is Pai Kwang-he, and he is a graduate of an upper middle school. There are five other upper middle-school graduates in the brigade, and some 20 from lower middle school. At Liberation, the brigade was almost totally illiterate. Few people reached the age of 60, for life was too hard and bitter. Pai Kwang-he's father, however, is 76 and still goes out to work each day, counting himself one of the 80 who work the land, have done the terracing and performed the miracles we saw. In the first years after Liberation, the brigade thought it did well to get 100 jin of grain a mou each year. In the Great Leap Forward this was raised to 300 jin. The 1969 harvest came to 430 jin a mou. It is hoped to do still better in 1970.

But the main work here has been in reclaiming the stony slopes of Horse Mountain and in converting them to rock-faced terraced fields. The mountain has to be cut into and flat fields of one or two mou each made, a front and some side walls built and earth carried in. For planting fruit trees, deep holes have to be sunk and filled with earth. As the grade steepens, many of the little fields are less than a mou — a sixth of an acre — in area. In the past three years over 200 mou have thus been reclaimed — and all by the work force of only 80 people, old and young, men and women, with hand tools and their bare hands, while carrying on the work on the rest of their land. This summer as we looked up at the terraces we found them lush. Apple trees, corn, millet, beans and so on all doing very well. The members have made a reservoir in one of the valleys and from this catchment they use an electrically powered pump to throw the water to a point above the terraced fields so that it can irrigate each one in turn. In the old days these were the very poor who found it impossible to get land, and hard enough to get work. So families came to this marginal land — which of course some landlord promptly claimed as his — and raised what little they could locally, while the menfolk went to other villages to hire themselves out for work. Quite often it is the group which has had the hardest time in the old society which does best in the new. Certainly, the way this particular one has pulled itself up by its own bootstraps has been an epic. No more relief grain is needed, and instead grain is sold to the state. There is a saying in these parts that if a commune gets over 400 jin a mou on an all-over count, it has crossed the Yellow river. If it gets more than 500 jin it is over the Huai, and if it gets 800 jin, then it has crossed the Yangtze, because north of the Yellow river the yields were always lower than 400, north of the Huai lower than 500 and north of the Yangtze lower than 800 jin. Paichia Paotze in 1970, with the aim of 550 jin, is determined to get over the Huai. Apart from the grain raised, there is the fruit which is sold to the state. Every one of the 56 households in the brigade gets a yearly income of 500 yuan from this source.

As the village is so small, a primary school for the smaller children only is operated by the brigade, arrangements being made with the bigger brigade of Liuchiapao down hill a bit to take the older children. All children between the ages of eight and 14 have schooling. The "barefoot" doctor who operates the brigade clinic has all households taking part in the cooperative health scheme. The task the group has set itself is to reclaim other mountain slopes like the one they have done already.

They are proud of being known as a vanguard brigade and quite evidently do not intend to let the name pass from them.

Horse Mountain and Paichia Paotze Brigade are not far from the buildings and permanent set-up of the Yangho reservoir which I visited a couple of years ago. So we went over to lunch there and see the cutting of a new and very adequate flood diversion channel on which 1,000 commune members were working, a number that will swell to 4,000 when the crops are in, ensuring that the whole task is done this coming winter. It is the water from this reservoir that makes for the rich crops down by the seacoast, so much rice being produced there that a modern paper factory is being erected by the county to make use of the straw. Some of our party went out onto the reservoir in a motorboat. The whole project, done by the hands and courage of the commune folk from the many communes downstream, is a monument to their tenacity and spirit. I asked a commune worker on the flood diversion channel how much grain a day he ate. "Two and a half jin," he said. For heavy work like this, a subsidy of an additional jin a day is granted to members.

Funing county has 401,000 people, and their number increases at the rate of about 10,000 a year. But increase in crop yields is now far ahead of the requirements of population, increase that in these last years is nothing short of phenomenal.

In all these places people have not only become economically self-sufficient, but a whole new spirit has arisen as people have changed in the course of their struggle.

There is still much to be done with housing and attendant comforts, but the main things have been brought in hand. The old folk — those over sixty are 90 in number — no longer feel they are unwanted and a burden, but eagerly take part in the communal life of the village. As for the cadres of each brigade, they all go off to regular study courses with other brigade leaders, so there is no danger of any narrow local patriotism developing, of what in China is called "mountaintop" mentality, or of feeling cut off from the mainstream of effort. Educational and health cadres do the same. Achievements like those of Paichia Paotze are an inspiration to all, and stories about them are taken back to other brigades to be discussed in detail by the membership. Throughout the countryside there is ever greater integration of the superstructure with the mass of working folk in line with Mao Tsetung Thought.

From Red Sand and Bare Rock to Grain — Dingchuang

In one of the counties administered by the Chinwangtao municipality in northeast Hopei there is Taiping Commune. Of its brigades, lying at the rear of the hills at Peitaiho, one is called Dingchuang and is rated as a vanguard one. Situated in a sheltered gulch amongst the hills, it had little land that could be called arable. The hillsides had long ago been deforested, and down the main valley was a wide, stony riverbed that filled with floodwaters during the rainy season, but which was dry all the rest of the year. The people lived mainly not on agriculture but on subsidiary occupations like fishing and servicing the big seaside resort of those days, growing only little grain for their own consumption from scattered fields around. Then when Land Reform came after Liberation in 1948, they found themselves with an allotment of 1,040 mou of hilltop, downs and gully, along with the riverbed. The population with its 237 households is today 1,047, with a 501-strong labor force. Three production teams are working on land cultivation, one does fishing — the brigade has 18 fishing boats — one works in the orchards, one specialises in side occupations like the machine repair shop, motor and pump upkeep, food processing and so on, and then there is one production team that has no land but is now working full time on cultivating waste bits of hillside that have been left to show what conditions were before reclamation. One is surprised that anyone would have the courage and spirit to try and make such a desert into crop-producing land. A coarse, red sand, heavily interlarded with rocks, over which sparse vegetation spreads, remote from any water supply, it certainly must have looked discouraging.

In the first years after Liberation much was done, but in the following years, when the Liu Shao-chi line for agriculture was being enforced, private initiative was encouraged, economism practised, private plots enlarged, all with resultant lessening of the collective spirit. With everyone wanting to make all the money possible, and side operations profitable, why bother too much about trying to get grain from such a place with its "three hills and six ridges"? The state gave relief grain, in amounts ranging from 50,000 to 220,000 jin a year in all the years from 1948 to 1967. But the more given, the less there really was. Livestock got steadily older and weaker. There was no pumping system for water, no attempt at a reservoir, the water running uselessly away each summer. The more given in relief grain, the lazier people became, too. They had planted some 6,000 fruit trees but did not cultivate the ground between them. The hilltops remained bare.

Then came the storm of the Great Proletarian Cultural Revolution, and out of it in April 1968 came a new Revolutionary Committee determined that they would follow in the steps of the Tachai model brigade in Shansi and convert their rough terrain into something completely different. For over two years now they have struggled with great intensity. They planned a reservoir that would give them water to pump up to the three hilltops and bring that land in. Reckoned it would take 100 days, but actually in 25 days they had completed it, together with its flood diversion channel. The riverbed below was cleared of stones, good earth brought in, and it was made into fields for dry rice. The hills were terraced, stone for terrace faces being cut from their own quarry. All spaces between fruit trees are tilled and planted and 17 electric pumps have been installed, taking 1,400 metres of high-tension and 2,000 of low-tension wire they have bought out of brigade funds. In 1969 they harvested 550,000 jin of grain. Out of their winter wheat crop in 1970 they have been able to sell the state 20,000 jin. The plan is to get a harvest of 800,000 jin in all for 1970, and to sell 150,000 jin of it to the state. They have aimed at withholding profits as much as possible to replace ageing stock, buy dairy cows, and so on. Yet they are able to allow 400 jin of grain and 275 yuan cash to each working member for the year, which is modest enough, but plenty to give a feeling of security. Families raise their own pigs, chickens and rabbits, but their private plots are now merged into the collective. Yet, as each member is entitled to a fraction of a mou of land for this purpose, the grain off that amount is given him free, over and above the regular grain allowance. The cooperative health scheme takes good care of the old and sick, the clinic being so bright, clean and business-like, it was indeed a pleasure to see. There is a six-year primary school, a well lit, modern building. We saw the pupils of the upper classes out planting tree seedlings on plots they have made, for the next leap forward in afforestation. Around 10,000 jin of compost fertiliser per mou is put out each year, and we saw new pits being dug for maturing it. There is no temptation to save the best of the pig manure for private plots, so everything goes into the collective. The fishing team sells all its catch to the state, as does the production team working in the orchard. Both these teams keep the rubber-tyred carts hauling in good earth which, together with compost and chemical fertilisers and plenty of irrigation, bring new life to once barren hillsides. The brigade has built a silo-like store to hold its own reserve of grain against any time of need.

One was most impressed at Dingchuang by the type of leadership that has emerged. Lu Ching-hai, the brigade leader, a man in his thirties, was obviously an able leader of immense energy and with a good mass line. The brigade Party secretary spoke in high praise of him, for he gave such thoughtful, clear leadership. Another cadre who left a deep impression was the young woman who is vice-commander of the militia group. She had the same good-humored directness as Lu Ching-hai, with considerable ability showing through it.

In all, Dingchuang is quite an epic. The human spirit militant pitted against seemingly overwhelming odds, and yet winning out. From the point of land utilisation, it is indeed a valuable object lesson. We left the clean whitewashed room of the brigade office with many pleasant impressions. Everywhere one turned there was something new. One especially liked the primary school children planting out the tree seedlings in plots they had so carefully prepared. Not in any slapdash way, but methodically and carefully. I was glad to hear that walnuts and chestnuts are amongst the trees being introduced now. Evidently the Dingchuang of five years hence is going to change its face again. Then it will be good to come and see how the trees have grown and what the land produces.

Hengshui and the Deep Wells of South Hopei

We left Shihchiachuang, capital of Hopei, one late spring morning in 1971, and going southeast passed the walls of Chaochow now being demolished, only a mound of earth marking their site, behind which rose factory chimneys of the new rural industrial enterprises. People were busy everywhere irrigating the fields of growing wheat, electrified pumps throwing up water into the canals from where it was conducted into laterals and finally down the rows of wheat. Winter work, as it has been over the winters of the past six years, has been on flood control, so that now it can be safely said that if another torrential rain over the Taihang mountains takes place as it did in 1963, the general flooding of the whole great plain of north China can be avoided without trouble. We passed across one of the dykes 2,000 metres long, now prepared to meet any such eventuality in the riverbed. All villages in its course have been removed and rebuilt in safe areas. Commune members come to farm the land as usual, pumping up their irrigation water from the straightened and now deepened river. It is all part of the Hai river conservancy project which provides new runoffs and outlets to the sea for the five great rivers and their mass of tributaries, and which once had to discharge through but one outlet, that of the Hai river at Tientsin. The project is one in which millions of commune folk have participated with immense elan through the winters of the past seven years, making it one of the great pieces of river conservancy in the history of man.

As we went through some of the counties of the Hsingtai prefecture, it was evident that the big earthquake of 1966 had also hit them, though this part was not the epicentre. There had obviously been a good deal of new construction making up for the losses then suffered. But the most striking thing in new construction noted on the journey was the stress being put on well-sinking. The success of the Hai river project having been assured and flooding having been mastered, attention now goes to gaining victory over drought. There was a good snowfall at the beginning of spring just before the growing season started, which was a big help, but now with summer coming on and the winter wheat growing, it had not rained since. The weather here also seems to have changed. Autumn lasted half a month longer and spring has come half a month earlier this year. Sweet water for these vast plains with their many millions is a pressing necessity. So all across country one noted well-sinking operations in full swing. There were the big wheels of the traditional type, and then also the new mechanised ones. On the highway, trucks, carts and tractor-drawn trailers were loaded with concrete pipes for well linings, trailers here usually drawn by the small Hsingtai-made tractor, a sturdy little four wheeler which seems well adapted to the locality.

We halted for a few hours in Nankung county of Hsingtai, one of 360,000 people organised into 32 communes. The administrative offices had grown around what was once a Confucian temple which later became a school, and then, after Liberation, a new teaching organ, for that is what the modern Chinese administrative centre sets out to be. Not to order folk around, but to educate them how to do any needed job themselves. A place with quite a history is Nankung. During the War of Resistance, only the county centre was held by the Japanese, the entire countryside being under the Eighth Route Army, so that with the departure of the Japanese in 1945 the whole county was liberated. Though yields are still not high compared with more favored lands, crops of cotton and wheat are over double now what they were in 1945. In the first

years of Liberation, around 40 percent of the land would be in cotton.
Now this has been lowered to 30 percent, with more acreage going into
grain. The general impression that Nankung gave was of a fighting
county of hardy people, making a gallant stand against the many difficulties that have to be faced.

We had left the macadamised highway some 60 kilometres out of
Shihchiachuang and now, soon after leaving Nankung, were on it again
going north to Chihsien and Hengshui in added comfort. Hengshui county
has 180,000 people, but it is also the seat of the prefecture which is the
centre of southern Hopei, encompassing 11 counties with a population of
over three million. In the flood of 1963 the whole area was under water,
and the population centres on higher land, cut off by surrounding flood,
could at first only be reached by airdrops from PLA planes and helicopters.
All surrounding areas came to the people's assistance with food and medical care, and everyone received a new impression of what it meant to
belong to a people's China where one man's struggle is that of everyone.
In the bad old days, at a time of natural disaster, the best that could be
got from a government was a grudging "remission of taxes" that could
not be collected anyway, accompanied by a proclamation stating how
generous the aforesaid government was.

Hengshui now has macadamised streets and many new administrative
buildings. Everything seemed to go on wheels. Workers off to their jobs
in the new industry, farmers out to the fields or into town. It is common
to see commune members riding in with an old mother, or a wife and
baby sitting on the bicycle carrier. At times a bicycle may have a rubber-
tyred handcart in tow, or else big baskets of goods tied over each side of
the carrier. Then there is the stream of heavy rubber-tyred carts pulled
by donkeys, mules, horses, cows, and then at times by stately camels
padding dreamily along. Early morning and there is the crowd of children off to school, all with shining faces, the girls with plenty of color,
while the boys wear a blue jacket and long pants. There is evidently no
shortage of cloth, for everyone has plenty. After eight in the morning,
however, the streets clear, and then it is mainly womenfolk going to the
market to make the day's purchases, old folk looking after small children,
and the usual passers by. Sitting at my window after arrival, I wrote
the following lines:

> Late afternoon
> and we come to Hengshui
> rising rural centre
> in south Hopei; a whole
> tree of white spring blossom
> smiles encouragement
> from outside my window;
> as dusk begins to fall
> on the street below,
> strides in an old peasant
> tall and erect, sparse

white beard, looking like
a patriarch; shovel on shoulder
and with a face reflecting
a life of difficulties,
fighting Japanese invaders,
floods, droughts, famines;
and beside him a lad
leading home a little flock
of sheep, coat wide open
to the warm air, chest
and stomach casually bare,
and a voice full of life and fun,
as he turns a laughing face
up at the old man, who tilts
his head and laughs back;
for the young one, the new
Hengshui will be an ever changing
home, giving more strength
and struggle too, yet increasingly
with ways to fight better; for
the old one, deep joy in seeing
generations rise, heading with
so great a spirit, such
sureness and gaiety into
dawn of a different day.

I had come to Hengshui principally to see the remarkable results gained by a commune brigade in Chihsien, an adjacent county. There had
been a stretch of especially poor country there on either side of the gully
of a dried up river called the Laoyangho where alkalinity had strongly
persisted. It was farmed by a brigade of Weitun Commune named after
its village, as is the custom, Hsiaohanchuang. The Hsiaohanchuang
brigade leader met us, as did the leading cadre of Chihsien. But in order
to get the remarkable story of this brigade into focus, it is necessary to
know something of Chihsien first. It is a county of 960 square kilometres,
with a population of over 300,000 people. It has 26 communes divided up
into 412 brigades. In ancient history it was called Chiangtu, "river
capital", for then many rivers joined here. In modern conservancy work
two of the big dykes in emergency riverbeds, one of which is the new
Pai river, now run through it. The Fuyang river is now so controlled
that it is not allowed more than a certain flow. Anything more is turned
off into one of the new canals that run straight as an arrow across the
countryside. Now with old rivers deepened and new ones being cut, alkalinity over the countryside has greatly lessened.

With the magnitude of the work they have done coming home to all,
the people have gained a new confidence in themselves and in their ability
to do things. Everyone is grateful now to Chairman Mao for his insistence
after the 1963 disaster that the problem of the Hai river and its tributaries,

affecting the whole Hopei plain, should be thoroughly solved. Now with flood, waterlogging and some of the alkalinity being met, lack of water and drought have to be faced. There simply has to be irrigation when wheat is growing if there is to be any crop at all. What to do when the skies do not respond? In the Great Leap Forward of 1958-59 better kinds of chain pumps were developed, hand, animal or motor driven. But in these counties of central Hopei, the water they brought up from shallow wells was often too alkaline to be of use for more than two or three seasons. Reservoirs to catch summer rainwater were tried but proved ineffective as they dried up too quickly. The countryside, moreover, flat as it is, does not lend itself to such construction, and much alkalinity still persisted. Then one-metre diameter wells were sunk to depths of 30-50 metres. However, salinity was found to be even worse than in the shallow chain pump wells. In 1966, a well-sinking apparatus was evolved that did better. Mechanised, it probed good sweet water at levels between 250 and 300 metres. Now the county has 40 teams working with such drills. Of the 288 brigades where deep wells are needed, 273 have been supplied already, a total of 860 deep wells having been sunk. Eighty percent of the heavily alkaline land has been washed clean and is responding with better crops each year. The wells are mostly lined with eight-inch inside diameter concrete pipes. Both types — those digging by percussion and the mechanized boring ones — are kept busy adding to the number of wells all the time.

To use the water well, the land has to be flattened and made into level fields. This is also important in the work of preventing waterlogging after heavy rains. Old flood disasters have left sand dunes, and these have to be levelled. The need for doing all this on a mass basis is ever with commune members, though they take agricultural land out of tillage only for a certain time to do the task. Good and bad land included, the average area per person for the whole county is around three mou. From that, folk must live, producing not only what they need themselves, but also what the state needs from them. Now 30 percent of the land is tractor plowed. The grain allotted for each person's consumption per year is 420 jin.

With this background, one returns to the people of Hsiaohanchuang. Leaving the main highway, one takes a short drive on a country road and finds the village set amongst a profusion of date, poplar and willow trees. It is one of just 76 families, 346 people in all. Noted locally once for having an especially high percentage of alkali in its soil, it was about the most miserable place around in the old society. No girl wanted to marry a lad in Hsiaohanchuang. Many families became beggars, many people simply ran away. Only the one landlord and the three rich peasants ever had enough to wear and eat. The landlord was the descendant of an official in the Manchu dynasty, and his son worked as an army officer for the Japanese invaders. The 798 mou of land averaged around 80 jin of grain a mou then, and 20 jin of cleaned cotton.

After Liberation in 1945, things went better as the organisation of people progressed, but alkalinity, drought and flood remained still. With floods taken care of by the Hai river conservancy, alkalinity and lack of sweet water remained. The line proposed by the followers of Liu Shao-chi for such places was against the struggle for self-sufficiency, and was in essence a conservative, reactionary one, amounting to "Don't try — you'll only be beaten!" The various attempts at using the shallow wells, then the 50-metre ones and finally the reservoir, gave reactionary elements a chance to say, "You see, we told you so. There is no way with this kind of land. It is hopeless. Let us not incur further losses. Each man for himself . . ." and so on.

Then came word of the success of the mechanised deep well-sinker, and of the likelihood of gaining good, sweet water that would wash out alkali and help to grow good grain crops. The question arose: should the brigade go after a loan to sink the first exploratory well, or should they try and finance the undertaking out of their own strength? People at the brigade meeting brought up the natural disaster of 1963, and many had such bitter thoughts they felt like weeping when they remembered it. Then some spoke of the high hopes placed on the reservoir of 1964 which enabled them to wash alkali from 400 mou of their land and get a better crop, but how in 1965 the reservoir had dried up in the drought of that year. Others brought up the subject of earlier well-sinking and losses incurred. How was it possible that new responsibilities could be undertaken after so many failures in the past? But Han Ping-chi and his supporters brought in Mao Tsetung Thought very effectively, so that they won out in the end.

It was in the late winter of 1966 when work was first started by the production team which brought the drill and equipment. Everyone did what they could to help. The venture was a complete success and, with the motor and pump installed, a fine stream of water flowing down the irrigation ditches greeted the spring. Many came to taste the water, youngsters leading grandparents to see, and old folk knowing what sweet water meant weeping a bit and unable to tear themselves away from the looking, while youngsters jumped and shouted for joy. The brigade now went ahead and sank three more wells. This was before the time concrete pipes were mainly used, and when the more expensive iron piping was still needed. Yet the total of 65,000 yuan raised was well spent, for in the next year a harvest of 620 jin of grain a mou was obtained. In 1970, as result of still better work being done on land levelling, seed selection and fertilisers along with continued washing of the land of its alkali content, 871 jin a mou of grain was gained, and 135 jin of cleaned cotton.

The target for 1971 is over 1,000 jin of grain a mou, utterly unthinkable once, now well within the realm of reality. Commune members have begun to build new houses. The brigade office which had gone through previous winters without heating, now had a stove installed. Trees were planted, piggeries extended. We visited the brigade food-processing factory, finding the oil press there had been pulled down for overhaul. As in all this cotton growing country, food oil needs are met by pressing cotton seed, with the waste seedcake going to the piggery. Very little land is used for planting rape or sesame for oil. Out in the fields, we found cotton seedlings being raised in beds covered with plastic sheeting. They are transplanted like rice seedlings, following the method established by a model farmer in Shansi. On most of the land put into cotton, seeds are sown the ordinary way, missing spaces in the growing crop being filled in by transplantation. Some land also is entirely sown by transplants. Down in the Laoyang riverbed, rice paddies were laid out.

Now the mood of the people has become confident, and unlike other times, the young men have no trouble at all in finding a wife willing to come and live in Hsiaohanchuang. In 1970, above the surplus grain and cotton sold to the state, the brigade built up a good grain reserve of its own, and in addition put 153,000 yuan into its funds. People now talk with appreciation of the strength of Mao Tsetung Thought, what it has done in carrying through the class struggle, in Hai river conservancy, and in promoting self-reliance. Relatively, the people are still poor enough, but they have grown in struggle and are no longer backward. In material things they are certainly better off than the old-time rich peasants. From being a wedge of rolling country, disfigured by big patches of glassy alkali on which nothing would grow at all, the land of Hsiaohanchuang is now set out evenly in flat, rectangular fields surrounded by irrigation channels lined with graceful poplars. The place presented a real picture on a spring day with the wheat, a deep rich green, being smoothed over by the breeze and the trees bursting into leaf. This year 330 mou was being put into cotton, and there were 300 growing winter wheat. Fifty mou will be in peanuts and then there will be some cotton and barley grown in alternate rows. More land is being reclaimed from the Laoyang riverbed and put into paddy, as work strength allows.

The brigade has a six-year school and a health clinic with a "barefoot" doctor. All homes have electric light. We went into one farmhouse compound where a number of women were shelling peanuts. There were school girls, nursing mothers and quite a few grandmothers, making up a happy, laughing bunch. There were no idle people to be seen in Hsiaohanchuang, yet the group work there seemed to be brimming over with vitality. Han Ping-chi said that though the brigade population had almost doubled since Liberation in 1945, yet one of the main problems still was a shortage of labor power. So many things ever pressing to be worked on, yet now with all pulling together, much could be done. When the decision came to sink the first deep well, the membership decided they would not go to the state for a loan to cover its cost, but would take 13,000 yuan from their own funds to complete the job. At that time they were not in the solid financial position they are today so this meant a good deal, especially as previous attempts to cure their problem of drought had not succeeded. Han Ping-chi, though with a growing family and many responsibilities in the brigade, preserves a youthful spirit, and is full of enthusiasm for the future. After he had told us about it, he said he hoped to learn more from Tachai and other good brigades in China, then too from the peoples of Indo-China, Korea, New Zealand and other countries. Then how he hoped that his people in their struggle would through it be better able to support the Chinese and world revolutions.

Local Industry

Small industry in Hengshui has grown from nothing to something in these years. In 1954, a number of small metal-working handicraft co-operatives came together to form a factory for making farm tools. Their production at that time consisted mainly of galvanised iron kettles, chimney pipes for stoves and simple tools. Then in the Leap Forward of 1958 it was organised into a regular metal-working plant, with 60 workers to begin with, and a start being made on bigger jobs. In 1961, however, the Liu Shao-chi line came into force, saying that expansion had been too fast, and so on. So the plant remained static until 1966, when with the start of the Cultural Revolution came the end of the Liu Shao-chi line. Workers, with their spirit burning brightly, now demanded the change to serve the people better, turning to and building better machines and making new products. Today the original plant has spread out and around, with 460 workers, 300 of whom are men and the remainder local lasses. In 1968 they made 400,000 yuan worth of products, and in 1970, 1,320,000 yuan worth.

Their well-sinking machinery is now much in demand. In Peking the present unit now being produced was demonstrated; successfully going down to water at 160 metres, 40 metres of which was rock. At Canton in the autumn fair of 1970, they went down 105 metres, 80 metres rock. The first drilling machine had a vertical set-up, which sometimes caused the drill to deviate. Now with the main drilling block in a horizontal position and with a gear box added, speeds can be regulated and control of the drill better maintained. The drill can reach a depth of up to 303 metres. The first drilling set weighed a ton and a half. The new type workers have evolved is but 260 kilograms, and can be easily loaded on one of the rubber-tyred carts common in the farming districts around. A 10-12 h.p. motor operates it, the working group responsible for putting down the well usually consisting of 15 people. Hengshui county alone has 60 such groups operating. The plant not only makes the well-sinking assembly, but also trains workers from the communes in its use, ever sending workers out into the country to help train fresh groups who are learning by doing.

The factory now has in all some 37 lines of production. Amongst the more outstanding ones is the automatic circuit breaker so important in spreading electrification. Others are mainly consumer goods important locally for all brigade marketing and supply stores. The people need strong, well made consumer goods — scissors and hair clippers for barbers, pocket knives, eyelets for shoe laces and a whole range of such things the now well-equipped factory can provide. No reason why these items can only be made in cities. In many cases the hinterland can support some of the needs of the cities for such things, as well as helping the export market. Before 1966, the plant had very poor tooling. A few old lathes and bench tools were about all. Now it has 85 modern tools and is making a series of new-type lathes for its own use. It already has the beginnings of automation in making some of the consumer goods. The trend will obviously increase as industrialisation goes into further stages. Wages are 50 yuan a month for the older workers, starting at 30 yuan for the youngest. There are two local cadres serving in the factory administration, one of whom is the leader of the factory Revolutionary Committee. There are no engineers or technicians, or graduates from technical schools.

I talked with Kao Feng-chou, a 50-year-old worker, who had come along with the plant ever since he was an apprentice in one of the small handicraft shops that went to make up the first factory unit. He has a family of ten, wife, mother and seven children, three of whom are already out working. He is leader of one of the shops, and obviously the type that workers like and will follow. I also spoke to a girl, Chen Shu-ping, 19 years old, who had come to the factory from middle school in Tsaochiang county a year ago. She has been back home once since coming, and is thrilled to be working on a milling machine. Then I talked to Chang Tse-chun, a youth looking 20, who came from a Hengshui middle school. He has two young sisters at home, and loves his work because everyone helps him and he is learning so much and happy that his long cherished ambition to become a machine worker is coming true.

One afternoon I paid a visit to the Hengshui power plant and the factory attached to it. The power plant, a coal-burning one, has three generators, all rather old, one Japanese and two German-made. Their rated capacity all together is 3,500 kws. In the Cultural Revolution, with added demands for power, the workers took a good look at the generators and wondered if they could get more from them. With no one like Liu Shao-chi to say them nay, they went into a huddle and then made new history. With some changes to the boiler and steam turbine, adding better cooling, and some other changes to one generator, they managed to increase its output 66 percent. Though rated at 1,500 kws, it did not usually give more than 1,200. When it was first stepped up, it ran at 2,500 kws but not so steadily. Reduced to 2,200 kws it went well. Now, however, with more problems solved, it runs merrily along at 2,500 kws all the time. Next will come the second and third generators, after the busy time for commune irrigation work is over. The power plant is also responsible for operating an electrical appliance plant, production at the time of our visit being mainly in transformers. All appliances go to rural electrification. Of the 324 workers 54 are women, and of the whole group 188 are under 25 years of age. The factory has a record of 2,000 days without an industrial accident. The plant is well set out on extensive grounds, the shops being spacious and well lit. It was first set up in 1959, and has gone ahead in stages since then.

A distillery is a convivial place to visit. The one in Hengshui we found to be making the famous local brand of white spirit, 67° proof as against 62° for both Maotai and Fen, two nationally known liquors. Other brands of different strengths are made, and also a medicinal cordial from a local wild berry named "kou chi", which is especially useful in treating some

diseases. For the white spirits, a sweet potato is fermented and distilled.
The residue goes off for pig feed. The season for sweet potatoes is the
five months between October and March, when the full 419 workers are
employed. In the off season various other products such as starch, alcohol,
insecticide etc. are made from agricultural waste. There is a good deal of
new mechanisation in the plant. Most of the spirits go up to the colder
regions of China, the Northeast and Inner Mongolia having a demand for
it. One felt that the "kou chi" cordial should have an export trade value
if brought to people's notice.

We did a little tasting in a pleasant room, with a wealth of spring blossoms out in the yard. Ideal surroundings for the task. In its present form,
the factory is one that was organised by bringing together 16 small distilleries operated by small capitalists. Production was low then, but after
mechanisation it was raised to 700 tons a year, then 1,200, on to 1,600, and
now last year, 1970, to 1,800 tons.

Well-Sinking

One day we went out to Mahweitai Commune of Wuyi county, east of
Hengshui, to look at some of the traditional type well-sinking there. The
wheat fields we saw looked somewhat dry. On some, chain pump shallow
wells were working, each of which could irrigate 20 mou. In this particular locality the water they brought up was not too alkaline for use. Localities, often quite close together, differ vastly in this respect. To work
those pumps, a donkey is blindfolded and a youngster keeps it moving
around in a circle.

But we had come to see the traditional percussion well-sinking method
which members of Tunghsiangting Brigade were using. We went across
country to where the work was being done at the tall timber structure,
lengths lashed together in the centuries' old style. A group of brigade
members would raise and drop the iron pipe plunger, taking hold of the
big handle to lift it, assisted by the bow rope from above, and then heave
it down again. When the iron pipe with its bit was clogged up with earth
and rock, members would get into the treadmill above and, turning it with
their feet, wind the bamboo-strip rope up, plunger attached, which would
then be cleaned. For relatively shallow wells this old method is quite
efficient, but when stone is met on deeper ones, driving through takes a
lot longer. The sinker takes about 1,000 yuan to build, and the concrete
pipe for the finished well together with pump and fittings would cost about
2,000 yuan. In areas like Mahweitai where there is no electricity yet, a
diesel engine costing around 1,000 yuan is needed to drive the pump. This
well had already gone down 170 metres and was expected to go to something over 200. Brigade members had been working on it for about three
months. As they are on workpoints, like other commune members, their
wages are not a serious factor in costs to the brigade. Some of the newer
rigs of this traditional kind now have two big wheels instead of one, which
is said to represent a considerable improvement.

We next went to Wudu Commune in Hengshui county and saw one of the new mechanised well-sinkers at work. It had already gone down 200 metres and was expected to go 50 more. There were 13 men in the team, the duties of those on shift at the time we called being in watching the machine operating. At the traditional type in Wuyi, two old peasants were in charge of the work. Men of long experience, they encouraged the members at what was really quite a back-breaking task. In this mechanised one, the team leader was a typical worker type, as were his team members. Most were youngsters in workers' overalls, learning as they went along. This mechanised well, including the iron pipe being used, will cost 13,000 yuan. The whole operation is usually completed in 15 days, and then the team moves on to a new site. Wudu Commune installed a similar well last year, and had raised production on 200 mou from less than 200 jin of grain a mou to over 500. They hope to go up to 700 jin this year, and on to 1,000 next. So naturally they are out after more deep wells for the rest of their land.

The iron pipes being used on the well have a screw fitting at each length end. Those for the deeper levels through which sweet water flows have holes in them to allow the water to seep through, the outside of the pipe being bound around with wire to keep out gravel. Sand is kept out by a thickness of stones being packed around the pipe. Iron pipe is a great deal more expensive than concrete. For a 250-foot well it would cost 6,000 yuan, while a similar length of concrete pipe would be only 700-800 yuan. It is too soon to say yet how rust will affect the iron piping, but it will certainly be a long-term factor needing to be dealt with.

We were most interested, then, to see the factory at Hengshui where the various types of cement pipes are turned out. It was an enterprise that started up at the end of 1966 in premises which before long began to be too small for the output demanded of the metre-long, 8-in. interior diameter deep-well pipe. There have been several problems to be solved in manufacture. The weight of 250-300 metres of pipe on the bottom lengths would be very great. But those going through the water-bearing strata would have to be made so that the water would flow through them, those at the very bottom being perforated, and only the top 100 metres solid. The extreme bottom lengths were made of reinforced concrete, short lengths of corn cob being inserted through the wire netting reinforcement so that there would be holes left after the cement was poured. The major portions of the lengths above the bottom ones were, except for the rims, made of concrete and gravel conglomerate through which water could easily pass. To be strong enough yet porous was the problem that had to be solved. So far, results have been most encouraging. More problems will come when still deeper levels are to be reached. Lengths have their joints tar-sealed as they are installed.

The grasp of all these problems that Cheng Hao, the experienced leader in charge of technical matters, shows is impressive. Himself an old construction worker, it has been he together with the other workers who have designed the machines and layout of the new factory started in 1969 and going into production in 1970. We spent an afternoon there visiting.

Some of the workers were busy constructing new staff housing, while in the production shops of the plant work went on with a determined swing. Local demand for the pipe is now being met satisfactorily. There are 278 workers, 27 of whom are middle-school graduates sent in from the various counties around. Present production runs at 1,200 pipes a day, six times the number being produced when the first plant was set up in 1966. The old factory, being beside the main highway, is now used as a depot for the communes to send members to and get their pipes, there being a constant stream of carts carrying them away to new well sites. At one place near Hengshui we passed a tall, shaggy white camel, majestically padding down the macadamised highway, his long wool flying in the spring wind, pulling a rubber-tyred cart piled high with deep well pipe lengths. A picture one does not see so often in these times of advancing mechanisation.

The days at Hengshui went swiftly. The evening before we left we attended a concert given by members of local organisations, mostly youth. The star piece was an act from the modern opera "Taking Tiger Mountain by Strategy" done by primary school children. Their youthful freshness gave the piece added piquancy.

There are several things seen in the China of the past few years that show well what serving the people really means. There is the pump turbine of south China, in its tens of thousands now, the cement boat of the lower Yangtze, and here in central Hopei, the deep well. These things have all made life so much richer, enabling so much more to be done. Before leaving Hengshui I wrote the following lines:

> *Over the years in*
> *the not too distant past*
> *have folk died bitterly*
> *on this great plain of*
> *north China; countless*
> *families wiped out by*
> *famine that followed droughts;*
> *how many eyes have stared*
> *hopelessly at parched fields!*
> *How many sighed it was their fate*
> *unchangeable, predetermined, not*
> *realising their own strength,*
> *minds stifled by feudalism.*

> *Today*
> *the people have come together;*
> *red banners flutter, as groups*
> *work amongst the green of*
> *swiftly growing wheat, irrigated*
> *by sparkling streams of water*
> *wrested from the bowels of the earth*
> *deep below; water which had*
> *always been there, unused and useless*

as long as people could not reach it,
while shallow wells often gave
but poor saline water, even if
they did not dry up.

Now mechanised well sinkers
save on human toil, driving
bits almost nonchalantly on
through rock and sand to
two hundred, three hundred
metres; the well is piped
and a power pump throws up
sweet water which washes out
alkali, irrigates and makes
the land live. City walls
which spelt security for
money lenders, officials
and landlords have crumbled,
but now high-voltage transmission
lines cross the land; transformer
stations send power to communes,
motors hum, rich harvests
come even in drought years,
a way has been found.

Deep, clear thinking
brings deep wells with
clear, sweet water to a people
organised and militant;
people to whom difficulties
now fall as grain before
the reaper, and marvelling
old peasants say, "It seems
there is now no limit
to what this land we have
toiled so long on, can
be made to do!"

Shihchiachuang

Four hours south of Peking by train, Shihchiachuang is now the capital of Hopei province. Paoting and Tientsin have both held that position in the past, but the growing Shihchiachuang, at the junction of the east and west lines linking Shantung and Shansi, with the north and south railway between Peking and Canton, and with an increasing industrial potential, seems destined now to be the permanent provincial capital. The centre of some of the best cotton growing country in north China, it now has six modern cotton mills. Arriving in the early evening, we saw the broad highways full of workers going home at the end of their shift. As both an industrial and agricultural centre, it is an up-and-coming worker and peasant city. There had been many improvements made since I last came here to stay a while, now six years ago.

The first improvement that comes to notice is the underpass the main boulevard makes beneath the railway. Organised townsfolk, giving voluntary service, completed it recently in three months of tough work. Another major bit of public works has been the laying out of a square and the building of a provincial hall of the people, a smaller edition of the big one in Peking. The guest house we came to was spick and span, shining with new paint, having recently been reconditioned. In Peking when we left, the poplar trees had not yet come out in leaf, but here they had already done so, while the ash trees were already starting to grow green also. The peach blossom brought to mind the masses of peach bloom each year at Shenhsien, a county town a little northeast of Shih-chiachuang. The peaches of Shenhsien and the pears of Chaochow are famous in these parts.

Chaochow, another county town 25 miles southeast of Shihchiachuang by macadamised road, is famous in Chinese and world engineering history as the place where in the Sui period, 605 A.D., a wonderful single-span bridge was built. It still stands, and today one may find copies of it in many parts of China where stone bridges are still being built to save on reinforced concrete construction. We took the opportunity to see it again. Now the Hsiaoshui river which it spans is dry, having been made part of the Hai river conservancy scheme, to be used as a runoff when necessary. The bed has been cleaned out and each bank dyked. The bridge itself is well cared for, foot traffic only being permitted, while heavy wheeled traffic goes over a new bridge nearby. There is a museum of stone sculpture in the well-kept gardens not far away, all in a good state of preservation.

We had tea in the little guest room of the curator, enjoying the mass of white lilac in bloom at the window. I was given a big bunch of it to take back to Shihchiachuang where it filled my room with its scent. The bridge has a span of 37.37 metres, and rises 7.23 metres. It has two spandrel arches at each end to take floodwaters, and its arch consists of 38 parallel lines of arch stones. Not much is known about its designer except that his name was Li Chun. The folklore about it has been subject matter for children's stories for generations, but such can no longer be sold, the youngsters simply snorting, "No such thing! Nonsense!"

Our first call in Shihchiachuang city was to the memorial park for revolutionary heroes. Since I last came, a new statue of Dr. Bethune had been erected in front of his grave. There was a large gathering of school children sitting under the trees nearby, while one of the memorial park cadres told them Bethune's history. They had hiked in from surrounding counties, but the little boy I asked stoutly denied that he was tired. The park looked very lovely with spring and early summer blossom.

A sad touch came when visiting the memorial hall and seeing there the picture of Dr. Kotnis, the Indian doctor I had gone with to Yenan in 1939. He had married in the guerilla regions, and his son lived on after his father died. In these last years the son, a PLA fighter, died too, so that his picture is also in the hall.

During the Japanese occupation, the name "Shihchiachuang" was dropped and the more high-sounding one of "Shih Men Municipality" adopted. With the victory of the liberation forces, however, the old name with its fine peasant association was restored. In those days there was not much industry. A small cotton mill, and then the pride of the place, the Chiaohsi coking plant which takes its coal from the Chinghsing valley, the corridor running from Shihchiachuang to Shansi. It was started in a simple way in 1906 at a place some distance from what was then the town. In 1925, German experts came to modernise it but did not finish before the outbreak of the War of Resistance in 1937, when they left. In 1953 it was producing but 30,000 tons of coke a year, and the ratio between the value of coke and chemical industry products then was seven to three. Now it has reversed to become three to seven, though today the plant produces 640,000 tons of coke a year, and with the putting into production of the new coke ovens the workers are now erecting will raise that total to 800,000 tons. "Even then," the leading cadre said, "we still will be, as we have always been, the smallest plant of our kind in China." Yet, in an age when petrochemicals are becoming more and more popular, there is still a place for coal distillation. The 890 workers here have shown extraordinary genius in developing the plant, in experiment and in innovations, well converting Mao Tsetung Thought into material advance. In 1970 they were able to turn over to the state 2,300,000 yuan. They have made do with old equipment, altering it, modernising it and raising its efficiency.

During the Great Leap Forward the plant was asked to make coumarin, but while some experts protested that it was not possible for a small plant to make what the country had not yet produced, workers rose to the challenge. Coumarin, the substance in sweet clover that gives mown hay its pleasant smell, is also a product of the distillation of coal tar and is an important component used in the rubber-tyre industry. To bring it from abroad costs around 8,000 yuan a ton. Here, the light-colored product can be produced for 2,500 yuan a ton, and the all-black one, just as effective where color is not a consideration, for 1,500 yuan. In its manufacture, workers created a new method. As they progressed they added some 40 innovations, pushing up the output to 11 times the original. The plant is producing or has successfully trial-produced 60 different products — from coke, fertiliser, dyes, phenol, naphthalene and coumarin down through a whole range of chemicals — some important in the manufacture of synthetic fibres, medicines, etc. Always workers have tried to use the materials they have in hand, ever raising efficiency and output. Over the past 12 years they have handed over 21 million yuan to the state, 50 times more than the total state investment in the plant. "Just a small place," the leading cadre said modestly, "with a lot of old equipment we have tried to make better use of. We have made many mistakes and have many shortcomings." To me, in going through the plant, their greatest triumph seemed in building up an able work force, resourceful and creative, capable not only of altering this plant as necessity arises, but to build still more advanced plants in what is now a rapidly industrialising society.

Shihchiachuang has another excellent example of what can be done when the spirit of workers is unleashed. It was seen on a visit to the cloth printing mill, where some 2,000 workers turn out printed cloth both for the internal and for the export market. The plant is a modern one set up in the Great Leap Forward of 1958-59, all of its machinery being made in China. Most of the workers are local folk, many of them middle-school graduates. The oldest workers are those who came to help the factory to set up, just a few of the many hundreds of thousands of technical workers Shanghai, that great hub of industry, has contributed to the development of the hinterland. Organised in the usual way factories were at that time, with a hierarchy of manager, assistant managers, engineers, technicians, division chiefs and what not, it was planned as one that would produce 400,000 metres of printed cloth a year, but up to the end of 1966 it had never been able to produce more than 360,000.

In 1968, a Revolutionary Committee was set up, and the old conventions were done away with. The Revolutionary Committee was organised of workers, cadres and technicians which set out to give rein to the creative ability of the working force and have it actively take part in advancing factory production. In 1968, so well did they do their task, that 800,000 metres of printed cloth were produced. In 1969 the total was 1,200,000 metres, which figure has been maintained since. In this last year, much attention has been paid to further technical innovations that will speed up the process in the future and make it still more economical. For instance, one enterprising textile worker thought of a way to size cloth with white clay, which has eliminated the need of using fine white flour for that purpose. The invention has spread. Two other young men, one who joined the factory staff in 1964 and the other in 1968, have invented a machine that cuts patterns on the cotton or nylon printing rollers, doing in a mere two hours a job that took a skilled worker two days to do by hand. The nylon printing rollers are another innovation, as is the use of plastics for many other things copper was once used for. Another young worker had produced a small transformer that changed alternating to direct current, and also regulated supply according to the machine's need. Now, no material incentives are given as was the old way, incentives that ever bred animosities amongst workers. Everyone helps the innovator, who himself or herself feels that what is being done is being done for the revolution. In the pre-Cultural Revolution period, workers would often put up an idea, but by the time it had gone through various offices it would probably have been tossed out as something that would upset the regular order of things.

We walked around the plant and saw what was being done. The average wage is 50 yuan a month, and each day there are three shifts of eight hours each. Workers study for an hour and a half outside work hours each day, usually finding a quiet shady spot on the grounds under the trees for this. The old flower gardens of the compound have been converted to grow vegetables, one portion being assigned to the clinic for raising medicinal herbs.

It had become warm by the time we were ready to leave Shihchia-chuang. The days had been pleasant, and one had learnt much. It was good to have come and it would be good to come again. Thinking of the visit to Bethune's grave I wrote these lines:

> Late April, and an early
> breath of summer; a park
> where against a background
> of evergreens, there blooms
> wisteria, lilac, peach and apricot,
> filling the air with sweet
> perfume; here lie the remains
> of many who served their people
> well, and died so that
> the generations who follow
> should have the freedom to work
> and live, to learn and to fight
> harder. Amongst these there stands
> a memorial statue to the doctor
> from Canada, who came
> to help when need was greatest;
> Bethune who worked and died,
> one with those who gave
> their all.

> A statue that lives
> a thin, eager figure
> bare feet in grass sandals
> representing the working
> people of the world, and
> an internationalism that is
> the hope of man to be.

> And all around the memorial
> cluster youngsters who
> have come in from the village;
> a good thousand or so
> of them sitting under the shade
> of trees just coming into leaf
> listening as the story of this
> revolutionary is told, a story
> so simple, yet so full of meaning.

Chinglung County and the Struggle for Self-Sufficiency

We came up the highway from Luanhsien in north Hopei again, over downs rich with summer crops, until we arrived at the Luan river crossing at Lungtoushan where an able crew of ferrymen got us over the silt-laden river despite the sand banks and the swift current.   Then at Chienan we halted a while, ate some of the good peaches grown there, and listened to a piece of the story of a county of 450,000 people who are now doing better than they have ever done before with grain production and general living conditions.   From Chienan to the Great Wall was not so far, and there at Lengkou, Cold Pass, we went through the ancient battlements and were in Chinglung county of Chengteh prefecture, once known as Jehol.   It is a county of hills, eroded in the past but now being replanted with trees, where some 400,000 or more people in 43 communes refuse to accept poor livelihood and are determinedly going about changing their county in the spirit of Tachai.

There was much of interest all along the road from Chienan north. As we approached Lengkou, we passed through a big village, once a Great Wall garrison barracks, called Chienchangying.   It has no fewer than 10,000 families — more than the county seat.   It is one commune of 28 brigades.   Some of the old wall at Lengkou Pass has been taken down for construction purposes, but its majestic sweep of tower and battlement over the hilltops on either side is still solidly impressive.   Coming up the valley to the county town we passed Shaho, a river where the local commune folk were busy with a big diversion scheme to utilise not only the surface water of the river but also that which runs in the sands underground.   Finally, driving on until we came to the county centre, we found over the main street at the entrance a big arch with the words: "We must learn from Tachai."

And what a beautifully clean little town it was, reminding us of the newly constructed Peitaiho we had left after an early breakfast in the morning.   Another surprise awaited us at the guest house.   The girl demonstrator Li Kwei-chen who had explained one of the models at the autumn 1970 Export Commodities Fair, a very moving one which showed some of the more dramatic pieces of work the county is doing, was there to meet us, as beautiful and alive as ever.   She is one of a commune family of seven, and quite an authority on progress in Chinglung. Actually, it was seeing the model she demonstrated so well that had made us especially anxious to see it all in real life.   Model of what a people, once so desperately poor, had been able to do for themselves once they gained the determination and organisation to do it.   They have had long experience of bitter times.   Under the long years of Japanese occupation, they were included in the puppet state of "Manchukuo".   One big area of the county was designated by the Japanese imperial army as "no man's land" where all homes were burnt and any living thing was killed on sight.   Yet they were liberated earlier than many counties in these parts, for the Eighth Route Army had penetrated the villages and taken over straight after the Japanese defeat.

Only one tenth of the 3,314 square kilometres of the county can be used for agriculture.   The rest is mountain and riverbed.   The highest mountain is Dushan, 5,400 ft high, and then there is a long ridge called Laoling, 4,200 ft high, from which one can view the sea below.   North is

Liaoning province, south of the Great Wall the counties of Tangshan prefecture. The biggest of the five rivers of the county is the Chinglung, which flows into the Luan river at Lulung.

It is called "Chinglung" or "Green Dragon", as once in the days when all of its hills and mountains were forested the river ran bright and clear, not carrying any of the eroded sand and silt it is charged with today. As erosion came the riverbeds widened, river flats were washed away, the climate became more arid and livelihood for the people became more difficult. In consequence, the settlers of today have an uphill fight in front of them all the time.

Kaoliang (sorghum) is the major crop, 200,000 mou being planted with it. Millet, corn, beans and sweet potatoes make up most of the rest. Newly recovered river flats are now doing well in rice. Pears, apples, apricots, chestnuts have been widely planted these years and give good crops. Medicinal herbs are found, as well as some minerals, plenty of iron ore, some anthracite and scattered deposits of gold, platinum and copper. In pre-Liberation times the highest yield of grain ever obtained was 113 jin a mou. That was in 1943. By the time officials and landlords had taken their share there was never enough to see people through the year. Many ran off to Heilungkiang in search of something more. Until the communes were organised in 1958 the area was always on relief grain. Then with better organisation, grain totals began to rise until they reached 200 jin a mou and relief grain could be done without.

During the Cultural Revolution, all-over average grain totals went up to 370 jin a mou in 1969, and 449 jin a mou in 1970. Some brigades got 500-600 jin. One 800 jin. In 1970, 20,600,000 jin was sold to the state, with 22 million jin in addition being put into commune reserve stores. To get these results, people have really had to work and plan. They have thrown up 2,183 dams big and small, turning the water into hundreds of li of irrigation ditches. Of the 44 reservoirs built or still in building, 21 are storing water already. Pump turbines have been installed in 106 places, 126 of them in all. Eighty-four small power plants have been set up, generating 1,215 kws in all. Sixteen more will be completed before the end of the year, which will bring the county total to 2,460 kws. All quite small when compared with the grid that runs over the flat country between big industrial centres. The Liu Shao-chi line thought that small installations were foolish. There should be a large state investment in a county which would do a big job, and people should wait for that. Or people should wait until the grid outside the wall had more power stations pumping into it, so that high tension pylons could come stalking over the mountains, and there would be enough wiring to bring electricity to every hamlet. How long they would have to wait, he did not say.

The Mao Tsetung line is self-sufficiency right away, with people training themselves as organisers and as technicians while they produce electricity, bring in irrigation and do all they have to do. Chinglung now has installed power plants on the county, commune, production brigade and team levels everywhere. Short of copper wire, they open a small copper mine and take six tons of copper to the Tientsin refinery where they get the value in copper wire and are in addition paid for the gold their product also contains. Short of cash to buy essentials, people weave baskets, sell fruit, pan gold in mountain streams, cut firewood to sell. They have asked the state for nothing, and through their struggles they have produced a new people. There are now 14 well-qualified electrical engineers trained by the county and over 600 commune electricians who come in groups to the county power station for additional courses all the time. For a new power station now being built two 800-kw. turbines are needed. They are being built locally in the county machine shops. Short of cement for power plant work, a vertical cement burning plant has been set up which produces what is needed. Before the Cultural Revolution, 15,000 mou had been irrigated. Now the total is 50,000 mou. The power that has been generated takes a big burden from the lives of the women-folk especially, who in the past spent so much time on grain processing, liberating them for collective work in their production teams. Now 32 of the 43 communes have electricity in at least some of their brigades — 110 of them so far. Twelve communes have radio broadcasting systems. Step by step, all work together bringing Mao Tsetung Thought right down to the practical things that people live by. The general idea of not taking anything from the state that the people can make themselves is now para-mount. Let the state use its resources for ever bigger things, they wisely say. It is our state, we made it, and we want it to succeed.

No explosives? So we will not go out to buy with borrowed money, but just make what we can ourselves. Explosive of a new kind that experi-ence has taught us how to make, and which does all that is needed. We keep all projects going throughout the year, though in busy times com-mune members in the main go out into the fields, returning in the slack periods. Stories are many of old men and women who refuse to be laid aside in retirement but who look after the children. Also many are stories of those who have braved sub-zero weather to get down into icy slush and do a job that had to be done. The struggle for self-sufficiency is revolutionary practice, and where there is a will there is certainly a way. The PLA men have brought in some new method, for instance that of breaking stone, which cuts out the wielding of heavy sledge hammers and does the job better with a simple rig. But as work proceeds, new creative innovations always appear. Only when people sit and wait for some upper authority to present them with what they need, suitably served, does the creative urge die.

Folk in Chinglung are very frank on their own shortcomings. They talked of the technical mistakes made so far, trying to irrigate before a proper land levelling was carried through. Not planning the situation of terraced fields well enough so that they could be easily irrigated, and so on. Each mistake, however, leads on to rectification from which all learn much, so well has the point been discussed in meetings. There are 130,000 working people in the county, who in the last year have put in 42 million workdays, 25 percent of which have been put into power, pumping stations, or general irrigation projects.

It was raining a little when we set out to go across country through many villages, until we came to a ferry crossing on the Chinglung river and went over it to Tunghaotsun Brigade. A fairly narrow river here, though very swift until big rains come and the denuded mountains which are the legacy of centuries quickly drain off into it making it into a great wide torrent that tries to wreak havoc. But today the crossing was easy, and soon we were sitting with Li Tsun-kiang, the brigade leader, while he told us something of the struggles of the past ten years. How the brigade had decided to dyke in a considerable part of the riverbed, and to bring in a canal to generate power for pumping and for commune use. How officials following the Liu Shao-chi line ordered the work to be stopped, and then how a big flood came and swept both dyke and power station away. Then how in the movement for socialist education the project was started all over again, work going on into the Cultural Revolution except for a brief stop during the struggle that raged for a while between opposing groups. The big stone dyke, over two kilometres long, has been completed and the women of the brigade have planted a wide swathe of trees inside it which now grow tall.

The canal intake has been strongly made, and 2,600 metres of canal have been dug to take the water to the powerhouse where an 84-kw. generator spins merrily and many machines turn, for food processing, fodder preparation and for the machine tools of the little repair shop. All homes and roads in the village are lit by electricity, and Radio Peking comes over loudspeakers. Electrically operated pumps irrigate the whole 1,200 mou of good land that has been enclosed by the dyke, and take water up to the lower hillside terraces as well. It all sounds rather idyllic, and on a bright summer's day certainly looks so, with tall corn planted between strips of young high-yield kaoliang, or else some low crop such as sweet potatoes. This practice raises crop production a great deal, letting in the light which plants need. With seed selection, better fertiliser, plenty of irrigation at the right time and people putting their whole spirit into the work, crop increases have been marked. They have gone up from 200 jin a mou in the 'fifties to 812 jin a mou in 1970. The 1971 crop promises to be higher than any ever gained so far. State grain quotas have been amply filled. The brigade carries a large reserve and has bought a new standard-size Loyang tractor and transport trailer, which we saw bringing in chemical fertiliser in preparation for the next season's sowing.

Chinglung as a county is a fairly new creation. Once it was largely forested, the flats being worked by refugees from Hopei. Before the mad ferocity of the Japanese invasion the three main troubles amongst the people were opium which was then widely grown, bandits, and bubonic plague, which at times swept away whole villages. The place was once administered from Chienan, south of the Great Wall. When the Japanese came in, another evil came with the ill-famed state of "Manchukuo". The poverty was indescribable, few peasant families having enough food and clothing for the bitter, long winters. It is good for children to run naked in warm summer days with a convenient stream beside, letting sunlight build bone and strength, but a bitter thing when snow lies thick and there is not enough grain in the home to stave off perpetual hunger.

When the first settlers came 300 years ago to Haotsun, it was overgrown with "haotsao", a common weedy grass here. They built their homes and tilled as best they could, but the name "Hao" remained as a reminder of their past history. In those bitter days, 78 families went off as refugees to the Northeast, while 28 families died out. In a big flood in 1930, 20 families with their houses were swept away. Today there are 342 families, 1,842 people in all. They live, and are living better all the time off 1,787 mou of land, not quite one mou per person. Grain allowance per person is 500 jin a year. It has not been easy to swing them all into line behind the idea of self-sufficiency, of course. There have been the old doubters, the conservatives and those inherently against the new order who would say, "Anyone who tries to get the better of the Chinglung river will come off second best. We are fools being led by fools!" But the majority were keen to show what they could do, and the doubters soon found that they had lost the argument.

When it came to raising the money for the power station project, many brought out their savings. It cost 130,000 yuan in all, 22 percent of which came from the state as a loan. Economy was the watchword in all that was done. Much extemporisation was put into effect until better practice could be used. For instance, the generator was first driven by a wooden wheel, later to be changed to a standard turbine. There are many tales of heroism amongst workers in their task of working through the cold winters. Wang Wen-hui worked at the power station and puzzled all the time about the right way to get the work done. In an accident he lost a good deal of the flesh from two fingers. Three days off, and he was back at work despite the pain. He was one of a little group of labor heroes who gathered at the brigade office to meet us. They were impressive. Two old men, one over 80 who entertained workers at rest periods with clappers, the other, a quiet 69 who with his long experience led in some of the more hazardous jobs that summer floods or sub-zero winters called for. Li Yun-hsiang whom people call the "mountain tiger" because he faces any danger, is a young militia man, now 20 years old. Then another was a tough, square-set peasant type in his early forties, a man of cool daring and great ability respected by all for his contribution to the construction work done. They were all good to meet.

The work that has been done at the intake of the water race is impressive. Taking advantage of a rocky promontory to swing the main force of the flooded river away, it is sturdily set with its sluice gate admitting all the water required. Down in the generating station we found many machines working away merrily. In the machine shops, there was a home-made power hammer pounding on the iron coming from the adjacent forge. Food processing of many kinds was in swing. Next door was a 100-kw. plant being installed for the commune, there being enough water to power both the brigade's plant and the commune's. It was curiously moving to see all of this tucked away amongst fields of tall sorghum and corn, in a place with so desperate a history behind it.

The visit to Haotsun was made in two stages. During the first came a call to return to Peking. The first thing done after return a few days later was to resume at Haotsun where we had left off, seeing all the things we had missed on the first visit. The trip to Peking and back over the mountains of Kwancheng county and then through Hsifengkou of the Great Wall to Hsinglung took us through some majestic scenery — great, tall red cliffs with a lone pine on top, swift rivers and waterfalls cascading down mountainsides. The rain and mist added to the beauty. Chinglung county, they say, is 80 percent mountains, 10 percent eroded riverbeds and 10 percent tilled land. Hsinglung on the other hand, they say, is 90 percent mountains, 5 percent riverbeds and 5 percent arable land. After passing through it going and coming, I wrote these lines:

> *Hsinglung of Chengteh*
> *called "Prosperity"*
> *perhaps because it just wanted*
> *to be that, but was not; now*
> *coming out of a past that was*
> *choked with bitterness;*
> *hungry children standing naked*
> *in winter snows; eyes staring*
> *from faces prematurely dulled*
> *by one tragedy after another,*
> *unable to lift them and appreciate*
> *the scenic glory they lived in.*
>
> *And now as we pass over*
> *a new highway, mists float*
> *in between tall mountain*
> *peaks; high on a lone red*
> *cliff stands a lone pine*
> *in all its delicate beauty;*
> *waterfalls cascade down*
> *steep hillsides, and in*
> *the valleys people set about*
> *making all they have over*
> *anew, finding better ways*
> *to make waters work for them,*
> *mountain slopes grow forests*
> *and orchards even while*
> *folk sleep, and now well fed*
>
> *children in summer*
> *like golden shafts*
> *of sunlight playing in*
> *rippling streams, or racing*
> *down hill paths amongst*
> *tall crops of corn whose*
> *leaves rustle together in*

the warm and pleasant wind;
these who will so soon
take up the struggle, clothing
their land of mountain and stream
in new verdure, making it
the truly lovely thing it
was surely meant to be.

Kwancheng county is one of 140,000 people, and Hsinglung has 250,000. One noticed a number of small electric power station projects, one of which had made a tunnel 200 feet long through a mountain, gaining enough power from its little hydro-electric plant to supply ten brigades. But with all these mountain counties the big problem is that of labor power. Crops have to be attended to first. Planting trees in spring and autumn means that holes have to be dug down into the rock, filled with earth, and then the young tree watered until it takes root properly. Irrigation work must be done and in the valleys protective dykes constructed to keep back floods, while incessant struggle must go ahead on bringing in more land, which means much stone cutting and building for terrace facings. So people need to be tough, high-spirited and resourceful to be able to put the policy of maximum self-sufficiency into effect and, taking into consideration their limited human resources, to tackle first things first.

Ulan Commune has a Mongolian name, meaning "Red". We halted by the road after leaving Haotsun in Chinglung to see where a water turbine down by the Chinglung river threw water up a hillside 500 metres away, where it could descend and irrigate the terraced land below. Then we went to Kanho Brigade where a considerable job has been done in irrigation and electrification. The whole commune has 2,830 families, 15,265 people in all farming 19,000 mou of land, 3,800 mou of which is irrigated, with plans for more now being made possible by local electrification. The present electric power station was started at the end of 1966 and completed on July 1st 1970. It cost in all 316,000 yuan, of which the state gave 100,000. The canal which serves it with water from the Chinglung river is 3,000 metres long, and in one place has to run through a tunnel. 310,000 workdays were put into the project, technicians learning as they went along, and having the advantage of being able to go to the already completed Haotsun project and compare notes. The county helped by having iron workers, electricians, carpenters and plasterers trained in a county class organised for the purpose. The project has been a success, and electric power now goes to five of the commune brigades.

A feature of Chinglung is the way children everywhere can sing long passages from the new model operas. One can hear groups of them in different parts of the town in the evenings doing so, and even kindergarten children in commune brigades put on a performance with them. One night in Chinglung the county drama group gave a concert, which we attended. The first part of the program consisted in dramatising topical things of everyday life — installing small hydro-electric power stations, irrigation, forestry and the like. The second consisted in selections from two of the new model operas faultlessly presented. No wonder the people of Haotsun and Ulan Commune sing bits as they go about their work. From Ulan Commune we went on to Shuangshantze Commune where at Wafang Brigade we visited another little power station generating 84 kws. It was made in the Chinglung agricultural implements factory. Shuangshantze Commune has 13 brigades of 12,558 people who farm 16,000 mou of the light, sandy soil below the mountains. The power station can already help the 31 production teams of six brigades. Two more generating stations are being built to help the rest with pumping water, power for lighting and food-processing machines.

The Wafang station is fed by a canal 2,126 metres long which comes through 216 metres of hill tunnelling. The whole project took around 50,000 workdays to complete. It powers a small repair shop with lathe and other tools made in the Chinglung machine shops. One of the things the new power station has made possible is the installation of some 3,000 loudspeakers in the villages, which helps people to keep in touch with what is going on. 1,200 homes have electric lighting.

This all in a countryside the people of which were classified by Japanese imperialism as third-class citizens, to be treated like animals, and living in what one writer of those days called "revolting misery and poverty".

Driving west of Chinglung town for 26 kilometres we came to the area of Wangchang Commune, which drains the waters coming down from one side of Chinglung's highest mountain, Tushan. Here in the Chaodaokou brigade area a power and irrigation project is being built with a dam 41 metres high and 68 metres wide, which will hold back two million cubic metres of water. Wangchang Commune has 1,573 families, 7,944 people in all, with a labor strength of 1,895. It tills 7,117 mou of land. The dam project will take 200,000 workdays, 50,000 less than planned. So far it has risen 29.5 metres high. When completed it will provide water for 168 kws of power. Other dams are planned for the upper reaches of the Tushan drainage system. Cut stone, despite the tough labor spent in obtaining it, is still cheaper for the commune than buying and hauling in cement, though a reinforced concrete foundation basework is best to have even on small dams. The county will soon have its own small cement factory, but that will provide for only some of the needs. Cutting stone blocks out on a hill face under a blazing summer's sun, as we saw being done, requires considerable fortitude which the local commune members evidently possess all right, for the tempo of the work kept on as we spent an hour on the site, admiring the fish already swimming in the reservoir, and seeing the exactness with which the stone construction was being done.

It is not only a construction site, but also a university in Mao Tsetung Thought. Like on all other county projects, a regular team keeps on with the task throughout the year, its numbers being augmented in the farmwork off seasons, mainly in the winter. The whole project will be completed by July 1st 1972. As in Haotsun it took some time to get complete understanding from everyone who had to work on it, so that they could throw themselves wholeheartedly into the task. The damage done by the Liu Shao-chi line in the years when it was paramount dealt a severe blow to the fine spirit that the Great Leap Forward generated, but with the Socialist Education Movement in the countryside and then with the Cultural Revolution, a deeper understanding of Mao Tsetung Thought as related to self-sufficiency gave new impetus. Hills could now be tunnelled, the river which had always brought death and destruction giving power to generators made in the county itself. Better crops provided the surplus with which to pay for them. Education in ordinary schools gave some general knowledge of electricity, so that it was no longer a miraculous thing, but one which could be made a servant. So the commune members working at Chaodaokou put up with fingers bleeding in the winter cold as they handled stone blocks and kept their working spirit high. The models I was told about were certainly heroes. Now they all say of their torn fingers, "That's nothing, when it's for the Chinese and world revolutions." Started in 1969, work here has been going on now for two and a half years, without any slackening. When the job is completed 12 of the Wangchang commune brigades will get power. Water already stored has been used to irrigate 5,000 mou.

Further down the valley, the runoff from the temporary power station which already uses some of the water and which in time will be replaced by the new one, has been put to work. It drives a 12-kw. generator — made in Chinghai, I noted — which had been brought to the county as a sample of what other regions find useful. It provides lighting for one brigade and moves pumps or food-processing machines in the daytime. It is a very neat, concise little plant, one of the many now being operated or planned in the county. We then went off to still another plant in the same commune, where a little dam had been made in a valley, creating a small reservoir used for raising fish, the water being taken down to a power station which gives its brigade 15 kws of electricity.

Chinglung county has its own "Tachai", a brigade that has followed close after that famous example. It is Kaolipu Brigade of Hsiaoyintze Commune, set by the Shaho river. We spent half a day there looking at the immense work that has been done in building stone-faced terraces that run up the hills on either side of the river, tier after tier of them. Not only have the members done that, but also they have pushed back the Shaho and reclaimed a sizeable area of land now transformed into rice paddy. At the same time they have brought in a 1,900-metre water race which operates two pumping stations to throw water up to the terraced land, as well as operating the brigade's food-processing machinery. The first plant put in was washed away by a flood. Now with added protection the people are confident that the second will fare better. Once a noted poor place, the brigade has now stepped out. In 1970 it harvested 577 jin a mou, 23 percent above the 1969 total. It now has 2,600 mou of forest it planted, 2,300 mou of terraced or hillside land, and the 325 mou of river flat below the village. 951 terraces have been made, the stone facing for which if put together would run for 50 kilometres. In addition to the terracing, check dams have been erected in the valleys to hold back erosion.

Surrounded by hills, it has 273 families, with 1,380 people in all, who have a labor strength of 458. Some of these go to work on state or commune projects, the 370 who remain being the entire labor force to make terraces, plant crops and look after the forest land. That the last-named task is no sinecure was brought home to us when we saw a man with a heavy wooden mallet striking trunks of young fir trees, so that many big sluggish insects fell to the ground for his killing. The pest he was after is an insect that eats the tree needles and which is able to make a whole forest of evergreens into pathetic dead trunks in a couple of seasons, if not checked. In the bigger forests up in the mountains there is a bird which feeds on such insects, the "fir crow" or "sung ya", but it is the only bird which will eat the pest. Chemicals can be sprayed effectively but it is not so easy to haul the equipment up high hills. The lad with the mallet is quite effective.

We spent a morning at two of Chinglung's young factories. The first visited was the machine shop. Big, modern, well lit and with plenty of space, quiet but for the hum of machines, it now turns out machine tools for commune repair shops, turbine pumps and other equipment necessary. It started in 1954 with 30 workers, increasing in the Great Leap Forward in 1958 to 310. Then it made such things as food-processing machines, fodder cutters and water pumps. In the Liu Shao-chi period following 1962, work staff was cut back to 24, who were told to make only things that could be sold quickly and profited on — chairs, tables, stoves and the like.

During the Socialist Education Movement starting in 1964, they began to make machinery the county needed, work strength rising to 218. With the coming of the Cultural Revolution, construction was started on pump turbines, which were already being used a lot in south China but had hardly come to the north yet. They did not have the right machine tools for some of the work and had to extemporise, but they turned out their first pump turbine in 42 days. They are now starting to make two 800-kw. turbines for a new county power station. The plant keeps two groups of workers rotating amongst the communes to help plan, instal and repair. They also help with the repair of diesel engines where such are used and other mechanisation right down to spray pumps for insecticides. The finest of their products does not yet compare with some of the products of city factories, but there have been no complaints on performance. Shifts are worked according to the need. One shop might do three shifts a day and another only one.

The other plant visited was one which called itself "Agricultural Implements Factory" but which now confined its production to motors and generators. Started in 1955 with 21 workers, it now has 161. In its earlier period it made spades, sickles and such simple farm tools as brigade repair shops now make. When its role changed as the Cultural Revolution came in, all kinds of generators and motors were taken apart to see just how they were made. With workers getting on well together, and the struggle having succeeded against the individualist who would try to keep his technique to himself and only dole it out in tiny bits, workers soon solve problems. Some have gone to big factories for a while to learn and take part in the work there. When they want machine tools, they make them themselves. The challenge now is to make the generators for the two 800-kw. turbines the machine works is building. Twenty-three of the workers are women, some of them being students from high schools who have come in. As we were in the main on this particular visit interested in small power plants, we did not go into the other county factories. The last afternoon in the city was quite hot, so we repaired to the river where a swimming pool had been made through which an offshoot of the main stream flowed. It was cold, clear water and very invigorating. A group of local school boys put on an impromptu exhibition for us, swimming in formation, diving, and full of fun. The new youth is certainly very different from anything the old order produced.

We had made many new friends in Chinglung and it was not easy to leave them when the morning of departure came. Here in this mountain county we felt a new front in the Chinese and world revolutions had opened up, and its people were ready and eager to meet the challenge.

We passed through Chinglung to Kwancheng county. Just before getting to the southern boundary at Tiehmen Pass we were going through a village when a small boy, suitably dressed in the nicest of summer attire, which is nothing, ran up out of a stream and, cupping his hands to his mouth, shouted "Have you brought the moving pictures?" We all laughed, and were still laughing when we passed over the boundary down into Tangshan prefecture again.

Thinking back on Chinglung, I wrote these lines:

> Battlements of the Great Wall
> at Lengkou, stream over
> rugged ridges, dreaming
> of past struggles that have
> surged beside them ever since
> Meng Tien, general and engineer
> of Chin had them built over
> two thousand years past; and now
> from the rolling downs of Chienan,
> we go over the pass into old Jehol,
> now Chengteh, past a village
> once the station of Japanese
> gendarmes who bullied any who
> had the temerity to want
> to go through.

>> Then change came on top of
>> change, until we are able to come
>> to a mountain county of deep
>> valleys and sparkling streams
>> where the old devils have been

laid low, old dragons spiked,
new banners raised; the urge
to be self-sufficient making
back hill villages put in their own
hydro-electric power plants;
reclaiming marshy valley bottoms
for rice paddy; carrying stone
fronted terraces boldly up
hillsides; planting new orchards,
new forests; setting up new factories
making turbines, generators, motors
machine tools; going on from
ideology to spirit, spirit to matter,
causing the people to raise their heads
and look around themselves, eyes
full of the light of dawn.

Hsiaokwanchuang and Beyond in 1971

Going south through the Great Wall from Kwancheng county in Chengteh (old Jehol) was a moving scenic experience. We went through the gorge and Great Wall at Tiehmenkwan, down south into Chienhsi, the largest and most mountainous of the 13 counties of Tangshan. As it was threatening rain and we had swollen fords to cross, we did not spend much time farewelling friends from our last place of stay at Chinglung, who had come to send us off. Rather did we press on to our immediate destination, which was a now famous brigade called Hsiaokwanchuang in Hanerchuang Commune high up amongst the hills. Hsiaokwanchuang has gained its name for its outstanding work on forestry, and for its ability to gain a self-sufficiency in grain by the making and utilisation of tiny fields terraced into the steep hillsides of its three valleys, in between forest edges and streams.

For a while we wondered where the road was taking us, for we had long left the main river valley and were going up a ravine with densely forested hills on either side of us. Finally the valley opened out, a hamlet came into view, and we were meeting the tough, sturdy people of the brigade and the tall, quiet farmer Chang Yu-ching who was their leader. He and his leading group had quite a story to tell. It went away back into the stage of the War of Resistance, when the gully had been an Eighth Route Army base and the people fought on, laying mines, cutting telephone wires, picking off enemy units and so on continuously right up to victory in 1945. Some people had their houses burnt nine times. The enemy declared the whole area a depopulated no man's land, and came frequently to try and enforce their kill all, burn all, loot all policy. But it never worked. The people did not run away. They simply faded into the forests and came back when the raid was over, salvaging all they could and planting crops on hillside patches once more.

After Liberation and land division they did better, but had to have government support with relief grain right up to 1967. In 1964-65 they learnt a great deal about the Mao Tsetung idea of self-sufficiency. Then in 1966-67 they learnt more about who are enemies and who are friends, and what the Liu Shao-chi line would have done to them if it had gone further. Some visited Tachai, others the Shashihyu and Hsipu brigades in Tsunhua county not so far distant. They surveyed their resources carefully. They had 84 families, 450 people with a labor strength of 128 only. There were 12,000 mou of forested hills, or hills they could afforest. Land available for tilling was but 282 mou — not much over half a mou per person. With hillsides too steep for carts, fertiliser, both compost and chemical, had to be taken out to the little terraces by carrying pole. More terraces could be hewn out, but that meant hauling down masses of stone blocks after they had been cut. However, fired by the example of all they had seen, they got to work with a will. Sometimes heavy rains would wash out what they had done, so that they would have to start all over again. One huge rock on a piece they were out to reclaim took 100 charges of explosive to be finally cleared off. An incredible number of workdays was spent on gaining this tiny strip, then that, so that those against the struggle complained mightily that the whole idea was nonsense. But the majority of the old poor peasants would have none of them, and they were struggled against fiercely. Work went on and the results have encouraged all. In 1964 they got 60,000 jin of grain. In 1970 it was 278,000 jin, 1,010 jin a mou. They fully expect to get over 1,100 jin a mou in 1971.

Going up the main valley to see something of what had been accomplished, we were astonished at the richness of the crops. And how they peeped out at us from belts of chestnut trees or ran along the edges of pine forests. Homes were not all down in the brigade village but were scattered over the hillsides as well, the brigade leader having quite a climb up a hillside path. We went into his home and talked with his very charming family, all so relaxed and so obviously full of confidence. 100,000 jin of chestnuts are sold to the state every year, as well as a fair number of walnuts and a goodly amount of medicinal herbs. People prefer traditional medicines here, and herbs not found locally are grown near the brigade village by the clinic staff. Primary school children are taught in the brigade school, while the middle-school pupils go to a brigade further down the valley where there is that facility. The brigade has 102 domestic animals like donkeys, mules, and cattle, and also 221 pigs.

"Now if all the strips reclaimed were put together in one line it would stretch for 40 kilometres, all the way to the county seat of Chienhsi!" they said, as if amazed at what they had done. So hard have they worked that their example has spread to the brigades around, the one immediately below them having also done exceptionally well with both forestry and land reclamation. The big problem that the brigade members now have is how to conserve the flow of little streams that run down its three valleys so gaily each summer. Most of the yearly rainfall comes in the summer, but each spring there is a dry period when crops on the light sandy soil badly need irrigation. Build a dam with cut stone? But there is not enough labor power for that. Dig holding wells? But there are too many fissures in the rock, and the water soon drains away. Pump up from the main river in the valley far below? Too expensive to think about yet, but perhaps someday when electric power is more readily available after the Luan river is harnessed this will be possible.

In the meantime they go on adding to their terraced fields and to their forest area, planting new groves of chestnuts all the time. They keep a flock of over 300 goats on one piece of hillside left especially for grazing, knowing well that goats and new forests are in strong contradiction and that the animals must never be let amongst young trees. With all the forest planting that has been done, the mountain streams that dance down the three valleys are all now more readily contained and all the remaining space in valley bottoms used for little fields. "We have only half a mou of grainfield per person," they say, "but we estimate we also have 40,000 trees for each one of us!"

Leaving them, we stopped down at the bottom of the valley a while at another brigade of Hanerchuang Commune, one called Taweichuang, where the people all have the name of Wei. They had made a stone-lined canal leading river water over nicely to drive two pump turbines which powered a 50-kw. generator used for pumping and lighting, as well as a whole battery of food-processing machines at which brigade girls were working, nattily dressed in white aprons and white caps. This brigade facility not only lights its own 800-people-strong village, but also a village of 300 folk who are their neighbors. Perhaps the following lines may give an overall picture of Hsiaokwanchuang:

> Moodily the wide Luan River
> swirls through the Great Wall
> at Panchiakou; still charged
> with the soil of ten thousand
> hills and mountains, denuded
> in the dreary past; a river now
> into which run streams, fresh
> and clean from forested valleys,
> up one of which we climb until
> we come to heroic Hsiaokwanchuang.

> Hsiaokwanchuang, where
> a handful of the poor made a base
> for the armies of resistance
> against an intruding imperialism;
> where in these years they have
> rebelled against taking relief
> grain from the state, and have
> with their own strength snatched
> plots of land from hillsides
> beneath the forests they have
> planted, beside running streams,

and under the groves of chestnut trees
— chestnuts they ground to flour
to feed resistance fighters on;
their cottages poked away in
side valleys where Japanese
marauders would be less likely
to find them, and now they
surprise all by garnering
massive crops that make them
self-sufficient in grain, even
though with so little land
to grow what they need; when
the spirit is there, miracles
can surely be performed; for
now they just raise hands
clenched around their tools
and the steep mountains
bow before them.

Chienhsi

On the road down to Chienhsi town we passed the rugged mountain standing out alone in the countryside called Chingchungshan. It has a temple of Ming dynasty foundation, a protected national relic, on its summit. Chienhsi town has a very broad main street, and everything looks neat and orderly. We spent the morning after our arrival with the Party secretary of the county who told us something of its revolutionary history and of its activities today.

Large in area, it is mainly hills and streams. Its biggest rivers, the Luan and others, come down from the Chengteh prefecture, and in flood times are liable to cause a good deal of trouble. It has 36 communes, 400 brigades, and 280,000 people in all. The Luan river flows in at Panchiakou, going through the county for 55 kilometres. 320,000 mou of its land can be tilled, though only 114,000 mou of that area is relatively flat. Hillside and terraced land account for the rest. The main crop is corn, with sorghum and millet coming next. A little wheat, cotton and peanuts are also planted. A large number of chestnuts are grown and exported, 12 million jin of them a year. Walnuts and apples are the other important fruit crops.

In pre-Liberation times, grain crops were small, 90-100 jin a mou for the best. With no way to get food, clothing or bedding, many of the people ran away as beggars or refugees. They cut down the forests and sold fuel. They carried, pulled and pushed, doing the work of draft animals, all for less than a reasonable livelihood. In consequence, when the Communist Party first started to educate in Chienhsi, it found many ready ears. It followed as a natural consequence that in 1928 a Party branch should be set up here with 14 members, and that in February of the following year of 1929, a county Party organisation be formed with 30 branches and over 300 members. Its slogans were anti-feudalist, anti-imperialist, against heavy taxes and crude oppression. At that time the county included Chienan and had that name. Then in the new Party organisation there arose a division and internal struggle, which resulted in Party branches being reduced to eight and the membership to 30. In 1933, the Japanese marched in from Hsifengkou. The Party now began to lead in the anti-Japanese struggle and, after the directive from the Wayaopao meeting near Yenan, organised an anti-Japanese army of 1,000 fighters, half of whom had rifles. It also organised a militia which gave the enemy so much trouble along the Great Wall that he declared the whole area one for the kill all, burn all, and loot all policy. This resulted in much indiscriminate murdering of civilians both in Chienhsi and also in Chengteh — then a part of the so-called "Manchukuo". The struggle went on furiously, a thoroughly aroused people putting all they had into the resistance. In consequence, by 1943 the Japanese were pinned down in the county centre and in a few redoubts. In 1944, they gave the area up as a bad job and withdrew completely so that the whole county was liberated.

After 1945, the county took part in the work of the People's Liberation Army. The Kuomintang columns drove in twice, but evacuated in very few days. The folk did not want them and showed it in direct action. Then came the liberation of the whole county, going on to Land Reform, and the various forms of people's organisation right up to the setting up of the communes. 1959 saw a bad spell come in, however. There was a prolonged drought followed by disastrous floods. The Liu Shao-chi line was put into effect, and much wrecking ensued. The new county industry was cut out and many other wounds inflicted.

Then came the Great Proletarian Cultural Revolution, and a very thorough criticism of all who had implemented the line so directly against Mao Tsetung Thought. The present Party secretary said ruefully that he had to undergo much criticism, and go through periods of self-criticism before he was liberated and confirmed in his post again. Now, looking back on it all, he realises how necessary it all was. The damage caused to the countryside by the implementing of Liu's ideas was immense. Forests were felled to sell timber, some people going out after enlarged private plots and neglecting their commune brigade duties. But not only was the thinking of the people clearer after the main struggles, they were also able to translate that understanding into spirit and put the spirit into gaining new production records. For a county that was the poorest of the 13 in the whole Tangshan prefecture to raise its grain production to over 500 jin a mou must have appeared miraculous. The spirit of many of the old cadres was magnificent.

A woman Party secretary of Lungtantsun Brigade of Hsinchang Commune by the name of Wang Chun-hua took all the criticism given her in a wonderful way, then at the same time went on with her work with increased strength and vigor, no matter what was said or done to her. Never backward in admitting where she and others had gone wrong, she served the people with such genuine warmth and ability that they all came to admire her in a new way.

Literacy in Chienhsi was not high in the old days. But with the coming of the Cultural Revolution the works of Chairman Mao, with quotations and pamphlets selected from them, came into every home. No fewer than 324,000 pamphlets were circulated. Many homes that had never had a book in them now had these, and literacy spread so that most folk could read and understand them, and learn from them.

Many brigades which had been on relief grain now began to have grain surpluses and sell to the state. New small power stations began to be built, electrifying villages far away from power lines. The doctrine of self-sufficiency began to take hold and become part of the process of living. It is expected that the 1971 grain totals will exceed those of 1970, and that plans for putting in small industry again will come to fruition. Already the small cement works stopped in the Liu Shao-chi period has been started once more and is now producing 30 tons a day for local use. With the addition of some machinery soon, it will raise this total. The county has now a reserve of 13 million jin of grain, and the people can turn more of their energies into such urgent problems as more afforestation, irrigation and so on.

They will have to face many problems, of course. There do come storms that play havoc amongst the chestnut trees — chestnuts that were the mainstay of guerilla fighters in fighting the Japanese in the bitter years of the War of Resistance — which are still an important part of local economy. A myriad streams flood when the waters come down from the deforested north, and transport is made difficult throughout the summer months. Pests and blights come and have to be dealt with — the current one for instance being "walnut black" which renders the nut unfit for export. Yet progress keeps on. There have been 22 small electric power stations such as the one we saw in Taweichuang Brigade put into production, and 24 others are in the process of being set up now. Lights go on now in one village after another, and the people know they come out of their own strength. The county operates a small copper mine — 14 tons a year — and can exchange the ore with a Tientsin copper refinery for suitable copper wire for its local electrification, saving much money. 240 big open wells have been sunk to help the task of irrigation. From them water runs in new irrigation canals. Small mining ventures, including some for gold, coal and so on, are successfully operated, thus adding to local self-sufficiency. In mechanisation, more engines and tractors are being bought and the county repair shops, now continuing with better equipment and technique, play their part as a necessary adjunct to all labor-saving devices.

As is the custom today, after the Party secretary had given us an account of some of the achievements made, he went on to talk of the shortcomings in all that had been done. Not enough new terracing carried through, not enough planting. A tendency by some to start work without being sure that it will be able to do all it was designed to do. Yet again, living at the mercy of rivers that are not yet controlled, they cannot fully guard against every emergency that might take place.

The town of Chienhsi was clean and neat, shops being set out attractively. Deforestation of the past has left a good many hills in the centre of the county bare, and on these there has been a good deal of erosion. Holes have to be dug into the rock, earth carted in and arrangements made to bring water to the young tree. Doggedly, work continues to be carried on. "We cannot pretend yet that we are as good as Hsiyang in Shansi or Linhsien in Honan, but people here have set their goals high, and having mastered the grain problem now feel that they can go on getting new results in the adventure of creating better livelihood," they said.

On to Tangshan

We went on through Chienhsi down into Tangshan. A modern industrial city marked by smokestacks as we came near it. We stayed long enough to visit one of the many potteries — there are state, provincial and city ones here. The one we saw concentrated in the main on export pottery, and was one I had last come to see at the beginning of the Cultural Revolution, back in 1966. It is on the site of potteries started here in the Yunglo period of the Ming dynasty, around the year 1407 A.D., now one of 20 units belonging to a complex that produces around 100 million pieces a year.

The factory we saw this time was set up in 1949 with 60 workers. It now has 1,500 who turn out 23 million pieces a year of household tableware. The continuous kilns are still fired with coal, though there is a plan to use the gas from another factory. The whole of the main shops is being reconstructed, section by section, the summer temperature being too high for workers' comfort. In the research institute, another unit of the complex, we saw designing being done by old and young craftsmen, meeting the demands of the 80 or more countries to which porcelain is being exported. One interesting item much in demand locally is an amplifier consisting of two round porcelain discs. Fixed on the back of a picture or in some other inconspicuous place in a room, they amplify just as well as the expensive metal amplifiers previously used. Production cost is ten yuan. They are being eagerly used now in households all over the area. Being delicate, they need careful handling, but once fixed they last well. Another product of this institute is the gold glaze that now can be sold to potteries all over the country. We left Tangshan on August 1st, Army Day. I have tried to recapture the scene along the road northeast in the following lines:

> August the First, 1971
> and in the cool of early morning
> we drove out of the growing
> industrial city of Tangshan.
>
> Long lines of rubber-tyred
> carts, animal-powered;
> convoys of trucks hauling busily
> for construction and industry;

two red tractors with trailers
packed with commune folk; a stream
of workers on bicycles; a column
of singing students marching off
to a meeting, celebrating
the day on which the Red Army
was born, forty-four years past;
and now the people, relaxed, confident
with meaning to life, because in
those past days some took arms,
fought back.

Today the Red Army
is named People's Liberation Army,
a force that increasingly
has become a great school for cadres,
a school that lives democracy,
its students one with the people,
born out of their midst, of and for
the fighting poor; understanding
the proper relation between officers
and men; between army and government;
army and Party; political work, then
military; well schooled in ideas of
serving the people, giving all
for them; technically able to handle
the equipment they need, and to meet
production demands for work in city
and on a commune; a new kind of army
is this, the common man militant,
knowing whom he fights and why; not
scared of bitterness or death,
a disciplined force, the new
Great Wall of China today.

Luanhsien

We spent a glorious summer's day at Luanhsien, 55 kilometres northeast of Tangshan. Once it was Luanchou, administering a large area including what is the Tangshan municipality of today. Then as time went on, other counties were carved out of its area and it was left with some 244 hills, a big river amongst nine others, and some 900,000 mou of land, most of which is light and sandy. Because of this kind of soil, it has become the biggest peanut producer in the province. It plants 210,000 mou in just this one crop. But the land, in order to stop wind erosion, has to have strips of trees planted at intervals across it, in addition to other windbreaks. The mulberry has been chosen because of its economic value and for the way it can be treated here. Cut down every winter, fresh shoots come up swiftly from the stump, bear leaves which are used for silkworm feeding in the four silk raising periods of each year, and then are cut for basket-making after the last crop is gathered. Leaves are not so big and luscious as those raised in south China, but the silk gained in the local silk factory is of fine export grade.

The factory is a new thing, a county venture started in 1968 during the Cultural Revolution and going into production in 1969. Prior to its establishment, cocoons had to be marketed a considerable distance away, and it was the Mao Tsetung idea of self-sufficiency that led to a plant being put up right on the spot. A move that was welcomed by the 430,000 people of the county and the 31 communes they are organised into. It was a joy to go to this plant with its 443 workers, most of whom are young girls fresh from school. 320 of the workforce are women. There are 18 staff workers and three doctors. The coming of the plant has led to a stepping up of cocoon production, for first-grade cocoons bring 1.40 yuan a jin, and seconds 1.20, which means considerable income to brigade folk. We went to one of the brigades, that of Mengchiatun, a big village of 3,200 people divided up into 21 production teams, where we found many homes raising cocoons, usually in the best rooms of the house. In one of these we entered there was evidently someone of considerable artistic ability, for the re-papered walls and ceiling had been decorated with quite charming paint-ings done in Chinese traditional style which light the place up wonder-fully. Experiments have been made in raising silkworms out of doors, shallow pits being dug for the purpose. This saves on wooden racks, basket trays, paper sheets, all that is needed being rice straw. So far the experi-ment has been successful, but it has not yet been tried for the whole four cocoon-raising periods of the warmer weather seasons. Here, a little bean-curd milk is spread over the mulberry leaves which, it is said, makes for a stronger worm and a better cocoon.

The silk mill is situated in the heart of the mulberry district some six miles out of the Luanhsien county centre. Everything is kept in first-class order. Silk from second-grade cocoons that do not come up to export requirements is spun and woven into fabrics here on modern automated looms constructed cheaply and efficiently on the premises from second-hand machinery which had been thrown out of a Tientsin textile mill. The factory has a useful small machine shop which has helped with this. Fabrics are dyed in the plant. This year, the mill expects to arrive at its planned capacity of 40 tons of silk a year. Seventeen tons were produced in the first six months, leaving 23 for the next half which workers are confident they can put out. The mill operates through all four seasons, cocoons in store being enough for this. Workers work in eight-hour shifts, two a day, one morning and the other evening. In China, there are engineers and technicians of various grades, then the eight grades of work-ers, but this factory has established itself without either engineers or tech-nicians, local workers going off to other silk filatures for periods to get the general idea and then coming back to teach others. As they become more proficient they can help their new pupils to advance more swiftly. In self-criticism, they say that they wasted a good deal of electric power in the beginning and perhaps spent overmuch on building construction.

The general impression on going around and meeting all those bright eager young people was that here was a school of a new kind, one devoted to putting theory into action, as all go into the adventure of productive living and studying together. There are only two university graduates in the plant. The one we met was a girl who had come from a teacher's training college. She was in charge of the testing laboratory.

So for the once sandy waste and barren hills of Luanhsien new things are coming into being. Chestnuts are being grown as well as mulberries, and already 80,000 jin of them are being sold annually. The silk mill cost 1,240,000 yuan to set up, but will soon pay for itself. Things are changing for the people of Luanhsien.

In Funing County

The last halt on this trip was at Funing county, one of 416,000 people organised into 46 communes, which last year gained an all-over average of 510 jin of grain a mou. Due to the fact that its Yangho water conservancy scheme was built in the Great Leap Forward period, a great deal of what was low alkaline marshland in Funing and Changli counties was converted to rice paddy. This in turn made large amounts of rice straw available for paper, material before used for fuel as a rule. But for carts to haul rice straw all the way to Chinwangtao, where the nearest paper factory was situated, took four days. In consequence, Funing county set out to build its own paper plant. 150 mou of ground was taken, therefore, and in November 1968 construction of a small paper plant was started. In September 1969 it started producing, with a planned production of 150 tons for its first year. It got 163 tons, and having by now trained its 163 workers and staff, went on for the next 12 months to full production of 3,000 tons of the brown packing paper required for the export industry. When its second paper machine is completely installed by November 1971, it will well over double — probably treble — this figure. Its workers work three shifts of eight hours each, and all live on the premises in staff quarters provided. As factory and staff buildings cover only one portion of the area, the rest is used for growing grain, fruit and vegetables and for raising pigs.

It is a pleasure to go around this plant. Well-lit, well-built, machines nicely spaced, it is spick and span, without any piles of material cluttering the place up; so the impression is gained of a quiet and business-like efficiency. When the plant started, almost two tons of coal were consumed for each ton of paper made. But now, with improved methods of stoking, this has been reduced to around three fourths of a ton. Waste water is treated so as to make it fertilise, not destroy, the land it flows over. The erection of the plant was done in the main by three adjacent communes, all of them rice-producing. With the plant so near, they can bring in four loads of rice straw a day with ease now. Twenty percent of the workers are women. The oldest worker in the plant is 31. They average 45 yuan a month wages. Some workers live off their wages, as city workers would do. Most others prefer to pass their wages over to their commune brigades and live off the workpoints and the grain allowance for themselves and families. Some of the staff cadres are county cadres who have been sent in. The machinery for the plant was constructed in the Northeast, except that in the machine shops where several lathes have been made by the plant itself. At present their aim is 30 tons of paper a day. They can market this for 600 yuan a ton. Then if more is required, they can easily make a replica of their present shops and instal more machines. They now have the know-how.

There is political study before and after each shift. At present they feel they are getting a good deal of help from their classes in philosophy.

Taoyuan Again

While in Funing county this 1971 summer, we drove over to see how Wu Chen was getting on in Taoyuan. The events of 1966-67 are beginning to fade from his mind a bit, being crowded out by the new problems that cluster around any brigade leader, but we did pick up a few items we had missed on other visits. How Wang Kwang-mei had managed to insulate the brigade against any outside news, making all mail and papers go through her offices. Thus the people of Taoyuan did not know what was in her book "Taoyuan Experience" until after she had been toppled, when there was general laughter at many of her stories. These stories brought out another thing — how putting over the Mao Tsetung line takes people of principle and determination. Then how the revisionists must rely on scamps as leaders and fools to follow. But the people of Taoyuan Brigade were never really fooled by Wang Kwang-mei or Kwan Ching-tung, and indignation was at the bursting point when along came the Cultural Revolution and the whole plot was exposed. For students of Tachai, the model for all China as a sincere downright expression of Mao Tsetung Thought, a trip to Taoyuan is important, to see the kind of thing that Liu Shao-chi was planning for Chinese agriculture. Communes run as Liu Shao-chi would have liked them to be run, e.g. in hock to city banks and these banks under Liu's control, would have been a gigantic step back to capitalism.

Wu Chen looked well. The Funing county Party secretary who also was removed by Wang Kwang-mei and has since been reinstated, was present too. Wu's daughter, he says, is now in a medical course, training to become a "barefoot" doctor for the brigade. Production results? The brigade gained around 200 jin a mou in the early days of Liberation, 1970 brought over 800 jin, and 1971 will bring more. I took pictures of some of the children and of an old man with two stalwart grandsons. The old man prided himself on the fact that he never missed a day's work, and though 70 could still keep up. Everyone was warm and friendly.

One More Visit to Yangho Reservoir

Driving around Funing city on the highway which has the old city wall for its base, we made yet another trip to the Yangho reservoir. When work on a dam is completed, this is just the first stage of a great deal more work. Main canals, with their aqueducts and laterals, then have to be built and the water distributed. This now has been adequately done on the east side of the river, so that the water gets to two counties and to Chinwangtao municipality as needed. But before the work on the west side of the river could be started, the temporary flood diversion channel had to be replaced with a bigger permanent one, complete with sluice gates. Over the past year this work has been done, the last stages of it, the installing of the three steel sluice gates in the headworks that have been built being in full swing at the time of our visit. Next year, work on the two rock tunnels and the 80-odd aqueducts along with all the stonework needed for the west side system will be on the way to completion also. Below the dam, fish hatcheries will by then be in operation, and more of the hills around the reservoir will start to show up green, new forests making a beginning of holding back the sand and silt that would otherwise go into the reservoir. We went out on a launch with the fishermen group and watched them pull in their nets. The first fish pulled up was a 30 pounder, a huge rainbow colored one. Soon more were flapping around in the fishermen's boat, until the load became considerable.

Quite a feature of the whole work at Yangho over the years is that it has been carried through by practical county workers, without much outside engineering help. The Great Leap Forward trained young local workers all over the hinterland, and now the outstanding ones are leaders on many a new development.

We asked about big floods in the Yangho river in the past. The biggest on record was in 1580, when villages and crops were swept away over a very large area and the death toll was serious. In modern times the worst one was in 1930, which the old folk remember well and have many tragic stories of. Now, due to the new irrigation, heavy crops are being harvested all the way from the mountains to the coast, and the old threat of flood has been taken away. Soon turbines will operate in the main outlet canals which, though only running for the six months' growing season of each year, will provide a welcome addition to local needs for electricity at that time, apart from the main grid system.

It is always good when visiting in the hinterland to be able to return to a place seen a few years before. The spirit and warmth of Pohai Commune down by the coast of Pohai Bay in Funing county, experienced in 1968, enticed another visit in 1971. And of the now existing 17 brigades of the commune the vanguard one called "Shuitien", composed of people of the Korean minority nationality, had its special appeal, for here one could see how well the nationalities policy of China was working out, and how enthusiasm had been maintained so well.

Pohai Commune has 38,808 mou of land farmed by the labor strength that comes from 4,325 families, 20,080 people in all. Once largely an alkaline waste of fen country, it now has rich paddy fields, 80 percent of its crop being rice. Today it averages some 800 jin a mou of grain, and 646 jin of peanuts a mou on the 1,500 mou it has planted with this crop. A workday averages an income of 1.50 yuan, and the commune's reserve funds are 4,280,000 yuan. The commune operates a tractor station, a hospital, six middle schools, and an old people's home amongst its various projects. All brigades have their own primary schools. We visited the one belonging to the Korean minority nationality Shuitien Brigade and, after hearing the leader of Pohai Commune talk on general commune affairs, had a plain, simple statement from the very direct young Korean nationality leader. He was accompanied by a quiet young man who was company commander of the brigade's militia, and an able woman who is head of the women's section. Half the workforce of the brigade are women. Of the total population now of 433, 75 are children in the brigade primary school and 35 are in a commune middle school. The brigade farms 1,058 mou of land with a labor force of 183. "We have enough grain in our brigade store now to support a battalion of soldiers if need be in any emergency," they say. They obviously take the slogan "Prepare against war and natural disaster" quite seriously.

The primary-school children put on an excellent concert for us out in the school yard, in dance and song, while the old men in white looked gravely on with much dignity and satisfaction. Then, after a feast of crabs brought in fresh from the sea that very morning followed up by the Korean speciality of sticky rice cake, we repaired to the compound where the brigade has its newly built office, meeting hall and clinic, where out in the open the older women gathered and danced for us. They obviously loved doing it, and were very graceful. The people too were clearly proud of them. Working women all of them who, though they had raised families, many with grandchildren, still retained their youth.

People's livelihood is good here. They have a grain allowance of 500 jin each per year, two bicycles per family, and a good deal else besides. They said that they had learnt much in the Cultural Revolution, being quite successful on one particular point. With them there had been the very bad custom of the men looking down on women. An occasion for sorrow when a girl child was born, rather than one of gladness. People would laugh if a woman rode a bicycle, or had much to say in a meeting. These old ideas have been pretty well demolished now, and the young women of the brigade are obviously a power and a strength to the whole group.

I wrote these lines about the "Omani" — the old Korean women who danced.

> Wrinkled faces toughened
> by work out in the fields,
> gnarled fingers that have
> always toiled; grandchildren

peeping around wide Korean
skirts, the working women
of Shuitien Brigade
smile invitation to each other
then come together in dance
full of the spirit of youth
and the dignity of age, moving
gracefully in time with
drum beats, then breaking
into song as they step so lightly
each movement definite,

> *dancing away the bitterness*
> *of the past, dancing in their*
> *hope for the future, lifting*
> *arms as if in benediction,*
> *for these who have given most*
> *surely have the right to give*
> *still more; these so great*
> *in spirit, so strong in will*
> *to make light of struggle,*
> *and in dance able to put*
> *meaning into every step*
> *they take, each bit of song*
> *they sing; these the brave*
> *sweet women of Shuitien.*

A North China Port City

With the impact of foreign imperialism on the coast of China, and the seizure of the Kailuan coal mines by British monopoly, there came the need for a port to export the coal to the rising industrial city of Shanghai. So the beginnings of a modern harbor were made at what had once been mainly a fishing port.   A historic spot, for the little hill at the promontory of a bay had once been an island before its rear became silted up, making it part of the mainland.   Named after Chin Shih Huang Di, the ruthless unifier of China following the period of the Warring States prior to the third century B.C., it lies a little south of the eastern end of the Great Wall, the famous Shanhaikwan gate.   Through this and nearby, frequently visited by foreign seamen who come to Chinwangtao and by summer guests at Peitaiho, is a seaside suburb of the municipality, about half an hour's drive from it by a good motor road.   Peitaiho was first built as a recreation place for the foreign businessmen and Christian missionaries of the China coast, who erected summer cottages there.

So much for background.   Today Chinwangtao is a thriving port visited by ships of many nations.   New wharves are being constructed in its now busy harbor to meet the increasing need.   Its industry goes ahead fast, serving not only its 310,000 people but also a good part of Hopei as well.

The first time I knew it, it had but two factories — one for bottling aerated water, which came from a famous water supply, and then the match factory. Both factories have been modernised and enlarged today. Then there is the glass works, which has gone on into making glass fibre used for fertiliser bags and such, and into other industrial plastics. It has now become a large-scale plant. Both the match factory and the glass works I had previously visited and reported on. But the plant we first visited in the summer of 1971 was a relatively small one, a printing works of 568 workers, 409 of whom are women. An interesting one for many reasons. Many of the original old-type platen presses and other such equipment is still in use. Then, too, there are big-size, highly automated modern presses from Shanghai and Peking. After the beginning of the Cultural Revolution it really came into its own, for then arose a terrific demand for complete editions of the works of Chairman Mao, the Little Red Book of quotations, and the various extracts from Chairman Mao's works in pamphlet form. Over three million Little Red Books were printed, and more than that number of Selected Works. More than seven million pamphlets were produced. At present, the main task is to get new textbooks printed for the schools. Among technical innovations, a good paste has been made from paper shavings, substituting the old flour-made paste which used up grain. The secret of adding the plastic coating for printing rollers has been mastered and is being used successfully. But one ever finds new ideas in operation in all factories visited these days. No fewer than 20 recent innovations are being used here.

We sat for a while in the factory reception room, a bright, well-lit one with one picture of Chairman Mao and a framed facsimile of his poem "Peitaiho". The other pictures were of the model operas, and then some Hangchow silk woven ones of scenery. There were flowers and some greenery. Out in the compound, groups of men and women workers were practising on a basketball court. The old labor union has been dissolved now, and its functions, including workers' health and factory safety, taken over by the Revolutionary Committee. Soon, however, a new workers' organisation will promote these undertakings. In addition to the Party group in the factory there is a Communist Youth League group with a membership of 110. We visited the factory clinic, with a doctor and two nurses in charge. Not only are workers served here, but also their families.

The factory visit took up most of a morning, but there was still time enough left to go to a kindergarten of some 240 children between the ages of four and seven, who entertained us with dance and song after a hearty welcome. Most knew Mao Tsetung's three short essays by heart, and older ones could all join in singing some extracts from the model operas. At seven, they go to primary school and learn actually how to work as well as play and study. In the kindergarten stage, they go out on little tours to watch workers in factories, on the wharves and in the fields as their earliest lesson in the work of the world, and something on which to base their first political lessons. A concert group from a nearby primary school came in to give us an item while we were with the smaller ones.

They had developed a good deal, and had an elan and technique surprising for such young children.

A few days later we continued with factory visits, starting off with one to a plant for making spare parts for tractors. It had grown from five small iron-working shops and had taken over a piece of land that had once been a Japanese open-air storage depot. There were only 100 workers in all at that time, turning out metal stoves, etc. for the consumer goods market. The plant grew in numbers to 367 by 1965, when a million spare parts for tractors were made. By 1971, production had risen six times. The last 12 months have seen an 18 percent rise over the previous year's figure, and there are now over 1,000 workers, 500 middle-school students having joined in 1970. Swiftly new equipment is being added that enables advanced method to replace old and speed up the process of manufacture. The two leaders of the Revolutionary Committee were both old cadres, while the younger ones seemed to be very able too. The leading cadre explained how they had all emerged from the struggles of the Cultural Revolution a good deal stronger, and now that self-sufficiency was the watchword they had out of their own strength made many things possible.

One problem came up in discussion amongst workers. There were those who said that the plant should not simply be one making spare parts for other plants, but should be one which made the entire assembly. These pointed to the need in a port city for a plant manufacturing marine diesels, and had actually started to construct one as a pilot. The argument waxed hard and fast but, in the end, the line won out that said that the present need was to support the mechanisation of agriculture by all means possible, and that the provision of oil pumps, fuel pumps, etc. for such tractors was an important duty. However, all agreed that the experimental building of one 400-h.p. diesel engine should be continued, in order to show what could be done if the necessity became paramount. We saw the completed engine, and watched it running for a time. Its makers were still observing its performance, correcting and testing.

Another department of the plant that is outside the general production plan is one where rifles are assembled for army use. They are trued up and put into sweetly running mechanical order, as part of the process.

The plant makes its own new machines, complete in every detail. The shop where ball bearings are put out also puts out ball-bearing assemblies of many sizes, both for tractors and for the new machine tools the factory makes for itself. Just the provision of ball bearings for farm mechanisation in so vast a country as China takes an enormous and growing number of factories to meet the demand. When looking at the big ball-bearing factory in Loyang some years ago, one felt that now surely China would be self-sufficient in this essential. But since then I have seen them being made endlessly in many parts of the country, and the process is just beginning.

We talked a while about industrial safety, wondering how rigidly the women, who make up 500 of the 1,100 workers, stick to their long braids, which are so great a danger amongst swift-moving machinery. But the factory reports very few industrial accidents have taken place in their plant, and none of a very serious nature so far. There is a factory clinic with two doctors and four nurses, which Dr. Ma Hai-teh who came with me on the visit inspected carefully and pronounced good.

In the bad old days of Chinwangtao port, as in other ports of China, waterside workers were simply dubbed "coolies" by the management. A "straw" boss hired and fired by the day. There was no regular employment, and no corporate life as workers. No responsibility for accidents on the part of the firms responsible for dock operations. No one cared what happened to their families or if they were faced with starvation. They were treated worse than horses or cattle. This was the case right from the beginnings of the harbor in 1900, through the British, Japanese and Kuomintang periods, right up to Liberation in 1948. Then the once despised workers took charge and all changed. Employed on a permanent basis, and with proper staff quarters, each worker averages a family of around five. Now able to bring their inventiveness into full play, they have helped a great deal during and since the Cultural Revolution in mechanising processes. For instance, in loading coal, it would take 300 men working for three days to do what automatic loading will do in 13 hours with 60 workers. Soon, with still better equipment, the time will be cut to nine hours, with fewer workers being needed for the job. No worker need fear being laid off in Chinwangtao. There is a shortage of workers everywhere. 40,000 tons a day of cargo was handled in 1970, while in 1971 the average is running at 100,000 tons. Learning from the oil well base of Taching, much is being done on the utilisation of waste materials for necessary improvements. The leading member of the Revolutionary Committee who took us around was once a wharf engine driver. He certainly had the whole situation at his finger tips.

Chinwangtao is a fortunate port in many ways. Typhoons do not affect it, and silting up is not a problem. It is ice free, and has plenty of room for extensions as may become necessary. We stood for a while, on the second visit in the summer of 1971, watching a Japanese ship loading soya beans and chestnuts, Chinese colliers loading coal and coke for Shanghai, Greek and Somali ships busy with their loading and unloading, in the parts of the harbor visited. It is not difficult to envisage a very much bigger port operating here in the next stages. Apparently ships of over 60 countries call, those of Greek registry being the greatest in number. Seamen sometimes take train trips to Peking, visit Shanhaikwan, or go in parties to visit communes in inland counties. The Seamen's Club in Chinwangtao is a big building with living, eating, recreational and department-store facilities.

The next factory visit made was to the Chinwangtao pottery. This is a plant 80 percent of whose production goes into the export trade. It was one of the factories planned for in the Great Leap Forward, but its beginnings were beset with difficulties as the then promoters tried hard to follow the Liu Shao-chi line of "big, foreign and complete" in every aspect. Their continuous kiln when built proved unsuitable for its coal gas producing assembly. The leaders at that time wasted large sums of money trying to make the unworkable work. Workers were not called in to give opinions and help out. It was the Russian imported one-line chain of command. Finally, after some struggle, the old leadership gave up and a new one using the Mao Tsetung line came in. They found that the continuous kiln would operate well if oil-fired, so changed over to that fuel. The struggle between the two lines, however, did not immediately cease. It continued through the Cultural Revolution, the victory of the correct line leading to production being raised from around one million pieces in 1966 to around three million in 1970, the number rising steeply again this 1971. Workers, except for 20 technical ones brought up from the Tangshan potteries, are all local folk, 187 of them women. A new department is that for the tiny porcelain fittings needed in electronics, which has specialised requirements of its own. The main line seems to be tea sets and dinner plates. All materials needed for working are obtained locally. Saggers are used 20 times, and the firing in the kiln takes 36 minutes. The pottery has well-mechanised conveyor belts and other devices ensuring a smooth production line. Workers have one hour's political study each day, and their spirit is obviously high.

From the pottery we went to see a factory that is quite famous in Chinwangtao for the high political standard of its workers and for the way they apply their theory to practice. It is the local knitwear mill which turns out a wide range of knitted goods for internal consumption, including underwear of wool, nylon or cotton; socks, gloves and such things that are needed all the time by people in Hopei counties. An exception are the white cotton workers' gloves which are exported to Japan. 280 kinds of products are turned out, now valued at 3,500,000 yuan a year. First set up in 1954 by bringing together two small dwelling-house industries, it has spread swiftly, until now it is having to build new factory premises to accommodate 720 workers, whose numbers increase as demand for their product increases. In the spirit of the Taching oilfield, model now for all industry, it is carrying through its extensions under its own steam without asking for more help from the state. Revolution is not just a matter of some inspired person leading a mass of cheering youth who battle gallantly with the police of the establishment, but rather a putting of revolutionary theory into real, down-to-earth methods of serving the people. 560 of the workers are women, who make up 80 percent of the work force. Many are of the 18-20 age group, fresh from middle school, for expansion has made it necessary to bring them in quickly. They look very beautiful in summer clothing as they work amongst colored fabrics in large, well-lit rooms. Despite their considerable achievement, one found them all very modest in talking about it, and also about the success they have had in the political field. It was pleasant to have had the privilege of being amongst them.

The next factory visited was one which made machinery for the building trade. It also made some of the machinery used in the Kailuan coal-mining industry. Its construction machinery goes to every part of China — grinders for crushing materials, hoists, and so on. Started in 1958 at the beginning of the Great Leap Forward with the workers of two small machine shops, one of which repaired bicycles, it then had 100 workers, a number which by 1969 had risen to 300. Now it has 600, 250 of them being women. It has built itself several modern shops and constructed the overhead cranes in them, as well as many of the new machine tools. Workers are in the main graduates of local middle schools, both girls and boys, who have come in during the Cultural Revolution. All are local. The oldest worker is a cadre over 60 who has been with the plant since it was set up. In the early 'sixties the Liu Shao-chi line held back progress a good deal, so that the plant could never meet the demands made on it. Now that demands have greatly increased, it still cannot entirely do so, but the way ahead is clearer and new shops are being built to cope with the new needs.

During the Cultural Revolution there was a good deal of struggle, but all soon settled down as groups came together and the Revolutionary Committee was set up. "We must struggle to raise our technique," the leader of the Revolutionary Committee said. "Our factory area becomes too small and we badly need warehouse space for our finished goods. But political training has raised the spirit of the workers, so that they now feel they can cope with anything. In factory administration we need to improve as our plant grows larger and our responsibilities greater."

He was pleased however, with the way that workers had made creative innovations in machine-building and in turning out machine tools they had never seen before. After visiting the bigger shops and watching work being done, we went to a small one where a special task was being carried out. It was the making of rifle barrels for army rifles. If each factory makes one or two parts for a rifle, and another assembles, there is a general carrying through of the slogan, "prepare against war", on a local, self-sufficiency basis, with workers being trained who can easily be added to. And with a working force now in the main a youthful one of middle-school educational standard, and well versed in Mao Tsetung Thought, progressive change in the future seems to be well assured.

Shanhaikwan, with its towered gate and the proud motto emblazoned over it, "The First Gate Under Heaven", is well known in history. From here the end of the Great Wall runs down to the sea, and on its western side shoots up over the mountains. The railway to the Northeast passes through here, and as a part of the railway building in the bad old days of foreign railway concessions, British interests which had gained the rights to build the Peking-Mukden railway, erected a factory for the making of parts for bridge construction. That was in 1894, 77 years ago. Following the British came the Japanese, then the Kuomintang, the area being liberated in November 1948, when there were 900 workers in the place. They made such things as machinery for alcohol distilleries, road rollers, and machines for small industry which they could sell. In a whole year, they would do but 30 metres of bridge sections, but as at that time most bridge parts were imported, assembly work was nearly all that was needed. Workers had to work 15 hours a day, and then get jobs after work pulling, pushing carts or rickshaws to make livelihood possible for their families, for too often pay would be held back so that when they did receive it, it had depreciated too much to buy essentials. Now there are 4,000 workers, with average wages of 60 yuan a month. 560 of them are women. They work in big new shops with modern machinery, and have provided the parts for the Wuhan and Nanking bridges, the Chengchow Yellow river bridge, as well as bridges in many parts of China and abroad. Their work has gone into Vietnam, Korea, Tanzania, Albania and Nepal, as well as to Cambodia before the U.S. decided to turn that lovely land into a hell on earth with their bombs. The factory has also trained Vietnamese for two-year terms, to do the work needed in their own country. Its buildings cover some 93,000 square metres of land. Thirty percent of its strength is composed of young workers. There are also middle-school students who come in to work during holidays and for certain periods during the school terms. In the plant there are 821 Party members and 535 who are in the Communist Youth League. Half an hour's political study is done before work, and one hour and a half in the evenings. Two half days a week, in work time, are also spent on study. Three 8-hour shifts are worked in a six-day week. In these last four years workers have made many technical innovations, which have rationalised processes and speeded up production. Already the present premises are being found too small for all there is to be done, and another shop has been started in a different part of Shanhaikwan.

Amongst shops we did see was one devoted to one section of arms manufacture, as is the custom with the bigger Chinwangtao factories, it seems. Here a group of workers turn out light anti-tank rocket launchers. To me they seemed a very useful weapon. "Prepare against war" is not an empty slogan. It is interesting that here, under the shadow of the Great Wall and its most famous gate, there should be a plant devoted to the cause of the working people's internationalism, their support going to so many parts of the world. In the enclosure, between the two gates of Shanhaikwan, there is a statue of Lo Sheng-chiao, the Chinese soldier who died rescuing a Korean boy in an icy river. Shanhaikwan then, is a place now symbolic of a great reaching out, of putting the precepts of working people's internationalism into solid practice.

The Chinwangtao Glass Works is a big concern. It makes plate glass, 70 percent of which goes into the export trade which it has with 47 countries. It also makes glass marbles which go into industry, some to the local glass-fibre factory. It is an old concern, having been started with Belgian capital and the son of Yuan Shih-kai, Yuan Ching-wu, as director, in 1921. It did not come into production till 1924. By 1933 it was found that Japanese industry was doing better with quality and price, so that in 1936 the whole plant was sold to them, they continuing in ownership until August 1945 when the Japanese were defeated. The Kuomintang flew in a manager who then put his own men in control. For the next three years the factory went into decline. Workers could not live on the depreciated currency they were paid in, while the management was lusty for any profit it might make for itself. Bad management and general Kuomintang corruption led to the closing down of much of it, so that the plant was in a sorry condition by the time the liberation forces came in 1948. Many workers had silicosis, serious accidents with shafts of broken glass were common, and morale was low.

New cadres came in. Another furnace was started. Workers grew in number from the original 900 to 3,700 working in three shifts, there being 350 women added. The assistant manager was a woman cadre, Li Su-ching, who has a limp and who had joined the revolution in 1938 in the Shansi-Chahar-Hopei Border Region. An able executive, she was reduced to worker status in the Cultural Revolution, but is now back in the equivalent of her old position, being vice-chairman of the Revolutionary Committee. The struggle in this factory was not as fierce as in some, however. Two groups were formed, and on the 21st of July 1967 battled together, students from the city, family members all taking part. In all, in struggles that took place, one student and one young worker were killed. The opposing sides used glass marbles produced in the works as ammunition for sling shots. The older men kept the plant running despite all, and there was no closure. With the grand alliance and the setting up of the Revolutionary Committee, things rapidly got on an even keel again, and progress was swift. Said Li Su-ching, "We all learnt a great deal. Know the way ahead much better. Workers can now better bring their initiative into play, as they have already done with many useful innovations on the technical side. Two reactionary persons have gone to the countryside for training, but those are the only cadres who have been dropped. The Cultural Revolution was good."

Actually, production has grown startlingly in these last two years. Glass is shorn off as it rises from the furnaces, millions of square metres a year. The campaign against waste makes for some interesting activities. For instance, workers' dependents come into the factory and cut up pieces of waste glass for glass windowpanes and the like for mass use. Sheets often crack down the middle and formerly were just pushed down the scrap chutes to be re-processed in time. Ashes from the coal-burning operations are made into a good, hard blue brick, and go out of the factory into construction. Workers are proud of the fact that Chairman Mao has visited the plant, and are touched by the solicitude of Premier Chou for those who had silicosis, prevalent at the time of Liberation but practically eliminated now. There were once a good many accidents with splitting glass, but mechanisation has cut down the number of people in the more dangerous spots and has greatly reduced the hazards, the big sheets being easily moved by ingenious devices workers have invented. Workers work eight-hour shifts, there being three shifts a day. There is half an hour's study before work, and in the evenings usually a two-hour meeting on current problems.

The Kuomintang, before they left, tried to destroy the plant, but the fires they started were not so strong as worker's spirit. In a few months after they left the whole plant was in production again. I asked if there had been any trouble with "May 16th" group operators, who used the red banner to strike down the red banner. This question had not been solved yet, I was told. At the time of the Cultural Revolution the factory was directly under the leadership of the ministry in Peking, and there was a good deal of coming and going amongst the younger ones at that time. Now leadership is in the Chinwangtao municipality. Now too, there is a thoroughly awakened work force, not a few of whom have come through all the hard times ever since the factory was started. Every aspect of the

Cultural Revolution has by now been discussed in detail. It is not so easy in consequence to fool workers as it was in the Liu Shao-chi period with its carefully controlled bureaucracy which more and more had the tendency to reduce workers to be mere cogs, to move as commanded without any feeling of responsibility or cohesion. If you worked well and pleased the management you got prize money.

The final factory visit made in the municipality was to the cannery at Shanhaikwan. It is a place that has come up through very simple beginnings, making such things as soy sauce and vinegar, then going on to aerated waters and sweets. Steadily it grew through the years until now it has 1,010 workers, 62 percent of whom are women. The factory works two 8-hour shifts a day, in five shops. It cans or bottles fruit, cans pork and chicken, fish, vegetables and so on, one quarter of its products going into the export trade. In season it makes a very good strawberry jam for which there is a strong demand. Automation is being carried forward well. Strict attention is paid to cleanliness. As local orchards come into richer bearing there is more raw material to work from. In the past there was not much encouragement to grow fruit, as there was so limited a demand for it. Now the establishment of such a factory right in the middle of a fruit-growing area means a great deal to local economy, as well as making summer fruit available to people down through the long cold months of winter, at prices they can afford or are increasingly being able to afford.

The dynamic head of the Revolutionary Committee of the municipality gave us a farewell in the shape of an invitation to see a performance of the Tsangchow acrobats. I had last seen them in Tsangchow at the beginning of the Cultural Revolution, and had not seen any acrobatic show since. They had a completely new repertoire which was much acclaimed by the crowded audience. Tsangchow has a tradition of acrobatics, going back into times when its performers were well known wherever temple fairs of local performances were held in the Hopei countryside.

One has the impression that Chinwangtao will become quite a large industrial city before long, and that it is only at the beginnings of its development. The excellent spirit one sees amongst the young workers now coming into its industry bodes well for a splendid future to which its position, situated as it is on the lines of communication and with a big hinterland to draw on, surely entitle it. The following lines may give some impression of the city.

> *Now does China begin*
> *to look at things anew*
> *so much theory having*
> *been transformed to spirit,*
> *spirit to the building*
> *of new factories, power plants*
> *highways, land reclamation*
> *irrigation, afforestation,*
> *and all the essentials*
> *the people need to pull*

themselves into line with
the best there is in
this planet of ours, enabling
them to better help all
other peoples to do the same.

And in just one relatively small
North China port town, the way
this begins to be done, excites
the imagination; plate glass
being crated for two score
foreign lands, porcelain for more;
glass being spun to fibre, parts
for engines being made; bridge
sections for rail and highway
being turned out; everywhere
the ranks of new youth, bending
over streamlined machines,
creating new strength, and along
with it, new people who never
for one moment forget the bitterness
their parents came through,
the evils of foreign aggression,
which still this 1971 stands
on the province of Taiwan; still
despite mounting world protest,
spends its treasure, the lives of
its youth, in killing and burning
in the bordering lands of Vietnam,
Laos and Cambodia, demonstrating
the utter necessity of being
prepared against war and against
all disasters; now in security
fishing folk set out from the bays
around Chinwangtao; in security
are the schools filled with children
and in security do the peoples
on both sides of the Great Wall
where it comes down to the sea
at Shanhaikwan nearby, grow their
crops, come together in meetings
planning their future in the spirit
of the Thought of Mao Tsetung.

Yet none for one moment
avoiding the responsibility
that has come to them
as they have taken power.

Water in Holiangshan village, Changli county, north Hopei.

HOPEI

Old type percussion well
sinker, Hengshui, Hopei.

Modern well sinker, Hengshui.

Ancient bridge of Sui period, Chaochow, Hopei,
built at the beginning of the seventh century.

New sluice gates, Hai river conservancy, Hopei.

Up go the dykes, Hai river conservancy.

Newly terraced hillside, Chinglung county, north Hopei.

New worker fresh from school, Chinwangtao factory.

Making electrical equipment, Chinglung county town, north Hopei.

Designers in a Chin-wangtao pottery, north Hopei.

Children in a commune brigade school, north Hopei.

Each face a study. Korean nationality children and school headmaster, Korean Brigade, Pohai Commune, Funing.

The *omoni* dance by working women of Korean Brigade.

Statue of Dr. Norman Bethune, Shihchiachuang, Hopei.

Dr. Bethune's tomb (*left*) and Dr. Kotnis' tomb, Shihchiachuang.

An old port, become a new port;
meeting place between workers
of many lands who go about
the highways of the world; an
old gate, become a new gate
leading to new understanding
between peoples; fascinating
the many who come and gaze
at its tower and battlements
now inspiring all with its
promise of greater things to be.

Chapter 5

Shantung

Shantung, originally the ancient area east of Mount Tai but now embracing part of the north China plain also, is a province of some 150,000 square kilometres in area, with a population of around 55 million. Half of the land is mountainous. Its biggest city is the port of Tsingtao, and its capital is Tsinan on the Yellow river.

The province is one with a swiftly growing industry, and too, one where terrific changes are being made on the agricultural front. Something of the strength of these changes may be gauged in a study of model brigades such as Niehchia in Penglai, and Hsiatingchia in Huanghsien. In 1970 it was reported that seven and a half tons of grain per hectare had been harvested in Wulien, once one of the poorest counties in the province, and about which a brief account is presented here.

Shantung is famous for its fruit, mainly apples and grapes. It accounts for a large portion of the peanuts produced in China, and is also a big producer of soya beans and cotton. It grows one crop of winter wheat, followed by corn or kaoliang as an autumn harvest.

226

In the days of the impact of foreign imperialism, Germany first attempted to seize control of the whole province; it was followed after 1914 by Japan.

Before and During the Cultural Revolution in Tsinan

We travelled to Tsinan by highway from the south on an early summer's day in 1966, coming up from Chufu through the green fields of wheat of rural Ningyang, Feicheng and Changching counties and then on through the hills down to Shantung's capital. It was good to see so many activities in the countryside. Water gurgled everywhere as we passed. Diesel engines and electric pumps threw it into canals up on hillsides, youngsters brought it up from wells with chain pumps. Production teams took it from dammed-up waterways across the wheat fields. People around these parts seem no longer scared of drought, and though the spring had been dry a rich crop was confidently hoped for.

On the first morning in Tsinan city we started out to look at the best of local scenery, going first to the Baotu Springs garden park. Tsinan is rich in natural springs, having some 72 of them. One of those in this garden is the source of the Lo river. It is a place that has been put into fine condition, with pavilions redecorated and surroundings beautified. In the courtyard a whole school of children were reciting the three short essays of Mao Tsetung: "Serve the People", "In Memory of Norman Bethune" and "The Foolish Old Man Who Removed the Mountains"; a few lines at a time were intoned by one small group, then the rest joined in, all going ahead with a swing. From here we went to what was formerly a very down-at-the-heel area that is now fast changing to become a beauty spot. It is mainly a big wide boulevard, over a kilometre long and tree-lined, that runs where the old city wall once was. Below is the moat which on this side of the city is fed from ten springs and has wonderful, clear water. The canal sides are being planted and stone steps laid down leading to the water. A new single-span bridge in the traditional style crosses the canal, over which we passed to see three of the more famous springs, the grandfather of which is Mohuchuan — Black Tiger Spring — whose water flows out through the mouths of three sculptured tigers. In the old days, when city improvements were called for country folk were pressed into service to do the job. Now all that is needed to be done is carried out in mass work by the cadres, students and street folk of the city themselves, and a very nice job they are making of it. Many came to work four days a week on it, including their day off. Tsinan today is hardly the Chichou it was in olden times. Its over 200 big industrial enterprises stretch well out beyond the confines of the ancient city. Its 1,100,000 people have changed. The doctrine of not just talking fine words, but getting down to put them into practice is becoming a part of people's lives.

Perhaps the most famous piece of scenery in the city is that around Daming Lake. During the Northern Wei dynasty, a temple was erected here called Damingssu. The lake took its name from that. Once a good deal larger than it is now, it is still over 100 acres in extent, enough for pleasure boating and to grow the lotus that brightens up a summer. The boat that brings one to Lihsia Island takes one on across to Peichike, a Yuan dynasty temple set high above the shores of the lake. Beside it is the temple used as headquarters for the last Kuomintang garrison, whose commander escaped as the people's forces entered, making his way to a village in Shansi where the local farmers, seeing his hands were not those of a man who had ever worked with them, turned him over to the government. In these latter years he has been pardoned and given useful work to do, after having been given a trip around the new China.

One has quite a sight from the top of the pavilion in Chinniu Park. It is a great wide pavilion under a roof of glistening yellow glazed tile, and below it is part of a forest planted in these past years. Beyond are the two rocky hills one on each side of the Yellow river, Chuehshan and Hsiaohuashan, with the Yellow river bridge between. The old steel bridge, which was repaired in the 'fifties, still takes the rail traffic. Road traffic has to go over the ferry at Lodu, where we spent a while watching the big junks going full sail upstream with a spanking southeasterly behind them. Down in the river mouth is a sandy island which the youth of Tsinan have by voluntary labor changed to one of greenery and which consequently can now be farmed. The number of trees that have been planted around the city in these past years is amazing. The big river dyke, now greatly strengthened, makes interior dykes not so important, and a lot of what was sand and little rocky hills has changed to become green in consequence. The Chinniu, or "Golden Cow" Park is on 200 acres of such land, some of which has been made into a zoo. Many of the animals can be seen in seemingly natural surroundings, as some of the small rocky hills jut out of the plain and have been utilised. It is really quite a majestic park, and the pavilion on its highest hill gives it the necessary splash of color to set off all the greenery.

Though Shantung was said to be having a drought, one would not have thought it by the look of the crops on the land we came through to get to Tsinan. But there are backhill areas with no water supply near enough, where the solution of the problem has meant a lot of struggle. One commune brigade of 1,000 people in a high, dry hilly region east of Tsinan that has always depended on spring rains had no rainfall this year. Its answer was for everyone who could walk to go with carrying poles and buckets three and a half kilometres, seven kilometres with the return journey, and bring water up from a valley. Steadily everyone in the brigade did this, day by day, all through the day and into the nights so that they are gaining a crop that at least will keep them, even if it does not give any surplus. "Stand up to the enemy and he will retreat," they say. The story of their fight has encouraged many other folk to put out their best and gain more also. This, they say, is really putting theory into practice in the way of Chairman Mao.

On a visit to the Shantung provincial museum in Tsinan I passed folk laying out gardens and a grapevine-trellised walk along the bank of a canal that has been widened. In the museum are several sections that deal with the economy of this province of 58 million people. In

the historical section, there was a fascinating Han tombstone with a tall
tree etched in its centre. There were also some good examples of
Lungshan ware found at a village around 30 kilometres east of Tsinan,
a fine pot of Tzechow Sung I liked well and some statuary of Northern
Wei. A sculptured relief of two wide-horned deer done in the latter
Han period was unique.

With more of a morning to spend I went into a people's marketplace
which has been created from a former slum area. The shop where
bicycles were sold seemed to be busier than most. Tsinan makes a wide
range of consumer goods, thermos bottles, aluminum and enamel ware,
along with most other daily necessities. After a walk around here we
went on to a small city park. In one corner a crowd of children had
gathered, so we went to see what they were watching. It was some
bayonet practice by Army men, done with all the dexterity of Peking
opera tumblers, and the precision demanded of a life-and-death struggle.
Lads from the communes of Shantung hills are naturally tough. Train
them properly and give them a way of putting their own creative ability
into a struggle, and the results are truly amazing. A sharp blow causes
one man's rifle to fly from his hand. He jumps high and turns swiftly
around a corner and then re-enters the combat with his entrenching tool,
swiftly pulled from his belt and opened, on hand. This he handles brilliantly. The practice was one of fast-moving incident, finishing abruptly
with the fighters forming up and swiftly wheeling off, helmets, armor
and dummy rifles on collapsible handcarts that suddenly appeared. The
park then returned to quietness, with small boys leaning over fountain
walls to reach down to the water and small girls sitting on parapets
playing games.

A drive through the city to the south brought us to the hill called
Chienfoshan, which has been reforested since the temples there were
used by the Kuomintang as barracks and the soldiers cut down the old
cypresses for fuel. The road up the slope is now remade, rest pavilions
built on the way, and as one gets to the summit the scent of lilac in
bloom is beside one. There are grottoes and Six Dynasties sculptures,
many of them somewhat battered due to the elements and to rocks
breaking away.

The temple is a Yuan dynasty foundation, repaired many times since.
Some of the halls have been used to store sculptures found around the
site. Looking down on Tsinan, one sees the apple orchards on the bottom
slope of the hill, some new forest plantations, and then the long lines of
college and university buildings that front it. Away behind them are the
smokestacks of modern industry.

I went out into the country for a few days, then returned to Tsinan
around mid-day on May the First. The streets were bright with red banners, carrying the slogans of the day. People were in a holiday mood,
though a cold wind had blown in from the sea bringing some rain. By
afternoon, however, it cleared, the sun came out and folk crowded into
the parks. I went to the hill on whose summit the monument to fighters
for the people is erected. Work was still proceeding on the structures

around its base, but enough had been done already to show how imposing it will be when completed. Trees planted on the stony hill at its rear are miraculously taking root. Shantung pines and cypresses seem to be able to drive roots right down through cracks in limestone and grow despite all.

Emergencies show up the spirit of the Shantung people well. The old folk remember about the wars of resistance and liberation, when the bitterness of struggle called for so much dogged heroism in the hills and hamlets around Tsinan. At the end of February 1966, there came another short, dramatic emergency. A cold blast came down the coast and froze the sea for several hundred kilometres on Shantung's northern shore. All the fishing boats, some 393 of them, were frozen in and the ice had to be broken before they could get out. In the meantime provisions and water had to be gotten to them. Concerted work all around brought complete victory, all boats, all fishermen, right down to two old men who were lost and cut off for five days, were saved. There is much exciting detail in the story, but the thing that pleased everyone was how well organisational work dovetailed between Tsinan workers, fishermen, Armymen, helicopters and all the rest. Putting theory into practice again, and making a bad thing turn into a good thing as everyone's understanding of their collective strength was raised.

The policy of making each area in China economically independent has demanded a good deal of thought and struggle. This was realised when paying a visit to the Tsinan pencil factory, which is one of 546 workers — 327 of them women — who turn out really first-class pencils in premises they have converted from an old brick and tile kiln into those of a modern factory. This has meant an enormous task in filling in great holes, levelling out the land, setting up in improvised buildings, then at last building modern workshops with machines that operate automatically. As they cleaned up the place they dug up 330,000 old bricks that could still be used which helped with material for the first workrooms. When they started, their pencils were only just good enough to be used in the local primary schools. Their 50 original workers were financed, in the first instance, as a cooperative relief project for unemployed. This was back in 1951. They operated as a cooperative until 1954, when the factory was made into a state enterprise and given assistance to modernise. By 1957 the production was seven times greater than it was in 1952 and six times as many varieties of pencils were produced. The factory went forward on its own steam, not needing government loans but modernising swiftly so that now a uniformly good pencil is produced that is much in demand abroad, 170 million pencils a year going to more than 24 countries. Though its product is up to international standard, improvements are being made all the time, now that a firm basis has been laid. It is certainly a sight to see the long production line of pencils being given the bright coating of plastic paint, labelled, and then packed in "Friendship" brand cartons for export.

A second Tsinan factory, this one of large size, I visited on May 2nd 1966. The day was a holiday, coming immediately after May Day, but the assistant manager was on hand to show us around. The factory is his work, his hobby, his evident passion, and the way he drives one of the eight-ton trucks that he and his fellow workers now produce shows his joy and satisfaction with the results that have been obtained already. He has a right to feel happy, for he was a worker in the guerilla arsenal that operated in the hills during the wars of resistance and liberation, and which he left only after Tsinan was freed to come and take over a small-sized late Kuomintang-controlled repair shop. His first task was to help to get the factory operating so that it could make spares for the vehicles that then existed in China, foreign models for which spares were denied by the blockade. With some years' experience of doing this, the idea naturally occurred to him and his co-workers, why not make our own trucks? They tried, but the first model of which but 20 were produced was a failure. This was in 1960 when the great drought had hit the countryside and things were tough. The future did not look so bright from a subjective angle, but still the workers were determined. They went in batches to Shanghai, and brought Shanghai workers to Tsinan in rotation. More trial and error. More headaches, more grim getting down to essentials. The country needs a heavy truck. We ought to be able to produce it. Finally by 1964 they succeeded and set themselves the first target of 100, but actually turned out 148. A big problem was how to make a press for the chassis. The Changchun automobile works in the Northeast had bought one from the USSR in the mid-'fifties that cost 2,500,000 yuan, with transport and erection costs along with the services of an expert in addition. The Tsinan factory had to do the job itself. Workers went into a huddle and in the end made one that cost 70,000 yuan, everything included. It takes 14 minutes to stamp out a chassis as against seven minutes for the one in Changchun, but as the factory is at present simply building a base for future enlargement, this additional time is of no consequence. 335 vehicles were made in 1965, and teams were sent out to ride with them and get the comments of workers on how they could be improved. The steering wheel was too heavy, the brakes did not act swiftly enough, and so on. Embodying corrections made in line with all suggestions, the 1966 model was turned out. A total of 600 was the target, which will probably be exceeded, possibly by as many as 400. The engine is a Shanghai-made 150 h.p. diesel, and some of the parts are made in other shops around Tsinan. The factory itself employs 2,800 workers, and has a part-work, part-study school for its rising technical workers situated in its compound. These work one week and study the next in rotation, all being lower middle-school graduates. They do a four-year course.

One feature I liked about the big eight tonner was that it had space in its commodious cab for the two men doing the loading, who in China usually accompany the truck. For them it is no longer needed to sit perched up on the cargo, out in cold and heat. It is a workers' land, and this was their request. In all, in the latest model, 170 changes have been made to fill suggestions workers have made. Naturally, the factory hopes to be able to go ahead in the future and to set up the factory of their expectations, producing the dream truck. For a while their product was the biggest truck produced in China, but now in Chungking one of 25 tons is already being made, so that they have to be satisfied with second place in this respect.

So came to an end a visit to Tsinan, with many pleasant memories of its spirit, its workers studying "The Foolish Old Man Who Removed the Mountains", as they took their factories on to higher stages despite all obstacles, its old folk looking back to the old days when first the Germans and then the Japanese tried to steal their patrimony, then all realising the need to protect it still further as the leadership of the old order now with different flags tried to encircle, apparently lusting for ever greater profits, prepared with the newest technique for genocide. It would be an act of sheer madness, however, for any invader to step into the hornets' nest he would find waiting for him in the Shantung of today.

Returning to Shantung for another visit after 18 months of the Cultural Revolution, one found that industry had kept operating through the stormy period and that production was now improving fast. No single industrial enterprise had closed down. The pencil factory was making more and better pencils, the big plant which turned out planers for heavy machine shops was busier than ever. Crop yields for 1967 were as much as 20 percent above those of 1966, which itself was a very good year. The truck factory was also doing much better than before and had started on the production of a new vehicle in addition to the old model. I asked if there had been any new industries started in Tsinan during the time of the Cultural Revolution. "Yes," came the answer, "it has been in this period that we have opened a new 50,000-spindle cotton mill that is now operating full strength. A big new fertiliser plant has also started production."

Driving out of the city the first morning after arrival I passed many busy industrial plants, most of them set amongst the vegetable farms of suburban communes. Such roads are always full of life and give picture after picture to think back on and enjoy. I caught a passing glimpse of a lad of 14 or less, helping his old father or grandfather to bring in a load of produce. The morning sun shone on his ruddy face and he laughed gaily as he fairly threw himself into the task of pulling. The unspoiled farm lad, accustomed to struggle and to working with others, is the salt of the good earth of China. I thought of him again when meeting more of his kind, now grown young men in immaculate uniforms, who sat around a table with me in the barracks of a tank corps. They were the fighters of a model unit, and each told something of his experiences in the Cultural Revolution. What it had meant to each and every one, and how it had affected the commune homes they had come from and the Army they had become part of. They too, like the boy on the road, had grown up in the struggle. They had been somewhat overawed by the heavy weaponry when they first arrived. Some got sick when the 33-ton tanks rolled and pitched. When they came to study all the "whys" and "wherefores" and understood the need for what they were doing and how a belief in it could give them added strength, then they began to understand the power of the Thought of Mao Tsetung. How much stronger this was than anything else! It created the spirit of the workers who built their tanks, and it made for the ability and determination of the men who operated such.

The political director, a lad who had come from Yangchow in Kiangsu, led well in discussion. All unit members took part, chipping in and carrying it forward. They described their daily life. They talked about their meals, their study and rest throughout the day. They told stories of how some of their number put the essay "Serve the People" into practice, all being very appreciative of one soldier who happened to be away at the time for the way he used to help others, truly serving the people. Another told of his village and of an old man there who really understood the class angle well, being able to trace the "operators" from the old exploiting class who would use fine words to come in and seek to perpetuate their rule in the new day, and how these would invariably follow the capitalist road. How important it was too to realise just what that road meant. Important for everyone, not just for a tiny handful of leaders. Only in this way would strength enough be found to meet the class enemy. How in the past so few had really understood why things were being done. How now it became the duty of everyone to know.

Fighters told how the study of the Little Red Book had helped them in their personal relations with others. How when a storm of hailstones had badly affected the family of one lad, others had chipped in and quietly sent money to help, without letting him know. "The success of the revolution is the success of the mass of common working folk everywhere," one said. "I thought I was someone when I graduated from lower middle school. Now I understand that being helped by the people to learn more is done in order that I can find ways to assist them more," said another. "An army like ours, a real people's army, must support the people in their revolutions everywhere. Why did Dr. Norman Bethune come to China? He knew our cause was the cause of all working folk, that's why." And so the explanation went on, in simple, direct language that carried a wealth of meaning, especially when one realised just who these people were.

We went around the compounds behind living quarters and saw the various service sections staffed by wives of the personnel — consumer goods store, food store, bank and tailor's shop where old work caps were being done up and made as good as new. There being a general campaign to save on coal, measures had been taken to cut down on the stoves used, and no one could have accused the staff here of leading a soft and over-comfortable life. Actually, it was quite spartan. We went to see the big tanks and then said good-bye to our hosts. We drove off back to the city again feeling that the trip had been very worthwhile.

While in Tsinan on this December 1967 visit, we visited an exhibition of the life of Wang Ssu-tung, a young soldier who was killed when removing repair work timber which had broken loose in a blizzard and had been thrown on the railway tracks on the Yellow river bridge. The lad removed the timber, but his companions were unable to halt the train in time from crushing him. He had a short life, being born in 1947, and was from a formerly poor farm family in Lichiachuang Brigade of Chihan county. He entered the Army in March 1966, and became very active in the Cultural Revolution which followed. Records of his diaries and letters and of his work at that time show that he was an eager fighter for the best he knew, throwing himself heart and soul into the daily work of his unit, whether helping the farm folk around, assisting the young Red Guards, or in his purely military tasks. Nowadays, it is the simple folk from the ranks of the people who have served the people well and have made the supreme sacrifice who are held up for youth to emulate. No longer is it the big militarist seated on a white horse, the bellowing demagogue, or the rich philanthropist who is held up as the type to model oneself on. Rather is it the Chiao Yu-lu, the Liu Hu-lan, the Lei Feng, the Li Wen-chung, the Wang Chieh, and the Wang Ssu-tung, men and women right out of the ranks of the common people who are proclaimed to be models for others to learn from.

In the exhibition, a corps of young girl Red Guards took it in turn to give explanations for each and every aspect of the life of this country boy who turned out to be so great a success, in the way that the world of Mao Tsetung judges a success in this day and age.

One artist depicted him, we were touched to see, on guard at the bridge, thinking of the struggle against U.S. imperialism in Vietnam, and of the ordinary folk there who were standing up so gallantly to the imperialism that would take their all.

I spent a morning at an unusual cotton mill. One of over 50,000 spindles and 2,000 looms on which construction had started in March 1965. In December of the same year, while building was still not yet completed, some sections of the mill were already in operation. Equipment was made in either Tientsin or Shanghai. Some of the new workers, many of them youngsters in their early teens, had three months' training in the cotton mill of Tsingtao. They then came back to Tsinan and trained still newer ones, so in all it has been a youth enterprise. When the Cultural Revolution got into its stride, some of the young rebels who stood out against the management were arrested and taken to the police. Later when things got to a more advanced stage, they were released and joined in the struggle between the two major groups into which the young workers had organised themselves. When the grand alliance of these was achieved, a 19-year-old boy took leadership, backed by all groups and those of the old cadres who had come over. Now 60 percent of the old cadres have been "liberated", and 80 percent of them are working, the rest still being in study groups. It is expected that most of these latter will be working again soon. To be "liberated" is a term that has come into use denoting the fact that the cadre has made an objective critical evaluation of his past work and has been accepted by the Revolutionary Committee.

Tsinan proclaimed its Revolutionary Committee in March 1967. Struggle between various groupings continued, however, through the four following months, with the result that production did not come up to plan in that period. When the grand alliance was completed however, production took a sharp upsurge, and by December 12th the plan for the whole year was met triumphantly.

Work on technical innovations has gone on well over this last period, and a clever device for raking away cotton from a long row of pressed bales, and then feeding it into the openers has been quite successful.

The last industrial plant we visited in Tsinan was a paper mill, the workers there being one of the first group to take power in the Cultural Revolution. It is a plant with over 1,000 workers, with quite a long history. Started by the Germans in 1908, it was later taken over by the Japanese, but until Liberation it never produced more than 240 tons of paper a year. Now it produces more than that in one month, and there are 60 varieties, different kinds of thin paper which will take printed photos on both sides and is used for good pictorials, paper for certain industrial uses, cigarette paper, and so on. During the past seven months workers have been hard at work installing a new paper machine of their own design which is much better than anything imported. They have changed one battery of pulp hollanders to a completely new design also, which has proved to be a great improvement. These are just some of the technical advances made.

The leaders of the Revolutionary Committee told us how the Cultural Revolution had affected the mill. Production on every machine kept on throughout all working hours, though a few workers did absent themselves at one stage or another. The early decision of the first secretary of the plant to join the rebels was a great help. Now the big majority of old cadres have been taken back into the fold and are working well. The grand alliance of all groups in the factory has been successful. One was impressed with the excellent spirit that permeated the place, marking it a concern that will play quite a part in the industrialised Shantung of the future.

Yentai and Penglai Today

It was after dark on a December evening when I left Tsinan for Chefoo, now called Yentai. The hard-class sleeper was quite full, but I had a bottom berth of the tiers of three. Sometime in the small hours of the morning I half awoke to hear the announcement, "Leiyang. 18 minutes' stop", and then drowsed off again thinking of the Lei, the Yi and the Kiau tribesmen of these regions in the second millennium B.C., wondering if they stayed in China and became part of the people or whether they joined the long trek across Asia in the direction of Europe. Anyway, they are commemorated in place names like Leiyang, whose up-and-coming youth, however, are too busy to bother much about the past. There is so much "past" in Shantung. Each locality is rich with it!

There had been heavy snow at Yentai which showed up in the moon-light as we came in. Not 5:30 yet, so I went off to the comfortable guest house to get an hour's blissful sleep before starting the day in the regular way.

Yentai is the Chinese name for the whole locality now occupied by the city and harbor of that name. Chefoo was the name of a little fishing village where a foreign settlement was set up as a pleasant summer resort for the rich, and also a missionary headquarters where quite a few foreign children went to school. From this port many of the tough farm folk set out to develop the northeast provinces, and in 1912 it was reported that 100,000 a year also were contracted to do seasonal work to open up Siberia for the Russians, returning home each winter. Chefoo, too, was made a summer station for units of the U.S. navy stationed in China waters, when it was said that the U.S. frontier ran up the Yangtze. At Liberation it had a population of 20,000. Now, with rail connections since the mid-'fifties it is a growing industrial town of over 160,000, with big wide roads and modern facilities. The beaches are as beautiful as ever, and as I write I look out over the circular bay. Right below me a group of boys are having a snow fight for the brief possession of this rock, that crag. They look and sound completely happy, delighting in the sun and the fresh morning air. On walls are slogans of the Cultural Revolution, "Struggle against selfishness, criticise revisionism". Shantung has done well in this struggle and all round the province improvement is now showing up.

Before leaving Peking, I had looked over old books to find something on Shantung, selecting one published by foreign missionaries in 1912. It was a heavy tome covering many fields, a book which I had not gone through before. It eulogised Gutzlaff, the German, later British missionary who first made reports on the Shantung coast in conjunction with British navy officers. It was on this information that in the Opium Wars the demands for access to coastal ports were made. Indeed, Gutzlaff had acted as interpreter for many opium running ships, and in the Second Opium War had organised the first foreign intelligence service on the China coast from amongst Chinese traitors to serve British imperialism.

Then when the coast was "opened" and foreign traders came, the first picked on the pleasant bay of Chefoo as being a salubrious place to live. The small fishing village there soon grew into a foreign settlement. Amongst the first traders who came was the missionary Williamson. His main interest seemed to be in things material, rather than spiritual. He travelled a lot through the Shantung peninsula and wrote about the province's richness in coal, gold, iron and so on. His book, done in conjunction with others and published in 1868, was so enthusiastic that it became the direct cause of the visit of the German geologist Baron Richthofen, who proceeded to map the province carefully, preparing the way for imperial German occupation of Tsingtao. German influence grew throughout the province till after 1914 when it was supplanted by Japanese imperialism.

Williamson gained the interest of a British diplomat, Alabaster, who followed in his steps. Then of the English consul Markham, who travelled with him. It was clearly stated that "all three of them were influenced in their judgment by their desire to discover minerals in which European capital might be employed in bringing to use". An enlarged edition of the book they wrote was published in London in 1873 in four great folios, "bringing in many more names of villages; projected railways, coal mines, supposed gold fields, etc. were marked on it". Church, state and commerce, again the unholy trinity. This pattern of missionary, diplomat plus gunboats, and the trader who hauled away the profit, was becoming more and more common in the China of those days. The voyage of Lindsay of the British navy and the notorious Gutzlaff led to the first traders arriving in Chefoo. British influence, however, was to be confined to the Weihaiwei area at the tip of the eastern promontory which they occupied in force a good deal later, and to its church mission district round Tsinan. The mission folk there deplored the fact that some 50,000 people a year would come to live in straw huts around Tsinan, trying to sustain life on a bowl of relief gruel a day. They also deplored the floods and the ever recurring droughts. Thought something ought to be done about the increasing number of grave mounds occupying arable land, but deprecated "any hasty legislation or unwise action" which might hasten their being cleared off. They were very much for the status quo, which gave them all a place to sit and vaporise from. "It will need foreign enterprise, capital and skill, before anything effective can be done", the book wails when talking of the alkaline sands "bordering the Gulf of Pechili which were then a vast waste; a howling wilderness yielding only weeds".

But actually it was the foreign enterprise, missionaries, diplomats and traders which brought chaos in their train. It was to be the Chinese people, increasingly grasping the ideas of Mao Tsetung, who were to make those alkaline wastes fertile, work the mines, build the industry, and make a new Shantung in which people could lift their heads and live. "What are you going to do when you grow up?" I asked a 12-year-old amongst a crowd of his fellows who surrounded me in a Tsinan park. "I'm going to work for the revolution," he answered without a moment's hesitation.

In the Yentai prefecture of 15 counties and two municipalities — Yentai and Weihaiwei — there are 8,130,000 people, who now have the highest living standards in all Shantung. During the Cultural Revolution no production enterprise has stopped in Yentai, and there have been steep rises especially in agricultural production. Whereas in Tsinan the surrounding hills and downs are part of the Mount Tai complex, here in Yentai they belong to the Laoshan group. There is a good deal of fishing done now with modernised trawlers, and a rich harvest of prawns comes in from the prawn beds off the coast. We watched local Yentai people fishing from the beach. They had made a small raft and put a sail on it. From this platform dangled multiple lines with hooks and bait. The wind would take the platform far out to sea, with a line attached. When the fisherman thought it had been out long enough, he would haul it in. One we watched had eight "pien dou", a kind of snapper, on the line when it came in, much to the fascination of the numerous small boys playing on the beach.

The old Army cadre with two young rebels who are on the Revolutionary Committee administering the area at present came to supper with us, telling us much about the movement as it proceeds in Yentai now, already with a good many of the old cadres "liberated", and with the prospect of practically all of them being so received before long. In the Mao Tsetung Thought training classes they have attended, they make their sincere self-criticism and give their understanding of revisionism and what effect it has on revolutionary activity. They study together and get a new evaluation of their comrades and their work in line with the thinking of Chairman Mao. As the Yentai area had long been an Eighth Route Army base, it possessed a good tradition of clear down-to-earth thinking, and this has helped in solving many of the problems that have arisen. For instance, it has been easier here to get mass action for the use of better fertilisers, seed, and irrigation than has been possible in many other places. Around 80 percent of the arable land in some counties is now irrigated, many big reservoirs having been built and wells dug down to the lower water levels. All communes in the area now have highway connection and every county has a tractor station, with substations in many of the communes.

Fruit is a speciality of the region. Yentai apples are now well known, and Yentai itself has varieties that keep right up to the beginning of the following summer. The use of bare hillslopes for growing date trees, of farm compounds for walnuts, and of suitable hillslopes for chestnuts is being worked on. In all, these 8,100,000 people of the Yentai prefecture were a good sparkplug for the 58 million in the province, though in the matter of the Cultural Revolution they hand a bouquet to Tsingtao, the industrial port on the coast: "Why, they already have over 80 percent of their old cadres 'liberated'. We have still some way to go to catch up with them," members of the Revolutionary Committee told me. Then, returning to the question of apples, they proudly said that just one brigade of a Yentai commune had produced 13 million jin this last season.

One morning I set out to look at a small local industrial plant which employs 357 workers to make compressors for fertiliser plants. Such plants are operated by communes, counties, prefectures and provinces now, so that the demand for this particular product is great. With technical innovations, the old models imported from the USSR have now been changed and less wasteful and more streamlined ones evolved. The factory was first set up in 1956 by combining some small local workshops, and re-equipping them with modern machine tools. Output this 1967 is 26 percent higher than for the previous year. Since the rebel group took over the management in April there has been a great raising of worker's spirit. The process of education in the Thought of Mao Tsetung has raised their political level so that they smile at the old concept of the simple, honest worker questioning nothing, waiting for commands and reverently listening to whatever the upper cadres expounded, whether such was in agreement with Chairman Mao's ideas or not.   Now they get together and criticise the 70 points for industry as put out by revisionists in power taking the capitalist road prior to the Cultural Revolution.   They are able to make this criticism only after a thoughtful study of the Little Red Book and by putting its maxims into daily practice.   Their study of "Serve the People" has made them more considerate of each other, more willing to help each other in problems of livelihood and work.   Their intensive study and memorisation of "The Foolish Old Man Who Removed the Mountains" has made them more and more determined to solve all difficulties and push ahead.   They reject the idea of bonus payments and such material incentives, now more fully awake to their own responsibilities as producers for the new day.   There are still many hurdles to be gotten over, but they know they are on the right path.

For around 25 years before Liberation there was a handful of small clock factories in Yentai that never turned out more than 30,000 clocks a year.   In 1954 these little enterprises were brought together, and by 1957 their combined efforts made for a total annual production of 220,000 timepieces.   By 1965 this had grown to 300,000; 1966, 370,000; 1967, 450,000. Now, with new lines of production, especially those for the export trade, the sky is the limit for the 1,060 people working there, over half of whom are local housewives.   We saw their products, from ship chronometers to the latest transistorised house clocks which run for a year on one dry cell.   There were grandfather clocks and then artistically made clocks for the foreign market as well as clocks for laboratory work, correct to a fraction of a second.   A boy apprentice of 16 was the youngest worker in the plant, which he had joined just nine days previously.   A bright, cheerful youngster, he came running downstairs to take part in the group saying good-bye to me, giving a warm and friendly handshake as we parted.   The leaders of the rebel group in charge, one of whom was the factory manager, pleaded for criticism, but what could one say except to congratulate them all for making so much headway in so short a time! Surely their premises, which looked as if they had once been some kind of a foreign hotel, were not very suitable for industrial work, but they have the advantage of being right in the central district where most of the staff live.   But there is no doubt that with the spirit the workers have now, if they want to do a thing they will find ways and means of doing it.   So the building of a more modern factory is only a matter of time.   Old Chefoo is full of buildings unsuitable for the present day — churches, mission houses, old consulates, traders' "hongs" and so on.   But the new Yentai is closing in on them now.

While in Yentai, my hosts were kind enough to invite me to a concert given by school children of the local primary schools.   Held in a truly magnificent hall, it went off with terrific zest and considerable ability. Items all had to deal with the Cultural Revolution and with the world revolution in one way or another, whether singing old Shantung chants with the words from Chairman Mao's works, doing an African dance, or with a boy orchestra playing the music of the day.   Some items were quite pointed, as for instance one in which members of two opposing political groups refused to cooperate and fought each other. Then, helped by an Army girl, they found it better to halt fighting and come together on the basis of principle. Not all at once, but little by little. Some of the things they said when they were fighting had obviously been heard before, judging by the uproarious glee with which the audience greeted them. When we came out of the hall into the clear steely air of a north China night, the snow-covered hills around reminded me of old Yenan in War of Resistance days, and coming out of a similar entertainment one winter there. Then it was Japanese and German imperialism. Now it is a new chief enemy. The spirit of youth is the same, and that is the thing that matters. The youth of a people who can no longer be trifled with, fooled or exploited.

The little, old Chefoo with its narrow streets and its European-China coast type of buildings now becomes more and more insignificant in contrast to the new city. For a time after Liberation it was an independent municipality. Then in the late 'fifties when two prefectures were combined, it became the prefectural seat, with a bright future as an urban industrial centre for a region that has been poor for just too long, and now does not intend to stay that way any longer.

My old book on Shantung says that in 1912 Chefoo owed its importance to its foreign trade and "all those goods from the East of Asia which come in European ships. Cotton goods and opium are among the chief of the imports. Besides these are metals and iron ware, also sea weed from Japan. The exports are trifling." It would be a foolish man indeed who even attempted to talk about opium in this day and age, let alone try to import and sell it!

We spent one morning while in Yentai going to the Chefoo winery whose four products, red wine, white wine, brandy and vermouth, go abroad to many countries. Started in 1892, it produced in a small way for China coast consumption. Since Liberation, however, it has grown into a large export business. Down in its cellars we walked through the great galleries where huge casks were stored, and watched the mechanised washing and filling of bottles. The whole place was scrupulously clean, and the 300 workers looked confident and happy in their tasks. The dry red and white wines are much appreciated abroad, while the brandy has now an international reputation. The winery has around 2,000 mou of vines but also receives grapes from outlying counties and from farm homes in communes around the city. Its bottles are made by the Chefoo glass works.

Just over the road from the winery are the premises that were once the gendarmerie headquarters during the Japanese occupation. No one I asked could remember what they were before that, but they are very large and roomy, and are now used by a handicraft workshop which turns out art embroidery in colored wool on a heavy gauze for the foreign trade. These products are used as pictures, upholstery for furniture and so on, and have a wide market. 270 women do some of the art work in designing and stitching, but there are also 1,500 local women working in their homes who bring in their products to this centre.

There are many other export lines. The prefecture which has as big a population as for instance Cuba, sells a great deal of surplus grain each year to the state; the whole of its textile requirements are taken care of by Shantung province itself, none having to be imported from other provinces. We drove up to the beauty spot on a hill where there was once a temple, to Yuwang, the great controller of floods. From here one can see all over Chefoo city the smokestacks of new industry, the terraces of workers' dwellings, the harbor and the scenic bay. On hillsides there are also the grape gardens of the winery we had seen, and terraces of apple orchards reaching far back into the countryside. Seen from here the city looks impressive; it is evidently a fast developing centre with a bright future. I commented on the sturdy, ruddy children seen all around us. "They ought to be. They swim and sunbathe in summer, eat apples in autumn and winter, and have plenty of good grain. The air is bracing and clean, and they look with confidence to the future," a friend said. The 11-year-old boy, who astonished us by his fine two-stringed violin, playing when we went to the children's concert, brought others of his group over to see me on my last afternoon in Yentai. They sat on the sea wall, and played and sang for a while. The 11-year-old was neither shy nor forward. So full of joy of life he was, it flowed from him and lightened all around. When he played his "er hu" he brought out the music in a gay, carefree way, yet giving new and richer meaning to it. We were grateful to local friends for the chance of meeting him again, and taking his picture. The whole group overwhelmed me by giving me their precious badges, an armband of their unit and their scarf.

I looked over the sea at Chefoo and wrote these lines to try and make impressions clearer:

> Too long
>> were the talons of imperialism
>> fastened here; yet
>> the long occupation did teach
> who friends,
> who enemies, then
>> going ahead in that spirit
> beginning
>> to look at even the revered past
>> with new eyes, wondering too
> if so many old things
>> like barren, treeless hillsides,
>> ancestor graves occupying arable
>> land, did not too belong
> to the enemy.
>
> Chefoo, once base
> for get-rich traders,

missionaries who carried the flag
and diplomats backed up by
gunboats,
a lazy watering place, where
the U.S. Navy played in summertime
and all around
poverty reigned supreme;

Now has this crust
of the other class departed
and the people have come in
building on the grand scale
new industry in a new city.

Of such things do I think
while beside me on the sea wall
sits a boy with his fiddle
bringing to life the song of the helmsman
and all it means to him.

On a clear winter's day with snow on the ground and the blue sea gleaming, the highway between Yentai and Penglai was a scenic one. Built during the Japanese occupation, it has lots of curves but is now being straightened out by the commune folk around, the new embankment, as straight as an arrow, cutting across the country. Folk working here and on the irrigation projects we passed often wore red woolen scarves and these, with the blue of their clothes and their ruddy faces, made a splash of color amid the snow. We stopped for a rest and talked to a man transporting 320 jin of outsize Yentai cabbage on a rubber-tyred wheelbarrow. Though growing so big, this famous local cabbage is wonderfully tender. It is also fantastically cheap — six jin for ten fen.

We got to Penglai, once Tengchowfu, in an hour and a half. Most of the old city wall has been made into a highway. The buildings of the Temple to the Blessed Isles remain overlooking the bay, but most of the walls of the water city have gone, and modern Penglai bears little resemblance to the quaint little old-fashioned city that came down out of ancient history almost intact to pre-Liberation times. The fables, legends and history connected with it have long been part of the heritage of China. From here, the Eight Immortals are supposed to have crossed to the Fairy Isles. From this region went Chang Chun walking across Central Asia to discuss Taoism with Ghenghis Khan in Samarkand, for Ghenghis had become a great Khan and felt he needed a religion of some kind to support him. There are so many tales about Penglai, but folk think it is high time they be laid to rest and new history be made by and for the young coastal folk of a new Shantung.

In the bays along the coast we noted many new diesel-engined trawlers. A good meteorological service now gives warning of bad weather so that hazards once faced by fisherfolk are fewer.

In Penglai we visited first the hill which overlooks the sea and, though the towers around the water city have gone, yet as we could see, some small boats still came in for shelter and the great gates still existed. East there stretched a wonderful beach which must be the delight of many thousands in the hot summer months. Due to weathering few of the old monuments on the hill can be read, the elements having erased the characters from the stone. The Kuomintang, before being thrown out from the mainland, swore they would make a stand from Changshen Islands in the north to Hainan in the south. This proved to be but an idle boast, as empty as the mirages often seen out at sea from the highest point of the Temple of the Blessed Isles.

Penglai is a peanut county. That is not to say it does not also have a surplus of grain to sell to the state, but just that more peanuts are grown here than in other Shantung counties. In the agricultural implements factory we visited, one of the production lines was a simple peanut thresher which does the necessary task of threshing so swiftly and efficiently that it is in high demand. The factory has some 400 workers who have been so fired with the political training of the Cultural Revolution that this year their production of spare parts for farm diesels has almost doubled. They have also reduced the price of some of their products to less than half. "To us, serving the people is serving farmers on the communes," they say, so they are doing their best to carry into practice the words "Everything for the people." This agricultural implements factory was started in the time of the Great Leap Forward of 1958, with seven workers. Many of their 76 machine tools they have made themselves. A determined group of people are these, grown more so with many difficulties surmounted.

At an evening concert I attended, a group of the workers of this factory did a very lively item of singing accompanied by their own orchestra. Interesting to see those I watched at their machines in the afternoon sitting on the stage at night. It was a concert rather different from that heard in Yentai, as it included items from the Army, from factories, communes and schools. A good touch, rolled-up sleeves, has been added and lightens up these Cultural Revolution concerts, which proceed at quite a fast speed. The bare arms add so much strength and vitality to the theme. The young people reminded me of their kind who are fighting so hard in Vietnam.

Morning saw snow-laden squalls coming in from the sea. We drove some 35 li up the coast to Niehchia Brigade of Peiko Commune right by the sea. Here I met the brigade leader, Nieh Chen-feng, and his committee, most of whom were also named Nieh, part of a community of 320 households, 1,530 people who are organised into ten production teams for agriculture, one for forestry and three for supporting industries. No, the village built of strong stone-walled homes, with tiled roofs, had not always been here. It was once a couple of hundred yards distant, but a big storm carried much of it away and a better place had been found to rebuild, for Liberation had come, the parasites had gone and the people had found their way ahead. They did not have so much to start with.

The principal trouble was a stretch of 2,000 mou of sand dunes which blew up in big winds and covered everything. The people had been desperately poor. They were determined to get out of the rut, and they did. They levelled the sand dunes, dug down through the solid rock until they got water, irrigated the wasteland and planted it with apple orchards and grapevines, with peanuts being cultivated in between.

A driving wind with plenty of snow in it accompanied us as we went to see what had been done. The fruit harvest was 570,000 jin this year of 1967. Over the rest of its farmland the brigade gained a total of 730 jin of grain a mou, which was less than expected due to a bad drought. The best harvest in pre-Liberation years would have been around 200 jin. A dry year like 1967, when only 300 mm. of rain fell instead of the usual 700, and that at the wrong time, would have meant many people leaving their homes and becoming refugees and beggars. This year however, with the strength of the thinking of Chairman Mao behind them, they have beaten back the sand, defied the weather and gone on with the Cultural Revolution. They do not have a single grown person idle in the whole community. Everyone has a job and is all the better for it. There is 100 yuan a year for every man, woman and child. By agreement, services like those of schools, clinic, barber, tailoring, carrying water, flour milling, are provided free for everyone. In the handicrafts section where bags for export are made from corncob leaves, and all kinds of basketwork done, the very old, the physically handicapped, have all found something to do. I shook hands with an 84-year-old man sedately clothed in padded black silk, who was keeping his fingers good and supple with a reeling frame. Talked to those at the piggeries, apple sorting and packing, those planting trees for new windbreaks, and then those who were digging new wells during the flurry of a snowstorm. This last task is a heroic one, entailing carrying up stone which has been cut out of a huge pit. This method of getting down to the water is an old one, but it gets results despite the depth to which operations have to be conducted. There was a woman working there who had eight children. An ex-soldier who was discharged after having been wounded. Two pretty young girls who carried up stone with unexpected strength. Old and young, all as one and all together they worked, in spite of hardship and difficulties. Without these wells it would not have been possible to meet last season's drought. Then without the mechanisation that made water lifting from them possible, they would not have been so much use either. It is a case of progressing on all fronts. The brigade, by the way, does have its own machine shop, which keeps its various machines in repair. It also has a very good wood-working shop where transport equipment is made.

I was pleased to find in its clinic a bright youngster who had been taken on as assistant to the brigade doctor, one of whose duties it was to see that this lad learnt everything the older man could teach. It is safe to say that this one brigade, situated on such poor land, now has more real facilities than a county city like Penglai had before Liberation. In the whole of Penglai then there was only one blacksmith, and he was too poor to rent a house, but had to ply his trade in the open. Surely there were some concepts followed after Liberation that were not in line with the aims of socialism. So, for instance, stress was often laid on immediate profit rather than on the long-term good, and similar other non-revolutionary policies were sometimes slavishly followed, now classed together under the general term of "economism". However, after an intensive study of the thinking of Chairman Mao, which has been part and parcel of living in these last two years, a much higher mass understanding has been gained. The leadership of Mao Tsetung Thought means now very much more than that of the once all powerful brigade leader who often rather looked down on his people and did not think they could really understand enough even to study politics. Brigade leaders who did think that way now have ample time and opportunity to reorient themselves and find out where they went wrong.

One of the things this brigade is proud of has been its trial in growing tea. Protected against the cold winds and snow, the plants look surprisingly healthy, and it will be interesting to see how the experiment of growing it in a place so far north will come through. Naturally enough, people seeing what incredible things their united strength can bring — digging one of these huge wells in seven months instead of the two years it took once before, raising crops three times as big as they were, making desert sands into arable land and so on — are somewhat impatient with the slow growing of trees, and with finding the right kind of evergreen fir, so essential in halting the spring winds that come before quick growing deciduous trees have put out their foliage.

Counting everything, grain per person for the people of this brigade adds up to something over 500 jin. A heavy surplus is sold to the state each year, and no one has to leave his home as a refugee and wander over the land. The brigade is out to store enough of its surplus grain, over and above what it sells to the state, to last it for a whole year, and this project is already well in hand.

Back in Penglai city, we talked over some aspects of the work in the county. Fishing is important, and a new harbor has been built for fishing boats to shelter in, much bigger than the old water city. Most of the fishing is now done by diesel-engined trawlers owned by a commune brigade, which also maintains a machine shop to carry out repairs. Every boat carries a transistor radio, so that it can get the weather signals from weather stations around the coast. Fishermen have gone south to Ningpo and learnt some of the newer trawling techniques from there. They now bring in 21 million jin of fish a year.

The county now has 12 middle schools of the regular type and 56 agricultural middle schools, together with 500 primary schools. There are now constant relays of classes studying Mao Tsetung Thought, which include cadres of all levels, commune members, townsfolk and workers as well. The old popular evening educational classes have been changed to political training. Everywhere there is a new realisation that politics must lead, and unless this matter is kept quite straight, nothing will follow on successfully.

We talked about irrigation for some time. One quarter of the land in the county is now irrigated, and as power comes from two small hydro-electric projects in the next few years, it will be possible to instal more pumps and raise water to higher levels on this land of rolling downs. By 1972, it is estimated, over half of the arable land will be irrigated.

In the past, due to the policy of economism which looked for quick returns, the cultivation of such valuable trees as the walnut, the chestnut, and similar ones which have a high food value, had been neglected. They took so long to come to bearing that they were not bothered with. The newer way will be to find a place on unused land for all these food-bearing trees. Gullies, headlands and so on will all be made to play their part.

The people of Penglai are in general a strong, healthy lot. The county has two full-size hospitals, and then also a chain of medical cadres that run down through the communes to the brigades. The training of new cadres who will make their life's work amongst the commune folk is more than ever being given the importance it deserves.

The peanut is an important part of the economy of Penglai; out of the 800,000 mou of its arable land, 270,000 mou is used for peanut growing. Running from the hilly country in downs to the sea, about one quarter of the farm land has to be terraced, which has meant a great deal of hard, slogging work over these past few years. Industries have grown, there now being over 40 plants of one kind or another. Boat building, cement, flour milling, and so on. With the new prosperity, people's livelihood has improved a great deal. Then again with a harvest three times that of the period of Liberation and with innovations coming in all the time, it is bound to be that way. And, believe it or not, the price of meat will be lowered 30 percent this coming Spring Festival! Where else in the world in these days of recessions will it be found that un-inflated income is being raised and the prices of basics lowered! This then, is a brief sketch of some of the things that are going on in this historic little county set in such picturesque surroundings on the Shantung coast. A county, too, that has much to teach the two thirds of our world where there is still hunger and oppression. A county that has caught hold of the spirit of Mao Tsetung Thought and has made it its guiding light in no uncertain fashion.

A great movement like the present one in China has its humorous moments as well as its serious ones. In a commune on the north Shantung coast, there lives an old couple. She thought he should not go out to meetings at night, and did her best to stop him. He, however, was adamant. Coming back home late one evening, he banged on his door, but there was no movement inside in response. Banged again, and still nothing happened. Then he shouted, "The old revolutionary general has returned." There was a tense silence for a few moments after this outburst, broken finally by his wife's quiet, level answer, "To rebel is justified." However all's well that ends well, and the old lady soon began to see the light and eventually was enthusiastically going to meetings along with him.

Modern Penglai is an inspiring place to visit. Before leaving on our last morning, I wrote:

Rich
in fable, part of the history
of Shantung, and of China
where one
climbs steep steps to the old
Temple of the Blessed Isles,
looks back over the city now
burst through its walls and
spreading into the countryside
around.

Yes
there is the site of the old
water city; boats can still
be kept there, but now for them
a modern harbor has been built
boats changing to be mechanised trawlers;
from watching workers over
machine tools, we went around
the bays to where a commune brigade
had taken sandy soil and brought it
to life again, where amongst 360 families
everyone was working, old and young
making something from nothing
cutting wells from solid rock
in the spirit of the Foolish Old Man
at Yushan.

These
learning that creative folk
working together with their kind
can really control
both heaven and earth
should they but find the way
and take hold of it
these
the true immortals of Penglai
people of the era
of Mao Tsetung.

Man Against Nature Amongst Shantung Hills

Picture some ranges of steep rocky mountains. Centuries of erosion following deforestation have converted valleys into wildernesses of sand and boulders. In some eight destitute villages, groups of people try to eke out a living. Perched up on little headlands, they grow sweet potatoes as a main crop, with little patches of corn here and there. If the young people grow up, many have to go off to the Northeast or somewhere else to search for a living. Out of their miserable income, families have to pay rent and taxes. The six months of cold weather means that they are cold for six months, because there is never enough clothing. They are always hungry. This is a picture of the hill valleys at the rear of Huanghsien in Shantung up until 1949 when change came and a new day began for the common man of China.

Hsiatingchia

It was a cold, bright winter's day when we drove up to rugged Hsiatingchia from the flat plain around Huanghsien. Snow lay on the hillsides, and on the higher levels rock pinnacles pointed skywards with white fingers. Four buses of people from Kiangsi in south China had arrived just before us, and representatives of organisations from that province were looking over what the new hill farmer of Shantung had been able to do. It was an amazing record, well worth coming a long way to see. The eight villages, with their 21 production teams of the Hsiatingchia brigade, farm 2,418 mou in all. As their total population is 2,800, this means that they have less than a mou each to live off. Then taking a look at many of their fields, one finds that these have been built up on solid rock, with earth that has been carried in, and are faced with a stone wall. The first group we came across as we went up one valley was one that included many old men, all over 60, the oldest 74. They were working with stone, a task in which their long experience counts well. To build a 15-foot wall fronting a terraced field and not have it collapse when the heavy rains come takes experienced hands. Now with new fields carved out of the mountainsides all the time, irrigation canals being dug and lined with stone, the old-timers are more important than they have ever been. They were a cheerful bunch working with a will, proud to be essential and appreciated.

It is through irrigation that livelihood has taken the biggest leap forward. We climbed up one gully, finding little dams across it in several places, each able to irrigate terraced fields beside and below. High up in a ravine another was being built, ready for spring rains. Barren rocky mountains were being planted with firs and chestnuts. The Shantung fir is a wonderful tree. Give it a start and its roots go down through rock crevasses and the tree grows, so that many of the hill faces are already green with them. Youngsters were high up above us planting more.

The villages have by and large been rebuilt. Everywhere winter wheat was growing well. In the old days no one even thought about growing wheat here, for with no irrigation the best that could be hoped for was corn and some millet. Now the fields produce what would be considered super-bumper crops out on the best flatland — 1,000 jin per mou a year. Apples and pears — the pear a yellow keeping variety that lasts right up until the next crop is ready — brought in a harvest of

1,800,000 jin in 1967.   The appeal for economic independence made by Chairman Mao has reached these backhill valleys in no uncertain way. They support themselves in a way their fathers would have thought impossible, and they sell a sizeable surplus to the state as well.   It has been no simple task to irrigate 75 percent of their hill terraces, but that is just what they have done.

In one place water is pumped 30 metres above the reservoir to a stone-built canal that takes it around a high level.   Most of the water, however, comes down hillsides and automatically flows into the fields between the rows of grain.   Fields themselves have been completely revamped so that they are much bigger than before, seven or eight little old ones being joined to make one big new one, and then where possible the big one being brought forward out into the wide old riverbed and faced with a new high wall, making a piece of land as flat as a tabletop that can be worked by the new mechanisation.   There has been no halt in struggle with successes that have come.   There is plenty of sheet rock hillside that can be cut out and filled in yet.   The children around look wonderfully sturdy.   They do tasks together in groups, then go playing as children everywhere do.   Whipping tops seemed to be the chief fun for boys on a winter day, preferably on some sheet of ice where the homemade wooden tops spin longer.   Outside the primary school, a group of girls had come in with baskets; they had been collecting material for compost heaps.   In one village three old men and one lad were busy with a blacksmith's forge, making new picks and shovels.   Another group was building a home of cut stone for a newly married pair.   Everyone was doing something.   1967 was not a good season from the point of view of weather.   In the old days a drought like the one this year would have brought much trouble in its train. But due to the water stored in reservoirs, the harvest was good.   Old folk remembered one bad period in the other days, when landlord bailiffs would beat and kill to try and extract rent that was impossible to give. This last year little rain fell, but the children continued to laugh and their elders went about their work in the usual way, all studying Mao Tsetung Thought together with great devotion.   They feel it is part of their daily lives.

Looking at one of the pumping stations, we noted that the line of pipes leading uphill from the reservoir was of plastic.   "All made in Yentai in our plastic factory there," someone said.   Each step made in the new industrialisation does lead further towards self-sufficiency these days.   Back in Huanghsien, in the quietness of a courtyard in the comfortable guest house there, once the mansion of the landlord family of Ting, one thought of the struggle those hill commune farmers were winning.   How other communes around were following in their lead, so that now it becomes as good to be a hill farmer as one out on the richer land.   Everywhere the straight, high walls enclosing the now level fields of hill farmlands could be seen as we went through the hills.   What the people can achieve with correct leadership is impressive.   The effort that has been spent is amazing.   The sheer doggedness and determination shown staggers the mind.

Huanghsien

Huanghsien is one of the richer counties of the Yentai prefecture.   It has a flourishing little port at Lungkou where commune brigades do much fishing.   Lungkou drinking water from its deep level wells is famous for its good taste.   Huanghsien is also famous for its apples, of which it has a very good keeping variety.   The population of the county is around 450,000, and in the old days 70 percent of the best land was owned by landlords and rich peasants.   There is the story of one beggar in the old society who at times got a meal from the bailiff of the head of the Mou family, who was one of the bigger landlords.   The meal was given only after a promise that the man defecate on the landlord's land. The man swore he would not add to so mean a landlord's compost heap any longer, but he would have to walk 90 li out of the city before he could find any field that did not belong to the landlord in question. Huanghsien today gains an average of 634 jin of grain per mou per year, so it has a very sizeable surplus.   The richest county in the whole prefecture, however, is its mountainous neighbor Chihsia, one of the two counties in the prefecture that does not border on the sea.   In the old days it was the poorest of all Shantung counties, with its rough hills and bad communications.   With about the same number of people as Huanghsien, it was a place from which a constant stream of refugees went to the Northeast.   It now has not only a high grain production but also the best communications, highways having been built into every big village, with fine modern bridges over its many streams.   It has done best with forestry, and its new orchards are widespread.

To come back to Huanghsien, the commune that has the highest yields of grain in all-over figures is Nanchongchiang.   In this 1967, it averaged 600 jin a mou for its wheat land, and for the whole year's grain crops 1,300 jin a mou.   Despite the drought, 1967 goes down as the year with its biggest crop in history.   Huanghsien has something over 600,000 mou of arable land, and 60 percent of its area is flat enough to be used. Handicrafts are now quite well developed, and the county has an income of over two million yuan a year from articles made from the outer leaves of corn cobs, once used only for fuel.

Thinking back on the drama of Hsiatingchia, the mountain village which is truly one of the most dramatic pieces of determined constructive work in China today, I tried to capture some of its spirit in the following lines:

Hsiatingchia
Rocky mountain sides
long denuded of forest
growth; eroded valleys
wide, boulder strewn

river bed; villages
where cold and hunger stalked;
this old Hsiatingchia
inherited by the new day.

> *Now, away high up*
> *on mountain faces one sees*
> *groups of youngsters*
> *planting trees; up from valley*
> *bottoms, old men placing stone*
> *by stone with practised hands,*
> *building new walls for terraced*
> *fields that will give new*
> *generations more grain; little*
> *waters conserved, each small dam*
> *giving life to growing wheat*
> *each spring.*

New homes built
new highways that bring in
those who would learn
from Hsiatingchia, and see
the Thought of Mao Tsetung
working as it must to change
the lives of men.

Leaving Huanghsien, we drove along the coast for a couple of hours, then struck south to the centre of Shantung. Yehhsien, once Laichow, was the last county in the Yentai prefecture to be passed through. People were busy with winter tasks, digging up old empty grave mounds and taking the bricks and big stone slabs back to the villages for construction work, carting fertiliser out to the fields, repairing irrigation canals or digging wells. Everyone was active. We stopped for a rest and talked with a tall lad wheeling a newly bought, small-size flour mill back to his village. They already had one but they needed another, and the new one would be able to run from the same motor they had. Yes, most production teams in Yehhsien now had such mills.

Weifang

It was evening when we came to Weihsien, now Weifang, the centre of the Changwei prefecture and itself a rising industrial city of 200,000. The Changwei prefecture is somewhat larger than that of Yentai, having eight and a half million people. It is largely flat plains and rolling downs.

The first morning in Weihsien we went out into the countryside to pay respects to the family of Li Wen-chung, the now famous Army group leader who lost his life saving young Red Guards in a boat accident in Kiangsi. It was in Kohsi Commune, Lichia Brigade where he grew up. In 1960 he entered the Army, his unit being transferred to Kiangsi in 1967. Twenty-five when he died, Li Wen-chung had known what cold and bitterness was as a child. As a boy he worked hard at school, and helped the growing family as well as he could, there being two brothers and two sisters following him. He married at 23, and his son Ah-hua — Albania-China — called so after a visit to his commune by an Albanian friendship delegation, is a lively child of two. His wife, Wang Pang-min, is a sturdy determined Shantung girl who is obviously a strong force in the brigade. She gave an account of her husband's political development and of his devotion to the ideas of Chairman Mao. Then another member of the brigade who had gone down to Kiangsi with Li Wen-chung's father and had heard eyewitness reports of the incident told of what had actually happened. How Li Wen-chung had been given the duty of seeing the young folk back to their homes, and then how on August 19th, 1967, he went to assist a large group to cross the Kan river at Yeluchukou. How two ferry crossings has been made safely, but then how the third, with mainly young girls aboard, most of whom could not swim, sank on the journey. The ferry boat was not in good order, for it was already leaking, but was put to use because of the press of traffic at the time. Winds raised the river waters which buffeted it, making crossing more difficult. All had to take to the waters at a point around 100 metres from the shore. Li Wen-chung ordered his group to push planks over to the drowning youngsters and in this way each saved several, the PLA men then assisting those on the planks to shore. With one rescued, Li would go back for another, but as time went on each trip became more difficult. Finally, in spite of his great fatigue, he went off after one more youngster and pushed his plank over to her to ride back to safety with, but then his strength failed and he himself went down. Two of his comrades and two factory workers who had come to help also made the supreme sacrifice after they had saved many lives. Brought up in the dry plain area around Weihsien, these Shantung lads were denied the early acquaintanceship with swimming that those in the coastal counties of the Yentai prefecture get, nevertheless they put up a fierce struggle, and by sheer determination saved many young people. The lad who told us the story dug down deep into his tunic pocket and brought out a piece of one of the planks used by the soldier lads. Though it had been waterlogged, it still carried a faint smell of the timber of the camphor tree so much liked by Kiangsi boat-builders.

After the news of the happening reached Li Wen-chung's home and his commune, the two rival groups who had been struggling, each dubbing the other conservative, began to look at themselves in a new way. Quickly they formed the grand alliance, and then swiftly carried on with the next steps. Li Wen-chung's 50-year-old father has now become the leader of the revolutionary group, and tells with pride what the brigade has been able to do this 1967 in its production work. His home is literally stacked with copies of Chairman Mao's works, statues of Chairman Mao and mementoes that have been brought by the thousands of people who have come to catch a glimpse of the family in which so famous a son grew up. One team of old women, for instance, all of whom are still working, came and gave a concert outside the home. The youngest of them was over 50. We took some pictures together with those of the children who were at home at the time. Li Wen-chung's younger brother has gone to take his place in the Army. The oldest of the sisters was out speaking to a visiting group about her brother, but the rest were with us. An unaffected group of quiet simple people it was a real pleasure to know. Shantung has produced many heroes whose names people will remember for a long time, and amongst these that of Li Wen-chung will stand high.

Wulien

Wulien county is a newly formed administrative unit, made up of mountainous regions which were formerly under the administration of various surrounding counties. A guerilla base in the War of Resistance and Army hinterland in the War of Liberation, it has done wonders in pulling itself up by its own bootstraps and becoming a place that gives good livelihood to folk who once found the barest essentials difficult to come by. Shantung highways are good, so that it took us a little under three hours to get there from Weihsien, driving across Anchiu and Chucheng counties. The short day of the winter solstice brought the great golden sun orb down behind the hills quite early in the evening, its last rays glinting on the ice of new reservoirs and over wide stretches of land sown to winter wheat. As we left the plains and came to the mountain areas of Wulien, we were surprised to find electric lights blazing in the villages and neat rows of homes built in a solid, orderly way. An unusual place, now in this revolutionary stage all the more so, as it shares the distinction of being one of the first in the land to have almost all of its old cadres who were in office before the Cultural Revolution back at work again as part of the new revolutionary group.

Chichiachuang Brigade

We set out one early morning from the county seat, driving some 50 li into the rugged country beyond. Long, sweeping hills lay above mist-filled valleys, and at their back jagged mountaintops. Everywhere terracing had been done and irrigation brought to the fields. Frozen waters of a big reservoir glistened in the sun. Lime-painted trunks of apple orchards could be seen everywhere, and behind them higher up on the mountain slopes groves of chestnuts. We turned off a highway, drove up a valley until we came to the village of Chichia Kwanchuang, the headquarters of the brigade of that name, which is part of Chiehchia Commune. Some of the brigade members had come down to meet us, a strong old woman of 74, an old ex-soldier of 64, proud of his Red Guard armband and of his task of looking after the brigade piggery, three very pretty little girls, and then the youngsters who were leading the revolutionary group in the commune.

As we sat around and discussed the situation in the brigade, the facts that came out were dramatic. One knew in overall terms what were the faults of the past administration and where it was going wrong, for we had gone through a year and a half of the Cultural Revolution. But here in this tiny mountain village through the simple words of earnest young people, everything was made so much more clear. The locality was liberated in 1943. Before that, there had been a terrible famine in 1941 when many people had died. In the best years then, 100 jin of grain was all that could be expected from a mou. Out of that the landlords and officials had to have their share. There were then 90 families, 300 people in all. By 1958, the best year after Liberation, 400 jin a mou was gained. Then came the new policies, and a reversal, a denial of the Great Leap Forward. The new policies enunciated by Liu Shao-chi called for more private plots, asked the people to seek loans, and so on. Class struggle was said to have been ended and everyone to be equal and united. In 1962, only 180 jin a mou was gained. Certainly there were droughts, but the trouble was worse than just weather. After the Cultural Revolution started, the people were helped to see things more clearly and understand where poor policy was leading them so that they not only made revolution but grasped production; in terms of grain, production rose then to 550 jin a mou. Now there are 141 families, over 600 people who are able to sit together and themselves criticise what has been wrong, from out of their own experience. Private plots under the revisionist leadership were increased from 100 mou to 310. The collective piggery had been gotten rid of and the pigs distributed. The three old landlord families got the three good sows because the brigade leader said that as they had most experience in pig-raising, they should have them. Poor families who did not have enough to feed themselves and who had never owned a pig, got the worst small animals, which of course promptly died. The landlord families then bred pigs and sold one jin of pork for three jin of peanuts. Then, when the price of peanuts went up at planting time, they would sell them at a good profit. The old brigade administration liked the ex-landlord and ex-rich families because they were always obliging. Better fed, they would always go out to do any collective work like hill tree-planting and so get full workpoints. They had experience in acquisitive practice, and quietly made the most of it. The poor man was often sick, and then would be fined heavily if he did not go out to work. Gradually the old rich got comfortably richer, the old poor much poorer. More time was spent on individual plots, less on collective land. Actually 300 mou of collective land was left untilled. A directive came down to increase grain production and get rid of new orchards in order to do so. So many flourishing apple trees were cut down. 1967 goes down as the first time in its history that the brigade really came together as a class-conscious group, knowing its friends and its enemies and acting as a true collective. For the first time it then was able not only to sell grain to the state, but also to store a considerable amount in its own granary. Wafer cakes, "po ping," made of the ground-up vines of the sweet potato are very pleasant to eat, and fascinating for an outsider to watch being cooked, but they need supplementing with other foodstuffs. How was it that the former landlord families always had good wheat flour when others were short? But oh, when private plots were increased from three to four and a half mou, the landlord families planted sweet potatoes, cut and dried the crop and changed it for flour on the open market. They could afford to feed some of the vines to the pigs too. Why was it that landlord families and some of the old rich would say "8-18-28" and smile? Was it because the end of that gangster jargon rhyme finished with the hope that Chiang Kai-shek would soon come back? People learnt that the class struggle still had to be fought, and that it was not yet a matter of all as one and all together. When the Cultural Revolution started the old rich said with almost one voice, and that raised in pious horror, "We refuse to make chaos with you!"

We attended a village meeting against revisionism and selfishness. It was a bright, energetic gathering, in which one speaker after the other got up to express what was in his heart, and how his understanding had been touched. Everyone is against waste now, and those present spoke in simple terms of their conservation of grain, cotton, and so on. Ninety-five percent of those able to work now go out to the hills for collective tasks. The poor now better understand what their role is, and they are not backward in taking it. Mao Tsetung Thought now evidently dominates the whole place, bringing it new light and hope.

Back in Wulien Again

Back in the Wulien county seat again, we met with the Revolutionary Committee which included some of the old cadres, especially the old first Party secretary. They told us more of the history of Wulien, how the first uprising had taken place in 1933 but was shortlived. Then how the next had come in 1938, leading to Liberation in 1943. How now there were 420,000 people in this county of hills and mountains, with 720,000 mou of arable land, 200,000 mou of which is irrigated. Out of its 16 communes, 15 now have the three-way alliance. Out of the 586 brigades only the leadership of 40 needed to come in for further study of the way forward, and of these 20 groups have already returned with the understanding needed. Eighty-two percent of the old cadres from commune to county level have come into the revolutionary groupings and more are coming all the time. All voice much gratitude to the work of the PLA in assisting revolutionary groups to struggle through.

Looking back on total overall grain figures in the county, which until 1956 had to be helped by the state with grain each year, 446 jin a mou was gained in 1964. In 1965, due to drought and to causes already mentioned at Chichia Kwanchuang, this went down to 341 jin. In 1966 it was 380 jin, and in 1967, 460 jin. In fruit 8,900,000 jin was harvested in 1966, and 16 million jin in 1967. 117,000 mou of the land had a new layer of earth put on it. Much of such terraced land is on rock, for deforestation and erosion had led to complete topsoil destruction, so new soil had to be carted up to fill the fields out. 551 ponds and reservoirs have been made since 1958, which means that people away up in these hills now have fish to eat. There were 90,000 pigs in 1964, and 200,000 in 1967. By and large, the soil is poor and sandy. In the valleys it was mainly swamp which had to be drained. In addition to drought, the area has to face frequent violent storms, with hailstones which some-times destroy the crops. Insect pests have always to be dealt with, and considerable proficiency has now been gained in this work. Apples are a new crop, there once being only chestnuts and persimmons. There are now tree nurseries everywhere, mainly for apples and chestnuts, and the firs needed for the higher rocky slopes. 700,000 mou of mountainside has now been planted in trees. Near Wulienshan, the mountain from which the county takes its name, there was once a big rich Buddhist monastery which had a hundred monks. The temple was also until Liberation a great landlord, owning the land in 72 villages.

Likutsai

We went on talking about the county for a long time and were about to disperse when a young man spoke up about afforestation around his village. It was a remote one where a great deal of other tough work had been done, flattening the tops of hills to make fields, building up new fields on a washed-out valley floor, all with an insufficient labor force but with a lot of determination. His production team had taken one piece of 40 mou, which had been divided into no fewer than 600 little plots, and had made it into three-mou fields. And how many people in this tiny village of Likutsai? Only 12 families, spread out over six and a half li! There were once 15, but three died out, the last men being too poor to marry. At Liberation, there were 36 people in the village. Now there are 68. Difficulties? There were so many. At Liberation there was no one who could read or write. "Our village head," and the speaker indicated a quiet man sitting beside him, "had to go ten li away and bring in a member of a landlord family to read documents. We started a school and," he said, pointing to the quiet man again, "this was our schoolmaster!" Then all eyes turned on Liu Tai-chen, a 37-year-old stolid farmer, now the father of a family of five boys. Liu Tai-chen is a personality. Quiet and with a dry humor he told of how when he first had to keep the books of his cooperative, he had to illustrate them with drawings, as he knew no characters. How difficult it was to see the difference between a '6' and a '9'! How he also had to start the school, first with five boys. Four mornings a week he would climb ten li over a mountain and down to another village where there was a man who would teach him ten new characters. He would memorise these as well as he could, get back home and give each of his pupils two of the characters with sound and meaning. Then they would help him to remember them the next day, and then all would practise the characters already learnt and put them into sentences. It was a mutual-aid school, and as all got over the first stages learning came more swiftly, so that they could go through all the books needed and, as time went on, prepare for examination to one of the new local farm middle schools in the county. On the day of examination he went with four of his first five who decided to make the try and waited outside like a father during his wife's labor, as he described it, rubbing his hands nervously and walking up and down. But all four passed, his first four. In the years to come there were to be many more, some passing through upper middle school, so that now the problem of literate folk for the new day in his tiny hamlet has been solved. In addition to his duties as accountant and teacher, he is also the keeper of the production team store and buyer for it. His store is one of the more unusual ones in our world today. People take what they want, weigh it, pay for it by themselves, just shutting the door when they leave.

He says that in his teaching of songs he was only moderately successful. When his first students went to other places, no one quite knew what songs they were singing, although there was something similar in the wording, folk said. A friend gave him a small pamphlet of "The Foolish Old Man Who Removed the Mountains" in 1958. At that time he could not read it, but he kept it with him, carrying it ever since. It was his school textbook and the first classic he learnt off by heart as well as being the one of Chairman Mao's works that influenced him most in his subsequent struggle.

His production team now is glad that they have been able to sell the state a surplus of 2,000 jin and to store 5,000 jin in their own grain store. We pressed him for more stories about his village, for he did not like talking too much about himself. Climbing over the mountain to get his schooling brought him quite a few adventures, once nearly being killed by lightning which hit a tree beside him, and once falling down a cliff in a snowstorm. Small things these, he says, and a privilege to have been able to do what he has done. Like any good schoolmaster he is enthusiastic about his pupils, and obviously likes them.

The stories of his teaching adventures are so many it would take quite a long story to pack them all in. Once in heavy snow he set off over the mountain, missed the trail and slipped back down the slope. The trip took him twice as long as usual, so that it was after dark when he got to his old friend's place. The friend asked him to stay the night and go back next day, but Liu said he had much to do in the morning and insisted that the old man teach him the necessary ten characters. Then saying them over and over, he set out to get over the mountain again. Everyone was asleep when he got home but he sent a boy around to wake up the other pupils to come and learn the ten characters, fearing that if he left them till the next morning they might be forgotten. The sleepy boys all came, and together on the kang they went over and over the characters and memorised them. At that time, the phonetic system had not penetrated back valleys like his, so he did not have that aid to memorisation. There are few people who have better claim to be what Lu Hsun called "a working ox in the service of the people" than Li Tai-chen. "I have never been a clever person," he said. "When I was a boy my father tried to get someone to teach me, but this teacher gave up and said I was just a clod, only able to push a wheelbarrow, and so sent me home again."

In Hsiatingchia the attack on wild nature and success in the struggle is easily seen in a relatively short time. There the mountains, there the ravines, there the rocks, and now here are the terraces and the trees, the dams and the new homes people have built for themselves. In Wulien the thing is on the grand scale. A whole big county of mountains, with a population approaching half a million who have set out to change their once barren environment, and who are carrying out the task with determination. One no sooner leaves the flat land of Chucheng county than one is amongst hills that once were so eternally drought-stricken that they seemed to be the place from which issued only long streams of refugees. Now in well over 500 villages, the people are finding a way to do things better. The recent changes have made some of those places that had the worst brigade leadership into some of the best. There is no doubt in overall figures: The start towards revisionism — taking the capitalist road — did make for an appreciable slackening of effort throughout these hills, where to maintain the momentum of advance it is essential to follow the line laid down by Mao Tsetung, the line of class struggle and relying on the masses.

There is no doubt that the once poor folk are now swinging together, taking over the leadership, and regaining better results than ever before in a most dramatic fashion. "Come back in ten years' time and see what we have been able to do," they said to me. Though the next ten years, when one is seventy, do seem somewhat uncertain, one accepted the challenge, with every intention of trying to meet it. Teacher Liu Tai-chen came down to see me off the morning we left. It was nice to see him again, and we took a picture together. A warm, friendly place, with a tough, dogged people now more determined than ever to stand up and be the masters of their fate. Better than ever the poor begin to understand that they have nothing to lose but their chains, including those of ignorance, superstition, slavishness, which too were part of the legacy bequeathed by the old order.

Weifang Again

Back in Weihsien, we spent the last afternoon looking at a very old handicraft. That of inlaying lacquer work with silver and gold wire. Around 200 people in all were working at this. The timber for the furniture is imported from Southeast Asia. It is inlaid and finally lacquered with six coats of the best Chinese lacquer varnish. It is interesting that on the Japanese market there has grown up an interest in Chinese revolutionary themes, including the poems by Chairman Mao, so that inlays of these have struck a new market. The factory had its own exhibition of the Cultural Revolution, with the more dramatic themes being displayed in cartoon and picture, then with specimens of the work of the factory alongside. There is now a new appreciation of what the handicraft worker can do. In an old 1912 book on Shantung, a Chefoo trader tells how good a business has been built up in hairnets in the countryside. They could then be made in so many villages at a cost of 50 cash, which at that time was a halfpenny, and would be marketed abroad for one shilling each! Hairnets are still made throughout the countryside in commune craft shops, but now they are taken by a state agency, a fair price paid, with ever wider markets being secured.

Coming back to Tsinan by train from Weifang one noted how swiftly industry had grown. Iron and steel, cement, and fertiliser factories dotting the countryside along with so many others. A new 45,000-ton-a-year fertiliser plant had just gone into production. There are still immense problems to be faced such as that of afforestation, but what is being done in this day and age is impressive, especially when one keeps in mind what is going on amongst all those tumbled hills in places like Hsiating and Wulienshan.

In Wulienshan these lines came to me, wondering how to meet the inadequacy of bald words in trying to tell such a story:

Wulien
> *Five lotus buds*
> *five mountain peaks*
> *opening out to the sky*

Wulien
> *mountains that lifted*
> *to the heavens, while*
> *below them, thin children*
> *scraped tinder from*
> *winter hillsides*
> *for fuel, and too many*
> *died in the struggle*
> *for bare livelihood.*

Wulien
> *base for guerilla armies*
> *that fought back*

Wulien
> *where revolutionary changes*
> *swept in, and slopes*
> *changed to become orchards*
> *valleys become reservoirs.*

Wulien
> *where the spirit of youth*
> *has helped to keep*
> *the revolution clean*

Wulien
desolation on desolation
mountain peaks raised
in supplication.

Wulien
with peaks like
arms raised in salute
Wulien
the impossible done
and a land
made over again
in the way of Mao Tsetung.

Old woman and grandchild, village in Wulien county, Shantung.

SHANTUNG

Park in Tsinan, Shantung.

Water gate of old Penglai, Shantung.

Village in Wulien county, Shantung.

Old men's team erecting terrace walls at Hsiatingchia Brigade, Huanghsien county.

Niehchia Brigade, Penglai, has recovered sandy waste and planted orchards.

Modern peasant bowls, Poshan, Shantung.

Old Poshan ceramics craftsman.

Boy from a propaganda group in Yentai, Shantung.

Old men keep on working in Shantung.

"When I grow up I am going to drive a truck!"

Shantung has many ancient relics.

Some of the many old cedars in Shantung.

Chapter 6

Kiangsi

Kiangsi is a central lowland province of 160,000 square kilometres, with a population of over 21 million. It is drained by the Kan river and its tributaries, the waters of which go into Poyang Lake and then down the Yangtze. Among the mountains that lie along its borders with other provinces is the famous one of Chingkangshan, which Chairman Mao made a base for the Worker and Peasant Red Army in the late 'twenties. In Kiangsi, too, is the old Red capital of Juichin, and the surrounding counties of the old Red areas.

Kiangsi porcelain has world-wide fame, the kilns being at Chingtehchen on the east side of Poyang Lake. Today, it is a rapidly industrialising province, with a web of new factories spreading out from its provincial capital of Nanchang. Its main products, however, are still cotton, food grain and citrus fruits. Many natural forests still survive amongst the mountains around its borders, and during my visits I was able to see some of the pioneer work done in them.

It used to be said that much of Kiangsi had no coal, and no salt. But in 1970, geological survey teams reported that great quantities of deposits of coal had been found and a big one of salt also. New sources of the wolfram that is one of its best known mineral products have also been located. The old coal-mining area around the Kiangsi-Hunan border city of Pinghsiang is still a big producer. It was here that Chairman Mao worked amongst the miners and brought so many of them into his revolutionary movement in the 'twenties.

Kiangsi is crossed by the east-west railway from Shanghai to Changsha. It has a good highway and river transport system. The scenic mountain of Lushan, on the west side of Poyang Lake, is well known as a rest place away from the heat of the Yangtze cities in the hot summers.

Around Nanchang in 1967

It had been raining heavily for a week in north Kiangsi. Poyang Lake seemed muddy from the air, and many of the paddy fields below were flooded. From the airfield into the city we noted many of the farmers plowing in red clover and flowering turnip as green fertiliser, the former on the lower level fields, and the latter on the higher. It was the beginning of the last week in April 1967, and soon the first rice crop would be sown. Nanchang's 700,000 people all seemed busy, and a trip through the suburbs watching the many things being done was much better than any movie or television show. Nearing the middle of the city by the broad boulevard known now as People's Road, there was plenty of evidence of the progress of the Cultural Revolution, with young folk pasting up posters or writing out slogans on the pavements and any other place they could find to put them. It was considerably warmer than in Shanghai which we had left in the early morning, and after a short rest we went out to see how current events were affecting one of the bigger factories.

Kiangsi Textile and Dyeing Plant

The Kiangsi Textile and Dyeing Plant has 7,000 workers. Tooled with China-made machinery, it has 100,000 spindles and over 3,000 looms. It produces 290,000 metres of cloth a day, and dyes or prints 220,000 metres. So it is not a small concern, though but one of Kiangsi's several textile mills. Its output mostly goes into local consumption. The whole plant was enlarged and streamlined in the Great Leap Forward of 1958-59, and looking back on that period workers feel that it was then that many old superstitions began to be broken, and they began to have confidence that things could be done by themselves. This change in thinking helped them to get over the bad years of 1960-61, when Soviet revisionism put such heavy pressure on China at a time when there was a great drought. The drought and the stepped-up drive for self-sufficiency also made all realise to what great extent they were dependent on the farm communes for the cotton and grain they needed. Seventy percent of their workers are from local commune villages, while the other 30 percent, including the leading cadres, were workers turned out by that great training school, the textile industry of Shanghai. Shanghai has not only built machinery as up-to-date as any in the world for cotton mills in the hinterland, it has also supplied the technique. The plant now turns out 70 products, 95.8 percent of them meeting the stiff reqirements of top quality grading. Designs are sent to many public places throughout the province each year to get the people's opinion of them, and only those which are received with approbation are used. Designers come from various art schools. They had just completed a new design and were out to get opinions of it.

Since the Cultural Revolution started, the mill has improved both production and quality. The chairman of the rebel group accompanied the leading cadre and myself on our rounds. Of the work force, 55 percent were women, many with families. Most lived in housing provided by the plant, working an eight-hour day and taking full part in study group meetings. Due to studying the ideas of Mao Tsetung, all have become much more conscious of the world revolution, of what revisionism really is, and where it would lead to. They are more concerned with the events in Vietnam than they ever were before. Political issues are now felt to be questions of personal responsibility by everyone. It is no longer "We are only workers. Major issues are not our concern. We leave such to those better educated than we are". Instead, the general feeling is now that the bigger the issue the more concern it is of everyone. So the struggles during the Cultural Revolution in Nanchang make for much serious effort on the part of all to understand and participate. The friend who entertained me the first evening in Nanchang said ruefully he had been criticised, but that he had finally come to realise that he was taking the wrong road, so was now doing his best to make the revolution a success.

Kian and Yunghochen

We went by car some 200 kilometres down the road to the city of Kian by the Kan river. It had been raining for over a month — the local yearly rainy season — and the first brilliant sunny day had come. People were out repairing the big Kan river dyke, plowing in the paddy fields, mainly with old style plows though occasionally by tractor. Youngsters going to school or taking care of buffaloes looked cheerfully at us and everything smiled back at the sun glorying. The 21 million people of Kiangsi now make one of the biggest contributions to state grain of any province, even though the soil they work is not of the best, demanding much fertiliser. We did not stay in Kian longer than to have lunch before we took a launch and went 20 li up the Kan river to the village of Yungho. A beautifully situated place with great camphor and tung trees in bloom, set along the river bank above a collecting station for rafts of timber and bamboo, where rivermen combined smaller rafts into huge ones that would make the journey to Yangtze river ports.

We came to see the ancient site of Kian ware, so famous in the Sung dynasty. Much of the mainstream of the history of China can be read through the products of the creative figures of the potter better perhaps than in court-written histories. Before the potteries of Chingtehchen rose to fame, those of Yungho, then called "Yaomenchen", were best known. Here black and brown wares were given patterns with other colors with remarkable success. The fragments that come out of the old kiln piles are often startling in their beauty. But the 19 main large kilns around and between which a pottery city with 72 streets once existed, are kept as a treasure for investigators of the future, and no more digging is allowed. Some of the piles are forested hills now, but most are just grass covered. The deep pool from which all potteries drew their water for mixing still exists. It was held that no other water would do.

One of the village elders showed us odd fragments he had collected, some of which were finely patterned. A group of children accompanied us, dashing up to the top of one of the big ancient kiln piles, and together singing "The East is Red" from the summit.

It was dark by the time we had finished our tour and had come back down the river to Kian again. I was excited at having seen the site of so famous a working town. Change had overtaken it, but it has left a record of its achievements in the big kiln piles. In modern Kian, change was also under way. There were loudspeakers and the sound of many voices, as there are throughout the whole of China today, where there is ever a seeking for the better way, a desire to pull down the decayed, and to plot the way forward.

At Kanchow

Coming down the highway from Suichuan to Kanchow in south Kiangsi, the last part of the 200 or more kilometres from Kian, one felt somehow that one was coming home, so deeply had incidents in 1938-39 and 1940 when I spent much time here left their mark. The great camphor trees, the people out planting rice seedlings, a brilliant end of an April day after a month of rain, the red azaleas on the hills and the busy villages. But Kanchow itself dispelled the illusion. It had changed completely. No longer a quiet walled city of some 60,000, it is now one of over 150,000 and growing fast. A magnificent bridge leads over the river on entrance. There are wide, macadamised boulevards and many big buildings. When we came in, we saw streets everywhere painted white with slogans, while slogans and wall newspapers covered every available wall, in today's Peking fashion, and loudspeakers were busy everywhere. It was nothing like the Kanchow of 1940, nor even like that of 1956, the last time I had made a visit. Now was still the high tide of the Cultural Revolution.

In the hills not far from Kanchow we passed a whole school out to collect pine seeds from the hills. The bespectacled headmaster even had a carrying pole and basket also. Shades of Confucius! He had the boys in long clothes, however, despite the fact that the day was very warm and farmers were in shorts. Though youngsters are out to work they must still look like students, seemed to be the idea. It is maybe not possible to eradicate all old ideas in one great swoop. As in all things, people must get rid of the main contradictions first, and in this case to make the gathering of pine seeds part of the school curriculum is already an immense advance, enough to make the Confucians turn over in their graves in surprise and anger.

Early Memories

Naturally, one thought over many of the past struggles. When we first came here at the end of 1938, five of us to set up the Gung Ho cooperative organisation in the Southeast, there was an epidemic of dengue fever and all in our little group went down with it. Once the incoming bus broke the ferry landing board and flopped us all in the river. I looked down from the high bridge we passed over on entering Kanchow city and contemplated the still intact landing place, the memory still vivid. But the intense activity was still the same. There was no industry here when we came in 1938 to try and establish our little wartime cooperatives. Our first machine shop was tooled with salvage from tiny machine shops whose machines had been buried to escape the advancing Japanese in Nanchang. We bought them, dug them up and brought them down to Kanchow.

Kanchow Today

Now there are 48 large state-owned modern factories and 87 cooperatively owned handicraft shops. The state factories employ 11,000 workers. There are three universities and colleges, and eight full-course high schools. There are, too, 24 primary schools with 19,000 pupils, as well as eight primary schools operated by the suburban communes with 1,000 pupils in all. Buses run on the city streets, and out on the east side of the city there is a magnificent highway bridge 600 metres in length, spanning the Kung river which runs into the Kan river near here. There are many new boulevards, and many of the old street names have been changed.

Chiang Kai-shek had hoped to make the surrounding area a base to fight back at the armies of liberation. His son, Chiang Ching-kuo, was the chief local official then. "Pockmarked Chiang", the people called him. But the PLA moved too swiftly, and the whole exploiting superstructure had to pack up and scuttle as fast as they could to Taiwan. Some of the rotten landlords could not bear to leave their land, so stayed on, hoping to live on accumulated silver in obscurity, ever expecting the big U.S. uncle would help their friends to return. Many of these were exposed by the young Red Guards, including one by the name of Wei, father of the Kuomintang "minister of foreign affairs" on Taiwan.

I looked over to where our "Gung Ho" office had once stood on a hillside but could see little sign of it. Then where our workers' hospital had been, but the site was hidden by big camphor trees. I thought of our doctor, Fritz Jensen, who fought in Spain for the revolution, came to look after our hospital here, and finally was killed when going with other correspondents to the first Bandung conference on the sabotaged "Kashmir Princess" airplane. But now a new generation takes over. There are eight modern hospitals in the city today, and services extend all the time. Friends were enthusiastic about the results achieved by the Cultural Revolution — a general raising of the spirit of the people, and a much deeper understanding of basic issues amongst them everywhere. Industrial production is 17 percent up over the 12 months following the start of the revolution. The seven communes in the city area, those which help to supply city needs for vegetables and grain, gained an average of 1,100 jin a mou last year, in place of their best result of 400 jin a mou in the mid-'fifties. They hope to still better their production this coming year. Better farm practice and local nitrogenous fertiliser helped in reaching this result. New varieties of sugar cane have been introduced for the area, resulting in steep rises in sugar production. New modernised sugar factories replace the tiny peasant ones, where one would buy in former days an old fashioned sweet made of local brown sugar and peppermint. Instead of being haphazardly mined by groups of exploited farmers, wolfram is now produced by modern methods, as are other ores the hills are rich in. Afforestation, as everywhere in hinterland China, will need more attention, despite all that has been done already in these exciting years since Liberation.

Following a heavy April rain, the translucent waters of the rivers in Kiangsi are soon muddy, a thousand little tributaries bearing down silt from the eroded hills. Sturdy efforts, but still only first beginnings, are being made to prevent this, and new tree planting can be seen on many sides.

Forestry Research Institute

We left the highway on one trip outside Kanchow and struck up into the higher ranges of hills to a forestry research institute. There was no one in the office when we came in, for all were out working. The director we found amongst seedlings. He washed his hands of earth before coming over to greet us. His institute has 50,000 mou of steep hill land for planting, and the spruce or China Pine is their main tree for experimentation and promotion. They have been operating for only three years, so their young forests are still small. But nevertheless it is fine to see hillsides of spruce shooting upward and whole hill faces of firs. They grow a good many tung oil trees and chestnuts with giant bamboo in suitable places, and even have some olives from Albania. I was interested in the comparative production of olive trees and tea oil bushes, but the olives are not far enough along for that yet. Despite the fact that for long it has been said "Kiangsi will not grow walnuts", all those that have been planted are doing well. An aniseed tree from Kwangsi is also growing quite nicely. Staff of the institute rotate amongst the forestry farms and hold teaching seminars amongst commune members to spread knowledge of their work. For many centuries past there has been continual erosion and a clogging up of rivers and lakes with silt. The time has come when folk must be led to rebel against the oppression and poverty that such continued erosion causes. We felt that the institute was making a very

gallant first step in the right direction, giving a down-to-earth example
to all.

A Chemical Complex

It was a Sunday when we went outside the city to visit a chemical complex
set up during the Great Leap Forward. We passed right by the spot where
our War of Resistance "Gung Ho" office had stood. It was burnt in the
Japanese occupation, and now wild roses bloom over crumbling steps and
piles of rubble. A little farther on, set on a hillside once covered with
desolate grave mounds, stood the plant we had come to see. It produced
industrial gases, carbide and a nitrogenous fertiliser from the waste.
Technically it was very much a going concern, its output having increased
a good deal this past year. It had been taken over by the rebel group
which included some of the old management, the army and the workers.
The old administrative offices were sealed off and closed, while new ones
were set up in what was once part of the factory garage. They were quite
simple. In 1958 when the plant was set up with Soviet experts, there was
an administrative staff of 220 and a working force of 1,000. Now there
are 79 in the administration, with 624 workers producing a good deal more
this year than last, and busy with technical progress all the time. The
workers are mostly local folk from the villages around, the technicians
having come mainly from Shanghai, where I remember seeing the industry
started in a small, under-capitalised way in the late 'thirties. All on the
administrative staff do two shifts a week as workers. The struggle has
been to eliminate Soviet-type organisation which gave all authority to the
management, no matter what workers' meetings decided, and also to
eliminate the clumsy technique these experts introduced, which took little
notice of workers' convenience or of working hazards. Most of the
dangerous processes have been automated, and the workers' spirit is higher
than it has ever been. Some of the cadres found manual work hard at
first, but this problem was soon solved as they found everyone eager to
assist them, letting them break themselves in slowly. They all now see
the inadequacy of the old kind of management which meant dictation by
order from a manager's office and which overrode all worker suggestions,
no matter what they were.

The factory site occupied a portion of an ancient pottery kiln. Spread
below were many others, huge piles of kiln waste material marking their
sites. In the Yuan dynasty, and then especially in Ming, a big pottery and
porcelain industry thrived here. Now homes of the local commune farmers
nestle in against the tall waste heaps, and trees grow from their summits.
House, yard and barn walls are made of earth and shards. The paths are
paved with them. They lie thickly all over the paddy fields. It is called
"Seven Li" Village, and is a remarkable storehouse of records written in
ceramics. The supply of local wood brush fuel probably ran out by the
end of the Ming era, and also by then Ching officials were promoting
Chingtehchen as the great Kiangsi pottery centre, so that the potters
probably moved up there.

A Brigade Primary School

More and more, the part-work, part-study type of education is becoming the model for the future. Not always easy to apply it to a primary school, but the leading group of the school of Tungwai — "Outside the East Gate" — Brigade has made a good try. A brigade school has to do everything for itself. Pay its staff, set up its buildings, make its own way entirely. This school started as a Leap Forward project in 1958 with four classes. Now it has nine, and as soon as it gets its new classrooms finished, it expects to go up to 11. It has 370 pupils representing the entire group of children of school age, which begins at six and a half years. The brigade, for which the school is responsible, has 280 families and a labor strength of 500. There are two terms a year, and a fee of 2.50 to 3 yuan a child per term is charged to help to pay teachers' salaries. The commune has given nine mou of land for the children to cultivate. Each class works one and a half days a week on it. At present there are 20 class periods a week, ten of which are spent in studying language and politics using the Quotations of Chairman Mao. Arithmetic takes up most of the other ten. Classes in the two more main subjects, bookkeeping and agricultural general knowledge, have been suspended for this particular period of the Cultural Revolution. Children have many out-of-class activities. Some half days they work with their own brigade. They also clean up the compound of a large adjoining factory and repair the road nearby. They put on small plays for commune members and help illiterates to memorise the three short essays of Chairman Mao: "Serve the People", "In Memory of Norman Bethune" and "The Foolish Old Man Who Removed the Mountains". Their school is a mass of wall newspapers they have written on the Cultural Revolution. They collect waste paper and sell it for school funds. They go to movies and have discussions afterwards. They invite elders to tell of their experiences in the old society, and they have a school excursion each school term out into the country. They all learn to swim before leaving school, some becoming ardent swimmers. As the teaching staff are all members of the brigade, they come into continual contact with the parents of their pupils and so everyone knows everyone else, making problems easy to clear up. For the new classrooms, the children collect bricks from sites around. Some come from the old city wall which is now pulled down, some from old graves which must give way for modern construction, a few from here, a few from there, and the pile by the construction site grows magically. Then, when the brigade can spare the labor to erect the framework of the new classrooms and put on the roof, the rest of the work of building will be done by the children themselves.

A child coming in at six and a half takes around eight weeks to learn enough "pinyin" or romanisation to get the sounds of the written characters right. In class two the child can read the phonetics fluently and is starting to use it to recognise characters. By that time also he has memorised the three short essays, and knows many quotations. In their third year, they can all read much of the book of "Quotations from Chairman Mao

Tsetung". In higher classes, background and meaning and the philosophical background of the quotations is taught.

It was raining hard when we came, so it was not easy to see everything. The brigade piggeries are near the school so we visited them, finding that fodder is mechanically pulped, and that the place was beautifully kept with the animals in good order.

Hsiangyanglou

A nice ending to one busy afternoon was a visit to Hsiangyanglou, a tower at one corner of the city wall overlooking the confluence of the two rivers that go into the making of the big Kan river. The tower was originally of Sung construction, dedicated to Lu Tung-ping, the Taoist immortal. It has a little museum of relics found mainly in excavations around Kanchow, including quite a few Stone Age artifacts. There are also some interesting pottery pieces, including specimens of the Nanchao period in the south. The tower has been reconstructed and the area below made into a park. There is a magnificent bell of the Yunglo period of Ming here that has somehow escaped being looted. The river view from this point is grand.

Kanchow Paper Mill

We spent the next morning at the Kanchow paper mill. To set up a paper mill in the hinterland in the other day was not so simple, for machines had to be made on the spot, and much had to be done with improvisation. With Liberation and better communications, a machine industry rising, much better results are now achieved. The new directing group of old cadres, rebels and Army men who met with me told how in 1948, when the former owner had gambled away his money, he tried to make the workers take their wages in paper that he could not sell. The works could produce but 400 pounds of paper a day then. In 1965-66 they produced 17 tons a day. In this last year, 1966-67, the workers have raised this to 20 tons, and expect to further raise it to 37-40 tons when the two new machines now being installed are running properly. Not only this, but they have also helped to set up another paper mill in the city which will have a similar capacity. They use rice straw, small bamboo, pine logs, sugar mill waste, and city waste paper for raw material. They make typing paper, writing and packing papers which go to many parts of the country. There are 700 workers, all local except for the few technicians who have come from Shanghai. All workers take part in the Cultural Revolution, and there was amongst them all a common determination against taking the path towards revisionism. One after the other group which met with me talked on various aspects of all these points, and when they had finished, we read four quotations from Chairman Mao's works together and then started our tour of the plant. All installing of the new machines was being done by the plant workers themselves, no one being called in to help. The new shops are light and airy, and the good spirit of the workers very evident. They have made many useful technical innovations, one of which has increased the capacity of a three-ton machine to seven tons.

Another plant I saw is situated on a hill some nine kilometres from the city on what was once red soil wasteland high above the river. Here workers from many different small metal-working and machine shops have been provided with a modern factory building and modern machinery to turn out a line of goods to directly assist the farm communes. They make pump turbines which now begin to stud many of the Kiangsi rivers, and power pumps. And now a start has been made on the production of a small-type tractor, really an enlarged rotary hoe. The first 70 have been manufactured and sent out to the communes in all the 18 counties of south Kiangsi to be tried out and criticised before the plant goes into mass production. Such tractors are sold directly to the commune and do not go to the tractor stations, which are for bigger size tractors only. The small tractor burns diesel oil and works a mou of land for around ten fen in costs for fuel and lubricating oil. Many young farmers have been trained already to use it, and it has proved quite successful in paddy fields. Used for hauling, the tractor can pull a load of around 1,000 pounds. Workers in charge of production are pleased with the sturdiness of their product and its performance, but are having a struggle in lowering costs of manufacture to those of the Shanghai-made model. Workers all live on the site, and their children have a wonderful time scampering around the hills, all so much better than in the crowded city. Trees have been planted everywhere. The entire body of 230 workers were all full of enthusiasm for their task, and for what they could do to serve the people in their own practical way.

Lilaosan Brigade

Land around Kanchow city in the old days was subject to severe exactions. Farmers lived poverty-stricken lives, many with no padded clothing or bedding quilts through the winter. Half of their income would have to be paid to the landlord. Grain and other taxes took half of what remained. To get through the year they had to supplement their grain with bran and wild roots. These were familiar memories to the older folk of Lilaosan Brigade, now in the spirit of the times with its name changed to "Eastern Brigade" of "The East is Red" Commune. Before we got to it, however, and going over the hills on the other side of the river from East Gate Brigade, we came across a huge arch erected over the roadway. It was now covered with the posters and slogans of the Cultural Revolution. I asked who had built so big a thing in such a place. Then was told that it was constructed with the funds contributed from around the world to Madame Chiang Kai-shek's wartime orphanages. It gave entrance to a so-called children's village, youngsters collected by Chiang Ching-kuo and trained as his own henchmen. Some were over 20 when finally the whole group was taken by Chiang Ching-kuo to Taiwan to be his personal followers there. In truth, many strange things are done in the name of charity.

Arriving at the commune, we sat in the tall cool room of the brigade office under a great camphor tree, a giant even amongst the big trees of the locality. The brigade Party secretary was convincing. Quiet spoken, making a clear point with every statement, and barefoot in the warm early summer weather like most others of his brigade, he obviously took a deep pride in all that had been done. He spoke of all the past struggles, and of how even in the bad three years of 1959, '60 and '61 they had gained 600 jin a mou as against the 460 which was the record before Liberation. Then how they had faced the floods of 1962 and the big one of 1964 which topped anything the oldest people knew of. They had now raised their dykes and installed seven pumping stations to pump out floodwater and to pump in irrigation water in dry periods. This they had done with their own financial resources, believing it better to put as much as they could into the welfare fund each year than distributing a higher bonus. Out of this welfare fund they have also set up their brigade school, attended by all brigade children of school age.

Brigade statistics are always fascinating. There are 157 families here, with a total of 836 people altogether, those able to work being divided into seven production teams. They own 796 mou of land, of which 660 mou is irrigated paddy fields, the water for which can be pumped up the hillside in several stages. Their average yield per mou per year for the years 1962-67 has been 1,008 jin. This 1967 they expect to raise the total to 1,600 jin per mou. In the past few years they have planted 130,000 trees, all of economic use, 30,000 being fruit — orange, pomelo, lichee, pear and persimmon in the main, the other trees being tung oil bearing, chestnuts and the like. Their plantations now rise high up the once barren red hills that slope above the riverbanks. They have 440 pigs, and families keep many geese, which even the quite small youngsters still in split pants can herd quite well with the aid of a long bamboo stick. Amongst handicrafts produced are fine sleeping mats for summer use, which a group of girls were weaving as we came by. As they spun and wove, they sang the songs of the Cultural Revolution. I asked what were the effects in general of the revolution on the brigade members. All agreed that there was now a much deeper understanding of Chairman Mao's thinking and a greater willingness to work for common goals. There had risen in the revolution a good deal of criticism of those who sought to enlarge private plots and put their best work into such. Criticism, too, of old landlord and rich-peasant families who did not join wholeheartedly in the stream of endeavor but who tried by various ways to gain advantages for themselves. A group of young folk from the city were busy pasting up slogans on the walls and sticking up wall-posters. They were evidently old hands at the process after a year's experience, dressed in their army-type suits of khaki, happy yet serious as they worked.

"Kouliang", the amount of grain per person each year, old and young, is 460 jin here. The brigade operates three rice mills. The rise in living standards and economic security compared to the times before Liberation, is astonishing. Now that revisionist tendencies, the tendencies towards "private enterprise" and "better use of personal plots" have. been halted, a further upswing is to be expected.

Mining Machinery Plant

I remembered that in Kanchow in earlier days there had been a small repair station for the trucks of the Wolfram Administration. At that time the Wolfram Administration was a group of Kuomintang officials who bought the wolfram which peasants on Hsihuashan and other hills around mined in small placer mines, and then transported it away. One set of officials would transport it through the enemy front line to sell to the Japanese. Another would take it to Chungking for transport across the Northwest to the USSR. Trucks were therefore of considerable importance. Trucks would have to make long journeys with poor lubricating oil and bad fuel, so constant repair was needed. With Liberation proper mining methods were introduced and a great demand for machinery arose. So the little repair shop rapidly grew in size to become a mining machinery plant. The workers formed their own organisations and added to their practical experience a theoretical education in the class struggle. They learned of the responsibility that the revolution put on the working class. In the 1952-56 period, new buildings were added to the old shops and 600 new workers brought in. 1958 was a hectic year for the plant, so much planned, so much done. Besides producing mining machinery, the workers started to smelt steel which was in short supply. Various kinds of steel alloys were turned out and much new technique introduced. In 1960 came the withdrawal of the Russians and the effort to isolate China, with the result that the will for self-sufficiency inspired workers immensely. In 1963 came a period of intensive political study that led to workers' productivity being increased three times. 1966 and now in this 1967 the 1,000 workers are bettering technique and increasing production in a startling way. They have taken full part in the Cultural Revolution and have gained much from it. Their plant is a beautiful one with fine grounds and big modern buildings. The tooling has come from specialised works of now famous machine builders in many Chinese cities, and the workers themselves have been trained in many parts of the country, bringing now much new life to old south Kiangsi.

Kanchow Fish Breeders

Chinese diet depends much on fish for its protein. In the past when the fish ponds of south Kiangsi needed fish fry, it had to be brought down from the Yangtze regions by plane at considerable cost. We went over the river south of the city to the fishbreeding farm of the Kanchow municipality which can now produce 15 million fry of the three best species of fish for distribution to the fish ponds not only around the city, but also in the counties of this prefecture.

The manager of the fish farm was a young enthusiast. He took part with his cadres and workers in the tasks of artificial propagation, all carried through under modern conditions. He had the big breeding fish measured for girth, their weight taken, and then calculated how much hormone to inject under one front fin. Children from communes around got a great deal of fun out of watching the process. Cuban frogs are also raised here for their meat. Their legs are nearly as big as those of a sizeable chicken.

On our way home through the countryside we passed much red soil hill land, which in this last year has been terraced and planted with tung oil trees. The daily plane from Nanchang lit on the old War of Resistance airfield as we passed, reminding us of the one-time contradiction between U.S. commanders Chennault and Stilwell — Chennault, servant of U.S. airplane manufacturing monopoly who thought that the war must be won by air power, and Stilwell, who said it was infantry that counted. The Japanese captured many of Chennault's airfields, including the Kanchow one, and Stilwell who wanted to aid the Communist armies where real fighting power lay was retired, dying soon after. But again, it will be infantry that will count in any future war, and the air base, no matter where it is stationed in Asia, will be the "sitting duck".

A Kanchow Beauty Spot

In my Kanchow days, I had heard vaguely of a famous beauty spot in the hills north of the city, but was told that it was occupied by Kuomintang soldiery. May Day 1967 being a holiday, and the city being given over to various mass meetings, we took the opportunity to go out to visit it. One cuts in from the main highway some 15 kilometres from the city and soon comes to a massive red sandstone cliff through which there is a natural tunnel, where people sit to cool off after climbing around the hills. It appears that the place was used by the Kuomintang as a storehouse for army explosives and was barred to the public. There are many natural grottoes and still some fine Sui dynasty rock sculptures here. In one place the faint lines of the head of a water buffalo, life size, may be seen, and there are some other interesting pieces of Sui design. Images of the later historical dynasties placed in the temple which were made under the rock shelf have been removed. Originally called "Tung Tien Yen" — "Cliff Through to Heaven" — it has recently been given the name "Cliff of Labor"; the old temples have been renovated and are bright with pictures of Chairman Mao and quotations from his works. The pavilion in which we rested here was said to have been made over to house Chiang Kai-shek's prisoner, Chang Hsueh-liang of the Sian Incident. But somehow plans miscarried and he was not brought here but taken direct to Taiwan, when the general dispersal of Kuomintang officials and those they wanted to remove started from the hinterland provinces. On top of the highest hill, reached by several hundred steps, there is a newly built pavilion from which a wonderful view of the surrounding country can be obtained. Many young folk from the city had walked or cycled out to spend the day here, but many more were in the waters of the Kan river cooling off when we passed by. Late spring turns to hot summer weather swiftly in southern Kiangsi, and the forested valleys around the scenic mountain looked cool and inviting. When we got back to Kanchow, the long lines of marchers with red banners and pictures of Chairman Mao had gone from the streets back to their homes or schools. The day gave them all a chance to come together and feel again the power and vitality of the revolution. A good stiff wind kept the heat within bearable bounds and made the red banners stream gaily, so that in all it was a May Day to be remembered.

Three-Ply Board

It was exciting to see a big factory making pressed board in Kanchow, its product going to various Kiangsi counties as well as to Shanghai and Lanchow in Kansu. Beginnings were made in 1959, but only with relatively simple machines. In 1963, the plant got proper equipment for the steam pressure process and the first 50 tons of large-size board were made. The present manager stressed that due to diligent political study, state-set targets were reached in both 1965 and 1966 in around 105 days. In the first two months of 1967, due to the demands of the Cultural Revolution on workers' time production dropped, but with March and April rose to an all-time high.

Of the 400 workers, 46 percent are women. All live in factory housing. Eighty percent of them are Kiangsi folk, most of the remaining ones being technicians brought from Shanghai. They have a modern, automatically fed boiler installation, a modern chemical research laboratory, and modern glue-making section. The bigger part of the timber treated and shaved off in such neat rolls is pine. But there is also camphor wood used for lining camphorwood boxes, chestnut and other woods that are beautifully grained coming off the production line. The management hopes to add a plastic paint to better bring out the wood graining when further improvements are made. Situated well out of the city and near its transport artery, the Kan river, it has plenty of room for expansion as the demand for pressed board becomes greater and greater. All its scrap goes into wood pulp for the Kanchow paper mill. No waste!

Dry Cells

One of the tiny handicraft industries necessary in hinterland centres cut off from the coast in the War of Resistance had been that of making dry cells for telephones, flashlights and so on. In 1956 two small old enterprises were brought together, 18 people in all, and given a disused winery at Chilitsun to start work. In their first year with some workers added, they produced 400,000 cells. Last year (1966), with 58 workers, they turned out 2,500,000. In the first three months of 1967 they made 800,000. Their planned total for the whole year is 3,500,000.

The enterprise is only half-mechanised. Children come in from school and for a while help mothers to do the work, making a good game out of it, then rushing off to their own games. There is quite a domestic air around, accentuated by the big spreading trees beside and the wide waters of the Kung river below. Their product is used in Kiangsi and goes also to many inland cities in other provinces. The brand is "Kungkiang".

Aluminum Bars

From the dry cell makers we went on to the smelters of aluminum bars. Their raw material comes from another province, and is brought here where electricity is cheap. The 300 workers have big, modern buildings to work in and a good wide hillside to spread out on. They were an up-and-coming enthusiastic group. As in the dry cell plant there was a pleasant mixing of workers, their wives and children outside the works, which made for a good, friendly atmosphere. Production has kept right up to plan over the past year.

Kanchow Match Factory

The Kanchow match factory is quite a modern one, rating as third best in China. It was started in 1945 as a privately owned concern with 100 workers and a yearly production of 5,000 cases. In 1967 its working force had grown to 328 and its annual production to 41,000 cases, each of a thousand boxes. It uses pine for the match box and a local softwood tree called "fa" for sticks — the only industrial use the wood from this common tree has. The automation that now enters every process has been carried out by the plant itself. Production in April 1967 was an all-time record for any single month in the factory's history. Fifty-five percent of the workers are women. To see them so deftly and swiftly plaiting the bamboo-strip containers for the final packing was fascinating. In Hunan a match has been produced which lights from both ends. For places in hills where transport is a problem, and for economical peasants this may be an advantage, so the factory is experimenting with the line to see if the people want such or not. The sticks are a little longer, the price two boxes for 5 fen. Two boxes of the ordinary kind cost four fen. It is thought that prices can be still further reduced when more automation takes place.

A Handicraft Cooperative

We called and spent some time at a blacksmiths' cooperative, the Kanchow ironworkers, finding 66 workers busy making tools for household and commune use. The co-op sends out people to the villages to see what the demand is, and then sets about trying to meet it. One of its most popular lines is the large-size kitchen chopper which goes from Kanchow to many provinces. Workers have made a good effort at raising the standard of the product, lowering the cost, and making the things that help the growers of grain on whom all society rests.

Air Compressor Factory

In 1956, I had visited what was then the Kanchow Agricultural Implements Factory, meeting up there with many old worker friends of War of Resistance "Gung Ho" days. On this 1967 visit, I found the factory had been greatly enlarged, with huge, modern shops where big machines worked with precision guided by the hands of the 570 workers making air compressors for fertiliser factories, which now find their way into all parts of China. Four types are produced. The old portion I had seen in 1956 was now making smaller fittings for the machines.

The factory has solved the problems of construction for some of the machines it had to have but which could not be supplied from outside. Most, indeed almost all, of the workers are local people. The plant has its own primary and part-work, part-study middle school, the pupils of which gave me a riotous welcome.

Without exception, every factory visited stressed what had been gained in the Cultural Revolution, and its determination to hold to the teachings of Mao Tsetung as a weapon for progress.

To Hsinfeng

Going south by highway from Kanchow, the seat of the Kanchow prefecture, we first passed through Nankang county. Then one drives on through dry, mostly treeless hills in vivid colors of red, brown and ochre, which have been terraced wherever possible to allow for trees to be planted, until one gets to the Hsinfeng county seat, built around an ancient pagoda. The pagoda is rather remarkable in that it has stood for probably six or more centuries, though the only mortar used between its bricks was the local red mud. The walls of the little old city of but 7,000 people have gone, and its name has recently been changed to Hungweitun — Red Guard Town.

The county had 260,000 people at Liberation, and has over 330,000 today. Second to rice, its main product is tobacco, for which the place is famous. It has 23 communes which farm its downs and valleys, and is drained by the Tao river, which in turn flows into the Kan river tributary called Kungkiang. Timber is floated down by raft to go on out into city construction in Yangtze towns. It is just 75 kilometres from Kanchow, a short trip by car over a good highway these days, but in one's memory of the War of Resistance period when I last came, quite a journey by a puffing charcoal-burning bus which had to be pushed up all the steep hills by the concerted efforts of all the passengers, in the manner common to those times.

This time we stayed in the county guest house, which had been taken over as the offices of the organisation for "grasping revolution and promoting production". It was evidently the cooperation organ of Army, old cadres and young rebels. We talked together on the achievements made in Hsinfeng in these years, of the five big irrigation projects started in 1958 and finished in 1966, which give 200,000 mou of once dry land the ability to stand a drought of at least 60 days. How the reservoirs also helped to hold up waters from flooding land along the Tao river. We talked of trees, and how the 23 communes had set up 80 forestry farms in the hillsides in these few years, while the county itself had been responsible for a big one at Chinpanshan, which has 700,000 mou of hillside to work on. Tree planting totals for the county over the past three years are

480,000 mou in 1964, 110,000 in 1965, and 80,000 in 1966. Pines take first place in planting, spruce second, and then the food or oil-bearing trees third. Chestnuts, pears, sour plum and tung are widely planted. Tree planting campaigns come in waves, the 1966 lower total being but a prelude to a still higher wave to come. In one county nursery seedlings for the autumn of 1967 now growing number 140,000. For the next year their numbers are expected to be much greater. Hsinfeng grain totals show an average of 600 jin a mou. Grain per person throughout the county averaged 500 jin a year.

To Bailan Irrigation Project

We went out of the city on the road south to Chuannan, branching off at the Datang villages and taking an earth road into the hills to go to the Bailan irrigation project. This was once the poorest part of Hsinfeng county, being perpetually drought stricken, with an occasional flood in between. In good years the people could get around 380 jin of grain a mou a year. Now they harvest 720 jin a mou. How has this happened? In 1958 a water conservancy project was planned. Done entirely by the local communes, it took until 1964 to complete entirely, a million man days being used on it, and a reservoir of 11 million cubic metres of water being formed. The leading county cadre came with us to see the work, pointing out the spot in the newly formed lake where once his old home had stood before the land was inundated. One of the 18 young people in charge of the dam and laterals came to the dam edge in a coracle with a load of fish he had caught that morning. These 18 support themselves, growing their own grain and vegetables, planting peanuts in the light sandy soil for their cooking oil. Fish from the reservoir sells in the town for 50 fen a jin. For local farmers the price is 30 fen. The pump turbine has come here also, and we noticed where in one place the water was stepped down from a main canal. We saw one turbine-driven rice mill milling rice for the people at 40 fen for 100 jin. In Hungweitun town the fee is 60 fen. The county cadre said that 125 pump turbines were already working in the county, and soon there would be more. Laterals from this reservoir called Bailan after the village nearest it total 70 kilometres in length. In 1966 there was a 95-day drought, but the total amount of water available for use in the reservoir was more than enough to meet the demand. Around a million jin of grain was saved from certain destruction. Construction of the laterals entailed the building of five long aqueducts over valleys and 11 tunnels, totalling 750 metres in length, all done with the tools of commune members and by themselves. This was just one of the five big irrigation projects which put the thinking of Chairman Mao in his "Serve the People" into action, as the head of the group at the project control office emphasised.

I was interested in how tea oil bushes had been planted along the roads amongst the new plantation of pine, and how well they mixed. Three counties in south Kiangsi are already getting their total supply of food oil from the hills of Ningtu and Hsingkuo and Juichin — old Red Army centres all of them. Hsinfeng hopes to emulate them in the near future.

The Tsoumalung Irrigation Project

The Bailan irrigation project was so interesting that we took in another one of the five in the district, this one in the southwest corner of the county in what was once a Red Army area. It had been much poorer and drought-stricken than Bailan, the people existing on a poor diet of dry-land grain and sweet potatoes — with never enough of that. Adding everything together and in terms of grain, they never averaged more than 180 jin a mou, and out of that rent and taxes still had to be paid. When Liberation came, state grain had to be brought in to assist them. Then in 1958, as a Leap Forward project, the Tsoumalung dam was built, 68 metres high and making a reservoir of 15 million cubic metres of water covering 86 square kilometres, from which water now runs quietly out on its task of irrigating 45,000 mou in three communes, changing it all into rich paddy and ensuring an average harvest of 752 jin per mou a year. The area has now already sold six million jin of grain to the state, and keeps itself well. The fresh crop of children here were full of bounce and made themselves into a hilarious escort for us on our tour around.

We admired the very fine view from the dam top, looked at the fish breeding ponds where the fry for local reservoirs is spawned, saw the newly enlarged flood spillway, and met all the young folk who now work on the control of the system. There are already over 100 kilometres of canals big and small to be taken care of. To get to Tsoumalung, one goes for 30 kilometres down the highway that leads over the border to Nanhsiung in Kwangtung, and then strikes inland over a commune-made highway. Twenty-two of the Hsinfeng communes, all except one, have built highways. First victories in the class struggle have taken the loads from many backs and have filled multi-millions of hungry stomachs.

In Hungweitun

The supper my hosts brought in on our return to Hungweitun looked particularly appetising. At this time when rice is being planted out and people stand in the water all day, a bowl of hot rice beer goes with supper. We had not stood in the water all day, but the rice beer was beside the fine bowl of Chingtehchen porcelain which was heaped with rice, and a dish of sliced mushrooms, onions and beancurd beside that, paired with another of fresh young Chinese cabbage. Kiangsi folk are kind to their guests. After supper I sat back and thought over the countryside as we had seen it today. Everyone was busy. Schools had their "busy time holiday". Lads planting paddy were often middle-school boys. All the old folk were doing things also, the men looking after animals, the women cooking. Older children looked after the younger, and boys helped to heat the water older folk would want to soak their feet in when they came in from rice transplanting. In Hsinfeng the custom is that the men do the actual planting while the women take up the seedlings and, selecting good ones, tie them into bundles and take them to the planters. All stand above their knees in water from dawn to dusk. No matter how often the weather turns to rain, the planting goes steadily on until in the end every field, big or small, is covered with straight lines of graceful young plants standing on their own for the first time.

I thought, too, of the steady work of maintenance and extension of water conservancy laterals that was needed to carry any project like this through to completion. New laterals are being dug all the time, and also a proper grid system of cross irrigation is now being put into use, ten of the 45,000 mou now being so supplied. All such work demands tenacity, care and devotion of a high order.

In the night a fierce thunderstorm beat over the town and one could not help thinking of the Vietnam that lay so close, where homes were broken and wet, wounded and sick were battered by the elements after being ripped by the maniacal power — thousands of tons of bombs a day dropped by the richest nation of the world on one of the poorest. It is the class struggle on an international scale now, all right. The "haves" trying to take all from the "have nots". But it was the dogged determination of peasant youth here in south Kiangsi which started defying the "haves" and, together with the workers and peasants of the rest of the country, built the China that now means so much to the "have nots" of the world today. Poverty and struggle do not mean that the people are rendered ineffectual.

Chinpanshan Forest Farm

Up amongst hills where once Chairman Mao tramped, as proudly stated by the folk who live there, is the Forest Pioneer Farm of Chinpanshan. To reach it, one goes east of Hungweitun on the highway that leads to Anyuan and then turns into a side road up a wooded valley where, after some 18 kilometres, one comes to the centre of the forestry farm there. It consists of 240,000 mou of land, 220,000 mou of which is hilly or mountainous. It includes 6,100 mou of paddy fields. About 10,000 mou of timber is cut each year and, as not only all felling is replanted at once but also bare hills that are the legacy of the old society are being put into trees again, the resources are really inexhaustible. The farm supports itself completely in food and money, and is responsible for the upkeep of a branch of Kiangsi Labor University as well as a tree seedling station.

We made our first visit to the branch of Labor University. It has some 500 students, 87 of whom are girls, in five departments — agriculture, forestry, accounting, irrigation and animal husbandry. Now, in the midst of the Cultural Revolution, classes and study courses have mostly stopped. The students rise at six. Until breakfast they do morning exercises and study Chairman Mao's works. Then all the morning is spent on military training, while two and a half hours in the afternoon are for practical work, whatever department they are in. Two hours in the evening is used for more study of Chairman Mao's works. Their normal course runs from two to three years, depending on what they are learning. They are aged from 17-24. There is a primary school attached. They have helped to instal the 13 pump turbines on the farm and so know something of that problem.

Shihpinchang

Up at Shihpinchang, eight kilometres further east from the centre, there lies the biggest piece of flatland on the farm, that was once, in the 1928-31 revolutionary period, the location of a village Soviet. It was then called Shihpei. "Shihpinchang" means "food factory", and it is here that rice is processed and made into a delicacy similar to red pickled beancurd. Sent out from here in large jars, it is re-packed and sold in small pots in both domestic and foreign trade. Fifty workers operate the factory. A modern piggery uses the bran from the husked rice to feed 140 pigs. Here in these valleys water can be laid on easily and effectively by bringing it down from hill streams or springs by giant bamboo pipes. Situated as it is at the end of the highways into the mountains, this village is also a collecting place for logs hauled down from the hills. In addition it has a big apiary.

Forest Products

Up in the old standing forest one sees many big chestnut trees in bloom. These often give a rich harvest and in season the nuts are steamed with rice for the table. They are the small chestnut, however, about half the size of the one demanded by the export trade, which are called "pan-li" here. The farm has planted 500 mou of the latter to meet demands, and all the young trees are doing well. We stopped for a while to look at the resin refining and packing plant, where resin that is tapped from the pines on the hillsides is made ready to go out into industry. I asked about walnuts, but found that they had not been tried out here as yet. The young people at the tree nursery would not let us go away without having a look at their work. They were a fine bunch of enthusiasts, keen on their job. It was after dusk before we saw the old pagoda of Hung-weitun rise up in front of us. It had been a long day, but one full of interest.

Yushan Forestry Farm

Back in Hungweitun we found that another forest farm had sent us an invitation to go and look at their work before leaving for Kanchow again. So the next morning we set off on a road that runs to Tayu county in the extreme southwest of the county, and after 25 kilometres came into the hills of the Yushan forestry farm. It was from here that the guerillas left behind when the Red Army marched off in 1935, operated until the War of Resistance started and they went to Anhwei to form the New Fourth Army. It was here, too, that a new guerila movement sprang up in the War of Liberation. Chiang Ching-kuo, son of Chiang Kai-shek, came here in his burn all, kill all expeditions, but nevertheless the guerillas gallantly held out until Liberation, and Chiang Ching-kuo could do nothing but run off to Taiwan.

Guerilla methods in this area were highly developed. On my return to Peking I talked with a leading cadre who fought here. He said that groups were of not more than ten each, as the forests would not support more in one place. But they interlinked, and could concentrate easily when an attack came that they estimated could be dealt with. The population supported them magnificently. The Kuomintang would arrest people and demand to know what they had seen and where the guerillas were. The invariable answer was "I ng shao" which is local dialect and means "I do not know". This dialect is the old Chinese language of the so-called Hakka people who came down from the central provinces and whose language is understood from Pingkiang in Hunan through Chingkangshan and the hills of southern Kiangsi, on into Kwangtung, at Meihsien, Hsingning and surrounding counties.

The Yushan forestry farm was started in 1957, with 500 cadres sent from Kanchow on a temporary basis to toughen up and do some practical work. They built themselves huts thatched with wild grasses and started in to open up roads, laying the foundations for the forest farm that now exists. The hills are neither so heavily forested nor do the forests cover so great an area as in Chinpanshan. There are 190,000 mou, 70 percent of which is wooded. About 21,000 mou has been planted in the past seven years, some on slopes burnt off by the Kuomintang. At present around 3,500 mou a year are felled and the same amount replanted. There is still quite an area of original, untouched forest on the higher levels. Replanting is mainly of spruce, tung oil trees, and tea oil bushes, grown together with pines. A new species of camphor tree has been discovered in the old forest and is now being propagated in the nurseries down in the valleys. It grows more swiftly than the ordinary camphor and has a much stronger camphor smell, as a forester showed us by breaking off twigs from both species and giving them to us to examine.

We visited two timber mills and watched the various mechanised timber-working processes, saw the excellent piggeries, the new reservoir and dam project which will give 600 kws of power for village use, and called on an old revolutionary who lives in retirement in one of the villages. He is Chu Chang-cheng, still with cadre rank and coming to action again at times when needed for mass work amongst the farmers in the county. The farmers in the valleys of the forest farm have seen great change come to their lives. With an ensured flow of water to their paddy fields, yearly yields are no longer only 100-200 jin of grain per mou but range now from 500 to 1,000 jin. With considerably more than they can eat, they have been able to sell 17 million jin of grain a year to the state over the last ten years, as well as much oil and many pigs.

Of the around 10,000 people, old and young, on the farm 5,300 are workers, 370 are foresters and 174 are cadres. The branch of Labor University has about 400 in it. Many of the students were busy pasting up big red posters or painting slogans at the time of our visit, for the Cultural Revolution was still very much in progress. The forest farm manager emphasised what a lot the study of Chairman Mao's works had done for the working spirit of the whole place over these last two years. Amongst the Yushan forested valleys, long arms of the Tsoumalung reservoir reached. In one place an island was left, which has been planted in chestnuts. As we came across country back to the county centre, we passed many of the canals from the Tsoumalung reservoir carrying water to places that had never seen it before in such quantity and just exactly when needed. On some places where there were check dams to let the water down gradually, pump turbines had been installed to throw water up to still higher channels around the hillsides.

I awoke early in the morning before leaving Hsinfeng county. The ancient pagoda at the rear of the place in which I stayed is quite an aviary, and with dawn is full of the songs of the flocks of birds who nest inside it. The leading county cadre brought his son in to see me. His given name was simply "Ping" — "soldier". He was 11, and liked to swim and fish in the Bailan reservoir, near which he and his younger brother and sister lived with their grandparents. Day after day he brought down 30 jin of firewood from the hills, and would also help in the rice harvest. His mother was, like his father, a city cadre so he saw her only when he went to town. He had come this time because of the school holiday. It was evident that he was learning well what the countryside was and where its strength lay, excellent education indeed for a young rebel ever out to change. No theory will ever be effective unless it is accompanied by sound practice, and practice can only be learnt by practising. Strength comes from the people, and only by actually living and working amongst them can that fact be fully realised.

Hsiniu Commune

On the return journey to Kanchow we stopped for a while at Western Buffalo or "Hsiniu" Commune. It is one of 13,000 people divided into 13 brigades. It has quite an area of rolling down country, foothills to higher mountains beyond. In 1963, a forest farm was started on these downs, and since then some 5,000 mou of the land has been planted in pine, eucalyptus, tung oil trees, tea oil bushes, and with various kinds of orchard trees — Chingtien pomeloes, Wenchow sweet oranges, pears and chestnuts. When their work of planting on the downs is finished, the group of foresters here will be able to begin their attack on the hills, 37,000 mou of which belong to the commune. At present they have a small agricultural farm operated by the forest farm staff, which provides more than enough grain and oil for their own use. They also plant tree seedlings for distribution amongst the farmers. 200,000 were given away in 1966. This number is not included in the county totals, as these trees are planted around villages, beside roads, and so on. Without the water that is led around the edges of the hills and then over the lower ridges all the way from the Tsoumalung reservoir, the forest farm could not be run on the scale it is today. It is certainly a valuable asset to Hsiniu Commune, as it provides a good base for a concerted attack on the barren hills around. Forests and dams make for rich paddy fields and better living, giving the people the strength they need to face any adversity the future might bring.

Shangyu County

Lying snugly beside the southwestern tributary of the Kan river is the little county seat of Shangyu. With its walls down it does not look much bigger than a village. A lovely spot just 60 kilometres from Kanchow, it is easily reached by both road and river. One goes a further 15 kilometres west to the hydro-electric power plant, which takes the name of the county. In the rating of such plants in China today, it is classified as small, with a capacity of 60,000 kws. Its dam rises 68 metres from the valley floor, in a very convenient gorge between two high cliffs. Though it is not a big station, yet it has quite a large staff, youngsters being sent here for practical experience, later going to other plants as needed. It has a number of unusual features, including one for bringing timber over the dam. Timber rafts coming down from the reservoir are raised by lift to the dam top and then run down a trolleyway into the river below. There is usually too much water in the three months of rainy season, April, May and June, but often not enough for full capacity in the three succeeding dry months. In the dry season timber goes off to Kanchow from the reservoir on 78 kilometres of a newly laid light railway. Until the hydro-electric project started here, the hills forming the basin of the reservoir were heavily forested and almost untrodden by the foot of man. We took a motor launch and went out on the big reservoir lake that has been formed, going placidly up flooded valleys where forests rose from the water's edge, passing wild duck and big fish leaping out to catch flies. It came on to rain, and the ranges looked magnificent across the lake. The place is truly a scenic joy.

Evening after the rain and coming down the valleys to Kanchow again, one saw the lines of commune farmers planting out rice with precision and exactness, bringing a pastel green color to paddy fields that had so recently been just mud. Strength showed in their bare legs and arms, and color from the plastic sheet or coat that hung down the backs of many from their shoulders — blue, red, white or green. Some groups of peasants still wore on their backs a palm-bark cape. It was interesting to note that a production team would wear either one or the other. No palm-bark coats seemed to mix with the plastic ones. The production team set its own fashion! In one village where there had been a little temple to a sylvan spirit underneath a huge camphor tree overlooking the river, the image and accessories had gone and the place been given over to a bespectacled village tailor who could raise his eyes at times and look out over the children and the waters below. Earth gods, tree gods, and all the assorted host of images that once demanded veneration and the spending of hard-earned cash on incense, have marched clear out of the countryside in front of the youth of the Cultural Revolution. New forests and new dams have taken their place. In every one of the 18 counties of southern Kiangsi there are irrigation works, and in most there are forest or pioneer farms opening up previously unused land. There are many branches of Kiangsi Labor University on the pioneer farms, where a good beginning is being made to produce the kind of student who can go right in and help the ordinary man to produce better. China's graduates no longer belong to a superior, administrative class which lives apart from the people; even their consciousness has changed and more and more they identify themselves with the common man who, as the warm weather approaches, can preserve his dignity while wearing a minimum of the clothing that formerly was the outward mark of difference between the rulers and the ruled. A bunch of workers getting logs up to a roadway in Chinpanshan, bronzed by the sun and wearing only briefs, were like a piece of good music in the harmony of their movements. A group of girls in the Chinpanshan afforestation nursery, bare feet and pants rolled high peasant fashion, did not look much like members of old middle-class families in south Kiangsi cities from which many had come. Only in carrying out Mao Tsetung Thought, identifying with the people and living with the aim of serving the people can real work be done. So do still more dams rise, still more forests spread amongst the hills of beautiful southern Kiangsi.

Kanchow to Juichin

The highway between Kanchow and Juichin in south Kiangsi has changed. At the end of the 'thirties I knew it quite well, having been over its 150-odd kilometres quite often by bicycle. At that time one never quite knew whether the wooden bridge at the bottom of a long slope was in repair or not, but it always seemed a pity to cut speed when the acceleration would take one quite a long way up the opposite rise. But I can remember being caught only once. Now new bridges are wide reinforced concrete ones, and even the old ferries over wide rivers are giving place to such.

Passing Maodientze, now surprising with a new sugar mill showing on its skyline, we halted at Yutu on the way. Yutu is a county city where Chairman Mao once held a meeting of 10,000 farm folk. We went to see the fertiliser factory, an enterprise being jointly set up by three old revolutionary counties, Yutu, Hsingkuo and Ningtu. It has taken over the pottery which was a legacy of the War of Resistance and will be soon turning out 12,000 tons of nitrogenous fertiliser a year. Its row of air compressors made in Kanchow was impressive. Most of the equipment has been made in southern Kiangsi, and even the rest comes from inside the province. Then we went on to some pottery sites near Tangtu, south of the river, but found nothing historical amongst remnants there. They were right beside some coal mines, so fuel has been no problem. Twenty-three of the 33 communes in the county now have their own coal mines, giving them ample fuel without cutting timber growth from the hills. All but four are connected with the main highways by good roads. Five reservoirs give water to 80,000 mou of once dry land, and the population of the county has gone up from 320,000 to something over 400,000 since 1949.

Juichin

Juichin, with its five pagoda-capped hills around, is a smaller county than Yutu, having around 280,000 people, 60,000 more than at Liberation. Average production of grain in both counties is around the same — 600 jin. Grain per person per year is 400 jin in both also. During the Red Guard visiting period in the last three months of 1966 and at the beginning of 1967, around two million youth came to the county, there being a permanent guest group of 80,000 all that time. They lived with the commune farmers in the 17 communes and ate "Long March" food, as they called the commune food they were given. One group would move on and then in would come another.

Around Juichin they had much to see. The sites of historical interest have been renovated, cleaned up and, where they had been destroyed, rebuilt in the original form. The first morning after our arrival we spent visiting them, going first to Yehping, where Soviet government was established. The original memorial to fallen fighters there was a plinth of red sandstone, surmounted by a white shell top. When I saw it first before it was finally destroyed by the Kuomintang, the red plinth was described as representing the masses of the people, and the white shell top the foreign imperialism that stood over their heads. The grey plastered renovation does not carry this idea. Rebuilt also have been the three-cornered memorial to Huang Kung-lueh, a people's commander who was killed after going through three of the enemy encirclement campaigns, and the foursquare one of Chou Poseng who brought over his army to the Communist side, finally being killed after fighting in four encirclements. The pavilion to the Red Army dead has also been replaced. But the biggest piece of reconstruction of old memorials has been that of the great hall of the people of those days — the assembly hall which was destroyed by enemy bombing. The reconstruction in its original octagonal form with a great high ceiling and plenty of doors for a sudden exit in case of enemy air raids makes an excellent modern theatre or assembly hall which is very often used.

We saw where Chairman Mao and others had lived in Yehping and then later in Shachoupa, in the latter place there being the little Lenin school opposite Chairman Mao's home. It still is used for two classes of the smaller children, the bigger now attending school in newly built classrooms nearby. There are many mementoes of Chairman Mao around. His words carved on stone at the base of the memorial at Yehping, the pool where he worked the paddle irrigation wheel, standing with the local peasants there fighting drought, his daily used articles, treasured in many a home and brought together after Liberation. The coming of the Red Guards in 1966 unearthed many village people's stories of things he had done, places he had visited, thus enriching the local repertory.

The Kuomintang burnt most of the forests on the hills around Juichin, so that there has been a consequent erosion and silting up of the river. Some 50,000 mou of low hills have been terraced in squares to prevent rapid runoff and have been planted in trees. I especially liked one stand of 70 mou of chestnuts which were doing well. Most of the trees planted are pines, often with tea oil bushes amongst them. The new stone bridge leading to the city was finished in 1962, reminding one of the newly built one outside East Gate at Yenan, the next Red Capital after Juichin. The old red stone arched bridge nearby is still in use. Many of the immense camphor trees around the city have escaped felling and give a very pleasant shade to the tall two-storied peasant homes during the five hot months. The children here look hardy, natural, and unaffected. There are ample schools and hospitals for everyone now, and quite a few old revolutionaries have retired to come and live here. Along one hillside is a branch of Kiangsi University, and near the bus station a four-floored hotel for travellers.

It is not far out to the nearest hills in Juichin. We drove through the yard of the sugar mill, which was preparing for its seasonal intake later in the year, and went up a slope to where the little power station is situated that supplies the town with light. It has two Chungking-made turbines with Shanghai-built generators installed by the Juichin technicians themselves. Each turbine gives 450 kws of electricity which supplies the town with lighting and powers pumps out on the flatland in the daytime, helping to resist drought. Soon another station will be built up the valley at the rear of this one which will generate 7,000 kws. This will be enough power for the area for the time being.

Mienkiang Forest Farm

We walked up to look at the hill lake that had been formed, lying so prettily with the shadow of one of the ancient pagodas reflected in its waters. Then we came down the hill and went up an adjoining valley to the headquarters of the Mienkiang forest farm, one of 326,000 mou, 118,000 of which consists of old forest, while 140,000 is in planted trees, 113,000 mou of these planted since the forest farm was set up 11 years ago. Of the latter total, 90,000 mou has been planted in spruce and 30,000 mou in pine. The area is the oldest Red Army guerilla area around Juichin, and the hills nearest the town were repeatedly burnt off by the Kuomintang. Many of these bare hills were those first planted, so that now quite large areas are becoming ready for the first timber harvest, and a highway is being built into the area to facilitate cutting and transport. Staff on the farm consists of 160 of whom 14 are cadres. They share administration buildings with Anchi Commune, which is adjacent. As one is immediately struck by the wide ranges of denuded hills in approaching Juichin from the west, it is gratifying to see how the problem of getting forests growing again is being tackled. A thunderstorm struck the farm as we visited, the high wind that came with it ripping branches from compound trees, so we did not get up the valley as far as we had hoped. But we did catch a good glimpse of the nursery beds with the young spruce coming up proudly in time for planting in the late autumn of this year.

Lungshan Reservoir

Running along the valley road below the Wuyi mountains that separate Kiangsi from Fukien, and before we came to Shihcheng county, we turned off and drove over downs, then into the hills to see the Lungshan reservoir which irrigates the previously drought-stricken higher fields of Yehping, Huangpei and Yingtien communes.

In his concluding statement at the Second National Congress of the Soviet Republic of China held in Juichin in 1934, Chairman Mao said: "We should help the masses to realise that we represent their interests, that our lives are intimately bound up with theirs. . . . Do we want to win the support of the masses? Do we want them to devote their strength to the front? If so, we must be with them, arouse their enthusiasm and initiative, be concerned with their well-being, work earnestly and sincerely in their interests and solve all their problems of production and everyday life. . . . Comrades! What is a true bastion of iron? It is the masses, the millions upon millions of people who genuinely and sincerely support the revolution." It is in this spirit that the six irrigation schemes already completed in Juichin and the two bigger ones now under construction have been undertaken.

The three communes irrigated by the Lungshan project often had to let their second crop of the year go unplanted because of drought. Their average grain production ranged from 100 to 200 jin a mou. Now with the waters that come down so freely, it has risen to 600 jin a mou. Once barren red ridges are now converted to pine and other tree plantations. Water pump turbines use canal water to mill rice and generate electricity. 200,000 fish fry were put into the 34,800,000-cubic-metre reservoir, greatly assisting village diet all around.

The project was a Great Leap Forward one, started in 1957 and finished in 1961. Of the 2,200,000 yuan needed to complete it, 1,400,000 was lent by the state while the rest was raised by the three communes whose members, coming from the 26 brigades and 179 production teams, did the labor necessary.

It was very quiet talking about it all in the project office, which is in ancient temple premises once used by the peasants to placate the Dragon God of the waters. When the land was so dry that great cracks appeared in it, when frogs perished in the dust, they would offer incense to the Dragon God and supplicate his assistance in their plight. But all the image could do was to look stonily and haughtily over their heads out into the distance. The images have all gone from the temple now. Wild ducks skim down to land on the surface of the reservoir, and castor oil plants grow on the face of the dam. The spillway for taking excess floodwaters was found to be rather small, so a tunnel has been driven through the rocks on one side to act as an additional safety device, and control gates have been installed at its entrance. It will be some time yet before the tree planting turns back the tide of flood and erosion that makes for bigger and bigger water flows from the barren hills each year. With the water that has been conserved already many tree nurseries and plantations have been started. More and more hills in accessible places can be planted with spruce and pine to be felled in 15 or 20 years for timber requirements. All this is a kind of gathering of strength for a final widespread attack. Natural forests have been preserved in some areas because they are inaccessible. They preserve the headwaters of rivers and reservoirs, thus performing an invaluable function. Should they be felled, the lapse of time before new forests grow would mean a good deal of erosion, and then too, the new forests would hardly compare in water conservancy function with the deep-rooted old. The best way out, it would seem, is the afforestation of all accessible naked hill country that now still lies waiting to be covered again.

Too big a task? But it was youngsters of Juichin who marched off in 1934 to make the historic Long March. It is they who have already built the dams, highways and new towns with new schools and hospitals. It is they, too, who will turn the tide of erosion back and have the rivers flowing clear and translucent again.

Old Folks' Homes

In several places around Juichin we passed old people's homes. The old society left many stranded with nobody to care for them. There are two of such homes to every commune, one for those who have been old fighters, and one for others. Seventeen communes, 34 homes, with fruit trees around them, and old folk who help to look after each other. The toll on Juichin people in the revolutionary wars was heavy. I talked to the cook at the guest house. He had five brothers. All went off to the revolution, and with none coming back it was left to him to look after his parents and bring up the next generation.

Shatzekang Nursery Farm

A pleasant afternoon was spent going to the nursery farm of Shatzekang, which occupies 1,000 mou of red lateritic hill topsoil. Six cadres, 21 regular workers whose number is supplemented by temporary workers from nearby communes at times, and 45 students of a small forestry middle school make up the community which has already done good work in promoting the growing of fruit trees in the communes around and in supplying young trees for many places, orders coming even from Kwangtung and Fukien. It was quite some time before the water they used was clear of the red soil and clothing could be washed in it without changing color. As they have terraced the hills, putting a water sump in each rectangular terrace to allow the water to soak down into the soil, and as they have planted vegetation alongside the streams, they now have reasonably clear water for use. There was a quiet woman technician here who was a very convincing person with an obvious interest in her job. Many kinds of trees are tried out to find those best suited to the locality. Quite a lot of eucalyptus is grown, since it is popular with the farmers as a tree which will grow well on high waste ground and is suitable for fuel. Though there is a good deal of coal in Juichin, farmers prefer to use wood fuel because they are used to it. Said one, "We do not have the custom of using coal." An old custom is not so easily changed. Frontal attack will not always do.

The nursery farm grows its own rice and has raised production to 1,005 jin a mou in 1966, with the plan of making it reach 1,080 jin in 1967. It plants a new, short-stalk, big-eared variety which all like. Peanuts are grown for the farm's food oil supply. The youngsters in the school, quite a few of whom are girls, look strong and healthy. They do half-time work in class and half-time manual labor in the nursery. When they graduate they will go back to their communes and help with forestry and orchard work there. The nursery farm is self-sufficient with regard to its upkeep.

Huichang

One morning early, we set off to go to Huichang, 47 kilometres south of Juichin, a place where the provincial government of the Kwangtung and Kiangsi Soviets had its offices. There is also the house where Chairman Mao stayed on his frequent visits to Huichang and where he wrote two poems, well known now to many. Maybe the one best remembered is one with the title "Huichang". It may be translated as follows:

> In the east, day breaks; do not
> say we have started too early;
> for we shall cross many hills yet
> before we grow old; here
> scenery startles with its beauty.
>
> Ranges rise above the walls
> of Huichang city, and run ridge
> after ridge down to the Eastern sea;
> our fighters, pointing, gaze down into Kwangtung
> where lands lie spread out
> still greener, still more rich.

This headquarters was set outside Huichang city, in a village of today's Chingchao Commune. It is called Wenwupa and consists of 33 families with 135 people in all, a production team of Huada Brigade. A meeting hall and museum have been erected here, the museum having recovered some of the documentation of that period of struggle, as well as seals and other relics people had hidden away during the period of Kuomintang return. It had been quite a poor area, and looking back one wonders anew at the strength and determination of this group of poor peasants who had the courage and belief to write on one of the old flags I saw preserved here, "Workers of the whole world, unite!" And thin-legged, hungry peasants they were in those days, too. Today, the production team does quite well, with ample water from one of the 28 dams and their reservoirs that serve the 23 communes of the county. Each of three of these reservoirs serves over 10,000 mou of previously dry land. In all, the county has 310,000 mou of irrigated land, 180,000 mou of which can now stand a drought of over 70 days.

We went around a few other projects, including a tree nursery of six hundred mou and a piggery operated by the county with cadres who were sent down to the countryside to work in 1957. The nursery was one of several in Huichang and was started in 1962. It had a good many difficulties to face, not the least of which were with regard to the five women technicians brought in from Shanghai who thought the place too poor and dreary. The intensive study of Chairman Mao's works, said the quiet, barefoot director with much sincerity, helped them to get over this difficulty. They have many fruit trees which have previously not borne fruit in the county, including bananas, which they have coaxed to cooperate. They are now sending out many seedlings of pine, spruce, chestnuts, and so on. Startling results do not come quickly in a nursery, especially one that has had to start off with a piece of country no one else wanted, build its own housing and grow enough grain for itself, as well as plant its first orchard trees. Its aim is to serve three communes and the town of Huichang.

The piggery keeps 84 breeding sows and three boars. There were 220 piglets when we visited, from 1,200 to 1,800 a year being bred. The place is scrupulously clean. A fleshy plant called "shuiholien" and grown on ponds is the main forage used. It is a kind of water lily. One mou of pond surface can raise 40,000 to 50,000 jin of this plant. For seven months of the year it is fed to the pigs. Bran from grain milling is a subsidiary food. For the three cold months a different pond plant is raised. It is called "hupang". Four Frisian milk cows are kept here also, the milk going to the county hospital for patients' use there. The piggery has its own grain fields, needed for the support of the 32 workers on it. With the help of pig manure in their composting, they are getting 1,015 jin of rice a mou.

Huichang started early with the installation of diesel-engined pumps to help irrigation. It has 97 of these now. The water turbine pump now comes in as everywhere else in the hinterland and competes with other power-driven installations. It is mainly a rice and timber growing county, 80 percent hilly. On the hills it has grown many tea oil bushes, so that in 1966 alone it gained 1,300,000 jin of tea oil, too much for local consumption, with the result that 60,000 jin was sold to the state. Land that once was used to grow rapeseed for oil now is used for grain instead. A certain amount of tobacco is grown, and some cotton. The county exported 1,000 tons of resin last year. As in the other parts of southern Kiangsi, the reafforestation of bare hills bequeathed by the old society is still a challenge to its youth, a challenge that is being more and more taken up.

Huichang city looked different to me when I caught the first glimpse of it from Nanshanling which one crosses in coming from Juichin. Some pieces of the city wall which act as a protection against flood have remained, but the city has spread out a good deal from the peninsula almost surrounded by rivers that made it so perfect a site in the days when there was only river transport. We watched a new 30-ton cargo junk being loaded to go to Kanchow and then on to Nanchang, boys swimming around it or fishing from the bank beside. But today there are also highways that lead down into Kwangtung and across to Fukien, all linking up with the national highway system, so that trucks and buses can be used for swift transport easily. The local dialect of Juichin is very like the Hakka dialect of northeast Kwangtung in the Meihsien and Hsingning districts, which makes communication easier.

The Weiyang Bridge

On the way back to Juichin we stopped for a while to look at the Weiyang bridge, a wooden one beside Weiyang village, over the Weiyang stream. It was here that the units of the Long March army gathered and over this bridge they went on up through Juichin city 35 li away, and then across China to the Northwest to lead the War of Resistance. The village folk were coming in from work, bandying jokes as they passed under the huge camphor trees that shade the paths near the village here. One had the feeling when watching all this youth that, if needed, a new Red Army could march out of Juichin at almost any moment and then, laughing and bantering, throw themselves against terrific odds, just as their fathers did before them.

The 1967 vegetable harvest around Juichin seems to be about the biggest in memory. Excellent cucumbers sell at three fen a jin, and the assortment one sees in the vegetable market would make many a northern city dweller jealous. The rainy season is April, May and June, so that there is lush growth in that time. The drought season comes in the second half of the year, and it is always the second crop that must be fought for.

Yunshanssu

We drove some 15 kilometres east of Juichin city to a little limestone mountain that stands up out of a valley floor. It is covered with vegetation and is capped with a temple building — dedicated to whom no one any longer remembers, for the images and so on were removed long ago. Here Chairman Mao spent the last two months of his time in

Juichin, some of it sick with malaria, and it was from here that he rode off on the Long March. Those months must have been bitter for him, for policies he knew must fail had been put into effect, bringing as he knew inevitably terrible losses. But from here it was not retreat. It was the seeking of a new front to fight from after getting right up into the Northwest, to put the Red Army into the van of the struggle against Japanese imperialism. The finding of a place from which to give leadership to the people of China. Much had been done at Juichin, but for the time being its day as the Red Capital of China was over.

Juichin town has changed a lot since I last saw it. Streets are cement-paved, shops bright. On the day towards the middle of May which was to be our last in Juichin the premises of the Juichin hotel near the bus station were being cleaned up, the by now weathered wall posters of the Cultural Revolution removed and the bamboo hoarding which had been provided for the overflow of these being taken down. The struggle was now entering a different stage, apparently, though in the town itself many new informative wall posters were still being pasted up. Throughout city and countryside, as throughout all southern Kiangsi, there are big hoardings, billboards and slogans or pieces of quotations from Chairman Mao's works. All quotations are the down-to-earth ones: "Who are our friends, who are our enemies" . . . "Do not fear hardship or death" . . . "The masses are the real heroes", and so on, including many other extracts of the Little Red Book of quotations, now common throughout China.

Juichin Dairy Farm

We spent the last afternoon at a small stock farm on the outskirts of the city, where 29 workers farmed 30 mou of land, kept a small herd of Frisian milk cows and 33 breeding sows among 180 pigs in all. For their early rice crop they had planted the new short stalk variety, which showed thick and green against the pastel shade of the old strains of rice beyond. Well fertilised, they say, it will bring in 1,050 jin a mou for the first crop. But for the second crop it will not be suitable, for the weather is drier then and local seed will need to be used. Like other projects of this kind, this stock farm is self-supporting.

Juichin to Ningtu

Leaving Juichin on a warm May morning, we went up 85 kilometres to the city of Ningtu, famous as one of the revolutionary centres in south Kiangsi. As soon as we arrived and had been entertained with tea we went out across country some four kilometres to the mountain called Tsuiweifeng, about which there are many stories. It is a fortress-like mountain set amongst other peaks, with a plateau on its summit. It can only be reached by one man at a time climbing a cleft in a steep, almost perpendicular face where steps have been cut. The Kuomintang had a well-armed garrison up there, and there were also Kuomintang officials and landlords who had taken refuge along with them.   The Army made an assault in 1931 but it was not successful.   Rather than lose more men, it was decided that as the KMT could do no harm up there and could be easily prevented from coming down, to simply leave them there and surround the place.   And so the battle of the revolutionary wars surged to and fro with this queer Gibraltar standing in lonely isolation.

In 1929, there was a certain company Party leader named Huang Cheng-chen.   Finding life with the Red Army tough, he defected and went over to the Kuomintang.   In the War of Liberation, when it became apparent to the Kuomintang that the south would also be liberated, he was made commander of the third KMT military area.   He chose for his headquarters the peak of Tsuiweifeng and proceeded to fortify it, even bringing in a small arsenal along with clothing factories, stores of grain and so on, all enough to last him and his troops for three years, by which time, the Kuomintang estimated, the USA would probably come in to help them in force.   When the People's Liberation Army reached Ningtu, however, with the whole countryside rising to welcome them again, they took one glance at Tsuiweifeng and sent out some men at six in the morning.   By three in the afternoon they were back, with the place taken and all its garrison captured.   Huang Cheng-chen could not have really expected to have any better fate than to be shot, for he had betrayed his comrades during their toughest time.   And shot he was.

Ningtu city is over 21,000 in population now.   The county had a population of 280,000 in 1949, and has one of 380,000 now.   Grain per person averages 480 jin a year.   Seventy percent of the hills which comprise 80 percent of the county are now forested.   We had meant to stay a while at Tapoti village on the road between Juichin and Ningtu, for Chairman Mao wrote one of his well-known poems on the struggle here. We passed a crowd of school children standing under a big tree and too late did we realise that these youngsters marked the place, and we had gone on too far to turn back again.   Ningtu has built no fewer than 500 dams for irrigation, big and small.   Twenty of them irrigate from 3,000 to 20,000 mou.   Seventy percent of the arable land is irrigated.   There are 4,000 mou in sugar cane here, each bringing in from 6,000 to 10,000 jin of cane a year.

Ningtu, Juichin, Huichang, Yutu and Hsingkuo counties comprised the heart of the old liberated areas of southern Kiangsi.   The Red Army which came down from Chingkangshan to occupy them and mobilise the people on their side made much history in the years from 1929 to 1934, forging a revolutionary force that was to carry the revolution into newer stages as increasingly it left its imprint on the China of that day.   No wonder it has attracted the young Red Guards of today on whose shoulders will so soon fall much of the responsibility for China's progress in the next stage.

We now leave our early summer 1967 Kiangsi tour and return to spring of that year — coming up from Kwangtung to the south Kiangsi county of Chuannan.

Chuannan

The hill county of Chuannan of south Kiangsi is on its border with Kwangtung. Once it was called "Chien Nan", the "Chien" being a word used in feudal practice, denoting excessive humility. It has now been changed to "Chuan" meaning "complete", or "all together".

We set off on an early spring day in 1967 by car from Tsunghua, the place in Kwangtung north of Kwangchow where we had been staying. Leaving after breakfast, we crossed north Kwangtung and got to Chuannan in Kiangsi by suppertime. It was a magnificent scenic drive, first around the fiord-like Luchi reservoir and then on up through forests, mountains, over valley streams, wondering just where all those 40 million people of Kwangtung lived, for we saw so few on the road. Around Hsinfeng and Wengyuan county centres there were somewhat wider valleys, rich with the brilliance of yellow rape in bloom. Then too, there were many homes lit up with the pink and white of peach and plum in full blossom.

At Kwangtu, after a picnic lunch, we strolled to the marketplace to watch a children's performance. They were singing the revolutionary songs of the day, and doing little skits on current themes, red banners and pictures of Chairman Mao much in evidence.

When we crossed over the dividing watershed between the two provinces and drove downhill to Chuannan, we found a town alive with construction. There had been a cloudburst in the hills last year, bringing down so great a flood that some of the old housing by the waterfront had been swept away. It was now being rebuilt on a higher level. Lines of permanent hoardings of well constructed brick were being completed to take quotations from Chairman Mao's works. On the hills around tall spruce trees were shooting skywards. Spring farm work was going on all around with great vigor.

As 81 percent of the county is either hill or mountain, all flat land here is important for cropping. At the county office, we were met by a little group of young folk who then administered this hinterland county. They included leaders of the Revolutionary Committee and also a member of the leading group of a provincial organisation in Nanchang. Amongst the group who received us was the young school teacher Chung Chi-fang, the man I had especially come to see. They appeared a confident, energetic group, and told me how at the moment their big concern was with making preparations for a successful spring sowing. Each year at this time a mass movement is generated by calling in all cadres from the 16 communes and two towns of the county and in going over agricultural plans with them. The county is one that exports grain, timber and many other local products.

Most youngsters of the new generation have big ideas of how they intend to put the precepts of serving the people into effect. Some like to dream of themselves as big engineers or generals, doing a very great deal. Youth likes to aim high, but actually what is "high"? As they go on they will learn that the humble ones also can do great things. Chung Chi-fang was a lower middle-school graduate when the time came for him to go out to work, first as an ordinary primary-school teacher. However, he still stuck to his idea of rising higher on the educational ladder, so in consequence had some misgivings when a new task was proposed. Chuannan is a mountainous county, but the place where he was asked to go was in the most rugged and inaccessible part. The proposal was that he organise teaching there to meet the demands of three production teams in some scattered villages where there had never been a school before.

A Mountain School

There were but 14 children waiting to be taught. There was no classroom. Chung Chi-fang is a native of Lunghsia Commune which lies in the hills and includes the production teams of the villages where he is now teaching, his home being only some five kilometres over the hills from them. After Liberation, at the age of 11, he went to a boarding school in Kiangkou, down by the river in the valley below. At 18 he graduated from its lower middle-school course. He is now 24, though he looks older. Tall, broad-shouldered, with a spare energetic frame, he walks with the loping stride that carried the men of Kiangsi on the Long March through China's hinterland. At 18, having had some education, his thoughts turned away from going back to the hard conditions of the countryside. He wanted either to go on to higher schools or else join the Liberation Army and see more of the country. Then when it was suggested to him that he should now repay the folk of his own mountains for what had been given him, he agreed but wondered just how he would go about it. He had studied the essay "Serve the People" and saw the justice of it all. It was simply that, from the practical standpoint, the difficulties seemed too many.

However, he went up to Changpei village and started in, getting the local people to help in fixing up a classroom, making desks and stools. Then borrowing a blackboard from another school, he began teaching. For himself, he fixed up a room in the loft of a cowshed, cooked his own food and carried his own water. Soon he became completely devoted to his work and now, six years later, when I saw him with a group of his pupils it was obvious to me that he is one with them. They respond to his wishes, which he is careful to keep at a minimum. He is not the "don't do this—stop doing that" kind of teacher, but rather one who encourages initiative and is pleased when he sees it in action. The children clearly like him very much. Being natural, he likes to sit for a while after a meal smoking a cigarette, in itself rather an unusual thing amongst the young cadres of today. On a fine spring day he will take his class out under the plum blossom and, hanging the blackboard up on a branch, get lessons done in the sun.

The general idea at first was that the children of the other two villages would come to Changpei in the morning and bring their lunch. But on the way to school one day the children heard the growling of a tiger. This was nothing unusual, for the region abounds with these beasts as well as with panthers and wild pigs. So three of the children from Lungtzekou, the second village, were told by their parents it was too dangerous for them to go, as they were too small. Chung Chi-fang promptly moved house himself to Lungtzekou, taking another space over a cattle stable, and himself brought the children to Changpei every day. Then again one more problem came up. The children found the slippery tracks in the rainy season too hard to manage, and their elders wanted them to mind buffaloes at least for half a day, as otherwise one of the older people would have to do that work when he was wanted elsewhere. So Chung Chi-fang set up another classroom in Lungtzekou, and taught there in the early morning and then again in the evening. In the daytime he went back to Changpei to teach. Then a similar situation arose in the third village, which he solved by teaching there in the afternoons. The people are full of admiration for him, calling him the teacher with feet of iron. Someone has estimated that Chung has walked 3,000 kilometres in the past two years, cheerfully and with determination. "If I wholeheartedly want to do a thing, then I do it." Nothing to brag about, but on the contrary a real privilege to be able to do what he wanted to do, he reasoned. "Here is a clear, definite way I can help people and it is within my power to make it a success." And that is how it has been.

The Fifteen Pupils

There were 14 pupils to begin with. Now there are 15. They are in all six grades, from beginners to the graduating class. The senior boy is Lai Chung-kwei, aged 15 by traditional count, which is from one to two years above the Western way. Chung-kwei is a wonderful child. Handsome, erect, quiet, yet warm and confident, he is the school monitor. "What would you do if the Americans came into China?" I asked him. The answer came back swiftly and in a matter-of-fact way. "Toss them out." And he would be the kind to do that.

Lo Te-wen is 13 by traditional count. "A tiger came near our place. It killed a wild pig, but could only eat half before our hunters chased it away," he said, his face alive with the excitement of it. Unspoiled creative children are these, able to manage a buffalo, climb a mountain. Not in the least awed by the presence of a foreigner who came in a car — a bit of gadgetry they had never even seen before they came down from their mountain village with Chung Chi-fang to meet me. Full of fun as is natural with well brought up children, yet not trying to dominate the picture when sitting in a group of grownups. It was a real pleasure to be with them. They talked about spring sowing, tree planting, minding crops from wild pigs at night as though it was all an exciting game they were playing with their elders. "Trees? Why you should see our big trees! They are so big that it would take two people even like you to put their arms around them!" Lo Te-wen said to me. They knew about wild life, and modern methods of agriculture. About Chairman Mao and the Cultural Revolution, and about the USA in Vietnam. They wrote their names and ages in my notebook with a flourish.

Having so many times seen the embarrassed faces of country youngsters and their elders too when confronted with their own written language, unable either to write or understand it, the nonchalant air with which the written language was used by these young people was itself a tribute to Chung Chi-fang's work. It was more fascinating to see him in action with his group, enjoying the spring sunshine with a class out of doors under the plum blossom. The job of the older children in the village is to mind the younger ones while the grown people go out to work, so pupils just bring the babies to the classroom with them, sit them down somewhere with a home-made toy while classes are in session. Babies that are breast-fed are taken to the fields by the mother, but when they get to the next stage it is the job of the elder children to take care of them. At the time of my visit, however, this duty was put aside, holiday clothes were taken out and red scarves put on. Two who were helping work in a nearby paddy field came over in their springtime clothing, pants rolled high, giving an everyday look to the pictures I took. I could not go to the highest villages, as the distance was too great for the time I had in hand, so representatives from each village class came together for a common class in a village I could get at. There are five pupils in each of the three villages, and the group I saw was composed of youngsters of each of them. They recited "Serve the People" and "In Memory of Norman Bethune" very well. They sang half a dozen songs, did arithmetic, and wrote out their thoughts on the theme of what we live for.

Then when the break came, Lo Te-wen had some stories to tell about a "tsai-lang", a kind of local wolf-dog that ate both wild pheasants and local chickens, and had very big jaws. Then about wild cattle in the forest that could be hunted and were good to eat. Lo Te-wen's father is a hunter, and he goes out with other boys to help as a beater in driving the game. I asked them which season they liked best, and they all said summer. You could have the young people's freedom of getting clothes off, playing in the streams, learning to swim. The other seasons are more difficult in the mountain country, as there are but tracks instead of roads, with mist coming frequently. There is also a good deal of rain. The teacher Chung Chi-fang walks over eight kilometres a day, each and every day, in between classes. From Changpei to Shangyen is not so far — only one kilometre. But the track is steep all the way, a 45-degree slope, so not easy in rain or snow, yet he has never missed a class because of the weather. He himself is of a poor peasant family who did not even own a home in the bad old days. Now he has his mother, who is still able to herd cattle, his wife, who is head of the women's section of her brigade, and his younger brother. The brother is a militia leader — an important function everywhere, but especially so in the high mountain country where a guard has to be placed around fields to keep off wild pigs at night. So he is proud of his revolutionary family, all of whom have found a clear way forward.

All of the people of his generation in the mountain country have become literate now, either with night classwork or through going to outside towns to learn. Many of the older folk have also learnt, and most villagers can recite Chairman Mao's three short essays, which are now universally known in China.

Chuannan is a lovely place in spring. In the valley land crops of rape light up the landscape with vivid splashes of gold. Up deep mountain valley, small terraced fields rise one above the other, and on the hillsides stand graceful spruce trees. The children of Chung Chi-fang's school climbed hills, legs apart, arms out and swinging, as if it was more important to go fast on the upgrade then on flat land. Chung Chi-fang, perhaps because of my white hair, kindly took my arm as though I might stumble, and as we went told me some of his problems. When he started, he related, other teachers in better schools rather looked down on him. After all, just a handful of children in three scattered villages, and his salary but 24 yuan a month! His wife was especially angry with him and wanted to divorce him if he did not quit school-teaching and come back to be an ordinary commune member, getting one yuan a day at least. She went to the commune office with her complaint, but the cadres there just tried to reason with her against divorce proceedings, though they could not convince her. Finally she and Chung Chi-fang did talk it out. His task was to change her whole philosophy of life. It took quite a few sessions to do this, but in the end he succeeded. A simple enough lesson — that not what we get but what we can give is what matters — but yet one that entailed so much! Their child had become sick and had died, a tragedy which had embittered her. For a time she would not mend her husband's clothing or cook him any good food. But finally his arguments won out and she made the turn, herself starting to take part in women's work until she was elected women's work leader. She lives with his mother in their little home in another brigade over the hills from Changpei, which takes a load of worry from Chung Chi-fang's mind, as his mother is over 70, though still keen to work.

Chung Chi-fang Runs the Store

Not content that he was doing enough with his school work, Chung Chi-fang looked around for something else to do to help people. He found that he had around an hour during the lunch break which he could use, so he opened a branch of the consumers' marketing and supply agency in his village, which saved people from having to walk quite a long way to the store in the nearest big village. Stocking articles like tobacco and matches, and common groceries, he sold them at exactly the same price as in the distant village, taking no profit for himself. The agency cooperated with him by carrying in the supplies and collecting the cash or goods to be exchanged, like skins or native herbs the people would bring in. This enabled him to meet people every day, and be of more use to them.

One problem he has not solved yet is that of living quarters for himself. The loft in the cattle shed smells strongly of cow dung, but all rooms in other buildings are occupied. People are very busy the whole year through, and it needs a cooperative effort from everyone to produce the grain targets set, so he has not asked for more work to be done on his behalf. Then, too, he has to mill his own rice by hand, not always with very good results. As he goes from village to village he collects firewood and carries it home on his back to do his cooking. In all, he thinks, he has been fortunate in being able to learn more deeply the real meaning of what Chairman Mao has said, and is now well content to do the work that has been planned. There is a good crop of children coming on to school age, so that he will have much good material to work on. His being in the village and his close contact with the people has enabled much of the old load of superstition still alive in hill villages to be tossed aside. In place of the ancestral tablet and the incense burner below it there is now a picture of Chairman Mao in every home. Earth gods, tree spirit gods and all the rest of the ghosts and monsters are heartily laughed at by the rising generation, who want the fascination of applied science instead. "How does it work?" they say as they look at the bits of gadgetry I bring along with me. A part of their education is to question everything and see if it runs along the line of being of service to the people.

We got on to wolf stories, of which everyone seemed to have a stock. Chung Chi-fang was chased by one pack himself. The boys capped one exciting story with another. "Ever seen a live tiger?" I queried. Sadly almost, they all answered in the negative, though all had heard one roar, and all had seen tiger tracks. I asked about sickness, and it was said there was very little of it up around those high mountaintops. Lo Te-wen could tell hunting stories with such dramatic intensity he carried his audience with him every time, despite his Hakka hill dialect. In the evening, when we were sitting around the charcoal brazier telling stories, it came through that the smallest pupil, Huang Pang-chin, was the son of the brigade barber. He had to look after his two younger brothers, bringing them to school each day so that he could keep an eye on them. The oldest boy, Lai Chung-kwei, also carried a younger kid to school on his back. He carried water for the home also, helped to cook food, carry fuel, look for missing cattle, mind buffaloes, feed pigs and, on the way to school, used his hands to weave baskets which could be sold to the marketing and supply agency. None are spoiled children. They all are full of fun, lively with their fingers. I gave them a brush to write some characters, which they did with good style. Then they made some drawings for me: a fish, a fruit tree with branches broken by a heavy snow. Lai Chung-kwei and Lo Te-wen were both Red Guards and had taken part in the class struggle in the mountains. "There was one very reactionary man around our place. He hated socialism and everything about the new order, and went around trying to make people unhappy with it. He was once the richest man in the mountains."

"Then what did you do?" I asked.

"We wrote a big 'dazibao' and put it on his front door. Then we told him to go to work honestly and not talk so much!" they said.

Wild Honey

Lo Te-wen then went on to describe how they took honey from hollow trees. They stuffed up the hole with an old hand broom, pushing it farther in as they cut the entrance hole bigger, then putting in a big tin containing a few human hairs. The bees would then all go into the tin, which was closed, thus allowing the work of taking the honey to go on apace. If anyone was stung, then garlic was rubbed on quickly, and there was no swelling. All so different from the New Zealand method of felling the tree, rushing in to stuff up the hole with sacking, then pushing in gunpowder fuse to smoke out the bee colony, and rubbing the blueing bag from the washhouse onto the stings. But the honey tastes about the same. It was getting late and Huang San-ying, a girl who had caught a cold, was sleepy. Huang Pang-chin, the smallest boy, sat listening until he too began to drop off to sleep. But the two elder ones kept on making us happy for another hour until we all turned in.

The next day out with them, I asked them how many jin of what in China is called tea (camellia) seed they could find in a day, because this is a job taking a good deal of ability, the seeds falling downhill, or amongst brambles or else becoming buried beneath fallen leaves. The biggest haul for one day with two children working as a pair, they told me, was 40 jin. A good average with plenty of seed is about 20 jin. There was a lot of fun in tea-seed picking though. All the cooking oil used in the mountains comes from it.

Hsiaoyehtung Forestry Farm

While in Chuannan, we went to the state forestry farm some 25 kilometres up a narrow mountain road. This farm, although started earlier, had developed only like so many other things that form a base for progress, in 1958 at the beginning of the Leap Forward. As we rose higher, majestic sweeps of spruce (China Pine) could be seen as if storming the ridges. The farm had been started in 1955 on 280,000 mou of hills with eight foresters in charge who camped in a tiny room and started encouraging the people around to come in their off-season to plant. There are now 104,746 mou of spruce, 60,000 mou in pine, and 50,000 mou in various other trees including tea seed, tea plants (for tea leaves), fruit trees, mulberries, walnuts, chestnuts and tung-oil trees. It is estimated that enough tea-oil trees can be planted here to supply the whole of Chuannan with cooking oil. All the grain the 470 farm staff need is now grown in terraced valley fields, and the farm asks for no money from the government at all. It has a steady income from young spruce cut out of the bigger standing plantations to give space to bigger trees. These are "chuantze" — the small timber used widely for house rafters. In ten years' time, 5,000 mou of big timber a year will be cut and sold. This will be a continuous process, for always 5,000 mou a year more will be planted. Four thousand mou of this year's quota has already been put in, as well as 24 mou of nursery seedlings to be ready for future planting out. It rains up in these mountains for about 100 days of the year, a good deal of the rain coming at spring sowing time, which makes for some difficulties. There has been no forest fire so far, but fire breaks are kept clean and ready.

On our way home from the forestry farm we halted in a valley to watch a tall local lass, pants rolled high, plowing the paddy with a buffalo. It was not so long ago here that it was held to be bad luck if a woman worked the fields, and it was supposed that the crops certainly would not grow. The women of this region make woven belts, one of which they wind around a kerchief which falls down the back of their neck. Quite a striking headdress, and one which suits them well.

In the forestry farm the Cultural Revolution had entered as everywhere else, and there were many wall newspapers and much criticism. The group in charge welcomed me. They were proud of the fact that they had kept up with all productive work at the same time as conducting their movement activities. They feel that, with the putting of their work on a strengthened theoretical basis, their progress in future will be swifter and better in every way.

Yao Minority Nationality

Not far from the forestry farm is a commune brigade the members of which are all "Kaoshan" Yao minority nationality folk. They say they have always lived in these mountains, and though they are cut off from the Yao folk of Lienhsien in north Kwangtung and the adjoining ones in Chianghua in Hunan, they have about the same customs. A hardy, able people, they rear tough children not scared of any kind of hardship.

We took two of the school boys from Changpei with us to the Hsiao-yehtung forestry farm, as it is called. I asked for their criticism. "Not such beautiful scenery as at Changpei," Lai Chung-kwei thought, "and the valleys are so narrow." Lo Te-wen said, "Not many bamboos here. How do they get on for bamboo shoots? We have so many on our mountain! Too many to eat even!" Soon there will be highways connecting the Lunghsia and Kiangkou communes with the outside. These are the only two of the 16 communes of the county so far not served by highways. Their surplus then will go down in trucks to the cities, and their incomes will rise. More people will come to live in back valleys, and there will be new schools.

Chuannan Schools and Hospitals

Schools in the county have shown a steady increase over the years since Liberation. Before 1949 there were no middle schools and but 12 primary ones in the whole county. In 1957 there were 23, and in 1966, 76. These are full-time primary schools. Primary schools operated by the communes number 288 already. One middle school was established in 1949. In 1966 there were 25, of which 19 were part-work, part-study. In the matter of people's health, there was but one medical clinic in 1949 operated by a traditional practitioner. Now there are four hospitals and 60 clinics, with 442 staff, doctors and nurses.

Industry and Agriculture

There was no industry in 1950, the region had only a blacksmith's shop and a tailoring shop. Now, in 1967, there are eight factories started in the Leap Forward, and all doing well. Agricultural implements, power generating, printing, timber working, wolfram ore refining, and so on. The population of Chuannan has risen from 70,000 in 1949 to its present 110,000. Rice production has increased by 53.3 percent in that time. That of edible oil has doubled. Two main crops are now the rule each year, where but one was reaped before. Sweet potatoes, peanuts and other foodstuffs have greatly increased. The use of better fertilisers has made for much change. Green manure is now plowed in everywhere. Pigs have greatly increased, composting is better done. The autumn droughts are being met by the use of water pump turbines in the rivers, and also with power-driven pumps. Soon, when the medium-scale reservoir now being built is completed, there will be a better supply of water and some additional power as well. Everyone enthusiastically tells of how the ideas of Mao Tsetung have penetrated into the minds of the people, giving them added strength. Now 80 percent of the people can read and have studied the three short essays. Thirty percent of them can recite them by heart. There are winter schools every year to enable people to study further, and some 30 selections from the book of Quotations have been set to music and are sung at big meetings, one group competing with another. The people do love Chairman Mao, as the present young leader of the county administration said, for if they did not, nothing would make them want to sing as they do about him.

Old Memories

They remember the time when the Kuomintang kept burning off the hills to get the Communist guerillas out, ruthlessly destroying the natural forest wealth from which so many lived. They remember the Kuomintang blockade on salt which was clamped on to bring the people to submission. How raids were made to seize conscripts for the Kuomintang army, with youngsters being roped together and driven off like cattle. They all have seen the pitiful old and lonely bachelors, with none to care for them. Hired workers who were never able to support a wife or family. They have all suffered from having the burden of superstition piled on their backs, the kind of "education" that sent them buying incense and paper money to help when folk were sick, and which denied schools to the common people.   Now they are all out to take the road forward together.

They average over 500 jin a year of grain each.   Some of this they put into their production team or brigade granary.   There is security even if there is a year without crops, security they have never known before. In the hills, food-bearing trees are being planted all the time, and those who live there learn better how to eat off that kind of country.   Their old isolation is now ended, and both road and river transport has been accelerated.

Local Theatre

A must in every county is an attendance at a performance of the county theatrical troupe.   Somehow or other, county performances are often even more full of spirit than those of larger places.   Members of the troupe are usually village youth who have shown talent.   The one at Chuannan was no exception to the rule, and its singing and dancing to the themes of the Cultural Revolution followed one after the other with ease and verve.   When there came an item with drums and gongs praising Chung Chi-fang he slumped into his chair as low as his big frame would allow as if to escape notice.   His youngsters who had come with us loved it, and little Huang Pang-chin literally shouted at the top of his voice in one place.   In all it was quite an evening.   The county hall seats 1,000 people and it was quite full that night.   Lai Chung-kwei and Lo Te-wen each took one of my arms and saw me home in good style.

Nankang Commune

Around 45 minutes' drive from Chuannan city towards the Kwangtung border lies the village of Nankang, which is the location of Nankang Commune, one of 8,000 people who farm around 13,000 mou of irrigated valley land and a vast stretch of mountainous country in between.   We came to see it and spend a morning with commune leaders, because in the past it was a place widely known as an area of half-starved people tilling some land for landlords who took away all their rice and thus forced folk to get along as best they could on yams and whatever else they could scratch in the hills. It was a place where contagious diseases would come and kill widely, without anyone being able to halt the epidemic, where flood and drought alternated endlessly, only punctuated by insect pests.   There are still droughts, and still floods, and still insect pests.   But there are also now irrigation systems, including a long, raised canal and aqueduct that presented some considerable technical problems, problems the people solved themselves.   More and more tree slopes are being planted, thus lessening the power of floodwaters.   There are spraying machines and insecticides to fight insect pests.   There is a hospital in the village with a competent staff.   The landlords have gone, and the conscript-hunting pressgangs of the KMT also.   The commune has been able to buy three tractors, put in three power pumps and three pump turbines, instal eight rice-husking mills, and supply power from its own power plant, erecting 16 kilometres of high transmission line to take power to where it is needed most. It has 991 head of cattle and 1,991 pigs. All brigades and teams use the three most common kinds of green fertiliser, red clover, broad bean and turnip leaf which, when plowed in, help the local kinds of soil. Twenty jin of lime are also put on each mou in addition to the house, pig and cattle manure, composted with green matter.

We went to one brigade which had built a block of two-storied houses and visited some of the farm families living there. They had gained over 600 jin of grain per capita in 1965, but adverse weather conditions in 1966 brought them a little less than 500 jin. Still enough and to spare. The children looked strong and very up and coming. They even enjoyed being photographed. And one of the commune women gave me a head belt, woven very beautifully in the family in a red and white traditional pattern. This commune prides itself on its success in the policy of self-sufficiency. It has been able to finance the buying of machinery, including the equipment for its tea-curing factory, out of its own resources. It finances two middle schools with 440 students, and sees to it that 97 percent of all school-age children are in primary schools. It gains revenue from the sale of timber, but is rapidly increasing its tree planting each year and seals off many of its hillslopes from any cutting at all, even of the long grass. There is enough local coal to burn its lime and also its bricks and tiles for house construction.

More and more of the farm folk are now able to afford a radio and buy at least one bicycle. It has not all been easy. To finish the main irrigation canal, for instance, took three winters and three springs, so much stone work had to be done. The commune leadership prided itself on the way the works of Mao Tsetung are being studied, and on the direct effect this study has on people's spirit and consequent production.

The Cultural Revolution in Chuannan

With the group in charge we spent an afternoon discussing the Cultural Revolution as it affected the lives and work of the people of Chuannan. The leader, a cadre in his early thirties perhaps, sketched the movement since its beginning with the revolt against the Teng To, Wu Han group in Peking, and how the movement started early in the summer of 1966, resulting in some 10,000 big character posters locally. How it developed, until people began to see what was meant by the kind of thing that led back to revisionism and so on to capitalism. How the local administrators were called on to answer criticism made against them. Many problems came up. Where does the money for good living come from? Is this the revolutionary way in line with the teachings of Mao Tsetung? Do some officials tend to become lords, though perhaps not quite realising it? Are their children spoilt, becoming a new class? Will China lose its revolutionary elan in the third generation as Western "sinologues" prophesy? Some people wanted to get richer by pushing others down. In consequence there has been immense questioning. Each says what he thinks. One might say, "I represent the Party. You are against me. Therefore it is you who are counter-revolutionary." Which in turn would bring the answer, "In the light of the teaching of Mao Tsetung we are empowered to criticise you. You say what you think. We shall also say what we think. Then the people will judge." And so the movement has gone on through the winter, and still proceeds this spring. The young folk said that only a few of the old cadres were following the wrong road, and that mistakes that would have led them to do so have now been pretty fully exposed.

I asked how spring sowing was going on, and how the basic work of irrigation had proceeded since the Cultural Revolution started. There has been an acceleration in the spring sowing work already, they said, and as for irrigation, more has been done in the 1966-67 winter than in any other winter since Liberation. They then took me out on a new highway constructed in October 1966, to their middle-size reservoir project that will store 85 million cubic metres of water and generate 2,500 kws of electricity. It was started last October and is planned as a two-year project. Some 2,000 youth, most of them Red Guards from the communes, were working on the site when we visited. The completion of the dam and the work of reforesting the hills behind should do much in preventing any flood of the 1966 proportions which then swept down the Tao river.

There is also a smaller dam which has already been constructed, which will come into use in the next dry season. Everywhere one sees more pump turbines, more dams to serve them, and more hillside canals being dug.

In the Cultural Revolution in Chuannan, it is worth noting, many of the youngsters of the former landlord and rich peasant families came out on the side of the revolution. They showed where their families had flags hidden in a plastered-over hole in the wall . . . where they had concealed this and that. . . . It has not been an easy time for everyone, but a great deal has been learnt, and there is no doubt that the new rural China which comes out of this furnace will be more highly tempered than the old.

Chung Chi-fang and some of his pupils came to spend the last evening in Chuannan with me. The children's dialect, a kind of Hakka-Kiangsi mixture, was too unusual to understand fully, especially when they got to the exciting parts of a pig-hunting story. But the animation in their faces filled out the picture for me, especially since I had a good knowledge of pig hunting in Taranaki, New Zealand. The children themselves laughed so much at the funny bits that they soon had everyone else laughing along with them, especially when Lai Chung-kwei told how one cornered pig grabbed the hunter by his unmentionables. Then they told landlord and peasant stories. How one landlord family would tell their grand-children, "See that hill over there. That hill is yours. And all the paddy land right down the valley! One day you will have it all back again!" Then they all laughed again, as if that was the funniest thing they had ever heard.

It came out that it was the same difficulty Lai Chung-kwei had in carrying the young one he was looking after, up and down the steep road between Shangyin and Changpei that made Chung Chi-fang take the third class up there. It is all very well to do the daily eight-kilometre walk for a week, or even a month or two. But when the same trail must be taken day after day, year after year, facing all kinds of weather, it is another thing. He has stood the test, and looking at the faces around me I felt that they were worth all the trouble he had gone to. His results are impressive. The children are cooperative, lively, able to create and analyse, and completely unafraid of difficulties, no matter how big these may be. In one short week I had grown very fond of them all, for they gave so richly in warmth and comradeship.

It was a brilliant morning when we left Chuannan and headed back towards Kwangtung. The early sun made the forest leaves glint and the spring blossom sparkle. The blue hills rose tier after tier in mystical grandeur. We passed through one of the two pioneer farms of the county and were soon crossing the Kiangsi-Kwangtung watershed again, and then returning through the hills down to Tsunghua.

Now from this Chuannan digression we go back to summer 1967 and proceed both from Juichin and Ningtu.

At Kwangchang

Leaving the old rebel centres of Juichin and Ningtu one day, we drove north to Kwangchang. I had come here once in the War of Resistance period, but then thought it too small a place to start up any little cooperatives and so passed it by. The old Red Army had come here in 1932 and had remained for over a year. Chairman Mao wrote a poem here in February, 1930 called "On the Kwangchang Road" which may be translated as follows:

> A white world, and a snow
> that lends urgency to marching men.
> High mountains above us
> and through the pass our banners
> stream in the wind.
>
> This time where do we go?
> Down through the storm
> to the Kan River for yesterday
> the order came for ten thousand
> workers and peasants to march on Kian.

The county population at Liberation in 1949 was 80,000. It is now 120,000. On the way in, we were much impressed by the way irrigation canals wound through forested hills, and how in one place one came across the highway over a tall graceful aqueduct, of a design I had not seen in China before. Then we passed a bright new brigade hospital set under some trees. Coming into the city, we found it now facing a great wide street with all buildings completely new. On a hilltop nearby a reservoir tank supplied high-pressure water. The guest house was set on a hill away from the town, quiet, simple, and very clean. After a cup of tea, we made the most of the rest of the daylight going out to see the Chintung reservoir and power station.

Chintung Dam

This was another Great Leap Forward project started in 1958. It has a 28-m. high dam which creates a reservoir of 12 million cu. m. of water, and from it canals wind through forested hills. The old riverbed below the dam has been changed and made into a series of fish-breeding ponds, some 500,000 jin of fish being marketed from them each year. The flood diversion channel does not affect the old course of the river, it having a different outlet through the hills behind the dam. A tunnel through the rock on one side of the dam brings water into a small power station which provides the town with light and powers some irrigation pumps in the daytime when needed. It is just one of 13 major irrigation projects that help to irrigate over 80 percent of all cropping land in the county. 160 water pump turbines have been installed, some using the water in the main canals of this Chintung project. 120 more are being installed now. They also give lighting and power to many villages. Of the 18 communes in the county, 17 have electricity now. At the Chintung reservoir, there is not only the regular staff which looks after the canals and laterals, the power plant, and the fish ponds, but there are also the beginnings of a part-work, part-study school whose practical side concentrates on what is being done on the dam. There are girls as well as boys, and together they make up a first class of 18. Soon, other classes will be added.

It was sunset as we returned to the town. In the stream a whole bunch of youngsters were splashing, the rays of the setting sun bronzing their suntanned bodies. In addition to the county nursery for tree seedlings, every commune has its own nursery, as indeed have many commune brigades. Every commune has its part-work, part-study agricultural middle school. There are ample educational and health facilities for all. As the masses of wall newspapers and posters around attest, the county has played its part well in the Cultural Revolution.

On the way to Kwangchang, when passing through the higher forested country, we wondered why many of the paddy fields in the valleys there had not been planted, quite a few not even plowed. When we inquired, we found that this land was watered from hill springs whose water was too cold for the early crop rice seedlings. In consequence but one crop a year is gathered from them, and planting does not come until early June. On the way into the hills of the Tsuilei pioneer forest farm the next day, we saw many more such fields.

The Tsuilei Forest Farm

The Tsuilei forest is one of 195,000 mou. It has three brigades of farmers working valley paddy fields, as well as 688 cadres and forestry workers, and then workers who operate a timber mill, a hydro-electric power station and other projects. The setting up of the farm was a 1958 Leap Forward project, originally pioneered by 196 administrative cadres who started the work of building a road in, constructing houses, and getting timber out. Since then, 90,000 mou has been felled and replanted, mainly in pine, spruce and giant bamboo. There has also been planted 604 mou of fruit trees, 3,000 of such trees of food value as tea, oil and chestnuts, and then 2,000 mou of tung oil trees. Paddy fields have been extended and irrigated by means of pump turbines, many of which have been installed in this last year. Hill villages get enough lighting from one turbine and generator without the expense of bringing in expensive high transmission lines and the use of much copper wire. By day, the pump turbine can throw water high up the hillside, or mill rice, press oil, gin cotton, grind flour. It is cheap to buy, easy to instal. So far the farm, whose main production is timber, has had to buy some of its grain, but with a concerted drive being made on that problem and a determination to get 1,000 jin a mou this next season they all hope to have this problem solved.

The crop of children is impressive. A good, sturdy bunch over 600 in all, who flocked out of the several schools we passed to see the unusual stranger. There is a branch of Kiangsi Labor University on the farm, with a student body of around 300. They have six classes, two for agriculture, two for accountancy, one for animal husbandry, and one for forestry. Operated on a part-work, part-study basis, the course lasts from two to three years. With 125 mou of paddy, the school supports itself in grain. In 1966 it averaged 960 jin a mou. There are tigers, wild pigs and wolves in the mountains, which are hunted at times. With regard to work with the domestic pigs in the farm piggery, the manager shook his head and said, "We must study Chairman Mao's works better and find out how we can improve this part of our work. It has not been so successful as other branches!" The farm operates a small machine shop which helps in the repair of the five trucks that cart out timber all the time and assists in general mechanical repair and installation. The long tail of the Chintung reservoir reaches up into some forestry farm valleys, so that plenty of fish can be caught to complement the diet. Another dam has been built in the hills to service the little hydro-electric power station, which has been beautifully installed and trimly maintained. Its reservoir is rich with fish. The 25-kilometre highway in from Kwangchang town is practically all uphill, so that in the hot Kiangsi summer the farm is quite a health resort. The last five kilometres we went over from the main centre has been constructed by the staff of the farm during the past few years. Cut out of solid rock, farm workers have gamely tackled one stretch of it at a time. We did not go further than this, as the road was temporarily blocked by a timber slide bringing down spruce logs, but we were told that the highway is still being continued well up into the valley beyond. On other projects, it is hoped that a small paper mill will be operated later. It will be the second try at this, the first one not having been found to be economical. The move-

ment to get young people back into the undeveloped hills of the hinterland and to bring up a generation that will develop such, has an immense
future in China, and in many ways the province of Kiangsi with its pioneer
farms and its Labor University has blazed a way forward in this respect.
There are many pioneer farms now, and most of them have a branch of
Labor University attached to them.

Leaving Kwangchang, we passed over what had been a wild expanse
of barren red hills. They have been thickly forested in pines, and
amongst the pines in one section at least we noted that spruce was already
growing. Spruce does best when sheltered in its early stages. As it
grows, the pines will be felled to make way for it.

Kwangchang to Nancheng

The next county north of Kwangchang is Nanfeng, where grow the small,
sweet oranges that are so popular in both Peking and abroad. The low
hills of the area around the county centre were a solid mass of orange
groves, and from this centre they radiate around through the villages. A
good many million jin of these oranges are exported each year.

From Nanfeng one proceeds northward to Nancheng, a place that
brought back many War of Resistance memories for me. We did not
stay here, however, but went northwest to Fuchou, once a small county
centre but now a growing industrial textile and machine work town of
around 70,000 people. By the time one gets to Fuchou the mountainous
country has receded into the background, and now on to Nancheng it is
comparatively flat, with low hills or just red earth mounds between the
paddy fields. The hot season comes around ten days later than in Juichin,
in south Kiangsi, where we had spent a week in really hot weather. Fuchou resounded with the songs "The East is Red" and "The Helmsman",
loudspeakers were busy everywhere and posters in many colors were on
the walls. Cultural Revolution activities were still very much in progress
here, as if still in their earlier stages. I learnt from local friends how
much the prefecture of nine counties which now centres here is indebted
to the Great Leap Forward, the basic irrigation work done on the many
dams built at that time now making it possible for at least 60 percent
of the once dry cropping land to stand a 70-day drought with ease. The
whole prefecture averages around 500 jin of grain a mou per year, all
kinds of land included. Its particular kind of soil responds magically to
phosphate fertilisers. Green fertiliser, too, is absolutely essential. Many
tea oil trees have been planted on the drier hill land.

One learnt something of the struggle that went into building the dams
that now exist, and of the new ones that are at present building. To
see a great lake of water imprisoned amongst mountaintops, and then to
watch main canals and laterals taking this water to wherever it is needed,
enabling so much to grow that has never grown before, has an unending
fascination. I thanked the prefectural cadres who invited me to come
again and spend time looking at what had been done, assuring them
that if the opportunity arrived, I certainly would arrive along with it.

Nanchang Again

Heavy rain covered most of the countryside as we went over the last 101 kilometres to Nanchang. Buffalo boys in their big palm capes and wide rain hats sat on their animals' backs and smiled at us as we passed. Primary school children under big umbrellas, and with vari-colored plastic raincoats, red satchels containing Chairman Mao's Quotations slung over their shoulders, splashed through pools beside the road. By the time we neared Nanchang the clouds had lifted and the sun shone again. The pupils of one school were doing a big cleanup, scrubbing all the school desks and stools in a newly formed pond nearby. They looked as though they were thoroughly enjoying the process, as they splashed amongst the floating furniture.

In Nanchang itself there seemed to be many more wall posters than there were nearly a month ago. Young activists were everywhere pasting up still more. In the middle of the city, loudspeakers were busy. There were crowds of young people on the streets. The plane trees that were just in bud when we left to go south were out in full leaf, shading wide boulevards. From the smokestacks of the hundred or so factories I could see from my room smoke rose and drifted out over the waters of Poyang Lake. On the main street below, one could see a long procession winding through the green leaves of wayside trees. The drums, the red banners, the huge portrait of Chairman Mao in the lead, and then frequent halts while one of the demonstrators made a speech. Youth has been given its head and is having its way.

Nanchang Tractor Factory

In Nanchang on this second visit we went to see the tractor factory, which was started during the Leap Forward of 1958. We had seen its products in the fields and on the roads in all counties visited, and were anxious to see the place they had come from.

Three capable young men met us, and bypassing the usual ceremonial welcome in the factory reception room, took us directly into the various shops. Total area of the factory site is 300,000 square metres. Shops are well built and roomy. There were 2,600 workers employed, and many of the newer machine tools they were using had been made by themselves. The big majority were Kiangsi people, a small minority being technicians from Shanghai. One of the first things the rebel group did after taking power was to bring in the wives of workers who needed employment and train them as machine tool operators. The experiment has been very successful. Two thousand tractors were made last year, and it is now expected that by next year the total will be from 3,000 to 3,500, climbing to 10,000 by 1970-72. The plant was designed for this number, but to get its product tested out and changed as local usage dictated has taken a good deal of time. Teams go out into the various counties where the tractors are being used to gather opinions and to make estimates themselves. It is a light 24 h.p. diesel all-work tractor that stands up to its tasks well. The factory does repairs free for an initial period of use and also carries out overhaul work later when asked to do so by the commune concerned. The repair technique of commune members was not high to begin with. Drivers learnt how to handle and maintain, but repair work takes a somewhat longer time to get hold of especially when there has been little mechanical background in the operator's life. Now, with more and more mechanisation coming into rural areas, the secrets of the internal combustion engine are no longer the mystery they were, so that more and more repair work can be coped with on the spot.

At the end of our visit a heavy downpour of rain covered the city. Back in my room, I looked down on the main street, seeing marchers and banners still passing despite the deluge. It evidently takes more than rain to halt the youth of today in Nanchang. Nanchang, the scene of that historical uprising on a hot first day of August 1927 that marked the beginnings of the Red Army, is still a revolutionary centre.

Nanchang Pioneer Farm

There are many pioneer farms amongst the hills off the highway leading from Nanchang to Kiukiang on the Yangtze. The one visitors who have some time to spare usually go to see is one that has taken over 300,000 mou of low hilly country between the bigger mountains and Poyang Lake. With irrigation work put in after the farm was set up in 1957 the downs have been planted in trees, 10,000 mou being in mulberry for sericulture, and 20,000 mou in paddy fields. Several thousand mou have been planted in fruit, nut and other oil-bearing trees, while the rest is going into pines. Before the farm started up there were some scattered villages whose rice production per mou was only 170 jin a year. These have been included in the farm now, which already has a population of 11,000. Average rice production per mou is now 650 jin a year for both old fields and all the new extensions that better irrigation has made possible.

We spent a morning going to watch silkworms eating mulberry leaves, visiting the piggery and seeing the Swedish White, the Yorkshire, Ukrainian, and Black and White Berkshire pigs that are kept for breeding stock, looking at the mulberry trees that are bearing, and then the seedlings which now are being sent out of this farm to many parts of the country, as far as Kashgar in Sinkiang.

The best part of the afternoon was spent in the silk textile mill which has been moved here from Shanghai with 1,000 workers. It fits well into the pioneer farm, for there is ample space to develop, a good supply of cocoons, and then too all the facilities a big pioneer farm that has been developing for a decade can offer. A good hospital, an excellent hall for cinema and theatre, both primary and middle schools, and also a 375-student branch of Kiangsi Labor University. The children looked in top condition, and a group of them, mostly textile workers' youngsters, attached themselves to our visiting party, providing a good deal of amusing accompaniment in the Shanghai dialect. One of the directors of the farm is an old Long March fighter who went from Kiangsi in 1934. He has been in the north so long that I noted when we lunched together he preferred steamed bread to rice. The farm can now not only supply its own needs in food but can also pass on 2,500,000 jin a year to the state, as well as two million yuan in profits accrued. The silk-weaving mill turns out 35 kinds of silk, weaving and dyeing ten million metres a year, mostly for the home market, though in 1965 five million metres were woven for the export trade. One wonders just how many factories, complete with machinery and workers Shanghai has already given to the hinterland! Their number cannot be small, and they make a new Great Wall of local self-sufficiency.

A Cannery and a Brewery

The last morning came, as last mornings must always come. The plane for Shanghai would not go until after lunch. There was time for one more visit, and where would we go? What about the meat works, where 4,000 pigs are killed a day by modern methods? But I was allergic to meat works today. What about another machine works? A cannery and brewery? I pricked up interest in the last named, and soon we were being met by a 48-year-old ex-Army man, who, with the leader of the rebel group, was managing a plant of 648 workers. We put on white clothes and rubber boots and went around seeing many appetizing things being canned — pork, curried chicken, duck, and so on. In the fruit season 1,000 local temporary workers are taken on for the seasonal work of canning pears and oranges. 1,400 tons of canned goods were made in 1965, 2,440 tons in 1966, and this year, 1967, the total will probably exceed 3,300 tons. In the period prior to 1962, much of the export trade went to the USSR and the East European Democracies. Now more of it goes to Hongkong, Singapore, Japan and other places in Southeast Asia. The brewery is a modern one, set some distance away from the cannery, but in the same compound. It is well maintained, and its product goes entirely into the Kiangsi market. Climbing upstairs to one of its top floors, we looked out at the wide expanse of factories around. "In 1957, mostly waste ground. Then came the Leap Forward, and they all mushroomed up, just as ours did," the manager said. He was insistent that we all taste some of the items produced. So we drank much beer and had quite a meal of steaming pork and chicken, rounded off by preserved pears and oranges. Then the cannery Red Guards decorated me with their armband and presented me with a book of the Quotations of Chairman Mao in English. On the wall beside us was one of these quotations in big red letters. "What is work? Work is struggle. There are difficulties and problems in those places for us to overcome and solve. We go there to work and struggle to overcome these difficulties. A good comrade is one who is more eager to go where the difficulties are greater." When we came back to the hotel, we did not feel the need for lunch after all our entertainment at the cannery, so made a final packing up of our bits and pieces and were soon moving out to the airport. The streets were a waving mass of red banners and enthusiastic youthful faces. And so ended an inspiring and instructive month in a changing Kiangsi. Our driver told us we had covered 4,000 kilometres. It had been well worth it.

Kiangsi in 1970 Summer

It was after midnight when our group came off the train from Hunan at the town of Pinghsiang in Kiangsi province. The next morning, Kiangsi friends told us something of the locality, which lies on the east-west railway 280 kilometres from the provincial capital of Nanchang.

It is a town of 40,000 in its urban portion, but the municipal administration is in charge of 930,000 people, which includes its suburban communes and various coal mines. There are 700,000 people engaged in farming and 200,000 in industry. Of the coal mines around, that of Anyuan is the most famous; here Chairman Mao made eight visits, coming over the hills from Changsha in Hunan, from the time of the First Congress of the Communist Party in 1921, to the end of the Great Revolution in 1927, when he left the region for Chingkangshan, 300 kilometres south of Anyuan, to build a revolutionary base. From then on until 1934, when the Red Army set out on its Long March, the agrarian revolution flared throughout much of the 117,000 square kilometres of Kiangsi. After Kuomintang occupation there were so many killings that the population figure went down from its 23 million in the 'twenties by so much that, in 1949, it had recovered to but 14 million. Today it is again over 23 million. Industry is swiftly developing and the new Revolutionary Committee in the leadership is keen to reach new production records. Tractors of different types are already being mass produced. In 1969 the first 500 four- or six-ton trucks were manufactured. Nanchang is giving leadership to both industry and agriculture over the whole province. All these reports brought back old memories to me and reminded me of the time when I came to Nanchang in 1938, just before the Japanese occupation. How I looked at first in vain for some machine tools to buy and to remove into the hinterland, finally finding that there were two tiny machine shops but that they had already buried their machinery. The lathes and so on we dug up, bought, and removed together with the workers south of Kanchow down the Kan river. It was all there was, but it was certainly useful, as the workers came along with it. And the Chinese worker, but given a chance, can make nearly anything.

First Foreign Group to Anyuan

As the highway is good, it took us only about 20 minutes to come by car from Pinghsiang. Our group was the first foreign one to come to Anyuan in its new setting. Soon, no doubt, there will be many more visitors, especially as a big, impressive exhibition hall has been built on the side of a hill in Anyuan, opposite the main coal mine shaft. Here, the different stages of the old working-class struggles in the mines are clearly depicted on paintings, in sculpture, photographs and drawings. This particular mine was at first German-controlled and later, following the First World War, by the Japanese, who took over many of the German assets in China. The big, roomy house of the old foreign manager stands high on the hill, arrogantly looking down on the small miners' homes below. The mines were opened in 1898, as part of the Hanyehping iron and steel complex — smelting works being in Hanyang, a part of Wuhan, the ore coming from Tayeh, and the coal from Pinghsiang. The mines were operated in the feudal manner then common, with one policeman employed for every ten workers. The mine administration had its own court and jail, and workers were ever subject to degrading search and ruthless exploitation. Wages were paid out in the paper money issued by the company, which could be spent only in the company store. To ensure that the workers were kept ignorant and superstitious, there were 24 temples in the 21 square kilometres of mine territory. In these temples the priests and their backers battened on the workers, scaring them into giving part of their pitiful wages for temple rites to ensure their safety at work. Miners who had accidents were simply fired. When one particularly bad explosion took place underground, the management did nothing, but simply sealed off the galleries where it had taken place so that all 92 workers inside were suffocated. The average worker produced coal to the value of 70 yuan a month. But in wages he received but 6 to 7 yuan. In the countryside around, landlordism was rife, so that destitute peasants, unable to repay landlord loans, were forced to take jobs in the coal mines, and then to try and save a little to pay back, despite compound interest. When Mao Tsetung came and took lodgings in a humble home, he found it easy therefore to make friends amongst the workers and to organise worker resistance. He told them that their sufferings were not predestined but the result of imperialism and a rotting social order.

If workers would unite, they could really master their problems. A workers' club was formed for railway men and miners. Then a night school was set up, and in February 1922 a Party branch. The organisation of a trade union followed, and on September 14th, 1922 came the first big strike, a five days' fight which was successful, all worker demands being met. This was a real victory for Mao Tsetung Thought, resulting in a big advance for the workers' movement in these parts.

How much things have changed! It seemed strange hearing of so tough a thing as a miners' strike when one looked at this big well-lit building, which was completed in 1969 at a cost of 445,000 yuan. It is a good school, however, and the money was well spent, for since its completion some 4,000-5,000 people a day have come from all parts of Kiangsi and Hunan to see its exhibits and listen to the demonstrators who tell their story so clearly. Those who come then go out to watch the mine operations, where work now is mechanised. With far fewer workers so much more coal is now produced.

Chairman Mao was the first man who really understood that in China, a semi-feudal, semi-colonial country, the workers' struggle was that of the peasants also. Workers and peasants came into the Red Army and joined many guerilla units, doing wonderful things in the Great Revolution and in the Chingkangshan struggles later. Mao Tsetung came again to Pinghsiang on September 20th, 1930, with a Worker and Peasant Army force, and talked to 30,000 of the local people at a meeting in Pinghsiang city.

We were reminded of that on the second day of our stay, when we were invited to take part in a big mass meeting of support to Chairman Mao's call for struggle against American imperialism. Over the radio came the voices of speakers on Tien An Men in Peking to half a million people, and I, sitting and listening to the speakers, penned these lines:

> A background of mountain
> ridges in blue haze, and
> in front of us a mass meeting
> bright with red banners
> and portraits of Mao Tsetung,
> who spoke here forty years ago.
> Today Anyuan coal miners,
> Army men, townsfolk
> school children, farmers and
> workers, the people militant have
> rallied here in response to
> Chairman Mao's statement
> in support of the world's people
> against U.S. imperialism;
> ten thousand bare arms, Little
> Red Books in hand shoot high
> as they shout for an end to
> aggression, and a way ahead
> for all peoples, so that we who
> have happened here at this time
> from Indonesia, Japan, Ceylon
> and New Zealand, join in with
> all our hearts.

> > Here in Pinghsiang
> > Come forward speakers from each walk
> > of life; once rising imperialisms
> > lorded it high as they greedily
> > looted treasures from the hills
> > along this Kiangsi-Hunan border;
> > today, a dying imperialism
> > lashes out crazily in Vietnam,
> > Laos and Cambodia, dragging in
> > its bought up henchmen; so here
> > this early summer's morn, all
> > meet in protest, as do also

the multi-millions all over China;
now no empty protest either
but that of an awakened people;
protest with a defiant ring,
protest with teeth in it.

One of the exhibition halls of Anyuan exposes the role of Liu Shao-chi. During the beginnings of the miners' struggle in Anyuan, he advanced what were in fact social-democratic slogans and spoke out against united workers' action, saying conditions were not ready for such: unity was not good enough and so on. But when he encountered, and was stymied by, the determination of the workers, he tried to weaken the struggle in other ways, asking the workers to "always behave in a civilised manner" in any strike action. He signed a secret agreement with the mine owners, promising to protect the pit, boilers, winch and other hoisting apparatus during the strikes. His deal with the mine administration was a de facto guarantee that there would be good order maintained in the mine and in the area around. Of the 17 strike demands the workers had put forward, Liu Shao-chi deleted four quite important ones. The first was that workers should have a day's rest once each week instead of only once in two weeks, the second that eating and sleeping conditions be improved, third that the mine should run on three 8-hour instead of two 12-hour shifts, and the fourth that contract jobs for work to be done should be cut out and straight wages paid. The whole story of his activities in Anyuan is too long to relate in detail, but his "work" there during the time of this first strike can be summarised in saying that he in every instance tried to put the brake on workers' activities to dampen the struggle and to compromise with the owners. Still, he was bested by the correct line and the practical work of Mao Tsetung, so that victory was won. After this victorious outcome of the strike, Liu Shao-chi moved to the field of arbitration and worked on setting up a wage control committee in the workers' club, now controlled by the mine administration. Miners who rebelled were jailed. Liu tried also very hard to destroy the worker-peasant alliance, keystone of Mao Tsetung's policy, and in 1927, it has now been discovered, he actually wrote to the traitor Wang Ching-wei to the effect that he would do everything in his power to lead the Communist Party to follow Wang's traitorous policy. How far divorced he was in spirit from the working class can be seen from his slanderous statement that workers had no revolutionary spirit and worked but to eat. He went so far as to publish articles in the reactionary press in which he lauded and supported the administration of the Hanyehping Iron and Steel Works. Very much in concordance with his activities during the period of the first strike, he pushed now for legalism and economism, he demanded that all trade union work be in the open and ensured that there were no secrets from the mine administration. This policy was the direct cause for the losses the workers sustained, when on September 25th 1925, the capitalists and warlords' agents launched a surprise attack on the workers' club, killing and arresting a great number.

The grave of a union leader, Wang Chin-yuan, then murdered, lies outside the museum. When Liu Shao-chi was in power in Peking, however, he had a museum set up to glorify his own work in Anyuan, and a painting he had commissioned to show him with workers took five years to paint. Now his memorial hall is sealed up, his real part in the whole workers' movement of Anyuan being carefully traced, documented and preserved as a negative example for people of the future to study.

We went around Anyuan village, stopped to talk with miners and their families, watching the coal trucks come out of the mine mouth that ran into the side of a hill. In the days when Mao Tsetung came so often from Hunan, and when he had his brother, Mao Tse-min, working in the consumers' cooperative here, there were over 10,000 workers. Today with modern, automatic mining methods there are but 3,000, producing 3,000 tons of coal a day. They look back with pride on the role Anyuan miners played in the Great Revolution, when they took a leading part in the worker-peasant alliance, organising 30,000 peasants in Pinghsiang county, armed with spears in the main, and under the red flag with its emblem of a plow on it. Later 1,700 Anyuan workers were in the second regiment of the first division of the Worker and Peasant Army. On September 12th 1927, they took Liling county in Hunan, and on September 15th planted their standards on Liuyang city walls. Many went all through the Chingkang Mountains struggles with Chairman Mao.

We went to the different houses in Anyuan where Chairman Mao had lived. Humble miners' homes they were. He came to Anyuan so many times, he became very familiar with the place. The next day after his first arrival in 1921, he went down the pits to see for himself the actual conditions under which the miners worked. In January 1922 the first workers' evening school was set up, and one month later the so essential underground Communist Party branch.

Pinghsiang Gas Engine Works

Before we left Pinghsiang, we spent half a day at the Pinghsiang gas engine works, a plant set up in 1954 by 20 metal handicraft workers. Established on waste ground outside the city beside hills covered with camellia bushes — the source of Kiangsi's food oil called "tea oil" — it is now a thriving concern with 400 workers, who turn out gasoline engines. Since the lifting of the Liu Shao-chi ban on industrial expansion on a wide scale, it has built or added 98 modern machine tools to its equipment, all in three years, this contrasting favorably with the 50 such tools added in the 12 years previous to 1966. Workers' innovations have made a great difference to production, a fact of which all are proud. Last year the factory completed its plan for 2,500 gas engines one month ahead of time. This year they are also running ahead of plan. In addition, in 1969 they turned out two trial truck engines in 35 days. This year they are putting in a production line for engines for the Peking style jeep.

One interesting aspect of the factory is that which deals with its part in giving practical education to local school pupils. The school concerned is one of 1,200, a middle school. Its older students, girls and boys, rotate in groups of 120 a time to the factory for three months, working six days a week, with one hour each day given over to political study out of the eight-hour work period so that all get this training before graduation. The school also sees that each one of its students gets at least half a month a year working out on farms in communes. Youngsters will in consequence have a much better idea of what life and work entails before they are sent out to meet it.

The plant is a good one to work in. Big, well designed buildings with plenty of space and light, they house a group which obviously has a considerable future for service to the people. A not unexpected thing to find in a town with the tradition which Pinghsiang has.

Anyuan to Yunghsin

It certainly was a scenic trip over the new mountain highway between Anyuan and Yunghsin. At times the road ran amongst the clouds on mountaintops, wound through forests, then when the mists cleared giving wonderful views of the carefully terraced land in the valleys below. We dropped down from the mountains and then drove through fertile country until we came to Lienhua, a place which got its fame as a revolutionary centre in the struggles for Chingkangshan. From now on, we were in the base area called in this stage of the revolution "Hsin-Sui", the character "Hsin" being taken from the place named Yunghsin, and the "Sui" from that of Suichuan over on the east side of the mountains. From Lienhua to Yunghsin was easy going. Despite the rain which fell intermittently, commune folk were all out in the fields transplanting rice. In Yunghsin, we put up in a very comfortable rest house for the night, and next morning went to see the home — an old ancestral temple — in which Chairman Mao had worked, and in which he had called a meeting on July 4th 1928, to discuss the request from delegates who had come from the Hunan Provincial Party Committee. They wanted the whole new Worker and Peasant Red Army to march into south Hunan. Mao Tsetung heard them out and then produced a carefully analysed reply, opposing the idea completely in seven reasoned paragraphs.

The delegates were unconvinced and went off to other centres where they ordered and persuaded different commanders to march into the south Hunan counties, an operation which had disastrous results. In order to retrieve the situation, Chairman Mao led some of his troops to Kweitung in south Hunan to save what he could of the defeated main forces, joining with them on August 23rd 1928. On the 25th, an important meeting to summarise the whole operation was held at Tanghsia in Kweitung. Points were thoroughly discussed by Mao Tsetung, so that all might properly understand. Yes, he realised there were many Hunan men who wanted to get out of Kiangsi and go home. But the main function of the Red Army now was not to fight positional warfare in adverse conditions against forces seven or eight times their number. It also was not wise to abandon all in the face of minor successes of the enemy. These policies had to be thoroughly understood and digested. The losses caused by this adventurous expedition were why much of the Chingkangshan base, including Yunghsin, which had so carefully been built up, was lost to the enemy.

Not much good for Chairman Mao to say then, "I told you so!" Stubbornly and methodically he went ahead saving what could be saved, then going on with the organisation of the people, ever conscious that the Army and people were like fish and water, and that the tendency of armies to become roving bands of adventurers had to be checked, while movements like those of agrarian reform and for bettering people's livelihood had to be promoted, if this great plan for having rural bases encircle the cities was ever to come to reality.

Yunghsin to Chilungshan

We went from Yunghsin to the Chilungshan area where, near the old stone bridge at Lungyuankou, a tough and victorious battle was fought with the Kuomintang on June 23rd 1928. We took pictures down by the old stone bridge and then climbed up to the new monument which overlooks a long valley. This valley splits the Chilung mountains into two long spurs. During the battle a pincer movement down these mountain spurs, made possible by an incredibly tough and long forced march by the Worker and Peasant Army from Ningkang and backed by local armed peasantry, resulted in a smashing victory for the revolution, making the liberation of Yunghsin possible and raising morale all around.

The enemy had attacked in considerable strength but now was sent reeling back. Over 2,000 rifles and many valuable supplies were captured, and both Hunan and Kiangsi troops were forced to withdraw from the area. I wrote the following lines as we rested near the village a while during our visits:

> A Red Army forged
> into two pincers of steel
> slipped and crushed the enemy
> on the ranges of Chishiling
> with the help of peasant
> militia, the victors gained
> some 2,000 rifles
> plus much equipment.

>> We went to the old stone bridge
>> where battle had raged, and then
>> to the tall monument commemorating
>> victory, and as we stood up came
>> a peasant boy, grandson
>> of one of the old fighters
>> who struggled here, and I asked

where is your home, and he pointing
to a quiet old house beside
the stream, said with laughing eyes
"See! It is over there."

To Sanwan

From the Lungyuankou battlefield we went on through the hills until
we came to a place where a newly made branch road struck up a heavily
forested valley to a little place called Sanwan, famous for its Maple Flat
where 1,000 men under Chairman Mao came on their march after the
Hunan Autumn Harvest Uprising. Their purpose was to reorganise and
to decide on the next steps to be taken. This was on September 29th
1927. They had left Wenchiaosze in Liuyang, Hunan, on September 20th
after listening to a speech by Chairman Mao, who had asked them whether
they had the determination to push the revolution through — to dare, or
not? Now in Sanwan, with autumn coming on, the same problem was
to be faced again. Chairman Mao told them that any who wanted to
go home could do so. They would be given travel money and the Army
hoped they would take part in the revolution back at home. Sanwan,
as they came to it, was simply a tiny hamlet of a few scattered houses
on forest clearings, with a river below. A quiet and beautiful place to
come to by car on a summer's day, but it must have been seen in quite
a different day by the battle-worn troops who, with their wounded, came
over forest paths to it. Rain is frequent amongst the mountains, making
paths slippery and the going difficult.

Chairman Mao, however, was full of revolutionary optimism in spite
of such tough conditions. He was in Chingkangshan. He had the beginnings of an army, and he had the people on his side. A careful and
searching discussion revealed the reasons for the past defeat and many
important shortcomings were criticised. The leadership of the Party over
the Army had not been properly established, old army types with their
experience in feudal armies were likely to waver in an emergency. Officers still cursed and beat their men in the old style. There had been
interference from some who followed a rightist line and from others who
advocated an extreme left opportunist line. The task now was to establish a completely new army, properly under the control of the Central
Committee of the Party. In the past, Party leadership had been found
only in the upper echelons. Now it was decided that each battalion
should have a Party committee, each company a branch, and each platoon
a Party group. The authority of the Party was to be absolute. The
inclusion of the Party at all levels gave the army a soul, a nucleus of
leadership, which would insist on the practical democracy needed to maintain good relations between officers and men, the right of soldiers to hold
meetings, express opinions, and get clear of old ideas about an officer
caste. Financial accounts of the army had to be open to the inspection
of all. Soldiers had five obligations. To have a representative take part
in the management of the army, to defend army discipline, to supervise

economic expenditure, to carry on political work with new recruits and lastly, to do political work amongst the masses of the people. Then there were the two powers all soldiers had. The right to submit suggestions, and the right to question. But of course there was no right to interfere directly or to veto Army decisions. The new Worker and Peasant Red Army was to have better organisation, discipline and democracy politically, militarily and economically. Organisationally and with immense confidence in its future, the name Worker and Peasant Army was formally adopted, the soldiers present being included as the first and third battalions of the first regiment of the first division. There were three companies in each battalion. Officers not immediately needed were organised into an officer reserve corps, and in addition to it a medical corps was organised, as well as a guard unit for special purposes. There were not great numbers to deal with, for after those who wanted to go home had left there remained but 800 men. But, because of the reforms that had been instituted, it was a much stronger unit than its predecessor.

When the nucleus of the Red Army first came to Sanwan, the people fled their homes and went out to hide. Chairman Mao ordered that until the villagers came back no one was to go into their houses. Shelters were built outside and soldiers cleaned up the place, carried water and fuel for the people. The local people watching from their mountain and forest hideouts soon saw that these soldiers were not like those they had known in the past who treated the people brutally; so gradually they came down, until by night all had come home again. The next day Chairman Mao asked the people to a meeting and told them that here now they had the army of the exploited, of the long suffering people, an army whose duty was to work for the people, die for the people if necessary, and try to bring happiness to the people. Then he asked them why it was that all were so poor. Who made a living from their labor? Afterwards he distributed some of the spare rifles to the villagers and gave them money and cloth, making all realise that here indeed was an army of liberation, indeed their own army.

On the third of October, the army assembled under the big camphor tree on Maple Flat and prepared to march to Ningkang, the people gathering to give them a hearty sendoff. Before they went, Chairman Mao told his men not to be scared because their numbers were few. A well-trained, politically awakened soldier was worth ten or even 100 of the old type if directed rightly. "So, multiply our number by ten and you will see we have a great force already," he said, half in the humor soldiers love and half in earnest. He also announced the three disciplines. Be kind and polite when speaking to people. Be fair in all buying and selling and, lastly, take not even a piece of sweet potato from the people. These rules sufficed until they were amplified at Lungshih on May 4th 1928. While in Sanwan I wrote these lines:

> 1. *Here in a tiny forest hamlet*
>   *set like a gem amongst*

green hills, came a thousand
fighters in revolutionary
struggle, led by the ever
undefeated in spirit, Mao Tsetung
to whom it was just one more
opportunity to learn, sum up,
organise better, change what
was left of an army too close
to feudal forms, to one that
would grow purely for and be
of the people; now at old sites
boy rebels of a new generation
stand with spears
on guard, taking their task
most seriously.

2. *A great camphor tree spreads*
    with a tall maple beside; it is
    Maple Flat, where the Worker
    and Peasant Army was formed
    by Mao Tsetung; tall trees
    standing in salute to fighters,
    waters of the stream below
    sparkling up encouragement;
    great setbacks there had been,
    but the spirit lived, and we
    a party with many Indonesians
    amongst us, heard here from
    the midday broadcast, the message
    of the Chinese Communist Party
    congratulating P.K.I. on its
    fiftieth birthday, then stressing
    the absolute surety of its
    final victory.

On to Ningkang

The first day's march brought the army to Kucheng, where some more organisational work was done; the move to Ningkang followed. Our group followed the route the Red Army had taken so many years before, but travelling over a modern highway it did not take us very long to arrive at Ningkang. Evening, and we were being welcomed by a group of young people in the guest houses which occupy the place where in Red Army days an Army school was established. Situated beside the Lung river on a scenic spot, it was the centre from which we made our visits around. The first place we went to lay some kilometres past Ningkang city. It was Maoping, which was Chairman Mao's Chingkang-shan base headquarters for many months. Here he established his Army hospital, and here he wrote his essay "Why Is It that Red Political Power

Can Exist in China?" It was here in Maoping, too, that we heard something of the epic of incorporating the Hakka rebel irregulars on Chingkangshan into the new army following decisions made at the Kucheng meeting on October 3rd 1927.

Maoping

In these last few years especially, there has been much careful research done by thoughtful historians bent on getting down to the correct facts of the so pregnant struggle of the Second Revolutionary period. Fortunately, many of the participants are still alive, so that the checking and analysing of each piece of struggle has made for a much clearer understanding, and has emphasised needed lessons. Old stories that are only stories have been discarded, and new appraisals based on fact made. The situation with regard to the rebel Hakkas is one that has been gone over and appraised again. These irregulars were led by an ex-middle-school student, Yuan Wen-tsai, and a tailor, Wang Tso. They plundered the Kiangsi landlords and officials and supported poor Hakkas. Chairman Mao welcomed them warmly, making common cause with them against the main enemy, giving them rifles and ammunition and taking some of their fighters into the Worker and Peasant Army, while sending some of his men into theirs. He got their leadership to understand that the struggle was one between classes, not between Hakka and local Kiangsi people. That a Hakka landlord was every bit as much an enemy of the poor as the Kiangsi native ones, so they should have a force that represented all the poor, not just the Hakka. In these Chingkangshan areas the Hakka people were not in such a majority as they are in the more southerly Kiangsi counties or in those of northeast Kwangtung. Contradictions between them and the local people, therefore, had been easily played upon by the officials and landlords, on the general principle of "divide and rule". The principles now enunciated of (a) forming a united front with all people's forces against the main enemy, and (b) carrying the class struggle into a minority group so that they could unite with the majority poor, were both basic ones.

In Maoping we met Yuan Wen-tsai's widow, still a sprightly woman in her seventies, well looked after by her large family and by the local authorities.

We visited six historical sites here, including the house where the hospital was once situated. There we were told how deeply Chairman Mao valued its work, regarding it as one of the essentials in the setting up of the base. As drugs were in short supply, the masses were mobilised to go up the mountains and bring down herbs which could be used. As an essential part of the hospital work there was the rule that one doctor out of three in the hospital be assigned for work amongst the peasant folk around. Even the sparse medical care available had to be shared with the people. Whenever the people made some present to Chairman Mao, such as a basket of eggs, he would send it to the hospital for the sick and wounded. Later Central Hospital moved to Small Well in the midst of the Chingkang Mountains, where it set up with 16 doctors. With limited supplies, it had to restrict its service to serious cases. For ordinary ailments, officers and soldiers were encouraged to look after each other and help each other. One function of the Army as its units moved around the country was to reconstitute Party committees dispersed or destroyed by the Kuomintang suppression, slaughtering and robbing. Kuomintang armies now lorded it over the areas where during the Great Revolution things had gone so well. In northeast Hunan alone 330,000 people were killed. In one rural area, that of Shuangtung, out of 3,000 people only 32 were left. As the Kuomintang approached the people's base area around Chingkangshan, however, their operations in the face of resistance in the seven counties there became more difficult.

In September 1928, after the disastrous drive into south Hunan which has already been described, a Party rectification movement was carried through in Ningkang and Yunghsin counties, which left the Party considerably stronger. The forces from the Nanchang uprising had, after their expedition to the south, joined up with the Worker and Peasant Army in April 1928 in Ningkang. On May 20th 1928, the meeting of county and special districts around Chingkangshan had been held in Maoping, and a 24-member special committee had been set up with Mao Tsetung as secretary to control the work in the whole region. Trade unions and peasant associations were set up, and agrarian reform went ahead. A good deal had been lost after the abortive south Hunan drive, but in the middle of September 1928 the Worker and Peasant Army had recaptured much of it.

We met some of the old men who had lived through those times, men now in their seventies, who still had a good story to tell of old times and old struggles. They remembered a good deal about the hospital, it being evident that this had made a deep impression on the local peasants. Then there was a time of grain shortage. Chairman Mao investigated, found out what the situation was, called in the Army and sent out investigation teams, then got the soldiers to agree to a cut in rations so that the people could eat more, and had the soldiers distribute the grain themselves. This made a further big change in the people's attitude towards the Army which they increasingly looked on as their very own.

During the time he spent with Maoping as his headquarters, Chairman Mao not only put a great deal of his energy into Party building, but also laid great stress on the political aspects of the organisation of the new army. Soldiers had to gain a new understanding of why it was necessary for them to fight, and to know whom they were serving. Daily training, therefore, consisted now of three periods for pure army technique, and two for lectures on political problems. Great stress was laid on giving an understanding of class struggle. Army life was rigorous. Even in winter there were but two layers of thin clothing. At night, the men often had to get up for exercise to restore circulation. For food there was red rice and pumpkin soup at the best. Wild herbs when grain was short. But these were the men who applied the political theory and generated the spirit and organisation that finally liberated the people of China.

Remoulding of Cadres

In Ningkang we met some of the revolutionaries of today. They were city people who were remoulding themselves so that they could face a future of service with courage and understanding, learning from the experience and the determination of the common man. Now, in many places in the China of 1970, May 7th Schools have been set up in order to give a changed outlook to cadres and intellectuals. There has also been a mass exodus of middle-school and college students to join in with the work on commune brigades or state farms throughout the country. In this area the system is to incorporate both students and cadres being remoulded into the "Chingkangshan May 7th School", made up of all who have come to the countryside. They started coming here during the last part of 1968, so that many have now had more than a year and a half in their new environment, and are already richer by new experiences. All go to work in the communes or elsewhere, just as Army units are sent out — a squad to a brigade, a company to a commune, and so on. They have time for meetings and study together, as well as with the masses they work with.

· Wu Ping, a cadre of the United Front Department of Kiangsi, and Huang Hsueh-chi were the two members who left the deepest impression on all. Wu Ping described how he had entered the Red Army when he was 12, and how he had followed Mao Tsetung through the years of struggle, fighting hard and learning much. Then how the countryside surrounded the cities and took them. Afterwards he became a cadre, rising higher as the years went on, the long period of peaceful, secure life making him forget the sufferings of other days, and much of the feel of the fight forward being undertaken in the villages. It was easy to forget revolutionary tradition when exposed to urban influences; to become scared of hardship and fatigue, with thoughts concentrated on how to obtain a better life, becoming ever more comfortable, yet still further separated from the masses. Now he had been able to realise that only the first steps in the Long March had been taken, and that old cadres must be on their guard against conceit, keeping up with the spirit of tough struggle, ready to face any hardship of fatigue necessary. He said all this frankly and openly without any kind of breast beating, his simple, quiet words showing the sincerity he obviously felt. Yes, he said, he had done his work according to the requirements of his organisation, but now looking back on it, it was not really in accord with Mao Tsetung Thought. In some ways it had not served the people, but had brought losses to them. He felt that now through hard down-to-earth work and identifying himself with farm folk through practice and study, he had been able to change his outlook. In October 1968 he had come and settled in Pailu Brigade of Sunchang People's Commune, living in a house that is right beside one in which in January 1929 Mao Tsetung held a meeting. It had subsequently been a grain store and is a very quiet, excellent place to study. Of his five children three are grown up and are out at work. When he arrived, he was given work sorting and selecting seed.

He noted that all the others in this team were women. Asking where the men were, he found they had all gone up the hills to cut bamboo. "But all commune work is good, I thought, and so I kept on with the seeds until I was used enough to the country to go up the hills with the men," he said. "Gradually as my muscles hardened I could work ridging paddy fields and strengthening walls in winter, transplanting rice in the spring despite sore feet and chapped skin. If one does not fear death, what else is there to be scared of?" he laughingly went on.

He felt that he was somehow now really working for the Chinese and world revolutions in a new and down-to-earth way. No one called him respectfully department head, he was just "Old Wu" to all. In the winter he was told to go up and burn charcoal. But as he had never done this before two young peasant girls came up and taught him. All the time it was like this — things that seemed simple but were not so when one came to do them, had to be mastered. All the time, he felt, he was learning, gaining not only knowledge but strength from the revolution. Once he had carried grain from Ningkang right up Chingkangshan, as Chairman Mao had done when he was helping the farmers with this, thus through practice bringing to life revolutionary tradition he had forgotten.

With a contagious sense of humor he told stories of how when he had first come with his wife and two youngest children it took him all day to walk 30 kilometres, and after it his back was sore, his feet weary. Once as a soldier he had walked 70 kilometres in a day and had fought battles at the end of it. Now after many years living under the Liu Shao-chi line he had softened all right, he thought. On arrival, the family had to learn how to cook and manage the home. In Nanchang, everything had been done for them. Now much had to be learnt all over again. But he had great faith in the masses and he soon found that they had great faith in him also.

Different was Huang Hsueh-chi, a young intellectual. He had had the kind of education which had persisted from the old society in China, and though he had come of a worker family, was soon made into a spectacle-wearing bookwormish student, anxious to pass exams and be someone. He had been sent to Morocco to study French and had stayed there for three years, perfecting himself in that language. Then on return he was assigned to work in the Foreign Affairs Section in the Kiangsi provincial government. He said, "I had become a great reader, and nothing pleased me more than to get a good book and settle down with it. With regard to my political status, I felt it was unquestionable. I came from a worker's family, I had been brought up under the red flag. I had made no mistakes in my school life. In fact, I was quite satisfied with myself. Then, at the end of 1967 I came to the countryside. Though I had read so much I had not read the works of Mao Tsetung, nor did I know much of the revolution at all. Now in the time I have spent in the countryside, I have learnt more than I learnt in all my long years of schooling. A great change has come to my thinking."

He went on to say that in all of his years of study, he had never dreamt that one day he would become a member of a farm commune. "Looking back now, I feel that my understanding was very narrow indeed. When people talked about unity, I felt that was a problem for others, not for me, for had I not been correctly educated and prepared?" he said, going on to state how he really had looked down on manual work, and simply could not imagine himself as a common toiler. Now his understanding had advanced so that he realised that without re-education there is no way to understand the people of the countryside who make up the great mass of the Chinese people, and that the people have much that is all important to teach about work, cooperation, and such basic things. When he came he sweated a lot and his legs trembled when he carried a load of 25 kilogrammes on his shoulder pole up country paths. He, a well-fed young man over 20 years of age, could not do as much as the average commune member who carried 70 kilogrammes and walked faster. Even a little girl of 13 was carrying more than he could. "So everything I had to do was a fresh test."

He realised that every difficulty had to be met and overcome if he was to be of use to the revolution. He talked of his struggles in learning to use an axe, grind beans, and so on, and how little use any sort of conceit was, how physical work and its problems make for sincerity, honesty and humility in the face of great issues. He has also learnt much of the continuing class struggle amongst the villages of the commune, and then of the difference between the capitalist road and the socialist one as exemplified in so many previously unthought-of little things. He was grateful for the patience and the care with which he had been surrounded, and for all the efforts folk had made for his better understanding. When he goes back to the work in which he has specialised, he will do so with better mental and physical health than he had before. He will go, too, with a new understanding of his place in society, and of the people it is his duty to serve.

Wu Ping, who had to go out on some business for a while, now came back and told us some more about himself. That he was 50 years old, and that in his city job he had suffered badly from stomach ulcers, often being in hospital. Now he no longer had them and could eat anything that was going and enjoy it. The commune had helped him a great deal, and he felt that he was able to do something for the commune also. He went to the Red Guard reservoir construction site, and was able to organise the youth in study groups of Mao Tsetung Thought with the result that work went ahead with terrific speed and spirit. How good it was, he felt, to see political and ideological work have so definite and stimulating a result on a practical problem. Putting politics first was always the best way, he found. Now in the commune, study has been reorganised and has been able to bring its strength to every part of daily life. In this work, all those being remoulded can take part with immense profit. Never put on airs, he said. Always be first at work. Struggle with the task as if it was a piece of revolutionary living, and adopt a completely new working style, that was his advice to those who like himself have come to take part in Ningkang's May 7th School. How long will they stay? Until the organisation calls them to go elsewhere, of course. Just now, there are no plans for moving, only to make the commune better and learn more. Yes, they had had a wonderful welcome in Ningkang when they arrived. They were part of a vast exodus from the major cities of Kiangsi and Kiangsu, a new contingent of youth and cadres going back to learn first lessons anew. When they came, the people sent them good things to eat, peppers, egg plants, and so on. Just sent without any names being given.

The Chingkangshan May 7th School

In the Ningkang detachment of the Chingkangshan May 7th School there are 460 old cadres and 698 young people, 500 of whom are students who have come from Shanghai. Every one of the 39 brigades in the county has its quota. Many of the cadres had their families with them, and it was obvious that all were determined to make the very best of this period of study and learning. A special committee, under the Revolutionary Committee of the county, attends to May 7th School affairs. It includes representatives of all the different groups and organisations concerned. Except in busy seasons, half-day study is scheduled on Mondays, Wednesdays and Fridays. Study permits better understanding of why they have all come, of the need to know the countryside and of being able to help it to advance. Such understanding is something that all cadres should have, for cadres are the wealth of the state, and their training is fundamental to any real progress. Mentally, they must be prepared to stay in the communes for the rest of their lives, glad to be able to do so. No other thinking will enable them to give their best. Some become "barefoot" doctors, others take part in scientific research, while others teach in brigade primary schools. "How do you keep up your French?" the student who had been to Morocco was asked. "I can read the Selected Works of Mao Tsetung in French whenever I like," came the answer. Some cadres and students help with innovations on agricultural machinery and have already produced good results with adaptations. But the main overall plan is to change the thinking of cadres, really remould them, with down-to-earth work being an integral part of their transformation.

Huangyangchieh

It was fascinating to go up Chingkangshan by highway from Ningkang. On a clear day there are great vistas of scenery spread below. One comes first to Huangyangchieh, one of the five passes into the mountain complex. It is on the north side and commands the view down to Ningkang. Here was fought a fierce battle on August 29th, 1928. The force that had gone into south Hunan had not returned yet and the enemy attacked, thinking to occupy the Chingkang Mountains before the Red Army could rally from its Hunan defeat. So he attacked with four regiments, there being but two companies of defenders down in Maoping. These were immediately sent up the mountain to reinforce the peasant militia there. The peasants had made their preparations and had filled the small paths with bamboo spikes, old men and children cutting and planting them by the thousand. Above Huangyangchieh they collected great piles of stones for ammunition, some held back by boards and ropes that, when loosened, would permit a whole pile of boulders to hurtle down. The people had their hunting guns, spears, and plenty of firecrackers ready to explode in kerosene tins. The battle went on all through the 29th and 30th, the enemy attacking continuously, but every wave was beaten back. As a final gesture the Red Army fighters brought their mortar up from the rear. It had three shells but the powder in two was damp, and only one went off. However, after it was fired, the enemy retreated pellmell onto the spikes set in the little paths. The Kuomintang retreat soon grew into a rout, for it was the fourth time they had pushed their troops into the attack, and now all wanted to get away to the lowlands as fast as they could. The troops of Yuan Wen-tsai and Wang Tso at Dalung intercepted many and either killed them or took them prisoner. The victory was a grand morale lifter after the south Hunan events, and the Red Army soon took back many of the enemy-occupied areas around the mountain base. Today, the battle site is marked by a pavilion in the form of a five-pointed star, while over it a big pillar representing a torch has been erected. Near the pavilion are the two trees under which Chairman Mao rested when carrying up grain from the lowlands.

To Big Well

We went on from Huangyangchieh to Ta Ching, "Big Well", one of the five wells of Chingkangshan around which villages have grown. Chairman Mao arrived here from Maoping to live in the house which has now been rebuilt after Kuomintang burning. While we were there, the May 7th group of Tsinghua University in Peking were visiting also. A tough, hardy group of ordinary farm folk they looked now, with well worn clothes, many with long suntanned legs and battered straw hats. The stone in front of the house on which Chairman Mao often sat in the evenings is still there. I was pleased to meet an old friend who had greeted me here on my 1961 visit. A one-time member of the guard group around Mao Tsetung when he lived at Big Well, Tsou Wen-kai looks very healthy still. I asked how his nephew Tsou Kwei-hsiang was getting on and he smiled broadly, saying that he was a cadre in marketing and supply work now. It was pleasant to meet Tsou Wen-kai again after the years, and find him so well. The people of Chingkangshan are a sturdy lot indeed. I once more was very taken with the children, so warm, friendly and confident. At Ta Ching, I wrote these lines:

> Here at Big Well
> amongst the peaks of Chingkangshan
> stands one of the homes

Mao Tsetung once lived
and worked in; a replica,
for a vengeful enemy burnt
the old one, but here still
stands the stone he sat on
and pondered.

So today around it
flocked the students
of a May 7th School
of a great Peking university
professors, lecturers
fellows, students, legs
tanned a deep brown, battered
straw hats, neatly patched clothes,
toughened faces;
intellectuals who now
learn from peasants, becoming
one with them, eating
something of their bitterness
in mountain rains and summer
sun; these pioneers
of the new education, as stressed
by him who sat on the stone
working out the way to bring
freedom, unity and strength
to the poor everywhere.

At Tzuping

We went on from Big Well to the big centre at Tzuping, where there was a comfortable guest house with modern facilities for us to spend a few days in, see the museums, go over all the old Chingkangshan struggles and discuss them together. In Tzuping the little old village with the old Worker and Peasant Army offices and supply organisations have been kept up nicely, so that one can see things as they were, and fill in the human portion from the stories one has heard of immense courage and devotion to the revolution.

In our meetings here we discussed the many aspects of the whole effort to make Chingkangshan a base. The immense economic difficulties, including the problem of how to get a supply of salt. How people would pull down old walls and grind up the weathered mud brick to get salt-petre from it, which was the nearest thing to salt they could find. How all wore so little, had so little to eat, yet with what spirit they fought on. Chairman Mao had a straw hat, a pair of grass sandals, a blanket for nights and only two thicknesses of clothing in the winter, sometimes sleeping on the ground with the soldiers, just a bit of rice straw underneath. He had a horse but usually gave it to sick and wounded soldiers to ride. From their meagre army rations soldiers would save food to help destitute farmers. Army discipline around the new rules which had been amplified after Sanwan where they were first enunciated was excellent and raised the morale of the people throughout the whole area. Organisations like those for children, the Little Red Soldiers, provided guards for the roads, inspecting the passes of travellers. Red Guards were formed amongst the people for auxiliary duty in village defence. It was good to have met some of the old Red Army fighters who are still alive. Now in their seventies, they still remember much. Yi Chin-kun, now 71, a tall, spare man who had been village head of Big Well, told how Chairman Mao had written the essay "The Struggle in the Chingkang Mountains" there. How the people had all become convinced that the Red Army was their army, serving them, and how well he had picked Chingkang as being the best part of the Lohsiao mountain ranges to make into a base.

The museum in Tzuping is very well set out and complete. We went over the earlier phases of the struggle around the mountain area again, and then came to the last period of occupation as a main base, that of September 1928–January 1929 when there was rapid expansion and enemy withdrawals. Then the main centre moved out across Kiangsi to Juichin in the southeast. Party building, an ever important task, was well done in this period and much was learnt, much accomplished. The theory of roving bands further discredited, that of deeper integration with the people emphasised.

Tzuping to Kian

When the time came to leave Tzuping one afternoon, we drove swiftly down the mountain slopes and valleys, past one old battleground after another until we came to Suichuan county, where we crossed downs and flats until we reached Taiho, where in the face of Japanese invasion the refugee Kuomintang government of the War of Resistance period had once established itself with one of its concentration camps for those suspected of being Communists. From Taiho we passed through low hills and scattered villages until we reached Kian, now a spreading industrial city, and river transport centre. Many changes were noted here since my last visit of but two years ago. More changes were evident on the highway north. May 1st, 1970 saw the opening of the big Kan river bridge here and the work on improvements to the Chingkangshan highway, so that the trip in future will be made easier for motor traffic. As we came into the outskirts of Kian we saw that road construction was evidently taking precedence and being swiftly completed. The next day, travelling up the highway to Nanchang, we also were to meet with fairly large-scale road work.

Nanchang to Kiukiang

It was early morning when we took the train from Nanchang to Kiukiang, where we rested for the remainder of the day, saw the sights and then in the evening went refreshed on to a very spick and span ship which carried us down to Nanking in some 20 hours of placid and pleasant journey. After coming on board and the next day, I wrote these lines:

> Out of Nanchang, on
> through Teh An and
> along the western slopes of
> Lushan we go, thinking
> of how the people from
> earliest times have loved
> this mountain, but too how
> it became the resort for
> the well padded, the gentry
> compradores, warlords,
> always carried up on sedan
> chairs by the very poor;

>> and now around the cottages
>> of the former bearers, we see
>> well fed children playing
>> happily; a new spirit of up
>> and doing, of putting Mao Thought
>> into definite practice, taking
>> hold of a whole countryside.

> At Kiukiang we board
> a river steamer, soon
> gliding down a Yangtze
> in full summer spate; to
> the north stands regally
> the mountains called
> Tapieh, and we think
> of Liberation Army drives,
> one from these mountains
> to Wuhan while the main force
> stormed across the Yangtze
> in junks, to free
> the Nanking we soon come to.

>> Nanking, where a great
>> bridge throws itself across
>> the Yangtze almost casually
>> it seems, though to a resurgent
>> people it is so triumphant
>> a monument to worker skill
>> and determination, making us
>> realise anew that victory ever
>> must be fought for, despite all
>> the bitterness of temporary defeat
>> and that now any people, organised
>> and in unity, cannot but win.

Pavilion commemorating a victorious battle fought by the Chinese Red Army at Huang-yangchieh, Chingkang Mountains.

The tree Chairman Mao planted at Ta Ching (Big Well) in the Chingkang Mountains.

KIANGSI

Chairman Mao stayed at this house at Maoping, Chingkang Mountains.

Where Chairman Mao lived in Anyuan.

Sanwan is a quiet and beautiful place, Kiangsi.

Weiyang Bridge near Juichin where the Long March started in 1934.

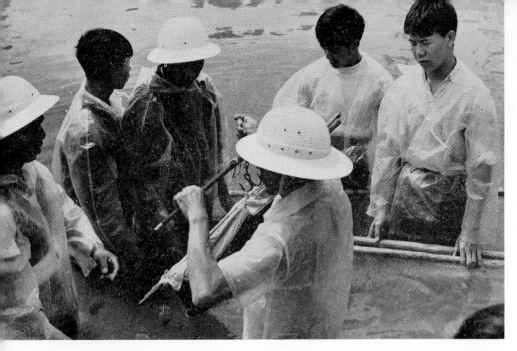

At a fish breeding station, Kanhsien, Kiangsi.

Golden carp from a reservoir at Hsinfeng.

Students at a factory school, Hsinfeng.

Chung Chi-fang, the model school teacher, Chuannan county, Kiangsi.

Ancient sculptures, Kiangsi.

Irrigation work at Kwangchang.

At the old Yunghochen pottery site below Kian.

Reservoir in south Kiangsi.

Worker in a Kiangsi factory.

Making three-ply boards in Kanchow, Kiangsi.

Looking back over the trip, we felt that it had given us many valuable pointers and taught a deep lesson on the method of building a revolutionary Party of the oppressed people, the way in which a people's army could be set up under the leadership of such a Party, and then the organisation of a Party directed united front of all revolutionary people to struggle against the common enemy. We thought back on the incident when the Hunan provincial Party representatives came to get the Red Army to march into southeast Hunan and how they in a superior, bookish way said, "You will find no Marxism amongst these mountains and valleys of Chingkangshan," when actually it was Mao Tsetung who by the practical application of his own correct interpretation of Marxism gave leadership to revolutionaries, first in his own land and now on a widening horizon everywhere.

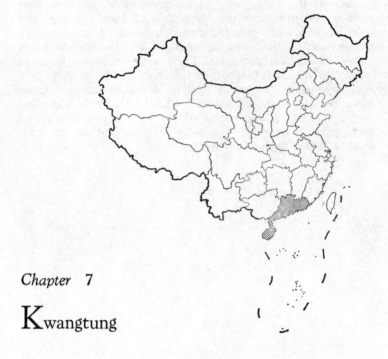

Chapter 7

Kwangtung

The well over 42 million people who live on the 220,000 square kilometres of hill and stream, valley and delta of Kwangtung enjoy a subtropical climate — tropical in Hainan Island — producing great quantities of rice, sugar cane and other food products. Much of the population is concentrated in the Pearl river delta and along the East and West rivers, so I have selected reports from communes in each of these areas and some stories from around the provincial capital of Kwangchow (Canton), where today there is a swiftly growing industry.

Kwangtung has been self-sufficient in rice since 1953, and actually was a rice-surplus province already before the Cultural Revolution. It also produces about 600,000 tons of sugar a year and over 50,000 tons of bananas, as well as a very considerable amount of other fruits.

Kwangtung produces silk and ramie. Nylon fibres make for one more new industry. After 1960 its fishermen from the coast and from its island territories out in the South China Sea gathered a harvest of around half a million tons of fish a year. In 1949 it was 150,000 tons.

The province has its own light and heavy industry, while handicrafts have been considerably developed. Steel is smelted, ships are built, and there is a considerable export trade in products of light industry that are manufactured in Canton — the sewing machine, the electric fan and the bicycle, to mention but some of the more important lines being considered well up to international standards for such commodities and much welcomed in other Southeast Asian lands.   Art pottery, carved ivory, wood carving, lace and embroidery work are amongst some of the more favored handicrafts that go abroad.

Kwangchow to Enping

It was an early spring morning in 1968 when we left Canton city and, cutting across the Pearl river delta, went west to visit the county town of Enping.   Soon we were passing the busy pottery kilns at Shihwan. Then, cutting across Nanhai and Shunteh counties, we watched farmers working deep in the mud of paddy fields, paddling swift little boats up canals or else tending the rich vegetable gardens that grow so well in this sunny, well watered south.   We went on into Kaoho county where I wondered why it should be called "high crane" until I was told that the word for crane had come from "Crane Hill" (Hoshan) county, and had been combined with "kao" which means "high", half of the name of a neighboring county when two were merged.   On all the three ferries crossed our luck was good, with practically no waiting at any of them. The last, over the wide seventh river, brought us near the boundary of Kaiping county from where, across broad fields of golden rape in bloom and alfalfa in red, we could see the central dome of the Toishan mountains some 20 kilometres to the south of us as we went west.   We halted a while for food in the big overseas Chinese hotel at Sanpo.   This place is one of originally three separate towns, now brought together by a bridge over a wide river.   Sanpo is today the county seat for Kaiping county.   We watched how, at small wharves, small locally made cranes were handling the cargo from sea-going junks most efficiently.   A group of overseas Chinese emerged from two buses coming from Canton.   A visitor passes quite unnoticed here, so different from country cities further north where the foreigner is such a rarity that he is fair game for all the small fry to chase after and catch a glimpse of.   Here, the youngsters could not have been more unconcerned by my visit.   They have grown up in the tradition of there being foreigners and foreign lands, foreign clothes and foreign ways, with so many of the folks going and coming from abroad over the past century.   So they see nothing strange at all in the lone foreigner on the street.

Villages and towns in Siyip, as Cantonese call this section of southwestern Kwangtung, have plenty of mementoes of the bad old society around them, for the high towers of the once rich, built as places of refuge against the rebellious poor, still stand many stories high with all the excesses of ostentatious architecture plastered over their tall top floors. Some of the tower tops are in the neo-classical tradition of Europe, others have caps like Norman castles.   Now they are all empty and deserted. Some have a decided lean, their foundations on one side having sunk.

Many were built with money sent from abroad by overseas Chinese. I remember being told about one old man who saved and scratched when abroad so that he could send enough back to relatives to build a seven-story tower, one floor higher than that of his landlord neighbor. But now these, as so much of the past, are just smiled at and ignored. In due course they will be demolished for any useful materials they might contain or for the land they stand on, and a generation will grow up for which they will be but a tale, told at times by the older folks. For youth these days it is the future and the future only that is important.

At Enping

We arrived at our destination of Enping during a demonstration which marked the coming together of various groups in county organisations following the successful setting up of the county Revolutionary Committee three days before. Banners, firecrackers were all in action.

The county guest hostel was being renovated, and the rooms given us were spick and span. At sunset we stood together on the balcony of the upper floor looking at the hills around Enping, a county seat which lies on the edge of the basin of a river that often overflows its banks. "Yes, with the Cultural Revolution now having come to its final and successful stages, we shall have to turn more attention to getting all these hills growing something again. The trouble is that they have been de-forested for so long that there is not much earth left on their slopes. But with men and trees we shall see what we can do," one of our friends said.

"But why go all the way to Enping, especially away down in Kwang-tung?" those who know their China may ask. Surely new roads and places not visited before always have their fascination. But why Enping in particular? The reason is that in this Cultural Revolution one of the Enping communes has done so well that it has excited nation-wide notice, like the famous ones of Tachai in Shansi, Hsiatingchia in Shantung, Mao-tien in Hunan, and so on. At the time of writing almost 1,000 people a day from many parts of China arrive to visit it. Here is Hengpi Commune, farming what can only be described as rather a poor stretch of country — light, shady soil in a thin layer on top of rock. But to go back a step or two in explanation. Enping is a county in Fushan prefecture with a population of 280,000 on 380,000 mou of irrigated land in its 13 communes. Farmlands are a series of basins set amongst hills, largely rolling country. Before Liberation, 71 percent were landlord owned, with an average grain crop of 270 jin of rice a mou per year. In 1966 the yield had reached 668 jin, and in 1967 despite a drought, some bad typhoons and an insect pest, it rose to 734 jin for rice only, not counting peanuts, beans, and so on.

To Hengpi Commune

The next morning after our arrival we went out of Enping going west, then struck down a branch road to the south, and after some 20 more kilometres got to the Hengpi Commune headquarters. The leader of the commune Revolutionary Committee, who was previously its Party secretary, met us and before setting out to explain the present situation took us around a very well displayed photo exhibition which showed the rise of the movement for the study of Mao Tsetung Thought, right from its beginnings during the struggle for socialist education in the countryside prior to the start of the Cultural Revolution. How the various team leaders for carrying the movement further amongst the ranks of the people were then trained, and what problems confronted them afterwards.

From the exhibition hall we moved on to the big roomy offices of the commune. The auditorium was crowded with visitors from Shaokwan in north Kwangtung, but we went to a spacious office on the top floor, looking out through gum trees to a wide vista of mountains beyond, and listened to the cheerful voice of the commune leader as he patiently explained. The commune is one of 19 brigades, seven of which border on the South China Sea. There are 228 production teams that farm the 60,000 mou of arable land. Through the storm of the Cultural Revolution, production work has gone on better than ever before, and everywhere there is a new awareness of the problems that await solution, everywhere a strengthened belief in Mao Tsetung Thought. Of the brigade cadres, 133 were struggled against in criticism meetings; none were thrown out. All of the brigade leaders except one have already been accepted back into their positions by the people. Criticism has been found to have many advantages. It educates the people, the critics often actually criticising themselves, a fact that the people are not slow to catch up with. At first, many of the cadres resented criticism very much but, country fashion, their friends would come to help them out. One brigade leader's wife managed to get her husband to accept the correct criticism that was given him. By pointing out many instances she showed him that he had been too impulsive, too impatient, not careful of political advance, and so on. He so sincerely thanked the people at the next meeting for helping him that folk accepted him readily again as a good revolutionary worker. The instructions that a cadre must be judged on his life's work and that the task is to change cadres' thinking, not to destroy them, has had great effect. In one brigade there was a Party secretary and a brigade leader who did not get along well. The brigade leader grasped the opportunity given by the Cultural Revolution to try and pull the Party secretary down. Then, in a study of the cadre policy, his conscience got the better of him and, following a sleepless night, he decided to make a clean breast of it all in front of the people. This he did, with the result that everyone was pleased, and his relation with the Party secretary became a new and warm one. Not only has the relation between cadres become better, but also that between cadres and commune members has vastly improved.

Whom Do We Work for?

The complete exposure of the revisionist line in agricultural policy made the people realise things in a new way. That they were not out just to get workpoints, but rather worked for the revolution. Fertiliser was needed. Members started carrying it in early in the morning before going

out to work with no regard for workpoints at all. Old retired folk began
to spend their days looking for composting material and carrying it to
collecting points. Those who had looked for some way to gain private
profit criticised themselves. One told how he had made 200 yuan in a
cow deal on the side. He returned the money to the brigade. Another
who was in charge of brigade stock owned up that he had let two commune
animals die because he used their fodder for privately owned animals.
Since his confession he has reclaimed three mou of waste hill land and
has planted it with fodder to help stock with in the future.

In the year 1966 a big flood swept down from the denuded mountains. Many people lost their reserves, but those who had not helped
the others so well that all had enough. In 1967, the people sold 2,000
piculs (100 long tons) of grain over the amount fixed for their commune
so as to help the state better. "We average 45 jin of rice a person per
month in our commune. That is enough. We perhaps could eat more or
use more somehow, but we will not go into that. The state needs grain,
we will give all we can," they say. Actually, with the rise in production,
not only does the amount of grain per capita rise but also the cash distribution at the end of the year. It was 49 yuan in 1963, 73 in 1967. Responsibility for defence comes home to people now in a new way. Now
1,000 young folk have requested to join in the work. There is a good
deal of scope for their energies in reforesting the bare hills, so as to
protect the eight reservoirs and keep the water supply steady. There
is to be a new drive to get bamboo grown wherever it will, which is very
wise, for giant bamboo is so wonderful a plant. The 130,000 mou of bare
hills that belong to the brigade are marked down to be afforested inside
the next five years.

The Revolutionary Committee of the commune is composed of 47
persons. Rather more than in other communes, where there are usually
less than 30 members. But Hengpi was the first to establish a Revolutionary Committee, so it had to blaze the road by trial and error. It is
composed of eight cadres, two workers, one student, one teacher and
35 peasant commune members, some of them members of the militia.
Although it is only a temporary organ of power, people in the commune
have paid a good deal of attention to the composition of its membership,
each member having to gain their approval. I asked what were some
of the more pressing political tasks.

"We must give leadership in the struggle against factionalism and
anarchism, and carry on with the work of the struggle against selfishness
and revisionism. A good deal has been done, but more remains still to
do," they said. Following the lead of Hengpi, eight more of the 13 Enping
communes already have Revolutionary Committees organised. Of their
total of 161 brigades only five have serious problems awaiting settlement.

Irrigation, Literacy and Housing

Eighty percent of the farmland of Hengpi is irrigated, water flowing into
the trunk canals from eight reservoirs amongst the hills. With regard

to literacy, more than 80 percent of the adults above the age of 40 were illiterate at the time of Liberation. Now there are six middle schools, one operated by the county, the others by the communes. There are 59 primary schools in the commune, county- or commune-operated. Living has become a great deal better in these years. In Hengpi village alone, eight pigs a day are slaughtered for local consumption. Springtime, before rice transplanting starts, is the time for house building, and this year there have been many more than usual put up, with so many young couples starting new families. Houses are strongly built of stamped earth, with tiled roofs. Whitewashed, they look very attractive.

Baiyun Brigade

On March 3rd 1968 we went out to Baiyun Brigade, and spent a whole afternoon there. The brigade is building its own new meeting hall, so we met with the political activists in a primary school. They were an interesting group. An old man of 84, entirely deaf. A 13-year-old girl; three sedate matrons. The brigade leader, and then a good many young people in their early twenties. The meeting was a lively one. The brigade is one of 2,200 people, and its leadership is keen to try and make it a real school for Mao Tsetung Thought. The old deaf man started the session by sketching out his previous life. How hopeless it was and how selfish he had been, always trying to grab some advantages as a kind of compensation for his affliction. Then he said, "When the movement for the study of the three short essays started, I memorised them all. Out in the countryside, I found that a big irrigation canal was in danger of breaking. I thought of how Bethune gave himself for the people, and so threw myself wholeheartedly into the task of mending it, thus being able to prevent much damage. This actually was a turning point in my life, and now I look at people always wondering what I can do for them. I thought of the 1966 flood, how at that time a good cadre neglected his own family and gave himself completely to the task of saving the community. Now I find rich meaning in Mao Tsetung's writings, so is there any wonder that I read what he says over and over again? And I strongly agree that all who have been liberated should work to liberate the rest of mankind. I believe too that we are right in getting rid of those old things that have kept us tied down. Not much sense in all those old things concerned with ancestor worship kept in our houses. We must look far, and think big!" To hear a deaf peasant in a Kwangtung poor soil hill county talking about constructing a new world on the basis of altruism and anti-imperialism is surely a new thing in our world of today. As he spoke of ways and means to get around and spread these ideas I looked out through the open door over the big irrigation pond beyond. A graceful tree framed the picture and a bunch of children playing under it lent it life.

"I got rid of that big rock that stood in the way of our canal digging. People wondered how I could have moved it, but I hit the brute so many times with my sledge hammer it just had to split and let me carry it off!" The deaf man was going on with his story. He has sold 400 jin of his home store of grain to the state, and people had questioned him why he had sold so much. Surely he and his family could have eaten more. He replied that he knew this extra sale to the state was not demanded, but he thought that if he gave more the country could do more, and that he was now arranging his life so that it fitted in with the needs of the world revolution.

Young at 84

Another man of 84 took up the discussion. He too was getting deaf, but he preserved a wonderful smile that lit up his rugged face. Not many teeth left, but determined to go on as the Yu Kung of "The Foolish Old Man Who Removed the Mountains" and get to be 90 at least. "If I show my determination, perhaps it will move people to do more! I can still carry stone for the lime kilns as well as anyone. I get the other men together and we go out after animal manure every day, carrying it into the brigade fertiliser dump. Then I can tell the youngsters about my life as a boy in the old society, of all the beatings the landlord gave me when as a boy of 13 I had to herd his buffaloes, cold all through the winter months and always hungry. Before the Cultural Revolution started, people told me I must not work anymore, so I just sat around all the time. Now I have a pattern of work and am much happier. I have lived through the rule of emperors and generals, but now we are in the era of Mao Tsetung and must listen to him and struggle against selfishness. The urgency of the world situation demands that we get the peoples of the world ready to fight for themselves, so we must study politics hard."

A 13-Year-Old Girl

A 13-year-old girl then spoke. She said that she had not been a very good child at school. Others nicknamed her "the fighting hen". But being a child with imagination, she listened in at meetings and paid particular attention when being told at school about those who had sacrificed themselves for the people. Once she was sick and could not go out with the other children to help with field work. Near her home was a large pond, and into this a small child fell. Hearing the shouts of other children she raced out, thinking at first to call some elder, for she could not swim and did not know if she could tread the bottom of the pool or not. Then she saw that no time could be wasted, so jumped in and grabbed the already drowning little one. Back at her home she made a warm bath and soon revived the youngster, who had been shivering badly. When the elders came in from the fields everything was in hand.

Yes, she was head of the children's brigade, but when the movement for criticism started, she first thought to drop the position. "Then I thought of Wang Chieh, Bethune and all the others, and I knew I must go through with it; I must learn to welcome having my failings pointed out to me," she said. "Unless we do this we shall never be able to keep our hills and streams red."

Five Eggs

Then a tall, middle-aged peasant woman rose. Quite simply she told how, before she read and studied Mao Tsetung's works she had been a very dull person. But then how life took on a new complexion when understanding came to her. "So many stories!" she said. "But maybe the one of the five eggs will illustrate best what I am trying to say. A neighbor's hen laid five eggs in the storeroom of our house. My little boy wanted to take them and eat them. But that morning we had been studying 'In Memory of Norman Bethune', so I told him how wrong he was. What he must do now was to see what hen came in, then when it went, to follow it home and find out to whom the eggs really belonged. We did this and the neighbor was glad, and everyone said, 'Just see how Mao Tsetung Thought has come into our village!' "

Then she went on to tell the story of one peanut, and the discussion around it. She asked a youth working near her on a peanut harvest not to eat the peanut he was just ready to crack. Then as others gathered around, she explained why. She said, "If we all eat as we wish, soon there will be none for the brigade to sell, so that both we and the country lose. If we believe in our country's future, then we must be careful of even the smallest thing."

A Brigade Leader

A thoughtful, middle-aged man followed on in our talk. He told how, when folk started doing things in opposition to the wrong thinking of Liu Shao-chi, they decided that big groups were preferable to small ones. So a brigade was formed of three small groups joined together, and he was voted in to be its leader. He had never been a cadre and was scared of the difficulties. His wife was very much against the idea, and told him that he would simply become a figure to be struggled against. Stay at home and lead the happy life, she advised. Against this advice, due to his growing belief in the ideas of Chairman Mao, he decided to take the job. Then came the time when his wife was giving birth, and an urgent message was brought for him to return home at once to be with her. But just at that moment he was overwhelmed with work, and so had to make the decision, brigade work first, or family first. "There are folk to look after my wife," he reasoned, "but my own task is clear. The people around me, I was happy to see, also appreciated my responsibility towards them."

The Blind Man

Folk at Baiyun told us about one of their activists who was completely blind. He was not there at the time of my visit, having been sent away for an operation that is expected to bring him eyesight. As a blind man, he once told fortunes and tried to make a living that way. After he got hold of the ideas in Chairman Mao's works he spent his time teaching others who were illiterate how to recite the three short essays: "Serve the People", "In Memory of Norman Bethune" and "The Foolish Old Man Who Removed the Mountains". He also told the people exactly how he had fooled them for years in fortune telling, exposing all the tricks of the trade to everyone's amazement and better understanding.

My knowledge of Cantonese not being enough, I had to have a translation into the common language, so I doubtless missed some of the finer points in these simple stories. Yet there is enough, I think, to show that a new spirit is being born amongst these Kwangtung hills. When we went outside after the meeting, the tall woman who told the story about the eggs sang to us, new words set to old west Kwangtung folk tunes. I was delighted to hear them, as they were quite new to me. The 13-year-old girl danced prettily and sang her own accompaniment. It was a fine ending for a fascinating day. As we went back to Enping in the evening, we saw the first swimmers of the season, two boys who popped up from the middle of a pool, looking very bright and fresh.

Hsiashan Brigade

The next morning we returned to Hengpi Commune again, this time going to Hsiashan Brigade where a feature has been made of a simple exhibition hall, which in four farmhouse rooms sets out to show some of the people's struggles before and after Liberation, and then during the Cultural Revolution. The whole thing cost less than 13 yuan to put on. The drawings were all done by the people or by visitors, then the whole was put together in an artistic way by the members of the Cultural Revolution group. Going over the exhibits, one realises how deep the new thinking has struck into the hearts of the Hengpi commune people. The picture of members sitting and looking at two big piles of grain, one good, the other less so, deciding which should be sold to the state. One set of pictures showed just exactly what the revisionist line being operated by some leaders in the past administration was leading to. Exactly where the poison lay. In another room the story of a local man was told. He is now 31, the only remaining member of a family of 12. It is a harrowing story of landlord despotism and cruelty, painful to hear, yet important that the young people do hear it and learn from it. Not strange either that the one remaining member is an activist in the cultural movement.

A Militia Exercise

The education of the militia is one of the important political tasks in the countryside. The militia member, whether lad or lass, has to understand politics, knowing well that politics controls the gun. We went to a militia exercise at the village of Chungchilin in Baiyun Brigade and listened in to an hour's discussion by the political instructor of the outstanding political problems of the day. The starting of the Korean War and China's role in helping that country, the seizure of Taiwan as a U.S. base, the U.S. drive into Vietnam, and the many provocations over China were all pointed out in clear, simple language that did not forget to call a spade a spade, and dub the present USA chief enemy of the peoples of the world.

The speaker went back into modern history and showed how people's war could defeat the Japanese, and how the PLA rose as the strong protector of the new society. He talked of the antics of the revisionists as well as those of old Chiang on Taiwan. The militia men and women must have heard the sentiments a good many times before, yet they were all attention. The instructor told them they must come to the ideas held by Dr. Bethune and fight for the peoples of the whole world who are oppressed. The USA wants to smash China. "It is they who decide when they will start to try and do this. It is we who must prepare ourselves and our folk to meet them. We must not lull ourselves into the belief that there will be no enemy action against us. An attack on us is always possible," he said. After he had finished, the militia divided into groups to discuss what he had said and how they could get more people to understand things as they were.

An "All Red" Family

One afternoon we went to see an "all red" family. They lived in part of what had once been a landlord's house in Hengping Brigade. The old tower still stands in the compound by the house and, quite naturally, a collection of people came in from surrounding homes to see what the visit was all about. The place was the home of an old widow of 61 named Ssutu Yeh-fang. Then there was her daughter-in-law, Kuo Yen-lei, who had three children, Liang Sho-ching, a girl aged ten, Liang Shu-liang and Liang Yu-liang, aged eight and four respectively.

After some polite exchanges we finally got seated and down to business. It was quite a story all in all. The daughter-in-law first spoke. Her husband had work elsewhere and was not often at home. She had listened to people discussing things and felt backward. Then she heard how some of the leaders of the capitalist world were saying not to worry over China — that after a generation or two China would be back on the old road and the revolution would be forgotten. This made her uneasy as she looked at her own children. Would these and their children turn against Mao Tsetung Thought? And if this was possible, what would make it so? She started to study more herself, and to have the whole family understand as much as they could. Then, as she went on describing the things she and her family had done to put their politics into action, I looked around the room curiously. Well built as were all former landlord houses, there was a treadle rice husker in one corner, and a grinding stone in another. The small low table we sat around was evidently used for meals and was spotlessly clean. Visitors had brought them so many portraits of Chairman Mao that these made a frieze around three walls. Against the wall on one side was a high table with the family's study materials on it.

The ten-year-old girl took up the story from where her mother left off, describing how much trouble she had in getting her grandmother to memorise the three short essays. "At first she would be cross with me always talking about Chairman Mao and his writings. But I said that I simply had to talk to her like this and be like a Bethune who gave everything he had for the revolution. But she said, 'I'm over 60. My eyes are no good. I have lived my life now. You're always talking about that Canada place where Bethune came from. Never heard of it before!' And then she would go off to sleep. But I kept on telling her about the need to struggle against selfishness and criticise revisionism as a first step, and then got her telling tales about her old life, so that I could relate them to what I had to say. It worked very well, and now she takes a great interest in everything. I myself was a very naughty child before I started on this study. The teacher of our school came and talked to Mother about me, and my mother used the wrong method to correct me. But one thing led to the next and soon we were all learning what Chairman Mao wanted us to know each and every day."

Then the old grandmother, Ssutu Yeh-fang, took up the story. She is a sinewy old woman with a good deal of determination, and told of her early days. How her family had to sell the children, how each year became more bitter than the preceding one. Then how, when the great change had come, she was given a good place to live and the way to earn all the food she needed. Her son had married a nice girl, and she had grandchildren now. Surely she had something to thank Chairman Mao for, she reasoned. Then how to thank him by doing his will? There were so many ways. The state was buying ducks, geese and chickens. Formerly when she had sold any such birds, she, like the other women, had fed them very well just before the sale so that they were paid for several ounces more than the actual weight of the fowl. Now she still took along her chicken feed, but fed the birds with it after they had been weighed in. The collector was vastly pleased, congratulating her on her application of political study. Everyone around felt better, and she laughed at herself for the time she had fed two chickens so well that both died. Then, too, at herself when she started learning the three short essays. Now, as her family has become knit together in a new way, all thinking of ways to get rid of old selfishness and to look out on the world in a new fashion, she feels younger. "Yes, I have grey hairs but my spirit is so much higher than it was, my days are more full, and my life happier all around," she says. We went out into the yard, and the children danced and sang, and we all laughed together. Somehow or other, the big landlord tower in the yard looked insignificant beside them, the people militant and alive with their better understanding.

Meeting with Cadres

We met with a group of six Hengpi Commune cadres to talk over the implementation of the cadres policy. The Party secretary of Hsiashan Brigade started the discussion. An able, energetic type, he looked back on his faults and discussed them quite objectively. No, he had not understood the consequences of the revisionist line that came down from above. Then, when the Cultural Revolution started, some operators and scamps sought to take advantage of the storm, and try to pull down real revolutionary workers. They often accused wildly and viciously, but the people actually did not pay too much attention to them. He had criticised himself and had asked the people to point out further faults. The scamps, however, brought up many strange things, quite unrelated to reality. Then again his decision in solving some of the contradictions amongst the people were attacked by those who did not benefit.

There had been a fight between two brothers and one got the worse of it. As brigade leader he ordered the victor to pay for medical attention to his brother. In any case, the doctor had reported that the hurt was not serious. The brigade leader was now accused of being the cause of the death of the brother who got beaten up. Actually, the row had been early in 1964. The man died at the end of 1966. "However," he said, "I decided to maintain a quiet and thoughtful attitude, and watch how the whole thing would turn out. After I had been through all this criticism, I realised that after ten years' work as a cadre, I seemed to be a failure. I became disgusted with the whole process. I went back home and decided to rest a while. My folks asked me about the movement saying, because it was the wish of Chairman Mao, it must be good in the end. I said that I had made mistakes, certainly, but that people should not treat me as an enemy. Should not try and destroy me. My folks wanted me to go back but I simply said, 'What would be the use of that?' Then there came an outbreak of contagious disease. The poor peasants came to see me and insisted that I return to take charge, but I told them I had given all the power over to them, and they ought to deal with the problem. However, I was worried and decided to go around the villages and see for myself what was doing. When the people saw me they smiled warmly and said, 'See, the movement has brought our Party secretary back to us!' So then I went to work and we got organised so that we were able to cope with the disease. My struggle with myself at this time was tough. It was hard for me to sleep. I reasoned that if I did revolutionary work I must at all times be prepared to give my life. I read and re-read what Chairman Mao had said. Finally I came to the conclusion that I had not believed either in the Party or in the people, and wondered how I could have been so blind for so long, just trusting in my own ability to solve everything."

As I listened to him, I realised how here in his quiet, sincere words there showed a frankness in explaining motives, an objectivity and truthfulness which would not be easily understood in the West. Each stage in his struggle for understanding was meaningful, and the fact that all stages led to a new feeling of confidence between the brigade members and himself, gave him a big lift. He felt a new appreciation of his own position — that he was really not so important, after all, yet in a new way more important to the brigade than he had been, giving leadership from within, not from above, and with a much better understanding of

the class struggle than he had had. He had found that honest criticism
by and large came from the poor peasants, the dishonest from operators
and opportunists with a bad class background. "All of my thoughts on
this matter, coupled with a new criticism of myself, I cleared with the
brigade membership in a general meeting. If one wants to go swimming,
one has first to get one's clothes off," he said, going on to say, "The
people were all very pleased and grateful for the Cultural Revolution,
all glad, too, that the cadre they trusted had no grudge against them.
They unanimously elected me to be head of the new production committee.
Then we started a family study group and now, along with the six other
cadres in the brigade, I have an "all red" family. Everyone now has
gained new understanding, all feeling better armed to meet the new tide
of endeavor that now arises. We are all out to make our once so backward
brigade the vanguard of a progressive commune."

A Hengping Brigade Cadre

The next to speak up was Liang Kuo-tsai, a small energetic-looking man
of around 40. He had been a cadre for ten years in Hengping Brigade
and had four children aged from eight to 15. When the movement started,
he had studied the Sixteen Points (Decision of the Central Committee
of the Chinese Communist Party Concerning the Great Proletarian Cultural Revolution, adopted on August 8, 1966) all right, but now realised
his understanding of them had not been deep enough. He first watched
the struggle in the Enping county centre, then in Hengpi Commune and
on down into the brigade. When it began to approach his production
team he felt dispirited. "Once we struggled against the landlords. Now
we just struggle against ourselves," he thought, and decided that perhaps
it was best not to be a cadre at all. So he prepared to leave his post.
Soon big character posters were stuck over his gate attacking him. "The
clever son of an old landlord family was pushing himself forward as
the next production team leader. So the head of the poor peasants'
union came to me with some of his friends, telling me that I must keep
on with my work but, too, that I must change. They said that most of
the people were good, and at least 95 percent of the cadres. Did I
believe in the people or not, was I part of the 95 percent or not? I grumbled, saying that in the old days the landlords made us eat bran, and
now there are people who want to make us eat the bitterness of being
called bad and reactionary." But nevertheless the others talked with
him, and he went to a poor peasants' meeting. When he came home it
was with a new light in his eyes.
   "I see now that what some people away up on top wanted to do was
to make us eat bran again. We are not revisionists. We are revolutionaries.
So I went home and with my whole family studied the three short essays
again, going over the benefits that the last 18 years had brought us,
understanding that it was the Cultural Revolution that was going to
keep our hills and streams red. For a while I could not sleep at night,
thinking over how mistaken I had been. Then we had a mass meeting

of the whole production team and I pointed out as well as I could what the revisionist line had done already, how we must see through it, denounce it, push it behind us, and how we must struggle against the selfishness that had held our brigade back."

Watching him speak, one realised that with this kind of man every word counted. He was expressing the voice of his fellows when he coupled landlord oppression with the revisionist advice to increase private plots, and so on. Now he knew that to rebel was right. Oppression was not right and the people must lift up their heads and stand against it. "I made all my mistakes clear, and folk accepted the explanation well. Everyone worked much harder, more cooperatively, and the year 1967 ended with us being able to raise the production on our land so much that our rice per person went up from 41 to 45 jin a month. And please remember that our land is some of the poorest in Hengpi Commune, most of it being very light and sandy. We hope to do still better with production in this year 1968, and better than ever put the Thought of Mao Tsetung into action."

The Militia Captain

A 22-year-old vice-captain of the militia was the next to speak. A handsome lad who had grown up in the years since Liberation, he was the son of a brigade leader, and had been very unhappy when in the first flush of the Cultural Revolution a storm of criticism was directed against his father. His head ached, he could not sleep, and he began to think that the best thing to do was to get out of it all by going to some distant city to work, and so forget the struggles of the commune. "Our militia leader, however, did not agree to my idea," he said. "Then the call came for us to send ten men to guard an airfield. I asked to go but was at first refused. Later I was told to take ten men and do the job. Foolishly happy with no longer hearing the voice of the people, I decided that I would try and stay away from the commune altogether. But then came a telephone call ordering me home, after only two days away. So I had to return. On my arrival home I saw my father being struggled against. I knew how hard he had worked over the years, never once taking advantage of his position. Now there were some who seemed right out to knock him down calling him a 'capitalist-roader', and an anti-Chairman Mao element. Again I could not sleep and wondered why people should be allowed to talk so much nonsense. My father had told us children many times how in 1943 he was a starving boy eating grass, and how other poor peasants helped the family out. Then, when the great change came, how we all put such hopes in working for a communist society. Surely, when our cadres make mistakes it is good for the people to criticise, I reasoned, but then again so many people are foolish in that they seem to think a cadre must be utterly perfect in everything, and by their own particular standards.

"At that time I turned again to Chairman Mao's works and read about the need to school ourselves in revolution, and to study hard. How we must always listen to the people, trust them, not be scared of them, digesting their ideas and getting them into perspective. Understanding the essential goodness of the big majority of them and ever gaining wisdom from them. Then on criticism. I had to ask myself, did I agree with Mao Tsetung or not? If I knew my father had his mistakes, then was it not my duty to point them out? So in the next people's meeting I did so.

"Back at home for the mid-day meal I asked father to eat, and he turned on me saying, 'You have nerve to ask me to eat after criticising me all the morning!' My mother backed him up. I said that I did what I had done because we all have responsibility to the people. I have not made so many mistakes because I have done so much less than you, but I surely have made plenty. But father would not eat, saying 'You're wrong. You've simply piled one wrong thing on top of another.' The only way I could reply was to tell him that it was my duty to say what I thought, wrong or not. Some people say the families of cadres do not follow Mao Tsetung Thought. If we want to sow good seeds for the revolution, we must be strict with each other. But still father said nothing, though he was evidently thinking a lot. Next morning he got up early and went around the villages to ask people to say more about his failings. He found the people very warm to him, and came home happily. After this we started our family study group, and though my mother was illiterate, she memorised the three short essays well. I then went through my own criticism, and in our militia company of 304 we received new spirit in our task of pushing production. My father says that only now, after having been brigade leader for over ten years, has he learnt that always it must be politics in command. The people have given us a certificate saying that all think we are a good red family, and we feel ourselves that we are not against them, but going right along the road with them all. My father has many new responsibilities now which keep him busy and happy."

A Wife

A small, determined middle-aged woman wearing the usual black clothing of the farm folk in these parts, trousers coming just below the knee, sunburnt legs and strong feet in sandals, toil-worn fingers and a small, bright badge of Chairman Mao on her tunic, told us that she was the wife of Hu Liu, the Party secretary of Hengping Brigade. In the past, she said, she had not been interested in collective work, only in the family private plot. Yes, and moreover she influenced her children to think as she did, and always to get what they could for the family. She did not like her husband going away to meetings all the time, and sometimes when people asked where he was she would angrily retort that she did not know, as he had been dead for years! Then other brigade members would say to her "Please keep your anger to yourself. Why inflict it on us?" Often she would grab her husband to stop him when he went off, always criticising him, never giving him any peace at home.

Cleverly she turned the children against him, too. In short, she was what could be called "bitchy" about the whole political side of living.

Then the Cultural Revolution came to their brigade, and her husband was struggled against. "On the first night he came home and I said, 'Now you see how right I was. You don't get any extra money for all the work you do. All you get is trouble. Stay at home. You'll make so much more and have peace as well! You have now got yourself into this mess. How do you propose to get out of it?' But then my 20-year-old eldest son, who had just returned home from middle school, called a family meeting and told us in detail about the Cultural Revolution. He stated everything very simply and clearly, so that I understood well. The next day some of the neighbors told me that there were many big character posters about my husband, asking me what I thought of them all, for they wanted to hear what I had to say, but I didn't say much. The struggle meetings lasted for three nights and four days. My husband was quite worn out and did not know what to do. I told him that he must think over all that had been said, and decide what was right in the criticism. I myself had changed and now did my best to help him. But he was so miserable he did not want to be a cadre at all, saying it was best to give up the whole thing.

"Then I talked to him about our bitter life before Liberation. How now our children were all alive and in school. How now we no longer worried about food or housing, and that he must be of good spirit. The next day he went out to help brigade members with rice transplanting. It was quite cold, so I heated plenty of water for him to bathe in when he got home, and bought some meat for supper. He was called to go off to the county town for a meeting, so I sold a hen and gave him the money for additional travel expenses. Now I began to have a new interest in life, trying to hold the family together on the basis of Mao Tsetung Thought, and not on the old selfish ideas I had before.

"After one period of study, we went out to dig a canal, despite the fact I had to take the smallest child along with me. To look after five children is not so easy, while digging irrigation channels as well. But now I was filled with the importance of studying Chairman Mao's works and of carrying his Thought through into action." She is 41 this year. Her husband, 42, who has since been made a member of the Revolutionary Committee of the prefecture in Fushan, is now away from home more than he has ever been, and is proud of his wife's strong support. She herself has become an activist in arranging and conducting study meetings. The whole family is happy in a new way.

I have put down these little sketches of a few people in Hengpi Commune of Enping as being indicative of what is happening throughout the countryside. New people are being created strong, confident and cooperative. It is good that folk around our world should know this. The fact is that to be hard working, devoted and energetic personally is not enough. Any cadre who loses that intimate touch with the people he works with, not carrying them forward with him in his endeavor, is not applying the first principle of leadership in a socialist society. To some cadres learning this lesson is hard, but when they do new successes come to their every endeavor.

Pottery Kilns

We spent the last day in Enping city going around various factories that were started in the Great Leap Forward in 1958, and which have continued since. I especially liked the porcelain and pottery kilns which make not only pottery for rural use but a fine white porcelain that is a pleasure to handle. Working conditions here were ideal. Set out in the countryside near the source of materials, there was plenty of space for everything, and work went on cheerfully in a fine practical way. In the county machine shops where most of the machine tools had been made by the workers, motors and transformers were being turned out by 204 workers, demand being greater than the supply available. County farm machinery was also repaired and kept in order here. The other factories were for cement and chemical fertiliser. All were doing well. Though there are overseas folk from 35 foreign countries in Enping, there are none in Hengpi Commune. Somehow or other, no one had been able to make the start of getting connections made with such places. We drove back to Canton through the garlic fields of Kaiping with the brave words of Hengpi Commune members still in our ears, feeling privileged indeed that we had been able to come.

> Tall ranges enclosing basins
> studded with little round hills
> of yellow clay, covering limestone;
> swift irrigation channels
> down which clear waters run
> swiftly; gum trees scenting
> the air, spring winds blowing
> through blossom, and cheerful shouts
> of the new generation mingling
> with the stamping of rammers on
> new walls, making homes for
> new families; lively children
> whose bare feet step so lightly
> and all around new tasks needing
> to be done, with the spirit
> generating to do them; here
> by the South China Sea, that washes
> Vietnam coasts nearby, people's
> militia does its exercises, and
> too carries the message into
> many humble homes on the way
> imperialism must be dealt with
> if the people are to take the next
> step; from one peasant home
> to another we go, seeing folk

*with new concepts of themselves
and of their future.*

> *Young bamboo bends
> gracefully; a spring
> of red blossom beckons
> from outside the wooden
> barred window in a thick
> farmhouse wall; so many
> facets to the business
> of living and working together
> so many human situations
> that impinge; so much
> soul searching before new
> trust in the people emerges
> from those who lead among
> the ranks of the people, all
> in the way of Mao Tsetung
> down in Hengpi Commune
> of Enping, west Kwangtung.*

To Polo County, East Kwangtung

In Canton rain fell in sheets, seeping through bamboo and palm, splashing to the ground. It was early in 1968 and the hills as we drove east were shrouded in mist. Tsengcheng county seat lay comfortably back in greenery beside broad waters. The flooded fields around had mostly been worked and on some, transplanting was already beginning. Lofushan, a more than 4,000-ft high mountain in Polo county, which was our first destination, was lovely with its cloud effects. It is a famous spot, not only for the beauty of its scenery, but also for the guerilla fighters both in the War of Resistance and the War of Liberation. But as we had come to see commune brigades, especially Lunghua Brigade of Lungchi Commune in Polo county, we did not have time to rest amongst the various beauty spots there. Rather we had a good long talk with PLA cadres who had been helping the communes after the directive which asked all cadres to grasp production while carrying on the revolution. Army units in the vicinity then went into a huddle, studying what they could do to help, then going off to the communes' production brigades and teams around to find out where to start. Of the 20 communes of Polo county there was Lungchi with its 8,263 households and 38,320 people divided into 19 brigades, of which Lunghua was one that, because of its grasp and application of Chairman Mao's works, has become nationally known as well as a living example to folk in the vicinity.

When Army cadres first came through the villages to help, however, the situation in Lunghua was serious. It was already the end of February 1967 and only around 8 percent of the land had been planted. The commune cadres were badly scared, and were unsure of the attitude of the people towards them and, too, unsure of themselves. The chief blackliner in power in the province had put out a directive telling the people to knock down all cadres. Landlord and rich peasant family groupings had quickly emerged to make hay while the sun shone. Many of the people who had not studied politics much and had minds full of conservative ideas were further corrupted by the economism line that had come down from Liu Shao-chi. Thirty of the over 80 cadres in Lunghua Brigade had dropped their responsibilities and were not working at all. The class enemy spread rumors. Someone collected all the sowing sieves and hid them on top of landlord family roofs, out of sight. Another would not open up the granary it was his duty to look after, even to let the people get the peanut seed they needed to sow. Evil rumors too were directed against the PLA, so when PLA men came around investigating, they were at times met with a door banged shut and someone spitting on the ground in front of them. It was evident that much had to be done.

So Army and militia lads came to every village, cleaning and sweeping, carrying water, bathing children, working in the fields. Some good training had been done in the villages in the Socialist Education Movement in 1964-65, so there was a base to build on when it came to getting the ideas of Mao Tsetung over to all. They began to get the people singing quotations and songs, carrying pictures of Chairman Mao to the fields with them along with a red banner, in the full understanding that every bit of good work done was carrying theory into practice. Then, as the correct cadre policy was explained, the cadres got to see their own mistakes and to trust the people. Together with the PLA men they could then start ironing out the contradictions. Sowing now went on apace, the people determined that they would make 1967 the best year for harvests in their history, which they did.

PLA men asked them why things were so bitter in the other days. Why was it that one girl now still living in their area was sold 18 times?

"It was because we had no power!" they said.

"Now what do you do with your power when you have so much?" they were asked. "Did this power just drop from heaven? Who gave it to you? Chairman Mao says 'Struggle against selfishness, criticise revisionism. Grasp revolution and promote production.' These things we can all do." And the people shouted assent. In the new and better relationship between cadres and members, the cadres realised afresh that they must learn from the people if they were to serve them well.

Leaving the main highway some distance from Lofushan, we went on a commune road across fields and streams until we came to the headquarters of Lunghua Brigade nestling amongst the hills. The commune secretary had come to the brigade to meet us and to tell us a few overall facts about the commune, which obviously is doing well in this progressive Kwangtung countryside. Last year it had 59,200 mou in early rice, and 72,400 in late. It also farmed 22,600 mou of dry land. It had 254 electrically powered units, 161 of them being pumping stations. Its ten tractors work 20,000 mou of its land. In the old landlord-ridden society, there was never more than 60,000 mou of rice altogether harvested in the area, and harvests were almost always affected by either flood or drought. Now dams and other water conservancy works can deal with the ordinary flooding. There have been many good results in the commune since the start of the Cultural Revolution. 1966 was a good year, but the 1967 harvest exceeded that of 1966 by 110,000 dan (One dan = 50 kgs or 110 lbs.). In 1966, the average income per family was 491 yuan. In 1967 it was 622 yuan. After the setting up of the Revolutionary Committee in February 1968, people have studied harder than before and are fully determined to make 1968 a success in every way.

Liang Chin-tang, the bright leader of Lunghua Brigade, told how his 15 production teams operated from 14 villages with their 615 families and 2,869 people on 6,700 mou of land. In the old days, he said, landlords owned 5,200 mou of this. In the bad year of 1946, 156 peasants hired themselves to landlords as long-term workers — really slaves, in many ways — 32 went off to beg, 26 families sold children, 136 became house servants for landlords, 21 starved to death, and 158 sold land and homes and went away. Of the 89 cadres in the brigade now, 42 were once long-term workers for landlords. In landlord times, production per mou ranged from 250 jin a mou of rice to 300 jin. In 1967 it was 996 jin. Brigade members get 50 jin per person a month of rice, and have sold 670 dan of grain to the state over and above the amount required of them. They have 1,711 dan in their own brigade store as reserve. They got 15,000 dan of sugar cane in 1966, 36,000 in 1967. Relative figures for other crops for the same period were: peanuts, 350 to 757 dan, beans 35 to 210 dan. They have a range of small factories, fulfilling the directive for local self-sufficiency in necessities, and 12 "green" hills on which 10,000 clumps of bamboo have been planted, as well as 37 kinds of food-bearing trees. They have 12 piggeries, eight poultry runs for geese, ducks and hens, six brick and tile kilns, four agricultural implement-making and repair shops, and so on.

A Brigade Leader Speaks

Liang Chin-tang thought that before the Cultural Revolution they were a fairly ordinary brigade, not very progressive, not so backward. It was when they decided on putting Mao Tsetung Thought into action that they pushed forward fast.

Now they say proudly, everyone in the brigade old enough to do so understands the outstanding points in the teachings of Chairman Mao. Even the blind, the deaf, and the quite old. Study is done in rest periods when out in the fields, in the family and in meetings. The strength of the message comes home to all, bringing them together in a new way. The effect of all this is to make everyone want to put his best foot forward in daily effort. Of the 1,650 people over 12 years of age, 90 percent can recite the three short essays. Once they have reached this stage, further developments are easier. The revisionism that so insidiously leads back to the old society is countered by intensive study of the

nature of Kuomintang rule, of what the Kuomintang soldiers did, of Kuomintang policy and which class it favored, and favored at whose expense.
Then in contrast, what the Communist Party stands for, its policy, and
how the PLA works for the people all the time.   These contrasts are
made very clear by actual experiences of people who have lived through
both societies, and by many historical facts.

People learn to ask questions: What did the old landlord families do
after the start of the Cultural Revolution? Why were they so eager to
have all cadres pulled down? Why did they come out against the Communist Party, spreading rumors and poison? People are easily won to
the side of revolution, but the class enemy stands in his heart of hearts
with the imperialists who would destroy us. How then is it possible to
unite with him? Now Chairman Mao has written a good deal, and it
is urgent that we study his thinking, so that we may find the correct line.

Ideas like these now circulate throughout the brigade. Activists for
teaching from the Little Red Book, and the important documents relating to the Cultural Revolution and the correct political line increased
from 16 to 98. The people's militia, learning quickly from the PLA,
spent their spare time helping the people out in every way possible.   While
Liang Chin-tang was talking, I looked over the table at the well worn
Little Red Books lying in front of everyone. It was evident that study
had been a real thing with all. Liang Chin-tang talked of the wonderful
way the PLA had come to help everyone, and especially what this had
meant to cadres, puzzled as they were at that time, with so much. Then
almost suddenly, as if after a storm, the skies cleared, and they found
themselves better able to discuss, better able to plan, better able to carry
through all the tasks that had to be done. They found, too, that they
were much closer to the people than they had ever been.

Production Team Leader Lai Ping-ho

The leader of the production team based on Lunghua village was the
next to speak. Like all commune cadres there he was barefoot, as Cantonese farm folk commonly and sensibly are, especially at this season
of rains. Unlike the others, however, he was not able to speak the common language. With a strong determined face and decisive wording, he
told of some of the problems he had encountered. Still in his early
thirties, he has come through a hard school already. He was made production team leader some time before the Socialist Education Movement
of 1964-65 came to Lunghua and was struggled against for some eight
months, many people not liking his then perhaps too commanding attitude.
He felt rather downhearted, telling his folks that it was really too difficult to be a cadre. So much criticism had always to be taken. Then,
as each movement came along, he must always prepare to be knocked
down. To be a cadre meant that one must always be a target for people's anger. Always living under the watchful eyes of so many, and
with so much less freedom than ordinary members had. He wondered

if he should not give up the whole cadre business, concentrate on his private plot, on profitable side business, making tools to sell at markets, and so on. He told his son, then a little boy of nine, never to be a cadre when he grew up. There was no future to the job at all! Then, again, he was sorry for himself that he had to deal directly with the people. If he was an upper cadre, he would just have to tell other cadres what to do, and they would do it.

When the Cultural Revolution came, some people treated him as though he were a pariah, saying he was conservative. His whole family was unpopular. For some time he was put aside from his work. Then the PLA came in and talked to both him and the people, exposing a clever but reactionary landlord family which had been agitating for a clearing out of all Communist Party members. As he talked with the PLA and the members of his production team now, after his careful, thorough study of Mao Tsetung Thought, he realised that he must remain as a cadre as long as the people needed him, and that not to do so would mean that he was not loyal to the best he knew.

So he now told his little son: "Father was wrong when he told you never to be a cadre. You must grow up always studying ways to serve the people. That is what we live for. For me not to be a cadre would be not doing my best to serve the people." Really, the cadres had not always been correct. Some had started on the road to revisionism — one setting up a little food shop, another on the side dividing up grain from one patch of land amongst the members who worked with him. One more paying too heavily for compost fertiliser brought in to get popularity, and yet another who would say to members, "Just do this extra bit of work and I will give you two jin of grain." Then, if the member refused, bargaining and saying, "Well, I'll give three jin, how about that?" So entered the wedge of economism, separating cadres from people.

Said the production team leader: "Now, looking back on the way all of this has been talked out in meetings, I can see how important it is to believe in the people, for without them we are nothing. Their future, the future of the mass of the poor, is the future of all of us. So I accepted the criticism of people when they said, 'Lai Ping-ho, you always kept things to yourself, never brought problems to us. Why do you not do things the way Chairman Mao says they ought to be done?' They were right, I was wrong."

Then he went on to criticise a certain black-line official who said: "Buddhist priests reading sutras and you reading the Little Red Book are all the same," saying how priests mumbled language they themselves did not understand for money, while the people read easily understandable quotations, every one of which they put into practice, every one of which they believed in.

"You know," he said, "not long ago, Li Cheng-cheng's daughter cursed me and wanted to strike me. So I went to her home and in a family meeting there cleared up her grievance. It took some time but it worked out well, and the people around were pleased at the way the incident was handled. I feel now that it is a privilege, not a headache, to be a production team leader. We have all learnt a great deal in this movement."

Woman Activist

One morning we went to Lunghua Brigade to meet seven activists who helped to spread the Thought of Chairman Mao. Two of them were men, five women. Of the women three were staid matrons, two were young. Chu Kwei, one of the women, started the meeting by giving an account of her own attitudes. She confessed that she had been a very individualistic woman before. That she did not like study. Good at business, she did what she could in a quiet way at it, with considerable profit. Her thinking at that time was that a horse belonging to the commune was not so important as one's own dog. The thing that really changed her was the criticism made of Liu Shao-chi, each turn of his policy being analysed by the women of the village as they talked together at work. It then became more and more clear that the basic trouble was selfishness. She had never realised how bad a thing this was until it was uncovered as the root trouble of so much. She could see how the innocent private plot could be enlarged to become the main interest in a family. Then how the selling of produce grown for private profit in the market would interfere with the strength of the collective. How simply thinking of ourselves would inevitably take us back to the bad old society, and how it would be the poor who would really suffer then!

As she spoke, I watched her strong, determined face, wisps of hair around her ears, which the light from the window behind played upon and lit up to go along with the light in her eyes as she went on to say how becoming immersed in the thinking of Chairman Mao had made so much difference to her life, giving her indeed a root for living.

A Geese Herder

As these village folk spoke, so full of conviction with all they said that evidently came right from their hearts and their experience, one felt with a thrill that here in our old world a new force was being born. Something the like of which we have not had before. Following Chu Kwei came a man of 67 who had lost his teeth but who could yet talk quite clearly. Yes, he realised he should have studied before, but had not. Thought he was getting too old for that. Young people with a future should, of course, concern themselves with such things. Yes, he herded geese all day. Before he had quite a fine flock of them belonging to himself on which he could have realised over 100 yuan by just selling the fat ones. But after he had gone to a study group he changed his mind and now he herds a flock of geese for the production brigade. His daughter, a 15-year-old activist, has taught him to recite the three short essays and many of the more important quotations and documents. All of this has given him a new interest in life. He feels that all poor folk, old and young, must come to understand the process of revisionism, and how to combat it.

Mother of Six

Li Li was an older woman of around 58, with six in her family. When the PLA fighters called and asked if there were any in the family who had studied the works of Chairman Mao, she was embarrassed. She herself was illiterate, and none of the others had done so. The PLA men invited her to attend a literacy class where they went into a deep discussion, criticising the old society in its various forms, relating their own experiences in it, and then stacking it all up against what they had now. She had advised her son never to become a cadre and have to suffer the anger of the people. Better to grow up happily. Get frogs and fish and market them. Do things for yourself and family. Never become a public servant. When she heard of people criticising Liu Shao-chi she was quite upset. "He is a leader. We should not talk of him in this way," she said then. Finally, along with some other members of her literacy class, she went to a model brigade called Huangshandung which was away up in the hills of Polo county. She saw how she had been hoodwinked by the chief revisionist's agents. When she came back she was full of fire for the new way. Her very backward husband grumbled, "You have stayed three days in Huangshandung, and now you come home just talking the language of Huangshandung!" But she kept on, and with the help of the rest of the family, and reminding him of the bad old days, she brought him over.

Speaking quietly, and taking each section point by point, Li Li went on to say that now of her six children three had become militia members or cadres. Now when she hears wild talk of wanting to kill this cadre or that, her vigilance is raised. "Who would say such a thing and why?" she reasons. "Who would use our movement for other ends?"

Sold 18 Times

Liu Hsu-niu is a dynamic little woman. She has an almost incredible record, having been sold 18 times in her early years. Like so many who tell of their early lives, she broke down and wept when telling some of the more terrible parts — when, for instance, a salt merchant stuck a hot poker into her foot so that it suppurated and did not heal properly for several years. An intense person, she would be a very good friend to have, but a very tough enemy. Every year at New Year she makes a bowl of bitter herbs and bran for each member of her family, to remind them how the poor ate in the old days so they will not forget the class basis of the revolution. Imperialism? She knows of that, for did not her father die after being struck on the head by a Japanese soldier in Hongkong where they had gone as refugees? The same Imperial Japanese soldiers who had killed two elder brothers and an uncle. So often sold, for two dan of grain, she had to do whatever her new owner wanted, while he in turn would sell her just as he wished. Now when she hears that Liu Shao-chi has said that exploitation has its good points, she realises that the class enemy can come back in new form, working on the inside of the revolution. This just makes her fighting mad.

A Lass of 26

Chen Sho-ying, 26 years old, is a leading young woman activist for prop-agating Mao Tsetung Thought in the brigade. Before the Cultural Rev-olution, she explained, the 11 landlord families in the brigade were treated the same way as everyone else. They stuck together and found many ways of prospering. Wang Di, one of these, would tell his children how so much of the village land was really theirs, and meticulously kept ac-counts to be presented when a change might come. She told how another, Tseng Ken-lang, kept arms and poisons in his house. How all the land-lord group were most active in trying to lead against the cadres when the Cultural Revolution came to the village. It was important that all these things should be understood by the people and, in helping them to assess things from a class viewpoint, it has been her duty to analyse and explain. Then the people themselves will be better able to judge who is with and who against them. Decide themselves how best to keep their hills and streams red.

Student Anarchism

The pretty daughter of the 67-year-old man who had spoken of his geese herding was the next. She was 15, and explained how in her middle school there had been a good deal of anarchism following the first changes of the Cultural Revolution. The students had taken charge and had made rather a mess of the practical work, not taking directions from anybody. "Then as we went on with our political study," she said, "and better understood the various directives from Peking, we realised that cadres are good or for the most part good, that we should study what they had actually done in their lives; that we had been foolish in mak-ing a good teacher an enemy. Certainly some teachers had been fooled by the revisionist line, but they believed now in the way of Chairman Mao. So we found ways to join with them and to build a real Mao Tsetung school. We criticised selfish students who had taken school tools to go back home and help with private plots there, and also those who had simply left the school to work out its own salvation, as if it was no business of theirs at all. So we have come out of the past two years really stronger than before, with improved understanding all around."

The Brigade Barber

We walked around Lunghua village visiting many families. Mists stole through the tall valleys of Lofushan. Fields were springing into green as transplanting got under way. Truly a land of beauty with its swift-moving eager country folk, who now so resolutely take the revolutionary way forward. One of the most interesting homes we stopped at was that of the brigade barber. He was quite a personality with his six chil-dren, two of whom were boys. Yes, he cut hair for a living. He did not get workpoints but depended on his trade. His wife worked in the tailoring shop. He never refuses anyone a haircut even if the client has

no money, and often in spare time goes out to the fields to see if any
need his services there, never charging them much. "People support us,
and we have enough," he says. He told how as a child he had been
sold by his parents over in Nanhai county and then had been brought
here. Then of his taking up the work of barbering, finding that people
needed him and he could make friends with them. Always he was scared
that his work might not be considered good, that he would not be able
to meet needs and so might make enemies. But then, after going to
study classes he realised that the better way of thinking meant much
to him, too. He was not successful in getting his wife to join in the
movement for some time; she thought it was not the business of an illiterate mother like herself. But finally, with the aid of the older
children, she came over, and now they had an "all red" family. And
what a talented family it was! We sat for over an hour watching them
dance and sing. The two little girls were quite extraordinary. Their
bare feet moving in time on the earth floor, songs that never repeated
themselves — dances that would credit quite a large stage in any city —
making them a fresh and beautiful group.

There has been a burst of house-building this spring, and the brigade
brick kilns have been busy providing the brick and tile. We went to
some of the little brigade factories — the oil press, the grain processing,
the beancurd making, and so on. Folk were quite proud that they could
do so much themselves. All were warm and friendly, and pinned so
many badges on my coat that it was ablaze with them.

Yuyeh Brigade

Leaving Lofushan one morning, we went to visit Yuyeh Brigade of Tieh-
chang Commune over in the southwest corner of Polo county. This
commune is a prosperous one of some 30,000 people, with its irrigation
secured by reservoirs up in the hills, so that good crops are the rule. In
the past, its one very poor group was a fishing brigade of boat people
who lived in their little sampans as they had done for generations, moor-
ing them somewhere near river banks, a hen or two kept in bamboo
baskets, a puppy tied up on the roof, a pot of flowers to brighten up
the cabin, and a square foot of garden in a box to grow some onions in.

In the old feudal days and until Liberation, they had not been allowed to come ashore to live nor to wear shoes. They were the "tan"
(a derogatory term meaning "egg") people who paddled boats with great
ability, and who manned the big long boats at the time of the summer
festival. Before Liberation they were pitilessly oppressed. Today their
brigade has 63 families, with 346 people in it, from which comes a labor
force of 144. Before Liberation, many of them were beggars, a prey
to loafers and gangsters. The brigade leader said, "In 1965 we started
to study Tachai, and decided that we would push for economic independence too. We had already built many houses by and for ourselves on
the wasteland allotted us, as well as our brigade headquarters. Now
we decided that we would purchase a fleet of transport boats, from seven

to ten tons capacity each, to do transport work to Shihlung on the railway south. So we cut the 75 yuan each family then earned each month to 13 yuan, just enough for us to live on, until we bought nine big boats. With these the brigade became much more independent. Then we set about digging and enclosing fish ponds on the wasteland and marsh, as well as making paddy fields, so that we can be responsible for at least part of the grain we use. Our 27 mou of paddy now brings us 400 dan of grain a year. Last year we sold 80 dan of this to the state. We have in addition dug 107 fish ponds, and raise both pigs and cattle. We have two brick kilns. Every winter 70 percent of our membership turns out to dig new ponds. We know we must help Vietnam as well as we can, and can do this best by creating more wealth than we consume. Our total assets in 1956 were valued at 8,000 yuan. In 1967, they were valued at 108,000 yuan. In 1965 average earnings for the year per person of total population amounted to 132 yuan. In 1967 it was 172 yuan. We have taken no state loans of any kind. In addition to our 63 newly built homes we have put up seven buildings for our brigade. We have gained strength of spirit and so we have been able to change this spiritual force into the material things we need, and we feel that our production can increase a good deal yet. There is so much more we can do still to raise standards, though we feel we have already come some way along on the path Chairman Mao has plotted for us."

A Lad of 20 Speaks

The various activists of the brigade came to tell us what they had been able to do, and how they themselves had felt the winds of change and had changed with the changing times. Hsu Hung-ken is a 20-year-old lad, tall and handsome. His grandfather is a retired city worker with a 26-yuan monthly pension. Now well over 80, he sweeps, fixes tools and does carpentering jobs at times. His eyes and technique are still good. Before the Cultural Revolution he helped the family by doing small jobs around, and he found a bit of waste land to make into a private plot. When the first study classes started, he thought everything in the political line was too difficult, and that it was the business only of the cadres to teach it. Then he realised that he too could learn and still do much. So he first memorised the most important passages and went amongst the fishermen, reminding them of what had happened to him in the old society. How his wife had died and he had no way to get her any kind of coffin. How he had to give one child away. Then later, the brigade wanted some work done on a storage building. At the same time, a relative also asked him urgently to fix a boat. Naturally, he wanted to help his relative, but the brigade came first and family affairs second. Only after the week or so's work, when the storehouse was completed, did he turn to the boat.

The lad told other stories about his family and then one about himself. He had gone to the toilet and found on the floor there a wallet in which were grain and cloth tickets and quite a sum of money. His first thought was one of happiness — now he would be able to buy many of the things he needed. But then he thought again, realising that to use such would be a betrayal of his new beliefs. So he looked for the loser and returned all to him. One evening, after the family had been declared an "all red" one, his mother asked at supper, "Is it that we have no selfishness now in our family?" No one answered, and then she went out and came back with two fish which his younger brother had caught on his way back home from school. "Go and take these to the brigade at once," she said. He went. In the other day she would have praised him. Now she used the incident to show all that words must have understanding, and understanding must lead to action. His younger brother later took all his fishing tackle to the brigade also, saying that now when he fishes, he fishes for all.

The Pretty Girl

Hsu Yun-mei, an attractive lass, came into the brigade as a young woman from a middle-peasant family, with selfishness deeply engrained, as she confessed. Her main desires were to eat well and wear good clothes. "So naturally I didn't make a very good impression in our brigade," she said. "Then, when the Cultural Revolution came, I took part in a study group, and was deeply impressed with the danger of selfishness in starting on the road towards revisionism. One night when I came home, I noticed a big basket of lime in the house and wondered why we needed to buy so much, with no way to use such a large quantity. Then I looked at it again and realised that, if we had bought it, it would be dry, whereas this was damp. So when the family met in the evening I asked them if this was not lime cleaned out of the boat after a cargo was brought in. They said it was, and that if they had not brought it home it would have been dumped in the river, which would have been a waste. I said that the only right course was to take it to the brigade where it could be properly used. The family was split for a while on this issue, but finally came to my way of thinking, and the next morning we carried the whole load to the brigade. It was a useful lesson to us all, helping us to realise better what selfishness was."

The Naughty Boy

"I was always a naughty, obstinate kid. I liked eating, fighting, looking at the opera and movies. At school my relation with other pupils was bad. I was always playing truant, going out to steal lichee fruit or cucumbers. Wherever there was anything good to eat or to be seen, I would be there. Once in a fight, I used a pocket knife and stuck another boy in the leg. The boy's father came after me and asked my father for damages. At school, the other boys nicknamed me 'Monkey King'. If I could not get in through the window of a theatre, I would worm my way in between people's legs past the ticket collector. It was either over or under. I always got in."

Speaking clearly and quite directly, Hsu Hung-shui, aged 14, sat across the table from me, live face and a good smile. "Then last year, my grandfather told me a lot about his history and the evil of the old days. He had waited to tell me all of this until I could understand. So I studied the three short essays better and learnt them by heart, realising that in the new day my life would only have meaning if I could serve others. Our family at that time did not all think alike. I used a school holiday to herd buffaloes for the brigade. My mother was not pleased, saying to me that if I did not bring fish home, she would not give me food. I continued working for the brigade, and if there was no food at home went to my grandfather's place to eat. Father was away at Shihlung at that time but when he came back he was on my side. When I had done 18 days of buffalo herding, my mother said I had better tell the brigade I had done 22. I refused, for such would have been absolutely against Chairman Mao's instructions. Finally, to make a long story short, we managed to convince everyone in the family, and I gave all my fishing tackle to the brigade." He was quite natural as he told the story, the first time he had spoken in public. Not in the slightest bit priggish or goody-goody. A lad obviously with a future in the service of his people.

Once So Ambitious

A 28-year-old cadre, Teng Su-kun, told how he had become a cadre because he thought then that some advantage could be gained thereby. It was a beginning, he felt, in an official career which could lead him high. He had gone to Canton once, spending ten yuan on a meal, buying 70 yuan worth of new clothes, and paying ten yuan a day for a good room at a fine hotel. His salary was but 70 yuan a month, so he took what he needed from public money he was entrusted with. He said, "This was the beginning of a very tough time for me. In the Socialist Education Movement people struggled against me, and in the Cultural Revolution all the old troubles came up for a second time. I wanted to get out of the ranks of cadres, and at home my wife told me I was foolish not to have done so long ago. Had I done so, she said, I could have come back as a rebel and seized power that way! Now, all I could do was to stand to one side, while the revolution went on.

"Then the PLA came and organised cadres into a Mao Tsetung Thought study group, and we began to realise that it was our duty to struggle through to the end, or else the revolution would not succeed. I had come from a very poor family, and I had been brought up in an orphanage in Canton, my parents having died really of starvation when I was nine. I was on the side of the revolution but I had not been true to it. Then, just when I was learning, the second great temptation came. I picked up an open cheque for 800 yuan. So much money would give our family new clothes, a sewing machine and so on, with plenty left over. But this time, Mao Tsetung Thought won, so I took the cheque back to the place where it was issued and felt that I had beaten my selfishness this time. The next time temptation comes, it will be still easier to resist,

I felt, and now, too, I have more confidence in my ability to serve the people properly."

Women's Section Leader

Wu Kwei-lan, a woman of 27, then took up the tale, saying how the other women of the brigade had wanted her to head the women's section, but because of her task of looking after three small children she had refused. But was it just the child problem?   Analysing, she realised that the main trouble was that she was afraid of being criticised, and of making enemies.   Nevertheless, she went to the study group and studied along with the rest of them.   In the past, boat women had not done heavy work, leaving that to the men, which is not the usual custom in Kwangtung, where women have the tradition of working quite hard.   Now she was able to help to influence the women to go out and help with the digging of fish ponds and bringing in land.   Finally, when the women again asked her to lead them, she realised that to serve them in the spirit of Chairman Mao, she must do what they wanted, so took up the task they gave her.

Down with Superstition!

Hsu Yu-mei was a mother also with some young children.   One child was rather poor in health, so she went to appease the devils which, her mother said, were the cause.   She honestly believed that if one did not appease images of devils and saints, they would follow one and do harm. At night, looking back and seeing a white stone on the road, she would think it might be a devil following.   The boat people had so many of these superstitions that they had a good deal of trouble giving reverence to them all.   Some days were good for fishing, some not.   Some places good, others not.   Images had to be bought and placated.   Money had to be spent on incense.   The ash of the incense could be made into a medicine that would cure all.   There was a whole mumbo-jumbo of such nonsense that had come down through the ages, which naturally cunning operators with an ability to talk would take advantage of to milk the people.   To try and cure her child by these means she borrowed 300 yuan, but they did nothing for the child's health.   The cure was finally effected at the local hospital at a total cost of two yuan.   "So it is good," she said, "that Chairman Mao leads us to get rid of old superstitions. For me, there came another testing time.   I had had a baby not many days before.   According to the old superstition, a woman at such a time should not let cold water touch her feet or hands.   There is also the superstition that if you save a person from drowning, the bad part of their fate will descend on you.   Passing by the river, I saw a child fall in.   I had to decide quickly whether to save it or not, and the words of Chairman Mao, 'utter devotion to others without any thought of self' which I had memorised, really pushed me into the water to save the drowning one at all costs.   When I got home all wet and tired, however,

I was met by angry family folk who upbraided me for being so bad as to go against established custom. I was sure of myself, though, when I recited Chairman Mao on Bethune to them, and succeeded in silencing them all. I told them about PLA heroes and how they had sacrificed their lives, so why could I not even do this one little thing? In the end, both they and the neighbors agreed with me, that we all had another experience in education together.

Family Song Groups

We walked around the homes that had been built. Families would come to the door and, with the smallest child usually leading, sing a song for us. The spirit of the place was infectious. Everyone for the brigade, even down to the smallest. Not that catching a couple of fish in the river on the way home from school is so bad, but in a fishing community the lesson must be learnt early that fishing is their economic base, and all fish caught must go to the whole group. As it is, there are not enough hands to do all that has to be done, and the struggle for improvement is a fight that all able to must participate in.

There is still some waste land available — marsh and red clay hillocks — that can be transformed into fish ponds and paddy, which will be the task for next winter. But the inner meaning of what I had seen in Lunghua and then again in Yuyeh Brigade was that, right here in the Kwangtung countryside, a new force is developing, one infinitely stronger than any atomic bomb. The experience of the people is at the same time full of meaning for the two thirds of the world that are still poor and exploited.

Thinking over the trip to Polo made me write these lines:

> *Rugged peaks of Lofushan*
> *waterfalls gleaming against*
> *dark rock behind, gaze*
> > *serenely, proudly*
> > *over fields and streams*
> > *below, and a people resurgent;*
> *a people*
> *who say to the children*
> *who will greet the year 2000*
> *"everything for others*
> *with little thought for self"*
> *shall be your way of life.*
>
> *And such children these!*
> > *a little one, perhaps five,*
> > *conducts with arms swinging*
> > *the whole family with precision*
> > *singing, "The East is Red".*
>
> *A song that wells up from*

each and every home, each
and every village, from
fishing boats, and from the slopes
of Lofushan, a song that carries so well
the ever hopeful spirit of dawn.

Communes and Schools in Kwangtung

It was the late spring of 1969 in mid-Kwangtung.   Women from the production teams are scattering extra compost fertiliser over the beds of rice seedlings that will soon be planted out in the waiting paddy fields, some already flooded and plowed, others having this done by the men stepping slowly through the mud, as they shout at the buffalo that pulls the plow.   It is terraced land running up valleys, with forested ridges above, so the fields are small.   Some production teams are busy bringing in new land high up on the hillsides for orchard or pineapple planting. We pass a forester going back up into the mountains after having brought a raft down the river.   Hanging from the end of his pole is a tiger trap he is taking back to catch a young tiger which has been bothering the production team in his village by stealing their small pigs.   Two 14-year-old boys pass us and put down the loads of firewood they have cut, for a rest.   They have already walked several miles, and it is hot.   They respond to our greeting and we notice that one has his knee bandaged. Going over to see the extent of the damage, we find that he has cut his knee open with his razor-sharp slasher.   We suggest he go into the commune clinic and have the wound cleaned and sewn up.   "Yes," he says, he will do that.   We say it must be very sore.   "Yes," he says, "it is very sore."   Then gamely he puts his shoulder under the carrying pole, lifts the load and is off at a limping trot, yet keeping pace with his companion.   They bring them up tough in Kwangtung villages!

Folk are not rich, but now they are very evidently on top of the situation to a far greater extent than they have ever been in the 42 years I have been moving amongst them. Proffer a sweet to a child and he will refuse it.   Offer a Chairman Mao badge, and he will accept with a smile and say "Long live Chairman Mao".

In Tsunghua County

After the Socialist Education Movement in the countryside, and now the three years of Cultural Revolution, people in Tsunghua county in Kwangtung understand well what are the two different political lines, and which of them will lead forward.   Many an opportunist, many an operator, has been thrown out from leadership.   More than at any time in their past they move forward together.   Looking around we find many things of interest.   The two big water wheels that so efficiently hoist water up to commune fields above have been repaired over the winter months and make a pleasant picture as they splash the water under the rays of a morning sun.   In the cooperative marketing and supply store, no sooner does one new consignment of bicycles come in than commune farmers arrive to buy and wheel the vehicles off. In all fields of endeavor, the people are taking greater responsibility for their own affairs, not only in agriculture but also in commerce, medicine, education and defence down at grassroot levels.

In the War of Resistance against Japanese imperialism, many visitors would go to Yenan to get a picture of what the future might be in the countryside. Now every county is a Yenan, full of struggle, and full of endeavor. Like old Yenan, too, there is a gaiety that goes along with such. We come down a road cut from a hillside. High up on the bank is a big tree, and amongst its top branches a small girl with a slasher in her hand is taking off some of the top branches. We shout, "Come down! It's dangerous!" as we watch her nonchalantly stepping across from one not so big branch to the other. She just laughs back at us, and her laughter follows us down the road. We meet a young man who does not at first reply to a salutation, then looks towards us and smiles, starting to explain his rudeness in somewhat incoherent speech accompanied by actions. He is a hunter up in the hills, and has been a deaf-mute. Now he is getting acupuncture treatment for his trouble, and has already learnt how to speak, and can hear a little. But old habits persist, such as walking past people without taking notice of them. He has never had acupuncture before, and thinks some of the needles rather painful, but marvels at their effect. We note that on the bulletin board by the cooperative is a notice offering free treatment to the deaf and mute as well as to polio-paralytics, by an Army medical unit at present in the locality.

Kwantsun Commune

One fine day with a pleasant breeze blowing, we took a commune-built side road from the main Tsunghua highway north, and after a few kilo-metres were amongst the hills. Soon we came to a fairly wide basin dominated by a scenic mountain amongst the stark peaks of which wisps of cloud glided, sometimes concealing one height, sometimes shyly reveal-ing it. In the centre of the basin was situated the headquarters of Kwantsun Commune, one famous in the region for its work in emulating Tachai Brigade in Shansi, and for the way it has carried out health work amongst its people.

At the simple but spick and span commune offices we spent some time talking with two quiet, capable barefoot leaders of the Revolutionary Committee, discussing the way the eight production brigades and 73 production teams of the commune had come through the Cultural Rev-olution, and then what changes their struggles have made possible over the 20 years of Liberation.

Kwantsun Commune has a population of 12,000 farming 12,000 mou of rice-growing land, the soil of which is rather poor and sandy. It also keeps around 12,000 pigs. Under the old society, the region was dominated by some 20 landlords, nearly all of whom lived in Tsunghua city or else

in Kwangchow (Canton), using bailiffs to collect rents. In the period of
the Japanese invasion the people suffered the loss of 220 houses burnt,
53 people killed and the women of 258 families abducted during the
many burn all, loot all, kill all raids.

The Kuomintang Rides High

When the Kuomintang returned, a big scamp was put into office by the
landlord group as district head.   He was accustomed to shooting people
just for fun, and instituted a reign of terror in the countryside around.
As no proper irrigation was done in the area, and as Kuomintang exactions
were so many, ever keeping the spirit of the people low, very few fields
gained a production of as much as 300 jin a mou.   Then two thirds of
all produce went in rent or taxes.   In addition every landlord had to be
presented with pigs, chickens or ducks on the main feast days of the
year.   The hills were infested with small bandit groups who would come
down and rape women, steal clothing and food of any kind.   In the
last days of the old order, still very much on the minds of the older
people, 465 families were forced to sell their children, 321 families went
off to become beggars, 577 people died of starvation, and 2,262 worked
for a miserable pittance as hired hands of landlords or rich peasants.
156 families lost their homes and dispersed because of Kuomintang con-
scription. There was but one school. An ordinary primary one, in which
the children did not stay longer than two years, and only the better off
ones at that. Never more than 200 in it, and most of the pupils managed
to get half a year's learning only. Some only a couple of months. In
consequence, illiteracy was high. There were no roads, only hillside tracks.
Two Kuomintang leaders had bicycles, but they were the only ones in
the place. It became a veritable living hell, each year becoming worse
than the preceding one.

Liberation Comes

Liberation brought swift change. Landlords and Kuomintang officials
were forced to face an angry people. Each year became better than the
one before it. Youngsters went off and took part in building a big dam
for a hydro-electric plant, and power lines soon came from it to all brigades
of the commune which by the end of 1958 had evolved. The Great Leap
Forward brought a spate of small irrigation projects to fruition, so that
by 1965 there was an all-over average of 600 jin of rice a mou. Many
orchards of lichee and sour plum had been planted on the hillsides above
croplands and were coming into production. Lichees are an important
crop in Tsunghua county, two million jin being exported yearly. The
sour plum, which is dried, goes all over China as well as to countries
in Southeast Asia.

Between 1960 and 1965 there was some halting in effort due to the
revisionist policies of Liu Shao-chi, all of which have now been thoroughly
exposed and repudiated. The Socialist Education Movement started to

turn people's minds again to the only real way forward, and everyone entered on a period of struggle, criticism and change which continued through the Cultural Revolution and was still in action while this account was being written. The results in better production and in construction work achieved since 1965 were impressive. Grain fields were now yielding over 1,000 jin a mou, well over three times the amount gained under the old order.

Irrigation Project

The lads who learnt in the Great Leap Forward hydro-electric plant construction drove a 368-metre tunnel through a hill, out of their own strength, and by mid-year 1969, after a smaller tunnel has been completed to connect with the main water supply, will be turning a permanent stream of water into a 15-kilometre main canal which the people have dug in these past two years and for which they have built many aqueducts across hillside valleys. We climbed up to see this tunnel and to admire the workman-like way it had been constructed, two metres wide at its base and two metres high. One hundred commune members took eight months to drive it through, using only the hand tools which the commune could provide.

Also in the past two years, the commune has built eight multiple-arch stone bridges for the highway going through their area which was built in the "Leap Forward" period. These have all been constructed with locally cut stone, all being entirely engineered by the commune itself. We stopped to take a picture of one of them, which was just then having the finishing touches given to it. Bridges of this kind are strong, are of fine appearance and make for considerable saving in both cement and reinforcing material.

Electrification

Electrification has become a reality in this commune. All homes are now lit with electricity, all brigades have electric power for doing their rice milling and other such needs, while nine pumping stations have been set up with motors for their pumps. All of this has been done with commune funds at the low expenditure of 500,000 yuan — much less than it would have cost had the commune asked outside authorities to do it for them. All 73 production teams have loudspeakers installed and, in a very short time after an important communique is issued in Peking, folk in all the hill villages are listening to it.

Grain Production

Rice which goes to the state is milled before leaving the commune in a special rice mill that processes 20,000 jin a day. Over and above the commune quota for grain, a considerable surplus is sold to the state each year. Commune and brigade stores are also kept full, while the people have a rice allowance of 660 jin of grain a year per person of population — too much for consumption. In consequence, homes store some and now usually ask brigades to sell their unused grain to the state rather than themselves disposing of it in the markets and thus making a profit from it.

The 16,000 lichee and sour plum trees already planted in the commune and the 8,000 clumps of bamboo are having their numbers added to very considerably this year. There has been a surplus, too, of the peanut oil used in cooking, this being sold to the state also. How is it that this commune should have become such a dynamo of effort?

Mao Tsetung Thought

In the 2,150 families in the commune, there are no fewer than 2,380 sets of Selected Works of Chairman Mao. Everyone over seven years of age has a copy of the quotations. All adults in the commune do political study for an hour a day. Every one of the 73 production teams has a Mao Tsetung study centre. There are 85 propaganda teams with 3,100 members, a third of whom are activists. All brigades run schools, and over 95 percent of the children attend, the school charging but three yuan a year per pupil as a fee. Upper middle-school courses are given in the regular schools set up for that purpose in the county seat. It is all practical class education, pupils helping to teach each other, and influencing their old folk at home in no uncertain way.

Commune Medicine

Before going out through the hills to the brigades we visited the commune hospital. Very spick and span, and very busy with patients who have come in. A good deal of traditional medicine is being used, including a great many formerly secret prescriptions that people have passed in to the hospital during the Cultural Revolution in the campaign against selfishness. "If Dr. Bethune, a foreigner, could give his life for the Chinese people, the least our family can do is to give the secret prescription it has preserved for so long for the use of everyone," one old man said. Practically all the herbs used in traditional medicine come from the hills and mountains around. In the acupuncture department, we saw a woman in her thirties getting treatment for deafness, the hospital having had considerable success with such patients during the past few months.

In the cooperative marketing and supply store, we found an array of goods much the same as one would see in a big city. Transistor radios, sewing machines, bicycles, all seemed to be popular. There are 2,380 bicycles and over 1,500 sewing machines in the commune already.

Shentien Brigade

We went over the hills to another basin where the land was farmed by Shentien Brigade. In a commune noted for its health work, this one is considered the best. As we came up to its housing area we saw a brand new Kwangchow-made tractor and waggon attachment standing outside, the small boys getting a great kick out of being allowed to sit in the seat and grip the steering wheel. The machine was all red and gold, and obviously everyone was proud of it. It had cost 20,000 yuan and was a recent purchase.

We went through a number of homes, pleased with the neatness and cleanliness of everything. The passages between rows of houses, so often full with tools and whatnot, were quite clear of clutter and were swept, and indeed scrubbed. Soon the brigade will institute the cooperative health service which has already been started by Lunhsia Brigade of the commune, where the total cost of medicines and medical help is taken care of from the brigade's welfare fund which members have raised to meet the need. In this way, it is to the best interest of everyone that there be as little sickness as possible, and all lend an ever more ready ear to public health proposals.

Here in Shentien Brigade lives a member who was a real go-ahead, individualist type. When Liu Shao-chi advocated an extension of private plots and reclaiming waste land for personal use, he planted many clumps of bamboo up on the hillside. From these, he calculated, he would be able to make a total of 640 yuan a year, which would be a nice help to his family. Having so much at stake then, he did not like talking about cutting down the enlarged private plots and passing reclaimed waste land to the brigade for the use of all, until at one meeting an old member got up and asked him how long his mother had lived after he was born. He replied that she was killed by the Japanese army just three days after he had come into the world. "And who fed you then?" the old member asked relentlessly. "Were you not passed around from mother to mother, all giving you milk so that you lived and thus were able to come through the hard times and be with us here today? Do you not owe everything to the collective strength of your fellows? Why then do you object to sharing all with them now?" The go-getter member dropped his face down to his knees, unable to face the people, just whispering, "I was wrong. Please, everyone pardon me! The bamboos belong to the brigade!"

There are many such stories of how deepening political understanding has affected people's lives in the brigades of this commune. Socialist morality has been raised, the determination to struggle along together deepened. A 76-year-old man in Nanhsing Brigade was pressed to stop working, but he said, "Chairman Mao keeps on working, why can't I? To work is to live!" And so he kept out on the highways and byways all day collecting animal manure for compost heaps in all weathers, always with a smile for the children around, and still getting a lot of fun out of life.

Brigade Primary School

It was getting on in the afternoon when we crossed a stream where the members were building a new arched stone bridge, and went up the hill to the brigade primary school. The pupils had gone home for their afternoon meal, after which they would go out to do practical work, but the 12 teachers were all around. So we went into an empty classroom with them and talked about the school and their ideas on education for life. They were equally divided between men and women. Of the six women, three were graduate students of the normal school in Kwangchow who had come to Tsunghua with the rebel group which preceded the present Revolutionary Committee there. Six of the teachers were local people. The school had an eight-year course, from primary up to and including the first year of middle school. There are 378 pupils, 165 boys and 213 girls. There were no halts at all during the three years of the Cultural Revolution. Now that the brigade has taken over the school, it appoints one of its Revolutionary Committee members to sit in with the teachers and supervise educational policy, and it was this representative who opened up the discussion. In the first place, he pointed out, a school must know what it is educating for. In the immediate post-Liberation period, most if not all the teachers had been educated under the old system. Many were children of landlords, for very few others could afford to put their children through teacher's training colleges. They did not want to educate for farming which they looked down on, but rather to prepare the cleverer students who would go on to upper schools in the cities. Now, after 20 years of Liberation, he said, we do not need to rely on the leftovers from the old days who refuse to advance with us. In our brigade we want our children to grow up as farm commune revolutionaries, knowing what that entails. We want them to be students of Chairman Mao. We want practice to run together with theory. Some of the leaders of the last stage propagated the line of Liu Shao-chi, a line based on material incentives for the individual. We want our youngsters to grow up thinking of their collective before themselves.

The headmaster discussed the subjects taught. General knowledge in science and agriculture was an important one. Old peasants, for instance, were brought in to teach how to distinguish between rice seedlings and those of a grass weed that to the unpractised eye looks exactly the same and which, if left, feeds greedily on fertiliser and then produces nothing but trouble later. Farmers after a lifetime of experience have much to teach, so that both students and teachers have learnt much from them. Expert local animal husbandmen come in to give classes on the way to care for water buffaloes, pigs and other animals. The teaching staff helps in making up lesson sheets from such lectures. The culture of lichee and sour plum trees is also a very important subject with many technical aspects, meaning much for the revenue to come in from the once unproductive hillsides. Bookkeeping and elementary accounting are taught, and the brigade health staff is invited to give health lessons. Classes start at 7:30 in the morning. At ten the children go home for the first meal of the day, and then come back for classes that go on until two, there being six classes a day for five days of the week. After their afternoon meal they take part in various tasks around the brigade until evening, when they do their preparatory work for the next day.

During rush periods in the brigade, both teachers and children halt classes for a few days, and all buckle down to help the brigade members with transplanting rice, the harvest, or whatever the urgency is.

On Teachers' Attitudes

One of the young women teachers who had come from Kwangchow spoke up for her group. She and her companions had thought they understood the revolution very well until they came and actually worked with brigade children and brigade folk in Kwantsun Commune. Now they are beginning to feel humble in front of those they have come to teach and learn from. Quite freely they discussed how difficult it had been for them at first to acclimatise themselves to local conditions. To go barefoot when that was the best way, to roll pants high and get into the mud as necessary. They were full of admiration for the way their pupils faced life and really tried hard to learn. Their ability and their courage. How lovable and how truly loyal to the teachings of Chairman Mao the people are. Then too, how patient, hard working and steady the peasants are in finding ways to counter difficulties. Realising all this, they had one great regret. It was that they were unable to do more to help. One spoke of how difficult it had been for them at first to rise over old city-bred ideas that to go to the countryside and work with the people was a step down, and how difficult it had been to change their preconceived notions of what education should be for. How in the beginning also they missed the comforts of the city and its crowds, its excitement, its seeming promise to the individual, but how now in these quiet surroundings, with their thinking undergoing change they were learning more than they had thought possible. She herself was named Hu Chao-ping, and her father is a worker in Kwangchow. She and her group had once envisaged themselves as becoming science teachers in a big city school. Now they find themselves amongst the mass of the people and are learning from them things they have never known in their past city environment.

Teachers spend three half days out working with the brigade, the headmaster explained, one half day in political study, and one half day discussing experience together.

From Theory to Practice

When we left the school, we went down to the bridge which was being built. The upper class pupils of the school were carrying sand for the mortar. All were swinging together in great style, really showing what the people militant could do. We stood and watched them for a while, and then as we left they all came to the top of a bank and waved us farewell. With the light of the afternoon sun behind them they looked as gallant a bunch of youngsters as one would wish to meet.

Kwangtung in Spring

Only 86 kilometres to Kwangchow, and a good road. A warm spring day when we left mid-Kwangtung. Through the trees surrounding a big fish pond we saw the golden bodies of half a dozen school boys, having the first swim of the season.   They were pulling tree branches down to the water and climbing up on them, some falling back into the pool and laughing, careless of how beautiful and free they looked with the sun shining through a tall eucalyptus in flower, and down on them.   No tabus to be bothered with here.   Just drop the baggy pants, toss off the short coat and dive in!

Further down the road a barber and his apprentice were out on bicycles to give barbering to any peasant they met who looked as though he might like such.   Of course, there are hairdressers in the villages and towns, but at times these take to their bicycles and do a round of country roads and fields, looking for people to serve.   The customer probably has no money in his pocket but never mind.   He can give what he likes or nothing at all.   In this case, the barber stood by watching while the apprentice did a very competent shaving job after the haircut.   The peasant's big load and carrying pole lay beside the folding stool the barber had brought and set up under a big banyan tree.   Country barbers now often do this one or two mornings a week, solving a problem for many a fellow with little time to spend in a barber's shop, and the barbers themselves gaining a new touch with the countryside.

Direct Rice Sowing

The spring of 1969 had been marked with many cold drafts coming down from the snowy north, so that in consequence seed beds for rice seedlings were set up a little later than usual.   Communes, however, have surmounted this problem by direct sowing of some of their seed in the paddy. We passed many fields that had been planted that way, the seedlings standing high and healthy.   In occasional places where seed had not grown, there would be a few transplants, but the overall appearance of the fields was good.   This method was tried out first in experimental plots, then in commune fields, and now this year is being done on a much bigger scale.   The method has many good points, and also maybe some negative ones, one of which is that it perhaps is not so easy to discover weeds as it is with transplanting, and by the time they have grown big enough to be spotted they have already consumed a good deal of fertiliser. The saving in labor during the busy season, however, is very considerable, and yields are reported as comparing favorably with those of transplanted fields.

The evening in Canton was an exciting one.   At 9 p.m. the city rose to a crescendo of sound, with gongs, drums, crackers, loudspeakers all going together.   The Ninth Congress of the Communist Party was opening in Peking, to make new decisions after the three years of the Cultural Revolution and its successes.   At 3 a.m. the next morning I awoke, and there were still sounds of celebrations coming into the room from the streets outside.

Tungfanghung Commune

North of Kwangchow city is the county of Panyu. After Liberation it was brought under the city administration. Near its northeastern boundary lies Tungfanghung Commune, one of 25 brigades, 60,000 mou (10,000 acres) of flat paddy field, with a population of 60,000 people. It was pleasant driving out there one early morning, even though it had been raining steadily for the past 24 hours, and it looked as though more was coming. An old stone bridge cast its reflection in the waters of paddy fields, and behind it was a low ridge of pines silhouetted through the mist.

As with many communes along the Luchi river, there were many bitter memories of the old society in Tungfanghung Commune. Alternating flood and drought, landlordism, Kuomintang soldiery, Japanese invaders. No wonder many of the people who once lived in this area went off overseas to try and find a living there. In that bitter past the only way peasants had of irrigating in drought periods was to carry out water in tubs by cart. No government bothered about river conservancy. A five months' drought such as the locality experienced in recent years would have then meant starvation and death for many. As it was, the new irrigation schemes took that drought in their stride, and good crops were harvested. Now it can be said that each year is better than the one before it. Dyke building, pumping stations, electrification, have helped to guarantee 50 jin of rice per person per month, 600 jin a year. There are over 10,000 bicycles and more than 5,500 sewing machines throughout the brigades, and all brigades have set up a scheme of cooperative medicine. In this, people pay 30 fen a month into the health fund and, except for a five-fen registration fee, have all medicines, treatment and attention free. We went to the commune hospital to talk about the health work of the whole county, finding a quite modern hospital set up in simple buildings, complete with X-ray section, operating room for minor operations, maternity wards, dental department, and all the rest. Included in the staff of 33 were both Western and traditional medicine doctors. We watched the group of deaf-mutes who had been brought in from the brigades, 23 of them. They had been in hospital for but 16 days, but after acupuncture treatment 12 had started to hear, while 15 could already make sounds near enough to speech for any to recognise that they were saying "Long live Chairman Mao". The 30 good medical cadres sent out to the 25 brigades have already trained 43 "barefoot" doctors from local young people, all of whom can now deal with the common sicknesses. In 21 of the 25 brigades maternity clinics have already been set up, and very soon it is expected the whole field will be covered. None of the brigades are far from the commune centre — nine kilometres being the most distant — so that it is easy to send in serious cases when necessary. The key to the success of the plan seems to be to get good medical cadres in each brigade who will train an increasing number of "barefoot" doctors, who then will be able to cover the whole situation entirely.

The commune operates a machine repair shop and has 11 trucks. Brigades have ten, or even 14 tractors. The usual rice mills and other food-processing mills are operated by motors from the power supply.

There are also street cooperatives in brigades where various consumer goods — knitted products and so on — are made.

The biggest second crop in the brigade is peanuts, the production of which has advanced from around 80 jin a mou 20 years ago to 250-300 jin a mou at present. In the old days, only a limited amount of compost would be added. Now a regular 200 jin a mou is applied as well as various chemical fertilisers, and green manure is plowed in, which is essential for good production in this light, sandy soil on a red lateritic foundation.

We found that one brigade, Hsiashui by name, had planted half of its paddy with the direct method this year. It has experimented in 1968, and had gained 500 jin a mou for one of the two main crops that way, so is satisfied to go ahead with the new system in a bigger way. One man can plant five mou a day by this method, while by transplanting he can do but one mou. With labor shortage always being a problem in the communes, never enough hands for all the work to be done, this is important.

Aikuo Brigade School

We went to see the Aikuo brigade school. This is a famous one for having been taken over by the poor and lower-middle peasant members of the production brigade, a procedure that has proved to be an unqualified success.

We were greeted by all classes marching out of their classrooms and converging across a green on which ten big maple trees towered. They certainly gave an impression of strength and revolution, did those children. Seven hundred of them from first year primary to second year middle school. Carrying banners and pictures of Chairman Mao, they sang as they came, marching into place with great precision. Individually, they were just charming Cantonese farm children. Collectively, the effect of their manoeuvre was stunning. Later we went through each and every one of their classrooms and watched study in progress, all very orderly but full of life.

We sat for a while with the poor and lower-middle peasant representative and were joined by the chairman of the school Revolutionary Committee. The peasant leader explained how it had become necessary to take over the direction of the school. He pointed out that under the past system theory and practice did not come together. Children were not clear what they were being educated for. Usually they had the general idea that they would go and be cadres of some kind or other in Canton or some other big city. The first years of Liberation had got the children into schools, but as that stage went on, more and more children were becoming individualists. For instance, two graduates of the school were sent to production teams to be bookkeepers. They quite soon started to steal team funds. There were many instances of children stealing from orchards or crops. Of older boys bullying little ones. But the teachers kept on with their cut and dried rules. School fees not paid, the child must leave school. No admittances over the age of ten. Worth gauged on examinations passed. There was a lack of discipline, pupils going out to play and not returning. All of these were trends in the general picture which had to be checked. There is no question now that this has been done. Old intellectuals have been helped to gain a new outlook and drop the bourgeois one they had picked up in the city. Relations between students and teachers under the new order quickly changed for the better. If teachers did not come on time, the matter could be brought up in the after-class meeting. Criticism could go both ways.

Little Red Soldiers

The Little Red Soldiers organisation, which now replaces that of the Young Pioneers, feels its responsibilities keenly and tries to meet them. Youngsters help each other in evening study and in turn help their parents. If girls have to look after little brothers and sisters, they can bring them along to school with them. If families are too poor to pay the school fees of two yuan per half-year term, then the charge is remitted. Children are judged on how they apply the theory they have learnt. For instance, Yeh Chih-an is considered to be a good pupil. He went to help a neighbor on one rest day to build a house. When he came home for lunch, his mother complained that the least the neighbor could have done was to give him a meal. He said they had offered but he had refused. His idea was to do something for them, not take anything from them. Later, the same boy heard that a girl had dropped an iron dipper from the end of a bamboo pole. It had fallen into the deepest part of a fish pond. Despite the cold day he stripped and dived in to look for it. The first try was not successful, but he kept on until, after the fifth dive, he brought the lost article back with him.

Another boy thought highly of is Yang Chih-hsing. The Kwangchow suburban bus station asked for some capable Little Red Soldiers to go in and help to line people up so that there would be no pushing to get into buses. Yang went. He was quite successful, and when a peasant came late, sick and in need of an operation in a city hospital, Yang in a few words got all the people to see the point and had the sick man put on the bus first, though he had come last. He worked all day, and only in the evening did the staff realise that he had not eaten all day. The bus drivers were so moved that they saw to it that he had a conveyance to get him the 16 kilometres home in the evening, which the boy had meant to walk. If "serve the people" is to be more than a slogan, this is what it entails in the lives of growing children. An essential part of their character building.

In the 25 brigade schools now there are over 9,000 children. Not all these schools have middle-school classes yet, and so send their middle-school students to the city-run middle school which is situated in the commune area.

Chienfeng Brigade

We left Aikuo Brigade and went across country to Chienfeng Brigade which has its headquarters at Panghu village, a place I was familiar with, having visited it twice before, to see the locality from which quite a few Chinese in New Zealand came from. As we drove in, great activity greeted us. A big stone bridge was being built across the Luchi river, 210 metres long and able to take heavy traffic. It was started in October 1968 and will be completed before this June (1969). There has been no engineer and but one technician employed. Eighty percent of the materials were paid for out of the brigade's welfare fund. They cost 100,000 yuan. With the cost of wages in workpoints granted the brigade builders, the total cost will be around 350,000 yuan. The commune and the state both helped out with this. The brigade is one of 2,500 people, with a labor force of 1,050. As there is no stone locally, members transported it on the river by boats. 380 tons of cement have been used. It is a nine-arch bridge built in the ancient Chaochow style, that has been so well adapted in Kwangtung.

Chiayen Rolling and Plating Works

It was 1969 and we were in Kwangchow city, with a spring rain pouring down in torrents. A good day for looking at a factory, we decided, so set out to make a call at the Chiayen Rolling and Plating Works, meeting a representative of the Revolutionary Committee, once Party secretary of the plant in the old organisation. He explained how the plant was set up in the Leap Forward of 1958 by combining a number of small enterprises, that now it had 1,597 workers, one of whom, Liu Chun-yi, who came two and a half years ago to the factory after service in the PLA, has been elected a member of the presidium of the Ninth Party Congress.

As we sat in the office discussing past and present in the factory, a fierce fusillade of crackers burst out, so that we had to be silent for a while. They were for the opening of the ceremony and entertainment that was being staged in the factory meeting hall to mark the opening of the Party Congress. Present were worker representatives, the pupils of the middle school supervised by the factory, and the factory's concert and propaganda team. There was no stoppage of production however, and all essential sections needed to keep work going were swinging along as usual.

Of the four previous leaders of the works, three have stood up and been accepted by the workers. Only one, an obstinate individualist who did not want to change, has been dispensed with. Of the 11 section leaders, four have been replaced as being old-time capitalist-roaders not wanting to keep up with the times. All other cadres in the works have come through. Some have made mistakes and been criticised, but have accepted this and come back to the task in hand.

One of the greatest changes made over the past two years is related to technical improvement. The factory engineer in charge before the setting up of the Revolutionary Committee said it was quite impossible for workers to undertake a technical change that entailed the replacement of a whole battery of direct-current generators by a single, compact, modern set of electrical equipment. The workers, however, set to and carried the project through with complete success. In addition, they have streamlined much of the production process and have brought new machines into use. The plant is proud that monthly production has risen from 40 tons in August 1968 to 210 tons in March 1969, with the cost going down as a result of technical improvement.

Some of the products are gold- or silver-plated sheets, some delicate metal foils thin as paper, rising to rolls or plates of brass, copper, or aluminum alloy. The plant was not built for its present capacity but has grown from small beginnings. Starting with old and primitive tools, the workers are fast reaching out to improved methods and high-quality products. Some of the lines are already reaching international standards. In the past stage, the leadership was becoming more and more cut off from the mass of workers as Liu Shao-chi policies for worker and management relations were enforced. Now since the Cultural Revolution, leaders are just referred to as "lao" or "old", a term of friendship — Lao Chang, Lao Li, and so on, and all leaders do practical work in the various shops with the workers for some time. No engineer now scoffs at ideas the workers bring up. All do political study together each and every day. Every time a new directive comes down from Peking it is mimeographed and sent around the whole factory area, this plant becoming a dynamo for activist work in the thinking of Chairman Mao in the district.

The factory has installed an efficient recovery plant for metal fumes, and as a side line makes copper sulphate for the chemical industry.

Kwangchow Middle School No. 12

We went with two of the factory leaders to visit the school to which the plant now gives leadership. The school was previously the Kwangchow Middle School No. 12, a junior middle school which gave a three-year course. Now in line with the shorter time spent in education, primary schools do five years instead of six, middle schools two instead of three, for both junior and senior.

The ex-dean, now chairman of the Revolutionary Committee, told us the story. He was introduced to us as "Lao Kao" by the factory chief representative, just as if he was their fellow worker. A Kwangsi man, he had come to the school in 1965. Briefly he outlined the struggles of the three years of the Cultural Revolution. The 1,600 students of that period have now gone on, 400 to upper middle schools, 40 to the factory and the rest to communes throughout Kwangtung. 2,500 new students have taken their place, coming from the five primary schools in the surrounding industrial district. They are divided into 48 forms, there being a teaching staff of 72, who together with 16 others make up the school cadre group. The factory keeps a propaganda group of 30 in the school, rotating it every three months. There are seven classes a day, with each class lasting 45 minutes. Teachers have from 14 to 16 classes a week. Parents have taken part in the meetings criticising Liu Shao-chi, and also take part in meetings in which the old society and the new are contrasted. Classes are quite large, 50-52 in each.

The PLA Comes In

In March 1967 the PLA came to the school to help to conduct study of the works of Chairman Mao and to criticise the Liu Shao-chi line. Then, on February 1968, the school Revolutionary Committee was set up with school delegates, cadres and PLA men. But the defeated did not accept defeat and, using red flags to try and push down the red flag, brought new problems. This went on until July 1968, when workers from the factory sent in a team which, by October, had helped to expose the trouble-makers and bring in order. Chairman Mao has said that the working class should lead all, but many of the opposition said indignantly, "The workers know so very little! How can they possibly lead a big school like this?"

The workers replied quite simply asking firstly, for whom is the school set up? Then secondly, on whom does the school rely? And thirdly, what kind of youth does it set out to train? Actually, 95 percent of the present student body are from working-class homes. Their future is to be working folk either in industry or else in agriculture. But under the domination of Liu Shao-chi, many thoroughly bourgeois intellectuals had come into the school and could influence some of the youth who had become jealous of others and who had gained inflated ideas. They were not loyal to the working class, and their ideas for the future were different.

Workers Join In

The coming of the workers was welcomed by the great majority of both staff and students. Students then went to work at times in the factory, and workers went with them when they set out to work with communes in the countryside. Truly, the workers brought in a new spirit, breaking down the old teacher-student attitudes wherein the students were liable to believe anything the teachers pontificated. Now teachers and students could quite naturally criticise each other, without hard feelings. The workers also helped a great deal to interest and educate the well-meaning intellectuals and get their cooperation, the intellectuals themselves analysing where they were right, where wrong. When workers started to teach some of the classes and held the attention of the students so well, the old teachers began to realise that a new day had dawned. Some of the students who were lazy and un-cooperative before got a completely new view of lessons. Workers so inured in practice can demonstrate industrial general knowledge dramatically. They know much of class struggle too. In consequence they have been a good, down-to-earth tonic for the school.

The textbooks of the past era have been discarded. New lesson sheets are now prepared for classes, and there is an exchange of freshly prepared material with other schools. School starts at 7:45 a.m. (8 a.m. in winter). Subjects are:

1. Politics, including Mao Tsetung Thought and the analytical method.
2. Chinese language.
3. Mathematics (cutting down on algebra and geometry).
4. General knowledge on industry and agriculture.
5. Revolutionary history.
6. Military and physical drill.
7. Singing.
8. General knowledge in history and geography.

Seventy percent of the time goes in class work, 30 percent in the factory or out on communes. There are no winter or summer holidays, the longest holiday being just a few days for the Spring Festival. Students help to edit teaching material and are also stimulated to help each other. Fees are five yuan a term. The school year has two terms. If the family of the student is unable to provide fees, they are remitted. If the parents are in real need, subsidies of from five to ten yuan a month are paid a student for his keep. For students both of whose parents are working, mid-day meals are provided at the school. Other children go home at lunch-time.

The school expects the students to be proficient in understanding Mao Tsetung Thought, to be activists in all progressive work, to always complete every duty assigned, and to observe school discipline.

Most teaching is in the Chinese common language but, at times, some teachers relapse into Cantonese in order to get a point across. All students can understand the common language, even if they are slow at speaking it.

The school has a clinic with two nurses for attending to minor complaints. Nearby is a suburban hospital which takes care of anything serious.

Before we left, the students put on a performance of songs and dances in their meeting hall. It was very bright and spirited, every item being awarded a prolonged burst of clapping, the youngsters themselves evidently thoroughly enjoying the endeavors of their schoolmates.

The educational system of China today is pioneering out into uncharted seas in which lie great discoveries. It is a brave thing to do, the only thing, if progress is to be made. Many around our world will watch the voyage with sympathetic interest and many, too, will learn from it.

The Kwangchow Truck Building Works

Before we left Kwangchow (Canton), we visited another factory whose workers, in addition to their own political and production work, had sent a team of workers into the big teachers' training college nearby, as well as taking over direction of the Middle School No. 55, one of 2,000 students in the city. It was the Kwangchow Truck Building Works where a start is being made, in addition to its regular line, of building small locomotives for mines, and forest narrow-gauge railways. Workers in this factory go to the middle school in groups which change over after set periods, and 100 students a time come into the factory for a six-week period of learning and practice.

It is good that they come to this particular plant, for it is one with an interesting history. In 1949, it consisted of a group of eight workers who repaired bicycles and pedicabs in the city. After Liberation its equipment of one motor and two old lathes on a total floor space of 60 square metres was enlarged, and more workers were engaged. The old capitalist manager who would sometimes ask workers to do an additional six-hour overtime on top of a 12-hour day, and then give them a present of but two bananas each for the extra time worked, went out into the limbo of the past. New machines were built, some for sugar mills, some, like cranes, for wharves. By the time the Great Leap Forward started in 1958, the work force had grown to 600, and the idea of concentrating on two lines had evolved. These were the small locomotive and the truck. A loan was secured, a big piece of waste land down in the Whampoa district taken, and a start was made in moving the factory into new buildings on the new site. Then, however, came the Liu Shao-chi revisionist line. The Leap Forward was a failure, he said. Factories should be cut back. Industry was growing too fast. This plant had better change back into a general repair works. If we want trucks, we can import them easily enough for the time being, it was said.

Again it was struggle between the two lines. Workers took much interest, for all wanted to make as big a contribution to China's progress as possible, and they were sure they could make trucks, if only given a chance. So they took loans and various machine-building contracts, cutting their cost so they were able to carry on with their plans. By 1964 all had moved to the new site, buildings were adequate, and they could keep up with the demand for their mine and forestry locomotives. In May 1966, they finally started to construct their first truck, a 3.5-ton vehicle for city use in the main. It was finished in late September of that year, a present for National Day on October 1st. During the struggles of 1967 no more work was done on truck making, it being started again in 1968 when eight trial models were made. One "expert" took a look at the product and gave his judgment that maybe it could make it to Canton city and home again. The workers' reply was to drive it all the way to Peking and back — well over 7,000 kilometres.

The Truck Evolves

In 1969 they will make 200 of these trucks. Then, with streamlining and some of the automation in the new shops now being built, they will start to meet some of the needs of Kwangtung for their product, finally going on from there. In the first struggles it has not been easy going. For instance, the production of one truck part, the joint below the steering rod, needed a special machine. The factory gave the problem to the engineers of the local industrial research institute, but these experts could not solve it. Then the workers themselves sat around in discussion and experimentation and finally constructed a machine that does the job perfectly. We walked through the various shops and around the spacious factory compound. The first shops built in 1958-59 are now too small, and the machines will soon be removed to bigger premises. The main task is still the production of the mining and forestry locomotive, but it is easy to see that workers have their eyes set on being able to turn out a good, strong and serviceable truck as their future main contribution to industry and agriculture in their province.

Students and Workers

One was struck too, as one went around, with the patience that workers showed in helping their middle-school charges to learn more, as well as being useful around the place. The students on their part are learning that, to be a worker, is to be an important person in the general scheme of things. There is a new unity amongst those who will be the creators of the next stage in China's revolution. One fact shows clearly: In the new stage we are entering, it will be the drive from the main working force that will carry industry forward to reach new production levels, rather than any "expertise". Workers fired with the determination their study of the works of Mao Tsetung has brought them.

Kwangchow in November 1970

Canton in mid-November 1970 was still warm, very lovely with flowers and green trees. The first day of my visit I spent in going to the art potteries at Shihwan, in the Fushan municipality. The place was an old favorite, visited many times before, but each visit bringing new respect for the quiet, careful hands of the potter and his creative design. The art wares here, especially the flame-glaze pottery, have a world-wide appeal. After admiring the new continuous kilns and the work being turned out, I went on to see an entirely new plant that means much to new industry.

Single-Crystal Silicon Plant

It was a bit of a surprise to young technicians after Liberation when industry started to catch up with modern standards, to find that there were many small things which seemingly just had to be bought from abroad — or were even sometimes unobtainable. For instance, they discovered that for only one kilogram of single-crystal silicon 50,000 yuan had to be paid. The only seller was the USSR which, in 1960, refused to make any more available. In consequence, it became necessary to be self-supporting. At first, one plant succeeded in producing it, and then, in the more industrialised localities, others followed. Chemical as well as mechanical technique is needed for its production, for the process entails silica stone being reduced to a gas, combined with another gas, and so on until the final product comes out of a furnace in the form of a small bar. This bar must then be sliced into thin sheets which are polished and cut up into tiny segments, and treated again. Certainly a good deal of the work is automatic, but then the machines employed, as well as the whole set-up have to be designed and built, and careful operators trained.

New Industry in a Rural Setting

In the countryside of Fushan municipality, not far west of the Pearl river from Kwangchow, one such task was given to a bunch of technicians to start on some time before the Cultural Revolution. They spent most of the allocation first granted them in going over other parts of China, studying existing plants, and trying to find ways and means of getting help. They failed so badly that they were disbanded. In 1969, two cadres and a group of workers were put onto the job of getting the plant set up and operating. They did not have much of a legacy to start with — a disused room in a school and some bench tools was all there was. Two of the group were potters, another a worker from a textile factory. The one who told us most of this story was a 20-year-old lass named Hsu Li-min, who had joined an Army acrobatic troupe in 1963 at the age of 13 and had been seconded to the factory with the first group, who started it in 1969. She was evidently a capable worker, alert and with considerable charm. Clearly she described the process, and then how the various difficulties surrounding its establishment were surmounted. Her old home, she said, was at Haikou, on Hainan Island.

The new group studied the theory of the process and went into practice together and with great determination. Local Fushan machine shops built them their machines. The chemical portion of the plant they made and adapted themselves. Although it does not look as streamlined as would be the case in a big, modern city plant, yet it gives the needed results. The plant now, with its 87 workers, produces all the single-crystal silicon Kwangtung province needs. Another link in the chain of self-sufficiency.

On another day, we went to visit Hsinhua Commune in Huahsien. One of the places we set off to see after being briefed on the present state of the commune was the Hung Hsiu-chuan reservoir (named after a Taiping rebel leader of a century ago), which has done so much to remove the threat of drought in its vicinity. Lying like a jewel set amongst fir or bamboo-covered hills, it preserves ten million cubic metres of water for brigades around. It was built in the period of the Great

Leap Forward, only one month being used instead of the planned three. It is just one of the commune's three reservoirs. In the bad old days, the villages of Huashan county suffered alternately from flood and drought. The government stole from the people but did not serve them, so that the only way out for many of the young Huashan men was to emigrate and struggle for a living in other lands. Today, the people of Hsinhua Commune have built a 40-kilometre irrigation canal running in from the Luchi river. Mass work over the off seasons has produced these wonders, and though the soil is light and sandy, very considerable crop rises have been effected. Thirty-three motor or electrically operated pumping stations assist irrigation or get rid of excess water according to need.

There were 80,000 mou of land under cultivation, 70,000 of which can be irrigated. The commune was formed in 1958 from 64 farm co-operatives, 13,500 families in all, now numbering 61,500 people. It has 22 brigades and 322 production teams. The main crop of course, is rice, but with peanuts following on. There are many fish-breeding ponds, and a good quantity of fish is raised in the reservoirs. Pig breeding is strongly promoted, for the light sandy soil especially needs the compost their manure helps to provide. The commune has 2,100 activists in Mao Tsetung Thought who have so helped to raise working spirit that very high yields have resulted. On land which in the early 'fifties did not produce more than 300 jin a mou, 975 jin was gained in 1969, with the 1970 crop certain to exceed 1,000. In the early days of Liberation, what with drought and flood, subsidy grain had to be taken from the state. Now, each year state grain quotas can be filled easily and an excess sold.

The commune offices were big and roomy, with shady courtyards which had stone seats set out under trees, convenient for small meetings. We heard much about the struggles that had taken place on the land, the experiments with broadcast sowing instead of transplanting rice; the beginnings of mechanisation; how the total of one pig per person had been reached, and then how small commune industries had been set up, and what a contribution to better livelihood these were making.

The Fertiliser Plant

Set well out in the countryside was the fertiliser factory which the county had set up. It made synthetic ammonia and ammonium carbonate, both used as adjuncts to compost fertiliser. It had a production of 1,200 tons in 1967, but this 1970 and up to the time of our visit it had already made 2,500 tons. The ammonium carbonate fertiliser is used on the land at the rate of 20 jin a mou.

The plant was first started by 13 workers sent in from a fertiliser factory near Canton (Kwangchow) city. These gradually took in poor and middle peasants, so that the working force rose to 283 who now take an active part in developing the work.

Other Commune Industry

The commune has a big brick-making plant, which uses waste coal that still has heating value discarded by the fertiliser factory.   Many of the workers here are young students from Kwangchow schools who have come to join the commune.   They laugh and quip as they wheel the brick forms into the continuous kiln, and unload those already fired.   Most of them were girls.

From the brick kilns we went on to see the lime-burning ones which were on quite a big scale.   The stone was gained from a deep open-cut mine, and went directly to the top of the kilns by wire-rope elevators, or else to the ground surface for wheeling away to a small cement factory nearby.   The exhaust gases from the kiln went on to an adjacent plant to help make calcium carbonate for the Kwangchow rubber industry. Coal for the lime-burning was dug from pits in the hill beside, for coal in Huahsien is frequent and in seams near the surface.   The scene around the kilns was a lively one, and the face of the leading worker who showed us around lit up as he described the way problems had been solved, and his plans to make the whole operation run still more efficiently.

Grain Harvesting

We stood for some time watching the last crop of rice being harvested. Foot-treadle threshers are used here.   Mechanisation was being tried out for harvesting but was still in the experimental stage, the production teams with sickles moving so rapidly still doing the major portion of the work. No sooner was one field harvested than big or small tractors came in for plowing to get it ready for winter wheat sowing.   In Kwangtung the land never rests.

Commune Hospital

Folk here are proud of their commune hospital. Not only for its daily hospital out- and in-patient work, but also because it is a centre for training the 112 "barefoot" doctors who work in the production teams as well as carrying through clinical treatments and preventive measures for their group.   The older doctors of the hospital also train the younger ones there and carry on research in traditional herb medicines.   The surgical work done is excellent. Dr. Ma Hai-teh of Peking who was with our party looked with interest at the hand of a commune member which had four completely amputated fingers rejoined, and was much impressed. We saw too, pictures of difficult cases which had been successfully dealt with — a clubfoot made right, a child crippled by polio able to get along almost naturally, and so on.   Acupuncture has been developed, and herbals are compounded and made up into easily taken preparations, many of which have proved to be highly effective.   The hospital buildings are simple, but with a good surgery and a small portable X-ray machine.

We would have liked to stay longer and see much more of Hsinhua Commune, but the early dusk of a November evening caught up with us, so regretfully we had to turn and take the highway back to Kwang-chow.

Shachao Commune, Shunteh

It was a perfect late autumn day in 1970 when we went over the Pearl river bridge and out across the delta with its fish ponds, mulberries and sugar cane, to Shachao Commune in Shunteh county. We drew up on the outskirts of a big village called Shuiteng, where the commune offices were situated in the front part of a modern meeting hall. I was rather surprised to find it equipped with up-to-date theatre seating, all perfectly maintained. As usual, we sat and had tea while members of the Revolutionary Committee told us something about their commune. It was one of 22 brigades, 14,600 families, 62,000 people in all. It had 32,000 mou of fish ponds, 16,000 mou of sugar cane, 12,000 mou in mulberries, 4,000 in rice and 4,000 in vegetables.

In the other days here, folk had suffered a great deal through recurring floods and drought so that, as in Huahsien, many were forced to emigrate. Now, during the past four years especially, a great deal of land levelling has been done, as well as dyke-building and irrigation in the communes of both Shunteh and Nanhai counties which adjoin. 160,000 mou of land has been recast into flat, rectangular fields, while some 10,000 mou of wasteland has been reclaimed and protected by a newly built dyke. Twelve pumping stations have been set up in the commune, and 190 kilometres of power lines have been erected. In addition to the electrically powered pumping stations, there are now motorised mobile ones, 539 of which are in use. Before the Cultural Revolution, there were 44 small factories being operated by the commune. Now there are 55. There has been a considerable struggle against revisionist ideas of personal incentive, as against those needed for socialist construction. For instance, some members wanted to plant the yam-like root called here "sa ke" — "di kwa" in some other parts of China — which would have brought in 200 yuan more a mou than the state-planned sugar cane did. In consequence, there came an opportunity for more education to be done on the necessity of building a socialist state. The upshot has been that in this 1970, the commune not only filled the state quota for cane but also planted an additional 1,000 mou in it.

Last spring, over 7,000 mou of mulberries were hit by an insect pest. The commune mobilised 5,000 people to fight it and succeeded in eradicating it in time, so that a rich mulberry harvest for the year was obtained. They got 250 jin of dry silk cocoons per mou this season, a 40 percent rise over the pre-Cultural Revolution total. Fish ponds yielded 350 jin per mou of pond, a rise of 22 percent over 1966. Sugar cane at 13,000 jin is 15 percent up, while rice at 1,200 jin a mou is 46 percent over the harvest of 1966.

The commune operates its own senior middle school, as well as 23 primary and junior middle schools combined. 54 youngsters have been sent out from the commune to specialised technical schools, and five to university. In buildings easy to convert to schools there is the legacy of old ancestral temples come over from the past. Spacious and especially well built in these regions, the bigger ones with their many courtyards are especially suited for conversion. The commune has 10,300 school pupils in all. From education we went on to talk about health. The commune has one general hospital and eight smaller ones, together with 22 clinics. Every production team has its "barefoot" doctors.

In production, commune brigades are not all of equal level, the narrator said. Shaotsung Brigade got 17,000 jin a mou of sugar cane. Others got less than the average of 13,000 jin. Food allowance per month per person in the commune runs to 26 jin of polished rice, as well as an allowance of three jin of fish. 30,000 jin of fish are brought in daily, half of which goes in tubs to Hongkong and the rest, above local needs, to Kwangchow city. Fish breeding is now more scientific than it was before, and considerable success has been achieved with imported Vietnamese carp, though the successful rearing of these does present difficulties in cold winter weather.

One can imagine what a nostalgia overseas Chinese who have had to emigrate from here must feel for their home place. On a fine autumn day Shuiteng is certainly beautiful, with light filtering through the big trees, children tumbling around in laughter, and the shining waters of the canal below. It has not always been so quiet and peaceful, though. Near the commune offices there rises a plinth of white stone on the spot where a Japanese imperial army post was. Nearby were buried some 200 village people slaughtered here. Another 1,000 of those killed lie under high ground over the canal, now planted in mulberries. Before the Japanese invasion there were 30,000 people in Shuiteng. In 1945, when a count was made, it was found that their numbers had been reduced to 8,000. Foreign imperialist aggression is not a pretty thing. Always the people pay.

A new method is being tried out in cultivating mulberry saplings in this commune. The old one, still being used in part, entails the grafting of a root onto a small piece of branch. The process now being tried out gives a tree with high yield, with no grafting needed at all.

We walked out over irrigation canals and flood protection works to watch the harvesting of fish from one pond. It was an exciting spectacle to see the net being drawn in and big fish sometimes succeeding in jumping over it or into the boats. Amongst the catch was a big killer fish with a long, savage snout, which lived on the small fry. The half dozen commune members employed on the task were very expert, and the fish went into the waiting tubs with great speed when the nets were finally drawn in.

From the fishing harvest, we went across country to see the silk filature, a medium-sized one in which 940 people work, 800 of them being women. There was a new-style central boiling plant from which the cocoons came back and then were processed in tepid water, not needing a worker to stir and manipulate with chopsticks before starting the reeling process. One worker, too, can now attend to 20 spinning reels instead of just the one of olden time. In the workrooms there is none of the heavy fatigue factor that used to come from the steam and heat of the old-time filature. We were taken around by a very competent worker member of the Revolutionary Committee. She was the young woman worker Liang Jui-lien, who said that there were 21 members in the Revolutionary Committee, 11 being old cadres and a militia representative, and ten being workers. Production is now three times as great as it was in 1966, and present improvements and extensions are expected to improve the growth process. Having occasion to use the lavatory, I was pleased to see one of the cleanest I have seen in any factory. But all sections of the plant were in like fashion. The hanks of finished silk so neatly packed and labelled, the children of the filature kindergarten so well nourished and full of life, with a work force that went at its tasks with immense spirit. The waste silk cocoons, those not suited for spinning, are sent off to a Shuiteng brigade workshop where they are processed for later use in the lining of winter clothing.

The average wage of filature workers is 45 yuan a month. Most are from families in the vicinity. We visited one of these families, that of the poor peasant Tu Yu-wei. His wife works in the filature and is a primary school graduate, now 28 years old. Tu himself is 31. Brought up in the thatched cottage of a very poor peasant, he is pleased with the solidly built brick-and-tile house he owns now. Family income is sufficient for needs. As a brigade member he raises six pigs a year, mainly to help the brigade with its composting material. His youngest daughter is five and is in the kindergarten, while her elder sister is already in primary school. As poised and confident a little family as one would wish to see. Tu himself, in his discussion with us, showed that he had a very good grip of the whole situation as it affected his commune and brigade, and that he had a clear understanding of Mao Tsetung Thought, and the dangers of the revisionist line.

Agricultural Implements Factory

Early one morning, with purple flowers lighting up the wayside trees and the big fronds of banana palms glistening in the morning sun, we went out of Canton (Kwangchow) city past Sanyuanli and came to a factory set up on a hill. Not a big factory, just one which had repaired agricultural implements and was now turning out the hand tractors that are becoming so common throughout China. It did not get permission to make the tractors until 1968, and before that, due to the Liu Shao-chi line, was not allowed to increase its workers. But when it did get permission, full steam ahead was the immediate answer. The engines for the tractor come from an engine factory, but all the 500 parts of the carriage have to be turned out and assembled with what equipment the plant has been able to make itself or adapt from its existing machine tools. Half handwork, half mechanical as its production is, the finished tractor is very convincing. The demonstration of the things the tractor could do, which one of the workers sitting on the implement seat replacing

KWANGTUNG

Cantonese farm boys are expert boatmen, Polo county, East River.

Gate of the old Peasants Institute, Kwangchow (Canton).

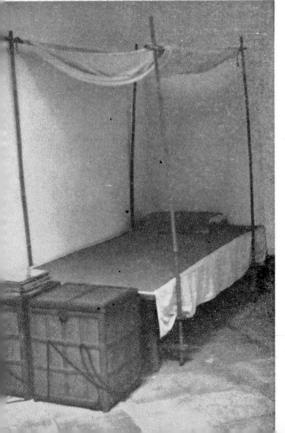

Chairman Mao's bedroom in the Kwangchow Peasants Institute.

School pupils from Aikuo Brigade, Kwangtung.

New bike in a farmer's family, Kwangtung.

Lichee trees with pines beyond, Tsunghua, Kwangtung.

Spraying young mulberries, Shunteh county, Kwangtung.

Women of Polo county move compost fertiliser onto fields.

From school desk to tractor factory, Kwangchow.

Tractors made in a Kwangchow factory.

Older pupils in Kwantsun Commune help build a bridge.

Part of the stone bridge built by Chien-feng Brigade, Tungfanghung Commune.

Commune headquarters, Kwangtung.

Enping city, Kwangtung.

the handles on the present model gave, showed that here was a machine most commune brigades would welcome.   With its three small wheels it can get around corners easily and is especially good for small areas. The plan is to make 2,000 in 1971, working up to 6,000 a year in the next few years.

Amongst the new workers in the factory are 110 students from Canton upper schools, and 109 women from homes around.   The students are already becoming workers, handling their machines efficiently.   Three hundred new machine tools, from milling machines onwards, were turned out by the workers in the 1969-70 period.   Actually, it took a good deal of time and thought to evolve the more difficult ones, such as the set-up for tempering to harden the cogs of gear wheels, while leaving the material in the centre of the wheel unchanged.   But as Peng Wu, the young worker member of the factory Revolutionary Committee who went around with us said, you can do most things when you really get down and try. There are nine members on his committee and all are full of optimism for the success of the project now in hand.   A city factory naturally has certain drawbacks when it comes to producing things for farmers.   Not so easy to teach handling technique, or for folk to bring in the implement when it needs repairs.   The problem of close liaison, however, has been excellently met here.   Tractor users and potential tractor users are brought into the factory school for a few months' training, during which they not only learn about the theory of tractors, but also take part in their assembling, gaining a clear knowledge of every essential part.   We watched such a class for a while.   The teacher was explaining the electrical system with actual parts and diagrams.   The trainees were completely absorbed, peasants evidently right out to gain as thorough a knowledge as they could before going back to use the tractor in their communes.   Then too, the factory sends its workers out to the communes that have already bought tractors, to help with operating and to get practical criticism on the machine itself so that improvement can be made in later models.

In wages, workers here average 40 yuan a month.   Living quarters on the site are provided for those who need them, but most of the workers live with their families round about and come in on their bicycles each day.   It is a hopeful factory, with a clear sense of mission in its efforts to bring in farm mechanisation, which is a vanguard task in the Chinese revolution.

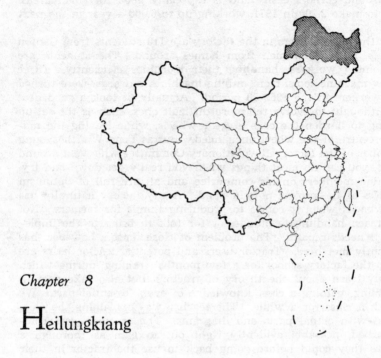

Chapter 8

Heilungkiang

This chapter takes us up to the frontier province of Heilungkiang in China's Northeast, the scene of much struggle in the first stages of the Cultural Revolution. Here the followers of the Mao Tsetung line won power very early, despite all that could be done against them.

Heilungkiang province with a population of around 21 million, is one of the areas of China where much land development can still, and is being, done. The spread of large-scale mechanised state farms has brought vast areas into production since Liberation. Mineral, timber and water resources are good. The main rivers are the boundary ones of the Heilung (Amur in Russian), Wusuli (Ussuri in Russian), Sungari and Nonni. Crops grown include wheat, sorghum, millet, corn, soya beans and sugar beet. The majority of the people are Han, with Manchu, Mongolian, Olunchun, Owenke and Hoche minority nationalities.

At the time of the visits described here, the provocations on the Chinese frontier by Soviet troops had not reached the proportions they did later, following the Chenpaotao incident. Yet it was a period when China had to carry through her Cultural Revolution and defend her borders at the same time, carry out her afforestation and keep her factories and farms running. Some idea of how she was able to do this may be caught from the following pages.

Harbin in the Late Autumn of 1967

A mid-September morning. Peking was waking to a magnificent autumn day, as we went out to the airport and were soon soaring over mountains, watching sunrise and mist effects below. At the fine new Shenyang airport we halted a while and were entertained by a Cultural Revolution song and dance group. Then, after viewing Changchun from the air, we landed at Harbin, capital of Heilungkiang province. It seemed to be as warm as in Peking. In Peking, though, the house interiors were still warmer than outside. Here in Harbin, in the high, beautiful rooms of the guest house, it was a good deal cooler. Some old landmarks had gone since I was here last. The colored spires and domes of the Russian church were among these. They probably meant a lot to the emigre White Russians, but to the ordinary Chinese they were just another symbol of Russian domination in a past that had seen vast Chinese territories seized since the "opening of Siberia". And with Russian imperialism still further encroaching southward from the time of the Boxer Rebellion onwards, and then fighting against Japanese imperialism in 1905, the Chinese people paid dearly and suffered terribly. Relics of that past, no matter how much they were liked by the Soviet experts who came after Liberation, are now too much out of tune with the feelings of a politically awakened people to be allowed so prominent a place. The northeastern provinces have been the playground of imperialism for just too long.

We went out along the banks of the Sungari river. In Peking our friends had warned us to wear warm clothing and to take padded garments along with us as well. But the banks of the river were still lined with youth sunbathing or going in to swim. Cooler than Peking, certainly, but still pleasantly warm. The old Russian summer houses on the island in the river here have been changed into workers' sanitaria. We went through parts of the city where in the old days most of the people one saw, especially in the evenings, were Russian. Now out of a city of 2,100,000, Russians number less than 1,000. They are all old pensioners. Harbin was once the administrative centre of the Russian-held railway, and its population of 800,000 at the time of Liberation consisted largely of Russians who have since gone elsewhere in the world, many back to the USSR. The Japanese were moved out in 1945 after the end of the War of Resistance. Then, as industry grew, Chinese workers came in from many parts of the country. There have been many struggles in Harbin during the period of the Cultural Revolution, but none that have halted industrial production. Checked it a bit at times, but never stopped it.

I asked about the 1967 harvest in Heilungkiang province. Everyone agreed that it had reached an all-time high. We passed through the educational quarter with its 14 universities, finding that the young trees had grown a great deal since I was last here. There is terrific fertility in this rich, black soil, and in the warm months it seems to want to show what it can do after being held back by snow through the long winter.

Like other big cities of China, Harbin has been thoroughly plastered with the slogans and big character posters of the Cultural Revolution, and meetings with plenty of red banners, drums and cymbals could be seen going on in many places all through September. It is evident that the people take the whole thing with great seriousness. The way forward must be found and there is no doubt that, through struggle it will be.

The Harbin Precision Instruments Factory

In 1957, I had visited the Harbin Precision Instruments Factory. It was then a factory which had been under the direction of some 40 Soviet experts who, having completed their task, were going back home. Today I found it to be much expanded, with a new, three-floored building taking a good deal of the more intricate precision work. There are seven shops with 4,300 workers in all. The factory is well pleased with the strides it has been able to make with precision instruments, the production of which took so long to evolve in the industrially advanced countries. Its workers smile when they recall the visit of a Soviet engineer around 1960 who told them not to try to make some of the instruments planned. "Why, we can't even do that in the Soviet Union yet. When we do, then we will sell you the equipment to make these things," he said. But problems when put to a well-picked group which works in unison have a way of fading out and becoming no problem at all. Looking at some of the different models produced in the evolution of intricate instruments, one realised this well. Production since 1957 has doubled.

There has been no shutdown since the Cultural Revolution started, though the factory has sent some workers to take part in outside political activities in an organised way. The old Party secretary did not want workers to study Mao Tsetung Thought. Said they did not need it. He was in favor of the Soviet "one leader" style of factory command, with a top order coming down to be obeyed everywhere unquestioningly. The new group came into office after a take-over in January 1967 and has been able to ensure that production keeps up, while going ahead promoting the revolution. The factory exports instruments now to some 15 countries, as well as supplying China's needs. Products of the time before and up to the end of 1957 look big and awkward compared with the lightweight, streamlined instruments of today, which are also much more efficient. In all, some 200 different kinds are turned out now, and a working force has evolved that can go on to meeting the more difficult demands of the future. Once given a start, and understanding the problem, the Chinese worker can advance with incredible rapidity, a fact clearly demonstrated in the progress made in these works. The Soviet machines that were first installed look clumsy beside the fine new ones that have come up from Shanghai, which do their task so much more precisely. There is still much to be learnt, but the important thing for the moment, all agree, is to raise the level of the political thinking of all workers. Only then can new strides be taken. Politics commands the machine. There is now no doubt in anyone's mind about that.

Political Groupings in 1967 Harbin

The overall political situation during the period of the Cultural Revolution in the province of Heilungkiang may be summarised as follows. In the first stage, from the beginning of June to August 8th, 1966, people studied the speeches and documents coming from Peking and wrote big character posters. From August 8th, 1966 (the day the "Sixteen Points" was issued) to the end of January 1967, groups formed. Some conservatives thought they could halt revolutionary change and, with their remaining power, they tried economism, fitting out workers in new clothes, sending them to Peking with plenty of expense money, and so on. Many workers were fooled and it took time to get them to understand just where the conservative line was leading them. When they understood, they came over, so that by the 31st of January 1967, the Revolutionary Committee based on a three-way alliance between old cadres, young rebels and the PLA could be set up. The radio, police, press, etc. were taken over, and five main committees with a general office were organised to administer the affairs of the province. Some of the old leading cadres came in and gave immense help. In the fourth stage, Revolutionary Committees were set up in the six prefectures and 62 of the 68 counties.

Study of Chairman Mao's works was carried into the villages with such zest that over 70 percent of the people took part. A new principle was enunciated for cadres. They would do office work a third of their time, inspect outside work for another third, and then go down to participate in actual physical labor with the people the last third. There is a new determination to halt the rise of any new bureaucracy that will hold back the creative urge of the people. A new determination to really serve the people in every possible way.

Naturally there have been difficulties. Conservative elements reorganised in a new way to become the ultra-left, which tried its best to halt work and lead the workers away from the new Revolutionary Committee. But as it did not have the support of the people it was doomed to failure.

In production, most industrial plants have kept up with their plan. In agriculture, the overall provincial wheat harvest of 1967 was 20 percent above that of the good year of 1966. Autumn harvests now being brought in promise to be at the same level. The 21 million people of the province have had more prosperity in these years than they have ever enjoyed in the past.

Foreign Imperialism

There is the nuisance of Soviet-provoked incidents on the Heilungkiang river which the Russians call the Amur — Russian launches running down

Chinese fishing boats and sinking them, and so on, but folk know that, though Soviet officials are against them, there are a lot of good people in the USSR on their side. They know too, that the Russians who by trickery ripped away yet another chunk of territory from China in 1865 have really never been able to develop it, and now are calling in Japanese monopoly to help them to do so. The same Japanese who once occupied Harbin and who erected a pagoda to their soldiers killed in the war, a pagoda that has now been converted into the main column of a parachute jumping tower for training young people.

The Harbin Tractor Parts Factory

The Harbin Tractor Parts Factory rose from a merger of four smaller plants which, in turn, had been built up by the combination of many privately owned small machine shops. It now has 1,145 workers, making such parts as tractor generators, assemblies for tractor auxiliary drives and so on. Most of the workers are old experienced hands, well able to carry through creative innovations and produce excellent results. Representatives of the Revolutionary Committee which had taken over met me. Of the 11 in the leading group after the take-over two were old cadres, three militia men, and the rest factory workers. Of the 72 cadres in the factory, only two had been laid off — the manager and the Party secretary. These two had been in collusion, and were really following a capitalist line so boldly that their mistakes showed up clearly from the very first. Their efforts to halt criticism and secure their position exposed them even more, so that the take-over by the rebel group became relatively easy. Since the take-over in January 1967, production has been raised quite considerably. Taking 100 as the figure for June 1966, August 1967 shows 157. The manager had tried hard to stem the tide by economism. Buying expensive winter coats and footwear for workers, raising wages recklessly, and giving free trips to Peking. But when the workers understood why all this was being done, they were angry and indignantly returned what had been put out to buy them over.

As the movement progressed, they spent more time on political study. There are over 40 study groups in the plant. There are also home study groups of family members and friends which they often attend after supper. The feeling that they have a direct responsibility for all that is being done is now much stronger with them, and they realise that to keep abreast they need to study all the time. Through study and that feeling of responsibility study engenders, workers have made many useful changes. To cut perforated disks for tractor generators they do not need to use good steel plate, for instance. They can as well use up the scrap from another factory. Instead of buying a new machine for 20,000 yuan, they can convert an old machine tool costing but 2,000 yuan to do the same job, and do it every bit as well. This they have done.

The old management used 324 workers in the administration. This number has now been cut to 110, with better and less bureaucratic work resulting. Out in the factory yard, I noticed a model plane running on a long wire stretched across the compound. "For our militia men to practise aiming at enemy aircraft," I was told. In the midst of their own change, workers have still to think of changes on the international scene which might well affect them. In one of the shops where some older workers were busy with precision tools, I noticed the windowsills were bright with colorful asters and other flowers, giving the place a cheerful touch. Older workers can make thoughtful use of experience and technique, as has been shown up well in their automation of the casting line in their foundry, which has really been done excellently with improved results and lighter work for all taking part in it.

Children's Railway

Most foreign visitors to Harbin visit the children's railway which has a two-kilometre run between two stations set in a park, one named "Harbin" and the other "Peking". The 14-year-old boy who was my guide was the son of a worker. He gave the general description clearly, as did the girl who operated the motorised locomotive that replaces the little coal-burning steam engine previously used. They certainly looked a bright bunch of youngsters, and it was fun to be with them on a warm autumn afternoon.

Politics in Command

During the time we were in and around Harbin, there seemed to be both daily and nightly mass meetings, attended by delegations from many industrial, educational and similar organisations. Crowds stood around the wall posters in the streets taking intense interest in what had been put there. The whole city seemed to be completely immersed in politics.

The old administration of Harbin had some grandiose ideas — for instance, building a huge railway station like that in Peking. A sports auditorium where all manner of sports could be enjoyed by some city dwellers in winter. These projects, begun but not finished, await completion at a date when other essentials have first been attended to. More stress on such things as tractors for state farms, fertiliser factories, and less on city amenities is the cry now. The country and the city must serve each other, and there must be no one-way traffic as demanded by the parasite city of the past.

Hsingfa Commune

A beautiful woman, simply dressed country fashion, stood in greeting as we came to the offices of Hsingfa Commune on the outskirts of Harbin. Harvest was going on, but most of the rolling hills were still covered with the brown heads of kaoliang (sorghum) that tossed gently in the breeze. An excited group of children rushed out of the red brick homes nearby to see who the visitor was. But the visitor was quickly ushered upstairs to the commune reception room, and over glasses of tea told something about the commune he had come to visit. The commune leader's name was Ai, the same one as the visitor used, so we laughingly greeted each other as members of one family.

Her commune covers an area of seven square kilometres, 106,000 mou in all, of which 53,000 mou is used for agriculture, 20,000 mou for grain, 30,000 for vegetables, and 3,000 for orchards. Then there is a large tree nursery. The rest of the land is either grassland used for pasturing animals, or else forest. There are 3,600 families in the commune, 21,000 people in all, with a work strength of 5,000. There are ten brigades and two animal husbandry units. Our visit coincided with a high tide of study of Mao Tsetung Thought and the struggle to go after basic construction such as the digging of deep wells, and so on.

This area was liberated in 1945. In 1946-47 Land Reform was carried out. Prior to Land Reform, 85 percent of the best land had been owned by landlords and rich peasants, 10 percent by middle peasants, and only 5 percent by the mass of poor. It was a great victory when in 1948 the first mutual-aid teams began to give more strength to the poor majority. But better working, it was soon seen, also made the better-off peasants richer, and ensured new forms of exploitation of the poor. The elementary cooperatives did not appear until 1952. But even in the co-operatives, the richer peasants did not always have to go to work in the fields as the poorer ones did. It was not until the cooperative of higher type was formed in 1956 that everyone worked, and all the horses and carts came into the collective. Yet again, the poor peasant was still at a disadvantage in many ways, a situation that was not really met until the setting up of the commune in 1959, when basic work of overall construction could be done in a proper way, and the people were welded together in brigades and production teams.

"With the development of our commune we feel victory will come," the commune leader said. She was proud of the 40 kilometres of canal and laterals dug to bring in waters from the Sungari river, and of the 40 percent of all land already irrigated. Wells have to be dug 60 metres deep here, and are then supplied with electric pumps. On the commune, 23 tractors do a good deal of the heavy work on the land, taking care of around 50 percent of the cultivation. Horse-drawn implements do the rest with some of the 1,800 horses owned by the commune. The commune operates 12 trucks and 350 rubber-tyred horsecarts. The highway into Harbin is a good, macadamised road, so the taking in of vegetables presents no great task.

In the nine years of commune working there have been many problems. The class struggle has appeared in many forms. With some who were able to get the power, the temptations offered by taking a capitalist line became too great and they succumbed. Such people came to like landlord and rich-peasant families because they appeared always so willing and so accommodating. Yet after the cadres had undergone a very strict examination, and everyone had said all on his or her mind, out of the 42 cadres in the commune only two were dismissed. Some of the others had made plenty of mistakes, but none that could not be corrected. At the beginning of the movement, 13 groups formed that soon came together in one, which then took power. In the early stages, a certain operator named Ma Yi-tsun took a good deal of prominence. He was all for getting rid of all cadres and all old organisations and "starting afresh" with his few friends. Someone made inquiries into his background and it was found that he came of a high Kuomintang police-chief family. Analysing his actions, the people decided that the things he was aiming for were different from those the masses of the commune wanted, and he fell.

We walked through hillsides of orchards, saw some of the 20,000 laying poultry, the big piggeries, the dairy herd, and the brick kilns that can turn out 50,000 bricks a day, then went off to a village where milk powder was made by a group of young women and girls, and bottled for sale. A smiling rich countryside full of hope and endeavor, good to come and spend a day at.

A Harbin Craft

In what had been a shop in a Harbin street, a group of some 40 city lasses worked at a craft that has been developed here in Harbin. In Swatow in Kwangtung province, pictures made from wheat straw have long been an article for export, especially to Indonesia and the South Seas. Here in Harbin, developing this technique further, pictures of birds and animals are made standing out of the picture, as it were, with a beauty all their own. It is a craft that has been welcomed in the export trade, all the products of this group being bought up by buyers from Japan, Italy, France and Africa. With incredible delicacy, straw is made to look like the fur of squirrel, or the feathers of a bird. An art form quite stunning in its effectiveness despite the simplicity of the material used.

Harbin Bicycles

Looking back at the post administration of the Harbin Bicycle Works, one can see well enough that it was led by the few who neither believed in the teachings of Chairman Mao, the potential of their workers, nor the future of their product. Rather, it would seem, they were after maintaining a tight little kingdom of their own. Not that they were "squeezing officials" of the Kuomintang type, even though the manager himself was the son of a traitor "Manchukuo" official. The Party secretary had been a Party member since 1937, but undoubtedly he was impressed by someone higher who probably set the pace. "Never mind what you do as long as you make the works pay," he seemed to say. A slogan which, if analysed, shows up quite strongly as a revisionist one.

Indeed the old leadership quite openly put production above politics. They did not want to have the workers study Chairman Mao's works. They promoted those who were loyal to them in every way, and kept others down. They went outside their plan seeking good paying contracts for small machine construction instead of improving the quality of their product and lowering its cost. There should have been little doubt as to the value of bicycles to the people, for the ownership of a good one is something that most every commune member and youth in China looks forward to. Had they been seeking a way to serve the people in the spirit of Mao Tsetung they would have had a clear, definite way to do so in their work. But the two chief responsible ones, manager and Party secretary, ran their little kingdom as they wished. Money was allocated, for instance, for an exhaust system around buffing wheels in order to prevent silicosis amongst workers. But they used the money for some other project nearer their hearts. Actually they degenerated politically. When the workers started to rebel, they organised their own group against them. But to make quite a long story short, when the workers took power, many of the cadres, including the assistant factory manager, came over to them. The workers' victory was not without a good deal of resistance from the old group, and from factories around in which the old group was very much in power still, all of whom were sticking together to halt the rise of the bicycle factory workers.

By January 12th 1967, however, the worker group was in command. Production had fallen badly. Under the old management, the factory had produced only 2,000 bicycles a month, with a working force of 1,350. This force was now reduced to 830, workers not needed going off to a factory short of manpower. In the last half of January, just to show what could be done, the new group produced 4,000 bicycles. By October 1st, National Day, they will have completed their yearly quota of 75,000, for they have been making well over 7,000 bicycles a month. The cost price per bicycle has dropped from 140 yuan to 80. Plans are being made for more automation. There is higher spirit all around, the study of Chairman Mao's works has become very much a part of daily working life. Ninety percent of the old cadres are now working under the new order, and supporting it. Many technical innovations have been devised and put into use by the workers, some of them doubling the rate of production for the part they are working on.

Harbin Zoo

It was ten years ago since I last visited the Harbin Park which contains the zoo. It was such a cold day then that even the big Manchurian tigers turned their tails to the wind. On the 1967 visit trees were still green, and country folk in to see the big city were going the rounds just as they do in the Peking zoo. It was a pleasant walk watching not only the animals, but also the young folk who were looking at them. One very small boy had made a friend of a deer which let him rub its head, much to the child's delight. We returned from the park to go to a 5:30 p.m. "ping chu" opera performance. The day shift in Harbin factories comes off at four in the afternoon. A theatre performance at 5:30 gives them time to eat something, and get there, then to get back to bed at a reasonable hour afterwards. Many of the workers had brought their children, for it was a thrilling opera about catching some Kuomintang bandits up in the snowy mountains of this Northeast. In the spirit of the times, and between every scene when the curtain came down, a quotation from the Little Red Book would be read over the loudspeaker.

Hsinfu Commune

The first county south of Harbin is Shuangcheng. Near it only nine kilometres away— is Hsinfu Commune, situated in one of the villages built in Manchu style that radiate a mile and a half from each other over the rich countryside. Seventy percent of the 28,000 people in Hsinfu Comune are Manchu, but they have become so like Han it is not possible to tell which is which. It is a commune of 17 brigades, 74 production teams, that farms 13,000 "shang" or hectares of land. One "shang" equals 15 mou, so that the commune has 195,000 mou of rich, black-earth country to till. It has 37 tractors and 350 horsecarts, a tractor station and whole range of small industry connected with the commune working. For instance, it makes the electric motor driven pumps that pump water up new wells being dug. It has a tractor station with all repair facilities. Electric power cuts chaff for its horse fodder and lights the homes of commune members. Turns potatoes into starch noodles — "fen tiao" — and processes grain. But it was rather to hear what has happened to a Heilungkiang rural commune in the Cultural Revolution that we had come to Shuangcheng, so we gathered in the commune office in a low neatly thatched building, looking out through the glass panes of the windows at the children playing as the tale unfolded.

Under the old administration, people had seemed contented enough. The land was rich, and even though grain totals did not increase, there was enough to get by on. The old commune chairman did not like members to study Mao Tsetung Thought. He said, "Work hard on production. That is good politics. You cannot eat Chairman Mao's works!" Until mass meetings that lasted but three short days showed up the line he was taking, many people would not have believed that he was really following the capitalist road. Yet it was amply proved that he had borrowed money so that he could help landlord families and those of rich peasants to get carts. He had lent money to a speculator in the city who paid him 20 percent of the profit made. He had protected a counter-revolutionary. He protected landlords who kept Kuomintang weapons and so on secretly in their homes, and who were already going into usury — "I lend you 100 jin of wheat, you repay with 400 jin at the next harvest," and so on. Employed a school teacher who tried to spread anti-government propaganda, always adding a picture of a setting sun to reproductions of Chairman Mao's writings. Wrote up poems like,

> "Our classroom is very cold,
> Nine out of ten are worried.
> Though it is not a prison,
> Yet it has suffering children in it,"

and so spread disaffection where he could. At the beginning, some cadres thought things would become too chaotic, so tried to stop the movement. But as they saw the enthusiasm of the people, they too became keen. The

old administration leader had protected the big landlord tombs that were
such a headache to drivers of tractors. He also protected the shamans who,
in the old Manchu way, still held sway over the minds of the people.
He looked with favor on Buddhist images and the ancestral shrines in
homes. He backed up the people in their conservatism, never pressing
for change to new ways, methods and thinking. They did not use chemical fertiliser. They did not use tested, better seed but clung stubbornly
to the old. However, the movement cleared away the shamans, the tombs,
the Buddhas, and all such. An agricultural research laboratory was set
up for experimentation and teaching. A new insecticide called "1059" that
dealt effectively with kaoliang pests was put into use. The best seeds
available were planted and, with the new wells dug, a 100-day drought
was beaten. Whereas in 1966 but 109 tons of wheat had been delivered
to the state, the total for 1967 was 450 tons. The main crops, however,
are sorghum, millet and corn. 1967 has seen a rise of 100 jin a mou for
all grain over the total area farmed. Only 120 jin of chemical fertiliser
was used in 1966. In 1967, 800 jin were used.

We walked out through a big schoolground surrounded by bright, well
lit classrooms where 400 children of primary school age in the village
study, to see a new well that pumps into a reservoir. It is the practice
to make fish ponds of such reservoirs, putting some beancake in them
before they are frozen over to feed the fish on until spring.

Some of the strongest supporters of the recent changes have been
the old men who were poor peasants under the old order, and who
have vivid memories of going through bitter winters without enough
clothing and having to live on beancake and bran in the main. The importance of the road forward having been explained to them, they could
see that it was not being followed, so they brought their full weight to
bear on the meetings. Homes that had studied Chairman Mao's works and
who could recite the three short essays were entitled to hoist a red flag.
Most of the homes, rich with strings of red peppers, golden corn and white
garlic, had this flag flying proudly in front of their yards. Everyone
was determined to see all the autumn harvest in before October 5th.
Plans were being made for windbreaks to be planted around every 100-
acre lot of countryside, the commune nurseries already having young
trees enough to start this program going.

We went through some cottage homes of commune members and met
the womenfolk and children there. All homes have glass windows, wide
kangs (brickbeds) and good heating. Household work in the autumn is
mainly in preparation for the long winter. The corn cobs have to be
good and dry, the potatoes put in the cellar, the cabbage pickled and so
on. In one home we visited an old-type Manchu cradle hung from the
ceiling, but the small daughter of the house had taken the baby from
it and was proudly playing with it. 520 jin per person is the grain allocation each year for this commune.

Amongst commune handicrafts we saw was one making the heavy
ropes for horse-cart traces. 350 rubber-tyred carts with several horses
usually in the lead need a good many rope traces, and their provision gives

steady employment to half a dozen commune members. Carters are used to working with such ropes, which have to be very strong and well made to stand up to tough usage. We learnt quite a lot at this commune in the all too short day we spent there. We also enjoyed their cornbread and millet at the mid-day meal, and really felt we would like to come again.

The Harbin Linen Mill

The Harbin Linen Mill was one that started work in October 1952, and so by 1967 had a history of 15 years. In the bad old days the Japanese imperialists made the people plant flax, or "yang ma" as it is called in the Northeast, and then sent the semi-processed fibre to Japan. In the Northwest, flax has been known for long, but there it has simply been used as a source of oil seeds, the stalks being used for kang fuel. It is called "hu ma" there. The Harbin mill was the first to use the fibre to make linen for domestic and foreign trade, and it has been the Harbin mill that has helped to set up other similar mills in Inner Mongolia, Ningsia and other parts of the country.

The Soviet experts left the mill and took some of their know-how with them, resulting in Harbin engineers having to put their heads together and make their own machines. This they did to great effect, devising much better methods. Their machine-building easily outclassed the Soviet technique and enabled Chinese to teach Albanians who, too, wanted to learn the intricacies of the process.

The existence of this mill takes up the whole flax production of nine rural counties around. Its 4,200 workers use over 8,000 tons of the flax fibre each year to produce their over 20 million metres of cloth. Some of the cloth goes into tropical clothing for abroad. Some is made into waterproof canvas for tents, canvas buckets, firemen's hose-piping, etc. During the Cultural Revolution many new innovations have been made and new production lines worked out. New machines are about to be installed to raise efficiency. There is no doubt that this plant which occupies so important a place in the linen industry will make even greater contributions to it in the future, as it takes one stride forward after another. Yes, workers have played their full part in the Cultural Revolution and are keen students of Chairman Mao's works. The labor productivity of workers in 1966-67 exceeded even that of the Great Leap Forward years, the manager proudly said.

X-Ray Tubes

The process of self-sufficiency in China is not a simple one. Take the matter of X-ray tubes, for instance. For a long time those needed in medicine and industry were imported from abroad. Prices were high, and the rural hospital in some hinterland centres could hardly afford to buy. A start on their manufacture was made in Shanghai and Hangchow, and then in this frontier province of Heilungkiang a small medical appliance factory that had been a Harbin cooperative but had expanded to occupy spare rooms in four different buildings, went into the manufacture. The technician who undertook the study had been trained as a Russian language interpreter but with the going of the Russian experts was redundant in that capacity. He was a practical lad, however, and a keen student so that before long he had grasped a good deal of the science needed. Practice taught him more. The factory manager is a dogged old cadre who believes in surmounting all difficulties in the spirit of Mao Tsetung. With a group of young folk around they built up a good combination of enthusiasts. First products were 70 percent failures. They went on through the early 'sixties and now, by 1967, have produced two products, one for a big and the other for a small machine, which are cheap enough and which can each be used for 3,000 hours. The price of an imported big one was 1,800 yuan. It now costs the factory 350 yuan to make such a tube. The small type cost 800 yuan imported, and 200 to make in Harbin.

Only two of the 40 workers and staff in this branch of the factory — which actually occupies the basement of a health training school — had ever had anything to do with X-ray. They were both operators of an X-ray machine in a hospital. All workers here are very pleased to be able to express the idea of "serve the people" in so practical and exciting a way — and to make something which it was said could not be made in China, especially not in a frontier province like Heilungkiang. Before too long the whole factory will be housed together. In the meantime they get along with premises they have.

Harbin No. 3 Tool Plant

It is good to be able to spend a morning amongst a group of such energetic workers as the one which sat with us at the Harbin No. 3 Tool Plant. The assistant manager, who was one of the rebel group now in charge of the plant, first gave me an outline of factory conditions. It was a unit of around 800 workers whose planned production is 2,500,000 files and 5,000 big timber mill saw blades a year. Previously operating as a number of tiny factories, it had been brought together as a cooperative in 1956, increasing its working force from 100 to 360 in that year. Then, as the city spread out into the country, it took over the headquarters of a commune, which gives it a fine large piece of ground enabling many new shops to be erected with plenty of space around.

The old general manager, it seemed, had come up from private industry and remained a merchant in his thinking. He was against the small units coming together, for he did not trust the workers and wanted to keep them separated. He went about things in a typically capitalist way, building up a group loyal to him because he gave them special benefits. The Party secretary degenerated, and as long as he had time to sleep in his office and then take his family out in the factory's car he paid little attention to political leadership. Yet, in the first part of the movement, only 100 workers stood with the rebel group. The rest the manager played with, organising them into various groups under various progressive names. The rebel group persisted, and soon workers who had been fooled began to come over to them.   One worker who had been sent to Peking by the manager and who was arrested there for disorderly behavior faced an irate family council when he returned to Harbin.   The father and mother reminded him of the bad old days, and the whole family threatened to beat him if he did not come to his senses. The next day his old mother took him to the rebel group and made him ask their pardon and get back to the job as one of their number. Workers set up their own study group and invited rebel worker leaders in from other factories to tell of their struggle, tying theory up with practice.   Out of the 49 old cadres only three were put aside, the manager and the Party secretary amongst them.   The feeling of the people is definitely one for unity on the basis of Mao Tsetung Thought.   In the No. 3 Tool Plant the first six months of operation of 1967 saw production running more than 20 percent over the plan.

Harbin Fountain Pen Factory

We found the Harbin Fountain Pen Factory situated in a block of once foreign-style flats in the old part of the city, a place where 429 workers manufactured fountain pens mainly for export.   In their political struggle they have an able rebel worker group as the leading committee.   All of the 23 old cadres are working, none having been laid off, though one of them is under investigation with regard to his past.   In the first half of 1966, 459,000 pens were made.   This number was topped in the first half of 1967 when the total rose to 692,000.   Some of the production is placed on the domestic market, but a good many are sold abroad in some 13 countries.

The production of a good modern fountain pen that does not leak, writes smoothly and is pleasant to look at, needs a great deal of care and ability.   Early Harbin pens were the very cheap kind sold for around 40 fen, which were common 15 years ago.   Now the demand is for a much more streamlined article.   Shanghai pens had the best name, so Shanghai workers came to Harbin to help in the modernising of the plant. Steadily work has gone on, and steadily new machines have been built to meet requirements.   Three clever innovations on the road towards automation have been completed in this last year and are now running smoothly and increasing production.   It is obvious that the present group in leadership will assure swift progress in every part of this expanding plant.

The New Czars

Back home in the guest house at the end of an afternoon, we talked of the curious way the Russians who have so comfortably ensconced themselves in the old Chinese territory north of the Heilungkiang river have unilaterally decided that, when the unequal treaty they forced upon China says that the Heilungkiang (Amur) river should be the boundary, it means that the Russians possess the river right up to the Chinese bank!   International practice when a waterway is a boundary is, of course, that the centre of the navigation channel is the boundary. The Russians seem to feel that the salmon which come up the river are their property, too, as are all river islands and the piece of land that lies between the Heilungkiang and the Wusuli rivers on which before a recent flood there were Chinese state farms. All most queer, as is the Russian invitation to monopoly-run Japan to join with it in the exploitation of territory seized from China. Queer, too, that Japan should make her appearance on the Asian mainland under the flag of the Russians she fought for the loot of Manchuria in 1905.

Harbin Railway Workshops

One thinks of the period of crude exploitation of Heilungkiang when one sees the changes of today during a visit to the railway workshops, built under Russian domination in 1898. They occupy 940,000 square metres of land and employ 4,800 workers who not only do repair work but also construct new rolling stock, particularly 60-ton steel tip waggons and big oil tank waggons. Workers here are proud of their revolutionary tradition. They joined in the Railway Strike of 1923 and were out for 40 days. All during the War of Resistance and in the face of incredible difficulties they maintained their Communist Party underground branch. In the War of Liberation, as the only big factory in Harbin at that time, they had the task of making munitions and arms for the Liberation Army. In the Korean War they sent in and maintained rolling stock for that country, despite every difficulty. They have been active in the Cultural Revolution and early came to the stage of unity on the principles of Mao Tsetung Thought. As many of the workers are old and experienced, they have been able to analyse well the 70-point directive for industry that Po I-po prepared for Liu Shao-chi, and now join in denouncing this as a thoroughly revisionist document.

The new administration was now going into a huddle on how to cut down the superstructure which has been burdened with the kind of administration Soviet experts liked during their period of influence. All cadres now do periods of work with shop workers, in the new fashion, and all are enthusiastic members of their study groups. And out of this period of analysis, study and change has come the 100-ton tip waggon, completed in the autumn of 1967 and then sent on to Peking for testing. There was a warm, comradely feeling about the place, that impressed one during the walk around the shops. A worker group that knew the way forward and was taking it sturdily and well.

Some Recent Harbin History

The name "Harbin" is a Manchu word that means "sunning nets", for here by the Sungari river there was always good fishing. Before the railway came there was a simple hamlet here called "the Fu family shop" "Fuchiadien", a name some old residents on the outskirts of the city still use. The Soviet troops who marched in before the end of the Pacific War recognised only the Kuomintang. So they passed over authority to some local Kuomintang troops who proceeded to get rid of the progressive Li Chao-lin who had been named head of the province. Li was a young man, able and strong. The Kuomintang thugs first drugged him, then murdered him. His grave stands in a little park, now called after him, in the city. We watched the children playing there in the evening, with the leaves changing color. The struggle for a People's China has not been easy, but step by step those things that give the people strength have been fought for and won.

Spare Parts for Oil Drills

The Harbin Oil Drill Spare Parts Factory is not a big concern. Yet its 437 workers have gained a good deal of political experience in the Cultural Revolution. It makes spare parts for oil drills and the oil industry generally. They are especially proud of the one part, previously a 2.5-ton job, imported from the USSR at considerable cost. The model devised in China and made in this plant weighs 200 lbs., costs a fraction of the former price, and is much more efficient.

But let us go back to the beginnings of this little enterprise. It started in 1953 as a group of local women who banded together to make straw and hemp rope. Then it became a cooperative making various machine parts with some simple machine tools. From this it graduated to become a local state enterprise, workers rising to 300 in number, and by 1960 able to produce 100,000 sets of ball bearings a year. People called it "the golden phoenix risen from a bed of straw", because straw was the main raw material in 1953.

The railway workshops already described in this story hold as a precious memory a visit to their shops by Chairman Mao and Premier Chou in 1950. The ball bearing plant has the bitter memory of a visit by Liu Shao-chi in 1961. Liu came in, had a cursory look round and gave the opinion it should be changed back into a cooperative for producing goods for the consumer market, relying on what it could sell to pay workers' wages. He told them to turn out moulds for making the plastic handles of tooth brushes, and also moulds for plastic shoes. The little plant was not tooled for this work, and most of the workers who had gathered around it were machinists. It appeared there was only a limited market for moulds, so many of the workers left and machines stood idle.

Bankruptcy was only staved off by orders for parts from the oil industry, which started to come in by 1964. Workers are proud of the fact that, since the beginning of the Cultural Revolution, they have not only maintained their planned quota but have exceeded it. Production for the first half of 1967 was 92 percent over that of the same period of 1966, while costs of the parts produced have been lowered by 21 percent. By October 1st 1967, the 1967 plan will have been virtually completed. All this sounds like plain sailing. Actually, everything that has been done has cost a good deal of sweat and tears. The onset of the Cultural Revolution saw the three top cadres working hard against the rise of the rebel group. Looking back on these three, one found their record as revolutionaries bad. The Party secretary had somehow entered the Party after being a Kuomintang Air Force officer, and before that an official under the traitor Wang Ching-wei. The manager had been a "Manchukuo" police officer. The Communist Youth League leader had many connections with the old order. Workers went to the city Party office and demanded change, which was agreed to. The new incumbents sent, however, were even more determined than the previous ones to hold the workers down, organising their own special group for this purpose, and practising the same kind of thing as reactionaries were doing in other factories. They denounced the rebels as "rightists" and "counter-revolutionaries". The struggle went on, but slowly the main body of the workers learnt and came over to the rebel side, though not without a good deal of struggle. At times rebel workers busy with meetings in the day would bring some food and work through night hours to fulfil their part of the plan. A horizontal drilling machine was needed. Right in the middle of the toughest time, the workers made one. They were determined to stand by Chairman Mao, cleanse their factory and be true to their class, and they are proud of their record in doing just this.

A University in Harbin

The Harbin Military Engineering College is a university of some 8,000 students who have come from all over the country. The Red Guard leader who was part of a group which came to see me was from Kansu. Others were from Anhwei, Hopei, Shantung, and so on. They had a sober, realistic attitude towards the Cultural Revolution, knowing that the 500,000 workers of Harbin would take the brunt of the movement from now on, as was indeed the trend at that period. They had a good, clear idea of the current international situation and China's position in the vanguard of the world revolution. They also understood the shortcomings of youngsters brought up in well protected surroundings without much struggle, and the danger of them degenerating into a new class that considered itself superior to the working folk of the land because of their better educational opportunities. A good, thoughtful group of youth, who have learnt much in this past year.

Last Days in Harbin

The Harbin that had been green when we had come was, two weeks later at the end of September, a glory of gold. Soon the southwest winds would change to northerlies and snow would drift in. Heilungkiang's first battles of the Cultural Revolution had virtually been won, and now the number of groups coming over into the new unity snowballed. Just before National Day on October 1st, figures were released showing that Heilungkiang in 1967 had an overall increase over the heavy crop of 1966 of 10 percent. There was a 30 percent increase in wheat yield, for last year more wheat was grown than ever before. Grain sold to the state was just double that sold in the corresponding period of 1966, the people's stores being already full.

At the end of September, Harbin resounded with the slogans from mass meetings being held to express unity. On the eve of National Day, posters were washed away from walls and windows and many hoardings taken down. The Cultural Revolution went into a new stage.

Among the Forests of Khinganling

We were up early on a late September morning in Harbin and down to the railway station to catch a local train for Ichun, northeast of Harbin and not far from the Heilungkiang river. We went in reasonable comfort in the hard class — no soft seats on these trains — watching the rich countryside stretching out towards the horizon, a great sea of kaoliang and millet now awaiting harvest. For around five hours we looked, punctuated by stops at every station, where many bits of daily life made fascinating glimpses. Youngsters climbing up piles of logs, people bringing in grain, teams of horses swinging along in unison. Up on a hillside a sturdy child of perhaps three still in his sun-tanned birthday suit, legs set firmly apart, waving farewell to the train. An old woman so tenderly, so patiently hanging up red peppers on the wall of her home, as she had hung them every autumn for her whole long life. Three small girls who had put flowers in their hair and were laughing at each other. A peaceful countryside rich in promise.

To Ichun

The last two hours of the journey took us amongst the hills of the Lesser Khingan Range that continue right up to the Heilungkiang river and run east with it. Trees were a startling red and gold, with the trunks of silver birch gleaming in the sun. We got out at Dailing, one of the "chu" or subdivisions of Ichun special district. This district has a population of half a million. Its administrative centre of Ichun town has grown from a little village 20 years ago to a sizeable community of 60,000. The district covers a considerable area, as big as several counties in most other parts of China. Its main production is timber, this being worked in 15 forestry divisions. Dailing, the place we had come to see and write about, is one of these. The township that has sprung up in Dailing is the centre of both the "chu" subdivision of the district and of the Dailing forest administration. With around 30,000 people it is quite a busy place, with many new big buildings amongst which is a foresters' training school. A new "main street" has grown up in the town in the past two or three years. Several of the bigger forestry divisions of Ichun have an annual production of 400,000 cubic metres of timber. Dailing produces 200,000. Forestry cadres come from all over China for refresher courses.

At the time of Liberation there were but 100 families living in Dailing. Most of them had poor homes, simply dugouts in the hillsides with a covering of forest branches and thatch. Now the town is a thriving one with all the amenities of a modern hinterland place. Good transport facilities. A good hospital, an old people's home, a fine big cinema, schools, a kindergarten, a dairy farm and so on. The whole Dailing area is under the forestry administration, farm commune brigades and all. There is a research station and a large-size nursery which provides the seedlings for the annual spring sowing drive. This takes place from May 1st to May 20th each year, cadres, workers, school children and house-wives all taking part, the target each year being to get around 2,500 (English) acres of hillside sown. This 1967 May, however, an all time total was reached with 3,572 acres being planted. Seventy percent of the trees in the forest here are deciduous. The most favored tree is the red pine, called so because of the tinge of red in its timber. It is "Pinus Koraiensis", the Korean Pine. In its first three years in the nursery, it takes careful nurturing, seedlings having to be covered with earth each winter, the earth being scraped away by hand the following spring. Then, in the hottest days they are covered by lattice mats to prevent sun scorch. Once planted out on the hillsides with grasses growing around, however, they need no more such attention. The Japanese oc-cupation of this region left a very poor legacy. All the hills adjacent to the railway had been denuded and the slopes had been set on fire. Wan-ton destruction of forest resources, after the very best pick had been taken of the timber, seemed to be their policy. The foresters they kept working for them were beaten, cursed and half-starved, never with enough clothing for the long winters. Since 1951, when forestry work was started, some 40,000 acres of land in the Dailing area has been plant-ed. Natural re-growth on slopes brings up the total of new forest to 50,000 acres. Timber over a little lesser area has been felled, only the good timber being selected, not leaving a totally devastated region as was the case with the Japanese cutting, but rather one that can be filled out with new planting amongst the many trees that have been left. Most of the work of cutting, loading and the transport of timber is mech-anised. Costs of handling have been drastically reduced. Next year the light railway will be torn up, giving place to a highway and heavy truck transport. The total area occupied by this Dailing forest division is 250,000 acres of the Lesser Khingan Range of mountains. These moun-tains are not high, the highest peak being Dachingshan in the Dailing forest area. It rises 3,000 feet. A good view of this mountain, now af-forested right to its summit again, can be obtained from the 50-acre nursery we spent a morning looking at.

Climate and Trees

The climate of the area is severe, though it is only 46-47 degrees north. There are four good growing months and seven cold ones, when there is a good deal of frost and snow. The first frost of autumn 1967 in Dailing town came in the middle of September. Another one arrived on September 24th while we were there. Mid-day temperatures in the hottest time range from 38° to 40° C. In mid-winter they go down to 38° C below freezing, and the earth freezes to a depth of six feet. Pro-duction brigades on valley flats are able to make the whole area self-suf-ficient in vegetables, as well as helping with the grain needed.

We spent some time looking at a forest of "leaf-dropping pine" (Larix Dahurica), a larch which rates as one of the five main kinds of "sung" coming under the category "pine" in Chinese. This stand was planted in 1953, and it is estimated that it will be cut in 1973. The long winter makes for slow growing. A spruce called Yungshan Sung (Picea Koraiensis) and another named Yulin Sung (Picea Jezoensis) also made some good stands which we admired much. One of the problems in the nurseries is to get supplies of tree seed. A big piece of land has been set aside for an experiment to graft branches from old seed-bearing trees onto young seedlings. It is expected that in this way seeds will be conveniently got from a pine after it reaches a height of only ten feet or so.

Silver birch and scrub oak are the most common trees to perpetuate themselves. Acorns are collected to sell to state buying agencies, not being used to make noodles as they are in some forest areas. Potatoes here are too plentiful for acorns to be used for that. People, too, have had enough of being made to eat acorn flour, as they were during the Japanese occupation.

Around Dailing

The town has modern machine shops capable of repairing tractors and timber-working machinery. The big timber mill handles some of the great sea of timber that collects around it, brought down by the light railway from the big forests further inland. Dwellings on the outskirts of the town are often dwarfed by the piles of timber scrap which are collected as winter fuel. Gnats and mosquitoes are a nuisance in the summer, and one sees workers on tasks like ditch-digging where these pests are plentiful, working with a towel covering the head and back of the neck. Then again, one will see many joyous youngsters nearby who have taken off their upper clothes in the warmth of the middle of the autumn day, tying them to their belts and then running and jumping without thought of pests at all.

I asked about walnuts here, and found that the Manchurian hill walnut prevalent is a long, rather thin one, encased in a thick shell, of the kind that old men in north China like to work around in their hands to keep their fingers supple. Not many are grown, however, they being rare amongst the 15 common kinds of trees in this part of the Khingan Range. Youngsters more often eat pine nuts, which are big, fat and very pleasant to the taste, even though one does have to spend some time extracting them from the shell. There are also many hazelnuts, though of a small variety.

We watched millet being harvested. With remembrances of the Northwest, I wondered how it could be kept dry and sunned throughout the winter, after it was threshed. Local folk smiled and said, "It is simply left in the fields in stooks and brought in when the ground freezes. The millet seed is frozen when it is threshed, and can stay frozen up to spring or until it is used." Which makes everything simpler. Kaoliang is threshed in the autumn, however, and stored.

China's Khrushchev, Liu Shao-chi, once came to Dailing and stayed for three days. He did not talk about politics but only about profit. Urged everyone concerned to get onto a profit basis. Seen in the light of his later pronouncements and his 70 articles for industry, it was evident that for him production, not politics, was very much in command. Ichun municipality now has the three-way-combination Revolutionary Committee in charge and feels that the future direction is clear. There is widespread study of Chairman Mao's works amongst forestry workers, town dwellers, children, and people in organisations. The amplifiers put over the speeches with just as much vim as they do in a big city. Drums and banners celebrate unity as it is gained, and the Little Red Book is everywhere. All are convinced that to follow the way of Mao Tsetung will help them to plant many more forests and maintain those in existence. The celebrations for unity increased in crescendo right up until the last night we were in Dailing.

Into Dailing Forests

It was heavy mist when we set out early one morning on a timber train hauled by a steam locomotive that goes some 47 kilometres on a narrow-gauge railway into the forested hills. At about nine the sun broke through and dispelled the mist, bringing welcome warmth, so that before we got out to look at this bit of forest or that bit of planting we shed some of the extra garments brought. At one point, we took another timber train, a diesel this time, and went up a branch railway to a timber loading and felling site. It was a magnificent ride through original native forest, the evergreens standing out against the golden autumn colors of the other trees. Timber men showed how fast they could fell their trees with their mechanical saws, cutting out a wedge in front and then dropping their tree with nice precision in the place desired. Mechanical loaders took over from the Harbin-made tow tractors when these brought in the logs, and lifted them up effortlessly to deposit them on the flatcars. The life of a lumberman is a changed one these days. At one job I asked a tough-looking old worker how old he was. "Sixty-eight, and still going strong," he said. "It is the good life now. We have all the white wheat flour we want now!" He gave me a cheery smile and a strong hand grip as we parted.

But most of the workers are on the young side, not becoming worn out through work as the poorly fed ones did under the old conditions, but taking a very real interest in the politics of the day, and their part in all that is being done. A leading cadre from the Revolutionary Committee of Ichun municipality who came with us explained that this whole Dailing forestry division was one of the smaller of the 15 other divisions in the municipality, most of whom had doubled the yearly production of Dailing. There were also other production organisations in amongst these Lesser Khingan Mountains. Mining projects, factories, and so on, and then, too, the almost completely new town of Ichun as a centre for them all. The main railway lines have pushed out so that all forestry divisions can connect with it on their light railway or highway systems. During the Japanese occupation, the invaders were busy exploiting forests beside railway lines so that the forested hills behind were left to the anti-Japanese guerillas who harried the enemy continually from their hideouts.

We visited many replanting sites. Improvement in technique has been responsible for some young plantations of red pine coming up at almost twice the rate of those planted with the Soviet technique used in the 'fifties. We saw some of the areas that had been felled and cleared, ready for the spring planting in 1968. There is no doubting the determination to push ahead with the new forests and have them cover all land available. There is also a growing interest in and liking for forestry, which is good to see. A schoolmaster must like his pupils if he is going to make much of them. A forester must like trees if he wants to obtain real results. We walked up into some original forest and admired the 200-year-old trees standing so gracefully and with such pride. Then as the warmth died out of the day and evening came on swiftly, we chugged down to Dailing town again, refreshed with the memories of a wonderful day and all the vivid, colorful pictures it carried with it.

Walking through forests gave some realisation of the perpetual struggle that goes on in them. In some places there were trees that had been struck and burnt by lightning. In others they had been blown down by summer storms. Roots do not go so deep here because of frozen earth below but rather spread out widely amongst relatively shallow surface soil. Occasional wild animals were seen, but tigers and bears now keep clear of valleys where tractors and trains make so much noise. Edible berries there are, and quite good fishing in some of the streams. Walnuts grow wild on lower forest levels, usually in places sheltered by other trees. The low scrub hazelnut, "chentze", is also found along many valley bottoms. There are wild grapes from which a very tasty red wine is made.

New Forests

We went out along the highway to Kirin to see where a pine called the "chang sung" has been successfully planted in marshlands. The cadre in charge of this forest and his technician came along with us and showed us their method: a little mound is made in the swamp and three pines planted on it, with a good space between them and the next planting. With this method, the take is quite successful and the trees grow much better than if they were just planted in rows in the usual way. We walked through a plantation of the "leaf-dropping pine". It had been planted ten years ago, and the same principle had been applied here, it being found that it worked well on a damp hillslope. These trees were just changing color and were very satisfying to walk amongst, in all their delicate beauty. On another hillside, red with scattered oak, a new planting of red pine was showing up well. We were invited to go further into the hills and see bigger and earlier plantings of red pine but, unfortunately, time did not allow.

Child Life

Child life in the villages along forested valleys was as fascinating as it is anywhere in China. One group of youngsters were watching a rotary hoe-type tractor with much interest, following every movement of the mechanic's hands as he repaired it. It will be they who will be responsible for the much greater mechanisation in the future. Even now as much hauling seems to be done with trucks and tractors as with horsecarts. There were many other pleasant glimpses of children. A boy on a bright blue bicycle held some of the forest berries and autumn leaves as we took a snap of him. A pile of logs seemed to be a favorite place for boy life to meet together here and to discuss the affairs of the day out in the sun.

Forest Research Station

We spent some time at the forest research station where many kinds of trees have been collected and grown in plots. A valuable institution for the practical education of youngsters in a forestry area. The leading cadre was a forestry enthusiast and pointed out many things about his trees that only a student of them would have understood.

Old Men's Home

Dailing has an excellent old men's home. So many Shantung workers came into these parts in the bad old days and were never able to set up families of their own. There are 68 of them, the oldest 88 and the youngest 68, in this place set apart for them. None has any family. All endured much bitterness during the Japanese occupation. They have a staff of 14 looking after them, and they themselves help in the vegetable gardens when they wish to. They also grow flowers in pots to brighten up their long winter and give them satisfaction. One perfect red rose was obviously the pride of their hearts, judging from the way they showed it to the visitor. They are also proud of the fact that they grew 7,000 jin of cabbage this year as well as 100 jin of garlic.

Near their home is a kindergarten, so that the old men often see the rising generation trooping past. We went in and listened to the children singing and then, for the final item of the day, climbed up to the big middle school and looked over the growing town. The cadres with me told of the work that had been put into fire prevention. They certainly had it all well organised right down to the children in the primary schools who were taught the rules and how to help enforce them.

On Trees

In all, it was an exciting thing to be able to come and see the tree planting that is so important in the fight against erosion and in water and flood control in China. What is being carried out here now will be expanded on a still greater scale, and will spread further beyond the con-

Forest of the Lesser Khingan Range, Heilungkiang.

HEILUNGKIANG

Forest boys and old forest worker, Heilungkiang.

Railway in the Lesser Khingan Range.

In the Lesser Khingan Range.

The author seeing experimental tree planting at Dailing, Heilungkiang.

Cadre inspecting the growth of seedlings, Dailing.

Felling a tree, Lesser Khingan Range.

Heilungkiang commune girls.

Heilungkiang commune lads.

Children's train, Harbin, autumn 1967.

Singers in a Harbin nursery, October 1967.

Old style cattle still work in Heilungkiang.

At Dailing, Ichun, Heilungkiang.

fines of Ichun into many parts of this great dominion of China's North-east. When I came to China 40 years ago I attended a lecture at which it was stated that north China was doomed to go back to desert conditions because of erosion following deforestation. The demands of the 18 years of Liberation on timber for construction have been heavy, and much of it has been met by the lumbermen of the Northeast. But on the other hand, billions of trees have been planted, thus halting what so many feared; but multi-billions more are needed throughout China so that no-where will there be marsh, desert or hill land. This work will actively halt erosion, the silting up of rivers, and all such attendant evils. The people of China have to wage intense struggle as they remake their land anew. Those of Heilungkiang know well that resources must be con-served and that at the same time they have to defend the frontiers. Chairman Mao has said that people ought to study the history of the last 100 years. That history on China's northern frontiers has been one of savage imperialist aggression and the theft of vast territory. Today the chauvinism of the new revisionists who cloak their dealings under the red flag of revolution, has to be watched carefully. Looking at the new generation of foresters growing up, one feels that here is a people who will not easily be trifled with. At the turn of the century, the Russians were the lords of Heilungkiang. They crossed the Heilungkiang river, which by unequal treaty they had forced the old China to accept as a boundary, burning towns and looting. They massacred, and they stamped in with the cry that they were bringing European civilisation to the "uncivilised" East, rather in the manner of the USA in Vietnam today. Now we can see that the superiority of this so-called Western civilisation is a myth. The Vietnamese are exploding it. Today the folk of Hei-lungkiang, too, are showing how they can do all the things that the im-perialists, Russians or Japanese could not. Give back to the land the tree wealth that is used. Weld people into one, and fill them with purpose in the spirit of Mao Tsetung Thought.

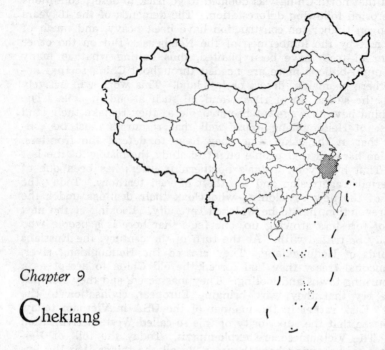

Chapter 9

Chekiang

Chekiang is a richly endowed and fast developing province on the south-east coast of China. Its main products are rice, jute, silk, tea and fish. It is also famous for its fruit, many of its oranges going into the export trade. It is mainly hilly, but with many fertile valleys and inland basins, as well as rich coastal plains. Its capital, Hangchow, is a world renowned scenic resort. With over 28 million people, the province is now diversifying its economy on the basis of an ever progressing agriculture and a rising industrialisation.

The fishing industry is modern and highly developed, especially in the Chusan Archipelago and also around Ningpo and Sanmen Bay. There are half a million fishermen.

With abundant hydro-electric resources and with the completion of the large Hsinan river project there is now power available for both the new industries and the communes.

Hangchow in 1966

I started coming to visit Hangchow, capital of Chekiang, in the late 'twenties. Saw it many times in the 'thirties, but then due to war not again until the 'fifties.   Now, in April 1966, it seems as if Hangchow which, up to Liberation, had relatively little changed from the fabulous city Marco Polo saw in the 13th century, is no longer the same place.   In the last decade changes have been immense, for now it is a swiftly rising industrial centre.   For the kind of bath-houses Marco Polo saw one would have to go to Japan, where their style and number have been well preserved.   From the old Sung imperial palaces nothing whatever remains.   Even the ugly monuments of the 'thirties of this century have now been removed and are forgotten.   Yet West Lake remains dreamy and placid.   Dredged, cleaner and with more trees, but still West Lake.   The willows and the peach blossoms are more numerous and as lovely as of yore in April, while the line of hills that change with each mood of the day are the same hills.   Marco Polo would get a bit of a shock, however, if he went a few miles along the highway west and halted at a modern state farm that has planted 1,000 mou of orchards — peaches and pears.   We walked amongst them and talked with bunches of girls from a junior middle school who were doing practical work in cleaning the trees of pests.

Famous sites of history and folklore still exist, but change has come amongst them.   There has been much renovation and cleaning up.   At the Jade Pool all seems new, but one can still pull up a table to the water's edge and feed the big carp as one sips the especially fragrant Lungching tea.   As to the temples of bygone great, today's youth looks to heroes of its own time, of whom there are plenty.   In this it is on surer ground, for there are many unanswered questions surrounding those of ancient feudal times, previously brought out of their historical context to be painted up as examples for a rising generation.   The cult of complete loyalty to a despotic feudal emperor hardly fits the needs of our time.

Back in 1927 the principal business was in the pilgrim and hotel trade. There were many hundreds of temples and many thousands of monks in the city and hills around.   Incense and silver paper for the dead went up in smoke all the time.   The wealthy families of the coast flocked here several times a year.   Shanghai gangsters had huge summer homes and even private armies of their own in the vicinity.   Many girls were forced into prostitution, and for the girls such a profession, pitiable as it is everywhere, in the old China was indeed far more horrible.   The silk industry was run down.   But yet the saying still went, "Heaven above, Hangchow and Soochow beneath", and was felt to be true by the wealthy.   Landlordism was rife.   As I sat in the spring of 1966 overlooking West Lake, children's voices rose in exuberant song.   They came from the few hundred youngsters of a school as they trooped out together for morning exercise beside the lake, a sturdy little girl of around 12 in the lead, carrying a red flag.   As soon as they reached the grassy banks of the lake they fell out and tumbled around in play.

Plenty more of these precious bits of the future were running up and down the steps of Liuhe Pagoda which overlooks the Chientang river. This is a stately pagoda of the "Six Harmonies" built first in the Sung dynasty and renovated through the centuries.   In late Ching a huge sum was spent on building its outside wooden covering, despite the memorial of at least one official who suggested the money be better used for education.

Lungching Tea

I went up a valley from the highway by the Chientang river to Chiuhsi, the "nine streams", a famous beauty spot, and then further to one of the brigades of Lungching Commune, whose main product is the famous tea of the name. Some years ago I had been to see another brigade of the commune, not far from the Linyin monastery. But the one seen now was easily the most prosperous and most beautiful. I watched the fresh tea of the season being expertly turned in shining iron pans, and then I visited the school.

It was well set on a high point overlooking the village with large, airy classrooms, all built by the brigade itself out of its welfare fund. The youngest class was exercising when I arrived. They had divided into two teams, each with a ball. Then the first two in line would race around two basketball posts at the other end of the pitch and pass the ball to the next in line, relay-race fashion. It was an exciting game, with the children shouting encouragement to the runners and getting ready to run themselves. No sign of regimentation here. I talked for a while with the brigade leader, one of a family of 11 which included his wife, and four young children all of whom were in the school I visited. Last year the average family in the brigade received 876 yuan. Counting 40 jin of grain each per month, a family would spend about 250 yuan a year on food grains and 30 yuan on sauce, oil, vinegar and salt. Tea and vegetables are grown by each household, so are free. They pay no house rent. They would have around 600 yuan a year to spend, not counting what they might gain through selling any eggs, pork and poultry they have of their own. The brigade consisted of around 600 people in 139 families. They had a labor force of 244, not counting part-time workers. Their primary school is full time, though when the tea crop comes in there is a holiday and a general mobilisation of all available fingers to pick the precious tips. In these past 15 years they have afforested those parts of their five hills they have not terraced for tea plantations, though their tea production is now six times as great as it was in 1949.

We spent some time at the spring from which the name Lungching or "Dragon Spring" derives. A restful spot, with pavilions for visitors, and like that at Chiuhsi, one of the "musts" for experienced Hangchow tourists who, through previous visits, know all the best places. Here one can sit for a while sipping tea and drink in the beauties around.

Scenic Spots

I went out for an afternoon on the lake, to visit some of the scenic spots. One of the West Lake boat women, whose mothers and grandmothers probably were boat women before them, took me expertly around. We first called at the Santanyinyueh or "Three Pools that Reflect the Moon" island and looked over to the ridge south of us which was once the boundary line between the kingdoms of Wu and Yueh, and which later overlooked the ancient palace of Southern Sung. Offshore here are three small pagodas standing dreamily in the water. The folk story says that once there were three deep pits below them up which evil spirits came, so that pagodas were built to keep them down. These pagodas make a graceful addition to a scenic gem. From the island one crosses to the Huakangkwanyu or "Watching the Fish in Huakang Pool" park. This is a much liked and very frequented place, now enlarged and even more beautiful. Many people who come down on the double-decker express from Shanghai to see the spring in Hangchow and to take pictures of their children before a background of peach or cherry blossom make this park their destination. The children especially never seem to tire of watching the shoal of big goldfish leaping for crumbs thrown them in the pools. Once this part of the lake was overlooked by the Leifeng ("Thunder Peak") pagoda, famous in folklore and to one-time Peking opera goers as the place under which the beautiful fairy "White Snake" was buried for 20 years as punishment for her sins preparatory to being made an immortal. The pagoda, built early in the Northern Sung period around 975 A.D., quietly crumbled to the ground on September 25th, 1924. It had been burnt red in the old days when Japanese pirates who raided the coast tried to destroy it, as it was used as a watch tower to warn of their arrival. So they set its outer wooden structure alight and it burned for three days and nights.

Hangchow is a city with a long history, one that has seen many changes. Marco Polo spoke of it admiringly as Kinsay, capital of the Manzi, the name by which the Mongols of the Yuan dynasty called the Han people. The city went through many vicissitudes in its long history. During the Taiping Revolution, Hangchow was liberated for a time from its Manchu court officials by the people. Today, as the capital of modern Chekiang province, it is more than simply an administrative centre. Old handicrafts have been revived and modern industry has come in. With all the area included in the municipality it has something over 900,000 people. It has excellent road, rail, waterway and air connections with the rest of south China. Today, a constant stream of visitors from the many delegations and groups who come to China each year from all over the world spend some of their time here.

No matter where you go in China, or in places abroad where many Chinese live, you will find a picture or two of West Lake somewhere on the walls. I have seen such in Sinkiang and Djakarta, Heilungkiang, and down in Oceania.

Linyin temple near West Lake is one of the greatest places of worship of Buddhism in China. It is wonderful, however, that it has survived at all, so many have been the wars and the fires it has passed through. I remember well the first time I saw it on an early summer's day and after a year of the bleakness of old Shanghai, how well then it seemed to me that it fitted the words written of it, "One foot below the Western Heaven". It was burnt in Sung times, in Ming, twice in Ching, was reconstructed in

1925, then was pretty well wrecked during the Japanese occupation. The first Buddhist monastic foundation came, it is said, when Hui Li with his pet monkey arrived here from India around 326 A.D. in the period of the Northern and Southern Dynasties. His monkey became very happy in sporting around a hill above a stream. Hui Li stayed and is said to have been buried under the stone pagoda that stands by the main cave entrance under the hill there. Depicted on the rock face nearby are sculptured horses, bearing on their backs Buddhist books. Then right on until the end of the Yuan dynasty and the beginning of Ming, sculptors added from time to time their conceptions to caves and rock faces. Around a great, happy Milo Fu in one of these places are grouped Lohan in very lifelike attitudes, and not giving the impression of being very holy men. This seems to be a favorite place for photographers to take pictures of their friends or guests.

On the opposite side of the stream rise the towers of the great Linyin monastery itself, the "Abode of Spirits". In its halls the massive red supporting pillars are now of reinforced concrete instead of timber so likely to rot in the middle, as was found to be the case with the big columns here in the past. There is a wealth of carved and gilded wood-work for which the region is famous.

We went away from Linyin across the lake and through the city to where we turned uphill to the top of the Wushan ridge. Here were once three temples, the biggest of them dedicated to the Hangchow city deity. This originally was thought to be the spirit of a judge named Chou who lived at the beginning of the 15th century and after his death was chosen to be the spiritual head of the city. But the cult of the city god became big business as the years went on, realising fortunes for the owners of the place. As a rule, unless upkeep is carefully maintained, traditional Chinese buildings do not last very long, and now all that remains of this temple are the broad wide steps leading up to the stone walled ridge top on which it once stood. Below, there is now a middle school, while another pavilion has been reconstructed where one can sit and get a good view of West Lake, the city, and the Chientang river. It is said that the old Sung city lay on the south side of the hill here.

One of the best known of Hangchow beauty spots is Hupaossu, "Haunt of Tiger Monastery". Folklore has it that once, during the Tang dynasty, there arrived a monk with the idea of building a retreat here. But there was no water, so he went into contemplation on the matter, and his need reaching Buddha, tigers were sent from Hunan to claw open a spring for him. The spring, said to be so miraculously derived, has a good flow and its water is generally considered to be the best anywhere for tea-making with the fragrant Lungching buds. As we sat drinking our tea, we watched a group of Shanghai workers with a glass full of spring water dropping coins into it, without the water brimming over. It is surprising how many can be dropped in before the water overflows. Most groups who come to Hupaossu try this out, and there is always much laughter and amazement as the experiment proceeds.

In the provincial museum one may see some of the specimens which have been found in various parts of Chekiang in recent years. Amongst them, I was interested in seeing a distinctive stepped-back stone adze, identical with those found amongst the Maoris of New Zealand. Although the Taipings were in Hangchow from 1860 to 1864, few of the relics of their rule survive. Most of such exhibits are from places in Chekiang outside Hangchow itself. Leaving the museum, we went through the park next door up to the hill ridge above.

Down on a greensward below this ridge children played merrily. They seem to especially enjoy the herd of lifelike deer that have been sculptured and placed amongst the trees above the lawns.

Hangchow's history goes back to very early times. Legend says that Emperor Yu came here on a boat, "hang" being the word for "boat". And Chin Shih Huang of the Chin dynasty in the third century B.C. is said to have tied his boat to a rock beneath the Paoshu pagoda. The estuary of the Yangtze then covered the Hangchow plain which, at that time, was still under water. We went over to this pagoda at the end of one afternoon and watched the big group of commune delegates who had a meeting in Hangchow coming from it down the wide stone steps lined by giant bamboos. It is also said that when the last of the Chien princes, Chien Shu, was summoned to Kaifeng by Chao Kwang-yin, founder of the Sung dynasty, he was scared that he would not be allowed to return to his fief. Chao Kwang-yin, however, not only sent him back but also gave him a roll of papers, only to be opened when he was on his way home. When Chien Shu finally did open them, he found they were memorials from court counsellors urging that the emperor detain him in the capital. He had the pagoda built on his return to express gratitude that, despite all, he had been permitted to come back to his beloved Hangchow. For many years there existed a "temple to the five princes" near West Lake, but in the wars of the last century it collapsed and has never been restored. These five princes ruled Wu and Yueh from 892 until 978 A.D., when Chien Shu died, and the place became the headquarters of a big military garrison under the Sung dynasty.

This perhaps was the reason why the Sung emperors, after their defeat by the Kin Tartars, moved their capital here from Kaifeng in the year 1130 A.D. They stayed until the Mongol armies of Kublai Khan took the city in 1276. Those with an interest in early Chinese science will recollect how Ko Hung, the early Taoist alchemist, during his experiments in Hangchow discovered many dyes, which caused his name to become revered by the dyers of Shanghai and Hangchow right up to modern times. The place where Ko Hung made his experiments was in the valley of Lungching where we had been to see the brigade of the tea-growing commune.

Of course, there is much more to be said about Hangchow. Its blossoms will bloom again and again in the springs to come, and more folk will come from around the world to write of its quiet beauty. A new modern industrial city is in the making, and the swiftness of its change will surprise even those who now plan it.

Two Years Later

Two years went past after the above had been written in April 1966. On May 16th 1968, I sat again in a boat on West Lake. Some of the pavilions in the gardens were being repaired and painted. A few old landmarks had gone, but the three stone lanterns still grace the lake, and the goldfish still scramble for tidbits beside the walk over their pond. There was a sunken boat under an ancient willow, and at its rear a whole bunch of youngsters were diving off grassy banks or swimming, their beautiful skins glistening in the sun. A new variation of the old Tang poem, with the new life graphically painted. The old poem says:

> In front of the sunken boat
> Stream on a thousand sails
> Beyond the withered oak
> Ten thousand saplings grow.

Suddenly from the city came the sound of shouting, of drums and cymbals. Over on the mountains at the back of Linyin, thunder crashed and a heavy rainstorm filled the valleys. The Cultural Revolution had gone through its first two years and the youth, on whom the responsibilities for the next stage will bear, were celebrating, with the heavens joining in. As we came down the highway we passed long lines of school children who had been out picking tea for the tea garden commune brigades. They take it in turn to do a week on this task and, going home, carry their packs on their backs, packs made up of bedding quilts rolled tight. Youngsters love the practical side of life, and obviously these were pleased with the fact that they had actually done something revolutionary together.

Hemp Bag Factory

I went out into the suburbs, along the southern terminus of the Grand Canal, to visit a hemp bag factory on a spot where during the occupation of the Japanese imperial army a concentration camp stood. Here many patriots were massacred, and when the factory, which started production in 1950, was being built, the skeletons of many victims were found. At that time, the setting up of a modern plant was not easy. First, the tools to make tools had to be built, for then none of the present machine tool plants existed, and there was a shortage of industrial essentials. But machines which previously could only be imported were satisfactorily constructed and the plant got under way. It now has 5,000 workers, 660 machines and 16,000 spindles. It produces hemp bags for export and as containers for Chinese rice for export, especially to Vietnam. A special line of small bags to hold 50 lbs., a load for one man, is also made as part of the Vietnam assistance program. Stopping in the plant to talk to a group of women workers, I met one who had been sent for a while to a similar plant in Hanoi, helping to train workers there. Her comrades were evidently proud of her, which was good evidence of the international spirit in action.

The whole plant was swinging along in a quiet, efficient manner, making it a pleasure to watch. I went to the factory nursery, kindergarten, past the schools where 1,000 children are taught, saw the swimming pool workers had made themselves, and visited the dining halls. All the work, I saw, was quite streamlined and efficient. Then I had a good long talk with my hosts. Factory production has gone up by 11 percent over the last year, and plans are being made to greatly increase output during the next stages. Nightshift workers work six-hour shifts, daytime ones six-and-a-half. Nominally eight hours, but time for meals and meetings is deducted.

An Old Cadre

The chairman of the Revolutionary Committee was under the previous administration first secretary of the Party group and so the most important leading cadre. In direct terms he explained how the Cultural Revolution had affected him. He divided his attitudes into three stages. During the first, he was disgusted with the heavy criticism he received, and with his being put on the side. "I have done my best to carry through the policies that have come down from above. Better now to become a simple worker, or else to go back to the countryside and help with farm production," he reasoned. Some people said he had killed himself because they did not see him around. "Then we tried to find out, 24 of us who were in my category, where we had left the people and why they were so against us. Later, as we met workers, they tried to encourage and help us, which touched us deeply," he said.

In March he stated his opinions in front of a factory meeting. "Then in April, various groups in the plant allied, and we were up for mass criticism which lasted for two months, and which was quite difficult for me to take. I thought to myself how hard I had worked to get the mill going, ever since its early stages. But also I thought of how Chairman Mao says we must always serve the people to the best of our capacity, and that we must change. I worried a lot, and could not sleep. Was I really loyal to the thinking of Chairman Mao? Was it not pure selfishness to think of my own dignity before the welfare of the workers? Had I really blindly and foolishly followed an anti-Mao policy? The reactionary line, put over as it was with all the power of Liu Shao-chi as head of the government, had been so deceptive, as I could see now. Slowly my thoughts clarified, and I could see that the workers were right. The highest incentive was to have the privilege of working for the revolution, in China and everywhere. Monetary rewards and the practices of economism were reactionary. That I could see now. I saw that really we had two lines in the factory, one revolutionary and the other reactionary, and that now the workers were rebelling against the reactionary one." So, from a mood of self-pity, Liu Wei was able to come to the idea of truly serving the people.

"Then came the third stage. I described my own contradictions to the masses in a meeting, and received much help from them. When the Revolutionary Committee was set up I was elected chairman. But then new troubles came. There were many problems but, scared of making new mistakes, I lacked the confidence I once had in dealing with them. This was quickly noticed by some members of the committee. 'Lao Liu,' they said, 'what's wrong with you? Don't you really believe in us?' Again I began to think that I had better get out of my position and be a simple worker. I told the Revolutionary Committee this, saying I felt I could not meet new requirements. But they said, 'Study Chairman Mao more. What is work? Work is struggle! It is part of your struggle to solve problems.' I then sat alone with this criticism, finally coming to the conclusion that, to serve the people, I had better use all my experience, all my understanding and the decisiveness necessary to make things work properly, not caring what happened to me or my own interests. By now I could see very clearly what the whole business was about. How it was struggle between two lines that by this time stood out quite clearly, the line of Mao Tsetung and the line of revisionism."

Obviously sincere, Liu Wei was making a success of his new task. Everywhere we went throughout the mill, we noted, he was received with smiles. On four days of the week he works on a shift with the workers as do all cadres now, over 90 percent of the old ones having returned to their jobs. In the other day, it was common for a few members of the administration to work with "pets", who organised small groups to support such leaders in everything. Sometimes these "pets" could be quite bad eggs, or people with a slavish mentality.

Workers' Families

Now with the new direction in politics there is no need or place for this type of cliques. Some of the stories of how the growth of understanding has affected the family life of workers are fascinating, whole families studying and making progress together. The ex-rickshaw puller and his folk, the old illiterate and his children. Many of the workers' families took part in the mass meetings during the movement and contributed much. I visited a little display the factory has set up of Cultural Revolution posters which groups or families have designed and made. Each bears the head of Chairman Mao, quotations and different designs. One big piece was entirely made up of the hemp the factory spins and weaves, and was easily the most artistic of all. When we went to visit one of the dining halls, an elderly woman, mother of a worker, came in with us. She was carrying a framed poster she had created, showing it to her friends amid general admiration. The point is that the people are doing things themselves, and are getting a lot of inspiration in so doing. "Before the Cultural Revolution, we wasted a lot of time sitting around playing cards," one worker said. "Our children copied us. Now we have too many things to do to bother with this, and the children too are finding things they can help with around the factory. We do not want to spoil them!"

Chaoyang Brigade

One morning I went east along the dyke beside the quiet majesty of the Chientang river, into Yuhang county, then branching off from the highway across country, until I arrived at Chaoyang Brigade of Chiupao Commune. The brigade farms 1,224 mou of land with a population of 1,340, coming from 274 households. The four production teams in the brigade grow hemp, rice, medicinal plants and peanuts as main crops. Before Liberation there were 219 families of whom 144 were poor peasants, and of these, 45 families had had to go out as casual workers, beg, and sell their children or else just give them away. Snail fever was rife amongst the people. One landlord and one rich peasant controlled a population then estimated at 800. The landlord had a high wall around his compound and kept seven fierce dogs. When the Japanese imperialists came they burnt and killed at will. Ninety percent of the people fled. The present head of the Revolutionary Committee, and previously brigade Party secretary, had seen his brother bayonetted by the invaders.

From Old to New

After the end of the Japanese aggression, the Kuomintang brought back the landlords and their gangs of scamps. During the Kuomintang times, the head of the "pao" was a person appointed by local officials and landlords, similar to village head, who was responsible for a group of peasant families. He could designate which family would have to send its sons to the Kuomintang army as conscripts, which family would have to quarter Kuomintang soldiers, and which would have to send in specified materials for army upkeep. He would excuse youth from being conscripted if they worked for him for nothing. Total production at that time was valued at less than 80,000 yuan. After Liberation the land was divided, but still the division between rich and poor remained and several of the poor actually had to sell land to live. Still some had to give away children, and many rented out part of their land. The older folk remember this well, and how such went on until 1954, so that the revisionist ideas urging return to that stage make them angry. The commune came, making the poor feel much better. But in 1961 a number of quite contrary ideas were spread, that production teams were too large and should be split up. That people should produce whatever sold best, without regard to any plan. That brigade funds should be divided up and then, if the brigade wanted cash for housing or anything else, they could go to the state banks for it. So the four production teams in the brigade were made into ten, much to the joy of the formerly better off. Then, in the 1961-63 period, while Chiang Kai-shek was talking so much of coming back to the mainland, another revisionist concept was handed down, namely that class conflicts were now no longer important, that class struggle was dying out and that all classes were now united, that the people should discuss grain, cotton and oil, not politics. It was evident that an attempt was made to oppose and undermine the ideas of Chairman Mao, for these hostile ideas began to permeate the countryside from many quarters.

The Socialist Education Movement had a good effect in 1965, and then came the Cultural Revolution. At 11 p.m. on the 28th of August, 1966, commune youth got up and raided the houses of the old landlord and rich peasant. In the landlord's home they found all the title deeds and the land surveys for his former property, kept to show ownership in the event of Kuomintang return. In the rich peasant's home they found five big boxes of clothing and some gold. A few days previously this rich peasant had been to the brigade office talking of his poverty and pleading for a loan of money to buy clothing. The "pao" chief who had said many times that he had thrown away all his old seals of office, was actually found to be in possession of them all. Much more evidence was turned up, educating all to the reality that old class distinctions were still very much alive.

New Struggle

Then came the struggle against selfishness and revisionism in the period from 1967 to May 1968. It led to a number of practical achievements. Six of the more important were as follows:

1. Previously certain plots of land were lying like enclaves in the area of other production teams. The production team would say, "That field has very good soil and it was given to one of our members during Land Reform. We should keep it, especially as the field the other brigade wants to give in exchange is poor." Now, after study, all agreed that the production team areas should be redivided in a scientific way, more conducive to good working.

2. Before, commune women would buy hemp from the brigade, hand spin it at home and then weave it. They made 6,900 lengths of it a year, each length being 36 ft. The state would pay the money directly to the people bringing in the product. Now all agreed that the brigade should handle the whole business, spinners and weavers getting workpoints, and the brigade keeping back a small percentage to add to its common fund.

3. The same thing applied to dried turnip. Before, households would buy turnips from the brigade and, after pickling or drying, market them — about half a million jin of turnip a year would be sold this way. The brigade, all agreed, should now take over this business and deal with it as with the hemp product.

4. In the yearly division of profits, brigade funds formerly benefited by 7 percent of the total. Now all agreed that the brigade should take 13 percent. In 1967 all decided that the brigade should have an emergency store of grain, which they had not had before. 1967 saw 54,000 jin put into it.

5. It was decided that the ten production teams be changed back to four.

6. Private plots had become bigger. They should not have been more than a small percentage of the total arable land, but they had grown to be 9 percent. It was agreed that this matter should be righted so that the brigade gained 50 mou more land. It was also agreed that all bamboo groves should in future belong to the brigade, not to private individuals.

The continued need to study is now evident to everyone. Production team cadres study half a day on the 5th, 15th and 25th of each month, brigade cadres on the 8th, 18th and 28th. On days when the weather is too bad to work, mass study meetings are called. At work, quotations are read and there is discussion during the rest periods. Work on sowing hemp that took seven days in other years, took half that time in the spring of 1968. Just one of the many instances that were given of the effect of study. There is also a resulting improvement in collective morality — people who find that they have been given too much in the marketing and supply agency give back what they do not consider is theirs. If valuables are found people go to much trouble to get them back to their rightful owners, and so on.

Folk are not rich by any means, but the crop of children look wonderfully well, none with the big stomachs and peaky faces of sufferers from schistosomiasis, so prevalent in the other day. The brigade clinic sends the seriously ill to Hangchow city hospitals, and for those who cannot afford to pay, the state provides not only free treatment but also helps with all other expenses, like food. Transport is free, and so on.

Fifty percent of the people have radios, and there are 190 bicycles. Before Liberation there were but two, both owned by the landlord. The allowance of rice per person per year is 563 jin. The brigade now has 65,000 yuan in its welfare fund, and 87,000 yuan in its accumulation fund. Amongst the collective tasks the people have carried out has been the digging of an 800-metre long canal, 24 metres wide, equipped with sluice gates. It is for both irrigation and drainage. The people say that in times of flood, before this work was done, they could wash their feet while sitting on the edge of the bed, as the water would be there right inside their homes. There is now electric light in every house and motors power their irrigation pumps, driving their rice and flour milling machines also. They say, "Before Liberation the Kuomintang looked on us poor people as just so much waste straw or reeds. Now Chairman Mao looks on us as something precious. What a difference!"

Embroidery Factory

One afternoon we went into the rather crowded portion of old Hangchow, down a narrow street to see an enterprise about 90 percent staffed by women. After Liberation some housewives joined together and made up two cooperative groups to do embroidery work. Later in 1965 these two groups combined to become an embroidery factory. They had a great deal of difficulty in getting what was necessary to start work, but by dint of determination and sacrifice they managed to overcome their early lack of resources and find an outlet for their products. By this time many other local women had joined them, and their strength had grown to 220. New technique has improved so much that 90 percent of their product goes into the export trade. Production has gone up during the Cultural Revolution, 1967 totals being 14 percent above those of 1966 and 28 percent over the 1965 figure. In the first three months of 1968, 75 percent of the planned output for the half year was completed. As all this was being told to me, I sat in the factory reception room whose walls were literally covered with embroidered pictures of Chairman Mao and of revolutionary scenes.

The Cultural Revolution, it was pointed out by the young man and young woman who were members of the Revolutionary Committee, has been an important thing for the workers. Before, they had studied very little and did not bother with politics. When the work force split into two groups, much discussion ensued. In May 1967, the grand alliance was achieved. Of the five leading cadres of the old management, four are now approved by the masses, and one of them has been made chairman of the Revolutionary Committee formed in January 1968. A great deal of dirt has come out in the washing, and morale has been raised to a new height.

The factory is building some new workshops and hopes to expand. "Come and see us again next year and see what we are like then," our hosts said as we left.

Hangchow Dry Cell Works

At the Hangchow Dry Cell Works I talked with a man in his late thirties, a greying woman maybe ten years older, a technician and a storeman. Graphically they told of the change of the past two years, first giving a brief history of the little plant. Set up by three small capitalists in 1938 with 17 workers, it made inferior quality dry cells. Because of the lack of these on the market the owners could still get a good price for them. There were no machines. There was no standardisation of product. With Liberation, the old manager of the plant, one of the three owners, was kept on and, as the plant expanded and with the backing of a handful of his own group, he maintained a hold on essential know-how. He ruled the factory as rigidly as he could. Extra pay for higher production, fines for any of his list of 15 offenses, and so on. His economism then, had all the flavor of the old order, and rebellion grew in the hearts of the workers. Even when they rose and deposed him he still would not give up his trade secrets, so a tall, thin worker named Yuan set out to find them himself. After 29 experiments and with the help of others he found the secret and the 126 workers threw themselves into their tasks in a new way. Mechanisation was swiftly added, and technical innovations brought in much automation. Productivity in 1967 was 18 percent over the 1966 figure. Monthly production during the first three months of 1968 went up over 28 percent from that of 1967. After a long period of struggle and criticism, of studying together, all of the 15 cadres of the old administration except the old manager and one other man were happily working again, filled with new enthusiasm. In addition to being asked to increase its production for both interior and export needs, the factory was asked to experiment with the making of certain graphite accessories for transistor radios. A small shop was set up for this work, the results being so successful that a full-sized shop is being built to enable 100 more workers to go into mass production on this line.

The Revolutionary Committee group gave many instances of how much the dusty thinking of the past was being rectified. How workers now became closer to each other and more considerate of each other. A man loses his watch. All help to find it and it is soon returned. Now, suggestions for better working come up from the ranks of the workers. The study program that is set for all is a rigorous one entailing a good deal of attention outside the eight working hours each day. But with everyone caught up in the momentum of the movement, it is willingly adhered to. "We live for the revolution. We are proud that some of our products go to help Vietnam," one said. In the struggle against revisionism there are plenty of homely examples everyone recognises from the last stage of factory operations. Then too, there is a growing awareness that collective effort on which success depends cannot be helped but only hurt by individual selfishness. So the slogan "Dousi Pixiu" — "Struggle against selfishness and repudiate revisionism" — has very real meaning to this working group.

Hangchow Rubber Factory

Buildings well set out, shops light and airy, green trees around and the smell of rubber in the air. A handful of young people met us at the gates. They belonged to the rebel group of the Hangchow Rubber Factory which specialises in rubber tyres, inner tubes for tractors, rubber half-knee boots for the villages, bicycle tyres, and rubber and canvas shoes for everyone. 1,135 workers in five shops work on this, enthusiastically throwing themselves into meeting the technical and production requirements of the new day.

The factory is one that was set up in the Great Leap Forward of 1958. Today its production runs to 2,000 or more tyres a day and 9,000 pairs of rubber footwear. The directive of helping the village as much as possible is strongly supported. Back in the hills, farmers ask for a tyre for their single big wheel barrow, then for half-length gum boots, and production lines for these are quickly set up.

In the struggles of the Cultural Revolution, one month's production was lost in 1967 and two months' at the beginning of 1968, due to intensive political discussions and struggle. The value of total production in 1966 was 21,950,000 yuan. In 1967 it was 21,750,000 yuan. In 1968 it will be over 22,000,000 yuan.

At the beginning of the Cultural Revolution there were 98 cadres in four administrative offices and eight section offices. Now two offices, one for political and one for administrative affairs, supplant all these. Section work is thrown back on the shoulders of production groups. Some of the older workers feared that such a drastic reduction would lead to chaos, but this has not been the case. The 36 cadres who were finally chosen from the 98 to continue administration have been picked mainly for their good political understanding. All others have gone back to the production line in the various shops.

The workers are very proud of their achievements with technical innovations. Already an automatic spraying machine has been made and installed which saves 30 tons of gasoline a month, spraying finely and evenly. A machine has now been perfected that makes soles and uppers in one, which will reduce the number of workers in the shop previously doing this from 300 to 30, while turning out a better and cheaper article. This type of machine has already been installed in some Shanghai factories, so that the worker groups making it in Hangchow were able to go and study how the problem has been met there and then incorporate certain improvements into the model they themselves have turned out. "We should have all new techniques and improvements in production that foreign countries have, and as for those they have not got yet, we must devise them too," a young technician said. The number of men and women workers in the plant is about equal. One of the women workers who was in the rebel group had been sent from the Dachunghua factory in Shanghai to train other women here after the factory had started operation. The program of political study is a rigorous one.

Support to French Students

On our way back to West Lake we passed the huge procession of people dispersing after a demonstration in support of the students in France who have rebelled. The leaf-lined streets were a mass of red banners and slogans. Most of the students and a fair proportion of the workers of Hangchow were there.

Hangchow Municipality

I learnt that of the around 320 communes in the greater Hangchow municipality which includes surrounding counties also, 300 had set up their Revolutionary Committees, and that the others were preparing to do so. In the municipality, the chairman of the Revolutionary Committee is the former deputy secretary of the Party. All leading cadres except two are back on the job again. The people are in the high tide of revolutionary enthusiasm, an enthusiasm that now expresses itself foremost in gaining practical results in work and study. Everywhere in early mornings and evenings one hears the strains of "The East is Red".

Hsiassu Brigade, Chienteh County

Swallows fluttered in the room we sat in. An old hat hung from one of the rafters made the beginnings of a nest for them. The rooms are high in west Chekiang, and this one was in Hsiangai Commune, Hsiassu Brigade in Chienteh county on the banks of the Hsinan river, half an hour's drive below the great reservoir and hydro-electric plant of that name. We had driven up through three counties from Hangchow in the rain, admiring the broad sweep of the Chientang river and mist effects in the hills around. But by the time we came to Hsiangai, all had cleared, golden summer wheat was just ready for harvesting, early rice making a carpet of green, and village streets were filled with laughing children. The leader of the Revolutionary Committee of the commune told me that it had 2,163 families, a total of 10,204 people. There were 11 brigades of 104 production teams, which farmed 7,790 mou of valley, down, and hill land. In the old days it was landlord ridden, and completely dependent on the weather. Drought years spelt borrowing money at high rates and often foreclosure by the landlord-moneylender. It spelt refugees trooping out into the hills, beggars who went around cities. Almost every poor family has paid in blood to the landlords, every old hired worker had an account to settle. From the area now farmed by one brigade, 555 young men were roped up and dragged off as conscripts by the Kuomintang, never to be heard of again. Eighty percent of the best land was owned by a handful of landlords and rich peasants, none of whom themselves worked.

The Irrigation Problem

After the bad drought years of 1959-60, the members of Hsiassu Brigade felt that the time had come to muster all the determination they had and solve the irrigation problem. Between them and the broad Hsinan river lay a range of hills. They carefully surveyed and found a place from which it was possible to drive a tunnel through 152 metres of a rocky hill ridge, to come out 50 metres above the river. With installation of a big motor and pump by the river they could then raise the water to run through their tunnel, around their terraced hills, and siphon it across to the terraced slopes on the other side of their valley, irrigating more than 2,000 mou of paddy field. It took three groups of members each of 14 men, one shift succeeding another round the clock, to do the tunnel job. By working hard they finished it in seven months and, the canal system being also done by then, the water went where it was directed. But troubles were not yet ended. The concrete siphon pipe, 50 centimetres in diameter, which was buried under several metres of soil, leaked at one joint. Water was urgently needed in paddy fields. To dig the whole thing up would take a long time. Then one of the members tried a way. Lying naked on a board, with arms in front and the board kept in place by a rope attachment men at the top held, he was let down the pipe. He did not know if there would be enough air at the place of the leak, so the first trip was short and experimental. Then he found he could stay down for about ten minutes, working at the joint with cement. At the end of each spell down in the pipe he would be pulled up to warm himself at a big fire built at the top. With determination, he finished the task, modestly saying, "Well, if Chairman Mao says one can do most anything if there is determination enough, I simply follow his words."

We climbed up the hill and looked at the siphon opening. It seemed to be an almost incredible story, but there it was. Then we went to see the tunnel — 1.2 metres high and 1.6 metres wide. Up on top of the hill there was a glorious view of the Hsinan river and the valleys around. We looked over to hills opposite, and folk said, "Those hills were all in trees up until 1961. Then Liu Shao-chi said to cut down trees and plant grain on hill terraces. This made for a mad scramble to cut forests, everyone for himself to get timber to sell and to try and bring in more land for private plots. Originally a tenth of a mou was allocated as private plot, but that big revisionist, Liu, declared people could have as much as they could reclaim. The result was that the common land of the brigade was neglected and some members spent all their time on private plots. The stress on these private plots also made some members encroach on common land. You take some, then I take some. He takes some. They take some. One six-mou field became a three-mou one, and so on. Sometimes there were tragic results. One old man who had an only son, a worker in Hangchow, brought the lad home to help him work his enlarged private plot, six mou of reclaimed hill land. The boy did not want to and went to his evening study class, keen on applying the ideas of Chairman Mao. The old man came into his room at night and beat him, the boy offering no resistance, the old man trying to make his son promise to help him. The more the boy refused the more the old man beat, all through the night. In the morning the boy took poison and died. Now the old man lives on with his misery, bitterly telling people what the revisionist line did to him.

But if one looks for instances of the evils rising from the wrong policy, there are so many! One brigade went so much into the private plot business that it had to be given relief grain by the state to support its people. In 1963 it was given 50,000 jin. In 1966 and also in 1967 the same brigade, after studying the works of Chairman Mao, repudiating the revisionist line and taking over excess private plots was able to sell to the state 120,000 jin, and in addition put 70,000 jin of grain in the brigade store for emergencies. In 1966, instead of cutting trees and bushes, it planted 300,000 of them. Tea, pears, chestnuts, pines and spruce.

Obviously the Thought of Mao Tsetung gets good results, while the opposite line does not. Tu Yu-ken worked hard on the private plot he had reclaimed, did not often go to collective work. He has seven people in his family and brought them all to oppose cadres. Finally, during the criticism of the revisionist line, he woke up and realised that he had been on the wrong road, and that without the brigade he would be nothing. He gave up his private plots and went to work, trying to make up with increased energy for his mistake.

Another member, Wang Chiu, who had been a Kuomintang soldier, used to make soap from certain tree seeds. He was so keen on following the revisionist line that he dug up river mud to make his private plot grow more sugar cane to sell on the market. After listening to the speeches in the mass meetings exposing revisionism, he went to work digging out mud as fertiliser for the brigade's tea plants. His profit on his plot of sugar cane worked out at 170 yuan a year. Because of his devotion in getting fertiliser to the tea plants, they produced an additional 6,000 yuan worth of tea compared with the preceding season. He has carried at least 7 dan (piculs) each and every day uphill to the tea gardens in rest periods or after work at night. Before, he was illiterate, but now he can write many characters, learning them from the book of quotations he memorises. "Now I know what 'serve the people' means," he said. "It means a new and purposeful life for all of us."

There was Tangping Brigade, following the revisionist "san zi yi bao" line, which means the extension of plots for private use, the extension of free markets, the increase of small enterprises with sole responsibility for their own profits or losses, and the fixing of output quotas based on the individual households. The brigade borrowed money, but as fast as it borrowed the money was used up. Then it borrowed more to repay loans, but still the people were poorer than before. At the beginning of the Cultural Revolution, they got together and, in 10,000 workdays, reclaimed 400 mou of waste land and irrigated it, not using a fen of the state's money. They have become self-sufficient and are now out of debt, with a clear road ahead of them.

One could go on for a long time telling stories like these which tumbled from the lips of the people here. They feel now that their commune is rapidly making progress. It has now 14 schools, a commune hospital and brigade clinics, power-driven grain processing machines, machine repair shops, and electric light in every home. There has been the mistake of following the wrong line, but now the essence of that line, its class basis and who was for and who against it, has become clear in their minds. Sixty-five-year-old Chang Kwei-ying, a woman who had not done any embroidery for many years, took out her needles and did a piece of silk with a red heart and the character for loyalty in it. As we left Hsiassu village the brigade leader, carrying a framed picture of Chairman Mao, walked in front. And behind the glass under the picture was the handiwork of Chang Kwei-ying. It was something like a procession of civic dignitaries in some European city, except that here it was a mountain village, and the participants were poor peasants, the spectators the families of every home on the way, old and young, who filled the big doors of old houses with life, ducks splashing in the little stream that ran beside the cobbled street, and chickens running underfoot. In every day and in every way, the people are more and more coming into their own. As we went off, the Revolutionary Committee waved their Little Red Books. The Hsiassu brigade leader raised the portrait of Chairman Mao he carried, and the lad with the red banner let it stream in the breeze. They made quite a patch of color, lighting up the hills that stood behind them in the pastel shades of evening.

Hsinan Power Station

When we came to the Hsinan Power Station, loudspeakers were broadcasting evening news. The space below the dam and in front of the guest house had been made into a pleasant garden beautiful with many trees. I had not been here since the dam was nearing completion in 1959, carrying in my mind a picture of a whole valley full of enormous activity, day and night. Now all was relatively quiet.

The next day we listened to the story of the political struggle here that has gone on over the past two years. There were 200 cadres of whom 109 were technical personnel. In the old administrative offices 120 cadres worked. Now there are only 53. Technical cadres are all busy, some having gone to help a nearby hydro-electric project, others staying in their usual positions. Of the old cadres in administration, a few are still being criticised, but most have gone off to work where needed. Out of the stiff course in political study has emerged the need for the struggle against selfishness and a thorough repudiation of revisionism, for they know that the revisionist line irrevocably leads administrators, no matter how efficient they may be in some things, onto the path of becoming enemies of the people, builders of a new and privileged class.

We talked for some time on technical conditions in the plant, then went to see the six big generators made in Harbin, all producing. The last three generators are now being installed. It was really something to get a 650,000-kw. plant operating in three years, and says a lot for the spirit of the workers who did the job. The long corridors of the power station, situated inside the dam, were cool and quiet. In the control room computers dialled output, and everything went ahead with the precision of a well-oiled machine. We took the elevator to the top of the dam and looked up the lake which stretched 160 kilometres to the west, being 70 kilometres wide in its broadest place. Bamboo rafts that came down were picked up by cranes and deposited in the clear waters of the river the other side of the dam. The dam produces so many fish that fish is the cheapest meat in all places around. Big fish with coarser meat ten fen a jin, smaller, good-tasting ones 20 fen. For any who have time to go fishing, none goes home empty handed. Fishermen putting out a big net have been known to get 160,000 jin of fish in one haul.

When the project was nearly finished, several technical problems presented themselves which made the administration want to postpone completion. Workers, however, were adamant that they must turn over the whole plant as scheduled and, working with the greatest determination, they did so.

Today, the massive great dam presents a gay appearance, with quotations in red and white painted everywhere, and in huge characters along its top the slogan, "Long life to Chairman Mao." Its power goes not only to communes and cities in Chekiang, but also to those in Kiangsu province and Shanghai city. Its strength raises the water into thousands of irrigation canals, lights millions of homes, powers many factories. There amongst the hills it is a powerful achievement of a revolutionary people determined to stand up on their own feet.

The PLA and the Cultural Revolution

In the Cultural Revolution in Chekiang province the PLA, as everywhere else in China, has played a positive and often decisive role in ideological struggles that have taken place. As a force drawn by and large from the ranks of the poor peasants it is one that is thoroughly integrated with the people, working with them in the fields and in the villages, learning from them and, at times too, giving them leadership. So it was a pleasure to sit and listen, while members of a small group of PLA folk told of how the Cultural Revolution had affected their lives, and what new understanding it had brought them.

Han Chun-tsai was a cadre in the Chekiang army headquarters. He admitted that at first in the Cultural Revolution he did not entirely understand all factors, but said that very soon things became clear. The Sixteen Points and, above all, Mao Tsetung Thought brought clarity as they were studied. With the negative example of the USSR before them, the fact that the first socialist country could slip back into the old system so quickly, quite obviously meant that something had to be done. The question was "where is the class enemy and how to combat him". They were from the poor peasant class with a simple love for Chairman Mao and had not lost the common touch. So when they organised the struggle against selfishness and for repudiation of revisionism they were able to see clearly the differences between the socialist and the capitalist road.

In one rural community where the PLA lived and organised such meetings along with the people, grain production had been poor, with state grain having to be sent in every year for relief. In 1967, however, the brigade with which they worked was able to sell 30,000 jin of surplus grain to the state. The people there were very warmhearted towards them. Old folk insisted on making shoes for them. They did not want to accept anything, but then one old woman member wept because they would not take the shoes she had made. Finally they took a few things as a token and returned the rest. While they were there, one of their fighters was breaking in a horse. Approaching the village on a narrow walled path, it took fright and bolted. Seeing some old village folk ahead, the rider threw himself off, and halted the beast. He was hurt but happy that the people in front had not been injured.

Huang Kuo-chan, a 23-year-old infantryman, native of Chekiang, went on telling how he wanted to be a soldier even when he was under age, but was always rejected as being too young. Finally his ambition was realised. "With two thirds of the world waiting for Liberation, we must stand on their side," he said. "And, first, we must stand on the side of the Chinese people in their struggle forward." Evidently quite an artist, he told of how he and his comrades had done woodcuts, wood carving, woven and embroidered pictures of Chairman Mao, and how they had written many poems praising him. Huang felt that in doing all this he was able to put the wishes of the people and his comrades into terms they could appreciate.

In all, they were a pleasant, warm group of people to meet, who gave the strong impression that they had caught hold of a new way of living that gave all new strength and great satisfaction.

Yanglin Commune

Tienmushan, Heavenly Eye Mountain, stands over 4,500 feet above the tilled valley lands of west Chekiang, a scenic place with many historical associations in the past, and still famous for the medicinal herbs that come from its slopes. At its foot and beside the great eastern gulch down which a pretty stream splashes gaily over big stones, lies the village of Yangchaotou.

Leaving the highway west at Linan, we wound across the country until we finally came to this village, where in the old house that had once belonged to a landlord, I met the leading members of the Revolutionary Committee of Yanglin Commune, whose 11 brigades and 63 production teams lie in the villages around. The gulch, which comes some 20 miles through steep hills, suddenly widens out here, and through the centuries floods have spewed out the bones of the mountains in the shape of great boulders, stones and gravel, creating a riverbed about a mile wide in the Yangchaotou area. Paddy fields run around the edges of this waste, and off them live 1,443 families, 6,700 people in all. In area they total 6,308 mou — a little over 1,000 acres. Eighty-three percent of this land, the best parts of it, were owned before Liberation by 80 families of landlords and rich peasants, though they totalled only six percent of the population.

As grain still accounts for 60 percent of production, a glance at the crop figures for the commune since 1949 is interesting.

    1949 — 280 jin per mou
    1953 — 327 „   „   „
    1956 — 420 „   „   „
    1958 — 640 „   „   „
    1966 — 767 „   „   „
    1967 — 770 „   „   „
    1968 — (expected on basis of results so far obtained)
       850-900 jin per mou.

Tea has been the second crop. The commune owns around 80,000 mou of hills, some of which are good for growing tea. In 1949, 280 dan (one dan, or picul = 100 jin) were produced. In 1967, 420 dan.

In 1963 a third source of income was put under way, the growing of mulberry trees and the raising of silk cocoons. In 1965, 93 dan of these were gained; in 1966, 572 dan; in 1967, 678 dan, and 1968, on the basis of the first of the four-crops-a-year of mulberry leaves, 1,000 dan is expected. Eventually, as more of the riverbed is reclaimed, many more mulberries will be planted until silk cocoons become the main crop.

It has been the reclamation of the riverbed land that has made people call Yanglin Commune the Tachai of Chekiang. The work that has been put in has been prodigious. Boulders and stones have been used to make walls around fields, earth has been brought in to add to the thin crust of soil there, green fertiliser has been planted between the mulberry trees to be dug in. The number of brigade pigs has been increased, for each pig is a fertiliser factory in itself. In 1949 there was one pig to five families, but now for the past three years the average has risen to 4.5 for each family. Reclamation had to be done at the same time as all the usual intensive farming of rice and tea, where production was also all the time increasing. Everyone in Yangchaotou turned out for the reclamation work, old and young, and the results achieved have been amazing. To facilitate work, they have built a suspension bridge over the river, and set up a part-study, part-work middle school where, on the practical side, the students all learn the technique of mulberry culture. There is still a large area that can be reclaimed but that must now wait until the big problem of water conservancy is met, for some unexpected flood from a cloudburst might well affect the reclaimed land. Five kilometres above Yangchaotou, near the village that is headquarters for Chili Brigade, a dam is being thrown across the valley where the waters from the gulch flow out. It will be 40 metres high in its first stage, over 70 in its second, thus creating a reservoir of eight million cubic metres and ensuring protection against drought and flood for the 870,000 mulberry trees already planted below it, as well as for grain crops. Folk have already had some experience on building reservoirs, for in the years 1958-63 they made 17 small ones, with a combined capacity of 890,000 cubic metres. Then in the winter of 1963-64, members of eight brigades reclaimed 2,000 of the 5,000 mou of riverbed planned to be done. The other three brigades at the same time made 850 mou of new tea gardens on the hillsides.

In that winter, part of the mulberry seedlings having failed, it became necessary to buy young mulberry trees for spring planting. People had planned to kill 310 pigs for their Spring Festival (Old New Year) but instead sold them and put the money into the seedling fund. Many withdrew their savings from the bank and put them into the fund, just asking that the money be returned to them when the brigade would be able to do so. People are no longer so poor now, though. In 1950 the average income per person was 30-40 yuan. In 1966 it was 79 yuan, and in 1967, 91 yuan, despite the drought of that year. Grain allowance per person was 200 jin in 1950, 360 in 1953, and 550 in 1967. All are now better off than the middle peasant of pre-Liberation times. The telephone connects all production teams and brigades to the commune, and the daily news comes over 250 loudspeakers in the 11 brigades. They now have 930 children in their primary schools.

On the political side, they have not always had clear sailing. At the change-over from mutual-aid teams to cooperatives, five were set up. But Liu Shao-chi's revisionist line directed at that time that four of them should be stopped. The people were told they were like children who had not learnt to walk yet, and so had to take it slow. In her anger over this one of the co-op members in Yangchaotou, a woman, cried for three days and refused to eat. Folk said, "When children cannot walk you do not kill them. You teach them by practice how to do it." On their own initiative the people went ahead and formed nine cooperatives of their own. The county leadership declared this illegal, but then came Chairman Mao's statement on cooperatives, and soon all were back on the collective road together again. In 1955 Chairman Mao said that some comrades in charge of rural collectivisation were going ahead like a woman with bound feet. So all cooperatives were reorganised and stepped out boldly. A year later, grain production had increased by an average of 105 jin amongst them all. Study of "The Foolish Old Man Who Removed the Mountains" started in 1963, before work on riverbed reclamation was begun. With it came new understanding of the class struggle, which has been heightened during the Cultural Revolution. In the two years of the Cultural Revolution the knowledge of Chairman Mao's ideas has been deepened. Of the 22 leading cadres of the commune 20 are back at work, the people having rejected only two of them as being unsuitable for their jobs.

While out looking at the mulberry planting, we met a lass carrying in a load of cocoons. They certainly looked very fine ones. "Usual high-quality cocoons have a thread 1,200 metres long. Ours are 1,700 metres," she said proudly. A couplet painted on red paper and pasted one each side of a peasant's front door said, "To be scared of difficulty means that nothing is done. The struggle for self-sufficiency brings fivefold happiness." The family evidently wished to have a slogan like that to add to the determination their political study brought, for the work was tough. To reclaim three mou, half an acre, an equivalent of 2,700 workdays was needed. Members said, "We must work until there is one mou reclaimed for each of our number." They did that and more. Now, with the purple blossom of the green fertiliser below and the broad rich green mulberry leaves above, the old riverbed looks different.

I sat for a while with one of the members in his home. It was a large, new house, still not finished inside. "Whenever I get some time I do some more to it," the man said. He had married late, after Liberation, for he was one of the poor hired hands condemned by poverty to remain single in the old society. He had four children, the eldest just 18. "On New Year's Day 1963," he said, "I gave my wife eight yuan to make clothing, and the children two yuan to buy sweets. But then we all decided to put this money and the 30 yuan all our other surplus amounted to, into the brigade fund for buying young mulberry trees."

In the Cultural Revolution, over 1,000 Little Red Books were distributed to commune members, and also the pamphlets containing Chairman Mao's three short essays ("Serve the People", "In Memory of Norman Bethune" and "The Foolish Old Man Who Removed the Mountains"), and other works. The peasants declared, "Study helped us to get over the droughts of 1965, '66 and '67. We had a dry spell of around 50 days in 1965, one of 73 days in 1966 and then one of over 100 days in 1967, when quite a few pines on the hills died." One big effect of the Cultural Revolution is that it has brought cadres and ordinary members closer together. Talking to one of the leaders of Chili Brigade I learnt that in the old days the people in his village often had to pound up roots from the hillsides for food, walk 100 li to Yuhang city to buy salt. Many strayed away as beggars and died on the road. In five years' time when the reservoir is finished, they will be taking in fish from it every year. "We feel that Chairman Mao has brought these things we now enjoy to us, so we are grateful to him," he said simply. His membership, amongst other things, had helped to put in 50,000 workdays building four kilometres of highway needed for the work on the reservoir. Everybody is naturally pleased with what has been done, feeling themselves part of a revolution that will continue and carry them to new successes.

It was evening with a thunderstorm blowing up when I said good-bye to the leadership of the commune and started off down the road back to Hangchow, my mind full of the stories of struggle and achievement I had heard all day. For here are people fighting for freedom from the uncertainties of nature, people who at last begin to understand their own strength.

Shaohsing 1966

It is hard to imagine doing anything more pleasant than to travel across a stretch of countryside south of the Yangtze in Chekiang province in spring, with the hills in blue streaming along beside the car, the vivid greens, purples and gold of the countryside and then the clean-cut white of house walls reflected in wide canals. It was especially beautiful when it happened to be the first warm day in April 1966, and farm folk had thrown off a good deal of cold-weather clothing to work the paddy, prior to transplanting rice. With Chingming (the mid-spring festival) fast approaching, the beds of rice seedlings under plastic covers were growing swiftly. The winter wheat was in ear already and would soon be turning to yellow ripeness for the first harvest of the year. The people one saw seemed happy and their land rich and lovely. No one was idle, it seemed. We passed a long file of Hangchow students hiking out into the country for their spring excursion. Soon we came into Shaohsing city which is one of around 110,000 people, and drove into the quiet courtyard of a guest house.

The first call, of course, was to the home of Lu Hsun, for it was the pen of Lu Hsun that stirred so many millions of hearts in the days when the need for basic change began to become more and more obvious. There is a good collection of historical material here on Shaohsing and on the early life of China's greatest modern writer. It was seven years since I had last come, and much had been added to the collection in the meantime. Pieces of furniture of his old home have been brought together, and the place has been restored as much as possible to what it was in his time. The bits that relate to his boyhood — the schoolroom over the canal in front of his home, the pictures and models of him with playmates and friends, these all have a poignancy of their own. The cobbled road outside his home has been renamed Lu Hsun Street, and a section has been made into a public garden. A sweet four-year-old girl danced up and said, "Take my picture," which I promptly did.

Shaohsing, like Soochow and other cities in the old Yangtze delta, is a place of waterways. Long low bridges of stone slabs cross the small lakes, and a tow-path runs beside the wider canals so that boats can be pulled instead of being propelled by the "yulo" oar at their rear. The standard of living is high in comparison with that of farm folk in most parts of north China. I remember how on my first visit here, somewhere in the early 'thirties, the most common sight at so many doors in the city was that of people sitting and hammering out paper models of silver ingots to be burnt at funerals. It was a trade that was then worth six million silver dollars a year. No one can say that China has not tried out the economy of waste! But Shaohsing of today is clear of all this. Some handicraftsmen were making brown felt hats for winter and spring use by farm folk. It is one made of wool, similar to that worn by country folk in the Tyrol in Europe except that it does not have the feather on one side.

Lu Hsun

The old city wall that perhaps Lu Hsun thought of in one of his better known poems has now gone. Part of its stone has been used to face the Sleeping Dragon hillside near a highway. Lu Hsun did not write so many poems, but there are two that most young people in China today know. One was written in the spring of 1931 in Shanghai, after 23 leading writers had been shot by the reaction, and may be translated like this:

> Often when I spent
> a long spring night restlessly
> I would feel how good it would be
> to return home, taking the family;
> now with greying temples
> I see hazily through my dreams
> my old mother with tears on her face,
> and the city wall, where now
> flags have changed; then
> coming back to reality knowing
> one must go on despite the fact
> that so many dear friends
> have been killed; I, burning
> with anger would be in the thick
> of the fight, writing these lines
> then dropping my head knowing
> that now there is no place
> they might be published;
> like shining water moonlight
> spreads over my dark clothing.

The second contains lines which are reproduced on the Lu Hsun memorial postage stamp put out by the new China. It runs like this:

> Now that my life has all gone wrong,
> what can I ask for? It could
> be said, do nothing
> when action brings trouble, but
> I simply wear a broken hat
> pulling it down over my face
> when I walk through busy streets;
> middle age, with some little comfort
> like a man with a pot of wine on a leaky boat
> in the middle of the river; yet
> determined that even though
> the enemy in their thousands
> point threateningly at me
> I will not heed them
> only bending my head and giving myself
> to be as a working buffalo
> led by a boy, ever in the service
> of good common folk; now only when
> I shut myself in my small attic room
> do I become ruler of all I survey

with no care for change of season
of heat or of cold.

Tunghu Beauty Spot

Shaohsing has a gem of a beauty spot. In its environs, there is a hill which for the past 2,000 years has been used as a quarry for the fine, wide stone slabs that are one of the exports of Shaohsing. Great perpendicular faces were formed down the side of the hill as the slabs were cut away and loaded onto boats in the canal below. Looking at the results, it is as if some big knife had shorn the hills down. Finally in the Ching period, under the hill a cave was found and in it a deep pool of water. The perpendicular cliff, over 70 feet high, was cut to the water's edge and one of the local scholars was seized with the idea of making the locality into a park with lake and pleasure boats that would wind through steep cliffs, past ornamental trees, pavilions and under bridges. This was done, and now the quarries operate on a different part of the hill. The park has become an attraction for the city folk from Shaohsing and is visited on holidays for rest and recreation. A new route has been cut for the main canal which is entered by passing under hunchback bridges from the scenic lake.

Three farmers had brought in a boat while we were there and were loading it with the rich mud they were pulling up from the lake bottom. This mud makes excellent fertiliser for the whole busy countryside, which is dotted with the white walls of electric power pumping stations. Some of the aqueducts for irrigation are made with the big stone slabs from the once too numerous graves that have now been removed to the hills. In 1959 in this vicinity I had watched many of them being removed with great spirit by the newly organised communes. The remains of the departed of so long ago were placed in glazed pots and interred amongst the red azaleas that bloom each spring on the hillsides not suitable for much else. There are a host of uses to which the finely chiselled wide slabs that once enclosed the coffins can be put. It will not be long before all graves have gone from arable land, with no new ones being put there. The 900,000 people who farm Shaohsing county and have already more than doubled their grain production since 1950 are going to need all the growing space they can get.

Shaohsing lads were well known all over China as good accountants. In the old imperial days, there would be a Shaohsing man in every yamen (magistrate's office) doing that kind of work. In the old society they became famous bankers, especially in Shanghai. But today there is no doubt about their ability to become also excellent farmers. We spent part of an afternoon out amongst them, watching them at work as we went on a visit to the temple by the tomb said to be that of the emperor Yu. The home of the rulers of Hsia, the earliest recorded Chinese dynasty, was most probably south Shansi. Local legend says that when the Hsia engineer King Yu was out controlling the waters over all China he came down the Yangtze and, on a hill by its estuary in what is now Shaohsing, he died and was buried.   There is a tombstone here over what legend says is his grave — a round stone like the head of a big fish, coming up from the side of the hill and now covered with a pavilion.

The Woman Li Shen-ying

In one of his powerful short stories, Lu Hsun wrote of a country woman who was a servant in his home.   It was not an uncommon story of life in the old society, but the way he was able to tell it made many think.   I thought of that story when meeting the 56-year-old Li Shen-ying, a woman who has five grown children and already seven grandchildren.   Small, yet with great natural dignity of bearing and a warm smile, she looks after the piggery of her commune brigade and takes a deep interest in the political life of the community.   Her husband is ten years older than she.   Not able to get married until he was 29, and she then 19.   The local landlord let them rent seven mou of his land.   Not very good land for which they had to pay 150 jin of rice a year.   Children came, four daughters and then a son, and still they managed to get along, though having to return to the landlord three mou of their land.   Then came the failure of one crop, and rice for the family had to be borrowed from the landlord to feed everyone. The landlord was of the kind who demanded 15 percent per month interest, so the debt swiftly mounted.   Soon it was taking more than all their produce to pay the interest payments demanded.   On top of this, the Kuomintang and later the Japanese demanded more and more taxes.   The eldest daughter was taken by the landlord to be sold as a houseslave in Hangchow, in lieu of one payment.   Another daughter was given away.   The two smaller ones were sent out begging.   The family tied straw around their limbs in winter to keep out the cold.   They often lived on grass roots and seeds.   The husband became a permanent invalid after a terrific beating by Japanese soldiers because he could not pay one tax.

When, after Liberation, a work team arrived to start Land Reform, they were all at the end of their tether.   The Land Reform team gave them two jin of rice.   They hardly dared accept, and had to go to a neighbor's place to cook it as they had nothing left of their own, having been evicted from their home. Then life took a sharp turn. In the past 17 years, Li Shen-ying says, she has become younger each year.   At a meeting of commune workers in Hangchow some years ago she told the story of losing her two eldest girls.   City workers helped to find them, and both are now happily married, as are the two youngest ones. The son is now a bookkeeper, having gone through a training course.   He is also a leader in the brigade militia. Is engaged, but thinks he himself should get more training and learn more before marrying.   A common enough story all in all, she says.   There were so many poor in the old days and they all had their story.   A real bit of Shaohsing, though, and I felt privileged to have met her.

Shaohsing Pottery

It was raining heavily the morning I went to see the Shaohsing pottery kilns.

Actually the area is amongst the most important kiln sites in China, for it was here that the celadons first reached some of the perfection they were later to attain when the kilns were removed to the wooded mountains to the south at Lungchuan. Later the kilns moved down to Chuchow, and finally back to Lungchuan again. The supply of brushwood for fuel was often quite soon used up in any locality, which may have accounted for the changes.

There are other kiln sites being found all the time. To the north of Hangchow, at Yihsing, just over the border in Kiangsu, deep green glazed fragments have been found on a site that is probably of the Sui dynasty. At Teching in Chekiang on the road from Yihsing to Hangchow, fragments of the tea bowls called Te-mou-ku in Japan have been turned up. Many fragments are found around the village of Chiayen on the road between Hangchow and Shaohsing. At Yuwangmiao (temple to Emperor Yu) there are plenty of shards showing that old kilns of the Five Dynasties time were situated around here. Further west from Shaohsing at Yuyao is Shanglinhu, a small lake, which is one more site of ancient Yueh wares as they were called. Shaohsing was once "Yueh Chou". Amongst the materials stamped into earth walls there one can pick out many a piece of Yueh ware of historical periods.

It is said that at Yuwangmiao, the first of the "bi-sur" or "secret color" glaze (often written "pi-se" in the West) was produced, as far back as in the Tang dynasty. Improved during the time of the Chien princes of Yueh, 902 to 978 A.D., it was still more developed in Sung times. It is said that when the last Chien prince went to the Sung court in 978 A.D. he took with him 50,000 pieces of the finest Yueh ware, which were much appreciated. The sites around Yuwangmiao were not discovered until the 'thirties, but then there must have been literally hundreds of kilns around the hills of Shaohsing in its pottery heyday, until the axe of the fuel collector turned the hills barren. The fact that the locality was once a great centre for ceramics became forgotten, though in Borneo, the Philippines and in many Middle Eastern lands prized specimens of its wares can still be found.

Ceramics then is an ancient craft here. The modern kilns were started in 1956 with 40 potters, a number which has now risen to well over 400. Daily use porcelain for the province is made from good local clay. Coal for firing the kilns has to be brought in, which is not a difficult matter in a land of fine waterways. The plant is modern, well managed and its various processes show a high degree of workers' creative ability in technical innovation, there being devices to cut out shapes quickly and cleanly, to glaze and decorate faster. Yet there is some work still done manually, like the 30 percent of food bowls which are decorated by hand, stencils and transfers being used for the rest. The lasses who paint hold two pens together and so do two rows of design at the same time, finishing bowls with incredible speed, yet all very finely done and with a sure touch. Over 40 kinds of products are made. Costs have been halved since the kilns were set up. In consequence, they are able to lower prices for their products all the time. They claim a breakage rate of only 2 percent. There is urgent demand for all their products.

Spiced Beancurd

From porcelain kilns I went to see a 300-year-old craft, that of making "mei dofu" or spiced beancurd. This is a delicacy that in its white painted jars goes all over the country and is eagerly bought everywhere. The old-style premises are very spacious and most of the workers have grown old in the plant. An increased demand for the product has called for mechanisation of its processes such as bean grinding, sifting and so on. The buildings stand beside a canal along which raw materials are brought in and the packed jars sent off to market. There was no evidence of a speedup here, one rather got the impression of sureness and confidence in a good useful thing being done skilfully and well.

Shaohsing Wine

Shaohsing, however, is best known around the China of today for the yellow wine it produces. A craft that has been operating in the district since the time of the Spring and Autumn period 2,500 years ago. Folk-lore has it that Wu Sung, who went out and killed a tiger barehanded, drank a whole jar of Shaohsing at a wine shop in Chingyangkang in Shantung before going to his self-appointed task. Some of the large jars of wine made here have a picture of the tough Wu Sung on the label, tiger in fist. As I stood in one of the shops watching the sterilising of the jar tops before the caps were put on, lotus leaf and bamboo leaves tied around to help in sealing them down, the manager brought a bowl of hot wine for me to drink. On a cold wet day, with feet already feeling a little numb, the wine went to the right place immediately and spirits revived noticeably all around. Some of the pressing of the sticky rice and wheat from which Shaohsing wine is made is done by a machine press, but most of it is still satisfactorily carried out by the traditional press seen in the woodcuts of old-time books. We halted for a time watching a worker operate several of these. He obviously liked what he was doing, pieces of wood seeming to flow from his hands as he fitted them into place and operated the big lever adding the weights. His spotlessly clean white head cloth, red shirt and light blue shorts seemed to be somehow interwoven with the task he was carrying out with assured deftness. The workers in this enterprise are now backed by a scientific research institute that enables standardisation of product and basic improvement in it. It has been found, for instance, why only the water of Chien Lake nearby will make good Shaohsing wine. Before, it was known that this was so but not the reason why. Five regular, standardised grades of Shaohsing wines are now made. Local people coming in from planting out rice in the cold spring mud like theirs hot. But this wine should only be heated, never boiled. If boiled it turns to vinegar, as it is likely to do also if heated in an iron kettle. It contains 15 to 19 percent alcohol, depending on its grade.   The wine-making time is from October to April each year.   Summer is too hot for it.   It is then that the waste from the wine-making process is used for producing a white spirit.

Leaving the winery, we halted on the bridge over the canal nearby, and despite the rain tried to get a few pictures of the wine-loading wharf by the canal below, from which the good Shaohsing wine goes out to so many places in China and abroad.   Then the car turned and we sped across country back to Hangchow again, glad to have had some time with the people of Shaohsing.

Shaohsing 1968

Two years of the Cultural Revolution had passed when, by the end of May 1968, I visited Shaohsing again.   Spring was over and the rapeseed was harvested, with production teams now out working the paddy fields or else transplanting rice shoots.   Wheat was ripening, and soon it would be cut, and the land also go into rice.   A busy countryside with everyone working, pants rolled high, bronzed legs set sturdily apart as they bent over their tasks.   In some production teams, tractors instead of water buffaloes were working paddy.   Soon overcast skies that kept the days cool would pass, and summer heat start.   Since my last visit, some fields were being plowed with electric power.   A motor each side of the field operates a winch which pulls the plow through the mud efficiently and quickly.   Commune brigades are pleased with the idea and it is spreading. But changes that have come to Shaohsing over the past two years are many, most being in the realm of the spirit that so soon translates itself into material benefit.

Shaohsing county got its Revolutionary Committee on March 12th. Shaohsing prefecture set one up the day before my arrival, on May 19th, 1968.   In the county are 68 communes, of which 43 have Revolutionary Committees established, with the remainder having theirs under preparation.   The big majority of cadres are back at work again, all of them now working at least a day and a half a week with production teams in the fields.   In 1967, during the progress of the revolution, the area went through a five-month period of drought when no rain fell at all, and many of the smaller canals dried up.   Yet the crop harvested that year exceeded the big harvest of 1966 by 13 million jin.   The whole population turned out to struggle against this natural calamity, and complete victory was gained.   It was an epic in mass work geared to one end, nothing like it ever having happened here before.

On the industrial side the struggle for better understanding was fierce, with a resultant opening of many eyes as to what revisionism really is. At the same time, many technical innovations were devised.   More export goods were made, from badminton balls to lace.   Both in the communes and in industry, mass meetings began to be run in better ways, starting on time, finishing on time.

Shaohsing Pottery Again

What a change to go back to the Shaohsing pottery after a two-year absence! Continuous kilns have been installed and various improvements made so that these, together with a better spirit amongst the workers, have resulted in a 98 percent production increase over 1966. Production and construction have gone hand in hand with revolution. With help from Shaohsing middle-school students and the PLA, the old management was successfully criticised and a Revolutionary Committee of nine members has been formed, two of whom were old cadres — the manager and assistant manager — together with seven young workers, one of whom was a girl. This committee has given highly successful leadership to the plant since. During the meetings the two lines showed up very clearly, and workers who were somewhat puzzled at the beginning of the movement were now able to see what was at stake and throw their whole weight in behind the change.

The export trade is now taking undecorated food bowls in quantity, the patterns being added in Hongkong. Big teapots with red roses on them that have been a feature of village life in this part of China for many decades are still made and are very much in demand. Most of the drinking mugs being turned out had Chairman Mao's poems on them. Chairman Mao badges in porcelain were also being made, and we visitors were each decorated with a specimen.

I stopped in for a while at Lu Hsun's home and school for one more visit. I picked up a shard there of green Yueh celadon on a thick base. The litter of previous cities literally covers all Shaohsing. When going to Lu Hsun's old school, a whole bevy of children accompanied us, making the place alive again. Museums about someone even as famous as Lu Hsun need something like this around them. The rooms in the old house were penetrated with the sweetness of mayflower of which there was a riot in the back garden.

I asked about the woman Li Shen-ying whom I had met two years ago, and was glad to hear that she was working hard in the Cultural Revolution and assisting those around her in the spirit of "serve the people".

Meishan Commune

To get to Meishan Commune one goes by boat from one of the Shaohsing city wharves and threads one's way through canals, until coming to a large sheet of water. Going down it, one finally branches off and arrives at the Kaisu brigade wharf. This brigade is one farming 896 mou of fairly good land, all of which is irrigated. It has 900 people who come from 201 families. At the wharf I received a warm welcome. Chen Chin-seng, the brigade leader, led me to the brigade offices where we sat with the Revolutionary Committee while Chen told us how in the drought of 1934, which was not so long or so bad as that of 1967, only 100 jin a mou was harvested. But with all cooperating and working with determination, the highest yield of history was gained in 1967 — 1,450 jin a mou.

When the four landlords and three rich peasants owned 600 mou, a good yield was 400 jin a mou.   Now the grain allowance per capita a year is 760 jin, which enables families to keep emergency stores in their own homes.   The brigade also has an additional emergency store of 200,000 jin, more than enough for five months' total brigade consumption.   Brigade members have decided that they will put 9 percent of their income into collective funds this year instead of the 8 percent of 1967.

In 1966-67 they installed several machines for common use — rice husking, flour milling, and irrigation pumps, all powered with the electricity that now comes in.   Twenty-two new buildings were needed and built by the members themselves.   Coming into the village, I saw that the crops that ran right up to the village edge had been protected against village chickens, ducks and pigs by a wall of tall stone slabs which had obviously come from old grave mounds, now removed.   Then a little later when listening to the brigade leader tell of instances in which selfishness was overcome, he spoke of the woman Ting Ah-san, who often would lose 50 workpoints a month in fines for letting her domestic animals stray into the grain fields.   In fact, the more she was fined the worse she seemed to get!

Then, in the Cultural Revolution, Ting Ah-san got hold of the idea of struggle against selfishness, criticised herself, and promptly took part in fencing off the village paths from the crops.   Actually, with all this kind of thing being done throughout the production teams of the brigade, one would have thought that the domestic animals would have become fewer. But in actual practice this has not been the case.   With better care they have increased in quantity and quality.   But there are so many instances of how people have changed — the idler always late for work, earliest to go back home, whose main interest was in his private plot; the bully who loved cursing people, fought with them, went off to the city to drink wine; the perpetual complainer and shouter when workpoints were being given — all these people who learnt that, with selfishness, there is no real future for any of the peasants and who changed so much as to become front rank people, the first to volunteer when something difficult had to be done, people who scorned workpoints and were ever anxious to do more.   One of these newly reformed and active people has been put in charge of the brigade piggery.   There was the man who was good at bringing back river mud for fertiliser but who, in his eagerness for more workpoints, took the easy way and brought as much water as mud in his boat.   He criticised himself and began to bring back the best heavy black river fertiliser the brigade had ever had.   The influence of the movement showed itself in all manner of simple things — sowing hemp, for instance, paid with results for more care.   Threshing hemp — more seed was obtained when a bit more muscular energy was put behind the task.   Old people who had retired and had given up suddenly found that they were wanted and useful, so came back to find work suited for them.   A new sense of belonging together and unity based on Mao Tsetung Thought has evidently been established.   In the struggle against selfishness, they say here, one must first criticise the selfishness in one's mind and after that go on to attack the revisionism that panders to it, and which leads away from the revolution which means so much to all. People know the effect of making production teams smaller, namely creating new contradictions and relations amongst all. Everybody offers many instances of such bad results during meetings.

I looked into each of the Mao Tsetung Thought study rooms of the production teams, peeped into their primary schools, watched village girls making lace for export, and listened to songs of the Cultural Revolution being sung everywhere. A busy village with everyone at work — threshing barley, transplanting rice, weeding rice — the long line of workers seeming to be almost swimming through the plants as they slushed through paddy water. The little village marketing and supply store seemed to do good business in Shaohsing wine which, when warmed up, must be very acceptable to a man who has worked for a whole day in the water. Electrification from the hydro-electric power grid of Chekiang has meant much, especially in powering pumps that did a great deal in helping to fight drought.

Near the scenic park of Tunghu is a state farm where I went to see plowing done by electrical power. For rectangular fields of several mou, unencumbered by grave mounds, as indeed most of the paddy fields now have become, the device is good. An innovation during the Great Leap Forward period consisted in pulling a plow on a rope over the land by manually turning a big wheel. At that time I thought it too clumsy and elementary to comment on, but out of that idea has now come this new, light device powered by an electric motor, with a steel rope and plow with double mould boards and shares, one facing each way. Transformer stations for supplying power to villages and pumping stations now dot the countryside and, as fields have to be plowed and cultivated three times a year, arrangements can easily be made to plug in. The set made locally costs 2,500 yuan, over double the price of a good buffalo, but the buffalo has to be looked after all the time and is idle throughout the winter months. The work is done five or six times as fast as a buffalo could do it. Costs work out at between 70 and 80 fen a mou. It takes three people to operate and a certain amount of technical know-how. The wire rope, for instance, might break and have to be spliced. The set needs to be placed securely and it then moves under its own power along the field-dividing path when side plates are pulled up. Two men can pick it up by handles provided and easily put it into a boat to take away, for the whole area here is criss-crossed by canals. It not only plows but also cultivates.

Wang Chin-yu

After a short row around the lake at Tunghu I went back to Shaohsing to meet a famous personage in today's Chekiang. He is Wang Chin-yu, leader of Shangwang Brigade of Hungshan Commune in the hills 45 li east of Shaohsing. He is also a leader in the Revolutionary Committee of his commune, being a member too of the Revolutionary Committees of the county, of the prefecture, and of the province. Still young, with a laughing yet very determined face, he has led a brigade through many adversities very much in the spirit of Tachai, with his fellows creating much that did not exist before. His brigade is one of 141 families making up 670 people in all, who have a work force of 312.

Shangwang Brigade

Before Liberation, there were only 85 families, tilling 105 little fields many of which were less than a mou. Almost every year there was drought. Good fields — all owned by the three landlords of whom two were active Kuomintang killers — would bring in around 300 jin of grain per mu a year, the poorer ones 70-100 jin. In one year 45 people starved to death, and many ran away. The main source for livelihood for the poor was carrying down firewood from the hills to the plains below. But even on that the landlords took their rake-off. For the people a pitiful place then.

Came Liberation, and the new owners of the land looked around themselves to see what could be done. They set up two cooperatives after their first beginnings of collective working in mutual-aid teams. But then revisionist policy directions came down from Liu Shao-chi and the two cooperatives were disbanded — part of the many liquidated in 1955-56 but later, on Chairman Mao's insistence, re-formed in late 1956 and then again, as higher cooperatives, in 1957-58.

After the disbandment 13 families organised themselves in the co-operative way, working their plots on what the folk around called "scabby head hill" because one piece was tilled here and another there. Old landlord and rich peasant families scoffed, saying that the 13 families were like chickens without feathers. 1958 brought the Leap Forward, and with it came the idea of making the tea gardens that are now the chief source of income for the brigade. Some old folk said the idea was not practicable but still joined the young ones in the venture. At that time, food was not so plentiful, the grain allowance being 300 jin. The commune was set up and the brigade leader had everyone study Chairman Mao's essay "The Foolish Old Man Who Removed the Mountains". In six months the people on the job, the oldest 73 and the youngest 13, had dug out 600,000 jin of tree roots from the 500 mou to be planted. The first year 12 dan (1 dan=110 lbs.) of tea was gained. In 1967, 600 dan, with 800 dan being expected in 1968, the first crop of the year having already given 400 dan.

When the brigade was formed 200 yuan was the average family income for the year. In 1967 it was 707 yuan. In grain, the people thought they had done very well when, in 1958, they had raised grain production to 470 jin a mou. But the 1966 figure was 1,697 jin. 1967 saw a five months' drought that made even drinking water a problem until a deep trench was dug reaching 20 feet down to tap underground water. A third of a mile long, it was six feet wide. To halt evaporation, it was covered with stone slabs. It provided all the water there was for both home use and irrigation at that time. The winter of 1967-68 saw many catchment pools and small reservoirs being dug against any future drought. During the drought, the water was brought up through as many as 18 different levels from the valley water supply, a wicker bucket on a rope being swung up from one level to the next higher one by two people. Now electricity has come to the brigade and pumps are installed. The coming of electricity has made the old wick lamp and the strip of pine used as a torch obsolete. Living standards have risen each year, and the allowance of grain per person is now 561 jin a year. "To think that we had the potential for doing all of this and never realised it! It took Chairman Mao to show us how," the people say.

Animal husbandry has been another thing that has been developed. Once only the landlords and rich peasants seemed to be able to afford pigs. Now the brigade piggery has 548 pigs and also looks after 300 Angora rabbits. Technique has not simply fallen down from heaven. It had to be found out after some mistakes were made in the beginning.

In the Cultural Revolution there was but one rebel group organised. The people had followed Chairman Mao's essays through the years and knew they were on the right road. The youth raided the old landlord's houses and, behind a Buddha in one, found land deeds and plans of lands the landlord had once owned. The fact that the old class-consciousness is difficult to get rid of was shown up further when another landlord, now over 80 years old, sitting outside his door, waylaid and killed a young pig that belonged to a farmer who had suffered from him in the old days, and who had criticised him bitterly after Liberation. The old man took the dead pig and threw it into the private plot of yet another person so as to make it appear as if that person had killed it when it was spoiling his garden. Quite a little intrigue, but one that did not work out as the old landlord had anticipated. The people suspected him from the beginning and then asked him outright why he had done it, knowing the answer, that he hated the pig's owner so badly. There were plenty of such instances in the locality, making the people aware that class differences were not at an end.

Income

In a commune, workpoints are given each day. Supposing an adult worked for 25 days in the month and was awarded 12 workpoints a day, he would then get 300 workpoints in the month. Each quarter of the year a meeting of members is held which decides how much to give for each workpoint. Usually around 13 fen, but this of course depends on the brigade income.

Naturally most commune members advocated a bigger division and less to the brigade funds — around 7 percent for that being common. This brigade, however, voted to put 16.2 percent of its income into brigade funds. From such funds it has already built and equipped its tea-curing factory as well as setting up its own grain-processing machines. A diesel-engined power plant has also been bought in case there is a power failure. Yet families cannot be said to be poor as a result. The total deposits in the local bank amount to 40,000 yuan. Spending money on equipment pays, as all can see. For instance, in the tea factory, it once took eight to ten people to cure 100 jin of red export tea. Now with machines the same work can be done by one person in half the time. The campaign against selfishness makes all want to put more into the brigade, worry less about workpoints, and gives teeth to the slogan "serve the people". The change in people's thinking during the movement has been dramatic, a fact which the brigade leader illustrated with many stories. "In the old days," he said, "the carrying-pole wore the skin off our shoulders as we carried down fuel. Our feet were cut and cracked, and our thin bodies could not be properly clothed in winter. There has been change."

To the Winery Again

Before I left Shaohsing this time I paid a call at the winery and listened to the story of the take-over by the rebel group, then went to see the new mechanically operated presses which replace the traditional ones I described after my last visit in 1966. They were certainly fascinating to watch then, but now the newly devised mechanical presses do eight times as much work in the same time, with just one worker attending. At the old presses a man was finished at 45, the work was so dangerous and exacting — wedges would fly out, big stones drop. Agility and swift technique was demanded. Now one of the workers at the new machine presses is 65 years of age and still going strong. The 1967-68 product is rated the best in the history of the winery. 3,100 tons were produced in 1966, and 3,200 in 1967. The next technical change will be to make a modern production line, ample space and buildings being available for such. The day of the old handicraft has ended. The workers both old and young welcome the change.

It was good to have caught up with things in Shaohsing again. Soon more changes will sweep in, exciting new changes that will make their creators into different people than they are now. Yet still people who will face the revolution with the courage and confidence their forefathers had, never letting their hills and streams change color.

To Hsiakaochiao Brigade

Tehching is a county seat in northwest Chekiang, about half way between the cities of Hangchow and Huchow. It is on a branch off the main highway, relying as it does for transport more on the internal waterway system than on roads. Canals carry most of the goods and people in these parts. Near the city we took a motor launch from a canal station and, passing from big canals to smaller ones, came at last into the area of Laidien Commune, one of the brigades of which, the Hsiakaochiao or "Downstream High Bridge" Brigade, was our destination.

It was a fascinating trip on a clear, warm autumn day in 1969, for the big waterways were filled with life and activity. We met big boats jammed with school children going out or returning from harvesting rice, small boats of old folk going home from the market, tugs pulling long lines of junks laden high with rice straw on their way to paper mills, and then too, boats carrying farm machinery to the communes. As we came into the branch canals, there was a passage left for shipping only in the middle, both sides being taken up for growing water plants used after processing as fodder for pigs and stall-fed sheep. Hsiakaochiao Brigade is led by a Revolutionary Committee and has 12 production teams with 520 families numbering 2,500 people in all. They work 5,000 mou of land, 3,000 mou of which is rice paddy and the remainder dry, on which mulberries, hemp, "pi-pa" (loquats) and other fruits are grown.

In the old society, the land was mostly owned by four landlords, the common people being held in a wretched, miserable state. During the period of Japanese occupation the Japanese army sent out kill-all, burn-all, loot-all columns, which completely razed the village, leaving nothing but ashes. The landlord families, of course, had by then withdrawn to their homes in Tehching city. By the time of Liberation many families had sold children, gone on the roads begging, or were hiring themselves out for a pittance.

Shortly after Liberation, the first steps towards collective working were taken. One of the famous pioneer mutual-aid teams in the region was that named after its organiser, a poor peasant named Sung Kwei-lin. I called on him, finding him to be a tough, healthy 48-year-old, now head of one of the production teams and an active Party member. After the first 12 cooperatives had been formed the Liu Shao-chi policy dissolved six of them and made for a good deal of local bitterness amongst the members who had worked hard to make them a success. Bitterness that was not forgotten and which later was brought up in the general criticism of the Liu Shao-chi revisionist line, in which so many disclosures were made.

As we came to the new, spick and span brigade office from the jetty, we passed down the new village street and could see quite a bit of activity. Electric motors operating grain processing machines, a bean-curd-making shop, a tailoring shop where the older village women seemed to be in the majority, and then a corner partitioned off for two barber's chairs, by one of which was a 17-year-old boy barber attending to his client. Then came the brigade middle school, with classes in full swing. Backing them all were the brick and tile kilns which had made the reconstruction of the village on the old site possible.

As we sat over our mugs of fragrant green tea in the brigade office, the head of the Revolutionary Committee explained that everything done has been carried through by the brigade membership themselves. The biggest piece of construction, however, is not the most showy. It has consisted in raising all the main dykes around brigade land and in facing them with stone, stone which had to be brought in from hills a considerable distance away.

"No," said he, "it has not always been easy to get understanding that the big thing to do is to follow Mao Tsetung Thought closely. Much poison has been left by the old society in the minds of people. Many wanted to get rich while others stayed poor. One of the former rich peasants, for instance, was keen that the brigade plant more sugar cane which, when sold stick by stick in the market town, was highly profitable. He did not want to put the main effort into the things the state needed. When others did not listen to him he tried to grow sugar cane on his own private plot, but because he had never grown it before he made a mess of it and his little crop failed." Another former rich peasant pushed the propaganda line that simply working as a collective was already socialism. He wanted his group to sell its rice straw to the highest bidder and then divide up the profit. Though this was quite in line with what Liu Shao-chi advocated with all his talk about "freedoms", the other members would not have it. Said he, "We are revolutionaries, working to put Mao Tsetung Thought into practice to make both the Chinese and the world revolution successful. Our fighting front is here!"

Major Aim

Evidently, getting everyone to see this has been the major aim of the Cultural Revolution. Yet it has not been so simple to get everyone's mind clear on the matter. There have been many meetings, long and heated discussions. The peasants have always sought the highest prices they could command for their produce. For a time it was not so easy to get them to see that it is not good if only some get richer and others get poorer. That one should not base one's life on the wretched profit motive, a survival from the times before the revolution. In consequence, it has been a constant struggle to put politics first and narrow economic interests second all the way through.

Sometimes it was not the formerly rich peasant who was to blame. An old-time beggar who had done many good things after Liberation worked out a way to buy himself a bicycle by doing some little business deals on the side. It took some time to get him to see that this was wrong. It is easy to say all this, but to make it the basis of people's thinking is another thing. The problem is serious when it comes to marketing produce in town. The state sets its price for buying each day. If private people pay more than that, folk realise now, then state business will suffer.

Yu Ah-hsiao told of how one member had taken in 200 jin of banana stalks for sale. A town restaurant looking for such stalks for making starch noodles was willing to pay quite a high price, but was surprised when our seller said he would not take more than the state marketing and supply organisation offered that day. It was a lesson to the restaurant keeper, and the story spread quickly all down the market canal side wharves. Said Yu, pointing to a massive sluice gate the members had made across some brigade canal, "If we open the sluice gate to capitalism, we shall have socialism flooded out."

Many other instances were given of how the brigade membership had stuck to the socialist way. A member taking only 18 fen for bamboo shoots when the street was offering 30. Another accepting only 80 fen for a jin live weight of piglets when someone wanted to give him 1.20 yuan. A woman who had brought in 83 jin of peaches taking only eight fen a jin for them when offers of 15 were made. "We will not sell out socialism," the brigade member declared. The membership thought it was a pity that bamboo shoots should be taken to the market town and there wait for transport to Shanghai, by which time they would no longer be so fresh for worker comrades in factories. They took the matter up with the marketing and supply depot in town, and came to an agreement that they would weigh their own produce and get it directly onto the boat trains going right past their village to Shanghai, so that it would not be more than a day old by the time it got there. Their credit was good as a revolutionary brigade.

Kao Yi-chu

Everyone here knows now the story of Kao Yi-chu. He formerly was a rich peasant who had a good deal to say in the 1961-62 period when the Liu Shao-chi line was propagated. Due to the fact that the funds of the brigade had been divided according to this line there was not enough money to buy the big round trays made of bamboo strips called "bien". These were usually made at bamboo workers' cooperatives in the county towns and cost from five to seven yuan apiece. Kao Yi-chu, however, had amassed a goodly store of these in his home, which he now rented out to the brigade for 80 fen each per harvest — and there are two rice and three silkworm harvests a year. In this way he could make 150 yuan a year without any other work than repairing the trays after use. It was quite a substantial side income for him, giving him capital to go into various other pieces of trade on the side. All of these things were brought out in the meeting which criticised him, the whole brigade learning much in the process.

Overcoming Difficulties

Back in the great flood of the Yangtze in 1954 the water rose so high that the dykes could not cope and the land was inundated. The only pumps then were the treadle-operated paddle pumps to get the land dry enough for crops again — long hours of work with slow results! In 1967, they told us, there was the worst drought in the locality, with many of the smaller canals drying up completely. "Yet due to the electric power and the mechanical pumps the state provided us with, we got the biggest crop in our history! Now who can doubt that our first duty is to support our socialist state? Nobody cared for us when the Japanese army was burning our homes and shooting us down! Who is doing the same thing in Vietnam and Laos today? Who other than U.S. imperialism, which our state keeps out of our borders? The new czars would like someone like Liu Shao-chi in charge in Peking. We are proud to be on the side of Mao Tsetung and we need our PLA to defend our frontiers."

Political study does have its victories, as our friends impressed on me in no uncertain terms. They told as an instance how the girls raising cocoons struggled to produce only superior grades, and of the measures they took including the borrowing of all the clean clothing their families possessed to nurse the worms over a particular stage. In consequence, their highly standardised product was most acceptable to the mills to which it was sent.

At the beginning of the Cultural Revolution, many of the former rich peasants came out with much criticism which had its roots in the Liu line. They clamored for a division of brigade assets which, they said, had been promised. "Our brigade assets are like gold and silver in the treasure house of an emperor. They can be seen but not touched," was one argument brought forward. They were especially angry with the brigade accountant and got support from the more foolish elements, as they presented their demands. The effect of this however, was to make some of the older ones who had once been activists sit up and take notice. "Why now, here is struggle. We are on the side of Chairman Mao and we should be in on this," they said.

One of these was an old peasant who was once a great activist but had begun to sit back as the years wore on. Around 50, he had three grown sons working. He bought a radio and sat back smoking and drinking tea instead of going to collective work or meetings so often. But he also began to get headaches and not feel so well, convincing himself that all this was due to advancing age. When he heard of the struggle however, he came out of his shell and began to take part in everything again. He asked for hard work and was assigned to tasks in the brigade piggery, where tasks are constant and exacting. His headaches went away as if by magic, and much of his old strength returned to him.

No Longer Poor

Today, the brigade is no longer poor. In 1968 and also in 1969 despite a scourge of insect pests it has harvested over 1,000 jin a mou. In 1949, it got less than a fifth of that amount. There is a yearly cash distribution now of over 1,000 yuan per family. The grain allowance is 650 jin per person a year. Reserve stocks in family and brigade stores are good, and a large amount of surplus grain over and above the set levy has been sold to the state. I went to the brigade farm mechanisation station where eight youngsters headed by an old experienced man looked after the equipment held there. Fifty-five percent of the plowing in the brigade is now done by cable winches operated by electric motors. Most of the remaining 45 percent is plowed by two diesel-engined tractors, 10 h.p., Shanghai-made, purchased some years ago for 2,800 yuan each including attachments. Sometimes the commune tractor station also comes in to help. There is a modern rice transplanter powered by a gasoline motor which has successfully operated over its first season. The earliest forms of rice transplanters, made mainly of wood, were crude in comparison with this streamlined all-metal model. It carries a driver and two operators and does the work of a whole team faster and better. "It makes a right-angled turn perfectly," the driver said. Only two buffaloes are now kept in the brigade; they are used for plowing small headland corners and other such jobs which present mechanisation does not reach. The problem of care of the machinery in the off seasons and its proper upkeep seems to be very well solved here.

Return to Tehching

The day passed too quickly. The brigade leader travelled with us on the launch as far as Tehching, for he had been called to a conference of activists in Hangchow. He was not long back from a trip to Peking where he had attended the National Day celebrations and had seen Chairman Mao and other leaders.

On the canals we noticed that a great many of the boats being used in transport were of the new reinforced-concrete type, so much more lasting than wood, cheaper, easier to repair and more serviceable. They are now made in many Kiangsu industrial centres as well as in some communes even, coming in as a new boon to a changing countryside.

To Huchow

Leaving Tehching our car went north to Huchow beside Taihu Lake, now a growing industrial city of over 100,000 people. It was evening when I came to rest in a guest house not far from the stump of an ancient pagoda that has long been a familiar landmark in that locality.

Next morning I got an early start and, going north into Changhsing county, cut inland towards the Anhwei border to Wushan Commune, going through the hills for some time, and then coming to a wide canal along which a motor launch took me to the commune headquarters situated in a pleasant village up on the canal bank.

Wushan Commune

We found that the commune was one of nearly 11,000 people, farming 20,000 mou of plowable land, and a big area of mountain country, only the foothills of which can be used for orchards and other trees of immediate economic value. In the old society 115 families of landlords and rich peasants owned 70 percent of the land — and all the best at that. As in Hsiakaochiao, the Japanese army had come and razed all buildings to the ground, the people having to escape for their lives up into the hills. Four hundred families became beggars. One thousand families precariously existed on the pitiful wages of hired landlord workers. In 1949 there was one mechanised pump which a landlord owned and rented out. Today there are 25 big electric pumps in 16 pumping stations. The commune has undertaken small mining projects, built plants for processing cotton and grain, and has constructed a reservoir all with its own resources. Despite the fact that there have been two floods in 1968-69 here, the average of grain fields, both on hilly land and on plain, showed 758 jin a mou for this period as against the 300 jin a mou harvest of 1949. The commune sold the state 1,700,000 jin of surplus grain over and above the grain quota for that period. People are calling such surplus "anti-imperialist, anti-revisionist grain" now. For local consumption, 600 jin of grain per person per year is distributed to commune members here, and 120 yuan each in cash for the same period. The place is particularly rich in fish ponds. Most families also stall-feed sheep, pigs or rabbits.

Fuyang Diesels

It is always refreshing to see a piece of the future in action. For anyone interested in the rational development of industry and agriculture, the trip I took in November 1969 to rural Chekiang was like a dream come true. The things I saw made about as clear as one could wish the difference between the two lines — one which follows Mao Tsetung Thought and the other which takes the revisionist way.

The place? In Fuyang county, up the Chientang river from Hangchow in Chekiang. The organisation was the "Fuyang County Agricultural Implements Manufacture and Repair Works", first set up during the Great Leap Forward in 1958. Chairman Mao had advocated local self-sufficiency as far as possible, the mechanisation of agriculture, and the setting up of industrial enterprises in the hinterland. He has always had a great belief in the potential of the ordinary peasants to do whatever necessary for their own advance. The group that started the works, however, had but few tools and little experience. Just nine blacksmith's hammers and two anvils to be exact. But gamely they set to work making ordinary farm tools and simple equipment for commune use, growing from the 62 young people who had come to join in to 300 workers. The range of the work finally done included the installation and repair of mechanised pumps and motors, the manufacture of simple threshing machines, rice hullers, and so on, and the provision of wheeled farm transport carts with rubber tyres and ball bearings. Major plans were being made to go on to the manufacture of small tractor engines, but when the cut-back that followed the enforcement of the Liu Shao-chi line in 1962 was effected the working staff was reduced to 62, and the manufacture of only the most simple farm implements was still permitted.

Then came the Great Proletarian Cultural Revolution with all its struggle, and workers demanded to know how Chairman Mao's plan for the mechanisation of agriculture could be carried through if the countryside had to rely on the big cities for everything. The workers were angry that they had been thought to be too stupid to make anything so precise as a diesel engine. They were critical too, of a line that fostered an attitude of widening the gulf between the ordinary farm commune member and the industrial worker. They themselves started to send out some of their own comrades to all communes in the county, to collect opinions on the best ways to advance. A good buffalo, they found, cost about

1,000 yuan. If a good, small tractor could be made for about the same sum, using cheap fuel, how much better this would be, the younger members insisted. The old folk, of course, often wanted to go on using animal power but the oncoming youth liked, even demanded, change. So when things were clarified in workers' minds and the sharp divergence between the two political lines was completely understood, the setting up of the three-way combination of old cadres, young rebels and Army men to carry through the Mao Tsetung line in their plant was easy.

However, there were still many problems to solve. The plan of making small diesel engines was still laughed at by many city technicians who did not believe that a county workshop could or should attempt such a thing. Yet the trial models which were subjected to exhaustive tests stood up well. Better than some city models, actually. A design similar in some ways to a small Japanese diesel had been worked out. It was lighter than the foreign model — 70 jin as against 90. It had done away with some 50 accessories also, including the oil pump. The expert who had to be consulted then said that even if the engine ran successfully for eight hours in the test room, it would not do so on the ups and downs of the hill valleys of Fuyang without an oil pump. The members installed their engine in a tractor frame and it passed the test with flying colors over rough ground the expert picked. It now is in serial production, over 400 having been made and put into operation the first year. The plans for the coming 12 months call for 1,000 to 1,500 units.

Self-Sufficiency

All of this has not been easy to do. The number of workers has now been increased to 200, one fourth of whom are girls. All are local Fuyang people. They have had to be trained to operate the machine tools the plant already has, as well as to help build new ones. The greater part of this new tooling has been made by the group itself, and as we went around we saw three sleek-looking modern drilling machines being finished off. We also saw the 300-ton press the workers had made stamping out engine pistons. Overhead cranes, heat treatment equipment, testing equipment and all the rest had also been set up by the workers themselves. Even new shops had been constructed. The original old workshops, now used only for simple agricultural machinery repair work, looked very much like any other rural construction compared with the spick and span new shops. The factory keeps on sending out its groups to the county communes, taking part in their living and working, and it frequently entertains commune members who come in bringing equipment for repair, making them feel at home with a warm welcome and food.

Political study has its part in everyday work, of course, and then there are also study groups which discuss methods of assisting the technical revolution, creative innovations and associated problems. "Yes, lots of people said our works were too small, our machines too bad; they said that no one could draw well, or work even from proper plans, that we were like frogs wanting to eat the meat of swans. They even told us, 'You can't pat the bottom of a tiger and get away with it. You have no capital, machines will have to be bought from abroad,' etc. We replied that if we lost our ability to be self-supporting and to do things ourselves, then we would lose a worker's real capital. Peasants said that they wanted an engine easy to handle, one with strength and precision. The Japanese one we got hold of for our first ideas gave five h.p. Ours gives seven h.p. It is air-cooled and certainly easy to handle. We have already trained many young farmers in successfully operating it, and we are always here to give advice, help with repairs, and so keep the machines operating. No matter when a commune member comes in with work to be done, at night or on holidays, we set to and get the job finished for him as soon as possible, whether it is a pump, a motor or a tractor engine, knowing how important the work in the countryside is. We do our best to translate the slogan 'serve the people' into direct and successful action. We now know very well that agriculture is the base of the revolution, and that it must be strengthened. We realise our heavy responsibility in this and try to meet the challenge. We just have to put Mao Tsetung Thought into practice right through.

Now we have eight small repair shops as our outposts amongst commune brigades to assist them in every possible way. There are some 300 electrically powered pumping stations in the country we help to keep in running order. All the time we try to prepare against natural disaster, against the eventuality of a war situation, and always with the idea in our minds to serve the people. When there was a big cloudburst amongst the hills last year, we all immediately went to the pumping stations to help. We felt this to be our duty. We ask for criticism from every commune group and try to meet such to the satisfaction of all. We feel ourselves to be part of the whole rural movement forward. When they told us that we would not be allowed to make tractor engines, we felt that something was radically wrong somewhere, for this was one of our main objectives and very much in accordance with the task of mechanising the countryside. Someone tried to take our objective from us. Now we know what the trouble was and we are determined to make our diesel engine program the success it needs to be."

This, then, is a digest of what the Revolutionary Committee members told me that pleasant autumn morning in Fuyang, with the sun glinting on the waters of the wide Chientang river, as we sat on its bank and saw the rich autumn rice crop being harvested in the fields. Fuyang in the old days had no industry except rural paper-making, done in individual farmhouses. Today some of the commune production teams still carry on the craft, but with the making of diesel engines in the county by the county people themselves all will soon undergo a qualitative change.

The Tractors Emerge

For the rest of the day, as one thought back, the final scene at the works kept coming pleasantly to mind. Two lads each sitting by tractor engines being tested, watching them intently. Then the row of engines already tested, fuel tanks a bright red, bodies black, ready to go out as a new kind of buffalo in the service of the people. The price of diesel oil is low, China being self-sufficient in petroleum products. The cost of a Shanghai-made diesel oil injector has now been lowered to three yuan. Inevitably now, mechanisation is coming to the countryside, releasing many hands to carry the work of construction still further. A simple, efficient prime mover in the hands of the Chinese peasants, which will increase his productive power many times over, is a revolutionary thing indeed, and will have vast consequences. The small, cheap, strong and simple diesel at Fuyang will probably not be the final answer, but it is a determined step in the right direction.

Difficulties Faced

Liu Shao-chi and his group wanted big centralised industry, high expertise, a tight-knit superstructure which bureaucratically would keep workers in check. There were good points about exploitation, he said. He did not believe in the potential of the common man, and used the full strength of his administration to put over the idea that the Great Leap Forward had been a failure, an idealist's dream. Mao Tsetung believed in starting industry all over the hinterland, going on from small to big. Learning by doing. He stood for local self-sufficiency and aimed at really helping agriculture in a down-to-earth way and promoting diversified industry.

Fertiliser Factory

In Hsiaoshan county, south of the Chientang river near Hangchow, I went to the hamlet of Puyen. Here, in the Leap Forward of 1958, were set up two small factories, one which at first made 10,000 tons a year of chemical fertiliser for the counties around Hangchow and the other which produced industrial chemicals, especially those for the paper and leather industries. They were adjacent to each other and went to work with a will to set up their plants, getting their workers from the communes around and from Hangchow city. There was not a single fertiliser factory in old Chekiang then, and only ten other small ones like theirs in the whole country. By 1960, both factories started to produce. But then in 1962 the Liu Shao-chi line came into force. Small fertiliser factories were out. Such work, the revisionists decided, should be done by giant factories in big industrial centres where there were all facilities. So a directive was sent to the Hsiaoshan fertiliser plant to cease operations forthwith and discharge its workers.

The revolutionary leader Ko Ching-shih in Shanghai, however, advised the workers to resist and keep on. So did some people in the Chekiang provincial administration. The two chemical factories promptly joined, with a combined working force of 800, and carried on under the name of a chemical combine, quietly improving as they went along. In consequence, when the Cultural Revolution came along, they were ready for it. The alliance between all worker groups was a fact by February 1967, and the three-way alliance between old cadres, young rebels and Army was complete and working by September of the same year. 115 administrative cadres were replaced by 25, and a Revolutionary Committee set up.

Production has soared. Fertiliser in liquid and powdered form is now enough for the seven counties around Hangchow and some communes beyond. Farmers were much surprised when they learnt that fertilisers were made from air and coal. The rising paper industry of the province is supplied with its chemicals from here also — 5,000 tons a year in 1962, 12,000 tons a year now. Intense political study has become part of the daily lives of workers, and shows its results in increased production, determination and higher spirit. Three eight-hour shifts are worked each day, with one day off each week. They had their study groups under the Party organisation, so that the whole 800 became a well-integrated working organisation. Staff quarters are provided, and new building construction of workshops goes ahead all the time, for though fertiliser production has now increased six times since 1962, much bigger increases are being confidently sought. Coming up the highway to the plant we passed many rubber-tyred handcarts taking away both the jars of liquid fertiliser and, too, the plastic-lined hemp sacks of the powder. Then, looking down on the canal, we saw boats going off laden in the same way. There is no problem of production disposal when the market is right at hand and there is so good a system of inland waterways that connects the plant with practically all of its customers.

During the Cultural Revolution political study has made for a much deeper understanding of major issues by everyone. Workers of poor peasant stock analysed why it was that they had grown contemptuous of the poor peasants around them. Technicians who had gone through college and who had never made great mistakes, as they thought, resented at first going to work with ordinary workers, but then found that workers had much to teach them. There has been a great levelling out, and new understanding of the meaning of life. There are many instances of complete sacrifice of self-interest for the good of the job on hand. For instance, the waste water, bad smelling and containing chemicals, is pumped up so that it runs down a long covered drain to the Chientang river. It has to be continuously pumped or else it will flow out over the farmland to adjacent canals, thus endangering the well-being of local farmers and their crops. Then it was found it must be choked at the intake. Immediate action was necessary. Though the water in the sump was rising fast and already over six feet deep, one worker immediately stripped and went in to investigate while others rushed away to bring clean water to sluice him down and get the chemicals off when he came out. He found the trouble, dislodged the stoppage, and came up victoriously, which all thought to be quite a sacrifice and a triumph. Steps are now being taken to deal with waste water so that it can be purified before discharge, as the effects of industrial waste even in a great river like the Chientang so near to its mouth at the sea are now being well understood.

Though the plant is still growing and bettering its products, the answer probably lies not in making this another huge one but in having more small plants located in suitable places, small plants which eventually grow bigger and which will make each area gradually self-supporting. A self-sufficient local economy is much more immune in times of war or disaster. Today there are already over 50 small plants like this one, all busy growing up and supporting the local economies in the China of today. There undoubtedly will be a great many more as the struggle for advance continues. While at the plant I noted that crops of vegetables and rice were growing in full health right up to the factory walls, with none showing any harm from the proximity of the plant. There, too, was an absence of bad smell.

Machine Tools and Children

I last visited the plant's machine shops, where I noted the many new machine tools being built to undertake still bigger tasks. Leaving the factory I said farewell to the new generation in nursery and kindergarten situated out by the factory gates. All of the youngsters looked fat and happy, and it was very pleasant to catch some of their note of hope. Out of their own strength, their fathers have built these works and have planned and built the machinery and equipment themselves. Some of their chemicals now even go into the export market for sale abroad. These children who inherit the fire of Mao Tsetung Thought — what wonders in their turn will they produce?

The Role of the Small Plant

Talking over the visit as we rode home, a friend said, "If we say small local plants are no good and that we must rely entirely on the huge factories of the cities, then we will probably come to the point of saying that our big plants do not produce as cheaply as do those in foreign countries, so why try to compete, just buy from abroad! Squeeze the people a bit more to pay, and so return to the semi-colonial status we have emerged from, a producer of raw materials only, and thus losing the revolution! The Hsiaoshan plant, with its 60,000 tons a year of fertiliser, and its promise of double that amount before 1972, is small all right, but it gives a new independence as a supplement to compost to around a couple of million commune farmers, and that is what we are after." So we agreed again that the Mao Tsetung way forward must be the one to follow.

Meichiawu Tea Plantation

Many visitors to Hangchow are taken to visit the Lungching tea plantations operated by Lungching Brigade of Hsihu Commune. One morning, however, our party set out and, going past Lungching valley entrance, struck off from the highway on a side road which led up another valley to the west. It was a brilliant autumn morning and the maples with which the branch road was lined were magnificent in their golds and reds. As we went along we could see the fine, round tea bushes of Meichiawu Brigade covering the valley floor and running up the hillsides. No spindly, dry-looking bushes these, but all well formed — big round globes thick with leaves. On one section the children of some city school which had marched out were at work doing a last picking. In other places some production teams were hoeing and cleaning around bushes, but the main activity of all working members of the brigade the day we came was in carting down stone from hilltops to lay the foundations for an addition to their already spacious tea-curing factory.

Brigade Leader Talks

We were met by the chairman of the Revolutionary Committee of the brigade, a pleasant woman in her forties, who very directly and without any unnecessary verbiage outlined the progress that had been made. First, she gave a brief sketch of the position before Liberation, when landlords and rich peasants owned over 80 percent of the land, while 95 percent of the people, the poor and middle peasants, had to be content with 20 percent of it. How the poor felled all the forests and carried firewood to the city, how poverty was increasing at such a rate that mass starvation threatened each winter.

After the take-over by the people in 1949 each family had a yearly income of 150 yuan. By 1965 it had risen to 900 yuan. And by 1969 it will be over 1,000 yuan in all. In addition, the brigade has been able to do a good deal of mechanisation, erecting a modern tea factory with electrical heating for curing, electric power for tea curling. A cable-way powered electrically runs across a valley and over a hill to a distant part of the plantation, so that 70-jin loads come down in 15 minutes instead of taking over an hour's hard travel by a carrier. In a hot valley lying into the sun this means something in the tea-picking season. The brigade also has a truck and several small tractors. It has 900 mou in tea gardens, 138 in rice paddy, 940 mou in forest and bamboo groves. All barren hills around have been re-afforested since Liberation. The income from tea is sufficient to buy all the rice needed, but the membership, anxious to take some of the burden of grain provision from the state, decided to reclaim some land for paddy fields — over 100 mou in a riverbed — by putting a dyke around it.

The spring rice crop of the first season had not long been planted when down came a big flood, washed over the dykes and swept all away. Nothing daunted, the membership planted a second crop. Again in the late summer another cloudburst came, and once more the waters swirled. This time however the whole brigade membership turned out and with sandbags halted the flood at dangerous places, saving everything. It turned out to be a wonderful harvest, giving the brigade rice enough for a whole month and a half. This winter more stone is being carried down, and it is expected that the dyke will be made strong enough to stand high water without any help. But the big task the brigade has now set itself in the field of reconstruction is to convert all hillside tea gardens into properly terraced land, thus doing much to halt erosion and flooding. The project will take the membership, who will work each winter on it, about ten years to complete, but it is expected to pay well in the end. Of course, the main work is in tending the tea plants, fertilising them, hoeing and spraying them. In 1949 the best yield was 30 kgs a mou. Now it is well over 110. This high yield was first reached in 1965; this year (1969) the harvest, to be exact, was 129 kgs per mou.

"No," the woman chairman of the Revolutionary Committee said, "the brigade did not want the three 'precious things' of Liu Shao-chi or his four 'freedoms' either. We did not need material incentives, and we were able to make the slogan 'serve the people' our motive. And now we also know, clearer than ever before, that we are part of the Chinese and therefore of the world revolution." Yes, many people came to help them. Sometimes in the busy season as many as 500 students in one day. There were 1,318 people in the brigade, and they felt that they had a frontline position on the production front. With pride she showed us the excellent brigade school, and then kindergarten. "We want to go on, not to fall back to where we were in 1949," she said quietly. "Yes," she went on, looking up to the ridges high on the hills, "we planted two and a half million trees up there. They have grown, and we have grown too — in many ways. We have learnt what Mao Tsetung Thought means, and that is a big thing for all of us, helping to fire our determination to do all that is needed from now on."

Silk Weaving Mill

The two traditional products of Chekiang are tea and silk. So after one has visited a tea garden brigade, the next suggestion often is that one go to see one of the many factories that deal with silk spinning or weaving. The one I set out on a fine bright morning in Hangchow city to see was the Hsiangyang Silk Weaving Mill, a concern of 2,146 workers, 45 percent of whom are women. When the great change came in 1949, it had but 56 looms, although it had been operating off and on since 1912. It was housed in old, badly lit converted dwelling houses. Like the sharp-pointed shuttles on their looms, the weavers' livelihood, as they said, flew to and fro as sometimes they worked, but were much of the time idle. And when idle there were no wages, so that weavers and their families starved. There were then but 254 weavers. Last year the 548 modern looms produced over nine million metres of brocaded or figured silks, most of which went on the home market, though some special items went into foreign trade. One interesting thing about the plant is that the average age of the workers is 45. There are plenty of white-haired old craftsmen still putting their rich experience into practice. The mill operates a part-work, part-study school of its own and last year took on 80 of its graduates, sending as many more to other silk mills.

Wages are from 40 to 55 yuan a month. It is impressive as a mill of old and young studying and working together. Three eight-hour shifts are worked, the hour for study each day being included in the eight hours. Most of the looms are automatic or semi-automatic, and technical innovations include one for tying threads and another for shuttle exchange. The former is an extremely ingenious device which works with great precision and ease. Manufactured in the mill's own workshops, it has now become standard for all silk mills in the province.

Changes

During the Cultural Revolution, after the formation of the Revolutionary Committee, administrative cadres were cut from 137 to 32, who are now in the three control groups. In political study, old workers can give many instances of the terrors of capitalist society from their own bitter experience. They are keen to learn, and not a few can recite long passages from the five now most commonly studied essays by Chairman Mao ("Serve the People", "In Memory of Norman Bethune", "The Foolish Old Man Who Removed the Mountains", "On Correcting Mistaken Ideas in the Party" and "Combat Liberalism"). All are now clear on one point. They do not work for wages. They work for the revolution, both China's and that of the workers of the world. They criticise the old administration for its system of rewards and punishments, and its inability to activate the mass of the workers.

As we went around the plant we halted a while at the boiler house, where foreign-made boilers installed in the 'fifties were being pulled out and more modern ones made in China installed. The foreign ones were not economical in fuel and not as efficient in working as the new Chinese types.

In all, going around the various shops, one gained the impression that this was a fast advancing enterprise. There were no signs of tiredness or lack of interest amongst the workers, all being obviously pleased with their work. Quite a bit of the new building construction the mill workers had done themselves, and a very nice job they had made of it, too.

Szechiching Commune

The wind lifted a fine, dusty sand, covering everything with it. Out of the haze came a long line of middle-school students shouldering tools on their way back to their mid-day meal after work. A group of commune members were cementing blocks in place along a dyke face and in the distance a great river flowed to sea. No, it was not a scene in the far hinterland but just one at Szechiching ("Green All Four Seasons") Commune on the outskirts of Hangchow. In the Chientang river a "bore" — a high tide that advances like a wall — comes upstream from the sea. It is especially high in some seasons, when it spreads out and inundates land on either side. To meet this threat, Szechiching Commune built a dyke 5,000 metres long, 20 metres wide at the base and three metres high, and then stone-faced it with rock brought in from the Hangchow hills. It took 200,000 man-days to complete and has, since it has been built, successfully protected over 1,000 mou of good land. Now in the spirit of the Foolish Old Man who removed the mountains, the commune members have gone far out over the mud flats and are building an even bigger dyke which will enclose more land and so help to make the commune self-supporting in grain. At present the commune supplies vegetables to the city and, in the main, eats state grain. The new big dyke is expected to take the same number of man-days to complete as the first one did.

Reclamation Proceeds

In addition to its dyke building, the commune has cut a channel between the Grand Canal and the Chientang river. With the help of sluice gates and big pumps, it can quickly deal with any surplus water which heavy rains might bring and carry in water in time of drought. Since becoming a commune the members have set up 24 fixed pumping stations and 37 moveable ones. No one commune brigade is strong enough to do this work, but with the commune organising all, it becomes possible. The commune is one of 10 brigades. It has a population of 20,300 and farms 8,544 mou of rich land. It also has 1,050 mou in fish ponds. Around 18,000 jin of vegetables a mou are produced each year. It also operates five factories, a mushroom-growing plant, and a garden of 20,000 pots of fragrant shrubs whose flowers are used in scented teas, a stud piggery and a dairy farm. It has 30 "barefoot" doctors, and has just completed a new commune hospital with a modern operating theatre. Its 12 middle and primary schools are oriented towards combining theory with practice. Students learn that their task is to serve the people and carry on the Chinese and world revolutions. The commune has its own broadcasting system with 2,000 loudspeakers.

Graduated to Commune Work

We talked with some of the young educated people who have come to the commune in line with the new trend. Two of them were graduates of an upper middle school and had been thinking of going on to more pleasant years in university. Now they find themselves in a very down-to-earth commune instead. Li Yung-ning is 19, son of a metal worker. He said that he came at first in response to the directive of Chairman Mao, rather feeling that he was making a sacrifice. Now, however, he finds life rich, happy and varied, with much that can be done and learnt in a revolutionary way. His friend, Chang Ching-hai, who is his senior by a year, is a tall, handsome lad, modest in speaking yet obviously sincere. He sees now why it was necessary for them to come. Not so much for what they have been able to do for the commune, but for what they have learnt. Both he and his friend Li were surprised and pleased with the warm welcome they received from the membership, and both now are proud to belong to such a commune.

Hill paths through bamboo groves, Hangchow.

CHEKIANG

Tea   factory,   Hangchow.

Commune farmer pulls up mud for fertiliser
from   canal   bottom,   Tunghu,   Shaohsing.

A production team busy at weeding rice paddy, Chekiang.

Electric winch plow at work in paddy field, Shaohsing.

Basket making at Hangchow, Chekiang.

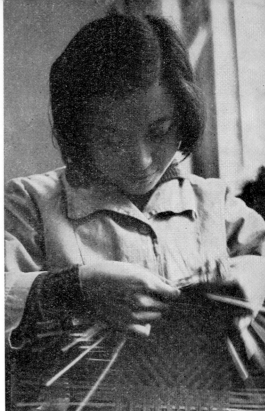

Hangchow handicraft designer.

Silk raised on reclaimed river bed, Tienmushan, Chekiang.

These steam sterilisers come down on top of the jars before sealing, Shaohsing winery.

Home-built suspension bridge, Yanglin Commune, Tienmushan.

Scenery on Chientang River, Chekiang.

Middle school teacher helping with harvest, Wushan Commune, Changhsing, Chekiang.

Wu Ai-tze, the teacher who
came to Wushan Commune.

Hangchow is a spot with many a lovely vista.

The next to speak was Sun Hsin-ming, one of the brigade clinic's medical staff who had just been appointed to work in the new commune hospital. He said that people in the commune were a healthy lot. There was no longer any schistosomiasis, malaria or typhoid. Very few scabby-headed children. Colds, rheumatic pains and intestinal troubles, cuts and abrasions were the most usual things dealt with. In the brigades, one "barefoot" doctor was on duty all the time. Others worked with the membership for half days, or attended health training classes. Most of their work was in preventive medicine. A good deal of acupuncture was used.

Hsiaoyinghsiang

Down in the older part of the city of Hangchow there was once a slum quarter called Hsiaoyinghsiang. Before Liberation it was jam-packed with the unemployed and the hopeless. One old house had 54 people living in it. Just before Liberation, 43 children were born but only 11 lived for more than a year. There were plenty of flies, mosquitoes and rats. After Liberation and towards the end of the Korean War, the health movement was entered into with great enthusiasm by the lane dwellers, to such good effect that the district became the model for the city and Chairman Mao, when he came to Hangchow, visited it on the fifth of January 1958. He spent some time in the area, calling on various people in their homes, and then resting for a while in one of the houses, which has now been made into a museum to commemorate the event. Very high standards of cleanliness have been admirably maintained over the years. There are now 694 families, 2,634 people, in this little sub-administrative area. A factory has been set up to employ some who were out of work. It makes transformers for radio sets and other small instruments in a well-lit and commodious workshop. There is a modern three-storied primary school with over 700 pupils. In 1960 a community restaurant was built where over 400 people come to eat each day. The kitchens are scrupulously clean, food fresh and good. A good deal may be had here for 10 fen. There is a public health station from where preventive medicine measures are carried out and where first aid is given when necessary. Twice every week the people meet for a two-hour period of political study, while every organisation and indeed every family has its own study group. The lane from which the area once took its name of "Hsiaoying" has now been renamed "Yiwuhsiang", or "January the 5th Lane", in memory of Chairman Mao's visit on that day.

During the Cultural Revolution there was considerable struggle which finally resulted in April 1968 in the setting up of the Revolutionary Committee, which is still in charge.

Too soon my time amongst the golden autumn leaves of Hangchow and its surrounding countryside drew to an end, and I was left with but the pleasant memories of all I had seen, refreshed too by walks in parks and gardens, the beauties of hill and stream, and the sight of a resurgent people so determined on taking the revolutionary way forward.

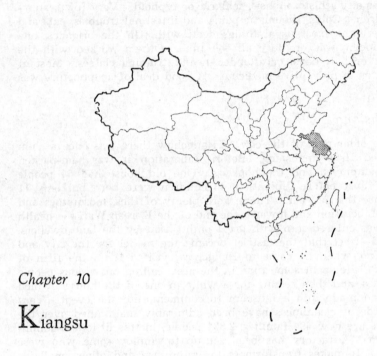

Chapter 10

Kiangsu

Kiangsu is a province of over 100,000 square kilometres, with a population of 44 million people. It contains some of the biggest lakes in China — Taihu, Hungtse and Kaopao. One third of its area lies south of the Yangtze river. This, including the Yangtze river delta, is mostly rich agricultural land. The two thirds which are north of the Yangtze have been devastated again and again in the past by the floods of the Huai river. Furthermore, as they approach the coast they include a good deal of saline fen country on which much heroic reclamation has been done during these past years, in the spirit that has marked the mastery of so many agricultural problems since Liberation. With new pumping and irrigation installations and a revamped Grand Canal which now goes straight north to Shantung, then through the southern portion of the province down to Hangchow in Che-kiang, many major difficulties have been surmounted.

Nanking is the capital of Kiangsu, and this chapter deals with two visits made to that centre, one in 1969 and then another a year later, when one was able to see demonstrated so vividly some of the results of the Cultural Revolution.

The new Nanking bridge over the Yangtze now brings north and south Kiangsu together in a better way. It is one of the more spectacular victories of the Cultural Revolution, representing similar big construction that has gone on throughout the hinterland in these years. In consequence, considerable space has been given it.

Shanghai to Nanking

We were on our way from Shanghai to Nanking by air. Pointing to the great stretch of Taihu Lake below, the air hostess explained that this was the locality of the story of the popular Peking opera "Shachiapang", which now plays all over China. It is a tale centred on the exploits of the New Fourth Army which spearheaded the struggle in these areas during the War of Resistance.

In Nanking

In Nanking, though it was mid-November 1969, autumn leaves were still in their glory. Kerbside plane trees had grown so that they formed a golden archway over many streets. The trees of Nanking were always beautiful, and now that the newer plantings have come to full maturity they are even more glorious. This year, however, the thing most people come to Nanking to see is the new bridge over the Yangtze, the bridge that foreign engineers in the old days said was impossible to build. When it was being planned during the Great Leap Forward of 1958, the Russian experts in China volunteered the opinion that there was no question but that any attempt to build it would fail.

Yangtze Bridge

When we went to see it, a whole school of children were exercising with their spears near the entrance to the bridge headworks, bringing a touch of old revolutionary China to the scene. Inside a glistening marble hall which we entered stood a huge statue of Chairman Mao. A modern lift, made in Tientsin, took us to the upper floors where in an exhibition room an able girl demonstrator showed us a model of the bridge and gave an outline of the struggle that went into the construction. When the first bridge over the Yangtze, that at Wuhan, was completed it was rightly hailed as a splendid achievement. The Nanking bridge is over four times as long, and its completion is now seen as an outstanding victory for the Mao Tsetung line over the old thinking. There were many who could only see difficulties and declared that China was not yet equipped to solve them. But workers replied: "What can be done in foreign countries, we can do here in China. And even what cannot yet be done in foreign lands, we can do here!"

Bridge Construction

Construction was started in 1960 and, as in all large-scale engineering projects, there arose many special difficulties that demanded original, creative solutions. In the final stages from 1966-69 these difficulties mounted, but by that time the Cultural Revolution had come into the picture and workers' spirit and determination to sacrifice for the job were raised. Work that had taken nine and a half months to do in the early stages was now done in 28 days. There were many acts of heroism in deep-diving work as well as in other construction tasks. Then, well in time for National Day, 1968, trains stopped using the ferry, and a rail-crossing took only two minutes as against the two hours the old ferry needed. From the highway bridge above, the people of Nanking could see what had been done. Many of them had participated and worked in volunteer labor brigades on earth-moving for the headworks. Everybody I spoke to felt that here indeed was a victory for Mao Tsetung Thought and for the Cultural Revolution. And it was realised that this triumph would have enormous importance for the economy of the region and the struggle for better livelihood of working folk.

The main part of the bridge is 1,574 metres long. With the approaches, the railway part is 6,700 metres long, and the highway 4,500 metres. At each entrance to the main crossing are massive groups of statuary. They were designed by the workers in folk art figures of Wusih, a Kiangsu city not far below Nanking. Soon the area below the bridge will become a public garden, with the temporary construction site buildings cleared away. There is no doubt but that the success of this daring concept has given great encouragement to the Chinese people who in consequence feel even more confident that the policy of self-sufficiency so forcefully enunciated by Mao Tsetung is the right one. The bridge also is a very good example for cooperation by the workers of the whole country, and amongst them one might name steel workers of Anshan who produced the special steel needed, and Tientsin workers who made a new variety of a special plastic paint that will last much longer than ordinary kinds and was used for the whole huge structure. A bridge that is a gesture of revolutionary defiance against the imperialisms that surround the China of our day. At night when all lights are on it is truly a sight, the big arches illuminated, the great red flags, each 15 tons of sheet metal, ablaze, surely a splendid sight for the once so down-trodden and despised.

Nanking Children's Drama Group

I had never seen any performance quite as good as the one a Nanking school put on. In had songs and dances, bits of opera, improvised plays, orchestral music, a program lasting two and a half hours, all done by the youngsters from the lowest grades to the graduating class. They did it with immense revolutionary elan, so that I thought of the boy and girl Taiping fighters of Nanking a century past, and of the youngsters of Resistance and Liberation Wars. The singing was really excellent, and the tumblers as agile as on a Peking stage.

Synthetic Fibre

On a 1966 visit to Nanking, I had visited the plant for artificial silk and wool fibres. The factory used as raw material the fluff around the cotton seed which was separated, baled, and forwarded from cotton oil-pressing works or from communes. As Kiangsu province grows very much cotton, there is no lack of raw material. When I came last, the factory had reached the production capacity for which it was designed: 5,400 tons of fibre a year. Three years of the Cultural Revolution, however, have brought the total up to 6,500 tons a year, and the target for 1970 is now 10,000 tons and considered easily attainable. When I asked for the secret, the group of young workers and technicians of the Revolutionary Committee were emphatic: One has to give full rein to the creativeness and spirit inspired by Mao Tsetung Thought. They told me that the old management had moved in forms well laid down, satisfied that they had been able to carry on and set up the plant after the Soviet advisers had departed with all the technical data for the new installations. The advisers had openly declared that after their departure it would take the Chinese at least 20 years to produce any kind of synthetic fibres. Actually the plant started to produce in 1961.

The 2,700 workers learnt quickly. Chairman Mao said that workers must lead in everything, and with the Cultural Revolution this was put into effect. In brief outline the technical process consisted in turning the cotton seed fluff into paper board which was then processed into viscose from which synthetic silk is spun. Workers have now devised a method whereby the whole paper-making shop will be rendered superfluous, and the pulp will go straight into the viscose-making production line. They have also eliminated a good deal of work in the production of artificial wool, transporting it by blowers instead of by hand. Now, too, that the factory is enlarging its shops, workers' creative genius is brought to bear still more effectively as new installations are built.

I went to see for myself what had been done and met a doctor of the factory clinic who was going the rounds of the day shift looking for any who would want to consult her. I saw the factory nursery with its many babies of women workers, and heard many stories of what had been done under the new leadership. "Look at that machine. It was being built by the leaders of the past stage. They did not trust workers enough to ask their help to complete it and they could not do it themselves, so it lay around for many months. After the workers took control, one of the first things they did was to carry the project through. Actually in just seven days they had the machine in production. Another process, designed to save coal and labor while increasing efficiency, had been projected and even started on once, but also had never been completed. The workers took 25 days to carry it through once the thing was put into their hands. It is not a small plant — there are 20,000 square metres of shop space, and some 70 kilometres of pipe lines — but workers showed high ability and understanding in their determination to carry theory into practice, regarding the factory as their field to fight the revolution through. If this is not serving the people, then what is, they say. Production is enough to weave cloth for ten million people. There are still plenty of problems in factory management, but the new set-up feels that work is improving all the time. Workers live in staff quarters set on a hill not far away from the plant. Last summer they constructed a new swimming pool for themselves which was greatly appreciated, for Nanking is really hot at that season. One problem now is that old workers especially are so keen on finishing a job that they go on working past working hours. "Chairman Mao tells us to use all our ability to serve the people. We are glad that he has given us this way!" they say. But they are urged not to work beyond their capacity.

October First Commune

Outside Nanking city, around a spot where there are many old sculptures of the Liang dynasty, 1,600 years ago, there is a commune which I had visited also in 1966. It is called the October First Commune. It is one of nine brigades, 15,000 people, who farm 15,000 mou of rich flat land and 2,000 mou of hillside. At Taiping village there is October First Brigade which Chairman Mao visited in the mid-'fifties, and where now a massive statue of him stands on the hill above the brigade headquarters. The head of the brigade Revolutionary Committee, a 41-year-old woman, Yu Fu-chen, told that she had been to Peking for the last October First celebrations, and that she had seen Chairman Mao several times. Chairman Mao's direction had been to use the hill lands, to plant fruit and other trees. These directions have been followed. We stood on top of the hill by his statue, and all around there were now flourishing peach orchards, while newly terraced land was being brought into cultivation, irrigated by canals filled with water from the Yangtze which a four-stage pumping system brings up from the riverbank level. With batteries of 40 h.p. motors operating the pumps, no one is scared of drought now. There is only 1,300 mou of valley land for the brigade population of 1,870 people, but now the newly cultivated 1,000 mou of orchards and hill terraces help. This year (1969) the average is 1,200 jin per mou in the whole brigade. We sat a while in the brigade leader's home and met a big bunch of city middle-school girls who had been working in the brigade for a month and learning something of country life. The house, like most others in the villages around these parts, was newly constructed of brick, with a good tiled roof. In the past, thatched cottages of the poorest construction prevailed.

Commune Headquarters

Back in the commune headquarters, we saw a meeting of "barefoot" doctors and all brigade medical staff having a discussion on traditional medicine and how to use it best. Many secret prescriptions have come to light, the once treasured possessions of individual families. Some of these are now being adapted for widespread use. One against dysentery is considered to be extremely effective.

The commune, taken as a whole, harvested 800 jin a mou of grain in 1966. This was held to be about the summit of what could be expected from land that once gave only 200-300 jin.   But 1969 brings an average of over 1,000 jin.   100-120 dan (a dan is 100 jin or 50 kilograms) of compost fertiliser is applied per mou of light land, 50-60 dan for the heavier.   Green manure and not more than 20 jin of chemical fertiliser per mou are also used.   There was some flooding last season from a storm up in the hills that brought down a great deal of water at a time when the Yangtze was at its highest, but the 42 pumping stations soon dealt with it, and the crop was not harmed.   The head of the commune Revolutionary Committee had been to Shansi to see Tachai Brigade and had learnt much from it.   He returned fired with new enthusiasm and ready to meet all difficulties.   Yes, his commune had once been noted for its poverty.   It is not yet noted for its wealth, but certainly its revolutionary spirit has grown, there is a widespread understanding of the value of Mao Tsetung Thought, and what the policies of Liu Shao-chi meant for all.

Commune Industry

We went to see some of the small factories the commune operates.   One turned out exquisite ladies' fans for export, black silk with floral designs on black lacquered bamboo, and also men's fans with cowhorn handles.   In the commune agricultural implements factory, farm machines were being repaired or made and contracts for parts from city factories filled by some 100 workers.   In the tractor station were six big tractors and 31 small ones.   So far they deal with but 40 percent of the farm work, animal power being used for the rest.   There are 300 mou of fish ponds.   Every brigade has its primary school, and there are two agricultural high schools which now rank as the equal of any of the city middle schools, a status they did not have before the Cultural Revolution.   The grain allowance for each of the commune population is 600 jin a year.

Nanking Machine Plant

In 1948 the UNRRA agencies in Nanking set up a little factory with 72 workers.   It was called with considerable flourish the Nanking "Agricultural Implements Company", but even the screws it used were imported from the USA.   It was in actuality simply a place to assemble U.S. material and distribute it to the profit of the purveyors.   In the time from Liberation in 1949 until 1958, the year when the Great Leap Forward began, the place became a machine-building plant and went ahead relatively slowly on lathe production to tool machine shops in the interior.   It was a period of gathering strength enabling the plant to exert itself to great effect in the Leap Forward which then presented its challenge.   New shops were rapidly constructed and tooled.   New products began to take shape.   The modern automatic and so highly sophisticated lathe that now goes to over 20 foreign countries as well as to all parts of China is a very different tool from the much simpler one of the early stages.   New shops are being built all the time, and soon the number of workers will increase from 2,000 now to 4,000, and another leap into the future will be made.   1969 production is 49 percent up over that of 1966, the first year of the Cultural Revolution.

Worker innovations which have improved production in that period have increased 100 percent. By mid-November 1969, when I visited, the year's plan had been finished and work on the 1970 plan commenced.

The Revolutionary Committee, set up in August 1968, has 23 members of whom three come from the PLA, five represent old cadres, and 15 come from the workers. All take their turn at the workbench — and so, as we went around the various shops, we shook hands with quite a few of them. There had been 200 administrative cadres. This number has now been cut down to 40, most of whom work on the production line at least one half day a week. We also met some university students who had become workers, as well as quite a few students from middle schools who had come into the factory as apprentices during the Cultural Revolution. There were also the graduates of the factory's own part-work, part-study school. In the future, those sent to universities will be those who have proved to be successful factory workers. This is the way started by the Shanghai Machine Tools Plant, a way which has received Chairman Mao's approval. Twenty-five percent of the factory staff are women. As in all other factories one visits, workers condemn the personal incentive motive of Liu Shao-chi and regard themselves as revolutionaries who are part of both the Chinese and also the world revolution.

Thermos Bottles

The rise of the thermos bottle in China over the last half century has been spectacular. First made in small shops around Shanghai in the mid-'twenties, it has now become the family hot water system of town and country alike, the row of big five-pound bottles up on a table or dresser being a familiar sight on entering a living room. With increasing use has come demand for a higher quality bottle, one that stands up to heat and cold. Carefully used, the ones made today last for many years, and keep water hot for 24 hours. In the old Nanking, there was a small factory for making them, situated behind some dwelling houses. It was taken over and expanded after 1949, but always suffered the drawback of having capitalist roaders in charge. One of the leaders of this group would say that communism was like a beautiful red flower, capitalism like green leaves. The two must go together. He carried some of his ideas into practice by setting up a little chemical factory on the side, which he called "Green Leaf Chemical Commune", which was really just an underground private factory.

The new Revolutionary Committee consists of eight people — three old cadres and five worker representatives, one of whom is a woman. The chairman of this committee is the previous manager, who followed after the fall of the "Green Leaf" expert. Yearly production is valued at two million yuan, and bottles go into the export trade to the South Seas, Western Europe, Vietnam and other countries. Sixteen technical innovations have been made by workers during the Cultural Revolution, five of them being basic ones speeding up automation and cutting down on the more exhausting labour.

I inquired why such innovations were not made before. The answer was revealing and important. The technicians assigned to the plant were university lads with much book knowledge. They knew in their hearts that they could not make improvements yet, and that probably the workers could. But if they let the workers have their head and carry changes successfully through, then they themselves would look foolish and become redundant. So they always found ways to discredit workers' suggestions and say the proposal would not work out. Now that they are back amongst the ranks of the workers themselves, they are being re-educated. The factory has many examples of how the Mao Tsetung Thought study groups have helped in giving understanding and kindled in people's minds the determination to improve both production and quality.

I saw similar results gained in the same way in one more factory I visited in Nanking. It was one which had grown from the practice workshop of a communications technical school into a modern plant with 600 workers that specialises in the production of automatic long distance telephone exchanges for the home market and export. At one time such an exchange would have been a bulky affair, taking up the whole side of a room. The modern product, transistorised, is about the size of the ordinary home refrigerator, easily installed wherever needed. The factory also specialises in miniaturised equipment for communications work, made under dust-proof conditions and entailing a good deal of work done under microscopes. We put on slippers and went from one workshop to another over polished floors, watching the workers in their white caps and long white gowns tooling, assembling and soldering incredibly small pieces.

Over 20 technical innovations have been made here during the last three years. The group which finally solved the problem of construction of the standard automatic telephone exchange was one of young people with an average age of 25 years. Three of this little workshop were college graduates, the remainder workers who had learnt their trade in the factory. The oldest worker in the factory is 55, but most are young people, 36 percent of them women. All feel that they have to continue to raise standards and that they cannot be content with successes already gained. Sixty percent of them live in factory staff quarters. On the Revolutionary Committee formed in September 1968 are four old cadres, two PLA men and six workers. They have been able to increase production fairly rapidly, producing 100 percent more than in 1966 and having taken on and trained 200 more workers since that year.

1969 Departure

The weather had changed, and it was in driving sleet that we stood for a while and looked up the long flight of steps to the Sun Yat-sen Mausoleum. A misty cloud advanced down the slopes of Purple Mountain. Trees around were a mass of late autumn color against the sombre green of firs and the verdure of bamboo. We left Nanking from the new railway station — the old central one is now "Nanking West" — and were almost immediately going over the great bridge, back to Peking again.

The Bridge Again

It was quite an event to come down to Nanking on a passenger ship with the Yangtze in full summer spate, and then to see the big new bridge looming up in front of us. On my former visits I had travelled mostly by train, plane or highway, but it had been some time since there had been the chance to do the trip in a comfortable, leisurely way by ship.

Now, as a member of a study group, I was here again by mid-summer 1970. We started off the morning by going on two chipper Army Command launches and circled around the bridge piers. "Take all the pictures you want," the friend who acted as a guide told us. After this boat trip we heard some explanations in front of the construction model, and then made a trip across the bridge on the highway — all as a preliminary to the serious task of learning and discussing what had moved workers to do so much, so fast, so well. There was Wang Chao-chu, a veteran worker on the Wuhan and Chungking bridge construction jobs, a member of the bridge construction Revolutionary Committee, and now elected to membership of the Central Committee of the Chinese Communist Party. He is a worker engineer in a Revolutionary Committee composed of workers, technicians and cadres. With him was Hu Pao-yin, who recently had been a foreign delegate himself, having gone to Albania with a workers' delegation. Then Liu Tsung-yuan, a Nanking man who led an important part of the building of the approaches, as well as half a dozen others with tough, weatherbeaten faces of the doers of this world. Wang Chao-chu had a serious mien which lightened up when he discussed the work, breaking into a real worker's smile only when questions were asked that brought back memories. Someone asked about accidents and casualties and Wang was describing how useful safety nets had proved that were strung up under construction jobs. "He ought to know," one of the other workers said, "he fell into one himself, once." They were a good bunch of men of action, and charmed us by the directness with which they made their explanations.

They talked of a puzzled old worker who when faced with an extremely difficult technical problem went home and asked his daughter to read quotations to him, for he was illiterate. "What is work?" she read. "Work is struggle!"

"That's it!" the old man said, and went off and solved his problem in spite of all obstacles. "Mao Tsetung Thought really has made the building of this bridge possible," everyone asserted.

Someone asked how many workers were employed on the project. The answer was: Between five and six thousand, not counting all the thousands sent in from the city and countryside around — the soldiers, the Red Guards, the country folk, all of whom would work for a period and then go back home again. Actually, pretty well everyone in and around Nanking had some part in building the bridge. The major part of the construction was done during the Cultural Revolution, the emergence of a Revolutionary Committee consisting of workers, technicians and old cadres assuring both speed and efficiency. The old style of work, with a chief engineer in command and the other engineers grouped around him, gave place to a new one in which workers were in the lead, well in a position where they could contribute their practical knowledge and revolutionary spirit. The old-type Chinese engineer, often with his narrow education and lack of practical experience, depended heavily on books, many of which were not up-to-date. The worker depended on his actual working experience and a working-class approach. The bringing of worker and engineer together in a new way has been one of the triumphs of Mao Tsetung Thought during the building of the bridge.

The view from the ground floor of the headworks on the Nanking side back through the colonnades supporting the railway approach is impressive. Both railway and highway approaches had to be built over low-lying land, at a considerable height and considerable length — 6,700 metres of double track railway and 4,500 of four-lane highway, to be precise, to reach the entrance to the bridge which rises 700 metres above the water of the river. The whole job was completed three months ahead of schedule. Each stage of the construction, of course, brought its problems, all of which were solved by the combined efforts of all who had directly to do with the job. To do electric welding down at the bottom of so fast flowing a river, to do deep diving, and have divers work effectively, to be economical in the use of material, yet to see that all structural work was up to standard, all this posed difficulties demanding solution. But the technical details concerning the whole effort have been already published in several journals. The outstanding fact is that here is a major engineering project, big on any scale, which was carried out for the first time in history under working-class leadership, with the workers themselves in actual control.

A Visit to Tungching Commune

We went over to the Kiangsu-Anhwei border to visit Tungching Commune. Tungching means "Copper Well" and the name derives from a small old copper mine there. It is a commune with 6,000 acres of land, worked by 16 brigades and supporting a population of 28,300 people. I remembered the place well from the mid-'thirties, having been halted by some bandits here who took what money I had on me. Then the place was pitifully poor, and a whole establishment of scamps battened off the people ruthlessly. The big landlord, Tung Pai-wan, not only owned the best paddy fields, but also operated his own jail into which he would throw tenants who could not give him the two thirds of the crop he demanded. Rates of interest on loans to the peasants were fantastic, often more than 10 percent per month being asked for and paid.

In flood years, a few people were forced to go out begging, and many died in the ditches. In 1931, 4,397 of them left their homes for the roads. It would indeed be a foolish person who tried to paint up the benefits of the old society to the poor peasants of Tungching.

With the new day, while rice and wheat remained the main crops, the call came for a diversified economy and all-round development. The struggle between the two lines of development, whether to follow a capitalist road or go in for socialism, has been severe over the past 20 years, but has brought much deeper understanding. In 1969, heavy rains swelled the river water to its highest level in 100 years, but far from forcing any of the people to become refugees, the flood was contained and the commune gained the best harvest in eight years of continuous good harvests, the total grain output that year being just double that of 1966, and three times that of 1949. Food oil totals doubled those of 1968. The commune has stocked up its own grain stores and sold a big surplus to the state. People's livelihood is continually improving. Before Liberation most families would have to live on less than 200 jin of grain per person a year even in a good year, and try to supplement that by catching shrimps or fish, hauling down fuel from the hills, and what not. We met a former poor peasant, Chen Yang-kwei. Of the seven people in his family, four of them were old and no longer able to work. Yet last year this family earned 5,000 jin of grain and 1,000 yuan in cash. The commune operates its own small industry, and we went to see an agricultural implements plant, a truck and tractor repair works, and a grain processing plant. It also owns eight tractors and 73 mechanised pumping stations. There are 220 electric motors and 55 diesel engines. Afforestation amongst the still mainly bare hills, orchard planting, and mulberry raising for silkworms, have all taken a leap forward in the commune brigades. There are 3,300 children in the 28 schools now operated by the brigades, some of them being long-term ones taking pupils up into middle school grades.

The commune does not rest on its achievements. Resolutely, it learns from Tachai and terraces hillside lands that can be used for cropping. 4,000 mou of new land have been brought under cultivation in the past three years. Of this, 2,000 mou has been irrigated and converted into paddy fields. We went out to one once barren valley where stone terrace walls were being built, and where some new small fields were already being harvested.

The moving spirit here was a sweet-faced matron, Yang Da-kun. She was over 70 when she started leading the people to reclaim this valley. "I realised that the days ahead for me were growing short, and I had to face a choice. Should I just live comfortably or should I get out and lead our folk to do this work? I studied the three short essays, I learnt about the wrong line of Liu Shao-chi, and I thought back on the bitterness of the old society, recalling how I had given birth to a child while collecting fuel up in the snow of the hills, and how the child had died. How often then we had only wild herbs to eat. There was so much bitterness to be thought over." She went on telling how her enemy, the head of the "pao" had sent his "running dogs" to beat her, not once, but several times. Had refused her permission to carry her daughter to the doctor when ill. "We were not looked on as people then," she said. "The Japanese army came and burnt down the thatched hut we had. But unless one had the land-lord's permission a new home could not be built. And to get that per-mission cost money. Now, though I am old, I feel young again in heart. My grandchildren criticise me when I forget to put salt into the food I cook for them, saying that I study so much I forget about them completely. But that does not stop me studying, and in trying to implement what I study by practice. I made 160 pairs of straw sandals last year, and also got in 156 workdays. I took no payment for making the sandals. They were my contribution to the brigade." Some other people joined in and told how last Spring Festival, when she had seen too much water in the pit for fermenting green manure, she had taken off her shoes and got in to correct the situation despite the biting cold. To do that, when you are in your seventies, is something.

There are many brave and thoughtful folk in this brigade. Another of them was a 15-year-old boy, Chu Ying-pao. He was a pupil in one of the new schools, but before the Cultural Revolution had been content to fix his ambitions on being a successful student, in the hope of getting his foot on the bottom rung of the official ladder and becoming a big cadre. His well-meaning mother told him to study well so that he would one day be a high official and thus earn a lot of money and be able to help the whole family. Perhaps he could become a famous scientist or engineer, and then his early teachers would be honored. He went on, "All this worked on my mind until I was determined to succeed for the sake of family and teacher, not knowing that this was all the kind of poison advocated by Liu Shao-chi. Then the Cultural Revolution started and young people from the cities began to come to the countryside. Seeing this, my mother thought there would be no future for me in the city but that it would be better to learn a skill and earn money right here in the country. So she scraped up ten yuan and entertained the master of a small bamboo and woodcraft shop, giving him some presents and so managing that I was taken on as his apprentice. Her idea was that I should get a lot for a small outlay and later be able to help the family more. Going to the shop and home again I had to walk five miles a day, summer and winter, hot sun or winter's rain. But mother consoled me by saying that the younger I started learning the sooner I would be earning money. So the idea was instilled into my mind that the all important thing to do was to earn as much money as possible. Then old Mrs. Yang Da-kun and a young girl activist Cheng who had come to our brigade from a middle school came to talk with my family and to conduct a political study class there. Mrs. Yang spoke the kind of language my mother understood, and the whole family was moved. The more I listened to them, the more I wanted to hear and understand. She told how she had been illiterate, and what a great thing it was for the poor and lower-middle peasants now to have schools for their children. The big thing for a young person was to get the tools for learning, not go after money. They made me see that I should be back at school helping classmates to understand better. But the master of the bamboo craft shop was not willing to release me, so we all moved into his home for meetings in the evenings until we got him to understand and agree."

Coming back to school again, the poor and lower-middle peasants along with the revolutionary teachers gave him much help. He was able to take a leading part in putting on revolutionary drama and to go with it out amongst the villages. He learnt about the wrong ideas held by USSR educators. Organised other school children to carry water and fuel for old people. Cleaned out latrines and pigsties, composting the manure, no longer afraid to get their hands dirty. "Together with my schoolmates we thought of ways and means to serve the people better," he went on, "getting out to fields in the busy season, carrying stones for the builders of terrace walls in winter, helping in the campaigns against waste and for better public health and so on." He was a clear, outspoken, farm lad, saying what he had to say naturally and without any affectation, only pausing when he thought what next to say. Mrs. Yang smiled at him encouragingly as he spoke, obviously proud of him as well she might be.

After he had finished his piece, the 19-year-old middle-school girl who had come to the brigade told of her struggles in getting used to hard work, but to which she was now quite accustomed. Planting out rice in the cold water of paddy fields in the spring, carrying earth bricks for building, stumbling and ashamed at first, but gradually learning how to do more. Months of sore backs and sore feet, sore shoulders and sore hands, yet all with a growing consciousness that as part of a struggling people her place was with them. She gained in self-respect, and she learnt at first hand of the problems of the great mass of the people whom previously, sunk in her study of higher mathematics, her memorisation of passages from many books and her struggle to "be someone" in the world, she had completely ignored.

It was evident that these three — a woman of over 70, a 19-year-old town lass and a farm boy of 15 — had changed so much in their outlook as to become a force to influence the many. Three ordinary folk who now could do so much to move their commune to undertake greater and bigger tasks and to follow the road of revolution, the road pointed out by Mao Tsetung.

I could not but think of the old Kuomintang days, when people like these three, people determined to work for the common good, were shot on the spot by local gangsters or else taken to Nanking and murdered at Yuhuatai. Only now people like these find their rightful place in society, and scope for work and study.

We spent all day at the commune, going to see the silkworm station, the big fish pond, the village amenities that have come with the new prosperity all have worked so hard for and have created together. Then, as evening fell, we drove back down the highway to Nanking.

Cinema Appliance Works

Out of Nanking, on the side of the former bare, but now wooded Purple Mountain, is an interesting factory in scenic surroundings. Here 1,000 workers manufacture film-projectors and other auxiliary equipment for use in China's wide countryside. China is a land of villages scattered through plains, hills and mountains, very many not yet reached by transmission lines. Some are collections of tents out on the grasslands, others up amongst minority nationalities on highland plateaux. To carry the big 32 mm projector up hillside paths and match it with a heavy generator is obviously too difficult. So the factory set about making a small, compact, easily handled 700-watt generator, just enough to power a 16 mm or 8.75 mm movie projector. Then it concentrated on making the projectors smaller. We could see that considerable success had been attained, for we saw a great number of small units going through their final tests. Two people with a carrying pole can easily transport the whole set, and it takes but one person to operate it. A new process of lens grinding and polishing has resulted in a new lens with greater sharpness and more light than before. For field trials the first projectors of this series were sent to the brigades of ten communes in the hilly portions of two counties of Kiangsu. They gave performances, and it was obvious that the masses approved, showing that approval in no uncertain a manner. The people were delighted with the so intimate documentaries, in which they saw their own leadership as if in real life. Heard the singing of opera as if the singer really stood in front of them, as they said.

It was not easy to put the whole new set into production. Sometimes workers stayed on the job for 24 hours, determined to produce the kind of thing that was needed and to get rid of all flaws. The factory has in its history of 18 years built up an experienced technical staff, anxious to produce new and better equipment. They are very pleased with the results thus far obtained with equipment for out-of-the-way places. As in every plant, and in every production organisation in the country, there is always a struggle between two lines, one, trying to keep to the old accustomed paths, the other determined to take a new road and to carry Mao Tsetung Thought into action and really serve the people who should be served first. Needless to say, it was the latter which took control here.

Militia Training

Early one afternoon we left Nanking with its tree-lined boulevards for a trip to Kiangning county where, in a natural amphitheatre surrounded by low hills with higher ones rising beyond, a people's militia battalion was drawn up. Its composition should have been enough to make anyone planning an armed adventure against China think again. For it represented a cross section of the people as they are found in every commune throughout the land. There were young boys and girls, their elder brothers and sisters, their mothers and their fathers. Not the people passive and exploited, but the people armed and confident. They proceeded to put on a show which demonstrated their mastery with their weapons. Technically, the performance was superb. Targets rose from amongst the grain fields, behind hillocks along country paths, and were speedily downed. Redoubts marked with white stones on hillsides were accurately mortared. Hand and rifle grenades shattered their targets. It all looked very real and most convincing.

Nanking Chemical Fertiliser Plant

To go to what was once the Yung Li Chemical Works, in Kuomintang times a capitalist enterprise that was Nanking's industrial show piece, one took a launch and went downstream — quite a journey in all, for the plant lies opposite Nanking over on the northern side of the Yangtze. Now it is no longer Yung Li but a vastly bigger concern, the Nanking Chemical Fertiliser Plant, producing a million tons of fertiliser a year, and occupying an area seven and a half by two and a half kilometres, the working staff and their families numbering 45,000 people in all, 20,300 being employed as workers. Like a self-contained town, the plant operates seven schools with a total of 9,000 pupils. In addition to fertiliser, other chemical products are made, the quality of all having been considerably raised and meeting exacting standards.

There are 530 activists in Mao Tsetung Thought assisting in political studies in the plant, such study being part of the daily schedule of all workers and staff members. The young woman who was guiding our small group was very clear and concise in her explanations. She told me in answer to my question that she was married and had three children, the youngest four and a half years old. As both she and her husband worked, the children cooked their own food, swept the flat and bought the vegetables, learning from an early age to be self-reliant. Our guide told us, "We try and clear the minds of workers of material incentives. Our task is to make fertiliser for the people so that there will be better crops, and thus assist not only the Chinese but also the world revolution." Here in the plant, everybody does his best to develop a creative spirit, and in 1969 alone 168 technical innovations were made which proved valuable when put into use. Up till the end of May 1970, 30 more have been devised, tested and accepted.

Formerly, when the plant was still the Yung Li Chemical Works, a great many of the raw materials were imported from abroad, even the coke had to come from Canada. Imported too were even screws and bolts, the excuse being that they had to be bought abroad because the local ones were of too poor a quality. In the period of Japanese imperialist occupation, conditions for workers were barbaric. The Japanese navy had a headquarters here, and the factory was full of secret agents who could kill, arrest, jail or fine workers at will. The Chinese capitalists worked hand in glove with the enemy. As long as they got their spoils, they were satisfied. There was an examination for new workers, for the worker turnover was large and always more had to be sought. Not a matter of questions and answers. A 25-1b. blacksmith's hammer had to be wielded 50 times. Then a tremendous load of fertiliser had to be carried around the factory twice. Poor, famine-stricken peasants would try, but have to give up. Some, over-exerting themselves, spat blood, and some died under the strain.

Han Pei-yuan was a very strong young man. He passed the tests and was put to work as a crane operator. But due to lack of safety devices on the crane, his left arm got caught and was cut off by the crane hoist. He was ruthlessly kicked out of the factory, with the result that he and his family became beggars. After Liberation, he was brought back and given light work. Now his two sons have become factory workers also. There are many such examples. The old workers have tasted imperialism, and they know well enough that imperialism will not die of its own accord, that the imperialists always seek some way of making a comeback. That is one of the reasons why workers study Mao Tsetung Thought and strive for self-sufficiency. "If a catalyst in the manufacture of synthetic ammonia is needed, why should we have to import it? We just set to work and make it. What others have made, we can make too. We have made capron, a synthetic fibre needed for turning out parachutes, good fishnets, steel substitutes, and so on. A certain German revisionist poured cold water on the idea that we could produce it, saying our plant was too dirty to turn out such a product. We should have to be as clean as a Western plant making antibiotics, he said. 'You just grow soya beans for us and we will make your capron,' was his idea. Finally, after some joint research with the Chinchow Chemical Works in Liaoning, we found the way all right, and swiftly went into production. The USSR had contracted to supply us with the necessary equipment, but the contract was torn up. We made what was necessary ourselves and of higher quality than anything we could have imported. In 1964, the Soviet ambassador came up to see for himself and was dismayed to find our machines operating perfectly.

"During the Liu Shao-chi period an agreement with a French company was proposed for making a nitrogen phosphate fertiliser. The proposed conditions were exorbitant. We felt that if we agreed, China could again be on the road to becoming colonised, so negotiations were broken off, and by 1963 the factory had succeeded in making its own product, which is well up to standard. A Japanese combine agreed to sell a certain fertiliser to China at $26 a ton. Suddenly they jacked the price up to $32. Our workers decided to experiment with making chemical fertiliser. In three months they succeeded, and we had no longer to import this kind of product. Such successes raise morale all around. It especially pleases all to know that every ton of capron synthetic fibre we have made equals the produce of 60 mou — ten acres — of cotton fields."

We talked with some of the workers. Amongst them was Tung Tsung-chih, the 52-year-old head of a cleaners' group which numbers 23 people, the youngest being 34, the oldest 67. He was once illiterate and a beggar and lived in utter destitution with the six members of his family. His father and elder brother starved to death, his elder sister was sold. He and his group now know enough Chinese characters to read the three short essays of Mao Tsetung and carry on with their study. Anxious to salvage all they can, they collect and recondition cotton waste, and make discarded piping and sheet metal into useful household articles such as chairs, buckets, dust pans etc. The waste material from so big a plant runs into a huge tonnage each year, and the utilisation of this has to be supervised and directed also.

Li Hsueh-hsing is a 5th-grade bench worker. "Just a very ordinary bench worker," he described himself. His father had died of bad treatment and hunger, but with Liberation the son was saved. He joined the Communist Youth League, then the Party. He said that before the Cultural Revolution all power in the field of technique was in the tight grip of a small number of people who thought of themselves as authorities, most of whom had been educated under the old order and so had a bourgeois political outlook. "So the line which was pushed in our plant was in reality a revisionist one and workers were unable to realise their potential. When the Cultural Revolution started, we set up a technical innovations group and broke down the monopoly of the authorities. At that time there was a call to make synthetic ammonia, so we put up a reaction tower for its manufacture. In successfully constructing this tower, we raised efficiency 40 percent and cut down the use of electricity by half. The old authorities laughed at us when we started. They used to say that workers are fit only to take care of machines, hands and feet agile but with minds of country bumpkins. However, in spite of all the difficulties we were successful. We workers are given power now," he said, "but we know well we must use it wisely."

Liu Chi-ling, who graduated from the Nanking Chemical Engineering College in 1962, took up the story. He is a technician. Very quietly and modestly he put his case. He was brought up to think that, as an intellectual, he would be in a position to tell others what to do rather than have to do it himself. Otherwise why go to all the trouble of studying technique all those years in college? After he came to the factory he buried his head in books, searching for better methods and paying little attention to the workers, living in a different world from them. He was put in a group of engineers whose task was to mechanise the process for making granulated urea. The group worked for a year and a half and did not succeed. Then came the Cultural Revolution, and his ivory tower of intellectual pride collapsed. He was forced by circumstances now to let himself be remoulded by the workers. They promptly revived the urea problem. With worker leadership it was solved in one month, the process has been in use since then and has proved successful.

Why were the old engineers and technicians unable to produce the goods? They had much too little practical knowledge. They were not out to serve the people but wanted to raise their own reputations. They wanted to carve out a career for themselves in the old way and were all the time only filling notebooks with advanced data rather than looking to the practical things going on around them. In our new grouping of workers, technicians and cadres we feel we can master all difficulties that crop up. The old engineers had been brought up in a society that still worshipped Confucius. Practice was not for them. Their hands should never be dirtied. Now, with a common approach and working together, we all do much better, he said, and then smiled and was finished. There were other stories but the theme was the same. Rely on the workers and trust them. Work with them and take them into your confidence. Let them lead, put your shoulder to the wheel, and then success will come.

Children's Propaganda Teams

Nanking is justly famous these days for the high standard of its children's propaganda groups, which have been formed in every administrative section of the city as well as being organised in the various primary schools themselves, as we had seen on our last visit to Nanking. We happily spent a whole evening with the Chaoyang area group in the guest-house meeting hall. It was a delightfully intimate affair, with high standards in both the singing and acting. Then there was the performance of yet another group, its items alternating with those of an adult acrobatic team which, though excellent in its own style, did not allow the spirit generated by the children to accumulate in the same way as a purely child performance did. There was one item at this performance, though, which would have graced any stage: selections from the ballet "The White-Haired Girl", accompanied by excellent children soloists singing in the wings. These groups now go out amongst the communes, factories, mines in or around Nanking. One, with an average age of 11, has already done 400 performances. These children moved me to write:

> *Nanking, whose massive*
> *city walls, now half*
> *hidden by greenery, enclose*
> *so many memories; rebel Taipings,*
> *imperialist massacres,*
> *fascist executions, Kuomintang*
> *terror, then finally the grand*
> *drama of Liberation.*
>
> *And in this Nanking where now*
> *the people hold power, there rises*
> *a fresh generation of youngsters*
> *successors to the revolution,*
> *growing up full of understanding*
> *and ability; learning that*
> *struggle must continue; helping*
> *to build a great bridge, or bring in*
> *commune harvests along with*
> *their classroom lessons; then, too,*
> *forming theatre groups to go out*
> *and tell folk about the thing*
> *that inspires them with so great*
> *a spirit; happy, gay young actors*
> *are these with voices*
> *that lift audiences; now many*
> *such teams have come into action,*
> *just one of which has already*
> *given four hundred performances*
> *mainly to workers and peasants;*
> *youngsters with an average age*
> *of eleven, doing big things for*
> *their own future and that of*
> *all children.*

All those eager little faces
lit with the passion of
their cause; the spirit which
really moves mountains; here
bare child arms that point
the way ahead; quick feet
that lead elders to it, steadying
many a heart, giving confidence
encouragement, and the feeling
of being truly one with
a glorious dawn.

Sights of Nanking

We did not leave Nanking before we had paid a visit to the tomb of Sun Yat-sen, beautifully maintained and now in the forest setting planned for it. We spent some time, too, up at the astronomical observatory on a Purple Mountain ridge, saw the old instruments which were taken away by the Germans during the armed intervention of the Eight Nations in the Boxer Rebellion and were only returned on demand at the end of World War I. We watched one of the telescopes that tracked China's first satellite and looked over Nanking city spread below us, its old walls where they still survived covered with greenery. The view led us to think that in 1864 it must have been somewhere around here that General Gordon looked on the city when he came to advise the Manchus, by then having become puppets, how to mine the walls of Nanking and blow them up with British explosives brought up from the Wusung forts so that the Manchus could enter and slaughter Taiping rebels. That was only around a hundred years ago, but few remember the story now. Still the process has not stopped, and imperialists give their puppets even in these days explosives to slaughter the working people in Indo-China and other parts of Southeast Asia. But the difference now is that it was a rising imperialism then, and today it is a dying one, lashing out in its last throes.

Life and Industrial Growth in Wusih

Wusih is situated in south Kiangsu province on the Grand Canal. It was once a little known county town without importance. In the twenties of this century, however, some industry developed with the establishment of then modern silk filatures. Wusih traders too invested their capital in the rising industrial city of Shanghai. They became a good deal richer from their investments and some of the profits flowed back to their hometown. The mass of the people, however, remained poor and exploited. Landlordism was ripe, and the cost of supporting a corrupt government and a rotting superstructure which included a host of Buddhist and Taoist temples lay heavily on them.

After Liberation, Wusih really began to spread. Modern industry came in. Suburbs reached out around the shores of Taihu Lake. Beautiful new parks were set up. The Grand Canal became a mass of busy shipping. A new day had come. The old city walls vanished, modern macadamised highways shot out into the countryside, wide new bridges were built, and everything expanded.

Today as a municipality of 600,000 people under the direct leadership of the province, it is becoming an industrial hub of considerable importance. Its diesel engines and its concrete boats and lighters are well known. Wusih machine tools are now to be found in many machine shops in different parts of China. The land around is rich, and with new methods, better seed, better fertiliser and better management, agricultural output is rising. On many grain fields there is a crop of wheat that might run to 400 jin a mou, which is followed by early and late crops of rice, each bringing 800 jin a mou, making up 2,000 jin a mou, which is 15 tons a hectare.

China is an old land, and every place has its history stretching a long way back. Here, for one instance, is Meitsun, now a village in Wusih county, which was once the seat of the kings of Wu, before the capital was moved to Soochow. Off the shores of Taihu Lake lies Mashan Island, famous for the prolonged resistance the people put up there in modern times against Japanese aggression, and for their stand against the Kuomintang reaction in the War of Liberation. It is now farmed by a commune of 8,000 people.

We stayed out in a part of the graceful Liyuan gardens, situated by Li Lake, which connects with Taihu. On my travels in this region I had each day a good opportunity of seeing something of life in Liyuan Commune as I passed through, as well as that on the waterways and in the city. In the commune, winter wheat was being harvested, and rice planted out in paddy fields. Students from many city schools were helping, little ones doing a job of gleaning after the harvest had been carted off. Tractors came in then, and the ground was prepared for rice. Tractors were equipped with paddles on their wheels to enable them to work through the mud of the flooded paddy.

Not so much land is left for mulberries as in earlier days, food crops taking priority over silk. The improvement in water transport (in quite a measure due to the coming in of the ferro-concrete boat), has enabled more lake mud to be brought in as mulberry fertiliser and this, together with digging under a crop of broad beans just before they come to pod, has made for a much richer crop of mulberry leaves. In the face of the big crops of wheat and rice gained in these days it is hard to realise that the place was once thought rich when it harvested 70 jin of winter wheat and 400 jin of rice a mou, back in 1950.

Despite the fishing grounds of Taihu Lake, fish ponds around Wusih are numerous. If the three varieties of fish for the deep portions of the pond are grown, the two for the middle and the two for the surface area, and all fed on the needed lake weeds, with the pond being cleaned out at set intervals, then 1,000 jin of fish can be gained for each mou of pond area. Fish is one of the main sources of protein locally, so there needs to be a steady supply.

In Liyuan Commune, adjacent to the highway we noticed three small modern factory buildings being erected. They were for the new small industry program of the commune. Passing by at night, we noticed that work was still going ahead on their interior finishing, under electric light. Out in the fields nearby, too, a high-powered electric light lit up wheat stubble on which farmers were working overtime to get the plots into paddy. Every day, every hour counts in this struggle, apparently.

One afternoon we climbed around the paths of a park by Taihu Lake. For scenery, Wusih in some respects compares well even with the famed Hangchow, for here the lake is on a much bigger scale and the park reserves are spacious. In the afternoon, with the fishing fleets clustering in and with the sun behind them, a picture of surpassing beauty is presented. Around the scenic hill fronting Taihu there was a glory of "huanghua", a golden bloom which comes in early summer. On weekends and holidays many Shanghai folk come up for the day. Parks these days in China are encouraged to seek as many means for self-support as possible, growing fruit trees and vegetables especially. There is plenty of space for this in most Wusih parks.

Chinese children are always fascinating, and Wusih was no exception. The way the rising generation is educated will determine the Wusih of the future. I had gone to Wusih this time primarily to see the building of concrete boats, the story of which is presented elsewhere. But high on my priority list was a visit to a local school.

Tungfanghung Primary School

Tungfanghung Primary School in Wusih was once called "Lienyuan", after the name of its street locality. One of 1,180 pupils, 80 percent of whom are from worker, poor and lower-middle peasant or soldier families, it has 51 teachers and staff. It has a small entrance from a narrow lane, but once inside, one sees that the compound is quite large, and the two-floored classroom blocks well lit and airy. Before the Cultural Revolution, it followed the usual Liu Shao-chi line. Study hard, pass examinations well, and be determined to rise high in society. Now as a work-and-study school, its aim is to turn out children who put Mao Tsetung Thought into everyday practice. For practical work, pupils do two and a half days a week in the school workshops, then two weeks in spring and two weeks in autumn helping commune farmers at the busy time. At intervals, they also take marches to famous parks, and the older ones out into the countryside. In class work, they have courses in politics, Chinese language, arithmetic, revolutionary art and literature which includes singing and drawing, general knowledge, and physical training.

They come to school at eight each morning. The first half hour is spent on the three short essays of Chairman Mao. At 11:05 they stop for lunch. In the afternoon there are two classes, except for two half-days a week when the teaching staff go off for political study with other organisations. Classes are of 40 minutes' duration. There are two Mao Tsetung Thought propaganda groups, and pupils are urged to join family or locality political study groups in the evenings. Some of these are led by retired workers or old soldiers and have considerable influence. Children take turns to stand at street corners helping traffic control. When the five-year training course is ended, the graduating class goes on to middle school without any examination. The school aims to have as deep roots in local community life as possible. Quite a few of its teachers are old pupils come back to work with the next generation. Pupils grow a considerable attachment for the commune brigade they go to work with and often wheel or carry out fertiliser from the city to the fields on Sundays or at other rest times. In games, pingpong takes precedence, and there are many competitions with other schools, it ever being stressed that it is not important whether you win or lose, but what is important is the spirit and cooperation shown in the game. I watched some of the games being played and was impressed by the technique shown. Going around the classrooms was an experience. Children were alert and responsive, obviously enjoying the classwork.

The school propaganda corps put on a very fine performance for us, which included pieces from the modern operas done with verve and precision. The other items captivated me entirely. The old woman teacher who is in charge of training the concert party told about how, for a period, the school dramatic group was in much demand in city and suburbs, organisations often sending a truck to take the children out to perform for them, so that some children began to get inflated ideas about their importance as outstanding actors, making for another problem that sessions of struggle, criticism and transformation were able to iron out. Always there is the need, she said, for youngsters to understand that one divides into two, and that of the two ways one is correct while the other is not. Ever the old questions are posed as children rise in their grades. What do we live for? Why do we live? What should be our role in the Chinese and world revolution? And there are certain principles children of the new society must grasp. There is, firstly, the class struggle and we must learn to be good, practical revolutionaries. We must learn theory from practice. Science is needed to make practice effective. We learn at school how to work, but we also must learn how to work more effectively. These are some of the ideas that are currently put into the teaching in the go-ahead primary school of today. "No wonder you were sent out of the drama group," said a teacher to a pupil in rebuke for a fault. The pupil thought it over and came back to the teacher after class, saying, "Teacher, the drama group is revolutionary work. So is classwork, just the same. It was not for punishment that I was sent out of the drama group, but because it was thought I needed more classwork. You were wrong to say what you did in front of our class." The teacher thought a little, and then confessed he was wrong and the boy was right. Next day in class he criticised himself in front of all, and all were comrades again. A little incident, but indicative of the relations between teachers and students in this school of today.

In the school's practical work there is a tailoring department with around 30 sewing machines. At the time of my visit they were cutting up waste cloth to make into bags for collecting Chinese herbal medicines, and also for finger guards for workers handling stone. They were handling the machines in quite a professional style, all deeply intent on what they were doing. Four girls were busy at the cutting table. In another section, waste cardboard was being made up into boxes for this product or that, while in yet another, discarded springs from some factory were being turned into key rings for the consumer market. Waste from cotton mills was being respun and woven into workers' gloves and mittens. "It is the idea of working that is important," explained the leading cadre of the school, "not the value of the product. And if we can get the idea over that waste is bad, waste materials can well be used for something, then we have taught another lesson." Work as a way of life is certainly an idea that is being inculcated here. Then too there is the idea of service, and the great privilege it is to be able to serve the people. Teachers go to the homes of their pupils and talk with their home folk, and then families send a representative to family and school meetings which are held three times a term. People help each other with problems that affect the children. Arrange, for instance, for the crippled child to be carried to school each and every day and be made to feel one with the rest. There are always ways to serve the people when there are so many people around. The children gave me a ringing farewell when I went off. I was the first foreign visitor they had had. It was good to have been with them for a while, and catch some of their enthusiasm.

The Wusih Diesel Engine Factory

I well remember seeing a number of small iron-working shops in Wusih in the 'thirties. These consisted usually of a couple of Shanghai ironshop workers with a few apprentices gathered around them. One of their products was a simple engine which was carried in a wooden boat, and which operated a pump that lifted canal water to irrigate paddy fields. These shops were brought together in a centralised factory in 1942, with 160 workers and 60 machine tools, still producing the old model. In the period after the end of the War of Resistance, the company was refinanced, and an American expert called in. He was not much of an expert, however, and the new management spent most of its time at feasting and gaming tables. The factory produced only 31 diesel engines a year, and they weighed three and a half tons each. Payment of wages to workers was always behind, the management complaining their profits were too small for them to pay.

After the War of Liberation it became the first state factory in Wusih. Work was stepped up on a better model weighing one and a half tons, and with double the number of revolutions the old model had. In 1953, a big change came in and several lighter and more modern models were turned out. The plant continued to expand, re-tooling with all China-made machine tools. Though this was the period when Soviet technicians were in China, none were employed in this plant, which went ahead producing 40- and 60-h.p. engines weighing less than one ton each. They were used for small town power plants, fishing boats, passenger and powered transport, and so on. This was the situation when I came in 1966. Coming again five years later, I was met by the same leading cadre who had met me before, and caught up with some of the latest improvements.

There are now 3,600 workers, of whom 580 are women, working on 301,000 square metres of floor space, including an addition of 10,000 square metres since 1966. Since the Cultural Revolution, the spirit of the workers has been raised, and Mao Tsetung Thought is being studied in depth. There are 207 study groups of workers. Over 50 old workers who were illiterate have memorised the three short essays completely. The old part-work, part-study school operated by the factory to train technicians has been discontinued and new workers are recruited from amongst the middle-school students who come to the factory to do practical work. When they become young workers, they go to night school for some years till they graduate in technology. Wages run from 33 yuan a month for young workers to 104 yuan for the oldest. There are over 50 university graduates from various national universities amongst the technicians. Eighty-three technical innovations have been made since and during the Cultural Revolution which have resulted in considerable progress. There have been five new models perfected, one of which, called "2120", is an air cooled 40-h.p. engine, lighter in weight than the old models, and more easily operated. This model went into production in 1969, when 100 were made. In 1970, 550 were produced and 1971 will see around 1,800. There were some V8 types amongst the new models, and one, a 600-h.p. one for big fishing trawlers, has passed its test and is being produced in series. We spent some time in the testing room, especially interested in one innovation which added an air compressor operated by waste gas. By pumping more air into the ignition chamber, the 80-h.p. engine had its power increased to 120 h.p.

In this big, roomy plant with well lit shops it was a joy to watch work on the final assembly line, and to see engines that will power heavy trucks, electric generators for the hinterland and inland water transport coming so smoothly off and being packed into crates for delivery to places where they will better arm working folk in their struggle. The diesel engine oil injectors are not made here, but in a connected Wusih plant not far away.

Wusih Clay Figures

An old craft of Wusih was the making of clay figures. In pre-Liberation times it was done by various poor folk who lived on the lower slopes of Weishan, their work being sold as toys for a few coppers at temple fairs, on the railway platform and so on. After Liberation, the old handicraftsmen were gathered together in one factory, with better designs and materials being supplied. The development has gone on over the years. In the main, however, the designs were still traditional. The Cultural Revolution changed that, and on this visit we saw many new pieces being produced, the main topics being the model operas of today and then, for the export trade which absorbs 50 percent of the production, many charming studies of China's wealth of child life. Some 200 kinds in all. On my visit in 1966 they had around 200 workers. Now there are 356. The leading cadre said that the demand for their wares could not be met yet. For export pieces, gypsum is used instead of local clay, but gypsum for moulds has been abandoned for rubber ones, which are cheap and give better results. The factory is set out near Weishan hill, good spacious workrooms in a compound with plenty of trees around.

The factory had the pleasant, homely look a place of arts and crafts should have. Some of the workers have been all their lives at the craft. An old woman with spectacles and white hair worked at one bench. At another, a 73-year-old craftsman worked on a new design. In one shop a woman worker had her child near her, the child busy making figures for fun from bits of waste clay.

Wusih Iron and Steel Works

In the Great Leap Forward, there was rapid industrial expansion in Wusih. As in other towns, an iron and steel works was set up and quickly went into production. With enormous spirit and determination, 6,000 workers set up a coking plant, an oxygen plant, iron smelters and Bessemer converters, a seamless pipe assembly, one for angle steel and one for steel wire. Progress was being made in all fields when, in 1961, down came a work team which proceeded to tell the management that the whole plant was redundant and all operations should be halted. The work team wanted to have the smelters demolished, but workers resisted. In the end, due to organised worker insistence, three sections of the plant were left, the oxygen, the seamless pipe and the wire-drawing, less than 2,000 of the 6,000 workers being kept on. The steel needed was brought in from other parts of China or from abroad. The Mao Tsetung idea of self-sufficiency was dropped. Through the nine years that followed, however, workers kept the iron smelters in order, painting them, stopping weather damage. They believed the Mao Tsetung line would win out in the end, as it did.

In 1970 the plant was put into running order again and, when I came to see it in May 1971, was a going concern in all departments. It had taken but 40 days of intense struggle to get the iron smelters going again. In Wusih alone, the Liu Shao-chi line closed down 83 plants of various kinds and halted the construction of any new ones that had been started. All over the land the small furnaces ceased to redden the nights with their glow. Today, as in Wusih, they start to operate again. Surely, as they begin once more, production will not be high to start with, but it will make local industry much more self-sufficient. The Wusih plant now is producing around 60,000 tons a year of iron, manganese iron, and alloy steel. But one thing leads to another very swiftly. In the Liu Shao-chi period they said that Kiangsu had no iron ore or coal. Now, however, ample supplies are being found in Yihsing just across Taihu Lake, where iron ore, coal, limestone and refractory clays are close together. A first target will be 200,000 tons of iron a year, while the present plant in Wusih will expand to 200,000 tons of alloy steels, both centres being part of one of the many small iron and steel complexes rising throughout the land.

It is not easy to cover all the essential parts of even a small iron and steel works on a hot, early summer's day. One watches iron furnaces being tapped, looks at the line of high-school students doing some of the earth-work for a new internal railway line, then goes over to the wharves to see how many of the lighters unloading are concrete ones, remembering that the plan for the new Wusih-Yihsing Iron and Steel Complex entails the use of ten tugboats, each pulling ten 40-ton lighters, all made of concrete and all produced in the Wusih Ferro-Concrete Boat Factories. In the steel-smelting shops one watches the girl high up in the overhead crane cabin nonchalantly picking up the melt and carrying it down to be tipped into moulds, and is fascinated by the automation in seamless steel tubes and wire making. There are the coke ovens and the ammonia recovery plant to remind one that each iron and steel complex is also a fertiliser factory for giving something back to the land. In the plant's office we stare at the many different forms and shapes of steel produced for Wusih's growing industry, realising well that today the way for new advances has been cleared and that each step forward in turn will create new people. There is little a people cannot do when it starts to work together in a principled way towards definite goals. It is safe to say now that, with the reversal of the Liu Shao-chi line, widespread small iron and steel industry will take a new leap forward, making possible the development of a great deal of other local industry along with it, and that there will be ample steel for all the new railways and all the big bridges that are needed to be built in the area for the new stages to come.

The Kiangsu Schistosomiasis Research Institute

We spent a morning at the provincial research institute against schisto-somiasis. Coming here in the early summer of 1966, I had written about it as follows:

"A plant which has a very direct bearing on the livelihood of the coun-try folk around Taihu Lake, and indeed on those of all Kiangsu province, is to be found in Wusih. One comes to it up steps through a wooded hillside to its fine, well-kept modern building set splendidly on a hilltop overlook-ing Taihu Lake. It is the research institute for dealing with the dread disease 'schistosomiasis japonica' which once in the old order affected many millions of people along the Yangtze, bringing great swollen bellies, weary limbs and then early death. The 'ting lo' snail which is the host for the parasite was once found everywhere. This institute, first set up in 1950 in some dwelling houses below the hill on which it stands at present, came with seven workers, only two of whom were doctors. By 1954, proper buildings had been constructed and the staff added to. Now there are 107 workers here, 50 percent of whom are university graduates. The hospital part of the institute has 100 beds to which patients can be brought from the countryside. On the preventive and curative side half of the staff stays out amongst the communes throughout the province investigating and educating as well as leading in the struggle against the 'ting lo' snail. They see that brigade clinics have supplies of the necessary medicines for any who get the disease, and of the ointment paddy field workers rub into their feet to prevent the parasite entering the pores of the skin. The disease has afflicted many generations since it was first written up in that very early medical treatise called the 'Nei Ching'. Traditional medicines do help, but when the sickness is too advanced for these or Western anti-mony compounds to deal with, there has to be an operation and the en-larged spleen removed. Around 1950, it was estimated that as many as seven or eight million people in the Yangtze valley were afflicted. The 'ting lo' does not do so well in provinces further south, apparently, the middle and lower Yangtze region being its home. Now it has been brought under control, and before long will be entirely eradicated. The scenic area along Taihu Lake, much used for swimming in summer these days, has been rendered entirely clear of the snail.

"The victory against it is like winning a major war against fiends for genocide. In terms of people, the victory gained so far has brought light and happiness into many lives from families of those afflicted with the scourge for untold generations, with none knowing its real cause or how to deal with it. Looked at under the microscope, the fluke seems a riotous little beast with two tails and incredible energy. Methods of dealing with its host, the 'ting lo' snail, have now advanced. In summer, for instance, one only has to spread straw mats on the water near the banks in infested localities for many snails around to congregate under them. They especial-ly like the crevices in and under old stone steps leading up from the water, or cracks amongst stone house-piles standing in the water. Certain sprays kill them easily. The presence of the fluke in water is now discovered with relatively simple methods, so that the attack on it can be directed on it quite easily. An afternoon spent at the institute with so much to be shown and so much explained passed swiftly, and one left with a feeling of deep respect for all accomplished. Knowing well, though, that it is the mass support it receives that makes all possible."

This was all true enough, but as the present leading cadre, a PLA man, explained, people were still getting the disease, certain communes in the province being especially badly affected. The battle had by no means been won. In the Cultural Revolution the whole problem of how an institute like this should be run came up for criticism and transformation. The old method of leadership was an upper-class, Western conception. It would never gain final victory over the disease. So the whole staff was divided into groups that went out into the worst affected parts of the province and stayed there for three or four months, coming back to the institute three times a year to sum up experiences gained. All underwent an intense period of struggle, criticism and transformation, during which the old concept of how to operate such an institute was completely demolished. Out in the field, they gave training to the "barefoot" doctors of brigades and the health workers of production teams, as well as the cadre especially allocated to each brigade for schistosomiasis prevention work. They saw to it that every person in the brigade, from the youngest to the oldest, had three stool tests at regular intervals, as well as other tests thought necessary. Saw to it also that the cattle and domestic animals were free from the disease, that all cracks in stones of embankments, bridges and so on where the "ting lo" snail might hide, were cemented up. That paddy fields were treated with anti-snail spray before being prepared for crops, that snail-infested canals be filled in and new ones dug. To do research on the spot rather than sit in an institute delving deep into academic studies of the problem, in the hope of being able to write a famous paper on the subject in some learned journal.

The problem was how to get rid of the disease in the shortest possible time, and in doing so to do research on the effects of the different drugs used, which has to be done right on the spot, all in the full realisation that only a collective attack can bring results. To get this collective effort, there had to be a bond of confidence established in the communes in which work was being done. Where this was done, results soon began to show up. Whole brigades without a single new or even uncured old case in them soon began to be reported. Research directed from above, a long way from the infected spot, might be listened to, and might not. But the only place to fight a battle is in the front line, and into the front line the researchers went. When they found local herbal remedies, they reported them and the institute in Wusih tested them, made tinctures or pills and sent them out. When a spleen had to be removed, as sometimes is necessary with long standing cases, this is done in commune hospitals. Very few patients are now taken into the institute hospital, for in Wusih itself the disease has been practically eradicated.

In herbals, two useful discoveries have been made. One is a tincture made of the leaves of the "feng yang" tree, a very common species growing especially by the roadsides, and the other a little hillside plant called "mao ken", the whole plant, leaves and roots, being boiled to get the tincture. "Feng yang" leaves given for 20 days effect a cure in 40 percent of cases treated, while "mao ken" scores 30 percent. Both are good for old people, as they produce no harmful reaction whatsoever. There are a considerable number of other remedies, but so far none so useful as the two mentioned. Generally, these herbals are tried before the Western medicines are. The use of "feng yang" leaves spread from Hunan where it had been found to be effective.

In schistosomiasis prevention, one commune production team vies with the other, and then one production team comes over and inspects the work of the other, and vice versa. The same thing with brigades. The people enter into the spirit of the game and enjoy it. Members go to the other group looking for "ting lo" snails in their area, or for any other lapse in the campaign against the disease. The advance of the small tractor for plowing in the countryside now cuts out many of the old water buffaloes, and with them also a schistosomiasis hazard.

We went around the various rooms in the institute where work was being done on chemicals against "ting lo" snails and where, too, herbals were extracted. In one section we saw Army medical cadres doing work on the effects of acupuncture in rabbits infected with schistosomiasis. One such rabbit was dissected during our visit and the liver was found enlarged, the blood vessels being full of parasites.

In the institute itself, the staff who remain and those who come back for summing up, together with their families, all take part in vegetable and grain raising on their hillside, to make it as self-sufficient as possible, and to keep in touch with actual working conditions. The whole institute was kept spotlessly clean and, with trees and flowers around, a very pleasant and workman-like place for the task. But its function is that of supporting a front-line struggle, a fact all now are well aware of.

To see something of how the new policy of the research institute was working out, I went to one of the Kiangsu counties, that of Changshu not far from Soochow, which had the reputation of being one of the worst affected counties in the province. And of the commune brigades which had been most affected by the schistosomiasis parasite, there was the example of Janting Brigade of Motsun Commune, which we visited one very wet morning. We found it to be a brigade of 1,780 people from 504 families. It farms 1,605 mou of rich, flat paddy fields. In 1970 it gained 301 jin of winter wheat a mou, and from later rice crops 931 jin. This year of 1971 they expect to get, in all, an average of 2,000 jin of grain a mou. Grain allowance per person is 550 jin. Then, after discussing all of this, we went on to talk of progress in the war against schistosomiasis. Yes, they had a health worker to every production team, and three "barefoot" doctors for their whole brigade. They had known something about the disease and that the "ting lo" snail was the carrier, so they went ahead and exterminated the snails. Drugs for the sick they could get but, actually, no one yet had organised the people themselves to eradicate the disease. It was all done from the top down.

Then, with the Cultural Revolution, change came. In April 1970, the brigades now being well equipped with clinics and medical workers, an exhaustive examination of every person was made, with three stool tests each for a beginning, 1,004 people were found to harbor the parasite. This led to a general mass attack on the scourge. Paddy fields were given a coating of lime powder before flooding. Medicines were prescribed, and in some older people where the infection was a long standing one, operations for removal of the spleen were carried out. Exhaustive tests made in May 1971 showed only 28 people still harboring the parasite. Soon they will be cured, and the brigade, once considered to be amongst the worst of all Changshu commune brigades for its health record, will join the increasing number which do not have a single case.

One of the three leaders of the brigade who spoke to us was a pleasant-faced, suntanned man in his late forties. Yes, he had been infected, so badly that his spleen had been removed in the commune hospital. He now felt better than he ever did. We went to the brigade school and looked at the children there. A healthier looking lot one could not find. Not a single pot belly amongst them all. The "ting lo" snail and the blood fluke is going, going, and will soon be gone amongst the working people in the communes of Changshu. Which, in all, is a very solid piece of revolutionary activity, and a victory to be proud of.

People in Wusih were still talking about the visit Prince Sihanouk had recently paid them, and how delighted he had been with the place. I sympathised with him, and tried to put down some of my thoughts in the following lines:

> A new Wusih that now has
> expanded, breaking clear of
> the grim encirclement of old walls
> increasingly becoming
> a place of beauty and wealth;
> beauty in its hills and lakes;
> in tall white sails sweeping
> down the Grand Canal; beauty
> in the sturdy efficient boats
> of concrete which slip so easily
> into waters from new factories;
> beauty in streamlined diesel engines
> created by the hands and minds
> of Wusih workers; beauty in
> the clay figurines that go out
> to many a land, bringing many
> a smile; beauty in the silks
> spun, woven and dyed, that
> please fingers passing over them;
> there is so much that is good
> to see in Wusih.

>> The vivid green of paddy fields
>> freshly planted; the sheen on
>> mulberry leaves; the old camphor
>> trees through which sunlight
>> filters, then above all, the rich
>> child life seen at its best
>> as summer begins; four small
>> school girls, plaits dancing
>> as they laugh and help sweating
>> pullers over a bridge hump; two
>> school boys in the briefest
>> summer wear, poling a boat
>> of manure back to commune land,
>> bodies as graceful and lithe
>> as the sweep of willows that
>> dance over the waterway.

> Beauty of spirit
> that creates wealth for all
> wealth and beauty
> that strengthens determination

> to defend it and all
> the gains the revolution has made
> along with all it struggles
> to make for the poor and wretched
> everywhere.

Soochow

The ancient capital of the Kingdom of Wu, Soochow is today a city administering eight counties, with a population of over eight million people in all. The city itself has 550,000 people, and is a rising industrial one. In the old days it used to be rightly said that there were more pagodas in the city than factory chimneys, but now the forest of factory chimneys spreads a long way up and down the railway line from the old city centre. Soochow is a name that conjures up many memories — stories of the Taiping Rebellion, of beautiful girls and the wonderful embroideries they produced down through history. Maybe it takes beauty to produce beauty, but however it is, Soochow embroideries are famous all over the world. Today the headquarters of the industry is beautifully set amongst gardens, and I was surprised when visiting in May 1971 to see how well the trees have grown, and what a serene and lovely spot it had become. In all there are four workshops set in different parts of the city, employing 1,500 people. Those in the central shops concentrate on exhibition pieces in the main. It was nice to have come and seen them all again. I had come last in 1961.

Insecticide Sprayers for Farm Use

We visited the Soochow spray pump works which was set up in 1958 at the time of the Great Leap Forward, and which has grown to be a plant of 803 workers operating in modern buildings inside the old city area. Their products go all over China and to many countries abroad — Cuba, Pakistan, Tanzania and others. In all they make between 300,000-400,000 a year, the majority being the knapsack type pump used for spraying under the leaves of the cotton plant, which sells for 22 yuan. A new type of power pump has been evolved which weighs but 8.5 kgs and throws its spray for 22 metres. It replaces one which weighed 28 kgs, threw spray only 18 metres and cost 950 yuan. The new type costs 800 yuan. It can spray 150-200 mou of rice land a day. The factory has sent teams to various parts of the country, from Hainan Island to the far Northwest, to get users' opinions on the spray pumps made, and demonstrating their possibilities for non-users. The 800-yuan type is also easily adapted in villages to do water pumping or for powering a generator to make possible an evening film or theatrical show. As there is a growing demand for the product, extensions of the factory are now being considered. To support agriculture as a base, they said here, was a first duty for industry. Amongst new models being experimented with is one operated by a storage battery, which appears to have considerable possibilities for useful service.

Soochow Industrial Porcelain Factory

This factory, set beside the Grand Canal out in one of the new industrial districts of Soochow, turns out insulators mainly for high voltage power lines, steam and hydro-electric plants and transformer stations. With modern mechanisation and a local oil-burning continuous kiln, it gives employment to 700 workers. In the old society it was a small plant turning out low voltage insulators, and employing but 100 workers, with simple equipment. In the intervening years, production has gone up 40 times over the old figure. Many of the products go into the export trade where they are well received. Quite a number of technical innovations have been made, very pleasing to see. All high voltage insulators go through a rigorous testing process before leaving the plant. When it was decided to change from low to high voltage insulators after Liberation, Soviet experts gave the workers heavy Soviet models to copy. In these years, however, following the Mao Tsetung line, old forms have been discarded. The new insulator of the kind weighs much less, and has increased resistance. The leading cadre was very modest in his own appraisal of work done, feeling that there was a great need for improvement in all sections. We felt that the work force had done great things, and that there was a bright future of endeavor in front of them.

The "Paotai" 53-Arch Bridge

As we were on the Grand Canal, we thought it would be good to run out into the countryside and look at the Tang dynasty "Paotai" (Precious Belt) 53-arch bridge there. It is one of the famous bridges of China and, kept in repair by succeeding dynasties, continues to serve the people. We sat and watched a while, looking at Grand Canal traffic going past. A concrete tug pulling a line of 40-ton concrete lighters. A fishing group with lines of cormorants on their boats. Some boat children, sturdy self-reliant four- and five-year-olds, busy making a model farm by the canal bank. They had ingeniously fenced off fields and were planting them with grass blades, making them look like a rice crop. Down the road came a detachment of workers from various factories going out to help commune farmers in the busy season. In the paddy fields beside the road small hand tractors churned their way, pulling plows through the mud. Here at the 53-arch bridge a big battle was once fought between the Taipings and the imperialists. But old battles are forgotten now, as newer ones loom up in front of the people: the battles to make an old land produce all that is needed and in so doing create a new man out of the fighters who take part in the struggle.

We had meant to have returned to Soochow and stayed a while, but after going to Changshu we had to return to Peking with our plan not completed. The following lines, however, may convey some impression of Soochow today:

> Bright flowers on
> the breakfast table

a giant magnolia bloom
set amongst green
outside the window;
sweet faces bent over
delicate embroidery, and now
an old city made over
anew; broad streets with
plane trees beside, and
spreading out into
the countryside the great
factories of the new order
built with so deep a passion
and now standing stolidly
each a redoubt in the fight
for people's livelihood,
chimney stacks
like exclamation marks
expressing determination.

Soochow girls were said
to be the loveliest in all China
but how many were taken as playthings
by purse-proud traders, greedy
officials? Girls who in this today
operate new machine tools,
their smiles as gay, yet now too
expressing confidence
in things that by working together
they can make come to be.

On to Changshu

It had been many years since I had come to Changshu, by boat over the lake from Kunshan. Then it was a sleepy county centre, a place where many of the exploited young apprentices in Shanghai's small industry came from. It was also the seat of a Kuomintang garrison and of the usual official bureaucracy of that time. Today it has a million mou of good, rich land, and around 900,000 people with 60,000 in the county seat. After Liberation it was found that 250,000 of the population had schistosomiasis. Now with a mass attack on it, this number has been reduced to around 20,000, and final stages of the battle against the disease still go on. A frequent slogan painted on farmhouses on the road from Soochow to Changshu is to the effect that the disease must be stamped out entirely. Changshu is 60 kilometres by highway from Soochow. It has good waterways, but no rail connection. Changshu cotton is especially good. Some 200,000 mou are planted to it, and the crop averaged 145 jin of ginned cotton a mou in 1970. Winter wheat now being harvested in this 1971 summer is averaging over 300 jin a mou. Rice last year averaged 790 jin a mou. A new product of Changshu is tea, which is now grown on the slopes of the adjacent Yushan.

Amongst the more important factories are a concrete boat and pipe factory, a ball-bearing assembly plant, a fertiliser plant, an agricultural implements plant and then many various textile factories. The city is kept in beautiful order, plane trees on the roads, their green leaves showing pleasantly against freshly whitewashed walls.

Ball Bearing Assembly Works

This is a plant which has much significance for the countryside. In the rapidly approaching mechanisation of agriculture, bearings are needed for each piece of equipment. The small hand tractor alone needs 30 sets, and it is a tool that will increasingly drive away the old water buffalo. The factory we went to see in Changshu was, up till the end of 1968, a simple plant turning out common implements now mainly done in brigade small industry. Beginning in 1969, it concentrated on two kinds of bearing assemblies, raising the number to 16 in 1970, and now in 1971 to 22. In its beginnings it faced many problems in technique, equipment and data, which it has solved as it has gone on its way. It has now 370 workers, over 100 machine tools, and 175 bits of other equipment made by its own workers. In 1969 they made 30,000 sets, in 1970 the figure was 140,000 and in the first four months of 1971 they have turned out 95,200 sets. They expect the total for this year to reach over 350,000. They still cannot meet the full demand made on them for their product, so are building new shops to expand into.

We went around the various shops, well lit, modern ones. From the shop where the balls for the bearings were made, on to the final assemblies, work went on quietly and efficiently with no signs of stress and strain. There were quite a few technical innovations which had been made, and which were being successfully used. A repair shop has been set up to take in bearings brought in by the communes for repair work. Factory workers often go to the communes also to help to repair tractors and with other mechanisation on the spot. At times, too, the factory sends workers to take part in ordinary farm work so as to keep in touch with the people. Bearings go to all eight counties of the Soochow prefecture, some also to the province (Kiangsu), to meet needs in other areas. The success of this factory so far would not have been possible without the help of other factories of its kind, and now that it has succeeded, it knows that it is its duty to help wherever possible.

The factory has a drafting section, a laboratory for testing the strength of materials, and a chemical lab. Tractors working in the slush of paddy fields have to have completely enclosed bearings, a need which is met amongst those produced here. The works is a good example of creating something from nothing, going from small to big in the service of the people.

Changshu No. 4 Textile Plant

Changshu has been famous for a long time for its cotton weaving. Now the craft is organised into modern factories spreading through the old city. One such was the No. 4 Changshu Textile Plant which weaves a good deal of the cloth used locally and in counties around, besides sending some into the northeastern provinces. It has 358 looms in its weaving shop, 150 of which have been converted for using compressed air rather than a shuttle to carry the thread through the warp. It took a little time to get the change working properly, but now all are satisfied with it, able to operate it, and looking forward to changing the rest. The old weaving shuttle has had a long history, but its day is ending.

Nine million metres of cloth a year are turned out here, and production has gone up 18 percent since the Cultural Revolution. All of this was explained by the very efficient leading cadre, a Shanghai woman textile worker who had come to Changshu and made her home here. She said workers were well aware of Chairman Mao's advice to gain quality as well as quantity and so do their very best to raise standards. They are aware too of his advice to keep on lowering costs and preventing waste, to study what the people need and try and meet that need. They have taken note of a popular suggestion that the common blue cloth needed for men's clothing should be wider so as to facilitate cutting, and are now weaving this in a 36-inch width instead of the previous 32-inch to meet the demand.

After going through the various shops we went to the kindergarten and played with the children for a while, and then, with the afternoon coming to an end, spent the remainder of it walking in the very beautiful park situated under one slope of Yushan hill, not far from the textile plant.

An outstanding worker in the textile mill is Li An-yu, who is now vice-chairman of the mill's Revolutionary Committee. She is also a member of both the county and provincial Party committees, and was a delegate to the Ninth Party Congress. She is a quiet, good-looking woman, modest about her dignities and obviously able.

Changshu Lace Factory

For the last half century, Changshu has been a famous place for lace making. The beautiful tablecloths that go into the export trade come from there in great numbers. The work is done out in the peasant homes in the countryside by people in slack work periods, or by womenfolk not strong enough to go out to the fields. The linen is cut in the factory which has been set up in Changshu. Here, too, it is marked with the pattern to be embroidered. If it is to be colored, silk thread is weighed out and added. When the embroidery work is done, and the neat cloth-wrapped parcel of work returned, it is carefully inspected, washed in a modern steam laundry, ironed and then packed for export. We visited the factory, finding it to be operating in modern, well-lit factory buildings, with 417 workers. There are some 500 kinds of products made, but pillow slips and table linen seem to predominate. 80,000 women in the villages become more independent now, with the progress of the craft. Workers are obviously proud of the beauty they create, and very happy to show it off to the visitors.

While in Changshu, we were entertained at a concert one evening by children of the local school. Pieces of the modern operas were the main items and, suitably for Changshu, included parts of "Shachiapang". . . . The locale of "Shachiapang" was in Changshu county. Changshu was a noted centre of guerilla resistance in the anti-Japanese war.

Changshu in the early summer was idyllic. Probably one of the best maintained county seats in China. I tried to put some of my feelings about it into some lines which run as follows:

> Changshu, set by the hill
> they call Yushan, in a countryside
> studded with lakes, crisscrossed
> with canals, where the guerillas
> of Shachiapang fought through
> the Wars of Resistance
> and Liberation; where now a people
> fight and defeat blood fluke
> raise rich harvests, truly
> making the green revolution come
> true; tractors churn through
> where once water buffaloes trod
> and in the city kept incredibly
> neat and clean, young industry
> blossoms and its products stream
> off into counties and towns around.

> Easy to fall in love
> with Changshu as it is
> today; city of a people
> who have fought through much
> and who now in all
> their quiet strength push on
> to greater victory.

Revolution on the Waterways of Kiangsu — The Ferro-Concrete Boat

"Serve the people" is a slogan that needs much practice to make it perfect. That is to say, to really serve them in a downright, creative way. Thinking over outstanding examples of such, my thoughts went back to farm boats made of ferro-concrete I had seen being made in Wusih and Yangchow in Kiangsu in 1966, and then also in both factory and commune in Shanghai in 1967. I had first heard of the idea of making ferro-concrete tugs and lighters for the internal waterway system during the Great Leap Forward of 1958. At that time an early model was made in Wusih. Then when the movement for greater support of agriculture came, a Wusih factory which had previously turned out reinforced concrete beams set out to make the cheap and efficient ferro-concrete farm boat. When seeing the first results in 1966, I had then written of it all in these words:

"After something over 100 experiments, the first standard type of farm boat was evolved. This was in 1963. Its designers travelled through 17 counties, talking to the folk of over 500 brigades of 100 communes, getting ideas from them of the best kind of boat to produce. In this part of Kiangsu, to get a crop or not depends on water — whether rain or irrigation. To get a good crop depends on fertiliser. And as some of the best fertiliser is the mud from canal or lake bottom, getting that fertiliser onto the land depends on boats. If one had told the local farmer of even a short time ago that he would be buying concrete boats at half the cost of the wooden, and that some of the workers making these boats would be his daughters, then sitting spinning by his door, he would have thought you mad. But the pilot plant that set out to master this problem, starting with a handful of workers, has now raised their number to 520, amongst whom are many lasses in their late teens from the villages around, who have come in to work as apprentices. So far, 4,000 of their boats are operating on the canals and lake in the vicinity, the number being expected to increase steadily as costs go down and automation proceeds. The three-ton boat is now mainly produced. Five-ton ones are also made, as well as seven tonners for carrying pumping plants for paddy field irrigation, and then the ten tonners for Yangtze river use. First models were sometimes found difficult to keep afloat when the gunwales became awash with lake fertiliser. Then air compartments were added fore and aft, so that now the craft is more buoyant than the wooden one. A wooden three-ton boat costs 750 yuan, a concrete one 420. The new boat saves on timber, and good timber is precious. It does not rot, is impervious to wood borer, is not spoilt when chemical fertiliser or wet house-manure is carried, and does not expand when there is high humidity. It can be easily repaired by the farmer himself at the very low cost of a few fen, whereas even a small boat repair on a wooden craft costs around 100 yuan, and a complete overhaul 300. It can be washed out easily, and because of its smooth surface goes a good deal faster with the same effort than the wooden craft. Its air compartments make it more safe, and because it is heavier it rides better, resisting wind and wave well. In a recent storm on Taihu Lake in a seven-degree wind, a wooden boat split and sank, an iron one was crushed, while the one of ferro-concrete sustained only minor damage.

"For some time now, teams have gone out from the factory demonstrating the usefulness of the craft to communes throughout the region. Local demand still cannot be met, but the factory is rapidly building up orders for the future. We watched the launching of one of the three-ton size, and the bolting of the wooden strips along the gunwales which will act as bumpers. The single big wooden oar, the wooden mast, and whatever superstructure is needed can be provided by the factory as necessary. But for the main purpose of moving in lake mud, no superstructure at all is wanted. As the mud settles in the hold and the water rises to the top, the boat can be tipped to one side and the water drained off.

"In the factory itself, processes are being streamlined. Fine steel wire is drawn and then woven into a close net for reinforcement. Soon the looms will be automatic, and joins needed when netting is fitted over the mould, now done by hand by boy and girl apprentices, will be done by welding. Care is being taken with the education of these apprentices, and they have night classes five evenings a week. They go back to their homes on Saturday afternoons and return on Sunday night, or in time for work on Monday morning. As the plant grows, so will boats from one to 15 tons be turned out, and in increasing quantities. The day of the wooden boat will end, and timber will be used for other things. Already the success of this factory has caused other boat-building concerns in different places to start in with similar construction. Many minds, continually pooling experiences and technique, will strengthen the foundations of this new and swiftly growing industry."

Now, five years later, I came to Wusih once more. The two cadres who had greeted me on my last visit were at the railway station to meet me again and, as we drove out to the Liyuan guest house by the shores of the lake, told me how the counties around Wusih had now set up factories for making farm boats of the smaller tonnages, how Wusih was too far from the Yangtze to make really big ones, yet how it was doing its best. We had halted in Shanghai on the way to Wusih, and had gone out to Machiao Commune where in 1967 I had seen a few concrete boats being turned out. But in place of the four tonners being made then, eight, 10 and 12 tonners were being constructed in the main, while lighters of 60 tons were on the slips. With all this in mind, then, we set out one late May morning to start on our journey through the concrete boat-building industry as it is in Wusih today.

First, we went to the plant we had visited in 1966. The same leading cadre who was in charge in 1966 met me. In these years the spread of concrete farm-boat factories into all counties around has brought in many of their new workers to learn, and at the same time liberated the plant from making the smaller craft, allowing them to concentrate more on heavier types, though the five-ton boat is still made in quantity. We saw a fishing trawler on the stocks, the first of 15 to be made this year. It is a 67 tonner with an 80-h.p. engine. Then some 20-ton lighters, and a tug that will take a 46-h.p. engine and pull 120 tons of lighters. Workers are not many more than there were in 1966 — now something over 600, one fourth of them women. The bigger vessels cannot be made here because of the bridges in the locality not having enough clearance for them, but the factory still cannot keep up with the demand for what they do make. Since they started making concrete boats they have turned out 20,000 of them and have established a process, trained a working force that ever creates new methods, and filled a very definite local need. We went out in a motorised 15 tonner and watched while 12 men came out on a five-ton farm boat, water filled to the gunwales. They came near us and loaded another ton of rock on the boat, which remained jaunty and buoyant. Then several men took a five tonner at full tilt against a rocky bank twice. The only damage was a small splinter off the wooden buffer bolted to the prow of the boat.

We went to the factory canal enclosure where commune farmers bring in boats for repairs and sat in our boat while a farmer's boat, which had developed a leak in the stern, had that part elevated by an endless chain, a worker clearing away the concrete from the damaged part, adding new, and then covering the repair job with a plastic wash. After a while the boat was lowered back into the water, the owner paid fifty fen repair fee and went off on his craft. It was the first repair he had had on it since it was purchased in 1965.

We went to the village of the first production team of Chinan Brigade of Chinan Commune, not far from the factory. They had eight boats — two small wooden ones and six five tonners of concrete. Sitting in one of the farmhouses watching a cat playing with its kitten, with children peeking in and mothers nursing babies, we heard something of the advantages of the concrete boat from people who used it in their daily life. They appreciated its low cost and the tiny cost of repair, its sturdiness and its steadiness in the water. In a favorable wind the old wooden boat, being lighter, went faster if a sail was used. But for tacking and side winds, the concrete one was better. Propelled with the single big oar, it slipped through the water better than the wooden one, but was not so easy to stop nor did it have the same springy feeling. For bringing in lime from the lime kilns it was much better. Unslaked lime often played havoc with wooden boats in rainy weather. Easier to handle than the wooden — three girls can take out a concrete five tonner, and manage it with ease. It is safer in the high winds and big waves that sometimes come on Taihu Lake.

An elderly man with a sparse grey beard felt that the ferro-concrete boat was Mao Tsetung Thought in action. A well-turned-out young man said it made work easier and more effective. A young woman nursing a baby said it gave women better opportunity to do things that men had previously done. And the boat factory, moreover, had made technical workers out of three of her friends from the production team.

The team has 35 families, 150 people in all. Another 100 from the village are working in Wusih industry or in various parts of China. In the team, they have a work strength of 60, with 17 youngsters just coming into work. They farm 80 mou of rice land from which they get 1,700 jin a mou of grain a year now. They have 32 mou of fish ponds, and 40 of mulberries. They average two pigs a family, and some families also rear stall sheep. Grain allowance per person runs at 520 jin a year, cash distribution at around 127 yuan. The well-turned-out young man thought that people understood much more now. Some of the old people had liked the wooden boats because they had always had them. But, he said, if one is to think in national terms, what a lot of tung oil it takes to keep wooden boats from absorbing water and rotting, how much timber can Kiangsu afford, and how much iron and steel, then one must be grateful for the concrete boat which has made self-sufficiency more real. The production team could not have afforded to buy and repair eight boats. It could not get good crops unless it brought in more manure, and the cheap five-ton boat made this possible.

Back in the plant, we looked at the innovation for spot welding, then at that for reeling wire. The automatic looms clacked away making the reinforcing netting, while at the end of the factory, where once small boats were launched, a big new canal was being dug to bring in enough water for heavier boats to be slid into. The leading cadre thought, now that the basis for advance in concrete boats had been made, there would be considerable advance. He had heard of a 600-ton concrete boat being made in Kwangtung, and that in or around Yangchow there are some 15 plants turning out craft of various tonnages. He also spoke of how the craft was spreading in and around many other Kiangsu towns.

Our next visit in Wusih was to the Kiangsu Provincial Wusih Boat Factory, one I had not seen before. It had some 900 workers and made not only boats and lighters but also the diesel engines that powered them. It has magnificent shops opening out on the long frontage of the Grand Canal it occupies. The Grand Canal here is rather like a busy city street, long strings of tugs and lighters, sailing ships, oared boats going past in never ending succession. A surprising portion of the tugs, lighters and powered junks are of concrete. But to return to the factory. It was first set up in 1956, with 170 workers who had been working in seven small boat-building yards. They erected simple bamboo lathe and plaster sheds and got to work. They had but seven machine tools run by overhead shafting and belts. Now they have over 400 modern machine tools and can make as many more as they need. Actually, 60 percent of what they have in machinery has been made in their own plant. At that time they did repair work for the interior waterway shipping.

After first experimenting by making a sampan of concrete and finding it successful, their first concrete tug boat was made in the time of the Great Leap Forward in 1958, and was called "5815". Powered with a 60-h.p. engine, it has worked well these 12 years. Then there were problems. Those who were taken in by the line of Liu Shao-chi, who did not believe in self-sufficiency, were against the plant developing its own type of marine diesels for powering its craft. A factory should make only one thing, they said, or a part of a thing. Concentrate on that. So there was considerable struggle against this line until it was finally demolished in the Cultural Revolution. There were, too, some mistakes in early design which had to be corrected as work went ahead. After the tough years of the early 'sixties, when all help had to be given agriculture, some nine kinds of boats were turned out for the farms, including those from two to seven tons. In the years following 1965, however, attention was mainly focussed on the 40- and 60-ton lighter, passenger and tug boats, trawlers and other craft. So much work could not have been done employing a new material for such without some mistakes being made. These were learnt from and the steady stream of advance maintained. Leaders were quite frank about their shortcomings and how sorry they were at having caused some losses to the state when experimenting with a substitute for the steel-wire netting for concrete reinforcement that did not work out. Going around the shops, we were impressed with the contrivance employed for launching the 40- and 60-ton lighters. After the netting reinforcement over the skeleton frame has been finished, the whole thing is moved onto a lift platform and concrete applied. A canvas tent now comes down over the lighter and a steam-heat drying process begins. This completed, the lift platform goes slowly down into an inlet from the canal, and the lighter floats off to have its work done on the superstructure.

On the netting reinforcement for the 40- and 60-ton lighter forms many high-school students had come to help workers. They evidently had been here many times, as their work seemed very good. We noticed them also in other parts of the plant, some intent on machine-tool work in which perhaps when they graduate from school they will come to take part full time.

A 40-ton lighter made of steel costs 18,000 yuan, one of timber 15,000, while a ferro-concrete one costs 13,500 yuan. Steel and timber are in short supply in Kiangsu. Sand and cement are not. The repair bill for a 40-ton wooden lighter would come to something around 5,000 yuan, repairs having to be done quite often. Steel lighters have to be painted and wooden ones treated regularly with tung oil. The concrete one does quite well without either, and may go on running for many years without any major repair being needed at all. One state farm reported that the six concrete boats it had used daily for ten years now have not cost more than 10 yuan in all to repair during that time.

It takes under 28 days to make one 40-ton lighter. Actually, the task can be done in 14 days if there is a rush order. In both boat factories seen in Wusih there were useful innovations in cement spreading, and both looked forward to perfecting a spray-on method. In this provincial boat factory, it is estimated that in the 44,458 tons of boat construction already done, there has been a direct saving of 5,220,000 yuan to the country in materials that would otherwise have been used. Plans are being made now for the building of a 200-ton boat, the first of many more to come from this plant in the larger sizes. We went through the engine building section of the plant, seeing its excellent tooling, and admiring the quiet swing with which everything went ahead. Most of the workers were originally from farm families around Wusih. Their wages average 51.50 yuan a month. Machine tool operators were mainly women, who make up one third of the factory's labor strength.

We went out to see "5815" still operating well, and then a line of 40-ton lighters not long completed and now awaiting delivery, watching the building of the superstructure on others. Each detail is carefully worked on, down to the provision of rice and other food store boxes for each boat kitchen. We looked into a concrete passenger boat that had come in for some engine repair, admiring its roomy seating arrangements and layout. Much is happening along the banks of China's most famous inland waterway, the Grand Canal, but it is only a beginning to what will happen in the next stages.

KIANGSU

Boats at one production team — only
one made of wood now, Wusih, Kiangsu.

Testing a concrete boat.   Eleven men,
one ton of rock and full of water, Wusih.

Concrete farm boat being launched, Wusih.

Doing wire work for concrete boat.

Forty-ton concrete lighter with load of coal.

Primary school child in school workshop, Wusih.

Weaving steel mesh for concrete boat.

Embroidery is an ancient craft in Soochow, Kiangsu.

Waste land made into good field. Production team at work at Yangchow, Kiangsu.

Bearings made in Changshu, Kiangsu.

Motors for spray pumps, Soochow, Kiangsu.

Construction college students at work, Nanking.

Iron smelters, Wusih, Kiangsu.

Children of Junting Brigade in Changshu once badly stricken with schistosomiasis, Kiangsu.

Nanking children's concert party.

Changshu County Concrete Boat Factory

To gain some idea of how the various county offshoots of the Wusih concrete boat factories operate, we went to Changshu county in the Soochow prefecture, and visited the boat-building work there. Changshu today is a thriving county 60 kilometres by road from Soochow. Once simply a rural centre, it is now the hub of a good deal of small industrial activity that is of direct assistance to the farm folk around. We spent a morning at the concrete boat factory, one of 224 workers who produce 1,000 five-ton farm boats a year. They also produce pipes for putting irrigation laterals underground, thus saving much land, and reinforced concrete cross beams for new farm home construction. Set below Yushan hill the various shops of the factory have sprung up one after another, and construction of a big modern shop is now going ahead. Demand cannot be met yet, so there will be expansion. With the "yulo" big wooden oar and some woodwork on top, the cost of a boat is 650 yuan. Half the workers are women. When the project started, a good many difficulties had to be encountered. No capital, no technique, no machinery and no buildings. But with the help of the concrete boat and other factories in Soochow and Wusih, all of these hurdles were surmounted, and today the industry is one that stands on its own feet, and has come to stay.

We watched one launching, an experienced woman technician being ably in charge. The boat was turned over by crane in the factory yard, put on a trolley which took it down to the canal waters simply and easily. The plant got under way in 1969, and is now able to carry out most processes including the repair of its construction machinery itself. It is just one county boat factory, of the kind that is now springing up over the whole of the Kiangsu countryside.

The Ferro-Concrete Boat Abroad

Ferro-concrete ships were experimented with in World War II, but then the idea was dropped. Recently came a news item in an American paper, how a Long Island boat builder had made a ferro-concrete pleasure boat in 1965 and how 10,000 people had come to see the launching, many expecting it to sink. How now the idea is starting to spread there in a mild way. But as in many other things, for advanced techniques in developing the ferro-concrete boat the researcher will have to come to China, where its application to people's livelihood has brought it into so great a demand that its numbers must now be counted in the many hundreds of thousands, with production going up rapidly all the time, and with that production, newer techniques in manufacture.

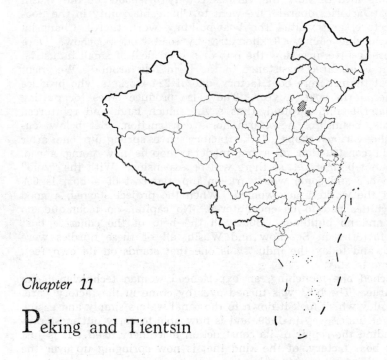

Chapter 11

Peking and Tientsin

The cities of Peking and Tientsin, with their surrounding counties, are special municipalities, under the direct administration of the Central Government. Peking in the Yuan, Ming and Ching dynasties was the capital of China, as it was until the Kuomintang removed the central administration to Nanking. As an old administrative and cultural centre, it was a city with many palaces, parks and gardens. With Liberation in 1949 it again became the capital, and also a rising industrial centre, with its own iron and steel industry, its coal mines, and its machine-building industry. It keeps its old craftsmen in jade, ivory and rug-making, but also now has big modern textile mills and a chemical industry. Geographically, it is a section cut out of the province of Hopei, covering an area of 17,800 square kilometres and having a population of over seven million. Now the old city walls have been removed, and the city spreads out. In the Western Hills much afforestation has been done, bare hills turning green again. There are new museums, exhibition halls and stadiums, with new parks adding to the old. Much electrification has come into the suburbs where vegetables and grain are produced for the city.

508

In Tientsin proper, there is a population of some 4,280,000. The municipality includes the surrounding counties, coming right up to the borders of the Peking municipality. The Tangku-Taku port area belongs to the city area now, and industry spreads swiftly on the base which has already been laid.

Peking to Tientsin

September 1969 in north Hopei was warm and clear. I travelled with a group of other visitors down the broad modern highway from Peking to Tientsin, in great comfort on a Shanghai-made bus. Crops on either side of the road looked excellent. Waiting to be harvested was the kaoliang (sorghum), which we noted was mainly of the short stalk variety with outsize, heavy heads of grain. Areas that I remembered as alkaline marsh had been converted to rice fields as a result of the water conservancy work carried out since Liberation. On fields already harvested, production teams were busy clearing up the land of corn stalks, bean bushes and so on, preparatory to winter plowing. Bright red tractors and animal-drawn plows were already turning up the black soil. More tractors this year than seen before. Long lines of Tientsin students who had been out working on the land were marching back to the city. The general impression was that of a working countryside.

As we approached Tientsin, factories became more numerous and we saw many more children at play. Country children all have plenty to do and while they work make a game of it. City ones have to find their own amusements and places to play and are as active as their country cousins, though their days are not so related to the collective work of their elders as is that of children on the communes. But the big thing is that workers are no longer poor and their children are no longer exploited in hell-hole factories as they once were in the old society. Arriving at our destination in Tientsin, we spent a good three hours of our first afternoon at the very fine exhibition on class struggle that the Tientsin Revolutionary Committee has organised. An exhibition which was located near an area that was in the old days one of the most dreadful scenes of exploitation of youngsters.

Santiaoshih

Once there was a stone-paved road in a city lane leading down to the bank of North Canal. Long years of iron-rimmed cart and wheelbarrow wheels had cut three ruts in its paving stones, so that the street and the area began to be known as "Three Lined Stones", or "Santiaoshih". A crowded, poor area where rentals were comparatively cheap, there mushroomed here, as China entered the first primitive stage of industrialisation, a whole chain of workshops that specialised in metal working. Actually, this was the cradle of modern industry in Tientsin, yet too, here untold suffering was endured, especially by the child slaves taken in as so-called "apprentices".

By the early 'forties there were 2,348 youngsters of this kind held in the various workshops of Santiaoshih. Whether in Tientsin, Shanghai, or any other coastal city, the story was always similar. A landlord-ridden countryside, beset by natural or man-made disasters, threw up wave after wave of refugees with no place to go but to the outskirts of cities. Here, in places dominated by gangsters in the service of factory owners, their children would be bought up. Outward forms were respected so as to save the face of the police and local authority. Contracts were solemnly drawn up and chopped with red seals, though anyone reading these through would see that the new owner of the body of the boy was absolved from any responsibility for illness or accident of any kind. Even if the boy died of the results of a beating or was forced into suicide, the owner was not held responsible. There it all was, down in black and white, whole sheaves of such contracts exhibited in the Santiaoshih exhibition.

The swiftly rising industrialisation was taken advantage of by scamps and loafers who were soon calling themselves "industrialists" as they reaped the income earned by virtually unpaid labor. Labor which was overworked with incredibly long hours, underfed, exposed to industrial accidents from old-fashioned unguarded machines, and then was literally kicked out when it was disabled, lost fingers in punch presses or got too sick to work. Workshops were invariably ancient dwelling houses, dark and unsanitary, and sleeping places were too often just extemporised lofts erected over the machines and reached by rickety ladders. A stifling place in summer, a cold and draughty one in winter. Clothing was too often a mass of rags held together with bits of string or coarse thread. Minor accidents the owner would refuse to take notice of, just cursing the boy for being careless, refusing to allow him to go to a hospital to be bandaged even, and ordering him to get along with the job and make up for lost time. All the owner needed was a fierce demeanor and the backing of the local street police, then so easy to buy up. He himself could while away his days with more of his kind playing mahjong or smoking opium, feasting, wining and what they would. The work of the boy slaves brought in the income.

The exhibition consisted of pictures and sets of models, similar to those of the famous "Rent Collection Courtyard" in Szechuan, excellently portrayed in the spirit of those times. One of the exploited boys was Wang Fu-yuan. After nine of his fingers were crushed and a thumb amputated, he was thrown out of the factory and became a rickshaw puller. A hard life, but he survived through to Liberation. At the time of our visit he was a vice-chairman of the Tientsin Revolutionary Committee, also being deputy director of the Santiaoshih exhibition in class struggle. His life story as shown in pictures and models was a harrowing one indeed. In those days when a boy was too small to reach the bench to work at a vise, a platform made of chunks of timber was supplied. The all important thing was for production to be maintained in the interests of the great fat slob who owned the place, and who lived so well from slave labor. Another boy worker who still lives was Kao Fu-ren, now also a director of the exhibition. He lost his sight in one eye in a nasty accident, which probably only saved him from dying of overwork.

The exhibition is a very complete one, down to models showing the quite usual procedure of the factory owner putting the clock back as knock-off time came along to get more work out of youngsters. There were the whips used for beating, contracts made with people who brought the boy in, clear statistics gathered from old documents and then the skeleton of an apprentice killed through a head injury. The workshops were really jails, from which youngsters rarely emerged to see even the streets of the city. But, although they were seemingly kept in submission through terror and beatings, sometimes they revolted and would smash up an owner's office. Half-starved and overworked, they were driven on until their usefulness was gone and they were left to die. Already a great many of Tientsin's population have seen the exhibition, which has been showing since 1958. In all, 1,300,000 visitors came during the year prior to our visit. All the time there were streams of people from Peking and other towns coming to study it. There is still a big job in front of it to carry through its demonstrational work, and it may be expected to become if not a permanent, then at least a semi-permanent piece of frozen drama of the class struggle, exposing as it does the rottenness of a decadent society.

When we left the place, quite a crowd of the people from Santiaoshih gathered around to see us off, for we were a group of assorted nationalities and people are always interested in other people. They were obviously relaxed, well-nourished, well-clothed, and gave us a warm farewell. People of the new era of Mao Tsetung.

Evening Meeting

The working-class district in which Santiaoshih is situated contains 530,000 people. The leader of its Revolutionary Committee kindly invited our group to exchange comments with seven one-time child workers of Santiaoshih, five men and two women. We consequently had a fascinating evening together as these old workers, now responsible political cadres, told us their stories and gave their comments. Wang Fu-yuan told how he had to fix up an arrangement on the shaft of his rickshaw so that he could pass his maimed hand through it and pull from his wrist, after he was kicked out of the factory.

Chen Su-yang, now vice-chairman of the Revolutionary Committee of Tientsin Technical College, had a face full of scars, results of a beating. "A hell on earth, was Santiaoshih," he said bitterly. "A place where we had to live like beasts. Where man ate man. Capitalism is an evil thing, any way you look at it." Teng Si-ping told how he was sold at the age of five, and had to start working, carrying and doing odd jobs for the manager's family, when he was six. He showed us some of the scars of beatings he had received, including a big one on his head, the result of a blow given him by the boss when once he dropped a bowl and broke it. The long bitter winters he remembered only too clearly. Never with the padded clothing so essential in the sub-zero weather of north China winters. But the worst of the many stories told came from a girl with a sensitive face, sitting opposite me. Going back over her tale, it was hard for her to maintain her level voice, keep control of herself, and not to weep. Her father had been beaten to death by a factory owner, and her mother was forced to sell both her and her young sister. Her new master tore her from her mother's arms and, flinging her onto a cart, took her away, a child of ten. From then on she had to fetch and carry for him all hours of the day and night, always being beaten, never with enough food to eat. Once out of pure exhaustion she slipped and fell, fainting as she lay on the ground. The master came and beat her for being lazy, breaking two ribs. He then pitched her into a small room so that she sustained further injuries to her hip. She would have died, had this not been just the time of the Liberation of Tientsin.

When revolutionary cadres came down to Santiaoshih and heard the many stories of oppression, she and others like her were sent to school and later took part in political work. Some years after, the Communist Party found her mother and young sister so that now they are reunited. "We feel that Chairman Mao has done this for us," she said simply.

Another former girl slave told how her 12-year-old brother, injured and ill, had been carried out at night by the owner and thrown into the river. When the Santiaoshih exhibition was first opened, it should be noted here, the Liu Shao-chi line was followed and there was an attempt to prettify the capitalists, trying to portray them as being "progressive" to some extent. Then Premier Chou En-lai came and protested, so that a more accurate depiction was made in line with Mao Tsetung Thought. It was one of the earlier open demonstrations of the great gulf between the two lines, inside the superstructure of that time. At our meeting with the seven workers, they told us not only many harrowing stories of the brutality of those times, but also narrated some episodes of resistance to the bosses. How they organised go-slow strikes, sabotaged machinery, and at times attacked and beat up bosses and their stooges, especially when oppression left them no other choice but action. They were proud that many workers had gone off to join the Liberation Army or the guerillas fighting for the people in the Wars of Resistance and Liberation.

Hopei University

From industrial Santiaoshih and its affairs to the serene halls of Hopei University, now situated in what was once a foreign mission college set up in 1923 in a quiet part of the city, is quite a way. The university buildings are strongly, heavily constructed, spacious and well maintained. There are 641 on the teaching staff, 500 on other work, and at the beginning of the Cultural Revolution there were 3,107 students. At present (September 1969) with the top classes having graduated and their places not yet having been filled, there are 1,124 students still in lecture rooms and workshops. There are nine faculties, history, biology, mathematics, physics, chemistry, languages, and political science being amongst them. The leadership of the university at the beginning of the Cultural Revolution was not in the hands of Marxist-Leninists but in those of a group of old intellectuals some of whom had been traitors, special agents for the Kuomintang, capitalists and landlords, while a very considerable number held strongly to revisionist ideas. As a group they cared little about serving the people, but rather concentrated on trying to become well-known figures and shine as experts in the academic world.

With the coming of the Cultural Revolution, however, things began to change. Red Guards rose up and took over. But then, due to various kinds of manoeuvres, the Red Guards themselves divided into two main opposing groups. In 1968, the PLA propaganda team arrived at the university and organised the leaders of both groups into Mao Tsetung Thought study groups, first asking each to criticise his or her own shortcomings. Then study of the evils of the old society was organised, illustrated by stories of the old society from workers who had come through it, visits to Santiaoshih and to the communes in the countryside around Tientsin. Political study then entered a further stage and the fight against selfishness and criticism of revisionism was undertaken, until at last the political level of all was raised high enough to achieve unity. Indeed by now group leaders had begun to wonder, after all, what it was that they had fought about so bitterly.

The three-way committee was set up of PLA men, old cadres and young rebels, and then the whole university went ahead with the task of cleansing the ranks. There were those who belonged to the ranks of the enemy, as the contradictions between them and the people belonged to the class of contradictions between the people and the enemy, and there were those whose contradictions with the people were of the nature of contradictions amongst the people, and who consequently belonged in the ranks of the people. Some people had worked for the Kuomintang in various capacities and had not reported it. Then they had somehow or other managed to get into the Communist Party after Liberation. Some of the most ardent supporters of the Liu Shao-chi line had quite a long history of pre-Liberation work with the reaction. The conservatives in the university used their influence to make the institution as similar to a Western capitalist university as possible, a place which would turn out a great number of graduates who were prepared to serve anybody who employed them, never feeling that they had been educated to serve the people. In short, to turn out graduates who had been indoctrinated with a whole range of false values.

Remoulding

In the cleaning-up process quite a few of the older professors were very obstinate. There was one who became known as the "cactus" because he was so prickly. He had graduated from a university in the

USA, and had been a Kuomintang official. He once said, "Before Liberation I lived in a palace like a lord, but now I live like a dog." He had influenced many towards a revisionist position. He had also said indignantly to questioners, "If you do not believe me, cut my head open and see what is there." For long he met all criticism with an immobile granite-like face. But then, as he began to understand, slowly he began to change. Before, he would not read the works of Chairman Mao. Now he became a keen student of them.

Many similar stories were told, the majority by professors and lecturers themselves as we all sat together in the big quiet, cool room, with the pictures of Chairman Mao, Marx, Engels, Lenin and Stalin looking down at us from the walls. One lecturer told how he had been educated on the idea that only riches make one happy, that it was easier for a rich man to find a wife than a poor one, that rich people should make friends only with the rich, that folk respected only the rich and looked with contempt on the poor. How strange this all sounded now that Mao Tsetung Thought had become so much a part of the lives of both faculty and students! One voice came after the other, and before we knew it, three hours had passed, and there were still many tales of struggle and change untold. But it was clear that thinking had changed and these people had grasped the fact that political work really and truly must lead, that professional training should only come in second place.

A Lecture Hall

We visited a lecture hall and heard a student raising questions on politics before a large audience, many of whom had a worker, peasant or soldier background. Then we spent some time in the university workshops where students had made the appliances for manufacturing transistors and other radio parts, and were pleased with their product. The transistors were used not only for radios, but also in industry.

Serving the People

It was evident that the present struggle in the university was aimed at educating the students (as well as the teachers) in a communist spirit, to fix in everyone's mind that acquisition of knowledge in a socialist society serves the purpose of enabling one to better serve the people, not to give one a privileged position in society. Before the Cultural Revolution such thinking, namely, that to study in an institute of higher learning would automatically set one apart from the common people and destine one to lord it over the "uneducated herd", was rather prevalent. In consequence, a first reaction of some who still lacked understanding was that it was a "come-down" to have to go to the country. "If I had only known I would end up in the country I need not have studied at middle school or university at all, just have stayed in my village," some said at first. But this attitude has changed and students are now eager to go to the countryside. University classwork is quite frequently halted to allow big groups to go out amongst the rural communes, helping with farm work in the busy seasons.

The chairman of the Revolutionary Committee summed up his expectations for the future by saying, "We want to liberate all of the old staff from their wrong ideas, so that they will join and work willingly with us. We do not want to produce a new generation who will become parasites feeding on the people, but young men and women who will serve the people. The future is bright, and the present situation in our university excellent."

He has good reason to be optimistic. The thinking of the university faculty has changed radically from that prevailing before the Cultural Revolution. The vast gulf that has separated the old intellectual from the people has been bridged. Professors and lecturers have worked in the fields and collected manure and rid themselves of the prejudice that by dirtying their hands they would lose position. They have felt the weight of the carrying pole on their shoulders, and have pushed carts along with commune folk. They have felt the bite of the sun in summer, and the bitterness of a driving wind from the north in the winter as they have worked out on the land. So now in consequence they have gained a new conception of what serving the people really means.

Mining Machinery Plant

A medium-size plant, erected out in the countryside on the then outskirts of Tientsin during the Great Leap Forward of 1958, turns out equipment for the coal-mining industry. It has 1,300 workers, and started production copying the various appliances that had been imported from the Soviet Union — chain coal conveyors, safety lamps, power miners' lamps, and all kinds of electrical mine equipment. Now workers here no longer copy the Soviet models, which were found to be of poor quality, heavy and difficult to operate. The Cultural Revolution here went through the same stages as in other factories in Tientsin and by January 15th 1968, a Revolutionary Committee had been set up which very soon had everyone studying Mao Tsetung Thought and putting it into action. A minimum of one hour a day for study was set for everyone. Problems of class struggle, material incentives, expertise, and so on were thoroughly threshed out. Production swiftly rose. Factory workers organised themselves into small groups which went around coal mines asking for opinions and suggestions for the improvement of their products from the miners actually on the job.

Back in their own factory, they cut down on overhead — the administration was reduced from 300 cadres to 40, working under the three divisions which the Revolutionary Committee promptly set up. 1968 output was as large as that for 1966 and 1967 together, while in the first half of 1969 as much was produced as in the whole year of 1968. The targets for 1969 were set high, but by August 80 percent of the plan has been completed, and it was expected that by October 1st the rest will have been done. "If we get hold of the right idea," workers say, "then everyone puts his whole heart into the job. When a whole group does this, a great potential is released and the results are startling. If service to the people is in everything the first consideration, work gives much more satisfaction. Miners, for instance, complained about the weight of the batteries for the headlamps they wore. The batteries of the Soviet model then in use weighed four kgs. Our new ones weigh half that, and give a stronger light for a longer time." The same story applies to the manufacture of alarm bells, sirens and other equipment. Now, too, electricians and mechanics devise new ways of automation and test them out, with coal miners coming in to see what has been done and to give suggestions. We walked through the various shops seeing the men and women at their work, the faces of the workers at the benches showing the interest in their task and the enjoyment they got from working together. Now with the miner at the coal face and the worker in the equipment factory both thinking of how to better the first steps towards mining automation, it is certain that big steps will be made to raise coal production in the future.

Hsihoying Brigade

Our last morning in Tientsin was spent out in the southern farming area of the municipality, an hour's bus ride from the city. Leaving the main highway, we cut across rice fields carved out from reclaimed swampland, till we arrived at the village of Hsihoying. Here in a newly built brigade meeting house, we learnt something of the story of class struggle centred around "Szu Ching" or the Socialist Education Movement in the countryside which started in 1963 and ran on into the Cultural Revolution.

At the brigade, the Revolutionary Committee of both men and women met us together with its chairman, Wang Fen-chen, leader of the poor and lower-middle peasants who is now, in addition to his local position, a member of the Revolutionary Committee of the Tientsin municipality.

Hsihoying Brigade belongs to Feichiakou Commune. It has 250 households of 1,300 members who farm 2,000 mou of reclaimed marsh as paddy fields. It owns three tractors and seven electrically operated mechanised pumps. In the old days, the area was noted for its famines due to recurring floods and drought. Now, however, there is ample food and the necessary clothing for all. In spite of the coming of the new order, however, the tail end of the old ruling class managed to get established as the leadership in this particular village. Under a man named Han Yo-ken, the Liu Shao-chi line was pushed and used to consolidate the power of the revisionist leadership. Any poor peasant who rebelled was liable to get beaten. Then Han Yo-ken, because of his well-known bad class background, thought it best to get out, and the woman Chang Feng-ching became leader of this tight little controlling gang of seven. The brigade membership had built up a grain reserve, but Chang Feng-ching's group decided to rely on Liu Shao-chi's line and divide it all up amongst members. She was able to store 600 jin of this for herself, hold it until rice on the free market (another Liu Shao-chi pet device) was high, and then sell it for 1.50 yuan per jin. This money, 900 yuan, she lent to the brigade at 20 percent annual interest, and it finally cost the brigade 7,000 jin of rice sold to the government at the set price of 12 fen a jin to pay the debt and interest off.

This was only one of her many thieving acts, and with the profits she made she had a nice cottage erected for herself, much better than anything in the village. But then the Socialist Education Movement started and the struggle began. She looked on Wang Fen-chen as her bitter enemy and sought by all means in her power to get him arrested. But the poor and lower-middle peasants protected him and prevented his arrest by the Tientsin city authorities of that time, who were hand in glove with Chang Feng-ching. The car sent by the black liners of Tientsin for Wang Fen-chen's arrest had twice to return empty. But still the struggle was to become even more acute. The main division between the two lines became apparent to the people, and finally they rose up. Chang Feng-ching and her gang were thoroughly exposed in a mass meeting and forced out of their positions of authority. That their intentions were not entirely peaceable was attested to by the discovery in their homes of a German-made automatic pistol and some U.S.-made hand grenades. Faced with all the charges brought forward, Chang Feng-ching could not but admit guilt, and the people could not but see that they must really hold the power and exercise it, not leaving it in the hands of the other class.

The experience gained at Hsihoying was similar to that gained in Taoyuan Brigade in Funing county, where Wang Kwang-mei, the wife of Liu Shao-chi, tried so hard by using terrorism and gangster methods to set up a revisionist "model" brigade, which was to be followed everywhere throughout the land. It failed miserably before the onslaught of the people activated by Mao Tsetung Thought, just as did the temporary Liu Shao-chi stronghold at Hsihoying.

These struggles of 1963-65 were precursors to the Great Proletarian Cultural Revolution, and show in retrospect how the struggle between the two lines broke into the open and the great debate started over the whole of China.

Brick-Making in Peking

It was a warm autumn day in 1969 when we left the highway at Heilungtan on the western outskirts of Peking, and struck across country to where in the distance a tall smokestack indicated like an exclamation mark the position of the place we had come to see. This was a large brick kiln operated as a state enterprise by the Peking municipal government. It is situated in the area of Yungfeng Commune, at West Liulitsun, and turns out ten million bricks and an equal number of big modern moulded roof tiles a year. After the trip it was pleasant to come into the office compound of the works. A cozy domestic air prevailed with many children around, the buildings of neat brick, and tall sunflowers together with summer greenery around, making the place

very attractive. Members of the Revolutionary Committee who met me
led me to their meeting room and discussed at length the various stages
that the works had gone through in the past three years of the Cultural
Revolution, telling in the manner of workers in terse language how deep
the struggle for criticism and transformation had gone, and what great
changes had already come to the thinking of the whole work force. Here,
almost all family dependents except the very old, the very young, the
children in kindergartens and those in school, work in the plant.

Peking Students

The factory includes 97 former middle-school students, most of whom
were graduates from the junior middle schools of the big universities in
the vicinity, now making up a total of 500 workers in all. There were
100 students at first, which was the number agreed upon between factory
and educational authorities six months ago, but three preferred to go off
to communes to work in the villages, so were permitted to do this. The
administrative staff is small. Half of the 32 cadres in the administration
in 1966 have either become kiln workers or have gone elsewhere.
Throughout the struggles of the past three years production has been
well maintained and the quality of products has not been allowed to
deteriorate, having been even raised in most cases. Especially since the
arrival of the students, many innovations have been carried through,
increasing the efficiency of the production line and making some bold
steps towards automation. We walked around the plant with a group
of the young school graduates. They told their story well.

Chen Ho-liang

Chen Ho-liang, the son of a Shanghai worker, is just 20 years old. Yes,
like the others he had thought that after graduation from a university
his future would be that of an upper cadre in the government. But now,
in the struggle that has gone with the Cultural Revolution, he has learnt
that revolution is not so simple, and that many things can happen when
revisionism appears on the scene and the wrong road is taken. He and
the others now laugh at their first disgust at being sent to so unromantic
a place as a brick kiln. "Why, just a common old brick kiln. And on
the outskirts of Peking, not far from home! We had thought of going
on a tough assignment to the frontiers, or else into some really big industry. But just an ordinary brick kiln!" But they had come, and as
they mixed with the people, heard stories of how the kiln came to be
built in the mid-'fifties, with the workers of many small kilns around
combining and erecting a modern production unit, they began to have
a new and ever deepening respect for their fellow workers.

The Kilns

As we walked along through the stacks of drying frames of the big,
complicated roof tiles, we stepped aside to allow transport trolleys which

drew their power from overhead lines to clatter past us. The long modern kiln, fired at one end while being unloaded through some of its 54 openings at the other, was operating with quiet yet obvious efficiency.

Chang Shang-feng

The young people told me, "We had read 'Quotations from Chairman Mao' quite a lot, but only now, when we come down to real practice, do we know how much there is really in it, and how important it is. We have seen here how many old kiln workers have of their own volition worked on through many holidays, just because they thought it would be better for the kiln, without expecting honors or rewards. How un-selfish they are in their daily lives, and how much they have really done to get rid of many of the bad aspects caused by selfishness, not in any effort at self-cultivation, but to better be able to serve the people. At first we did not think we had much to learn from them but their bit of technique. Now we find that not only is there a great deal of quite complicated technique needed in order to make good bricks and tiles in quantity, but also that, politically, the old workers are our superiors in so many ways. We are still very much the learners, and we hope to go right on learning in this kiln for a long time to come." Chang Shang-feng, whose father is an Army doctor in Szechuan, and who at 22 is the oldest of the group I talked to, said, "The revolutionary lessons we have learnt and are learning may seem pretty elementary to some. Yet, if we are to be really useful in the Chinese revolution, we must learn them — and we certainly did not learn them while in school. We have worked hard, not sparing ourselves, and in our political discussions we have been able to focus on certain points much better when we study them after our hours at work. Our attitudes, outlook, all have changed."

New Improvements

I watched the new improvements on the automatic production line, talked to the stokers up on top of the kiln, and felt the heat in the portions of the kiln being unloaded. Here the work was hard, but the big, Peking-made powered fans gave much help. Then, declining the lunch so kindly offered, I went off back to the city.

It was a pleasant visit that I like to remember. I could not help wondering, of course, what the work force would do when the clay re-sources in the vicinity finally gave out. Enlightenment on this point came when I made another probe into the countryside in the Peking city environs. Just a week after this brick kiln visit, I set out one morn-ing, passed through Tehshenmen in the north of the city, and turned off from the main highway into the countryside a mile or so past the vil-lage of Chingho which is not so far from the Ming Tombs. There had been heavy rains, but by now the bright autumn days had returned and the big leaves on tall poplars by the roadsides glittered gaily in the sunlight, while in the fields the heavy heads of millet bowed gracefully low.

Peking Metal-Fitting Factory

We passed through a village and then came to what had been still one more brick and tile works once owned by the local commune but, after the clay reserves gave out, had been taken over by the city government and converted into the Peking Metal-fitting Factory. There were quite a few well constructed buildings on the extensive site, which made the change easy, while there were plenty of bricks left around to build whatever else was needed. The change to making metal parts was carried through in 1963, and work had gone slowly ahead, there being but 100 workers by 1965.

Students Come In

Now, in 1969, with 175 students from middle schools sent to work here, it has been enlarged and has now 500 workers, a lot of new machinery and a swiftly rising output. After having seen 30-40 years back so many even then outmoded factories of the same kind in Shanghai, usually set up in crowded alley-ways amongst dwelling houses, I felt how magnificent it was to have nail-making machines, with their coils of wire beside, set out with so much space around, punch presses too, so well separated, wide open windows beside, through which tall sunflowers peeked, and a cooling breeze filtering in, carrying with it some of the freshness of the commune crops nearby. The gates into the factory, while not so imposing, were brightened by quotations from Mao Tsetung in red and white, with bright flower gardens and trees around. I visited the newly built students' dormitories, finding them neat and clean, airy and bright with a spartan simplicity. In the various shops, old workers worked along with the young, happy to be able to help and teach them. In visiting a factory or a school, there is always a certain "feel" about the place. In this one, there seemed to be a complete lack of any stress or strain. I admired the machine-shop section where new machines for the plant were being made or repaired. Saw the modern plating and painting equipment that is being used, and watched house or luggage fittings, as well as various building accessories coming off the production line and being expertly packed. Then, with six girls and two boys from amongst the former middle-school students, we went off to a quiet room to discuss what they thought of their new job.

Students Explain

I asked each of them to keep from reiterating what the others had said, and only to add new aspects, yet each and every one of them felt it necessary to stress the fact that the two weeks' courses of intensive study they had gone through when they first came to the works, coupled with their months of working experience, had all gone to deepen their understanding that the task of making hinges, latches and construction materials was a task set by, and important for, the revolution. And that it was the Chinese and world revolution they were out to support. All of them, too, had something to say of the ideas of Liu Shao-chi on personal incentive and self-cultivation, theories now thoroughly discredited in their minds. A member of the management told me that the coming of these youngsters with their youthful spirit and keenness on new methods had been applauded by the old workers, and that these young people have already been responsible for quite a few useful technical innovations. As one talked with them, it was easy to see that, though they were all quite different in makeup, they were all now clearly animated by strong class feelings and had the right spirit towards their work and the revolution.

Cheng Ke-lao

Their leader was the 22-year-old Cheng Ke-lao, an upper middle-school graduate of a girls' middle school, daughter of an electrical worker, and of a family of nine people. A girl with a serious, slightly worried face that lit up when she smiled, she talked a good deal of the struggle to understand workers' problems, their difficulties, and how important it was for the new group to press on in their quest for understanding, not simply to be satisfied when having learned a little and then resting on their laurels. To be a group leader, she felt, entailed more responsibility for self-criticism if the idea of serving the people was to be really carried through. Work results, she felt too, really showed up one's thinking. To put the ideas of Mao Tsetung into action should be the aim of youth, all the time.

Yen Kang

A very neatly dressed boy, the 17-year-old Yen Kang, son of a Tientsin printer, took up the story saying that he made hinges, and that it was important to study the hinges already produced to see whether there were any faults, and what improvements could be made to turn out a product that would do a better job. That was his duty in order to serve the people better. Another problem was to turn out a product that is up to standard, and to lower the number of rejects. This was brought home, when it had been pointed out that on one bad day 600 hinges had been judged not up to standard. Said Yen Kang, "We all sat down together and discussed the matter, then finally finding that not paying enough attention meant that indeed the class viewpoint was lacking in some of our work, we were able to cut out such losses. Then we found that a good deal of paint was being lost in paint dipping and drying, and finally ran the trouble down to the same cause." He finished with "You may smile when we say that we make hinges for the revolution, as an expression of working-class consciousness, determination, and ability, but that is how it is actually."

Li Chen

Li Chen is a tall, sweet-looking girl of 18. When she smiles she shows a roguish dimple. Tall and strong, she was assigned to bench work in the machine shops. It seemed simple, but when she started to use the tools, they somehow or other seemed to move clumsily in her hands. On her first day with file and vise, she broke four parts she worked on, then was most grateful to workers who came around and helped her, encouraged her, and taught her. "When you have a thing to hit with a hammer, you must look at the object with all your attention," she said. "If you look at your hand, then you will hit it, and it will be very painful. My father is an old worker, and when I got home I told our family of seven about my experiences, so that he laughed and said, 'Yes, you have to keep your mind on the main thing, not bother about personal safety.' " I had watched her at her work on the bench when going around the shops and now, hearing her speak, admiring her poise, directness and understanding, it came home to me anew that these young folk were probably getting about the best education in our world of today. A world that certainly must have revolution if it does not have war, and if it does have war, will certainly have revolution following hard behind.

The Last Two

The last two were Li An-fei and Chang Ke-sang, both around 20 years of age, both modestly saying that they merely wanted to add something to what had been said. Li An-fei said that she had felt that life was a series of hopes, some of which proved to be empty, others overfulfilling their expectations. Coming to the factory was one of the latter. She said, "Formerly only men and boys were allowed to do the work we are doing now. Now we can struggle, dare and do along with old workers, and so can clear up our old thinking, making us more able to serve the people." Chang Ke-sang with her good quiet, strong face, thought that a new realisation had come to all. What was clean and honest, what was dirty. How workers had honesty and clean minds, helped each other, and never complained. How so much that old intellectuals talked about was simply frothy nonsense. That beautiful clothes have very little to do with a person's real worth. "Here in this factory we have learnt already how dirty a thing selfishness is, and what an enemy it is of the working class. I am a graduate of an upper middle school. I thought I knew a lot. But when I was asked to make some calculations about the amount of wire needed for nail-making machines, I did it wrong and was corrected by an old worker who had never been to school. To make book learning useful one has to learn to do things with one's hands, things that will serve the people. I feel that I am still learning, still at school, and I hope I go on learning through the rest of my life."

When I left, I realised well that these young people were happy in their work and had an entirely new outlook on life and the role of educated youth in society. No question that they felt they were learning a great deal, and that they looked on their factory work as a preparation for bigger tasks in the field of production and revolution in the future.

Peking Gear-Cutting Factory

Following the trail of students into industry, I visited a well-known Peking factory, famous for its successes in the field of technical innovations during the past three years. It was the Peking Gear-cutting Factory, which employs 1,880 workers organised into seven brigades. Set up in 1960 to make spare gear wheels and gear assemblies for cars and trucks, it had been planned as a plant to produce 360,000 gears a year. But by 1966 it had not reached half that amount of production. This 1969 the production figure will be 600,000. In 1970 it is expected to produce 800,000, with the next target being a million. In 1966 there were 360 cadres in the administration, a number now, under the new Revolutionary Committee, cut down to 78. It was with some members of this committee that we went around the plant.

Students Enter

Eighty students from middle schools had been admitted this year as apprentice workers. Their first pay was 18 yuan a month, which rises at the rate of two yuan a year until they reach worker grade — usually within three years, and depending on the opinions of their own work group. The highest pay in the factory is 100 yuan a month. Food costs ten yuan a month on the average. Work clothes, hair-dressing, medical care, bathing and transport fares are all free. House rent for workers' homes costs seven to 10 fen a cubic metre of space per month. Apprentices could either go home or stay in free apprentice quarters. There are three eight-hour shifts a day, with political study classes before and after them.

The Shops

I went around the various big shops, finding work going on quietly and efficiently. Over 280 technical innovations have been introduced by workers in the past three years, 60 of these being major ones that have made for big increases in production. The principle of self-sufficiency has led workers to complete machines on which work had been halted by the past administration because of lack of materials. One large grinder, for instance, was completed in this way with materials already in the factory's possession, and is now doing a very much needed and excellent job. There is a growing surge to enter the age of automation, and production lines are being streamlined to make this possible. There will be plenty of scope for enterprising workers to express their inventiveness in this regard for a long time to come.

We watched new students at work. They looked poised and happy as they managed their machines, already different people from the time they left their schools so short a while ago. Thinking over the immense difficulties of hinterland truck and car drivers over the Wars of Resistance and Liberation in China, when the replacement of gear parts presented so great a problem, one felt happy that here in this factory they were being produced with such efficiency. Workers now laugh at the prize money once distributed for innovations in the pre-Cultural Revolution period. In 1965, 2,000 yuan was thus distributed for 36 small improvements suggested by workers. "Now we do not need material incentives like that. If we invent something, then it is our glory to be able to serve the people better," they say. Today all cadres in administration do regular time with other workers on the production line, so as to keep in better touch with actual conditions. I looked down the big shops with their rows of modern machines, looked into the faces of the workers who are so interested in the things they have been able to do, so keen to discuss the future developments in their plant, and felt that the lot of the new students coming here would indeed be a useful, happy and revolutionary one, fulfilling their fondest hopes.

Not all factories can take in students, as they may already have a regular system set up for adding young workers. Or they may have had a particularly intense struggle in the Cultural Revolution, necessitating a good deal of change in factory organisation not yet entirely concluded. Yet even these units maintain close contact with student youth, though in other ways.

Peking Diesel Engine Works

Back in the early 'fifties I visited a plant making agricultural implements, east of the old city. I did not come again until one bright autumn morning in 1969, finding that it was now a place where diesel engines for tractors, and gasoline engines for light trucks or jeeps, were turned out. Set out on a large area of 46 hectares, its buildings cover 200,000 square metres, over half of which are modern workshops. There are 5,100 workers, with an average age of around 30. A competent, already tested working force.

We went through six of these shops, seeing the various adaptations being made, some nice automation especially in the shop where crankshafts were being stamped out, then on to the painting and assembly sections. The value of the total output was 30 million yuan in 1967, 45 million in 1968, and will be 100 million in 1969, while it is expected to be 156 million yuan in 1970. There were 1,913 diesel engines manufactured in 1967, as well as 958 gasoline engines. In 1968, 2,459 diesels and 1,575 gasoline engines, while in 1969 there will be 5,000 diesel and 5,500 gasoline engines turned out. It is confidently expected that 1970 will see 8,000 of each type coming off the production lines.

One of the leaders of the Revolutionary Committee explained how before the Cultural Revolution there had been 1,300 cadres in the factory administration, which was subdivided into 22 sections. Now the sectional administrations have been abolished, and the overhead staff cut to 92.

There are three groups organised under the Revolutionary Committee, one for production and planning, one for livelihood and one for political study. Every worker does an hour's political study each day outside work time. Three eight-hour shifts are worked, but when workers become keen to finish some special job they often voluntarily stay on the job as long as they are able without extra pay, despite the factory leadership urging them to go home and rest. "We are working for the revolution," they insist. "The revolutionary people of the world look to us!"

So they put their all into building for the revolution in no uncertain way. They are pleased that they have been able to produce engines that are showing up well in tough work over hills and streams, and they are full of spirit to go ahead and try to carry that progress further. Three hundred of the workers are organised into Mao Tsetung Thought study groups. From these study groups, a team was organised to take over and lead a middle school of 2,000 students situated in the neighborhood. Workers regularly rotate in this kind of student work, all Revolutionary Committee members also take time to do actual work in the shops and maintain close touch with the main working force. Workers have made many technical advances and many proposals to improve production. As we went around the shops, we noted quite a few groups of students intently watching some of the more complicated processes. It appeared that they had come from the workshops and classrooms of Tsinghua University and the aeronautical college on regular and planned visits to the factory, this being another aspect of the factory's program to assist education. At the time of our visit, too, there was the movement to produce better results in honor of the 20th year celebrations of October 1st, National Day. So there was a new high tide of effort running through the shops that surely communicates itself to the students the factory is leading, and to those who come to learn by seeing how work is actually being done.

On Work and Learning

One could keep on going from factory to factory, big and small, throughout China, and find many new stories amongst them illustrating how the new ways are working out in practice. There is no question now that the working class is coming to control everything, and that workers have new inspiration, determination and spirit that is being passed on to a new generation. The links between workers who have come up from the old society and those who have been born in the new, are being strengthened. Workers have immense tasks in front of them. They must increase their political and technical understanding, as well as carry through their new responsibilities. The education of the younger generation that has to fill the ranks of the working class grows in importance, for there must be no turning back to the values of the old society. Though there are so many aspects to this problem, yet in a socialist country the underlying rules are the same everywhere, and the problem of how to further educate for life and carry a socialist higher education to the masses, remains a main one. Surely it is being realised by many in our changing world that the old ideas on education need a good deal of revamping and are no longer relevant even in a capitalist society. That the now out-of-date cycle of examinations and pure book learning, academic snobbery and bobbery, while perhaps pleasing those who are immersed in it, are remote from the real needs of the people who pay for their youth to be educated. So far, the process of rebuilding a system of teaching in China from out of the old one which has been shattered by the great Cultural Revolution, undergoes changes while it grows. It it too early yet to say what the final forms will be. But the principle that all education should be in the interests of the working people, and that the working people should be those who benefit from it, shows up well in what has been done already. The young middle-school and university students who have gone to work on state farms and communes in the hinterland, those who have entered industry or who are about to do so, have already found out much about the life of the people which previously they were completely ignorant of. As the struggle goes on, work places will become more and more the new universities, and the once honored names for places of higher learning will apply to the workers' world where they so justly belong. In the new day, all will be learners and all will keep on going to school.

Huangtukang Commune

Huangtukang, or "Yellow Earth Mound", is the name of a well-known commune in Tahsing county south of Peking which I chose out of the many good communes around to visit, for some of its brigades have much to show in the way of dramatic change. The area consisted once of sand dunes and marsh. It lies outside the former, once famous, Nanyuan walled-in Imperial Hunting Park. "Yellow Earth" could be better called "Yellow Sand", which in spring and autumn rose in great clouds whenever the winds blew. The land here was then farmed by the very poor, who lived in wretched conditions, rarely getting even 100 jin of grain a mou per year, and having to pay out a good deal of that in rent and taxes. Most of such people were families of city rickshaw pullers, cart pullers, or fuel carriers. Their lives were usually short and bitter, many of their children dying in infancy or growing up to be conscripted as warlord soldiers. Crop raising was really often just a sideline, covering only a small portion of living costs, the remainder having to be found by working in the city, begging or by carrying. One of the corner redoubts of the old Nanyuan wall which still survives is actually in Huangtukang Commune, and it was from this, once standing so high and proudly, that the present name of the area came.

The commune today is one of 7,000 families which, with the normal average of around five persons per family, make up the over 34,000 people who farm its 45,000 mou. It is divided into 11 brigades of 106 production teams. The brigade in which I spent a very lovely autumn

day in 1969 had been given the task of reclaiming sand dunes and alkaline marsh, and was in consequence called "Hsinfadi" or "Newly Opened
Land". Seventy percent of the brigade land had been unused wasteland
before it was reclaimed. High winds would send the sand flying to
cover neighboring fields. In the periods of flood, frequent in late summer as there was then no control of waters from hill valleys debouching
onto the Peking plain, the place would be a lake with sandhill islands
sticking up from it. Then, in drought, it would be arid but still plagued
with mosquitoes coming up from the marsh. There were no modern
roads, just muddy cart tracks. Deforested by fuel carriers, winds blew
unchecked. Only 19 percent of the land was cultivated at all. Poorly
irrigated and fertilised as the land was, it was only the dogged spirit
of the Chinese peasant prepared to battle against any odds which kept
agriculture here still going.

Land Utilisation

Today, as I could easily see, 95 percent of the land had been irrigated,
the sand dunes levelled, the alkaline wasteland converted to rich rice
fields, and even the higher land all planted. Many deep water wells
had been dug, all powered with electrical pumps, giving ample water
when irrigation is needed. Windbreaks have grown, highways lined with
tall poplar trees been constructed, while orchards, vineyards, vegetable
gardens and grain fields now cover the whole area. Production totals
for grain are six times higher than at Liberation. It is intensive farming
all right, with its 3,003 people in the brigade cultivating just 4,300 mou,
and making most of its fields bring in three crops a year of either grain
or vegetables. The last crop before the sowing of winter wheat was
of turnips for winter pickling. The late rice stood looking magnificent.
The lass who led me around the orchards had been a poor peasant child
sent by the brigade to an agricultural university and after graduation
had come back to teach a staff of six younger ones the science she had
learnt. That she had succeeded was shown by the lines of apple, pear
and peach trees. The apples were especially good, the well-pruned trees
a mass of fruit laughing up at the autumn sun. Results of the quality
of her work are shown in the steady rise in orchard and winery production, but still she plans to increase the crop several fold in the future.

Health Work

We went around to see the various services operated by the brigade.
In the clinic, we found a young doctor who had worked already some
years in his profession. His training had consisted of various short
courses designed to allow him to deal with the more common diseases,
and in the prescription of traditional medicine — nowadays often done
up in modern packaging. He is training six young girl commune members as "barefoot" doctors, one for each production team. The girls also
go in rotation to short-term classes, and their service is becoming increas-

ingly valuable to the team members, as they lead in public health work and institute a system of cooperative medicine. They are able to discover illness in its early stages and can get members to city hospitals when necessary. They also help with health classes in the brigade primary school with its 600 pupils. If not busy with these tasks they go to work in the fields with the other production team members. "Life is very full for us," one of them said to me.

From the clinic we went on to the livestock breeding section where a vet who had had ten years' practice interspersed by several training classes was dispensing medicine to a young stallion. The dispensing vehicle was an ox horn cut in the traditional way of Chinese veterinary medicine to the shape of a big spoon. Medicines were mainly traditional herbal ones perfected through centuries of trial, though in some cases injections of Peking-manufactured antibiotics were used.

A Farmer's Home

I had lunch in the home of an ex-poor peasant, who had had considerable difficulty to make a living through the years of the old society. Only one of his sons survived, and this boy was even able to get a little schooling between the ages of nine and 12. Then however, he had to go and help his father with transport work, for there was not enough for the family to live on. Due to malnutrition during growth he remained stunted, and had many bitter memories from the time before Liberation.

Selected as a cadre to work with youth, he soon began to learn a good deal. His wife, a determined-looking woman, very quickly grasped the incoming ideas on women's emancipation, and thus naturally resented his old feudal hangovers which frequently showed up in regard to the role and rights of women. In a rather lordly way he would say, "I go out to the fields with the production team. You can have it easy back at home. I will do the work for you all."

But while he had a good deal of spare time to go out and amuse himself, she was always busy. Then she said, "Do you believe in the equality of men and women?" and he was forced to say of course he did. So then she demanded that she go out with the production team and he take a spell of doing the house-work, looking after the cooking, the cleaning, poultry, the pig, the children, do the washing, till the private plot, and go to his meetings as well. He tried hard enough, but meals were not cooked in time, washing not done properly, the domestic animals were not well looked after, and he was always late for meetings. It was quite a lesson to him, and thereafter both went to work in the production team, and both took part in the work about the house, and grandfather smiles as he goes into his fourth big steamed bread, dipping it into the cucumber and egg soup, for most of his teeth are gone. He looks after the brigade stables, and is at it all through his working hours, never stopping. The grandson, now in the brigade school, came in while we sat on the kang. Tall, erect, and physically well near perfect, he had grown to his 14 years with good food, good sunlight, fresh air, and an affectionate family around him. Now he learns about Mao Tsetung Thought, and it will be on the shoulders of those like him that the next stages will depend.

Marketing and Supply

The brigade marketing and supply agency is situated in a cozy house surrounded by courtyards and sheltered against the winds, with plenty of sunflowers around to make it cheerful. It held a good range of consumer goods and was, like most commune and brigade stores, a favorite meeting place for members. The brigade has three trucks which run to the city with vegetables and other produce, as well as one big tractor and several small ones. But though a beginning has been made to join the old small fields, level them and combine them into big ones, not enough has yet been done to make the work convenient for tractors and replace hand and animal labor. We sat for an hour or so in the brigade meeting room, listening to many stories, showing with what determination people went out to save harvests that were threatened by hail, to save beds of seedlings from which high midnight winds were blowing away plastic sheet coverings, and of how much struggle improvements had cost. As we sat, I looked out over the land outside the window. An old brigade member was watering the vegetable crops, letting the water run from laterals onto the field. A small granddaughter of maybe ten in shorts and print blouse came and took his hoe for a while. Then when he grabbed it back she danced a few steps and laughed so that he laughed, too, and the sound came into the room where we sat.

The Two Lines

I have seen many farm communes in different parts of the country since communes were first set up in Honan in 1958, and have been able to learn something new on every visit. Here in this commune brigade, the leaders were at pains to tell us about their experience with the pitfalls of the Liu Shao-chi line which, by building on personal incentive and ideas of personal advance, took away spirit and determination from the collective. The three years of the Cultural Revolution have been a great experience for all brigade members, demonstrating the existence of, and difference between, the two class lines. This experience also showed the need to maintain the struggle against the reappearance of the defeated classes and bourgeois thinking in all fields of endeavor. Mao Tsetung Thought, they felt, was important whether they were trying to set a record for planting potatoes, harvesting wheat or any other activity. Something one needed in all spheres of work. Workpoints are rated at 10 fen (one tenth of a yuan), and all people are properly housed and warmly clad through the severe north China winters. In this brigade I found amongst the members a general understanding of their role in a revolutionary world, and what the hungry and oppressed in other lands expect from them. Today they have never been surer of themselves and their place in the world to be.

A Peking Shirt Factory

The poem "Song of the Shirt", which so well exposed sweated labor in the European industrial revolution, could well have been applied to much of the industry that grew amongst old dwelling houses in the coastal cities of China before Liberation. Big city shops would contract work out to poor folk who worked fantastically long hours under miserable conditions. Such workers usually were brought together in cooperatives when the new order came in, and living standards consequently rose. The next step was to organise state factories, and it was then that three cooperatives in the eastern suburbs of old Peking city got together, during the Great Leap Forward in 1958, and established themselves in a modern factory especially built for them and situated on an ample area of ground outside Tungchihmen, the old East Gate of Peking. They were not sorry to leave their old premises, some of which were in centuries' old temples or courtyard dwelling houses whose roofs leaked in the rainy season. For lack of better housing all the old cooperatives used such buildings, which were badly lit and unsuitable for modern industrial purposes.

To make a long story short, however, the three cooperatives combined into the Peking Shirt Factory, moved out to their new premises and started on modernisation. The old scissors for cutting out gave way to modern cutting machines. Workers quickly invented technical improvements, power-driven sewing machines were bought and new workers trained, so that the work force grew to 690. This despite the fact that a fifth of the old workers had been assigned to other plants of the same kind which needed their technique. In the old cooperative days, working hours would spin out — 9, 10, 11, 12 hours a day at times. Now, in a regular factory eight-hour day, the workers raise production ten percent a year, and have steadily done so all through the Cultural Revolution. Quality has also been greatly improved, and 50 percent of the output now goes into foreign trade. There are only two lines of production, shirts for men and blouses for women, but several grades of product for the export trade, depending on the quality of the material used.

Staff Reduction

During the struggles of the Cultural Revolution, an administrative cadre force of 54 was reduced to one of 17. There are now 12 members in the new Revolutionary Committee, some of whom are workers, some old cadres.

Group Struggle

I heard many good stories of the struggle during the Great Proletarian Cultural Revolution. Some were like those in other factories, but one stood out. There were the leaders of two main opposing groups who were so angry with each other they would not speak when they met.

When the call for unity came, however, they were prevailed on to explain their positions. The older one started the ball rolling. Ruthlessly he criticised himself, calling on all to help him to find more of his faults, and help him to change. Then the younger one followed suit, and said how his ideas of trying to get power were bad. The final upshot was that unity was achieved and the two of them began to look at each other with new eyes, in the end becoming the best of friends.

A Modern Shop

It is quite an experience going around the various shops. Everything is neat, spick and span, with well-lit spacious workrooms and workers keen on their various inventions that speed up the work so well. At certain intervals a worker will stop his or her machine, get up and read one of the quotations from the Little Red Book, then sit down again and go on with the job. Then someone else will call for a song, and all will join in, the sound floating out of open windows and rising through the graceful weeping willows that line the courtyards. I stopped and talked with an old worker. He said he had been tailoring for 40 years, but only now, in this time of Mao Tsetung, did he realise how enjoyable work could be. Some of the old ones have never been to school and were illiterate. But all can recite the three short essays, and all have learnt quite a few characters in the process. Sixty-nine percent of the workers are women, and two thirds of the whole work force still live in the old city, the rest in the commune villages around Tsochiachuang where the factory is situated.

Mao Tsetung Thought

From the moment one enters the plant and passes a big bed of gay dahlias by the main gate, one is impressed by the cheerfulness of the place. The working conditions are good, the machines good, the materials good, the product high quality, and Mao Tsetung Thought activates all. It is right, then, that they should feel as they do. There are many study groups. Those in the factory, and then those set up in the homes of workers with family members attending. The old workers who remember the bitterness of capitalist society and what being at the bottom of the social ladder meant, tell their stories so that the younger ones know and can compare. Said one old worker, "Liu Shao-chi divided us, class brothers though we were, but Mao Tsetung has brought us together." Many of the cadres and workers go out on propaganda work amongst the people on Sundays as one of the volunteer tasks they set themselves. One of them created a record by visiting 22 families in one day. A few cheery words to each, some discussion of problems, and then some ideas of how Mao Tsetung Thought would help, to each and every one. Explaining the slogan, "Struggle against selfishness and criticise revisionism", leads always to a good talk. This is also something the workers really know about and where they bring in down-to-earth illustrations. "Prepare against war, against natural disasters, and do everything for the people" is another slogan which serves as a point of departure in this type of discussion. The workers of this factory are evidently a group that not only produces shirts but also ideas that stir people, put in a way that the people accept.

By the riverside, Tientsin.

PEKING & TIENTSIN

Peking brick kiln.

Student giving a demonstration in class,
Tsaochangti Middle School, Peking.

Helping to harvest the wheat.

Students of Red Star Commune at class, Peking.

Teacher helping with
practical work after class.

Leading commune members in a song, Peking.

Students' propaganda team performing during work break, Peking.

"My apprenticeship has finished. I am now a 2nd grade worker." Tientsin.

"I am starting work as apprentice soon," says this Tientsin boy.

"It is good to be a worker now. I
was an apprentice in 1962." Tientsin.

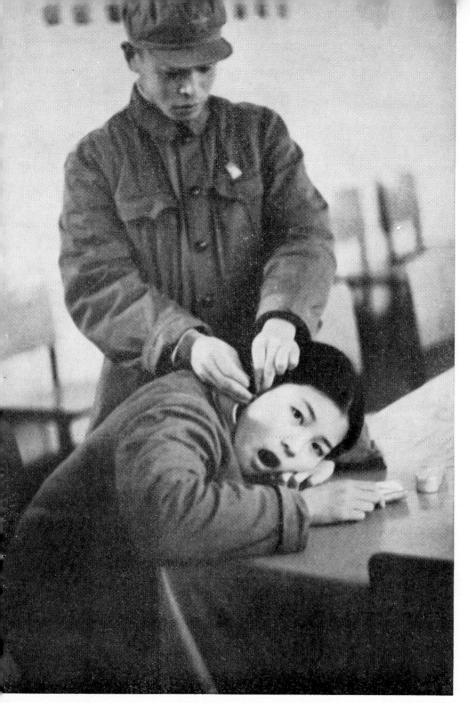

Peking deaf-mute school pupil having acupuncture.

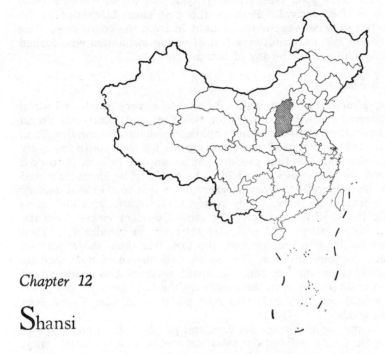

Chapter 12

Shansi

Mountainous Shansi province, with its tough, hardy people, was a famous battleground during the Wars of Resistance and Liberation. It produces in the main grain and cotton, and now, radiating from its capital of Taiyuan, industry is quickly enlarging. Its mineral resources are considerable, and its communications good. I arrived in Taiyuan on a hot July day in 1967.

Taiyuan, Shansi, 1967

Two years had passed since I last spent a couple of months in Shansi. Two years in which much had happened. Outside the hotel where I stayed for the first night a bus had been converted into a loudspeaker unit, and on its roof six trumpets put out news of the Cultural Revolution, competing with another set over in the public gardens opposite. All public buildings and shops were thickly plastered with big character posters, so that one could hardly tell which was which. Big groups of youth clustered around the buildings of the city Party office, now occupied by the provincial Revolutionary Committee. City trees had grown, and through their summer foliage chimney stacks of the many factories of the place pierced the sky. Peking had been damp and cool. Taiyuan, though so much higher, was hot and dry, with a real feel of the Northwest in the air. Crops in Shansi this year were good everywhere, friends told me as the first topic of conversation after arrival. Perhaps the best since Liberation. The streets were full of fresh vegetables brought in from the communes. The canals, rivers and lakes around were full of young swimmers who looked brown, healthy and full of the joy of living.

Shoe Polish Factory

After a rest, I made my first visit. It was to a very small industrial venture. Fifteen housewives and one or two men had jointly set up an industrial cooperative, at first making naphthalene balls and candles. Then a request was made by the local marketing agency for shoe polish to supply the provincial demand. The first product was a complete failure. It cracked open, it turned the shoes grey, and had to be collected by the agency and sent back to the cooperative. Then workers were sent to a Peking factory to see how it was made there. They stayed a very short time and came back thinking they had the answer. The second product leaked from the containers in hot weather, and was also returned as unsaleable. Then workers went to Shanghai to see how the task was done there, and on return put out the third product. But again, this one could not stand up to weather conditions and, in running, spoilt some of the goods stored around it in the shop. When on the fourth try they did get a proper product, people would not buy, as it was now widely said that Shansi boot polish was no good.

Then the women went out on Sundays and polished shoes and boots in public places, resolutely defying old tabus on such a thing — "Just fancy, my wife out polishing the shoes of strange men!" — and then, with every pair of shoes polished, the selling text: "Our Shansi polish. As good as any in the world now." It really was good polish. Then as an encouragement they got some orders for export polish, black, brown, tan and white. I took a tin of brown polish away with me. It was fine. The brand is "Butterfly", and the product is quite up to international standard. The women are experimenting on a new multiple filling machine, but have not succeeded yet in perfecting it. They have had so many reverses, however, that a first defeat no longer staggers them. They take it in their course.

Their Own Builders

As their production grew, the need arose to extend their little workshops. This they did by collecting waste material from big factory yards and hauling in brick from the old city wall. Their yard was low and became a pool in the summer rains. Working nights, they hauled in debris from old redoubts left over from the wars and raised the level enough for water to run off. They needed a carpenter to make factory benches and stools, as well as wooden packing cases for their product. But at that time they could not afford to pay wages to a carpenter, as there was only just enough money to pay everyone a livelihood allowance. So one of the women learnt carpentry and fixed up a small carpenter's shop. She told me, "The main thing about doing things is to follow Mao Tsetung and just believe that one can do it. Then put your whole self into the task, and it will come out all right." The young housewife who was the acting manager at the time of our visit said to me, "We started work as an enterprise in 1958. Some said the Leap Forward was a failure. We were determined to hold to its spirit, and not have our part of it fail. This is why now we have come through from nothing to something. We are proud of our cooperative, and the people around are pleased with us." Just a small group of housewives who have stepped out into the van of a working society by putting into action the slogan of self-reliance and doing something that many said could not be done.

Changching Commune

We went some 40 kilometres south of Taiyuan to Yutze county, and then ten more on a commune road to Changching Commune. A young man in his early twenties welcomed me in the commune office. Then, as the leader of the housewives cooperative had done, he led in the reading of some quotations from the Little Red Book. After that he spoke of the progress the commune had made during the last years before we went out to see for ourselves. On the way into the village we had passed some spirited bands of children marching with tools out to the fields. They were some from the five part-work, part-study middle schools of the commune which have specialized in this kind of education. Seventy percent of the commune land is irrigated either by wells or else by the 900 canals or laterals which have been dug and which total 1,120 kilometres in length. The wheat crop this year was good, and now the second crop was coming along well. Ninety dan of compost was applied to every mou as well as 15 jin of chemical fertiliser for the last main crop.

The commune consists of 4,960 families, with 21,600 people. It has a work force of 7,200 men and women divided into 24 brigades and 170 production teams, and farms 70,000 mou of flat land. Grain allowance per person is 500 jin a year. Wheat, kaoliang, millet and corn are the principal grains. Vegetables and cotton are also grown.

Commune Facilities

We stopped for a while at the commune hospital. There were only 20 in-patients, as at this time of the year little sickness is encountered. Around 60 people a day come to the clinic.

In the stock-breeding station, horses, donkeys and cows are bred. In the machine shops not only the ordinary agricultural hand tools are made, but also assembly frames for power pumps for the wells. The four tractors the commune owns are also serviced here, though not the tractors which come in from the local tractor station, which does the maintenance work itself. The oil pressing, flour milling and cotton carding workshops which every up-and-coming commune now possesses, are doing things collectively that were once part of the peasant's household tasks and which then demanded a good deal of physical effort. The commune has 55 kilometres of high tension wiring of its own and 45 kilometres of low, with some 30 transformers. Such electrification has become characteristic in Shansi since the Great Leap Forward in 1958.

I asked how many new farm implements were in use in the commune, and was told the number was now 580. People are certainly becoming accustomed to having things done the quicker way, and this especially applies to the pumping of water from wells, once so slow and laborious a process. More deep-level wells are being sunk, and now more attention also is being given to tree planting with emphasis on walnut, date, and chestnut trees. It is realised that the really bad years are the ones that have to be prepared for, and that, if in every home there are big earthenware jars of nuts, dried dates, apricot kernels and so on, these will help to balance diet in the spring days when vegetable crops have not yet grown.

New Use for Highway

The highway between Taiyuan and Yutze is a main one. We were interested to see that a commune on the way had turned the traffic off onto a parallel cart road for about half a mile in one place. The highway, cement-paved, was being put to use this day for drying the recently threshed wheat before storing it away. That food is the basis for everything is well understood in China, and no one demurred.

Taiyuan Opposing Groups

In Taiyuan city itself, the young people in the Cultural Revolution had divided into two main groups, and the evenings were taken up with speeches over loudspeakers, putting over the different points of view. Shansi province was one of the first to form the three-way alliance of Army, young rebels and old cadres. This assisted to keep up production and to maintain the general run of things. The problems the industrialisation of China poses are not small for, indeed, they involve basic social and political principles. From the quietness of a guest house out by the beauty spot of Tsinssu, I would come into the maelstrom of struggle each day and return to sylvan surroundings well away from the medley of sound each evening.

Knitting Mill

One morning in Taiyuan I spent out at a knitting mill along the Yutze highway. Once situated in the city, the factory had expanded so swiftly that it had erected three big modern shops out in the suburbs, in which 2,000 of the 3,500 workers now worked.

There had been no physical struggle in the factory during the movement. The old administrative group struggled with the rebel one, but the rebels obtained so much worker support that they were able to take over easily. The faults of the last administration were then thoroughly exposed; its stress on production and technique to the exclusion of politics, its whole system of prize-giving, its practice of using economic incentives in order to win support for itself amongst the more conservative workers. These were all found to be highly unpopular amongst the workers. A new spirit shows itself in production, which has increased and is from 10 to 45 percent higher than planned. Costs have gone down 29 percent. Instead of having some specially selected "pet" workers getting higher pay the whole work force is using its best effort. There have been several valuable technical innovations in the past six months, and six kinds of new lines have been passed for production, 37 others now being tested. Eighty percent of the old cadres are back at work in their jobs and have joined the rebel group. Actually only three people in the top management are not yet working at all. Two Army men have come in to help with study and in assisting the completion of the great alliance. One of the six shops, situated in the city, still had some differences with the rest, but all are confident that this situation will soon be straightened out.

The factory was originally a small private undertaking, becoming a state-private enterprise in the mid-'fifties, before it became all state-owned. Some of the original workers at the time of the rebel take-over and during the subsequent debates, wept when they understood what the road back to capitalism really meant, and how unwittingly they had been following, or were being led to follow, such a path. Said one, "In the old society I had to sell my five-year-old brother, whom I loved, to save him from death by starvation! That was capitalism. We want no more of that!"

Transformer Factory

The Taiyuan Transformer Factory was an organisation in which the Cultural Revolution was overdue. Established in 1958 during the Great Leap Forward in its newly built present premise on the basis of a state-private enterprise once operating in the old city, it was part of a projected plant which was to employ 4,500 workers. Buildings for 1,500 were built, but then the policy put into action by opponents of the Great Leap Forward during the hard times of 1960-61 cut it down to 400 workers, at the same time leaving an overhead staff which contained not a few who had been capitalists in the old order. These joined together and strenuously opposed the study of the works of Mao Tsetung. They fostered personal profit incentive in various ways, paying for piecework — a system the workers hated. When the Cultural Revolution started they forbade the workers to take part, and were against the putting up of big character posters. Then, when the old guard saw things were beginning to go badly for them, and that a strong group of 13 workers had joined together to expose mistakes in the plant, they organised a force of 168 Red Guards of their own and put some in every shop in order to control the others. Still it proved impossible to keep the rebel workers down. Each move of the old forces was counteracted by the worker rebels and, in January of 1967, they seized power after a five months' struggle.

The young man who told us this, a second-grade worker (workers are graded in eight steps), was quite sure of his politics. Yes, they had won over most of the old cadres, and now the factory was running better than it had ever done, with the national plan for the first half of the year exceeded. They were very pleased that they had been able to put in two transformer panels — one for high and the other for low voltage for their own use — at less than a third of the cost allowed for. 100,000 yuan had been allocated, but the task was done for less than 30,000. In this year also, they had perfected an advanced welding unit which is now in demand by other factories. The 1967 plan entailed a 21 percent rise in production. They all meet each morning at 7:40 and study Chairman Mao's quotations until eight. Then on Wednesday afternoons in work time, they do detailed study, as they do on two evenings of the week. Under the old management, they were not allowed to discuss class struggle, and study periods were not properly organised. When held at all, usually inconsequential business was dealt with. The workers I saw were a warm, well-knit group, both men and women. Their shops are beautifully maintained. The old administrative superstructure was particularly poor in providing and organising the essential features which make for a successful enterprise in a socialist society. The new one, which contains the best elements of the old management and the cream of the workers, knows where it is going and is determined to get there. Transformers are made in all sizes, but the main output at present is destined for communes which are being electrified. In addition to the over 400 workers, at times some 30 wives of workers are given temporary employment; they clean up the compound, or do temporary or relatively unskilled jobs. This group decide on their own pay per day, within the accepted standard limits. They are not so often called in, however. As they live in workers' quarters nearby, it is always easy to get them at short notice, and they are glad to come.

Railway Workshops

An important struggle centre in Shanghai was the railway administration on which the economic life of the city depended. It was the same in Taiyuan, for here too, the old leaders did their best to use their power to halt the rebels. During my visit I was able to talk with the new leaders, and it became clear to me as the tale unfolded that the change was not before its time. The leaders of the group which has now been relieved had gone to no end of trouble to hold up the Cultural Revolution and to stop the study of Chairman Mao's works. They had tried by introducing material incentives to build up their own group, and in the period from December 1966 to March 1967 had interrupted services and at times almost brought rail transport to a stop. The railway administration looks after 1,280 kilometres of railway here, with 108 railway stations, the whole being divided into 37 sections for working purposes. The administration runs its own hospitals and sanitaria, as well as 25 schools, from higher technical down to primary. It has 23,000 workers who average some three dependents each. The old method of administration was by "one sheet of paper", as it is called here, an idea introduced by the Soviet experts in the early 'fifties, which means that an office order is the last word on anything. It was part of this system that an extraordinary load of regulations was put on the ordinary worker. A passenger guard had no fewer than 106 to follow. But if he was clever and knew how to operate he could by-pass any rule, and by this type of opportunism bring himself to the notice of his superiors as a very diligent person, and thus come in for the extra salary then awarded to clever operators. Some received extra allowances which were more than double what others in the same category were getting.

New Administration

The old leading group was frankly upset when the Cultural Revolution broke. They issued orders that all big character posters had to be gone over by three offices before they could be displayed, and then they were only to be put up in certain designated places. But although they tried in many different ways, they did not succeed, and now the administration is in the hands of one group of old cadres, rebels and Army men. We visited the shops where locomotives were overhauled, saw the railway control system operating, and listened while the young rebels described in considerable detail the struggles they had been through in getting the railway system back to normal. Some of the very difficult problems in railway transport, previously said to have been insoluble, have now been solved, simply by determination and collective work. Future progress will be rapid, since there is a new willingness to work hard and solve problems in an unorthodox way.

Taiyuan Middle School

"So far, we have taken but the first steps on our Long March," said the vice-principal of Taiyuan Middle School No. 20, as she talked to us, surrounded by the staff and youngsters of the school Revolutionary Committee. It was a school that might be called an intermediate high school — offering a three-year course after primary school and then, on graduation, students go either to a technical school or else to be apprentices or young workers in industry. Actually, under the former administration, it was a school to which the less hopeful were sent — "hopeful" according to their ability in passing examinations in set subjects. But amongst the middle schools it has been one of the most progressive in Taiyuan, one that has learnt to adapt itself to the new requirements and get on with its task in the swiftest possible way. All classes we found to be in progress, though in the regular subjects a recapitulation was done of the lessons learnt at the time the Cultural Revolution started, and which were then dropped. The library and storeroom for teaching appliances were beautifully maintained and in capable hands. The whole place was clean and the full body of students was attending. One would have quite a hard time to imagine all that has been gone through in the stormy months by just looking at the faces of the Revolutionary Committee seated around the table at which the assistant principal made her report.

One of the committee members, a typical Chinese Northwest boy seated opposite me, had a real tough but likeable face set in a good-humored grin. When he stood up to walk around with us I saw he was crippled, so he already knew what suffering was. Like most others in the second grade, he was 16 years old. During the long report, one of his schoolmates turned to take a few long looks at the blank pages at the end of his Little Red Book where he had pasted in some of the new postage stamps with Chairman Mao on them. They were still boys, though they had been called on to do an adult job. Yes, there had been rough times. Some of the conservatives had tried to smash up the school and had to be halted. There had been many long debates, not all entirely peaceful. But out of it all there came a feeling for the need of unity, that their school was essential to them all in their life's work and that they must all be quite clear about what they struggled against and why.

Struggle

It was, in a measure, easy to talk to them, for as a school they had been discriminated against, and wherever there is oppression there is a fight against it. Yet at the beginning, most of the school, both pupils and staff, went along with the line dictated by the then Party secretary who, in turn, relayed the dictates from above. Yet the rebel groups did organise and, after the Sixteen-Point program (Decision of the Central Committee of the Chinese Communist Party Concerning the Great Proletarian Cultural Revolution, adopted on August 8, 1966) was announced, were able to feel that they were on more solid ground in their struggle, and the vision of a real people's school began to come to them. Autumn 1966 had begun before they were able to get together openly and criticise the old leadership. The 30 groups into which the school had become divided now began to unite, until at last there were but two opposing sides. The arrival of Army cadres to assist in study and military training helped no end, and PLA prestige is high with the whole school now. Then, on March 1st, the Revolutionary Committee could be organised and classwork start again, cutting out from it those features which the newer education feels to be unnecessary. Some of the political classes are now conducted as debates, with groups taking their discussion very seriously. In one of the classrooms we found the girls lined up against the boys, the girls sitting straight in rows, the leading boy speaker nonchalantly leading from the other side of the room.

It was pleasant living out at Tsinssu. The hills at the back of the beauty spot were now beginning to show up with the forest planting that has been done. I spent a whole morning strolling around the park there with its old temples and pavilions and sat a while writing these lines:

> *Tall poplars, leaves turning lazily*
> *in the breeze, glinting in the sun*

after rain, then parting to show
straight white trunks pointing upward
in their strength; ancient cypresses
and a garden of hollyhocks making
a splash of colour, birds that fill
the morning with symphony, coming sweetly
to one deafened by the cacophony of cities;
now hills with new forests showing green
grace Tsinssu; children play by clear waters
that flow with a smile in every ripple;

> *here a place where throughout history*
> *one lord battled with another, with now*
> *but crumbling ancient city walls showing*
> *through new apple orchards, to remind any*
> *who care to be reminded, that the struggle*
> *forward is long; a place where in our today*
> *workers on their weekly day off come to*
> *rest and debate, voices at times rising*
> *angrily, then simmering down as emotion*
> *expends; says one, "there is but one*
> *criterion: does it serve the people?"*
> *and the silence of acquiescence follows*
> *before words start again.*

To Hsinhsien

The highway from Taiyuan north to Hsinhsien is a modern one, so we did not use all of one morning going over it. After leaving Taiyuan, one soon comes to the loess country with deep gulches, terraced fields and parapets of desiccated loess standing above scattered villages.

Hsinhsien had a magnificent towered entrance gate, and inside the city one sees the same teeming life, everyone going about his or her appointed task as is evident in other Northwest rural centres. A Revolutionary Committee, a combination of Army men, rebels and old cadres, now administers the prefecture of Hsinhsien, which has 16 counties with 2,400,000 people. Here some of the toughest conditions in Shansi are met. It was with considerable interest, therefore, that I went to see the training school for cadres in medical groups that will penetrate the highest mountain village, the most desolate valley in the province. They were a bright and interesting group of young people, each picked by his or her own commune, each county being represented. These young people will be put through a three-year course by the state. It is a course that includes obstetrical and pediatric training, some simple surgery, and diagnosis and treatment of the more common diseases of the region, as well as acupuncture, which is very useful in dealing with many of the troubles that farmers get.

The school is a part-work, part-study one of five classes. It has 199 students and 54 teaching and administrative staff. As its work runs parallel to that of the commune, there are no long holidays. Eight months' study and four months' practical work fill up their time.

Students in Practice

When the Cultural Revolution started, the students went to Peking, joined in the activities there as Red Guards, and returned to carry out revolution in their own hometown. That they have been able to go through each stage of the revolution from beginning to end and attain unity in their whole group has been a remarkable achievement, though one remembered that they were all the children of poor farmers, down-to-earth people who know where they are going and why. The top class graduates next March, and wants to make up for lost time through intensive study. But they have faced their responsibilities gallantly through all the heat and struggle of the movement, taking part in local as well as provincial struggles in no unsure way. They are a group now as self-sufficient as such a group can be, even down to their own tailoring shop where the more able lasses sew and patch for the others. The old headmaster, they say, has "stood up", and with the rebels' help has joined the group in charge. In fact, they have been able to win all the old cadres over. The Army is represented on their control committee by one militiaman. Everyone now feels that he or she understands the revolution better than they have ever done, and that the struggle has been well worthwhile.

Changes in Thinking

At the beginning not all students were in favor of change. Now that they have been through the tempest and for several months already have been back on a steady curriculum, they can analyse and feel with one mind that Chairman Mao was right — the rebellion was necessary. The struggle the first group of young rebels put up was intense. When they had taken power the common sense of the Chinese peasant wanting to get on with the job stood them in good stead, and the central directives were closely followed until unity was finally gained. It is this unity that now enables them to go ahead with their studies and learn practical and needed things, so that their coming after graduation is anxiously awaited throughout the countryside. Now too, they begin to look at each other with a new respect born of the tough period they have been through together. This school has shown the way ahead to many other schools, and naturally its experience is now studied by many.

Chitsun Brigade

Driving southeast from Hsinhsien out into the country and on through many villages, we came on one hot summer's morning to Chitsun Brigade of Chitsun Commune. The power in this brigade was taken over by a rebel group on February 20th 1967, in a three-way alliance, consisting of members of the militia to represent the Army, old cadres, for example the deputy Party secretary, an old guerilla fighter, and rebels, amongst them a young girl, the driving force of the Red Guards. This girl, Wang Ying-ao, turned out to be my host and spent the whole day with me. She had incredible energy. She also knew well how to use it to the best advantage. She took me over the countryside to the big canal six kilometres long which the members dug last winter to bring summer flood waters into the brigade canal system, and then to the two big open wells dug like ponds, with high stone sides from which fresh water is pumped electrically into the rapidly expanding canal system for those times when there is no flood water. People like the flood water most as it brings down silt and compost, so is invaluable for flooding the 1,000 mou of sandy wasteland reclaimed this past year. The new canals into which water is pumped are lined with concrete slabs to prevent leakage. The new group are proud of this work, for the old office incumbents said contemptuously, "Now we shall see what the children can do! They will not be able to do anything!" But the "children" have done a great deal this year, spurred on by such remarks. That the people like the new set-up can be seen on the faces everywhere in the village. More than ever it is their show now.

About the Brigade

We went to the piggery which has been set up. The old one went bankrupt through management that was really heading towards the capitalist road and, in consequence, got very little popular support. The new one has 70 pigs in it this year and plans to rear 400 by next. But let us introduce the brigade a little more clearly. Situated 45 li from Hsinhsien it has 1,120 families, 3,891 people in all, and farms 8,400 mou of land. Before Liberation there were four landlord families and 73 rich peasant ones. They occupied 4,700 mou of the best land. On the sandy, alkaline land the 448 families of poor peasants tried to scratch a living. In the past 17 years the population has grown. So has production. Average grain per mou harvested is around 300 jin. The amount of grain per person is 357 jin. Both totals would have been thought quite impossible in the old society, and even more impossible would have been the reclamation of the land that has now been carried through. The first big project done was a Great Leap Forward one in 1958, when a deep canal was dug by 10,000 commune folk through winter, with the result that all the alkaline land in the commune area, previously not farmed, was brought under cultivation. The irrigation work of 1966-67 brings the remainder of the former wasteland under cultivation now. It is estimated that the harvest for 1967 will reach an all-time high of 400 jin a mou.

One of the many counts against the previous leadership of the commune was that they bureaucratically decided that cotton could not be grown here. Now, with cotton an important material in the countryside, successful experiments were made in 1966, resulting in 720 mou being put into cotton in 1967 and a projected 1,000 mou for 1968. Youngsters criticised the old leadership for always putting a damper on any useful suggestion for change, refusing to study or follow Chairman Mao's teachings, and of not putting politics in the forefront.

I had a most enjoyable lunch at Wang Ying-ao's home. Her father is an old revolutionary, and there are five other girls in the home, four daughters and one daughter-in-law. There are also two young sons. We sat up on the kang and stuffed ourselves steadily and with much relish from the fresh, wonderful tasting food. Going around the 16 little productive enterprises operated by the commune, we admired the basket weavers, who use willow grown on the commune, the flour millers, and so on. Went out to see how well the crops were growing and the water was running, and then listened to a very detailed report by Wang Ying-ao on all steps taken in the revolution to consolidate into the grand alliance and to have things not only running, but also going better than they have ever gone. To put it in a nutshell, whatever Chairman Mao wanted, the revolutionary youth would carry out. That came out during her speech very clearly a number of times, and there can be no doubt that she and her fellows thoroughly meant it. At the moment they were all having a spot of trouble with an insect pest, but again the mass line, the people working all through the night with 60 sprayers in their hands, were doing wonders. The old fighter, previously deputy Party secretary, said, "We want to make things better for our commune, for Shansi, for China and for the whole world revolution!"

Hsinhsien Transport

One of the things that has changed China's hinterland drastically in these years since Liberation has been the development of bus service over the highways. Bus lines now run to all manner of tiny places, bringing them in touch with bigger areas. In some parts of the hinterland during the Cultural Revolution, the usually beautiful finish of the passenger bus has for this past year given way to posters, becoming an extension of town and village walls plastered thick with big character posters. Here in Hsinhsien, however, there is one of the current slogans painted in bold golden characters on the side of the brilliantly red bus, but no other sticking that would ruin the paint and, from the point of view of propaganda, probably be less effective.

Bus Repair Works

The group from the 350 transport workers who service the 800 kilometres of highway transport and bus lines in the Hsinhsien prefecture were more interested in raising technique and lowering costs, after taking power and putting proletarian politics in command. They have not yet reached their three-way alliance, as the old management had used the militia group to stand against the rebel one, and the militia now has to be reorganised. Of the 13 in the rebel control committee now, eight are workers and five are old cadres. Workers here have to put their politics into practice in a very definite way, for they have to take their buses successfully into many inaccessible villages amongst places whose names ring loud in revolutionary history, especially that of the Resistance War period. Pinghsingkwan, Wutai, Yenmenkwan, and so on.

Equipment and Materials

For most of the buses all lubricating oil, gasoline and spares are locally produced. Some of the heavy trucks bought in these past few years from the USSR came without spare parts and these have to be made in the transport section shops. "Looks as though the sellers hoped we could not operate their trucks," one of the workers said. Going through the workshops, I saw many creative innovations the repair men have made that save much money and time while doing the job better. In this year of 1967, costs have been drastically lowered, while bus and truck mileage has been increased. Ninety-six percent of the vehicles in the station are on the road seven days a week. Only for about 15 days in January of 1967 was production lower. That was when the workers' struggle was at its height. Since then, it has bettered 1966 totals. The average distance covered by each bus per day is 160 kilometres. Whatever the people in back villages want is delivered where possible. Last winter one lonely old man wanted a load of coal. The bus attached a trailer full of it, and up it came through the hills right to his door.

Political study is a must amongst the workers in this stage. One shop had halted for such a study period as we came around. This is not a strange sight these days but rather an accepted way, and a sure means of getting good results.

Back to Taiyuan

Days at Hsinhsien were too short, and I did not make all the visits folk had kindly planned for me, for there was a timetable to be adhered to, and too soon the time came to go. It was a magnificent ride back to Taiyuan, looking over great swathes of rich cropping land in the lush green of a good harvest. The perfect pictures one does not get a chance to photograph, for they come in an instant and then are gone, showed tantalisingly. Two little girls in sleeveless cotton print tunics and short panties of the same material, flowers in their hair, which was done in tufts on each side of their heads, looked about as lovely as one could see anywhere. Then there was a group of boys herding cows and enjoying every minute of the long summer's day, as were another bunch seen down in the riverbed, sleek suntanned bodies with lines not spoilt by bathing costumes, who almost seemed to be part of the loess-colored flood waters themselves, diving in and out like seals. A long way apart from the Cultural Revolution, the scanner of these lines may say. Yet to me these are good things, a proper basis for the new culture based on the ordinary working folk of the land, and very much part of any appraisal of China today.

A Link with Japan

Purely for the pleasure of going there at such a season, I took a day off and went to the hills some 55 kilometres south of Taiyuan and there climbed up a steep gully to the beautiful temple called Hsuanchungssu. It is a place to which Japanese visitors often come, for it was from here in the dynasties of Northern Wei, Sui and Tang that Buddhist priests went to Japan, and it was from here that Zen Buddhism was brought.

It is a lovely spot. A white pagoda tops a commanding cliff and, on a ledge below it, the temple lies, facing into the sun. In summertime it is surrounded by a riot of flowers. Its vegetable gardens grow well, and its orchards are rich with fruit. Japanese friends have brought some fine scrolls for temple walls, and the temple itself possesses some excellent Ming dynasty ones of its own. In the reception room there is a magnificent Chienlung period rug on the floor. Images and everything about the place have been wonderfully preserved.

We had a lunch of melons and dried beancurd, beef, and cold fritters under an apricot tree below the temple, at a spot where the little pagodas that mark the graves of ancient abbots stand thickly surrounded by cypresses. The old woodlands here have been felled down the ages.

His father was a guerrilla fighter
in the War of Resistance, Shansi.

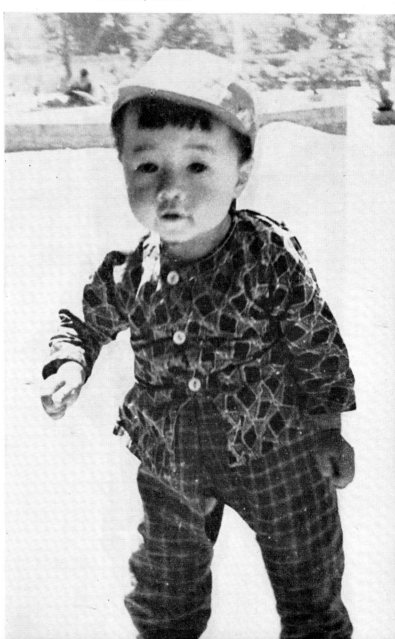

Corn cobs in Shansi.

They all helped to build this canal, Hsinhsien, Shansi.

Canal built in 1967.

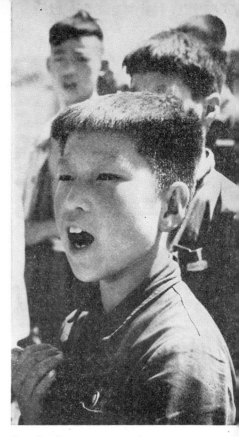

Summer in Hsinhsien.

Boy leading a song.

In Shansi under the warlords, there were few schools and many hungry children. Today youngsters are different.

At Tsinssu near Taiyuan.

Girl student, Hsinhsien.

Housewives make boot polish here, Taiyuan, Shansi.

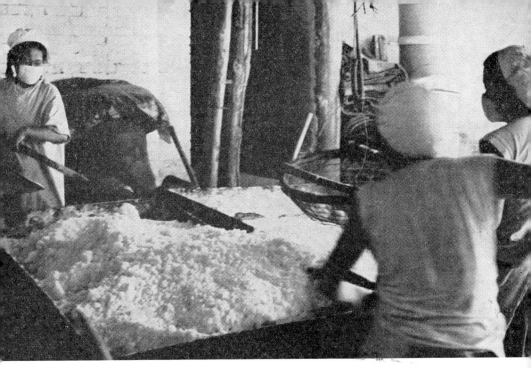

Extracting useful chemicals from factory waste, Taiyuan.

A neighbourhood tailoring shop in Taiyuan.

Winter scene in a Shansi commune.

Propaganda playlet — students denouncing revisionist line during the Cultural Revolution, Shansi.

Chapter 13

The Cultural Revolution in Education

Prior to the Cultural Revolution the part-work, part-study agricultural and industrial middle schools had been set up in deference to Mao Tsetung Thought, but these had not been extended in any serious way, and were looked down on by the educational pundits as being rather second-rate education. At the beginning of this chapter an account is given of some of the best of these seen in the late spring and early summer of 1966.

As the Cultural Revolution went on, however, it began to be seen that this dovetailing of theory and practice was the way all education should go, from that of primary schools on through universities and still further into cadre training. A revolutionary is always a learner, always going to school. Society is a factory, and the whole of society is a school, too. So here we have part-work, part-study starting in the lowest grades and going right on through to the May 7th Cadre Schools now a feature throughout the whole country. The selections I have made of places visited try to reflect some of the things tried out in various educational institutions on these lines. Needless to say, the picture is a changing one. One thing, however, is sure and certain. The old educational system has been shattered to smithereens, and a new one is being courageously and thoughtfully built.

First Steps Towards Part-Work, Part-Study Schools, 1966

The Chinese revolution is like a great river, sweeping onward. When something gets in its way, waves surround it and, little by little, the difficulty is washed away. Such an obstacle has shown up in the old educational system which, it can be seen now, has not produced the kind of person adequately fitted with working theory and working practice, immediately able to better production whatever sphere he or she is assigned to. If there is no proper relation of theory to practice the result will be study for study's sake, theory for theory's and art for art's sake, poets and writers without any roots amongst the people, engineers who do not want to work in factories but only in technical institutes, doctors who do not want to dirty their hands on patients and the growth of a new class of the privileged, who will want those who dig and hew to support them as superior beings. In other words, the emergence of a new class, instead of the abolition of classes. So in these days there has been much stress on promoting the part-work, part-study school as a basic revolutionary task. Not so easy as it sounds, for the older group of the teaching profession has itself been educated in the old way — accustomed to a rigid syllabus, memorisation, cut and dried textbooks and all the rest. It rather took for granted that the best in education was to be found in a combination of the Confucian school and the European one brought in by a century of Mission schools to the China coast, revamped again and then streamlined after Liberation, though without completely altering its basic nature.

The part-work, part-study school brings an entirely new kind of youngster to the fore. One who can make and create and understands the need for work and study in terms of his duty to society as well. Practice accentuates the political line that teaches the dignity of work, the greatness of the person who can sacrifice most, the emptiness of personal heroism, the value of the collective, the sin of waste and the need to keep in close contact with the masses. A political line that takes into account the need for class struggle as long as there remain classes, and relates every human effort to the struggle for socialism and a socialist and communist ideology. In consequence, one looks at every attempt of the part-work, part-study school these days as an expression of the true pioneering spirit, venturing out on an entirely new path. I felt this when accepting the invitation, while visiting Hangchow in Chekiang province in 1966, to go and see one of these pioneer schools in the old city.

Hangchow Handicraft School

One could feel it was a good school the minute one stepped inside and watched the youngsters at work. They were happy, poised and keen, quite evidently doing the thing they wanted to be doing. Not much of a school building to look at, in these days of splendid new educational plants. But equipment, spit and polish do not necessarily make a school. The place had once been a local command post of the Japanese gendarmerie during enemy occupation, but since that time a broad modern boulevard has swept through the old city, leaving this house on a cobbled lane well below its level. It has some big, brightly lit rooms, however, as well as courtyard space at the back where classrooms for the students have been built. Then again it is not a big school, nor has it been running for long. Just 64 lads and lasses, graduates of a lower middle school who showed proficiency in drawing or handicraft work, sons and daughters of city workers in the main, only 15 percent of them being from the once privileged class. They work and study together for four years and then go out to the handicraft factories of Hangchow as all-round workers capable of gaining new ideas and of putting them into practice. The school started up in 1960 and does not aim to enroll more than 200 students in the future. At present it is divided into several classes for work — wood carving in the rich Chekiang style, stone carving, basketwork and over-all design, which entails a high standard of drawing. In classroom work which students do one week off and one week on, in rotation with their practical tasks, they study politics, literature and applied arts. The staff consists of 20 teachers and technicians. All technicians work with the students at the same benches, hard to distinguish from their pupils as they, too, are young folk, graduates from this school and various other art schools. In the early 'fifties, when China began to pull in all the old handicraftsmen and get them to train others, most of the old-timers were already well over 50 years of age. Now those of that gallant old band who still wish to work spend their time in the quiet of the Research Institute for Applied Arts, just coming to their benches when they feel like it, yet being useful even after the end of their working days.

The field is now open to the new youth. In this school, trainees go through all four practical sections to get an all-round knowledge, since it has been found that all of the first graduating class have been able to fit in well in all places they were sent to, and that all have been able to help increase production in no uncertain way. In some instances they have been able to organise and help with an extension of the work their unit was engaged in. Factories welcome them and value them more than graduates of art colleges who do not have such all-round training. In its teaching, the school has to prepare its own practical work lesson sheets, for there are no textbooks which are suitable as yet. After the school was set up certain difficulties amongst students arose from a widespread wish amongst them: they wanted to be great artists, not just handicraft workers. Then too, many thought that so small a school was second rate, operated under poor conditions and would not have much to offer in the way of teaching. Some of their family folk backed the youngsters in these views though they later came to understand better. Hard as it was to retain good students, it was still harder to get teachers, for at that time very few were available. But with a great deal of stress on political study, the first group was gradually welded into a good working whole. The school has two terms a year, with a total of six weeks' holiday in between.

Like everyone else, students go at times to join in farm or other work in the countryside, to keep them in touch with reality and raise their creative urge. There are now similar schools in that particular line in both Shanghai and Soochow, so that the experience of these can also be drawn upon. One difficulty is that commercial orders given the school are too often for just one line and do not allow diversity in creating new forms needed in the training process. But the part-work, part-study school is a new thing, and ways and means have still to be found to meet such situations as they arise. That there has been success in doing so is evident from the fine general spirit obviously prevailing. With politics in command, the main objective is teaching and learning, and this has been made a first requirement, with the school contributing as much as it can to its own support, and not relying on public funds more than absolutely necessary.

Agricultural Middle School, Wusih

In many parts of the world, there has been a steady drain of the best brains of the countryside into the cities. Country folk are supposed to be stupid "country bumpkins" unable to enjoy the finer things of life, their task being simply to go on producing food, silk and cotton in the same old way for city use. And this supposition is in a feudal or bourgeois society in essence mostly true. But in China today, the "same old way" will no longer do. By and large it was the man in the countryside who fought the revolution and on him the success of the revolution still depends. As the revolution inherited a semi-bankrupt countryside, it is a government policy not to build up too comfortable a life in the cities, which would easily lead to constantly growing standards in town life while those amongst the primary producers would slip back. Such a way would be the sure way to chaos and would lead to the emergence of a new middle class.

These things were in my mind as I walked out over the countryside with friends one fine afternoon in the outskirts of Wusih in Kiangsu province, to see the agricultural middle school of Hsinan Commune, which operates on a part-work, part-study basis. We crossed bridges, wound through village paths, went alongside canals until we came to what was once an ancient temple. To the original buildings four classrooms had been added, three for the three classes of the junior middle course, and one for the senior middle-school course, recently started. Everything here was simply done. There were around 100 lads and 68 girls studying. They learn about wheat, rice and barley, mulberry culture and silkworm rearing, animal husbandry in outline, including some veterinary general knowledge, farm implements, soils and fertilisers, bookkeeping, health and political economy. They do around 170 days a year in classes, and the rest in practical work during the busy seasons of rice transplanting, wheat harvest, mulberry picking, and so on. The longest period they are away from their classwork is in May and June, which is the busy time. They get workpoints for their practical work, income from these going into school upkeep, so that the government has to meet only around 30 percent of the operating cost. The rest the students supply through their work. There are no summer or winter holidays, as city middle schools have. Classes run for six full days a week. There is a staff of ten, some of these are graduates of agricultural, some of other schools.

I watched one class for a while. It was studying plant diseases. There is no lack of new textbooks in these fields, but the students' notebooks were beautifully kept, it being very evident they all wanted to learn and were deeply interested in their subject. Another class was busy with seed selection, the technician going from desk to desk, pointing out the mistakes made, as the little piles of food seed were finalised. Along the walls of the classroom was a row of baskets of herbs cut for pig feed by the students on their way to school in the morning. On the way home in the evening they would fill them to the brim. Only 20 lads lived in the school, since they were from communes some distance away. The others went back home to evening jobs and to preparing their next day lessons afterwards.

The school is equipped with a dozen good microscopes, and students bring in many kinds of specimens to the research desk maintained in one of the staff rooms. There is a warm, comradely atmosphere about the place. It was set up in 1962, starting with 30 youngsters on a short course, then going on for three years with 120 students, who were given a junior middle-school course. Those who have graduated from the first groups have gone to work, and have been received gladly by their home brigades, production teams and different organisations. I asked what they were all doing and learnt that four had gone to the Wusih Agricultural Development Station as technicians, two had become heads of production teams, one had gone as a student assistant to a veterinary station, seven were brigade bookkeepers, six worked in health clinics, two were technicians for the distribution of electrical power, while six have become leaders in Communist Youth League work and six take part in the militia. Ten had gone on to senior middle school for training elsewhere. The rest were highly thought of commune workers, it being felt that their know-how had raised the general knowledge of the whole community, for the whole family is interested in "our boy" or "our girl" and listen to what he or she has to say with a respect they would give no one else. The youngster has books, but they are written in understandable terms and treat of things that have to do with daily livelihood. The home folk are fascinated.

After school is over, I noted, the students do not stay around very long. They play a game or practise long jumping, which they seem to especially enjoy, and then pick up their bag of school books and their baskets of fodder, and with an occasional stop to wrestle, cut fodder, laugh and sing a bit, are off. Two of the girls swung past us. They had put their fodder baskets on a carrying pole and then, with it on their shoulders, stepped fast and lightly. It was a pleasant group to have spent an afternoon amongst, and really a most significant one, for here was a preview of the way education will go in future.

Factory School in Wusih

While in Wusih I went to a third part-work, part-study school. This was a very modern establishment well laid out and with all facilities, set in the industrial part of the city. It was under the leadership of the nearby Wusih Diesel Engine Factory, a large establishment of over 3,000 workers.

I found it to be a school of 900 students doing a four-year course, all having come as around 16-year-old graduates from lower middle school. Soon another 100 students will come, and it will be the 1,000 it expects to maintain as its regular number. It has a working staff of 202, these being teachers, cadres, technicians and workers. It teaches the ordinary school subjects — politics, mathematics, physics, Chinese language, mechanical drawing, and then the technique of the plant the students will go to. Sixteen percent of the time in class work goes to political studies. The school does one week at practical work, and then one week in the classrooms, an arrangement that is being experimented with still. The only long holiday is the two weeks at Spring Festival. The off-day comes on the Tuesday of each week, as does that of the parent factory. Payment for the work the students do in their eight practical work sections is enough to operate the school. Students provide their own clothing, except the work overalls the school supplies. The school also gives free medical service and entertainment such as cinema shows, etc. Classrooms are modern, light and airy. The 14 well-tooled workshops likewise. There is a complete absence of any kind of artificial speed-up, the whole place seeming to go with the precision of the sets of wheels in the diesel gear boxes some students were assembling in one of their shops. Another line they were making were pumps for the diesel engines.

Twenty percent of the students are girls. Practically all students come from town homes including those of workers' and cadres' homes in the city. The son of the leading cadre of Wusih is one of the students busy here with his hands and mind, learning how to become a good worker. When they graduate they will have reached the standard of a third-grade technical worker, though to begin with they will only get second-grade status. Their basic education, however, will help them a great deal to rise to become technicians or engineers if they wish to continue their studies. They are an important part of a generation of educated workers stepping into the new industry for tomorrow. Watching them busy over their drawing boards and at their machine tools, there could be no doubt of their interest in their task and in life in general. Watching their faces as the teacher in politics spoke, it was evident that they were following intently. At times when there is rush work or something special to be done in the parent factory, some of those on practical work go to assist there. They get up at six a.m., do exercises or running, and then at seven have breakfast. At 7:30 they start classes or practical work, going until 11:30. Afternoon classes are from one to three o'clock. Then preparation, games etc., and another 50 minutes' prep after supper. Lights out at 8:30 p.m. Usually on their weekly holiday they like to do something useful for the community. Plant trees, work on city improvement or do something else of the kind. They learn all the time that a real person's purpose in life is to be of service to others. Their daily work demonstrates the necessity of combining theory with practice.

Yangchow Industrial Middle School

In Yangchow, in northern Kiangsu, we went in mid-1966 to a part-work, part-study school which had newly been set up, in September 1965. It has a staff of five and a student roll of 60, a number which it plans to raise to 160. At first it did two weeks' study, then one week's work in its parent factory which is the Yangchow Ferro-Concrete Boat Factory. Then it changed its system to one week on the job alternating with one week in class. It is realised that half a day at work and half in the classroom is probably the best system, but so far it has not been possible to experiment with it. Students are graduates of local lower middle schools.

When they first came they were disappointed with the simplicity of the school buildings, the smallness of the student body, and wondered whether it would not have been better for them to simply become workers, rising to the second or third grade in the four years they would otherwise spend in the school, and moreover getting their wages themselves for that time. Then as these questions were faced in the light of reality and of political theory, they realised that, with their better knowledge, they would help to raise the level of their class, and also be better able to meet the new demands that industry would be making in the future. Soon too, they found that between them and their teachers a new relationship was growing, for the teachers worked along with them in the factory. By working together, everyone felt closer to each other, and studies took on real meaning. The whole 60 of them were doing drawings of ferro-concrete boats and boat parts when I called. The precision of machine-drawing is one of the essentials in making the change from the old peasant mentality to that of the modern industrial worker who must work to fine exactitude. The student group was clearly absorbed in their task.

Other subjects taught are the usual upper middle school ones of politics, mathematics, physics, language. But some technical courses are added that deal more specifically with their daily work. They have one hour at preparation each evening, one day off a week, two weeks in mid-summer and three weeks in mid-winter. The factory manager acts also as headmaster, the full-time dean of studies being the actual leader in the school. Of the 60, 15 are from the villages, 19 are girls, and the rest boys from Yangchow city. The factory that gives them leadership is a rapidly expanding one, of the kind that will be duplicated elsewhere. Students on graduation will be allocated to work by the Ministry of Construction of the provincial government of Kiangsu. Students eat with the 800 or so factory workers in a big mess hall, the school buildings being part of the factory premises. They are well-lit and airy and with plenty of space around. Most of the big plants around Yangchow have now started similar schools so that there is much experience that can be drawn upon.

Commune Middle School, Yangchow

While in Yangchow, I went to see another one of the rural schools. This one was in Ssuchao Commune in Hankiang county. It has 220 students and 14 teachers. It took in upper primary school graduates for a three-year junior middle school course, and in addition had an upper middle school course of two years. Started in 1958, it has already had 700 graduates who have been very well received by the communes around, not a few of them having become brigade or production team leaders. Communes say they are more precious than gold to them. Certainly they have been responsible for some startling production rises.

The school is simply built by the students themselves. A row of new classrooms in grey brick has recently been added, but with paper or plastic sheet windows and tamped earth floors. Approximately the same as the homes of the farmers around. Forty mou of experimental land belongs to the school, on which different wheat strains are tried as well as other crops. While we were there, the only students remaining at school were a group working on a bed for rice seedlings. The others were on a tour of production teams explaining some of the newer technique they had learnt. Students who come from nearby villages live at home. Those from more distant places stay in the school. They work for 178 days a year with their communes, do 153 days in class, and have 24 holidays, which are those of the old lunar calendar observed by the farm folk. Their classes include politics, language, mathematics, bookkeeping, statistics and problems of agriculture, and some chemistry and applied physics to go with it. In the senior classes, more is learnt in these things, with courses on plant diseases, soil and fertiliser, seed selection, elementary meteorology, problems of irrigation and so on all having their place. Teachers work 120 days a year on practical work with the students and live in the same dormitories. A nice touch was the clothes-mending shop the students operate themselves, and a barber's shop, in which they not only cut each other's hair, but also the hair of many of the village children around the school. They also keep 30 pigs.

In all, the impression I had after visiting them was that this group of youngsters acquired knowledge which would be of immediate use to their communes and brigades and would help to bridge the gap between the educated and the common man in China. It will be quite some time, of course, before a new system of education evolves a universally accepted road. Most teachers have been educated in the old way, and it is not possible for all of them to change the whole of their thinking immediately. In their heart of hearts some do cling to traditional forms, ever waiting for the chance to say: "We have tried part-work, part-study and it does not really work, you know!" They may perhaps still prefer a set curriculum with examinations that allow an easy classification, one more based on aptitude for book learning than on aptitude for, and attitude to, work. Then too, there are perhaps some people who will wonder if, from the immediate factory production aspect, the apprentice system is not as good as the part-work, part-study plan. But this attitude is based on the long-standing division of labor into physical and mental. Way back in pre-history, the potters and other manual workers were exploited by the chiefs and wizards who decreed that only their own sons were fit to be chiefs and wizards in turn, and that the common folk must work with their hands. In early historical times in China, the Confucians elaborated on this, and became great supporters of feudalism. It is only in our day that we have leaders who believe that theory and practice interwoven together can make a new man and woman capable of working practically in every field of endeavor. The part-work, part-study school is one of the expressions of this belief.

The Need for Change

Ordinary middle schools and universities have so much inherited prestige, fine buildings and so on, that they cannot just be dismissed as of no longer any importance, but after a visit to a part-work, part-study school it becomes quite clear that here is the way for the future. For anyone who believes that a school is made up of students and teachers working together, and does not simply consist of buildings, that its function is to prepare youth for a future in which much change will have to be met creatively, there is a lot to be learnt from a close scrutiny of the part-work, part-study school.

Many of the school leaders I spoke to agree that the part-work, part-study school on the industrial side will probably be at its best when practical work is done for half a day and study the other half.   Four hours work a day does not tire the active, growing youngster.   He is happy to sit in class the other half, and his mind is more ready for evening preparation work than it would be if he has done a full day at the machine.   The daily impact of both work and theory helps the mind in its formative stage.   Progress is usually in this way faster even in theoretical studies than in a full old-time middle school.   But again, this system has yet to undergo more trial.   Different places have different conditions.   In the commune rural school, naturally, production must fit in with rush periods and the classwork must be concentrated during the slack seasons.   Here, however, the problem of integrating theory with practice is easier.   As a rule, the student lives at home, daily taking back newly acquired school knowledge and daily doing some practical work around the house and fields from which everyone benefits.   If he lives in the school, he works on the school experimental plots and is in touch all the time with farmers around, where topics of discussion always centre on things he is learning.   Progress in this way is fast and makes the youngster avid for more knowledge all the time.

One important aim of the part-work, part-study school is to keep growing youth from contempt for manual labor, and to avoid the artificial division of the working class into a white- and a blue-collar group, a division which allows in the old society the capitalist to perpetuate the exploitation of both groups and would in the new society give occasion for the rise of a new bureaucratic exploiting class.   Once education is thought of as a ladder towards personal progress and a means to avoid physical labor, a new distinction between a "higher" and a "lower" type of labor must of necessity arise.   And special privileges, city flats, country summer cottages, face, fame and fortune will become demands of those who are feeling that they are doing the "important" work of society.   The part-work, part-study school teaches that both types of work, physical labor as well as brain work, are equally "important" and equally meritorious.   The new society demands of its citizens the willingness to serve in any position when needed, and from its schools to prepare their pupils for service and not for personal advancement.

Combining work with study is now being advocated throughout the whole of China.   It is possible to see already a qualitative change.   One does not clear away the inheritance of traditional Confucian thinking in one day or even in one year.   A friend who worked in the educational field 50 years ago once told me how impossible it was for his students to take off any clothing while working hard to plant trees in their forestry school.   Even after Liberation, for a long time students would try to keep looking like correctly dressed students when they worked. Even by the way they handled their tools it was easy to see that they were not workers. In the summer of 1966, in the first stages of the Cultural Revolution, out in a Peking park with a friend, we came across one school digging an irrigation ditch to carry water to newly planted trees. They were of upper primary or lower middle school grade. The boys had their shirts off, looked like workers, worked like workers, and evidently wanted to be that way. They now handled their tools expertly, throwing the weight of their shoulders on the point of the shovel, and they obviously enjoyed the sunbath as they worked. The teacher, the administrator, the professional man of the future will have learnt through work to feel as the mass of the people feel.

The part-work, part-study school faces another challenge, namely to create more technical workers and progressive farmers who will be free of the old tabus, who will be able to apply theory and who will be able to meet new situations, new machines, newer methods with clear minds and able hands. Who will not be scared of hard work, tough living conditions or bitter struggle. The speed with which better ways are now being evolved will demand much from the youth which now steps in to continue the revolution in China. It is not going back to Confucius. It is, in the spirit of the teachings of Mao Tsetung, looking forward into and preparing for the brilliant future that can be theirs. The development of the part-work, part-study school in China will be observed with both sympathy and interest by all concerned with the basics of education for life in our world of tomorrow.

Chekiang University

Some years passed. In 1969 I spent an afternoon in Chekiang University. The chairman of the Revolutionary Committee there was an old professor, and with him were both lecturers and students. The chairman outlined the five stages of the Cultural Revolution as they affected the university with its body of 8,000 students. A technical university, it has five faculties, and its Revolutionary Committee was finally set up in April 1968 after quite a period of struggle between two of the rebel groups. In the past two years, horizons have widened. The students have gone from a beautiful university campus back into factories and communes, taking part in work and study, realising better where their future lies, and naturally criticising the defects of an educational policy that had divorced them from the life and realities of China. "We stay so long at school, study and memorise, trying to pass examinations but getting farther and farther away from the daily life and toil of the people with whom our future should be bound up. We come out shortsighted and often with a student's stoop, the white hairs of worry already showing in our hair — little old men," one said.

"Three years is enough for what we need — maybe only two and a half," said another.

"What has happened to all that stuff I learnt at middle school? I have forgotten most of it already!" said a third.

A lecturer said, "Of one whole class we sent to the hinterland frontier to work, no one stayed there. They all ran back!"

Another said, "I worked and worked. Slept four hours only. Studied, studied, then studied more. But it was all unrelated to the needs of the people. It was simply related to passing well, to social status, and in helping to enlarge the group of privileged people, who in turn would bring up children who would demand more privilege, more 'freedom' at the expense of working people. Then we would be like the USSR after 50 years. Our people would still be poor and backward, for they would have to support us in big cities."

A young student said, "When I went home after being a while in the university, I was shocked at how dirty the village was. In so short a time I had grown apart from it, and was already beginning to look down on it. Chairman Mao has made it plain as to what our duty is in serving the people. How can we serve them if we are conditioned to look down on them? How many of us have been thinking of better villages, how best to help them with constructive change? Learning mechanical engineering from books is one thing. But to see a machine pulled down and made to work again teaches in a clear, concise way. We go to school at seven years of age. Then, at 25 we emerge and go out to work, having to start learning from the practical beginnings. We were not taught the necessity of class struggle at school, for in actuality we were becoming part of a new privileged class. After we have been through all the ritual of the memorising grind, all that is creative in us is flattened, battered out. . . How, then, can we meet the needs of a changing world, catch up with the most highly industrialised countries? We must be able to create, able to analyse. Education in China from time immemorial has been in the hands of the exploiting class, stressing the individual rather than the collective. So much in the old textbooks we studied was already out of date. If we have the tools of learning and the freedom of spirit that does not inhibit our creativeness, then we can really serve the people."

From these and similar ideas the students brought up as the afternoon wore on, it was evident that all felt the need for change, but exactly how to go about it, how to bring practice and theory together to enable them all to live up to their potential and give leadership was still in the experimental stage. They were all sure however, that working in the spirit of determination and sacrifice, they would help to build a new educational system based on Mao Tsetung Thought.

Schools in Wushan

My main reason for coming to Wushan Commune in 1969 was not so much to look at its economic improvement, but rather to see for myself the results it has gained in its efforts to put new educational theories into working practice. I talked with four former poor peasant teachers, a regular professional teacher who had come to a brigade primary school, the commune cadre in charge of educational affairs, and a middle-school boy of 13.

All of these, except the middle-school boy, were mainly concerned with primary education. There are two commune-run middle schools, with 42 regular teachers. The commune primary schools have 220 teachers. Their students have gone up in numbers from 880 in 1966 to 2,100 now. The chief reason for this has been that the peasants now realise that education will not drain their children away from home to the cities, that the education given will help everyone in the struggle for living and that now, also, education is necessary for a revolutionary. The principle of bringing in older poor peasants as "barefoot" teachers and to have the control of the schools vested in the brigades, has also helped to make the schools more popular with the commune members.

Chen Ching-teh, a middle-aged former poor peasant of Tumen Brigade, was the first to tell me about himself and his work. Quite a few commune members here are from families who have been refugees from Honan province, mostly from the once famine-stricken counties of Lushan or Kunghsien. They managed when they came to make a sort of living growing vegetables on patches of waste hillside land, and somehow bring up their children. When he was nine, Chen Ching-teh, who was from one of these families, was given to a landlord to be a buffalo herd. He had never been inside a school until he came to teach in one. But he knew as did others who were determined to follow the Mao Tsetung line that, out of seven brigade schools in the vicinity, six had been in the hands of people who came from the families of rich peasants or landlords, and that Liu Shao-chi ideas were prevalent in all of them. What, he argued, was the use of schools if they did not bring the main issues to the understanding of the pupils? Do we educate for the revolution or do we set out to produce ambitious place seekers? So he felt it important not to refuse the invitation to come at times and teach about class struggle to the new generation which needs to know about it as they join in the battle of life.

Li Sheng-fen is a poor peasant from the hilly section of the commune, his brigade having the same name as that of the commune, "Wushan". He talked a while on the old idea prevalent amongst poor peasants that they and schools had nothing in common. "Best to keep clear of them. How can we with hands stinking of compost possibly go to school? But then, especially in this stage we are forced to ask ourselves, are our schools going the Marxist-Leninist way? Are we watching our children to see on what principle they stand? Are we at one with the teachers, helping them with their problems of livelihood and understanding? Then too, what can poor peasants do to teach what they know so well? How can we in a practical way help the work of the teachers, keep close to them, encourage them so that they go along with their task with a quiet mind? As ever the questions rise, what do we work for, do we have unity of purpose, and what is our plan for living? Then what do we require of teachers? We first want to be sure that they follow Mao Tsetung Thought. That they are practical and not scared of hard labor. We also want them to have a good style of work, carrying the people along with them. Have they cleared their minds of old ideas and are they ready to go the people's way? Can they help to produce the new educational material needed for the new age? When we say prepare against war and against natural disasters, what does this entail in teaching? Now our poor peasants meet with teachers three times a month, on the 1st, the 11th and the 21st, so that ideas can be exchanged. Poor peasants themselves take classes twice a week. In our brigade there are eight of us who do this work, so that we are able to do our part in succession, not boring the students with too much reiteration."

The next I spoke with was the regular teacher who had come to take charge of the Tumen school. She was a woman named Wu Ai-tze, aged 31, a graduate of Huchow Normal College. She had felt that she was sacrificing a lot to go back to the village. Coming back to a brigade school is different from being a secure salaried staff member of a city school. The brigade may have no proper school buildings, and her income comes only on workpoints like that of any other commune member. She is married and has three little children, one of whom, the smallest, is a cripple, unable to walk. Her husband is a middle-school teacher in the city and could not come with her. However, she bravely made the step, never dreaming how good things would be for her in her new job. The first inkling came when she was met at the Tumen jetty, the brigade school youngsters with drums, cymbals and banners to escort her to her new home. And when the brigade fell to and cleared a piece of waste land of ancient graves, building a bright new school on it, as well as two light, airy rooms for herself and her family. People took a positive delight in bringing things to her, so her place was furnished in no time with simple but useful peasant furniture and kitchen equipment. Water and fuel were never a problem. Someone always brought them in. What folk had, they shared with her. Never had she felt so much a part of the community around her or had so full a life.

At the first Spring Festival she lived in the village, she and her family were invited to the home of Chen Ching-teh, the former poor peasant teacher. Her husband had come to spend the holiday with her, so that the family was five in all. They rather expected that their host would put on a bit of a spread for them, but when dinner was brought in it was found to be bran cakes and bitter vegetables, in memory of the other days when such was the best food a poor peasant could have at that time of rejoicing. The two youngest children did not like it, but their eldest and both parents saw the point, and took the lesson in the good spirit with which it was given. After the meal, all went to the school and joined in mass building work. An unusual Lunar New Year's day, but a meaningful one. She had many stories of personal sacrifice members had made to help both her and the school, all of which obviously touched her a great deal, for she wiped an emotional tear or two from her eyes as she told about them. "One gets the feeling here," she said, "that we are on the first steps of a long march to world revolution, when we shall be really free of the threat of imperialism and all the deviltry of the old society."

Cheng Tien-ping, a grey-headed man from Hungshan Brigade, took up the story. "Our children were quite badly poisoned by the Liu Shao-chi line in education. They looked upon going to school as a kind of a race. The clever memorisers who won would go on to middle schools and then to colleges. We asked the local school to train us some production team bookkeepers. But the youngsters did not want to go back to production teams. They wanted to escape from country life. They were struggling for an education which would enable them to enter a different world from that of their parents. They did not believe that we could make a better world right here. They did not include service to ordinary working people in their scheme of living. Rather did they think it better to wear pretty clothes and strut around and be important.

That they knew and cared little for the work of peasants was shown in our locality when a number of school boys started playing with the irrigation system and ruined some crops with flooding. They felt that they should be allowed to do anything they liked if it amused them. They had grown quite apart from their own people, and did not want to even understand farm technique. Even down to thinking that it was beneath them to understand such. Now we want our children to do good things, but not to boast and be conceited about achievements. We want them to help the old people in the brigade simply and naturally, as a thing they ought to be doing, cutting fuel for them, carrying in water. We want them to be vigilant politically and not allow abuses to creep into our life. To maintain a good class attitude. One of our boys was going to school the other day when he saw the line leading to the brigade loud-speaker had fallen and had broken. Knowing that if this was not fixed, people would not get the news, he went back to the brigade office and asked for someone to come and help him fix it properly. This made him late for school. The teacher criticised him for not coming on time, but he did not speak back. It was only when other boys spoke up and told what had happened that the teacher said, 'I was wrong. I should have investigated the thing better before scolding you.' People speak about these things at home, and all take lessons from them. In our brigade we too have built a new tiled-roof school. We had but 49 pupils in it before the Cultural Revolution. Now we have 147. Today no youngster thinks that being a student absolves him from working. Teachers and students all work together on collective tasks, and school holidays are geared to the busy seasons when there is always a great deal for everyone to do."

Fang Sze-ying is a first year pupil in middle school. Just 13, he is a sturdy chunk of a boy, friendly and natural. He is a good speaker, direct and unaffected. He was proud that he was a Red Guard now. He commented on the vast difference between the two lines, and criticised the old education with its many stories of ancient heroes, most of which were designed to make intellectuals feel as though they were a cut above ordinary people. "We got tired of hearing that old story about Ssuma

Kwang breaking the jar of water to save the boy inside. It is better to hear about the revolutionary heroes of our today," he said. In his own family there was no one who could read or write. Once he and his family thought that things like war and peace were all something very distant and had nothing much to do with them. Now he has realised that such things are a part of life and have to be met by everyone. "Today, if war does come," he declared, "we young people will fight along with our Liberation Army. When we criticise the Liu Shao-chi line, we must know very clearly what it is, where it would lead us. Now it is good that former poor peasants come to our school to tell us more of class struggle. We all go to work in the fields for half a day regularly every week, and also take part in mass work during the busy seasons."

The commune cadre in charge of education mentioned that commune teachers were actually better off than they were on salaried posts before. He said that teachers were integrated with their pupils and their pupils' families as never before and that new methods were being worked out as new situations were faced. He said in summary, "The main object, an object which is being achieved, is no less than a new education for a new countryside, a countryside that has gigantic tasks to face."

I spent an afternoon going around the fields that were being harvested. The middle-school teachers and students were working hard. One group of teachers and peasants worked cheerfully together at a rice-threshing machine. The primary students' "Little Red Soldiers" force had planted its spears alongside their work place and were reaping with a practised hand. Teacher Wu Ai-tze was working along with a class, hoe in hand, on another field being prepared for late autumn planting. She came over to the school with me where only the infant classroom was in use, other classes being out in the fields. Two of her children, the crippled little one and a sister two years older, were sitting together in one seat. The class sang us some songs with great gusto, and we went off with some of their spirit and warmth. With considerable pride the teacher showed me her two nice rooms, and then I went visiting some of the ex-poor peasant homes together with her and others. They were of people who either taught or else helped with the running of the school — now their very own school, a part of their community in a new way. So did one marvel at the way that so much has now come right down into the basis of society as a result of the application of Mao Tsetung Thought. Everyone is learning, and a new appreciation of what change can bring is coming home to all as new results are obtained. Certainly no one is going to meekly submit to any reversal to old conditions. For it is no longer the same countryside, and the people are not the same.

A Shanghai Primary School, 1970

In the eastern industrial area of Shanghai I paid a visit to a famous primary school in Szeping Road. In the pre-Liberation period it was called Pingming School, was privately operated and had 200 pupils in six classes. Naturally enough, it grew swiftly after Liberation. In 1965 a new, modern building of three floors was erected, where 81 teachers now teach 2,350 children organised into 40 classes. Seeking tasks on communes and in industry, the school gives practical as well as scholastic training.

The leader of the Revolutionary Committee told how, before the Cultural Revolution, the teachers were mainly concerned with examinations, marks, memorisation, and so on. Actually what they were doing, although they did not realise it, was educating youth away from their class, holding out all kinds of material incentives in the shape of honors, awards, degrees for the successful, and never caring what the child's thinking was, how to prepare him to better serve the people, or carry on the revolution. To give but one, and almost unbelievable, instance of attitudes. There were two very poor illiterate people, a man and wife who had married quite late in life, people of the kind the revolution had been fought for. They had a son, and when he was nine they brought him to the school asking for admittance. He was not well dressed, and his parents did not know how to speak nicely, but they wanted him to have some education. He was refused admittance with the excuse that rolls were full, but for seven years afterwards, once each year when new students were being taken, the old couple brought him and each year they were again refused. By the time of the Cultural Revolution the boy was already 16. The rebel group in charge of the school immediately took him in, arranged for special teaching, and the lad's progress has been so fast that he is already in the fourth class. The capitalist roader headmaster of earlier days did not like poor, what he considered dirty, badly clothed pupils. The new stage taking the Mao Tsetung line welcomes such pupils with both hands.

On the school committee I met were some of the teachers led by the young chairman of the Revolutionary Committee, a worker representative from factories around, several old retired workers of the locality, who had had a lifetime's experience in work — a white-bearded man of 76, another of 63, and a retired woman worker. There were also two local housewives and four school pupils. They all take an active part in school life, and have regular meetings. The whole school was organised in the way of the People's Liberation Army, and can turn out in quick time when necessary. The last directive from Chairman Mao came late one night. Without being told, children of the propaganda group jumped up from bed, dressed, assembled from lanes around and were marching with drums and cymbals in a very short time. We ourselves had an experience of how swiftly the school can assemble when we went out on to the playground to see a "prepare against war" practice. The whistle sounded, and suddenly the dust began to fly and there, suddenly drawn up in correct ranks, was the whole school, some of the older classes with wooden painted spears and red tassels, others with wooden guns, tree leaves as camouflage around heads. An air raid siren sounded, and everyone was flat on the ground as imaginary bombs fell. Then the call to say that planes were in range, and everyone fell into groups aiming anti-aircraft fire at attackers. Other manoeuvres were done very realistically. Wriggling under obstacles, jumping over hurdles. Imaginary wounded were being given first aid and carried off the field, then all kinds of mass-drill movements followed.

After we had seen all of this, we went back into the school, where the propaganda corps put on items for us which were fresh and full of spirit. In one of them the dancers wore the red turbans of Taiping fighters of the last century. One could not help thinking back to old days at Yenan, for here was the spirit of Yenan so much alive again, right down to the youngsters with spears and the good patched clothes of working people.

Chenhsien Primary School in Nanking, 1970

The Chenhsien primary school is an ordinary Nanking city school with four kindergartens and 22 primary classes, 1,100 pupils in all. There is a staff of 50, and it was set up in 1957. A workers' propaganda team lends assistance in school affairs and has its representative on the school's Revolutionary Committee. Buildings are modern, and the playground large. Five subjects are taught. Mao Tsetung Thought, socialist culture, military and physical training, revolutionary art and literature, and lastly labor. Socialist culture comprises Chinese language, arithmetic including the use of the abacus, a foreign language, geography and history. Before the higher grades finish school, they must have put in time amounting to one year in either industry or agriculture. Lower grades must spend 10 percent of their time on this. Pupils are taught to follow the good points of a soldier in the PLA for they, too, have their Little Red Soldiers organisation which today replaces that of the Young Pioneers. Qualifications are: to be good in political ideology, good at carrying on the revolution in education, good in mutual aid and forging unity, good in the three rules of discipline and eight points of conduct of the PLA, and good in daily life. A good deal of practical political education is gained by excursions to the countryside, helping with harvesting and in other busy seasons. Sitting in at commune meetings they learn much of the class struggle in a down-to-earth way. The fundamental problems of purpose in life, whom to serve, can then be brought forward in a living way. There are six classes a day, each class lasting 45 minutes. If a pupil cannot catch up, he or she can stay in the class for another year.

We went around the classrooms, fascinated by the youngsters at their studies. The teachers let the pupils participate by calling them up to take over the class lesson. In the kindergarten classes, old folk stories such as those about Br'er Rabbit and the like have given place to those about modern heroes in struggle, those who have worked and sacrificed for the people. The ideology of the teaching staff has undergone a great remoulding in these years, and a much better understanding now exists of the place of education in the life of working people. Education always serves a class, and in China that class is the working class.

After we had gone the rounds, the school propaganda group of pupils staged a lively concert for us, which we all enjoyed. The youngsters put their whole heart and soul into the performance, which speeded ahead with laughter and melody — the orchestra of Chinese violins ("er hu"), guitars, flutes and drum music being remarkably effective.

Nanking Engineering College

In the afternoon of the same day we went out to a construction site for blocks of flats, where students of Nanking Engineering College were doing the building themselves. They had drawn up the plans and were now carrying them through. College lecturers and staff who welcomed us were dressed in the same overalls as the workers. They showed us a new style hollow brick they had devised. Two bricks do the work of three, and can take a heavier load. Students, teachers and ordinary workers helping out with the job were indistinguishable. All were builders together. After watching work swinging along apace, we went to the college itself, which has 2,500 students. Some have entered in the usual old way through examinations, but now a growing number come in after having been workers in the field of construction, picked because of their political understanding and practical ability. We spoke to some who had been workers for 15 years. Consequently there are now a number of older men learning. Ages, one learnt, ranged from 22 to 43 in the student body. Lecturers have had to alter their style of teaching. Be more direct, able to accept criticism as it comes, and learn from the practical experience of the students as they all advance together. Many of the new students have had but a primary education; only some have gone through middle school. Yet, here they were over their drawing boards producing complicated plans for new buildings most efficiently. "When we started," a lecturer confessed, "the new students sat glumly and simply said they did not understand me. Then they asked me questions I could not answer. The more tense I became, the more difficult it was. Then I asked some who had understood what I had said to explain it to the others. The others saw the point immediately. After that I re-shaped my teaching methods. Same content, but given in practical terms as used by workers. I now enjoy teaching, and do so with ease."

Those of the student body who have gone through regular schooling in the old way, are a different set now. They have been toughened up by work in mine, factory and commune, and now return to their classrooms with new ideas and great vigor.

Sun Mei-kun, a lecturer in mathematics, in talking about his experiences in the new type of education, dubbed himself a "typical three-door cadre" meaning that he had gone out of the home door to school, then from school through the door of an organisation, without a period of practical training in between. He did not think that he had been sufficiently remoulded yet, but he was trying hard and learning a lot from his students. He had once loved to fill the blackboard with formulas which were hard for anyone to understand. Now with the new look he tried to adapt his teaching material so that it could be easily understood, rather than showing off his own brilliance. He spoke appreciatively of the way physical labor had helped him to re-evaluate things, and to see workers in a new light. At first, the lecturers were inclined to sneer and say that worker students had so little education that nobody else but they themselves were to blame for their slow progress. But the real trouble was that the lecturer was liable to "talk down" to his new students, not see things from their point of view. Yes, he had tried to remedy the situation. Once he compiled a whole lecture, had it printed and distributed amongst the workers in class. He thought it clear, concise, with good working plans attached, and that the workers would be very happy with the effort taken, would praise him and ask for more like this. But actually, they were not at all satisfied, and gave him a lot of criticism that left him with a red face and feeling unhappy. The upshot was that lecturers had many meetings with the worker group, who did not apologise for their lack of understanding one whit. Their criticism in the main was very simple, surely they had not been taught as old intellectuals had been, for the old educational system had barred them, but if a thing was said plainly enough, there was no problem of understanding. "So we rewrote the lecture with their assistance and, following it, many others so that there was in the end general satisfaction," Sun Mei-kun said.

"We were once held down by force," said the workers. "What force was it? This is a thing we must all understand together." Others spoke in somewhat the same vein. A woman lecturer in structural design caused a good many laughs when she described her experiences. Yes, she had found that there was a class line in architectural design too, but had not seen it until the workers she taught pointed it out. She no longer prepares her lectures behind closed doors. Instead, she goes to the construction site and discusses various points with workers there, no longer relying entirely on books. Workers encouraged her, asking her to keep on with her struggle as they needed her, and that her lectures were just what they wanted. So with all of this she took heart. She now realises that, before, she had pretended to know things that she did not really know, but now this whole period has been a bright new one of learning and teaching together, she feels, on the solid basis of Mao Tsetung Thought.

The New School Emerges

Many of Peking's primary and middle schools are now running little factories, so as to put into action Mao Tsetung's thinking of coupling theory and practice in education. From April to the middle of July 1970, over 160 middle and 90 primary schools in the city had set up industrial work. Amongst the things produced are machinery, hardware, textiles, electronic equipment and optical instruments. There are, too, printing, carpentry and handicraft shops. Reports from other cities show that in middle schools new insecticides, transistors, and many other products have been turned out. In all, this change in education that now takes shape so rapidly is of immense significance to opening out young minds, and thus making for scientific development as it sweeps across the land.

It was a wet afternoon in September 1970 when I went to visit one of the Peking middle schools. It was Middle School No. 31, situated in buildings that were once used by Chungteh School, an English Christian mission school of pre-Liberation days. It now has 1,500 students, and a staff of 138. There are 30 forms.

Before the Cultural Revolution, there was a lower and upper middle school, each giving a three-year course. Now there is a straight four-year course for everyone. Instead of 33 classes a week there are now 24. The 11 subjects now taught are politics, mathematics, literature, a foreign language, physics, chemistry, geography, history, basic agriculture, physical training and revolutionary culture. Each year during the busy seasons, students go for one month to a commune production brigade in Shunyi county, ten kilometres outside the city. Each student spends another month in the school factory, and two weeks on military training in addition to classroom work each year. The school factory works in two four-hour shifts, one in the morning, one in the afternoon, and each student works only one shift.

Sitting in with us in the discussion at the school were members of the school Revolutionary Committee, including two Red Guard students. One of these latter, in explaining the difference between the present education and the past, said, "Before, we did study, but we did not apply. Then only the staff took part in political activity. Now it is no longer just them, but students and staff together. Our aim is to become more able to serve the people, and to carry through Chairman Mao's ideas about education."

An older teacher in explaining the present said, "People, now that they see the new way and how well it works, are amazed at the blindness and obstinacy with which the old road was so closely followed before. Now, since the new system has been working, over 200 students have graduated from the school, going to various factories, communes, border regions; some join the PLA. All are much better equipped, politically and practically, for the tasks which face them. After they have become workers, farmers or soldiers, those who study and work well will be selected to take university courses, but in front of all will lie a revolutionary life, with much scope for service to the people."

We went through the various workrooms of the school factory, amazed at what has been done. Taking off our shoes and putting on slippers before entering one set of workrooms, we found students working with delicate parts under microscopes, operating electrically controlled small furnaces, in well-lit, airy rooms. They were making parts for transistors. In another workroom the students were making printed circuits. The camera they were using was a home-made one for which they had simply bought the lens — a second hand one — for 30 yuan, making the rest of the camera from wood in their own shop. Mounted on a little trolley line, it works very well. In the machine shops the machine tools were cast-offs from modernised factories, but with some adaption they do their task quite efficiently. Besides the transistor parts, the school also makes two parts for the Peking two-ton delivery truck, now a common sight on the streets as well as being exported to some half dozen foreign countries. The parts are the oil line from the oil pump, and the wiring for the electrical distribution system. The different wires are covered in different colored plastic. Models and blueprints are on the walls, while each work bench where the wires are bound together and connections added has the diagram done in the specific colors of the wires. Students are proud of an innovation they have made for soldering on the U-connection. It does the job better than the soldering iron, with less risk of damaging the plastic of the wire. Whatever the number of trucks a year the parent factory produces, the students say they can produce the same number of wiring systems ready for installation. They are thrilled to know that some of their work goes to foreign countries, giving them a practical hand in the promotion of proletarian internationalism. Whenever they see a Peking two-ton delivery truck running down the street they look at it and feel, "some of our work is in that!" Which means a lot to all.

Many of the staff of the school also take part in factory work. Forty-eight of them, to be exact. "See him? He teaches history. That one? A Chinese language teacher," and so on, they said as we went around the shops. Working together with the students bridges a great gap, and there are also always staff members working with students out on the fields of the commune production brigades.

When students first started going to the commune, they had no knowledge of the countryside at all. Patiently commune members showed them which were the weeds in the cornfields, and which were the corn shoots. Yet imagine the chagrin at the end of the first period of work when it was found that corn shoots had been pulled up in many places, and weeds left. Patiently again, the commune members got the students together and showed them once more, explaining how every corn shoot pulled up meant the loss of one jin of grain to the commune, and what one jin of grain meant in the struggle for livelihood. Now, the whole of Middle School No. 31 knows the various crops as well as their weed enemies; knows how crops are grown, what has to be done with fertiliser and working the ground, seed selection, irrigation and pest control, before a harvest is gained. Then, back in schoolroom classes, problems in arithmetic and other subjects can be related to both politics and production. How much wheat, how many tons of sweet potatoes, bushels of peanuts, winter vegetables does a mou of this land produce as compared with a mou of land with less compost, and less irrigation. Comparisons in production figures before and after Liberation. The difference between rice production on some low-lying marshy land, and the production it gained before rice was introduced four years ago. In physics classroom work also, the operation of the more complicated factory machines is explained, so that each and every one understands how they work.

Actually, factory work was started in the school during the Leap Forward of 1958-59. Then came the Liu Shao-chi line, very much against Chairman Mao's thinking on education. "A school is a school. A factory is a factory. You cannot mix them," said the followers of Liu. So, in consequence, most schools halted their industrial work, though No. 31 kept its factory on in embryo all the way through until the Cultural Revolution, when work was enlarged.

"Since Marx, the educational problem has not really been solved," the chairman of the Revolutionary Committee said. "The ideas of Soviet revisionist educators we reject completely. We must build an educational system based on the needs of our people. The old student, through the way he was educated, was liable to leave the correct road forward, to leave production, and leave the people. Now our school propaganda group, with its songs and musical instruments, knows better what to propagate. Each and every member of it has already dovetailed much theory with practice. In the chemistry textbooks we used to have was a picture of a foreign scientist of great fame who got the Nobel Prize worth so much, and so on. We do not want to hold such a person up as an example to students. To worship those who strive after money, profit and credit for themselves. Now that education is in the hands of working people, what do we do with this great power? Certainly we will not use it to educate for landlords or revisionists!"

Work on the industrial side of the school is made easier because of its connection with outside industry. There is no problem of distribution or of looking for raw material. Factory technicians come in to teach the process and help to get things started. Some of the workrooms are already too small, and rebuilding will be necessary before long. Students all live in the locality and come to class each day. When they go to work on the commune they live in peasant homes, each group marching out there carrying its own bedding, Army style. It is certainly a very different school from the one which existed before the Cultural Revolution, and one felt after seeing it that here was truly a beginning of the worker, farmer and soldier school of the future.

Labor University at Hsinchien, Nanchang, Kiangsi, 1970

In Nanchang I went to see the Communist Labor University in Hsin-chien county. In order to get there one had to cross the Kan river bridge to the west of the city portion of the municipality. This university, an institution with 5,000 students, is the centre for the whole network of the Labor University of Kiangsi, branches of which have been set up on waste land or in distant forested valleys. Students come from every county in the province, and are of poor or middle peasant origin. They may be graduates of middle or primary school, or even illiterate, and their age varies from the earliest 'teens to the late twenties. The youngest I met told me he was 14. But the majority appeared to be in their late 'teens or early twenties. They study intensively for a year in six subjects that are of the greatest use to them, the first, of course, being politics and the remainder technical. They have recovered a large area of waste ground in the vicinity on which they raise enough grain for themselves and even a surplus to give to the state. They have piggeries and orange groves, pear orchards and vineyards. But what they are perhaps most proud of at the moment is their industrial side, in which students under worker leadership have turned out 15 large-sized jeeps during the past year and have now made all preparations to produce 150 this year (1970). After that, they say, they hope to be really able to expand. We went through classrooms, listening a while to one lecture on cotton raising, another on diseases in rice, and yet one more on politics. Quite a number of the students were working on digging a new irrigation canal, working every bit as well as do the peasants in the counties they have come from. The school course is a concentrated one, there being none of the old-time regular school holidays. The spirit is evidently quite high, with all out to gain everything possible from this opportunity of learning together.

Peking University in November 1970

It was a calm, cool autumn day, with the leaves turning gold in the beautiful campus of Peking University. A group of us were meeting in what was once the home of the former president of Yenching University, now amalgamated with "Pei Da" as Peking University is called. The purpose of the visit was to catch up with what is being done now in the university, after four years of the storm of the Cultural Revolution. We had been to visit at various stages of the Cultural Revolution, so knew something of what these entailed, from the first poster to the downfall of the Lu Ping administration, and the rise of the rebel groups.

The quiet voice of the narrator of events told how before Liberation the university was used by the reaction to educate their willing slaves, and was out to make a bridgehead to suppress the revolution. How progressive students and staff had started to rebel, and how Mao Tsetung had come to the university in 1918 and 1919, contacting Teng Chung-hsia and other progressives, adding to the student ferment that led to the May 4th Movement with its anti-imperialist slogans, and its burning down of the house of the traitor official, Tsao Ju-lin. Then how, through all subsequent years until Liberation, its rebels remained a force to be reckoned with. Not only did many take part in the Wars of Resistance and Liberation, but also in the Korean War of the early 'fifties. Students also went to the provinces during Land Reform. All this was the prelude to the great change inaugurated by the Cultural Revolution which led to the complete smashing of the old educational structure. The students however formed two separate groups and, hoodwinked by bourgeois factionalism, for a time lost a clear idea of who was friend and who enemy, and spent their time attacking each other, both verbally and physically, instead of going on with their real task of struggle, criticism and transformation.

This situation was corrected by the arrival on August 19th 1969, of a worker propaganda team which, with the team of the PLA, now brought the opposing forces together. After some 50 good talks together, the students could see how little they could do by themselves, how important it was to have practical, down-to-earth workers helping them. Now the process of struggle, criticism and transformation could go ahead easily. On September 27th 1969, the new Revolutionary Committee was set up with 39 members, seven from the PLA, six from the workers' team, nine of teachers, six revolutionary cadres, seven of students, three of workers in the university factory, and lastly one of the dependents of the university staff and workers. In shaping the new educational road, there was already the experience of an adjoining university, that of Tsinghua, which had already taken the first steps. But the educational line of Mao Tsetung Thought was clear enough, arousing teachers and students to mass criticism of the old feudal and bourgeois system, and to an understanding that now all must serve proletarian politics, setting out to advance morally, mentally and physically to become workers in a developed culture, training successors to the revolutionary cause. How the university should become an outpost for the Mao Tsetung revolutionary line against imperialism and revisionism, and bourgeois culture. How students should be inculcated with loyalty to the revolutionary line of Mao Tsetung and struggle to uphold it, ever serving the people wholeheartedly. With the leadership of the working class, with practical work on both factory and farm, and with a student body that have come up from the "doers" rather than from the pure "talkers".

It is an exciting change, in which revolutionary staff join in with enthusiasm. Feng Yu-lan, a well-known professor, now over 70, does not want to retire. He feels he has grown in understanding and wants to keep abreast. The staff now rotates, one third being on the school May 7th farm, becoming tempered in work, one third in factories and communes, and one third on the job teaching. This entails a larger staff than formerly, a need which has been met by the taking on of some 300 old students. In June and July 1970, the first batches of new students began to come in, replacing the 8,000 old ones who went out to work. At present they number 2,667, all being workers, peasants or soldiers with practical experience. Twenty-nine percent are women; 21 years is the average age, most being activists in the study of Mao Tsetung Thought; 90 percent coming from the working people. The steps to gain enrolment are for students to voluntarily ask for it, then to gain the recommendation of the masses in the places where they have come from, with the leadership of the local organ of power agreeing, and then sending the application on to university leaders, who will re-examine it and make the final decision. Examinations are out.

The university now reaches out into society in a new way. Society itself becomes a factory. Students and staff go out to help in running classes in factories, hospitals and schools. In August-September 1970 they set up a study group in the Peking Knitwear Factory, studying "On Contradiction". More than 200 attended, from old workers in their forties and fifties, down to a 12-year-old Red Guard. When the university folk find someone who has an outstanding grasp of problems, he or she is invited to the university to give a lecture there.

Today in the university there are 18 departments on the literary side, including those for philosophy, Chinese literature, politics, history, international politics, Eastern languages, Western languages, library training and law. On the science side there are eight departments including physics, radio, hygiene, geology, geography, biology, mathematics and mechanics.

The working people, from whom 90 percent of the new student body is drawn, are from the families of former poor or lower-middle peasants. Only 10 percent of the places are reserved for the children of cadres who, however, must have shown in a period of physical labor in factory or farm, the same as the others, that they follow Mao Tsetung Thought wholeheartedly.

We went to one of the factories operated by the university. It is one that turns out pharmaceuticals by quite a complicated process. The students get a great deal of satisfaction from being able to get good results. On the floor of one of the factory shops a chemistry class was sitting around in a circle on little stools, while a teacher explained the chemical equations used in the process. All eyes were on the blackboard and on him, none giving so much as a glance at the passing visitors.

On the literary side, the young students who go out to factories and communes now feel that they have plenty to write about. More material than they can use, actually. Now, the more all go the road of revolution in education the more preposterous does the old system seem. The kind of classroom education that set out to solve everything but actually very often solved nothing, only helping to produce minds like tape recorders which at examination time would scoop all the prizes, yet really understood so little. Workers coming into the picture make a lot of difference. An article written in the old days using 15,000 words is much improved, workers say, when it is cut down to 3,000 written in direct, easily understandable language. The college course is now cut to two years, and then graduates go back to the organisations they have come from, whether commune or factory, unless they are needed elsewhere. In teaching method, the discussion form is now widely used and the stress laid on giving a basis for self-education that will go on after the student graduates. There will no longer be one-sided emphasis on academic achievement or high technique which have to do with individual advancement, but more on an all-round development which enables the trainee to serve the people better in line with China's socialist development. The school too, is a factory, they say. Its task is to produce the kind of people who can fit into a swiftly evolving society. It was stressed, however, that present developments are experimental, and that there will be many changes as they are needed and as the situation develops.

One of the old professors, Chu Teh-hsi, told how his 20 years of teaching experience had amply demonstrated that the past system was divorced from practice. Now, since the storm of the Cultural Revolution and the great mixing that has taken place, he has come to a new realisation of the needs of working people. He spoke of the need for constant study, constant learning from which no one was absolved.

Canton Deaf-Mute School in 1970

We went some 15 kilometres outside Canton (Kwangchow), and drew up at a modern school building. It was a deaf-mute school, originally planned for 500 pupils and a 10-year course. Now the stress is laid on getting the deaf and mute children to speak and hear when possible, and then on getting them out into society to mix normally with other people. Now too, the acupuncture methods used are also common in the rural counties around Canton, so that treatment can be given there, and there is not the same need to bring a large group together. At present there are only 300 in the school, and these will graduate when they gain speaking and hearing ability, and pass into ordinary schools. We found the teachers and the PLA medical team intensely interested in their work and full of optimism about the results they were gaining.

In the Cultural Revolution the deaf-mute students here divided into groups and struggled against each other, as happened in other schools. Then in came unity, and with it the medical team of the PLA. Cures began to be effected with the new-type acupuncture treatment, amongst those whose hearing was not permanently impaired. They were taught to speak and, indeed, went out in concert teams and gave many performances. As in all schools, only the common language is taught, so that the cured child often goes home and criticises the family for being able to talk only in the Cantonese dialect. As far as is possible, youngsters are not sent out to work in factories with handicapped people, but rather to those where normality is the rule. Some learn lip-reading but the main help comes from the acupuncture course and, later, speech training. The acupuncture especially assists the majority of the deaf-mutes, whose disability has come through such childhood illnesses as measles or polio. The needling is not painless, and sometimes youngsters complain that it is hard to open their mouths and eat normally for a time. But all encourage each other to keep on with the treatment, especially as good results begin to come. The idea that the youngster must struggle to help himself and not give in to his disability is always kept to the front. Medical workers who give the acupuncture treatment all have tried the needling on themselves first. It is a fighting process. When hearing first comes, just what do all those sounds mean? Teachers have to speak slowly and in a high voice, using the sign language at times as an assistance to understanding. But results are being gained, and more and more graduates are going out into the world to fight their battles there.

The school concert group put on several items for us, singing and dancing. Then they did some little one-act plays. One about a boy who was reluctant to be needled, scared of the pain. Another about a doctor of the other day who, with a great show of superiority, would simply tell the boy that his case was hopeless. We left as evening came in, with the strong impression of having been with a courageous and happy group.

Red Torch Primary School

Situated in an industrial area of Canton city, Red Torch Primary School is a modern, well-built facility with 1,500 pupils. The buildings were constructed in 1958. Before that time it was quite small, 400-500 pupils in all, classrooms being in converted dwelling houses.

We visited it in November 1970, first going to the office and sitting in front of well-scrubbed desk tops set in scrupulously clean and simple surroundings. The vice-chairman of the Revolutionary Committee gave us quite a long talk, describing how the present school differed from the previous one, how well the dangers of the Liu Shao-chi bourgeois line in education were understood now and avoided, how the emphasis now was not so much on strict order and discipline, or on the "Peking duck" type of education. (For those who might not understand this image, the Peking duck is force-fed, with ever additional food being pushed down its throat.) The main aim now is to give pupils good, new ideas, not just those of eating and dressing well, once discussed so much, but ideas of work and struggle, why we live, how we can serve the people. The school now sets out to change the pupil's world outlook radically and to bring it close to life. With the help of members of the working class and the PLA as well as from the families of school children, much has been done in this respect already. More still remains to be done. By going out into the rural communes to work with the people and by going to city factories, valuable lessons in class struggle have been learnt.

The PLA itself is a good model, with officers teaching soldiers, soldiers teaching officers, and soldiers teaching each other, all becoming political activists in Mao Tsetung Thought, keen on physical education and ever trying to bring theory into practice. One very big problem, the speaker felt, was how to continue to raise the political level of the teachers. The worker propaganda team members who come in from factories help a good deal with this, as does actual physical work.

In school, children are encouraged to mend broken furniture, both at school and at home. Cut each other's hair, mend clothing and set up physical culture groups. Some pupils form groups to go out and do public service, cleaning at the railway station, sweeping lanes, helping in people's homes where help is needed, and so on.

Some of the pupils who had joined our meeting gave their impressions. How good it was to march out to the Ershatou production brigade of Meipu Commune and work there. How many things they found out that were not in lesson books. Care of fish, how to feed animals, how peanuts and water chestnuts grow, and so many other things a city child does not have any knowledge of, but at Ershatou can be learnt through practice!

After listening to the children telling us their side of things, we went together to look over the various small workshops the school maintains, watching the youngsters managing tools and machines, some evidently with considerable understanding, others who went more slowly.

Back in the office after making a tour of the classrooms and listening in to the various subjects being taught, we were entertained by some of the pupils putting on vocal items for us. It is a seven-year school, the last two years corresponding to the junior middle course of the last period. Eight hundred of the 1,500 pupils are boys. There are 62 teachers and usually around 50 pupils in a class. Children do two weeks a term in the school workshops, half days only. Primary classes do one week a term at the Ershatou production brigade, and the middle school classes two weeks each term. There are two terms a year.

Middle School No. 32, Canton

Middle School No. 32 in Canton (Kwangchow) was the next school visited. When arriving, we were met by the vice-chairman of the Revolutionary Committee, an old teacher, and some boy and girl students. It is a school of over 4,000 students and 160 teachers, first set up in 1954 and greatly enlarged in 1958. In the Cultural Revolution, it was the first school in Canton to set up its three-way Revolutionary Committee. This was on February 20th 1968. From that time until November of the same year, studies were done outside the school, in communes and with the PLA. Then a branch school was set up in the countryside and a small factory established in the school for turning out chemicals and parts of electrical equipment. In this way it was possible to have class work, production and scientific experiment run together.

As things are at present, classroom studies take up 70 percent of the students' time, and practical work the remainder. The course is a four-year one, two years for lower middle school and two for the upper, replacing the old six-year course. Boys and girls are about the same in number here. The branch school is out in Huahsien county, has 30 mou of paddy and 70 of hill land, with three fish pond reservoirs.

In the chemical workshops the students work over material discarded from factories in the city, extracting valuable chemicals from it. Material that otherwise would have been dumped, making for a pollution hazard. They also make alcohol by distilling fruit waste.

We watched the students at play and then, too, at militia work, for military training is one of the school subjects, in line with the idea of preparation for any emergency. It was stressed, however, that what has been done so far is by no means considered perfect. Everything is more in the nature of experimentation, on the way to carry through Chairman Mao's directive for future education.

Tungfanghung May 7th School in Peking

After the first two years of the Cultural Revolution, it began to be seen that throughout China for many cadres, old and new, a general remoulding was necessary, so that all would clearly understand the correct way forward and, in line with Mao Tsetung Thought, thoroughly identify themselves with the people. In many organisations a more rational system of administration led to the possibility of sending cadres to other places where they were needed, a process which required much preparation. Those allocated to communes had to learn how to do manual work again. Chairman Mao said that a good way for cadres to remould themselves would be to work along with ordinary poor and lower-middle peasants, learning from them.

In consequence, 1969 saw the rapid spread of May 7th schools throughout the land. Most organisations have their own, usually situated on wasteland that can be reclaimed through work. In most of these places cadres have, under the guidance of local commune members, built their own housing and other facilities. All manual work is done by trainees whose families, in most instances, remain back in the cities with the cadres' usual salaries being paid them, so that no financial hardship is entailed.

It was a cold February morning in the spring of 1970 when I went with a group of foreign friends out of Peking city by bus south to Tahsing, a county which belongs to the Peking municipality. An hour and a half later we entered the area of Tungfanghung (The East is Red) commune, once frequently affected by summer floodwaters of rivers coming through the eroded mountains of Shansi. These floods had left many sand dunes and quite a fair amount of wasteland, on some of which Tungfanghung May 7th School is situated, and which its trainees were reclaiming.

The trainees gave us a warm welcome, and soon we were sitting in a long warm room in one of the sturdy, newly erected blocks of buildings, listening to the leader of the school Revolutionary Committee, Liu Jen-san. He was a man with a strong, weather-beaten face with a good deal of kindliness and understanding in it, a veteran of the old revolutionary wars. I asked him later where he had originally come from, and he said, "Fuping, Hopei," which was once part of an old Eighth Route Army base. Then I asked him if he had ever seen Dr. Bethune, who had worked there, and he replied that indeed he had, twice.

But to get back to the meeting. Liu Jen-san invited us all to sit down, and then big bowls of peanuts and glasses of tea were brought in. "Our own peanuts," he said proudly. "Eat up!" Then going on to tell us how 1,400 cadres had come here on October 30th 1968, for remoulding, 600 of them Communist Party members and 100 more members of the Communist Youth League. Trainees ranged in experience from veterans of the anti-Japanese war with 30 years' experience behind them, though the bulk were those who had become cadres in the 'fifties. Another minority were the younger cadres of the 'sixties. Most had been administrative or Party functionaries in the county, only a few from further afield. Coming to the school, they had been first organised on army lines into six companies, with one additional unit directly under the school leadership. On arrival, they first simply lived with the peasants, but construction of the school started right away, many of the bricks having been carted into the country-side from the old city walls of Peking, now under demolition to make for expansion. At the same time, work was started on land reclamation. Moving sand hills into marsh and building up land that could be tilled. Already they had reclaimed 1,000 mou and produced good harvests from this land, 400 mou producing high-yielding rice, while the rest has grown corn and peanuts. To increase the supply of animal manure for compost the school has gone into pig-breeding with considerable success, as well as doing some duck-raising.

They have set up agricultural implement manufacture and repair shops, making the implements they need, such as threshing and winnowing machines, machines for rice hulling and chaff cutting. "Our support has come from the May 7th directive of Chairman Mao, and then from the help on the spot by the PLA and the farmers of the local communes," Liu said, going on to tell how old peasants who had lived through the hard times would come and tell of their experiences under the cruel exploitation of that society. "As this area was once inhabited chiefly by the very poor, there are still many such stories current that are good education for the student of politics. We have also followed the practice of having some of our trainees always take part in the work of production teams in the local brigades, the school having already given them 20,000 workdays. None of the land we cultivated for ourselves was brigade crop land. We simply demanded grain from the wild sandhills and surly saline marshes," Liu said, "and they gave in, faced by our determination. Always we had the example of the anti-Japanese "Kangta" University of Yenan, and the production brigade of Tachai before us as models for our work. So despite all, and even when the surface of the land was frozen, we went on with levelling and other work. The wind blew sand in our faces and we thought of Chiao Yu-lu in Lankao in Honan who, by his leadership, tamed a whole county of wild, ever-moving sandhills, and made its alkaline marshes bear well."

The first productive activity trainees went through was the weaving of baskets for carrying earth. Next came the making of carts and wheelbarrows, then the school furniture and so on, and even agricultural implements, using waste materials from big city factories. "We have planted trees and amongst them a vineyard and an apple orchard we expect to be bearing by 1972. We have dug drainage ditches, sunk wells, grown our own vegetables that at first we had to buy. Wondering what to do with our surplus of rice straw we have devised machines to twist straw into rope to sell as packing material in the city."

These are all things that can be reported on with facts and figures. Not so easy, however, to report on matters that affect the spirit, except to say that all trainees do one hour's study of Chairman Mao's works each day, and two full halfdays each week as well. In addition, poor and lower-middle peasants come in as lecturers, and trainees go out among the communes to help in mass criticism meetings, in propagating the results of important Peking meetings like the Ninth Party Congress, directives and other matters which are of concern to all. "We try to help get the idea over to the people still more deeply that all are farming for the success of the revolution." Then also 18 months have passed in which to judge the effect of the May 7th School on cadres. Certainly all have improved in health and strength. Old ones realise how, by being enclosed in offices, they had been isolated from the people and could no longer meet them in the same way as before. How now in the May 7th School the old spirit of fighting the enemy together returns, and life takes on new meaning again. One such old cadre, now in charge of the piggeries, has put so much devotion and care into his work that the project became a great success. Six hundred of the first group of trainees have gone out into the communes to take part in regular commune and production brigade work and help to raise political consciousness amongst the people. The 800 left in the school are able now to do much more than when they first came. For instance, Lin Yun, a girl, learnt how to use one of the big rubber-tyred wheelbarrows the school made, which can carry 100 jin of compost across paths between the fields. Over a distance of not much more than three li, or a mile, back and forth she could manage but three trips a day with it in the beginning. Now, she can do 21 trips a day with the same load, pushing the wheelbarrow in all something over 70 li, or 23 miles, and still having plenty of energy left.

After we had gone out of the meeting room and faced a cold north wind which drove the sand from big dunes still standing scudding over the frozen earth, we watched trainees working with shovels, throwing themselves into the task with a will and a way.   Then we saw some of the 800 ducklings and specimens of the 100 piglets, visited the tailoring department where clothing was repaired, the cooperative marketing and supply shop, the implement shops, then looked into the spick and span dormitories, finally finding ourselves comfortably seated in the big assembly hall.   Here an excellent meal cooked by the trainees and served by them appeared promptly in front of us which we, being somewhat hungry, all set to and consumed with great relish.   Then tables were cleared away, and we watched a performance of the school's propaganda team that goes out amongst the brigades to give performances.

They put on a rapidly moving show full of spirit, singing some of their songs pleasingly to the air of Hopei opera — "Hopei Bangtze" — that local peasants love so well.   Next, we all went back to the meeting room in which we had spent much of the morning and listened to the careful accounts which two of the trainees gave of how the training given over the past 18 months had affected them.

The first was a man, Liu Ju-ken.   He told how he came of a poor family in this area.   How from six to 13 he lived the life of a beggar on the streets of Peking.   How at 13 he was taken as apprentice by a shopkeeper, but was beaten so much that he ran away at 15, and had finally made his way to the Eighth Route Army, which he joined in January 1939. After being sent to a training school in Yenan he worked with self-supporting groups, spinning and weaving cloth, growing millet and vegetables, helping peasants with their work, and digging caves in hillsides for living quarters.   Then, everyone worked hard.   Manual work in the daytime, office work and study at night.   Sometimes when office work accumulated, it actually went on all through the night.   He was so full of spirit in those days that he was cited as a labor hero.   When the call came to go to the front he was always in the van.   With his comrades he then felt that the greatest thing to do was to knock down the old world of oppression and build a new one on its ruins, as the words of the "Internationale" had it. He became a Communist Party member in 1940, and maintained a strong spirit of solidarity with the people amongst whom he worked and lived.

Then after the liberation of Peking he returned there.   Chairman Mao had warned that this was but a first step in a great new Long March.   All should beware of the sugar-coated bullets that could be more deadly than the nickel-coated ones of the enemy.   "But like others," he said, "I changed over from the old system of livelihood in which what was needed was supplied, to that of a salary.   At that time, many Liu Shao-chi ideas were circulating.   We had won the revolution.   Now was the time for construction.   A cadre ought to be successful.   He should achieve fame and a place for the future.   I looked around me and found that cadres who could write well most easily became famous.   So then I tried to find ways of getting a quiet position that would give me time to write more and become a theorist.   I finally managed to be included in a course at the higher Party school.   At that time, the revisionist Yang Hsien-chen was one of the leaders there.   The school encouraged students to write articles that were divorced from reality.   I, like others, had memorised many passages in early Marxist classics as my stock in trade.   Now, I had but to fit them into passages I would write.   More and more I became divorced from reality.   I came to admire many old middle-class intellectuals, and especially thought that Liu Shao-chi's writings pointed out the way ahead.   Without realising it, I had left the people and was actually working against them!"

Liu Ju-ken, as he said this, became a little emotional and his voice shook.   Then, recovering himself, he went on, "The Communist Party had saved me, but I had not understood properly and now I was leading people back to the vicious old society."   He realised that he had not been true to the pledge he had given on becoming a Party member, and that he had to start over again.   He had not lived up to the expectations of the people from whom he had sprung.   The Cultural Revolution came and all of this became crystal clear to him, giving him much bitterness of heart.   Then came the May 7th School, and a second chance for him to re-dedicate himself for service to the people.

Living in a dormitory of comrades together, a whole flood of memories of Yenan days came over him.   Listening to the old peasants who, too, had been beggars on Peking streets, he was greatly moved.   How well he understood them!   This was reality!   This was not playing for fame, or for self!   This was something that had happened to them and to himself too and, unless the right way ahead was taken, would happen again.   "Now as I look back," he went on, "I despise the way I sat in comfort in Peking while so many things were waiting to be done everywhere.   In consequence, my advance has taken a zig-zag course instead of the straight one it should have.   I can only say how grateful I am to the thinking of Chairman Mao for the strong help it has been in catching me up in time and making a new revolutionary out of me," he said.   It was evident that now he was for the revolutionary road, and that the one of peaceful evolution had ceased to have any appeal for him, despite its allurements of material comfort for the enterprising.

The next speaker was Hsu Kwang-hua, a woman in her early thirties, who told how she was a "May 7 fighter" now.   How she had been an office worker in educational administration since Liberation, coming from a rich landlord family and being a university graduate.   She had never worked much with her hands.   In revolt against the criminal old society, she had joined the Communist Party at the liberation of Peking.   Despite the fact that her work was connected with country schools, she had never learnt how to distinguish the different crops, or mastered any of the knowledge of what went into making them grow.   She had applied to come to the May 7th School, and had been accepted with the first batch. When she came she suffered a good deal with blisters on her hands, sore back and sore legs, as well as from the sand and dust.   Most of the others in her group were from a peasant background and so did not have all the difficulties she had, but she would say grimly to herself that this was part of the price she had to pay for having been brought up in a home where there were 22 maids and hired workers, and where everything was done for her. She said, "If one comes over from the exploiting class to that of the working people, the transition must cost something. This is just part of the process of transformation. So I stuck to it. The blisters healed, the palms became hard and horny, the legs and back stopped aching, and I could keep up with the others quite easily. I forgot my dislike for the sand that filled ears and nostrils on windy days, and no longer wrapped my head in a silk scarf."

She then gave some amusing accounts of how she had managed to get over her distaste for country smells, and what she had been brought up to regard as dirt. She had a strongly inbred aversion to many of the things that the working person accepted quite simply as part of the task to be done. She also had to break with old landlord family attachments, reminding herself that now she had joined the working class and that the class struggle was still being fought. "I needed to remember always," she said, "that in the old days everything we ate, used, or wore came to us at the expense of people who were dying for want of such. Now that I have joined the revolution, I must be thorough in my joining, not ever looking backward. So I turned more and more to the people, and with their help transformed my outlook. I began to really understand that the group meant more than the individual so that, when my team was able to pull 92 carts of earth in one day, instead of the high target of 85 set, I felt that this was really something, even though each of us was tired and dirty, with hair and ears full of dust.

Old habits, however, die hard. Continually I have to pull myself up in many a little thing. To take just one instance. We were at a meal eating bean sprouts. Everyone but I ate the whole thing, skin and all. But I carefully removed the black skin from each bean, and when the dishes were cleared away, there stood a little hill of black skins on the table by my place. No one said anything, but some certainly looked as I swept them up hastily and took them away. It was not that they tasted bad but only that they were black in color and that put me off. But for poor peasants to throw away any edible skin was waste. And now I was one with the poor peasants. Even in small things like this we must take our stand."

Hsu Kwang-hua came from a class in which the ability to talk well was common, so that she made her statement with considerable effect. Most of the trainees, however, were from the class that expresses itself simply, not wasting words, or thinking so much of the impression it is making on the audience. In this school, there must be many good stories of cadres who have changed their outlook since the years of the Cultural Revolution. Now in the May 7th School they go ahead quietly and thoughtfully after they have been faced with a clear demonstration of the difference between the two lines, the two roads. The atmosphere they have created together is a happy one. The work, dealing as it does with real things, and done in conjunction with the farm folk around, is satisfying. To recapture the old Yenan spirit is a real challenge, and the sense of mission amongst the trainees is high. They all crowded around our bus as we pulled out in the evening dusk. Three of the women cadres had small babies hoisted on their shoulders, fat, laughing little ones, whose faces left a pleasant memory with us. For it is to help the children of the oncoming generation that all this struggle is taking place. The victory of Mao Tsetung Thought will affect many generations of the once poor and exploited not only in China, but also the whole world around.

Chapter 14

Conclusion

The main aim of the Cultural Revolution has been to keep the Chinese quarter of humanity sturdily on the revolutionary road. To do this, it was necessary to expose trends towards restoration of capitalism and modern revisionism that had arisen, and to demonstrate the necessity of continuing the class struggle in its various forms under the dictatorship of the proletariat. One consequence of all that has been done is a start in bridging differences, those between town and country, between the relatively highly paid and those on low wages, between the worker and the intellectual, with this general idea becoming paramount: "We are all in the revolution together to serve the people." The superstructure has been drastically reshaped and streamlined to fit its socialist base; bureaucracy is under heavy attack, and the potential of the ordinary working person is more and more being given a way to express itself. Scientific experimentation and creative innovations are the order of the day. Representative Revolutionary Committees replace the former administrative organs.

The Cultural Revolution has been essentially a high tide of the class struggle, and during this time the slogan in effect has been, "Get out amongst the working people, study their needs and build on what they know, live along with them and each day learn from them, go over their problems with them in all humility, take them to your heart and give them all your love . . . these things lead to a beginning of understanding." With the Soviet experience before their eyes, Chinese revolutionaries try and take the long view. They have come to understand well how important is the training and education not only of the present generation but also of the second and third, the "successors to the revolution". Revolutionising the rising generation has become an overwhelmingly important task.

But the old educational system was built to measure for the old order, and so it had to be pulled down and a new one erected that would educate for life, not for "education". All learning had to be tied with practice.

Another important new feature is to teach the rising generation how to create and analyse, and not simply enforce memorisation of book learning, in the realisation that knowledge acquired by rote can well become a trap. Education must teach "why" as well as "how" and "for whom", so that down-to-earth service to the people becomes more possible, and the part-work, part-study principle becomes universal from primary grades right on through university.   Education must promote revolutionary aims in the spirit of Mao Tsetung Thought. As a result of all this, the youth of the whole of China now takes a new look at itself, with oncoming generations leaping to the challenge. It has not been a question of peaceful transition, but one of revolutionary method.

> In the old society
> poor workers, poor farmers
> had to pay taxes
> to send the children
> of the rich to school,
> universities, for they
> were of the class the poor
> were privileged to care for.

> So were produced, as
> the brains and apologists
> for their class, the learned,
> the scientists, the intellectual
> pundits, some just proficient
> in memorising, others even
> cheating or buying diplomas,
> for cash counted heavily;
> the cream went on to more
> universities around the world;
> got well-paid jobs abroad;
> the less fortunate joining in
> the rat race at home, slick brains
> angling for privilege and profit . . .

> "I was trained an engineer," slyly
> said one old society Shanghai compradore.
> "And I as a scientist"
> laughed his fellow. "But as no one
> would pay enough for our skills, we are
> here in business, doing quite well, ha, ha!"

> Today the people of China
> still pay, but now they are out
> to get full value from their investment
> in bringing help to working hands
> helping puzzling minds to catch up; they
> deciding on what must be taught, and how;

who shall be trained and why; education
along with doing, not just pie in the sky
but education becoming an essential part
of the total living of a people who will
be ever learning, ever on the move out
into the unknown, bending nature to
their destiny.

Chinese provinces are as big as the greater European countries. Szechuan with its 68 million in the west, Kiangsu lying along the lower reaches of the Yangtze with its 44 million, then the plains of Hopei with 41 million, Kwangtung on the south China coast with its 42 million, and then Heilungkiang on the northeast frontier, these and all the great provinces that lie in between have all during these last five years had their centres of intense revolutionary struggle. China, with the motto put into action by the Cultural Revolution, now makes self-sufficiency possible at all levels. Indeed maximum self-sufficiency in all that is needed has become a way of life. With the idea of doing things themselves, multi-millions of children are growing up more sure that they can make their land produce all that is needed to support their work and future.

The strengthening of the organisation of working people on the land, brought about by the continuing success of the people's communes, which have given a lead in educating people to put out of their minds the profit incentive and to work for the common good, makes it possible to bring socialist morality into the tens of thousands of villages throughout the country. The new production brigade schools play a good part in changing the pattern of thinking away from the old and into the new, so that Man To Be begins to emerge in no uncertain manner. Who can say that this is not a victory for all mankind?

In these pages we have seen how adequate medical attention is now getting to be an available thing to the ordinary folk of even the smallest hamlet amongst hinterland hills. How now also mechanisation begins to give additional strength to hands, enabling more attention to be given to wasteland reclamation, afforestation, irrigation and also to hinterland industry.

For the new art and literature that will inspire to still greater efforts, it is too early yet to venture prophecy, except to say that as it does arise it will follow Chairman Mao's Yenan Talks on the subject, so that it becomes devoted to the needs and inspiration of the working people. The model operas and plays that have been produced have shown the way for the theatre.

In science and technology, new beginnings have already been made, and as industry reaches out, so will these keep pace. One has but to go to a few trade fairs in Canton, or to see industrial exhibitions like that in Shanghai, to realise what enormous strides have already been made during these last few years. How today China is really entering a new though unheralded "Great Leap Forward".

All in all, then, the record presented in this book is simply one of "I went, and this is what I saw." Due to China's physical size alone, most of the major developments in the hinterland have not yet been publicised. But I hope that enough has been covered in this account to enable the reader to gain some idea of the changes that are taking place in this ever-changing land. It has not all been just plain sailing. As one invariably divides into two, the two-way struggle has of course appeared in every bit of revolutionary endeavor. When people progress they invariably come to a crossroads, and there arises a problem. Which way will take us to our destination? Which will lose us? The struggle to find the right way may be quite a bitter one, in which some may suffer injustice for a time. Then, with victory for the correct line, things right themselves again.

With all this having been said, there no doubt will be those who will ask, "The cost of the Cultural Revolution must have been very high. Did you not see something of the negative side of things for, to understand the positive, surely we must know something of the negative also?" One sympathises with that point of view, but actually on my journeys I have put down pretty well all I have seen.

There were in urban areas, of course, many cases especially of some youth groups making struggle an end in itself, losing revolutionary perspective and embracing anarchistic tendencies, so that in the end they turned into their proclaimed opposite and were fighting each other; with them, a gang mentality replaced revolutionary consciousness, and partial interests were put ahead of the common good. In some of these unprincipled struggles people even got killed. But in each and every case that came to my notice the background to this kind of happening was more complicated than would appear at first notice. A bourgeois family background and bourgeois thinking was still very strongly represented amongst college and university students and for that matter also in other segments of society. This often made it possible for certain scheming individuals inside the Party organisation, who secretly held to the Liu Shao-chi line, to make these groups their own instruments in attacking the Party line. These people hoped to win power in China by mouthing ultra-left slogans, building up a widespread secret organisation parallel to and in opposition to the Party, pulling down each and every Party cadre not belonging to their own organisation. As a deliberate policy they tried to create havoc in China's foreign relations and to paralyse economic life in the country. In spite of these dramatic aims, very little success attended their intrigues, as can be seen from these chapters. Standing one day during the latter stages of in-fighting with a worker friend who had originally come from a poor peasant hinterland village, we listened outside the campus of Peking University to the sound of breaking windows and smashing up of equipment that came as steel-helmeted and spear-armed students struggled in violence together. The big majority of students had gone home, leaving the leading elements of opposing groups to fight it out. They were doing exactly the things that Chairman Mao had asked them not to do. "That is the people's property they are smashing, paid for by the struggling people of China," my friend said. "We would like a good new school in our village, but here these young gentlemen are smashing up all we have given them! It's just disgusting! Who do they think they are?" It was disgusting all right, and the damage was soon brought to a halt by teams of factory workers coming in and bringing opposing groups together. The contending students of that stage have now gone out to work, and the university, like so many others, has started again with a completely new student body of worker, peasant and soldier youth.

In some hinterland areas the struggle to gain unity and understanding was more difficult. The ultra-left, that arm of the ultra-right, worked in many devious ways, using all the powers it possessed to stop unity from coming at all. Prominent was the May 16th group, which took a fine name for a bad cause, and which was organised by some important people. Ruthless in a counter-revolutionary way, it became for a time the most powerful one. In addition, there were other local groups who fooled youngsters to join in with them, making for fierce fighting for a while. The old does not give up until it has exhausted every way it has to preserve itself. The strength of Mao Tsetung Thought, correctly applied by the great mass of common sense, down-to-earth working people, prevented the reaction from gaining the control it aimed so ambitiously for. As these pages of travel observations show, the people went steadily on with the work from which they had to gain their livelihood. China today is a system of interconnected groups of working people, and it is safe to say that in each and every group, whether on island, plain or amongst the hills, whether in city or up on high plateaux, the struggle for the transformation of man, started in the Cultural Revolution, continues.

As this conclusion is being written towards the end of our period of 1966-71, Party committees have been re-formed in all provinces, regions and municipalities. Each stage of the Cultural Revolution has been and is still being carefully analysed at the formation of each committee and mistakes and successes thrown into highlight, so that there has been a considerable rise in the whole political level. Naturally many of the things seen in 1966-68, when the revolution was at its height, have gone. By now, the words of the three short essays are well engraved on all hearts, and the oncoming generations learn them in school. There are pictures and statues of Chairman Mao still, but not the vast number there were during the earlier years. The whole mass of the people have had an intensive study course in Mao Tsetung Thought, and the guidelines for the future have been set. Now is the time to continue with the Great Leap Forward and make for the kind of economic independence that will enable China to carry through her own revolution and, at the same time, assist the world revolution.

One can say in summary that the Cultural Revolution set out to halt the growth of a new exploiting class recruited from amongst the superstructure. To create industry for the people, not people for industry. To educate the mass of ordinary folk so that "we" became more important than "I". To lessen the differentiation which had been increasing between city and countryside. To narrow the gap between educated and non-educated people, between physical and mental work. To make education possible for all working people, and to open the universities and high schools of learning to those once considered "non-qualified" — workers, peasants and soldiers. To bring in the most advanced industrial technique, and to take medicine, science and art down into the ranks of the common folk. To prepare people to resist natural disasters, and to prepare against war. To carry industrialisation to higher stages and accelerate farm mechanisation.   To revolutionise that part of the superstructure which had remained in the hands of "old-type intellectuals" and make it further serve the needs of working people; to carry the study of Mao Tsetung Thought into every home in the land, every school, every factory, every commune, every organisation. To clear minds from the inhibitions of old customs, habits, traditions, and to build an educational system based on the needs of the people in their struggle forward. To make self-sufficiency at all levels not just a slogan, but a way of life. To eliminate waste in productive processes, and to stress work on experimentation and technical innovation.   To keep the revolution clean and purposeful, maintaining its momentum, and having all understand not only their place and their responsibility in the Chinese revolution but also in the world revolution.

These, then, have been some of the things stressed, each one of them full of struggle and meaning. When we say, for instance, "prepare against natural disaster" in China this means vast work on river conservancy, afforestation, and other anti-erosion measures over great areas, demanding devoted, self-sacrificing work from multi-millions of people. Such work is imperative and can only be carried through if the spirit of the people is raised high enough to tackle it. That this spirit has been greatly raised in these few years is evident to any visitor. One finds it as strongly expressed in remote hinterland mountain villages as out on the richer farming land; actually, it is very often found that the tougher the local conditions are, the higher it rises and the most outstanding examples of success and self-sacrifice are to be found.

The struggle to solve the massive problems that face China today is a challenging one, one still in its formative years. Every success helps in the solution of other problems. Fire the creative imagination of a whole people, give them correct leadership and the deep conviction that power lies in their own hands and there is no need to remain poor or backward, then indeed earth-shaking changes begin to take place.

Never in all China's long history has an educational process been carried so deeply amongst the masses of the people as has been done during these past five years of change. As the end of 1971 approaches one can look back and make some beginning at a summation. First, Chairman Mao Tsetung's sensing and seeing the trends of a socialist revolution being taken over and diverted back to the old capitalist ways, and his initiating and leading the Great Proletarian Cultural Revolution. Then the exposure of the Liu Shao-chi line as a completely revisionist one, and the downfall of Liu's highly organised superstructure which had accumulated so much power in its hands. There were, too, many other mistakes, most of which were allied to the Liu line and needed correction. What took place, then, was necessary and wholesome. Then, when it became clear that some of the self-styled rebels, while posing as super-leftists, were in reality just another echelon of the Liu Shao-chi group, the struggle against these counter-revolutionaries had to be joined and another educational movement carried out to expose this stage of the class struggle and what it really meant. Even at the end of 1971 it had not yet been entirely carried through. But with internal unity already strongly re-established, minds clear as people throw themselves into the new economic surge forward. The people, too, are now able to turn to the remaining problems of China's relations with the rest of the world at this time. Determination to see the liberation of China's province of Taiwan has grown, as well as support for the three peoples of Indochina in their struggle against imperialist aggression.

All through the passion and struggle of the Cultural Revolution, as can be well seen from this narrative, creative work in both industry and agriculture did go ahead. From theory to spirit and from spirit to material advance. With the old educational system completely demolished, a new one began to be built swiftly on the people's needs, not on tradition. Metaphysical ideas were dropped, and Marxist ones took precedence. Closer study of the Marxist classics and Chairman Mao's works is being carried out at all levels. It is still too early to make a complete assessment of all successes gained, for there is yet much to be done on consolidation and preparation for new stages. But a better basis for change now exists, policy is more fully understood and the way ahead made clear. The problems that confront China are as vast as her land, but with a heightened political consciousness the people are better ready to tackle them than they have ever been. When one quarter of the world starts moving with such determination there is much that can be accomplished. Perhaps the following lines may convey the central point of the Cultural Revolution period.

> *The Chinese revolution*
> *dealt heavy blows to all*
> *the old order meant*
> *bringing down landlord gentry,*
> *warlord generals, thieving*
> *bureaucrats, bloated*
> *compradores and their like;*
> *yet deeply rooted, ego centred*
> *thought patterns persisted*
> *along with an educational*
> *structure evolved in the past.*
> *Around these dead, bygone things*
> *tended to rally a new elite, creating*
> *a new privileged class.*
>
> > *So came, as it had to come,*
> > *a Cultural Revolution; one*
> > *dividing into two, showing well*
> > *how in all struggle there persisted*

two classes, two viewpoints
two roads in the continuing
revolution; exposing both
the old ideology which would
preserve the worn out, and too
the counter-revolutionary who
would use the red banner to
smash the red banner, in
ruthless struggle for power
and to restore the old.

Throughout the whole land
struggle raged; in factory
in commune, in school, and
in office; so was the road
cleared for advance again,
and the people could see.

Hands now turned to fashion
newer machines, and to make
the land produce still more;
increasingly irrigation waters
flowed gaily over once
barren fields; more fertiliser
plants arose; more steel mills;
new railways cut their way
through rugged mountains; teachers
and doctors learnt new lessons
by living together with
hinterland people where
the need was greatest; ever
the struggle between the two
lines continuing, ever new ways
of doing things evolving,
and ever too understanding
deepening of the role
of a revolutionary people
in the new world to be.

中 国 见 闻

路易·艾黎著

*

新世界出版社出版（北京）

1973年（小16开）第一版

编号：（英）10050—748

00800（精）

00740（平）

10—E—1299

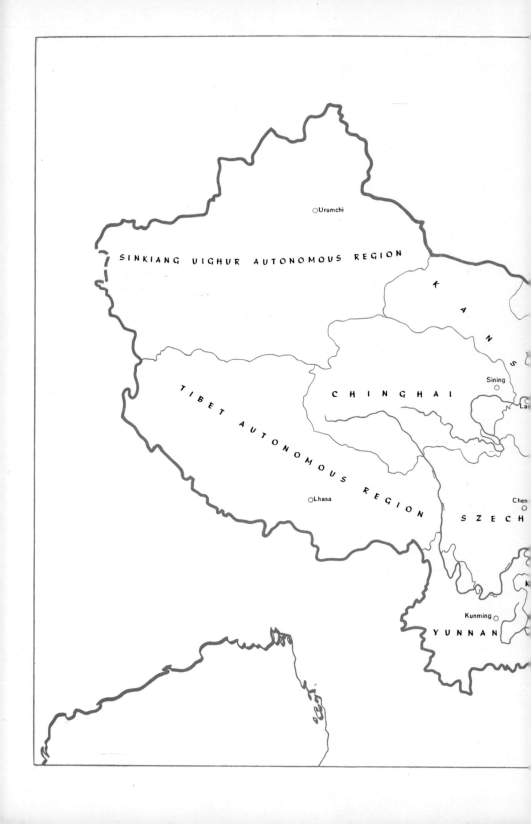

HEILUNGKIANG

○Harbin

KIRIN

○Changchun

INNER MONGOLIA AUT. REGION

Shenyang
○

LIAONING

Huhehot
○

Peking   Tsunhua
○   ○
             Chinwangtao
Tientsin

Hsinhsien
○
HOPEI
Taiyuan
○
Shihchiachuang   Yentai
                   ○
SHANSI
                Yellow River
                ○Tsinan
                SHANTUNG

Sian
○
SHENSI   Chengchow   KIANGSU
          ○
          HONAN

              ANHWEI
              Hofei   Nanking
              ○   ○
HUPEH   Soochow○ ○Shanghai
Wuhan○   Yangtze River
              Hangchow○
              CHEKIANG
      Nanchang
      ○
   Changsha
   ○
Shaoshan○ KIANGSI
HOW HUNAN
ang   Chingkangshan Foochow
            Juichin○ FUKIEN
                     ○

KWANGSI
HUANG AUT. REGION
        KWANGTUNG
○Nanning Pearl River Kwangchow
                       ○

TAIWAN

South China Sea Islands

○Nanning   ○Kwangchow

              Tungsha Is.

                    Chungsha Is.
    Sisha Is.
    ○

                    Nansha Is.

    ○ Tsengmu Reef

South China Sea
Islands